Mastering
Microsoft® Virtualization

Tim Cerling

Jeff Buller

Chuck Enstall

Richard Ruiz

WILEY

Wiley Publishing, Inc.

Acquisitions Editor: Agatha Kim
Development Editor: Dick Margulis
Technical Editor: David Hanna
Production Editor: Rachel McConlogue
Copy Editor: Linda Recktenwald
Editorial Manager: Pete Gaughan
Production Manager: Tim Tate
Vice President and Executive Group Publisher: Richard Swadley
Vice President and Publisher: Neil Edde
Book Designers: Maureen Forys and Judy Fung
Proofreader: Publication Services, Inc.
Indexer: Ted Laux
Project Coordinator, Cover: Lynsey Stanford
Cover Designer: Ryan Sneed
Cover Image: © Pete Gardner/DigitalVision/Getty Images

Library of Congress Cataloging-in-Publication Data

Mastering Microsoft virtualization / Tim Cerling ... [et al.]., — 1st ed.
   p. cm.
  ISBN 978-0-470-44958-5 (pbk.)
  1. Microsoft Windows server Hyper-V. 2. Virtual computer systems. I. Cerling, Tim, 1952-
  QA76.9.V5M36 2009
  005.4'3–dc22

                                     2009038771

10 9 8 7 6 5 4 3 2 1

Dear Reader,

Thank you for choosing *Mastering Microsoft Virtualization*. This book is part of a family of premium-quality Sybex books, all of which are written by outstanding authors who combine practical experience with a gift for teaching.

Sybex was founded in 1976. More than 30 years later, we're still committed to producing consistently exceptional books. With each of our titles, we're working hard to set a new standard for the industry. From the paper we print on, to the authors we work with, our goal is to bring you the best books available.

I hope you see all that reflected in these pages. I'd be very interested to hear your comments and get your feedback on how we're doing. Feel free to let me know what you think about this or any other Sybex book by sending me an email at nedde@wiley.com. If you think you've found a technical error in this book, please visit http://sybex.custhelp.com. Customer feedback is critical to our efforts at Sybex.

Best regards,

Neil Edde
Vice President and Publisher
Sybex, an Imprint of Wiley

Acknowledgments

This book is the first published work for each of us. The staff at Sybex has been great at gently coaxing us in the finer points of what it takes to deliver a good Mastering series book. It has definitely been a learning experience that we could not have gotten through without their patient coaching.

A special thanks goes to our technical editor, David Hanna. David has done a great job of reading the book like a technical guru (which he most certainly is) while at the same time reading the book like someone who needs a simplified explanation of the technology. Hopefully we have all followed his guidance in order to bring you a book that provides the technical detail required to understand Microsoft virtualization technologies, while making it easy for you to understand and build out the examples in your environment.

It is great to work for a company like Microsoft when it comes to something like this. Our management has been very supportive and encouraging in our efforts. Anytime we have a question on a particular topic, it is easy to reach out to the product managers and engineers to ensure that we are getting the right information.

It almost seems obvious to thank our spouses for their patience for all the time we have had to spend researching, typing, reading, building labs, and doing all the other things that went into getting this information into the book you are holding. Until you have actually gone through the process of writing a book while still holding a normal job — if you call working for Microsoft normal — you just do not realize how much time you need to spend away from your spouse and how understanding they have been.

About The Authors

Tim Cerling

Tim Cerling is a server and virtualization technology specialist working for Microsoft. He has been a customer-facing Microsoft employee for over 10 years and in the IT industry for over 35 years. Yes, he remembers keypunching assembler code into Hollerith cards and loading hex addresses via console switches in order to load a bootstrap loader program to get an operating system running on the first computers he worked on. Before joining Microsoft in 1999, he worked for Digital Equipment Corporation (later Compaq) from 1980 to 1999. At DEC and Compaq, Tim focused heavily on understanding and implementing DEC's clustering technologies, on both DEC operating systems and Windows NT. He was part of the NT Wizards group started by DEC that focused on helping customers deploy Windows NT for datacenter applications, particularly on the Alpha platform.

His degree is in computer science from the University of Iowa, and he graduated in 1974. During his schooling for operating systems programming, he actually had to write a couple of basic virtual machine managers and a simple timesharing scheduler to enable running multiple programs at the same time on a single operating system. So he has seen a little bit of change in the industry, and though his schoolwork was not called virtualization, it was where he really started working in that space.

Tim began working with the VMware Workstation product for a couple years before Microsoft purchased Connectix and released its own desktop product — Virtual PC. At that time he jumped into Microsoft's solutions and now tries to keep up with all the releases and changes that Microsoft is providing in its various virtualization products, with his heaviest focus on Hyper-V. He wrote the opening six chapters on Hyper-V.

Tim was raised on a farm in southwestern Wisconsin, so he loves being outdoors. Some of his favorite outdoor activities include fishing and camping in the Boundary Waters Canoe Area Wilderness in northern Minnesota, hunting and camping in the mountains of the West, and in-line skating marathons around the Midwest. He has also been married for 35 years to a most patient lady, who is willing to put up with his quirks and who mothered his computer programming son and bookstore manager daughter.

Jeff Buller

Jeff Buller is a virtualization specialist for Microsoft Corporation. He has worked at Microsoft for 18 years and been in the computing industry for 24 years.

Jeff grew up in Moline, Illinois, a small town in the northwestern part of the state. After high school, he went to college and later joined the U.S. Army. It was during his military service that Jeff became interested in computer technology and decided to make it a career.

After his four years of military service, Jeff went back to school and graduated from Central Texas College. His first computer job was working for a small computer consulting company in Texas that supported small- and medium-size businesses. He then moved to Minnesota and worked as a systems engineer and consultant specializing in operating systems and computer networking. During this time he worked with many Fortune 500 companies across the country, assisting them with server and networking design and implementation.

A few years later, Jeff joined Microsoft as a systems engineer supporting enterprise customers with Microsoft operating systems, networking products, and database solutions. During his career at Microsoft, he has held many technical positions, covering the spectrum of Microsoft's enterprise products and technologies. In his current role, Jeff is responsible for leading Microsoft's virtualization solutions business in the North Central District, working with enterprise customers and partners in that area.

Jeff has been greatly blessed with a wonderful family, wife Julia, and children Jessica and Jacob. During his free time, he enjoys spending time with his family and friends, serving at his church, playing and watching sports, camping in Minnesota, and traveling abroad.

Jeff wrote the final three chapters covering MED-V and VDI.

Chuck Enstall

Chuck Enstall is a network technology specialist with Microsoft Corporation. His entry into the technology field began in high school when he worked as a custom programmer on accounting packages on CP/M systems and other computers of the period. He enlisted in the U.S. Navy in 1982 and served six years of active duty in engineering. After the Navy, Chuck began implementing point of sale systems and Novell networks. He began working in early 1997 as a systems engineer for an Apple education reseller, focusing on cross-platform networking. In November of that year, Chuck founded a company to provide consultative services to the education market. That company grew into a regional concern and was eventually acquired by a larger company in 2003; he remained as the director of engineering until joining Microsoft in 2005. He holds numerous industry certifications and is a member of Mensa. Chuck is currently pursuing his private pilot's license and plays bass guitar (in a band for too many years). Chuck is married to Julie, a personal fitness trainer and photographer, and has a four-year-old daughter, Sophia. Chuck wrote the four chapters on Remote Desktop Services.

Richard Ruiz

Richard Ruiz is a virtualization specialist working for Microsoft. His primary focus currently is in desktop virtualization technologies such as Virtual Desktop Infrastructure (VDI) with Hyper-V, Microsoft Enterprise Desktop Virtualization (MED-V), and Microsoft Application Virtualization (App-V). Of greatest interest is the management of these new enabling technologies and scaling them up to global enterprise deployments.

Richard came to Microsoft with the acquisition of Softricity, a small Boston-based company responsible for some of the technology underpinning Microsoft Application Virtualization. Richard worked as an engineer and consultant with the product, then called SoftGrid. Prior to that, as an analyst with various public-sector agencies, including the Los Angeles Superior Court and the California State University System, he gathered real-world experience deploying and appreciating the benefits of application virtualization. Richard has relished sitting back and watching computer models swap over the years from being server based to client based and back again in the search for a silver bullet. Richard believes that with virtualization layers the war may end in an uncomfortable truce, enabled by technology, enforced by cost, and ultimately divided by user type.

Richard's interest in computing began with writing games for the Commodore 64 in 1984 when he was 10 years old. Later, his interests expanded into early multimedia software with photo manipulation and MIDI music scoring. Richard is an active member in the open source community, writing code for projects in areas such as investment trending analysis and bioinformatics.

A recent transplant to Colorado, Richard spends much of his free time with his wife, Carolyn, and two sons, Richard and Nicholas, enjoying snowmobiling, target shooting, and stunt kite flying. Richard's hobbies include Latin jazz piano, 3D modeling and animation, and video games.

About the Contributing Author

David Hanna is an infrastructure specialist currently working as a Technology Solutions professional at Microsoft. While David's first foray into the world of PCs was with a Commodore 64 in the early 80's, he started his IT career in 1995 when he installed his first peer-to-peer network at a small export firm. From there, he went on to participate in two large corporate PC rollout projects in Atlanta, GA. After achieving his first MCSE certification, he took a job that involved deploying, managing, and supporting infrastructure solutions at Cox Communications. While still at Cox, David went on to manage the Windows Infrastructure team, and finally, to work as an Infrastructure Architect where he helped build processes and procedures for a new architecture team.

In January of 2005, David began work at Microsoft. As a Technology Solutions Professional, he works with large customers to provide them with in-depth technical information, architectural designs, and proof-of-concept environments for Microsoft's infrastructure solutions. David specializes in Windows Server technologies and server virtualization with Hyper-V, but he is involved with a wide range of infrastructure solutions including Windows optimized desktop solutions, server management, high availability and disaster recovery, web, directories, and enterprise storage. David has spoken at several major launch events including Windows Server 2008, Hyper-V, and Windows Server 2008 R2.

David holds a B.A. from Cornell University in Russian Literature. David is ITIL certified, and holds a Six Sigma Green Belt. He currently holds MCSE certifications for Windows Server 2000 and 2003, and several MCTS certifications on Windows Server 2008 and Hyper-V.

Currently, David lives in Simsbury, CT with his wife Sara and two amazing children, Elias and Sofia. David spends the cold months of the year coaching and playing ice hockey, and the warmer months fishing at every possible opportunity.

Contents at a Glance

Contents

Introduction

In the last few years, the word *virtualization* has been a topic of discussion in most, if not all, IT organizations. Not only has it promised to save organizations money, but it has consistently delivered on that promise. The first area that this has generally been applied to is the server space. Organizations often take three, four, or more physical servers, create virtual machines running what previously ran on a physical server, and run those workloads on a single physical server hosting multiple virtual machines. Reducing the number of physical servers saves the cost of purchasing, maintaining, powering, and in some cases licensing those physical servers. Server virtualization is one of those technologies that has had a major, some might even say revolutionary, effect on how IT does its job.

But too often, virtualization has been interpreted to only mean running more than one operating system environment on a single physical host. That definition is a little too limiting, particularly when seen in light of all the virtualization technologies that are available from Microsoft. Microsoft takes the approach that different requirements are best served by different technologies.

For example, if we look at the simple understanding above, Microsoft does have a capability (Hyper-V) designed to efficiently run more than one operating system environment on a single physical host. With Hyper-V, we can look at virtualization as a way to abstract the physical resources of the host system in such a way that multiple software partitions can be created, and each partition can simultaneously run its own operating system environment. Hyper-V creates and removes these partitions via software, so they are very dynamic and can adjust to changing needs. This is different from hardware partitioning, where a physical machine is partitioned into two or more physical machines from a common set of hardware resources, creating fairly static operating system environments.

But Microsoft goes beyond just that definition of virtualization. Figure I.1 shows those virtualization products from Microsoft that are covered in this book. The center portion of the figure shows Management. That area is not covered in detail, but it is mentioned throughout the book. Management is a key component of any virtual environment, but its many capabilities will need to be covered in another book.

For many years, Microsoft has had a feature known as Terminal Services that has been included as part of the Windows Server operating system. This is another virtual abstraction product. In Terminal Services, a single physical host runs copies of applications and sends just the displays of those applications to client machines. The presentation of the application is abstracted from where the application is running in a physical environment. The application is installed once on the server, and then multiple desktops can use this application simultaneously. Terminal Services began to be referred to as presentation virtualization in Windows Server 2008, and then was renamed to be Remote Desktop Services in Windows Server 2008 R2 to better define some additional new capabilities.

Hyper-V and Remote Desktop Services (RDS) are roles that are available as part of the Windows Server 2008 operating system. Not all virtualization has to take place on the server, though. Microsoft has extended virtualization capabilities to the desktop environment.

FIGURE I.1

Server Virtualization
•Windows Server 2008 R2
•Microsoft Hyper-V Server
•Virtual Server 2005

Management
•System Center
•Active Directory

Presentation Virtualization
•Windows Server 2008 R2
Remote Desktop Services

Desktop Virtualization
•Microsoft Enterprise
Desktop Virtualization
•Virtual PC

Application Virtualization
•Microsoft App-V

Application Virtualization (App-V) is another method that allows for a single installation of an application that can be shared to the desktop. But this goes a step beyond what is available via RDS. RDS requires that a desktop be connected to the network in order to access the resources of the server. App-V enables a desktop or laptop to cache the application locally so that it can be run either while connected to the network or when disconnected. Updates and patches are still made to the single installation, and those changes are streamed to the client system the next time it is connected to the network. Application Virtualization also solves the classic problem of DLL and registry conflicts between applications and different versions of the same application (application coexistence).

There is also the situation when an application might conflict with the operating system itself — commonly referred to as application incompatibility. This has been an issue with applications that are coded specifically for a particular operating system, or to use a deprecated subsystem. If a client needs to run an application that conflicts with the operating system, it has sometimes meant that a user may need two computers to perform their job. Microsoft has developed a capability that enables the incompatible applications to run seamlessly on an operating system for which it was not designed. This is delivered in the MED-V product.

One of the latest areas that many organizations are investigating today is virtualizing end-user desktops. The industry term for this is *Virtual Desktop Infrastructure (VDI)*. Since so many organizations have had great success with applying server virtualization into their environment, they are investigating whether they might be able to obtain similar benefits by virtualizing their desktops.

VDI, in its simplest implementation, involves converting a physical client operating system environment into a virtual machine and accessing that virtual machine over the network. However, Microsoft, with its broad suite of virtualization capabilities, can provide more than that. Yes, it can utilize Hyper-V on the backend as the virtualization engine to run virtual machines with client operating system environments. But with the addition of RDS, App-V, and MED-V, it can mix and match specific requirements to provide a more flexible and cost-effective VDI environment.

Who Should Buy This Book

This book is intended for individuals who have a working knowledge of at least the Windows operating system. It assumes that you generally know how to install and run applications and services on the operating system.

With that understanding, it presents each of the various virtualization technologies and their capabilities. The presentations are technical in nature, so that people not familiar with virtualization technologies can get started with them, but detailed enough to help more advanced individuals learn how these technologies work. Nearly every chapter provides step-by-step guides to assist you in installing and setting up the technologies.

This book is a resource for individuals who want to gain a good understanding of the various virtualization technologies from Microsoft and learn how to apply them to different environments. Planners as well as implementers will benefit from this book.

The Mastering Series

The Mastering series from Sybex provides outstanding instruction for readers with intermediate and advanced skills, in the form of top-notch training and development for those already working in their field and clear, serious education for those aspiring to become pros. Every Mastering book includes:

♦ Real-World Scenarios, ranging from case studies to interviews, that show how the tool, technique, or knowledge presented is applied in actual practice.

♦ Skill-based instruction, with chapters organized around real tasks rather than abstract concepts or subjects.

♦ Self-review test questions, so you can be certain you're equipped to do the job right.

What Is Covered in This Book

Here is a glance at what is in each chapter.

Chapter 1: Understanding Microsoft's Hypervisor presents an introduction to hypervisor technology and how Microsoft implemented Hyper-V.

Chapter 2: Installing, Configuring, and Managing the Hyper-V Host presents the basic information necessary to set up the physical machines for a Hyper-V environment.

Chapter 3: Creating and Managing Virtual Machines presents the basic information necessary for creating and managing virtual machines.

Chapter 4: Storage and Networking for Hyper-V presents how Hyper-V virtual machines interact with the physical storage and network on the host and how to configure Hyper-V for use by the virtual machines.

Chapter 5: High Availability and Hyper-V presents the information necessary to set up a highly available environment for both the physical Hyper-V hosts as well as the highly available virtual machines.

Chapter 6: Planning a Virtual Infrastructure with Hyper-V presents a methodology for analyzing your physical environment in order to build a plan to move to a virtual environment.

Chapter 7: Understanding Microsoft Application Virtualization and Streaming gives you a brief overview of both what Microsoft Application Virtualization is and when it would make sense to deploy it.

Chapter 8: Creating Virtual Applications walks you through creating a virtual application as well as best practices garnered from creating thousands of them.

Chapter 9: Deploying Virtual Applications covers how to deploy, customize, and scale an App-V solution.

Chapter 10: Introduction to Remote Desktop Services provides a history and overview of the technology and highlights use cases.

Chapter 11: Installing and Configuring Remote Desktop Services lays out exactly how to get a RDS environment off the ground.

Chapter 12: Deploying and Accessing Remote Desktop Services illustrates how to get your end users connected into the RDS environment through a number of means.

Chapter 13: Load Balancing Remote Desktop Services identifies the mechanisms to ensure an RDS environment that can survive component failures and still be there for your end users.

Chapter 14: Introducing Microsoft Desktop Virtualization introduces Microsoft Desktop Virtualization solutions, specifically Microsoft Enterprise Desktop Virtualization (MED-V) and Virtual Desktop Infrastructure (VDI).

Chapter 15: Deploying Microsoft VDI provides an overview of considerations for planning a VDI deployment, reviews Microsoft server and client VDI components, and provides guidance for installing and configuring a Microsoft VDI solution in a POC and test environment.

Chapter 16: Deploying Microsoft Enterprise Desktop Virtualization provides an overview of the MED-V architecture and required server and client solution components.

Appendix A gathers together all the Master It problems from the chapters and provides a solution for each.

Appendix B lists Microsoft virtualization tools and resources.

How to Contact the Authors

We welcome feedback from you about this book or about books you'd like to see from us in the future. You can reach the authors by writing to us at the following email addresses:

Tim Cerling   tim.cerling@live.com

Jeff Buller   jeffbu@live.com

Chuck Enstall   chuck.enstall@live.com

Richard Ruiz   richardruiz@live.com

Part 1

Hyper-V

Chapter 1

Understanding Microsoft's Hypervisor

Just about every business today is either evaluating or implementing server *virtualization*, or partitioning a physical computer into multiple virtual computers. With hardware systems becoming so powerful, many applications do not require all the available horsepower that comes on a commodity server today. As a result, many companies are viewing server virtualization as a way to either save money by consolidating several underutilized systems onto larger, more efficiently utilized servers or create a dynamic data center that allows movement of virtual machines from one host to another as the needs dictate.

Consolidation will enable companies to save money on physical hardware purchases, possibly some licensing costs, and definitely power and cooling. From a development and test environment, it also speeds up the ability to set up test environments and restore to earlier points to rerun tests. These scenarios promise cost savings of various amounts. Other companies are looking at how virtualization will make it easier and faster to change their infrastructure as their business environment changes.

Windows Server 2008 provides everything needed to support server virtualization as an integrated feature of the operating system — Windows Server 2008 Hyper-V. Hyper-V is Microsoft's next-generation hypervisor-based server virtualization technology, following its earlier Virtual Server product.

Before getting into the details of various aspects of Windows Server 2008 Hyper-V, it will be helpful to understand a little of the history of virtualization and the architecture of Hyper-V. As with any software product, there are new versions and capabilities in the works. In fact, we started writing about the version 1 product and needed to add content to cover version 2. This is a very dynamic time for virtualization products.

In this chapter, you will learn about:

- ◆ Microsoft's history in virtualization
- ◆ Monolithic versus microkernelized virtualization architectures
- ◆ Hardware requirements

Virtualization History

Today, full server and hypervisor virtualization are being implemented or investigated by nearly every company. Based on this recent interest, you would guess that this is a new technology. But it is not. In the early 1970s, IBM released their first commercial version of full operating system environment virtualization on their IBM System/370 and named it VM/370. They had been running the precursor to VM/370 in their labs, and they even had another unsupported product they distributed to customers in the late '60s. VM/370 was an implementation of what is known as full virtualization, or a complete virtualization of the underlying hardware in software enabling the execution of all the software that could run on the physical hardware. If you want to read an interesting article about some of the early work done in virtualization, read the paper titled "Formal requirements for virtualizable third generation architectures," published in 1974 in *Communications of the ACM*, the Association for Computing Machinery journal. ACM is a professional computing organization formed over 60 years ago. You can see that the virtualization roots go deep. If IBM was selling this technology over 30 years ago, why is it only really taking off now?

Other examples of full virtualization exist. For many years, device manufactures have been developing their software on virtualized instances of their devices. For example, take out your cell phone. Do you think that someone is actually writing code and debugging it directly on that device? Obviously, that does not seem likely. The phone manufacturers virtualize that operating system environment on another platform that has human interface devices such as keyboards and monitors and that can run powerful compilers. Think of all the computer chips that are used in computers and graphics cards and all those other devices. Do you think that the engineers who design those chips are actually creating physical chips as prototypes? No, they have massive CAD programs that allow them to put the circuits together inside a computer and then execute the logic of that virtual chip in the memory of another computer. Once they have built the virtual environment of that chip, they will transfer that design into a physical prototype, but most of the development work is done in a virtual manner.

So what makes the current versions of operating system virtualization so intriguing? IBM had a very good product with VM/370 — they still do, though it is now officially called z/VM. However, it runs only on IBM hardware and clones of IBM hardware, such as Fujitsu systems. This product works very effectively and is still in use today, but that is not where most of the servers are today.

x86

More recently, virtualization has moved out of the specialized use cases and into the general marketplace. IBM has a great product, but the number of IBM mainframe systems pales in comparison to the number of systems running the Intel x86 architecture (x86 refers to both the 32-bit and 64-bit processors from both Intel and AMD that are based on the original x86 instruction set). Millions of x86 systems in the world today are running Microsoft Windows and various Linux distributions. Those hardware platforms have continued to get more and more powerful as Intel and AMD continue to produce faster and more powerful chips. In fact, the Intel and AMD systems today are far more powerful than the IBM systems on which the original VM/370 was developed. The availability of excess capacity in the commodity systems of today has created the interest in virtualization.

When organizations first started running business applications on the x86 architecture, neither the hardware nor the operating systems were as robust and stable as the IBM mainframe and other minicomputer operating systems. As a result, it was common practice to install a single application on a server instead of running multiple applications on a single system as organizations do on IBM mainframe and other minicomputer systems. And, because the x86 architecture systems cost so much less than the mainframe and minicomputers, organizations did not see a major problem with this.

As the x86 operating systems and hardware systems became more powerful and robust, organizations wanted to start running more applications on a single host. However, some limitations in the development and runtime environments on these systems could potentially lead to application conflicts. To mitigate some of these potential issues, many of the independent software vendors wanted to support their applications on stand-alone systems, that is to say, on systems that were running only their application. Application development has improved to the point that it is possible to run many applications on the same system, and some organizations do that. But there may still be reasons for keeping the application systems separate. That is a completely different discussion that we will not go into here. Suffice it to say that there are millions of systems in use that run a single application.

When you have a powerful system and it is running a single application, the system is most likely not running at a very high capacity. In fact, many surveys have shown that it is very common for the majority of x86 architecture machines to be running at under 15 percent of the available capacity of that machine, some even under 5 percent. That is a lot of wasted potential. Combine that with the cost of housing these machines in expensive data centers and the cost of the energy needed to power and cool these environments, and it is easy to see why organizations are looking at ways to lower costs and make better use of the resources they already have.

So why not virtualize several of these individual hosts that are running single applications and put them on a single host that is capable of running virtual operating system environments? After all, if an organization can consolidate two servers to one server, they can save half the costs associated with hardware acquisition, energy consumption, and cooling. But why stop at 2:1 consolidation? In fact, many companies achieve consolidation ratios of 10:1, and even higher ratios are being looked at for the server environment. Ratios of 25:1 and higher are being attained when consolidating desktop systems onto servers. That is exactly why several software companies are providing software products that enable companies to virtualize physical x86 systems to consolidate their physical infrastructure.

Today's Virtualization Market

Connectix was founded in 1988 and was one of the early leaders of virtualization. It developed a Virtual PC product that enabled a Macintosh system to run a Windows desktop operating system. They then enhanced that with a product that was supported on the Windows desktop operating system so that one could run multiple Windows operating system environments on a Windows PC. Connectix was purchased by Microsoft in 2003, and Microsoft continued enhancing the Virtual PC product. Microsoft made several significant architectural changes to the Virtual PC product, releasing the Virtual Server 2005 product designed for running server operating systems. Most recently, Microsoft has added a Type-1 hypervisor product, Hyper-V, to its lineup. Types of hypervisors are explained in the section "Virtualization Architectures."

Another major player in this space is VMware, a company formed in 1998. They also started with a desktop-based product and developed server virtualization products. They became the market leader as they enhanced their emulation product, VMware Server, into a Type-1 hypervisor solution for the x86 architecture.

There are several other players in this market space with various implementations of hardware system virtualization technologies, such as Citrix with its Xen hypervisor and various implementations of KVM from Red Hat, Novell, Sun, and Oracle. But the combination of Microsoft and VMware comprise over three-fourths of the market. Since Microsoft has entered the marketplace, it is looking more and more like the various server virtualization products will become a commodity market because companies like Microsoft and Citrix do not charge for their hypervisor products. This will force the virtualization vendors to differentiate themselves based on the added value they bring to their engines.

Microsoft's Server Virtualization Products

Microsoft offers three different products meant for virtualizing server operating system environments.

- Microsoft Virtual Server 2005 (hosted virtualization)
- Microsoft Windows Server 2008 Hyper-V (hypervisor)
- Microsoft Hyper-V Server 2008 (hypervisor)

Microsoft Virtual Server 2005

Microsoft Virtual Server 2005 is a hybrid or hosted virtualization product. It is written as a software service to emulate a specific hardware environment on which desktop or server operating system environments run. Virtual Server 2005 runs as a service on the Windows operating system, which in turn is running on the physical hardware. It was a groundbreaking release from Microsoft as it got them into the server operating system virtualization environment.

Virtual Server 2005 was Microsoft's first product as a virtual machine manager for the server operating system environments. They had obtained the Virtual PC product when they purchased Connectix in February of 2003. Virtual Server uses many of the components that Virtual PC has, except that Virtual Server was designed specifically to address the needs for virtualization as a service instead of as a desktop utility. Virtual PC and Virtual Server are good products that are still in use by thousands of companies around the globe. They work on both 32-bit and 64-bit versions of the Windows operating system prior to Windows 7 and Windows Server 2008 R2, but they support only 32-bit guest operating system environments.

Though the products are quite effective at what they do, there are some constraints in the software implementation. First, the execution environment is defined in software. This restricts operating systems and applications to the capabilities of the emulated hardware. For example, the software-emulated hardware is a motherboard that contains a single processor. That particular software implementation of a specific hardware constraint limits any virtual machine running on Virtual Server to a single processor.

Also, as new hardware is introduced and deployed, it may not be fully exploited. An example here is that the software-emulated network card is a DEC 21140, a four-port NIC. This was picked because it was a very common NIC, and nearly every x86 operating system has a driver for the DEC 21140. But those drivers did not support newer technologies that are being implemented in most organizations, such as VLAN tagging.

Lastly, the software-emulated motherboard was a 32-bit motherboard. In order to move into the 64-bit world, an entirely new software emulator would need to be written that would emulate an x86 64-bit motherboard. Rather than write an entirely new emulation package, which would still be limited due to the very nature of emulation, Microsoft decided to proceed down the proven path of the Type-1 hypervisor.

Microsoft Windows Server 2008 Hyper-V

Windows Server 2008 Hyper-V is what is sometimes known as a Type 1 hypervisor because it runs directly on the hosting hardware platform. This helps minimize the virtualization overhead. Though more efficient than a hybrid hypervisor, every form of virtualization has some level of overhead. It is much easier to minimize this in a Type 1 hypervisor because it executes on the hardware instead of being one level removed.

Hyper-V is a role of the Windows Server 2008 operating system. Microsoft has been driving toward making the operating system very modular with well-defined programming interfaces for interaction among the components. Windows Server 2008 is a major step in delivering on the goal to create roles in the operating system that can be added or removed or changed as needed with minimal to no effect on other roles. The release of Windows Server 2008 came in February of 2008 with 17 defined roles, one of which is Hyper-V. When Windows Server 2008 was released, Hyper-V was still in a beta state of development. In other words, features were mostly complete, but removal of bugs and additional performance work needed to be done on it. When these last tweaks were completed, it was released to the public in July of 2008 as an update available through Windows Update. This is a good example of Microsoft's goal of being able to change a role of the operating system without impacting the other roles.

Hyper-V can be installed as the only role on Windows Server 2008, or it can be installed in conjunction with any of the other 16 roles on Windows Server 2008. We will get into this in later chapters, but for production purposes, it is recommended that the Hyper-V role be the only role installed.

When the Hyper-V role is installed on Windows Server 2008, it inserts the hypervisor binary code between the Windows operating system and the physical hardware during the boot process. Installing the Hyper-V role also sets the hypervisorimagelaunchtypeboot Boot Configuration Database (BCD) setting to auto. If, for whatever reason, you want to disable the hypervisor, simply use the bcdedit command to change the parameter to disabled. Windows starts to boot as it normally does, but when the Hyper-V role is installed, the boot process inserts the hvboot.sys driver into the process. This launches the hypervisor while the rest of the Windows boot process continues.

Remember that if well-defined functions can be moved into hardware, performance can be improved. Both Intel and AMD have built technologies into their chips that make virtualization perform better. Hyper-V exploits some of these capabilities to ensure optimal performance. In fact, it requires that the 64-bit chip on which Hyper-V is installed have either the Intel-VT or AMD-V hardware-assisted virtualization technology. More information on this can be found in the section on hardware requirements.

Microsoft Hyper-V Server 2008

Though Windows Server 2008 Hyper-V can handle nearly any situation where x86/x64 virtualization is required, there are some instances where people do not necessarily want all the capabilities of having the hypervisor as a role of the operating system. That is one of the reasons why Microsoft released Microsoft Hyper-V Server in September of 2008.

Hyper-V Server is not a Windows Server operating system environment, but it is built on core Windows technologies. The easiest way to think of it is as a Windows Server Core installation with only the Hyper-V role installed. This is not entirely accurate because Hyper-V Server does not contain the full Windows Server operating system, but it is easier to comprehend if you think of it this way. To understand this, you need to know a bit about how the modularization of Windows is coming into play here.

During installation, you can choose between two Windows Server 2008 installation options. One option is what everyone is familiar with — the entire operating system with all its capabilities available. A second option is to select a Windows Server Core installation. The Core installation under Windows Server 2008 removes half of the available roles, and it removes the graphical user interface. All the core services like networking, security, file services, and RPC are still available.

Microsoft Hyper-V Server 2008 takes this a step further. It uses the Windows kernel and the Hyper-V role, but no other roles are there — the required components to support them are not even part of the distribution. Using the Windows kernel ensures that all the device drivers supported by the full Windows platform are available for use by Hyper-V Server. And, because the GUI is not available, all management of the host is done with remote management tools — the same remote management tools that are used for managing a Windows Server Core or Full installation. There is a command-line capability, and much can be done with these commands, but it is expected that this system will generally be managed with the remote graphical management tools.

The architecture of the virtualization stack in Windows Server 2008 Hyper-V and Microsoft Hyper-V Server 2008 is the same. It is simply packaged differently for different markets.

Virtualization Architectures

There are three primary forms of system virtualization. Figure 1.1 illustrates these three architectures.

FIGURE 1.1
Virtualization architectures

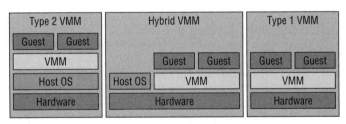

The Type 2 architecture is implemented with things like Java Virtual Machines or Microsoft Common Language Runtime environment. It provides a runtime environment in which commands or processes can be run, regardless of the underlying operating system. There is a dependency on the virtual machine manager to understand the underlying operating system, but the language used to create the process has no dependencies on the operating system. Type 2 focuses on process virtualization, not server virtualization. Therefore, we will not spend any more time discussing this form of virtualization.

Hybrid and Type 1 architectures deal with hardware virtualization. In the hybrid (also sometimes called full or hosted) environment, the virtual machine manager runs alongside the operating system. It is installed as an application on the operating system and emulates an entire physical environment. This enables virtualizing the whole operating system environment in the virtual machine. Microsoft's Virtual PC and Virtual Server and VMware's Workstation and Server products are examples of hybrid architectures.

The Type 1 architecture is what we are considering with Hyper-V. In this case, the hypervisor runs directly on the hardware without the need for an intervening operating system. This is the most efficient way to virtualize an environment because it has the least amount of interference between the hardware and the guest machines.

Since hybrid and Type 1 hypervisors provide similar capabilities, one operating system environment running one or more additional operating system environments, we need to look a little bit at the different implementations. First, remember that we said IBM's VM/370 is a full virtualization product. This means that the entire hardware environment is emulated in software. Connectix and VMware built their initial products this way. Microsoft's Hyper-V is implemented as a Type 1 hypervisor, which is defined in the "Hyper-V Architecture" section later in this chapter.

From the brief history given above, it is easy to see that most of the historical virtualization has been done in the full or hosted virtualization method. That is the method where the entire hardware system is emulated in software. This method works and provides a great deal of flexibility in the operating system environments supported by providing an emulated hardware environment with devices that are supported by many operating systems. But that flexibility comes at the cost of performance. Every access to hardware is emulated in software, requiring the execution of many software instructions to emulate what would be normally handled by the hardware.

The Type 1 hypervisor improves that environment so that the operating systems executing in the partitions have more direct access to the physical resources of the host on which they are running.

Hyper-V Architecture

If you really want to understand how a product works, it is often helpful to understand the architecture of that product. And understanding the architecture is easier if regularly used terms are defined.

Hypervisor   We like the definition of hypervisor that Microsoft uses in its device driver kit on MSDN (`http://msdn.microsoft.com/en-us/library/bb969710.aspx`).

> *"The hypervisor is a layer of software that runs above the physical hardware and below one or more operating systems. The hypervisor's main purpose is to provide isolated execution environments called partitions. The hypervisor provides each partition with the partition's own set of hardware resources (for example, memory, devices, and CPU cycles). The hypervisor must control and arbitrate access to the underlying hardware.*

> *"The hypervisor is a single binary that contains several components (for example, scheduler, partition management, and virtual processor management)."*

Guest   The operating system environments that run in the partitions are referred to as guests. They are also often called virtual machines, or VMs. These terms are used interchangeably in this book. One of the goals of the hypervisor is to be agnostic to what sort of operating system environment is running in the guest.

Parent Partition   In general all partitions created by the hypervisor are equal. However, you will see as we get deeper into the specifics of Hyper-V that the parent partition (sometimes called the root partition) acts as the owner of all the hardware resources. The ownership of physical memory and logical cores presents a special case. When a child partition is created, the parent partition allocates physical memory to the child and then the child partition manages it. Similarly, virtual cores are allocated to the child partitions and then scheduled by the operating system running in the child partitions. This is different from the architecture of VMware ESX, as in that architecture the hypervisor owns the hardware resources. This difference is explained in more detail later in this chapter when the differences between monolithic and microkernelized hypervisors are discussed.

Because the parent partition in Hyper-V owns all the hardware resources, it also handles other system functions generally thought as being part of an operating system. These include things like booting the system, creating and managing other partitions, Plug and Play recognition, hardware error reporting, and so on. This is different from ESX, which handles all these functions in the hypervisor.

Hardware Virtualization   Hardware virtualization is the act of providing multiple logical instances of physical hardware for use by the operating system environments running in the partitions. For example, on a system with only two cores, it may be possible to run three or four virtual machines, each with two cores.

Emulation   Emulation is the process by which a virtualized device mimics a real physical hardware device so that guests can use the typical drivers for that hardware device. This means that a well-known hardware device, like the DEC 21140 network card, can use the device driver that is included in nearly every operating system. Emulated devices are less efficient than synthetic devices, but emulated devices provide support for operating systems that do not have integration components installed.

VMBus   The VMBus is a high-speed memory bus that was developed specifically for Hyper-V. Any I/O traffic that passes to/from a child partition to the parent partition traverses the VMBus. This special kernel-mode driver is installed when the Hyper-V role is installed. Requests for access to physical devices, such as disks and network cards, are transmitted over the VMBus to achieve the highest possible performance.

Synthetic Device   Synthetic devices are purely virtualized devices with no physical hardware counterparts. They function only in the context of virtual machines running under Hyper-V. Drivers for synthetic devices are included with the Integration Components for the guest operating system. The synthetic device drivers use the VMBus to communicate with the virtualized device software in the root partition.

Emulated or Legacy Device   Hyper-V provides the ability to run operating systems that were written to run on physical hardware and have no knowledge of what virtualization is. This applies to older operating systems, such as Windows NT and Windows 98. These are known as legacy operating systems. Hyper-V provides emulated or legacy hardware devices. A given device's functions are emulated entirely in software in order that the legacy operating systems can access whatever the physical device is on the host computer. For example, the legacy NIC is a software-emulated DEC 21140 network interface card. By providing this legacy network interface, legacy operating system environments can still operate under Hyper-V even though the host environment might have a totally different physical device.

Integration Components   Integration Components are a set of services and drivers that improve the integration and performance between the physical and virtual machines. These components enable the guest operating systems to use the higher-performing synthetic devices instead of emulated devices. This reduces the overhead required for the emulation of devices. Integration Components make use of the VMBus directly, thereby bypassing any emulation of a physical hardware device. Performance of synthetic devices with Integration Components approaches the performance of a physical device.

Integration Components provide the following capabilities to the supported operating systems:

♦ Synthetic devices (IDE, SCSI, NIC, video, mouse)

♦ OS shutdown

♦ Time synchronization

♦ Data exchange

♦ Heartbeat

♦ Volume Shadow Copy Services

Table 1.1 shows the operating systems with varying levels of Integration Component support. This can change, so it always makes sense to check sources at Microsoft. Microsoft publishes this information in the Hyper-V deployment document, but it is not in a tabular format. Be sure to refer to that document (`http://go.microsoft.com/fwlink/?LinkID=124368`) for the latest information.

Virtual Processors   Each child partition has one or more virtual processors, sometimes called cores or logical processors, associated with it. A virtual processor is a virtualized instance of an x86 or x64 processor complete with user-level and system-level registers.

Hyper-V does not use hard processor affinities, so a virtual processor may move from one physical processor to another, depending on how the individual thread gets scheduled. Hyper-V schedules virtual processors according to specified scheduling policies and constraints to try to maintain locality for better performance, but there may be situations that move a virtual processor from one physical core to another.

Address Translation   Any virtual memory system provides each application with a zero-based virtual address space. It then has a page table in memory that is used to map the virtual addresses to the physical addresses in the host.

A hypervisor introduces a second level of complexity into this. Because it allocates chunks of physical memory to each virtual machine, it needs to provide a physical memory virtualization facility to allow each partition to have a zero-based contiguous physical address space. Virtual processors support all the paging features and memory access modes that are supported in the physical environment so that the virtualized operating system runs the same in the virtual environment as it would in a physical environment.

To put this into practice, the hypervisor needs to implement two levels of address translation. The first level is what comes "out of the box" with the guest operating system environment. This is done via standard page tables maintained by the guest. Again, because we want the guest to run unmodified, this works exactly the same way as it would if the guest were installed on a physical host, except that the guest is writing to virtual memory instead of physical memory.

A second level of address translation is provided by the hypervisor without knowledge of the guest. This allows the hypervisor to virtualize physical memory, mapping guest virtual addresses to system physical addresses. The guest physical address space is defined at the time the partition is created.

TABLE 1.1: Hyper-V Integration Component support

Server OS	Synthetic IDE	Synthetic SCSI	Synthetic Network	Synthetic Video	Synthetic Mouse	OS Shutdown	Time Sync	Data Exchange	Heartbeat	VSS Support
Windows Server 2008 R2 x64	Yes	Yes	Yes	Yes	Yes	Yes	Yes	Yes	Yes	Yes
Windows Server 2008 x64	Yes	Yes	Yes	Yes	Yes	Yes	Yes	Yes	Yes	Yes
Windows Server 2008 x86	Yes	Yes	Yes	Yes	Yes	Yes	Yes	Yes	Yes	Yes
Windows Server 2003 SP2 x64	Yes	Yes	Yes	Yes	Yes	Yes	Yes	Yes	Yes	Yes
Windows Server 2003 SP2 x86	Yes	Yes	Yes	Yes	Yes	Yes	Yes	Yes	Yes	Yes
Windows 2000 Server SP4	Yes	No	Yes	Yes	Yes	Yes	Yes	Yes	Yes	No VSS support

OS										
SUSE Linux Enterprise Server 10 x64	Yes	Yes	Yes	No	No	No	No	No	No	No VSS support
SUSE Linux Enterprise Server 10 x86	Yes	Yes	Yes	No	No	No	No	No	No	No VSS support
Client OS										
Windows 7 x64	Yes	Yes	Yes	Yes	Yes	Yes	Yes	Yes	Yes	Yes
Windows 7 x86	Yes	Yes	Yes	Yes	Yes	Yes	Yes	Yes	Yes	Yes
Windows Vista SP1 x64	Yes	Yes	Yes	Yes	Yes	Yes	Yes	Yes	Yes	Yes
Windows Vista SP1 x86	Yes	Yes	Yes	Yes	Yes	Yes	Yes	Yes	Yes	Yes
Windows XP SP2/SP3 x86	Yes	Yes	Yes	Yes	Yes	Yes	Yes	Yes	Yes	No VSS support
Windows XP SP2 x64	Yes	Yes	Yes	Yes	Yes	Yes	Yes	Yes	Yes	No VSS support

Monolithic versus Microkernelized

Monolithic and microkernelized are the two primary approaches to creating hypervisors. The difference is in the functions that are considered part of the hypervisor. A monolithic hypervisor contains many more functions than does a microkernelized hypervisor.

MONOLITHIC

This implementation is less complex than writing a complete operating system because it is not likely to provide all the device drivers that a full operating system would have, but it is still a quite complex implementation. Figure 1.2 is a simplistic graphical representation of the monolithic architecture.

FIGURE 1.2
Monolithic hypervisor

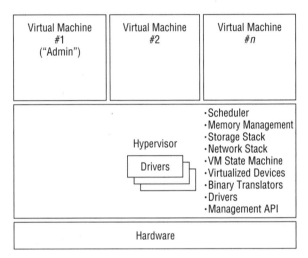

With this architecture, notice that the various hardware device drivers are part of the hypervisor, as well as many other components. This is needed because the monolithic hypervisor is really an operating system. It handles all the functions that one would generally expect in an operating system, such as scheduling, memory management, file systems, the driver stacks for all supported hardware, management interfaces, and so on. What are missing that you would find in a general-purpose operating system are those components for handling regular program execution.

MICROKERNELIZED

Microsoft's Hyper-V uses what Microsoft calls a microkernelized hypervisor. The terminology comes from the work that Carnegie Mellon University scientists performed in the late '80s and early '90s when they developed the concept of an operating system kernel that contained just the bare minimum of functions that needed to be performed at the highest privileged execution mode of the hardware. They called their kernel the Mach kernel. Figure 1.3 shows a simplistic graphical representation of the microkernelized architecture.

Notice that in the microkernelized architecture, only the functions that are absolutely required to share the hardware among the virtual machines are contained in the hypervisor. The scheduler provides the shared access to the physical cores or CPUs of the hosting machine, and the memory manager guarantees that no two virtual machines try to access the same physical memory. The other required functions of an operating system are found in the parent partition. With Windows Server 2008 Hyper-V, the parent partition runs the Windows Server 2008 operating system. This is how Microsoft gets Hyper-V to support all the systems and hardware devices that are supported by the Windows operating system.

FIGURE 1.3
Microkernelized
hypervisor

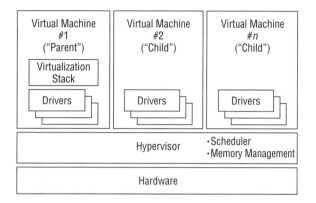

To understand why this is important, we need to look at how a typical operating system runs on x86 hardware. Execution of different functions is performed at different levels of the processor called rings, depending on how much access to the hardware is provided. The x86 hardware provides Rings 0–3. See Figure 1.4 for a diagram of the way Windows uses these rings.

FIGURE 1.4
Security rings

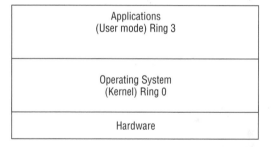

Generally, the lower ring values designate a higher level of system access privileges. Operating systems running on the x86 hardware architecture have used Ring 0 to designate the kernel of the operating system — the portion that requires direct access to the hardware. User code, or applications, is designated as Ring 3. User code has to talk to the operating system to gain access to the physical hardware.

This is important from a security perspective because we do not want a general-purpose user to have direct access to a resource that is shared with other users. That creates a major security hole in a system and major potential for instability. It also means that code that runs in Ring 0 must be very careful in how it executes in order to ensure the stability of the system. Most of the time when a system crashes, it is due to a problem in a device driver. Device drivers run in Ring 0.

This works quite well when there is only a single operating system running on a system, as it can arbitrate requests from multiple applications. But in a virtual environment, there are likely to be many guest operating systems. There needs to be a way to maintain control of all platform resources in order to ensure smooth operations. In order to maintain this control while multiple operating systems are running on a single physical server, the control should be placed at Ring 0, the highest privilege level on the CPU. However, all of today's operating systems are written to have their kernels run at Ring 0.

It is possible for software solutions to mitigate this. One method would be to insert a virtual machine manager that runs in Ring 0 to take control of the CPU whenever the guest operating system executes an instruction that could potentially cause conflict. The other method would be to modify the guest operating system prior to running it in a virtual environment. Both of these have been implemented, but each has shortcomings. Inserting a management component to trap instructions causes execution overhead. Modifying the operating system means you need to have a different version of the operating system for a virtual environment than is used in a physical environment.

AMD and Intel came to the rescue on this. They built hardware virtualization technology into their chips that allows specially written software to run at a level below the traditional Ring 0. Though the initial Intel architecture for the x86 family of processors did not have any levels beyond Rings 0 through 3, by placing certain components into some of the x86 64-bit family of processors, this critical control for sharing of resources can now be handled at a Ring-1 level. This ensures that the guest operating systems require no modification whatsoever in order to run, and they run very efficiently. This is known as the AMD-V and Intel-VT technologies.

Microsoft wrote its Hyper-V hypervisor to execute in this new ring. But since it executes at an even higher privilege level than the kernel of the operating system, Microsoft made sure that only those components that absolutely need to run at that level are running there. Figure 1.5 shows how this looks.

FIGURE 1.5
Security rings

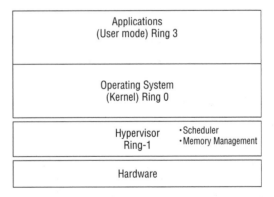

This implementation requires that Hyper-V be very tight code. No third-party code exists in the hypervisor. The code has been very carefully inspected by Microsoft and by outside security firms that Microsoft has brought in to review the code. This is to ensure that the code is as secure as possible and has a very, very low probability of breaking.

This implementation leaves the third-party code that comes in the form of device drivers in the kernel of the parent partition. In other words, the device drivers that are used by a Hyper-V system are the exact same device drivers that are used by a Windows Server 2008 operating system. Hardware vendors do not have to write a different set of drivers for Hyper-V, and they continue to write device drivers using the same tools and operating environments they are all familiar with. With the monolithic hypervisor, either the owner of the hypervisor needs to write new device drivers or the kernel needs to be opened to device driver writers.

The microkernelized architecture helps achieve three goals:

Isolation and Security   Hyper-V provides a high degree of isolation between partitions. Data that is in one partition cannot be viewed or manipulated by any other process except through well-defined communication paths, such as TCP/IP. In the next section on the parent partition, you will learn how the VMBus provides a path between the parent and child partitions. This is a special path that is used only for I/O to and from the physical devices owned by the parent partition.

Efficient Virtualization   Hyper-V supports efficient virtualization of processors, memory, and devices. The "virtualization tax," or overhead required to virtualize an operating system environment, is minimized.

Scalability   Hyper-V must provide scalability to large numbers of processors. The first release of Hyper-V supported 16 host cores. A patch increased that number to 24 host cores. Hyper-V R2 supports 64 host cores. As the number of cores in commodity servers increases, Microsoft will likely keep pace.

Parent Partition

Hyper-V provides isolation between the various instances of the operating systems by means of partitioning. A partition is a logical unit of isolation in which operating systems run. Hyper-V requires a parent, or root, partition running Windows Server 2008 x64 Edition. (As noted earlier, Microsoft Hyper-V Server 2008 is not a Windows Server, but it does run the Windows kernel.) The virtualization stack runs in the parent partition and has direct access to the hardware devices in order to share them among the child partitions. The root partition communicates with the hypervisor to create the child partitions that host the guest operating systems.

The parent partition is very important in the Hyper-V implementation. Until the Hyper-V role is installed on a system, there is no parent partition, and the Windows kernel operates directly on the hardware. See Figure 1.6 for a picture of what this looks like.

FIGURE 1.6
Operating system

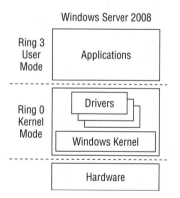

Installing the Hyper-V role on Windows Server 2008 causes the hypervisor to be installed between the physical hardware and the Windows kernel at system boot time. This immediately changes the installation of Windows Server 2008 into this special parent partition. This partition still owns all the physical resources of the system, but it now needs to provide additional services to the other partitions, known as child partitions. See Figure 1.7 for a detailed diagram of the way this environment now looks.

FIGURE 1.7
Parent partition

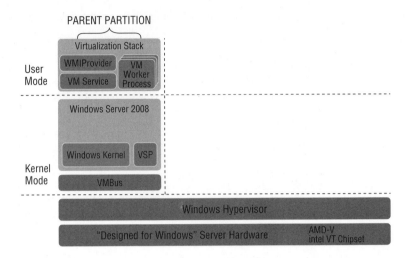

You will notice that there are now quite a few new pieces in the picture. Let's again start at the bottom and work our way up.

VMBus The VMBus is a high-speed memory communication mechanism used for interpartition communication and device enumeration on systems with multiple active virtualized partitions. If the host is running only the parent partition, this is not used. But when other child partitions are running, this is the means of communication between those child partitions that have the Hyper-V Integration Services installed.

Child partitions do not have direct access to the physical resources of the host platform. They are presented with virtual views, sometimes called virtual or synthetic devices. Synthetic devices take advantage of special Integration Components for storage, networking, graphics, and input subsystems. Integration Component I/O is a specialized virtualization-aware implementation of high-level communication protocols (such as SCSI) that utilize the VMBus directly, bypassing any device emulation layer.

Operating systems running in the child partitions make requests to the virtual devices. These requests are redirected via the VMBus to the devices in the parent partition, which handles the actual requests. This makes the communication more efficient but requires a guest that is hypervisor and VMBus aware via the Integration Components. Hyper-V I/O and a hypervisor-aware kernel are provided via installation of Hyper-V Integration Services.

The VMBus provides the means of communication between the virtual service provider, or VSP, in the parent partition and the virtual service client, or VSC, in the child partitions.

VSP The virtual service provider provides support for the synthetic devices, instantiated as VSCs, that are in use in the child partitions. The VSP is how the child partition gains access to the physical device on the host system. A synthetic device is the way to provide a guest an abstracted version of a well-defined device interface that can be mapped via the VSP to the physical device that is on the host system. This is the mechanism in the microkernelized hypervisor that ensures support for the full range of hardware platforms available to Windows Server 2008 instead of limiting the number based on specific device drivers included in a monolithic hypervisor.

Windows Server 2008 Kernel   The beauty of the microkernelized hypervisor is that the operating system kernel remains unchanged. The kernel, VMBus, device drivers, and VSP run in Ring 0 in the same manner on the hardware that the kernel and device drivers run in a nonvirtualized environment.

VM Worker Process   A VM worker process is created for each child partition that is created. This process is used to provide virtual machine management services from the parent partition to the guest operating system running in a child partition. The Virtual Machine Management Service spawns a separate worker process for each running virtual machine.

VM Service   The Virtual Machine Management Service is what creates the child partitions in which the guest operating system environments execute. It creates a separate process for each created child partition. Management tools communicate with this service to obtain information about the child processes.

WMI Provider   The VM Service exposes a set of Windows Management Instrumentation (WMI) APIs for managing and controlling virtual machines. This provides a common management interface to both physical and virtual machines, meaning you do not need to learn a different set of tools in order to manage the virtual machines.

Child Partitions

Child partitions contain the various operating system environments. Hyper-V accommodates three different types of partitions:

◆   Windows partitions with Integration Components

◆   Linux partitions with Integration Components

◆   OS partitions without Integration Components

The use of Integration Components is an optimization technique for a guest operating system to make it aware of virtual machine environments and to tune its behavior when it is running in a virtual environment. Integration Components help to reduce the overhead of certain operating system functions such as memory management or disk access.

There are Integration Components for several components that can be installed into operating systems via a menu option or command line. These Integration Components do not require changes to the operating system source code. Here is a list of the various services provided by Integration Components:

◆   Synthetic devices (IDE, SCSI, NIC, video, mouse)

◆   OS shutdown

◆   Time synchronization

◆   Data exchange

◆   Heartbeat

◆   Volume Shadow Copy Services

Figure 1.8 shows what a child partition running a Windows operating system environment looks like when it has Integration Components installed.

As you can see, the child partition does not have the various service providers and management components that exist in the parent partition, but there are pieces that act in parallel with components in the parent partition. Let's start at the bottom here and work our way up again, just as we did for the parent partition.

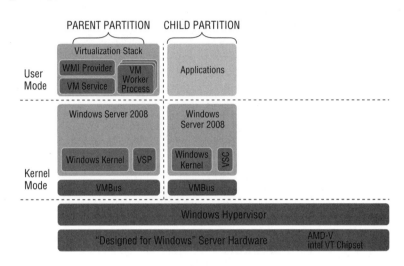

FIGURE 1.8
Integration Component
Windows child partition

VMBus   Any time Integration Components are used in an operating system environment, the VMBus will be used to provide the interpartition communication at a very high speed. The VSC communicates via the VMBus to talk to the VSP.

VSC   The virtual service client is the synthetic device instance that resides in a child partition. Installation of Integration Services or Integration Components (Microsoft uses both terms in their documentation) installs the VSCs, which then communicate over the VMBus to the VSP in the parent partition.

Windows Kernel   This is the off-the-shelf Windows kernel that is installed when the operating system is installed on physical hardware or in a virtual machine. No special code or special drivers are inserted into the Windows kernel to enable it to run in a virtual environment. The device drivers that are used are the device drivers that exist in the parent partition. The installation of the Integration Components installs the synthetic device drivers (VSC) for those operating systems for which Integration Components are available. Starting with Windows Server 2008 R2 and Windows 7, Microsoft includes the Integration Components in the distribution, so it is no longer necessary to install them separately.

Notice, too, that with the Hyper-V architecture, the kernel continues to run at Ring 0. Nothing is changed in the virtual environment from a security and isolation standpoint when compared to the physical environment.

Applications   This is what you are really interested in. Sure, it is fun to virtualize an operating system, but operating systems are there to control the running of the applications. The applications are the useful parts of the computer environment. Applications run in user mode, or Ring 3, just as they do in a physical environment. Applications make the same sort of requests to the operating system as they would in a physical environment. In other words, the applications will generally not even know they are running in a virtual environment. The exception to this would be when applications make calls for specific devices that may not be supported, such as USB dongles or fax boards.

One of the primary reasons for the lack of support of some of these types of devices is that when Microsoft was architecting this environment, they were looking at it from the standpoint of what a server environment needs. When you look at specialized devices such as a dongle, those are primarily used on desktop applications. Other devices, such as fax boards, are not supported because they are installed on such a small percentage of servers.

Some devices, such as smart cards, may be able to be passed through to the virtual operating system environment by making use of a remote desktop connection using the remote desktop protocol. Microsoft has built into all its operating systems the ability to remotely manage via the remote desktop protocol. Built into the client that uses this is the ability to share local (desktop) devices with the host to which a connection is being made. So, if you have a requirement in your environment to use smart cards on your servers, you can share your smart card via the remote desktop connection.

If you have a need for a USB or serial device for your application, there are companies that market network adapters for these devices. One such company is FabulaTech (www.fabulatech.com). I have not used any of these devices myself, but I have talked with others who have had success using them with Hyper-V.

Now let's look at another type of child partition — the Xen-enabled Linux kernel. Xen is another hypervisor designed for the Linux community that is quite similar in architecture to Hyper-V. This Linux child partition running in Hyper-V is very similar to a Windows child partition with Integration Components.

Figure 1.9 shows an architectural view of a child partition running a Xen-enabled version of the Linux kernel.

FIGURE 1.9
Xen-enabled Linux child partition

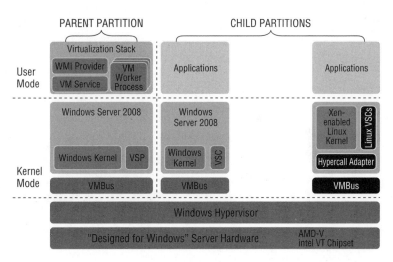

Notice that this is very similar to what a Windows child partition with Integration Components looks like. We have already covered the VMBus, so now we will examine the features that are unique to Xen-enabled partitions.

Hypercall Adapter   Nearly every capability Microsoft puts into its operating systems has an application programming interface (API) for communicating with that service. The APIs for Hyper-V are referred to as *hypercalls*. These are native in the Windows Server 2008 environment. When they are ported to another environment, such as the Xen-enabled Linux kernel environment, an equivalent package of tools needs to be built that talk to the defined inter-faces of the API. The hypercall adapter is that section of code for use by our partners to enable non-Windows child partitions to access the hypervisor.

Linux VSCs Since the Xen architecture is quite similar to the Hyper-V architecture, it is possi-ble to build a suite of VSCs for any distribution of Linux that has the kernel changes required to enable that distribution to run on the Xen hypervisor. These VSCs operate in exactly the same manner as the VSCs for the Windows integration components.

As of this writing, the Linux VSCs are available for SUSE Linux Enterprise Server 10 for both 32-bit and 64-bit. Work is under way on the Red Hat distribution. More changes are likely to occur as time goes on, so be sure to check `www.microsoft.com/windowsserver2008/en/us/hyperv-supported-guest-os.aspx` for the latest information about which distributions are supported.

Microsoft recently submitted code to the Linux kernel under GPL V2. This code provides the Integration Components with the synthetic drivers for upcoming versions of the Linux kernel. When incorporated into the kernel of any Linux distribution, this will provide VSCs for that Linux distribution.

Okay, now we will take a look at the last type of child partition. Figure 1.10 shows the struc-ture of an operating system that has no knowledge of virtualization. These operating systems are sometimes called legacy operating systems, particularly when talking about older versions of Windows such as Windows NT Server or Windows 98.

FIGURE 1.10
OS child partition without Integration Components

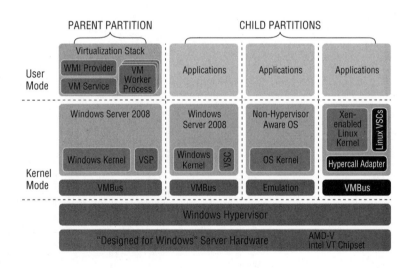

Child partitions without integration components do not have access to the VMBus or VSCs. They are called legacy because they do not have support for the synthetic devices to improve performance or minimize the virtualization tax. Hardware components are emulated in soft-ware, like the hybrid hypervisor explained earlier. The emulation layer provides the translation from the device drivers in the operating system to the parent partition. As noted earlier, soft-ware emulation of hardware devices is expensive in terms of performance. What may take a few instructions in hardware may take thousands of instructions in software. As a result, you will likely see systems operating at a lower level of performance than their brothers and sisters running with Integration Components.

Hyper-V Technical Specifications

One of the beauties of making Hyper-V a role of the Windows Server 2008 operating system is that it can make use of all the hardware and software innovations that are continually being developed for the host platform. To start with, Hyper-V is a role in Windows Server 2008 Standard Edition, Enterprise Edition, and Datacenter Edition. Depending on the specific need, the proper edition of the operating system can be deployed and still be used to provide virtualization capabilities.

Let's look at the specifics of what is required to run Hyper-V. Then we will look at the capabilities that are available.

Hardware Requirements

To install and use the Hyper-V role, you will need the following:

- ◆ A Designed for Windows x64–based processor. Hyper-V is available in x64–based versions of Windows Server 2008 — specifically, the x64–based versions of Windows Server 2008 Standard, Windows Server 2008 Enterprise, and Windows Server 2008 Datacenter Editions.

- ◆ Hardware-assisted virtualization. This is available in processors that include a virtualization option; specifically, Intel VT or AMD Virtualization (AMD-V). Hardware virtualization is defined in the BIOS and needs to be enabled, as it is typically off by default.

- ◆ Hardware Data Execution Prevention (DEP) must be available and be enabled. Specifically, you must enable Intel XD bit (execute disable bit) or AMD NX bit (no execute bit). As with hardware virtualization, DEP is enabled in the BIOS.

- ◆ Enough memory (RAM) to run the Windows kernel (at least 1 GB, but 2 GB is better) and to run one or more virtual machines.

DESIGNED FOR WINDOWS

Hyper-V requires an x64 system, a 64-bit hardware platform that is built with the x86 instruction set. Supported systems are limited to those systems that carry the Designed for Windows logo in the Windows catalog. Go to www.windowsservercatalog.com and select the server category. From the Server page, you will find a category specifically for Hyper-V–capable systems. This gives the customer the broadest possible selection of supported host systems. This also ensures that any storage and network card that are supported on those host systems can be used by the virtual machines. This is significantly different from a software-emulated environment, which limits the execution environment to the hardware that is emulated by software. It is also different from some other virtualization vendors that limit the selection of host, storage, and network to those particular systems and devices for which they have written their own device drivers.

HARDWARE VIRTUALIZATION

Both the major x86/x64 chip vendors, Intel and AMD, have worked to include features in their chips to provide hardware-assisted virtualization. These features offload to hardware some of the things that would have been done in software to streamline execution and boost performance. Intel's implementation is called Intel-VT (for Virtualization Technology); see `www.intel.com/technology/virtualization`. AMD's implementation is called AMD-V (for Virtualization); see `www.amd.com/us-en/0,,3715_15781_15785,00.html`.

Hyper-V requires either an Intel-VT or AMD-V chip. Several years ago Intel and HP developed another 64-bit chip called Itanium, and its architecture is often referred to as IA64. Hyper-V is not supported on IA64 platforms. It is only for the x64 platform.

DATA EXECUTION PREVENTION

Microsoft is very serious about building security into its products. Intel and AMD are also concerned about building whatever capabilities they can into their chips to enhance security. Both chip vendors have implemented a feature called Data Execution Prevention. In a nutshell, this feature prevents the execution of instructions in areas of a program that is defined as containing only data. This is a common way that hackers can cause problems in code with things such as buffer overflows. Hyper-V requires either Intel-XD or AMD-NX enabled on the chip.

Real World Scenario

SHERMAN, SET THE WABAC MACHINE TO 1973

When I was an assembly code developer, which was well before the days of the Internet and script-kiddies, I would regularly define a block of data as my patch area. Because it took so long to compile code back then, it was generally much quicker to find the offending instruction, change it to a branch instruction to branch to the patch area, put in the corrected code, and then branch back to the regular code by using binary patch methods. (Believe it or not, this was even sometimes done with punch cards when punch cards were used to start and control execution of the program.) In fact, this was such a common procedure that COBOL even had an ALTER statement that could be built into the code and could be executed if certain conditions were met. Hackers learned to quickly exploit the ability to execute instructions that existed in areas defined as data. A prime example of this sort of exploit is called buffer overrun.

Early exploits, and ease of doing this, showed the need for a stricter definition of what was data and what was code in a program. As that got better defined, it became easier to implement capabilities in the hardware to enforce the data execution protection. Therefore, Intel implements what it calls XD (for execute disable). AMD implements what it calls NX (for no execute).

Hyper-V Capabilities

There are many ways to define features or capabilities. Many of the other chapters in this book about Hyper-V will explain various operational features and capabilities and how to use them. In this section, we will look at the technical features, generally thought of as how one can configure virtual machines. First, we will look at what sort of system is supported for the host. Then we will look at the options available for configuring virtual machines.

HOST SYSTEM

Microsoft has two different ways of implementing the Hyper-V hypervisor. There are slightly different hardware requirements for the host systems.

Windows Server 2008 Hyper-V

- Designed for Windows x64 host
  - AMD-V or Intel-VT hardware virtualization in the chip
  - Data Execution Prevention
- Recommended processor speed: 2 GHz or faster
- Windows Server 2008 Standard, Enterprise, or Datacenter Edition
- Up to 16 processors or cores
  - KB956710 increases this to 24 cores only for those systems that have Intel's 6-core chip.
  - The maximum number of cores supported by Hyper-V is the same for each edition of Windows Server 2008, but the maximum number of physical processors varies according to edition:
    - Standard Edition — up to 4 processors
    - Enterprise Edition — up to 8 processors
    - Datacenter Edition — up to 64 processors
  - Windows Server 2008 Hyper-V R2 increases this number to 64 cores.
- Up to 1 TB memory for Windows Server 2008 Enterprise and Datacenter Editions. Standard Edition supports a maximum of 32 GB of memory.
- At least one network interface card (NIC)
  - Recommend one NIC for host server management
  - Recommend at least one NIC for virtual machine communication
  - Recommend at least one NIC dedicated to iSCSI if using iSCSI storage
  - Recommend at least one NIC for cluster communication if the systems are configured in a failover cluster
- Storage to host the parent partition, virtual machines, and associated data
  - Direct-attached storage: Serial Advanced Technology Attachment (SATA), external Serial Advanced Technology Attachment (eSATA), Parallel Advanced Technology Attachment (PATA), Serial Attached SCSI (SAS), SCSI, USB, and IEEE 1394 (sometimes known as FireWire)
  - Storage area networks (SANs): Internet SCSI (iSCSI), Fibre Channel, and SAS technologies

Microsoft Hyper-V Server 2008

The hardware configuration options for a Hyper-V Server host are very similar to those of Windows Server 2008 Hyper-V in that the host supports the Windows-certified hardware components. Since this is designed for a more restrictive set of uses, there are some limitations when compared to Windows Server 2008 Hyper-V.

- A host with up to 32 GB of physical memory

- A host with up to four physical processors (maximum of 24 logical processors)

- Guest with a maximum of 31 GB of memory

Because this is not a Windows operating system (it is just the Windows kernel), it does not support features of the operating system such as failover clustering. In order to ensure that it fits within a corporate environment, management agents such as antivirus and System Center Operations Manager can be installed. The hardware limitations are the same limitations that exist for Windows Server 2008 Standard Edition.

Microsoft Hyper-V Server 2008 R2 significantly increases the capabilities.

- A host with up to 1 TB of physical memory

- A host with up to eight physical processors (maximum of 64 logical processors)

- Guests with a maximum of 64 GB of memory

- Support for Failover Clusters and Live Migration

SUPPORTED VIRTUAL MACHINES

A point that often confuses people is the word *support*. The term *supported* can easily be misconstrued. Microsoft defines *supported* to mean that it either owns the code or has a support agreement with another organization that does have access to the code so that errors can be fixed at the source level. For example, when Microsoft says that it does not support other operating systems, it means that it does not have a way to gain access to the code in order to change it. That becomes pretty obvious when you consider any product that is not owned by Microsoft. Since Microsoft does not own the code, it cannot make changes to that code if a problem occurs. This does *not* imply that simply because it is not supported, it does not work. So, the list of supported operating systems that follows includes those operating system environments to which Microsoft can make changes or have changes made.

- Guest operating system support

    - Windows Server 2008 and 2008 R2 x64/x86

    - Windows Server 2003 SP2 x64/x86

    - Windows Server 2000 SP4 x86

    - Windows Web Server 2008 and 2008 R2 x64/x86

    - Windows HPC Server 2008 and 2008 R2 x64

    - SUSE Linux Enterprise Server 10 and 11 x64/x86

    - Red Hat Enterprise Linus 5.2 and 5.3 x64/x86

    - Windows 7 x64/x86

    - Windows Vista SP1 x64/x86 (not Home editions)

    - Windows XP Professional SP2/SP3 x64/x86

◆ Always check www.microsoft.com/windowsserver2008/en/us/hyperv-supported
-guest-os.aspx for the latest details. This list will change as more operating system
environments are tested and added.

◆ Nonsupported operating system environments

◆ Hyper-V has the ability to run other x64 and x86 operating system environments.
Though some of these other operating system environments may run fine, Microsoft
has not done any testing on these environments, so they do not fall under the support
statement defined above.

◆ 1-, 2-, or 4-processor virtual machine

◆ Up to 64 GB of memory for each guest, depending on OS

◆ Up to 12 network interface cards (NIC)

◆ Up to 8 synthetic

◆ Up to 4 legacy

◆ Static or dynamic MAC addresses

◆ VLAN support

◆ Disks

◆ IDE

◆ SCSI

◆ iSCSI

◆ Virtual hard drives (VHD) up to 2040 GB in size

◆ Pass-through disks (direct connection to disk connected to the host) — size limited by
operating system. Windows currently has a limit of a 256 TB volume.

◆ USB devices

◆ Mouse

◆ Keyboard

◆ Disks and NICs connected to the host (more detail on this in the chapter on storage and
networking)

◆ Hyper-V does not provide direct access to any USB devices, other than the keyboard
and mouse. Some nonsupported USB devices, such as a smart card reader, can be used
in a virtual machine by using the USB device-recognition capabilities of the remote
desktop.

◆ Documented Windows Management Instrumentation (WMI) interfaces for scripting and
management. For more information on the WMI interface, see http://go.microsoft.com/
fwlink/?LinkID=108564.

◆ Snapshots of at-rest or running virtual machines. Up to 50 snapshots per VM can be taken.

- Virtual CD/DVD drive

  - A virtual machine has one virtual CD/DVD by default.

  - Virtual machines can be configured with up to three CD/DVD drives, connected to IDE controllers. (Virtual machines support up to four IDE devices, but one device must be the startup disk.)

  - A virtual CD/DVD drive can access CD or DVD physical media or ISO files. However, only one virtual machine can be configured to access the physical CD/DVD drive of the host system at a time.

- Virtual COM port — Each virtual machine is configured with two virtual serial (COM) ports that can be attached to a named pipe to communicate with a local or remote physical computer. This is software-only access — no access to the physical COM ports on the host.

- Virtual floppy drive — this is a software-only floppy drive used for accessing `.vfd` (virtual floppy drive) files.

The capabilities shown above are the basic capabilities that come with the Hyper-V. In subsequent chapters you will learn about more advanced capabilities such as Live Migration, snapshots, Cluster Shared Volumes, backup of running virtual machines, built-in high availability, hot add/remove of storage, and more. As you learn about these capabilities, think of how they can be applied in your particular environment to help you implement a dynamic virtual environment.

The Bottom Line

Microsoft's history in virtualization   Microsoft has introduced multiple products for virtualizing the x86 architecture.

> **Master It**   List the three products that Microsoft has released that provide the capability to virtualize the x86 or x64 architecture.

Monolithic versus microkernelized virtualization architectures   Monolithic and microkernelized are the two primary approaches to creating hypervisors. The difference is the amount of code between the virtual machine and the physical hardware on which it is running.

> **Master It**   List the components that exist in the monolithic hypervisor. List the components that exist in the microkernelized hypervisor.

Hardware requirements   Not all systems are capable of running Hyper-V.

> **Master It**   List the minimum requirements of the host system for installing and running Hyper-V.

Chapter 2

Installing, Configuring, and Managing the Hyper-V Host

When dealing with server virtualization, you have two different environments to install, configure, and manage. You first have to build the host environment. Once that is accomplished, the virtual machines can be built. Building your server virtualization on Microsoft's Hyper-V platform provides a number of similarities between the physical and virtual setup, because the host often uses the exact same commands to set up an environment as the virtual machines do.

In this chapter you will learn about:

◆ Installing the Hyper-V role

◆ Remotely administering Hyper-V Server

◆ Backing up Windows Server

Installation

When I was writing this book, Microsoft was reporting more than 1,200 server systems certified to run Windows Server 2008 x64. Of that number, over 95 percent are certified to run Hyper-V. This points out that, even though most OEM servers support Hyper-V, you need to be sure that the system you plan to use for running Hyper-V is capable. To make this easy, Microsoft keeps a web page (www.windowsservercatalog.com) of all the hardware and software that has been certified for use with Windows Server. If you are purchasing your hardware from a mainstream vendor, it is easy to look up your particular model on this list to check that it is has been certified to run Hyper-V. Microsoft even has a section devoted specifically to those systems. Go to the above-referenced URL. In the middle column, under the heading Hardware, select Servers. On the left-hand side of the page that comes up, you will see the heading Additional Qualifications. Select Hyper-V from those qualifications for a list of all the certified systems submitted by vendors.

This makes it easy if you are purchasing a certified system. But for testing purposes you may be installing on a "white box" or a system that you have built yourself. I actually do most of my work on a laptop, and I have never seen a laptop on the list of certified Windows Server platforms! If this is what you are doing, you still need to meet the same basic virtualization prerequisites of the fully certified systems. You will not have a fully certified system, but you will most likely have a system that will run Hyper-V just fine.

Hardware

Hyper-V requires specific hardware capabilities:

♦ An x64 (64-bit) processor from Intel or AMD that supports hardware-assisted virtualization. This is available in Intel VT and AMD-V processors.

♦ Hardware Data Execution Prevention (DEP) must be available and be enabled. Intel calls theirs the XD bit (execute disable bit), and AMD calls theirs the NX bit (no execute bit).

These two requirements are absolute. Hyper-V will not run if you do not have both of these hardware features.

♦ At least 1–2 GB of RAM for the parent partition, plus enough memory for the number of virtual machines you plan on running.

♦ A minimum of 10–20 GB for the system drive, but a recommended 40 GB.

♦ At least one NIC, but two or more are preferred.

Windows Server 2008 was released with versions that run on 32-bit processors and both types of 64-bit processors — the x64 and the IA64. Hyper-V cannot run on a 32-bit processor or an IA64 processor. Neither of these processors has the hardware-assisted virtualization capability. Then, once you have selected an x64 processor with hardware-assisted virtualization, you have to ensure that it has DEP. Not all x64 processors were built with this function. Generally speaking, x64 processors installed in server systems built in the last couple of years are okay. But there are quite a few earlier x64 processors that did not have either hardware-assisted virtualization or DEP, and both of those functions are required. Also remember that Hyper-V requires a 64-bit Windows Server 2008 operating system. The x64 architecture can run a 32-bit version of the Windows operating system, but the Hyper-V role cannot be installed on that 32-bit version.

BIOS Settings

Not only does Hyper-V have specific hardware requirements — hardware-assisted virtualization and DEP — but those requirements must also be enabled on the system. Both hardware-assisted virtualization and DEP are turned on and off in the BIOS of the system. It is not always obvious what the BIOS settings are, though. Different vendors name these options different things. And, to make it a little more interesting, DEP is sometimes on by default with no option to turn it off or on, or it is tied to the hardware virtualization setting.

To determine if your particular system supports these features, check with the manufacturer of your system or the BIOS on a homemade system. Or, there are free utilities available from the Web that can run a quick check. Some examples are CPU-Z (`www.cpuid.com/cpuz .php`), Securable (`www.grc.com/securable.htm`), Intel Processor Identification Utility (`http:// downloadcenter.intel.com/Detail_Desc.aspx?agr=N&ProductID=1881&DwnldID=7838`), and AMD Hyper-V Compatibility Check Utility (`/www.amd.com/us-en/assets/content_type/ utilities/AMD-V_Hyper-V_Compatibility_Check_Utility.zip`).

If you run one of these utilities *after* you have installed Hyper-V, the output will indicate that the system does not support Hyper-V. Why is this? Well, remember the architecture discussion from Chapter 1. When you turn on the Hyper-V role in the operating system, the parent partition becomes simply another virtual instance, albeit a special one. Hardware virtualization is not available inside a virtual instance — it is available only at the physical hardware level. When you run the utility, you are running it in the parent partition, and the parent partition, as a virtual machine, cannot identify hardware virtualization.

I would give instructions on how to get into the BIOS settings of your computer, except they vary so much from one motherboard manufacturer to another. Generally it requires depressing a specific function key early in the boot process. Please see the manufacturer's documentation on your motherboard for information on how to get into and modify the BIOS settings.

Once you have made the appropriate changes to the BIOS of your system, you need to power-cycle the system. For these particular BIOS changes, simply restarting the machine does not make the changes. The system has to be completely powered off and then powered back on. I have not had this happen, but I have heard multiple reports of certain systems that even required the power cord to be removed before the BIOS settings would take effect.

I have also heard of some AMD systems that do not have a BIOS option to turn on AMD-V. They already come with AMD-V enabled and there is no way to turn it on or off. So you can use CPU-Z, Securable, or AMD's utility to determine the system's ability to run Hyper-V.

Host Operating System

Once you have prepared the system by making the appropriate BIOS settings, you are ready to install Hyper-V. These prerequisites, chip set and BIOS settings, are exactly the same whether you install on Windows Server 2008 Full, Windows Server 2008 Core, or Microsoft Hyper-V Server 2008.

When Microsoft released Windows Server 2008 to the market, they released multiple stock keeping units (SKUs):

Windows Server 2008 Datacenter Edition

Windows Server 2008 Enterprise Edition

Windows Server 2008 Standard Edition

Windows Web Server 2008

Windows Server 2008 for Itanium-based Systems

Windows Server 2008 Datacenter Edition without Hyper-V

Windows Server 2008 Enterprise Edition without Hyper-V

Windows Server 2008 Standard Edition without Hyper-V

All these editions, with the exception of Itanium, are available in either an x86 32-bit (sometimes known as IA32) or x86 64-bit (referred to as x64) version. Itanium is Intel's brand name of the IA64 architecture. As mentioned earlier, Hyper-V is not available to run on either 32-bit editions or the Itanium (IA64) editions of the operating system. Nor is it available to run on the Web version. It is available to install only on x64 Standard, Enterprise, or Datacenter Editions.

Now, even though I said it is not possible to run Hyper-V on any of the 32-bit editions of Windows Server 2008, the 32-bit SKUs also come with and without Hyper-V. What this really means is that you can install the Hyper-V Remote Management tools feature to manage Hyper-V from a 32-bit platform that has the "with" SKU, but you cannot manage it from a 32-bit platform that has the "without" SKU. Confusing? It is a bit, but just remember that if you want to run or manage a Hyper-V environment, be sure to obtain a SKU that does not have the "without Hyper-V" tag in its name. With the release of Windows Server 2008 R2,

Microsoft recognized some of the confusion caused by the "with" and "without" SKUs, so there is no longer a "without" SKU in this release.

One last note about the 32-bit version of Windows Server 2008 is that this is the last 32-bit release of the Windows Server operating system. All future releases, starting with R2, will be 64-bit only, either x64 or IA64. For a couple years now, the mainstream hardware vendors have been producing only 64-bit server hardware. Yes, it is still possible to install and run a 32-bit operating system on x64 hardware. But the demand has been changing because of the power and scalability of the 64-bit platform, so Microsoft is changing with the industry.

Microsoft Hyper-V Server 2008 is a separate, free download that installs a kernel based on the Windows kernel with the Hyper-V hypervisor. It is not considered a version or edition of Windows Server 2008, but its installation procedure is quite similar to installing Windows Server 2008 Core. Even though it is not considered a Windows Server operating system, it has the exact same hardware prerequisites as Windows Server Standard Edition. Microsoft Hyper-V Server 2008 increases some of the limits, such as number of processors and amount of memory supported, to more closely match the limits of Windows Server 2008 Enterprise Edition.

It is important that you decide up front what you want your final installation to look like. If you install Microsoft Hyper-V Server 2008, there is no way to upgrade that to Windows Server Core or Windows Server Full — it takes a complete installation that wipes the initial installation and replaces it with the new installation. The same is true when you upgrade from Windows Server Core to Windows Server Full. There is no upgrade from Core to Full, nor is there a downgrade from Full to Core. If you want to change, you have to do a complete install. Lastly, if you installed a SKU without Hyper-V, it is not possible to simply copy some files over and make it into a regular Windows Server installation. That, too, requires a complete installation to make the change.

Installation of the Windows Server 2008 operating system is the first thing that must be done before installing Hyper-V as a role on either a Full or Core installation. There is plenty of guidance on Microsoft's website to assist you in this. Besides, Microsoft has actually made it so simple to install via its installation wizard that even a neophyte should be able to do the base installation fairly easily. The next sections explain how to install the Hyper-V role onto an existing installation of Windows Server 2008, either Full or Core. I've also included instructions on installing Hyper-V Server 2008, even though its installation is a one-step process of installing both the operating system and the integrated Hyper-V role.

SELECTING THE APPROPRIATE HOST OPERATING ENVIRONMENT

Before you learn to install, you need to learn the different options you have on what to install. As you can see, Microsoft provides several options for the host platform. With the Windows Server operating system, you can choose Standard, Enterprise, or Datacenter Edition with the Hyper-V role and install that as either a Full installation or a Core installation. Or you can select Microsoft Hyper-V Server as a free download. How do you know which to select?

There are several factors that will help you decide what to run on the host hardware platform. There may be others that different businesses bring into their selection matrix, but I believe these to be the primary ones.

◆ Scalability — how many virtual machines you may want to run on a single hardware platform.

◆ High Availability — virtual machines running on one node in a cluster are automatically restarted on another node should the original node fail.

♦ Manageability — install with the full graphical user interface for managing the host locally or use the core installation without the graphical user interface and manage remotely with graphical tools.

♦ Licensing — some of the legal constraints to ensure you have properly licensed your environment.

Table 2.1 shows some criteria for helping you decide what should be installed on the host.

TABLE 2.1:   Host limits

	PROCESSORS	MEMORY	HIGH AVAILABILITY	RIGHT TO RUN
MS Hyper-V	4	32 GB	No	0
Standard	4	32 GB	No	1 or 1
Enterprise	8	1 TB	Yes	4
Datacenter	64	1 TB	Yes	Unlimited
MS Hyper-V R2	8	1 TB	Yes	0
Standard R2	4	32 GB	No	1
Enterprise R2	8	1 TB	Yes	4
Datacenter R2	256	1 TB	Yes	Unlimited

Scalability   The number of virtual machines that can physically be run is dependent on the hardware resources available. For example, every virtual machine requires memory. Enterprise Edition supports more physical memory than Standard Edition does. If you have a small environment, say a remote office, and you want to run only one or two virtual machines, you will most likely not need more than four processors and more than 32 GB of physical memory. It could cost you less to choose Standard Edition instead of Enterprise or Datacenter Edition.

At the other end of the spectrum, if you are going to be running 10 virtual machines, each one of them requiring 4 GB of memory, that is more memory than Standard Edition can use. In that case, you would have to use either Enterprise or Datacenter Edition.

High Availability   High availability provides you a capability to have virtual machines that are running on one host to automatically restart on another host in a cluster should the first host fail. Microsoft's high availability option is also the basis of the ability to move a running virtual machine from one host in a cluster to another. This is covered in more detail in Chapter 5. This option is available as part of the Enterprise and Datacenter Editions of Windows Server 2008. With the release of R2, Microsoft also included this capability as part of Microsoft Hyper-V Server.

Manageability   When installing Windows Server 2008, you have the option of selecting either a Full installation or a Core installation. The Full installation is what you are most likely used to with Windows. It provides a graphical user interface for managing the environment and for running additional applications. The benefit of running Hyper-V on the Full installation is that it provides you with the GUI you are familiar with for managing your environment. It also allows you to run any other server role/feature that is available for the operating system.

The Core installation includes the core components of the operating system, such as security, networking, and file services. But it does not include things like Windows Explorer or Internet Explorer, nor does it contain the framework to run many of the graphical management programs.

By eliminating the graphical components, Microsoft provides an environment that requires fewer patches and fewer reboots. However, it also means that you will either manage everything from the command line or use remote tools for graphically managing a Core installation. If you do not feel comfortable managing a server without a GUI management interface on it, by all means use the Full installation.

Microsoft's recommendation is to use the Core installation with just the Hyper-V role installed. This ensures that the entire system is dedicated to running the virtual workload. And by having fewer reboots, the host system will not cause as many additional interruptions to the virtual machines as would occur when running a Full installation that has more reboots.

These are just some of the considerations for using a Full installation versus a Core installation. Many companies will develop additional criteria.

Licensing   Lastly, how are you going to license your environment? When it comes to licensing, the basic piece of information you need to use for planning is that licenses are not assigned to virtual machines; they are assigned to the physical host on which the virtual machines run. To make it easier to license in a virtual environment, Microsoft includes the right to run a certain number of Windows Server virtual instances for each Windows Server 2008 license you purchase. For example, looking at Table 1.1 you see that Enterprise Edition comes with the right to run up to four Windows virtual instances. This means that you can install the Enterprise Edition on the host system, install the Hyper-V role, and legally run up to four instances of Windows Server as virtual machines. If you want to run more than four, you have three options:

◆ Purchase additional Standard Edition licenses and assign them to the host, receiving the right to run a single virtual instance for each additional license.

◆ Purchase another Enterprise Edition license and assign it to the host, providing up to four more virtual instances.

◆ Upgrade to a Datacenter Edition license, which gives you the right to run an unlimited number of Windows Server virtual instances.

Since Microsoft Hyper-V Server does not come with the right to run any instances, this means that you need to either transfer existing licenses from their current physical hosts to the Hyper-V Server host or purchase the appropriate Windows Server 2008 license to cover your planned virtual instances but simply install the Hyper-V Server.

This is a very simplistic explanation to give you an idea about how to decide which platform to run on. Microsoft has a complete explanation of their licensing at www.microsoft.com/licensing. My explanation here does not cover it in the detail you need to know in order to be legal, so I would suggest that you go to Microsoft's site and download their Product Use Rights for a complete explanation.

WINDOWS SERVER 2008 FULL

As mentioned earlier, some benefits of the Full installation include the GUI you are used to and the ability to run any other server role. Even though any other server role can be run, Microsoft does recommend that you run just the Hyper-V role. Since you are running one or more virtual machines on Hyper-V, you will not necessarily want to have required maintenance on other roles that might require a reboot to negatively impact the up time of your virtual machines.

Manually installing Hyper-V on a Full installation of Windows Server 2008 is pretty simple. This is one of the beauties of the way Microsoft has defined specific roles for different capabilities of the operating system. They have also provided a wizard to make it even easier

One thing needs to be noted, though. If you are using media from what Microsoft calls the release to manufacturing (RTM) version of the operating system, the version of Hyper-V on that media is a beta copy. In other words, the binaries for Hyper-V are not the final binaries. In order to get the final binaries, you need to install a patch that comes as KB950050 of the release version of the Hyper-V technology for Windows Server 2008 (http://support .microsoft.com/?kbid=950050).

If you are using media that contains Windows Server 2008 SP2, it already contains the KB950050 patch. This means that you do not need to install that patch because it is applied if you start with an installation that includes SP2. Similarly, if you install Windows Server 2008 R2, you will immediately have Hyper-V R2.

When deploying Hyper-V on a small number of machines, it is not too difficult to manually install Hyper-V and install the patch. But if you are going to be repeatedly installing across a larger set of servers, you will want to look at some automated ways of installing. In the next sections you will find out how to install both manually and with some more automated tools.

Server Manager Wizard

Server Manager is the default management console for a Full installation of Windows Server 2008. By default, after you have installed Windows Server 2008, Server Manager starts automatically whenever you log into the administrator account. If you have disabled that, you will have to manually start Server Manager. Click Start, and then click Server Manager.

1. In the Roles Summary area of the Server Manager main window, click Add Roles.

2. The Before You Begin page comes up. This explains the Add Roles Wizard. Click Next to continue to the next step in the wizard. (If you do not want to see this introductory window pop up anymore when you select the Add Roles Wizard, click the Skip This Page By Default box.)

3. On the Select Server Roles page, click Hyper-V.

4. On the Create Virtual Networks page, click one or more network adapters that you want to use for virtual machines.

   ◆ Though it is not an absolute requirement, it is highly recommended that you have two or more NICs on the Hyper-V host system. One of these NICs should be reserved (in other words, do not select it) for the purpose of managing the host over the network. The rest of the NICs can be assigned for use by the virtual machines, if desired.

   ◆ If you have only one NIC, or you assign all NICs for use by virtual machines, you will lose network connectivity to the host when you confirm the installation. This is because any NIC selected for use by virtual machines unbinds the physical NIC from the IPv4 and IPv6 protocols and binds it to the Microsoft Virtual Network Switch Protocol.

5. On the Confirm Installation Selections page, click Install.

6. The computer must be restarted to complete the installation, because installing this role adds the loading of the hypervisor into the boot process (remember the explanation in Chapter 1 that describes where the hypervisor runs). Click Close to finish the wizard.

7. Click Yes to restart the computer. After the computer restarts (it actually reboots twice), log on with the same account you used to install the Hyper-V role. This ensures that the Resume Configuration Wizard completes the Hyper-V role installation. Click Close to finish the wizard.

8. Whether you are installing Windows Server 2008 RTM or R2, a best practice is to run Windows Update as soon as possible. In particular, with Windows Server 2008 RTM, you must run Windows Update to get the update for Hyper-V (KB950050). If you do not apply this patch to RTM code, you will still have the beta copy of Hyper-V.

Hyper-V is now ready for configuration.

But before we get into configuring Hyper-V, I want to give an introduction to some other tools from Microsoft that assist in deploying operating systems in more automated ways. The tools work on both physical machines and virtual machines. I will go into a little more detail on one tool, sysprep, because it is often used with some of the other tools.

The first tool makes use of imaging — making a master image of an installation that can be used to repeatedly install the operating system environment without the need of going through all the steps you just went through above. The second method is called unattended installation. With this method, you basically capture the manual steps into a control file, and the contents of that control file drive the installation. This is introductory material, and I provide pointers to where you can learn more from Microsoft's website.

Imaging

Microsoft has built deployment tools to assist in rapidly deploying many copies of the operating system. For more information, go to www.microsoft.com/downloads and search for "deployment toolkit." You will find detailed instructions and a suite of tools to automate the deployment of Windows operating systems.

I am going to explain how to use one particular component of the imaging process. The concept behind this is to create a master image of the operating system you want to deploy. This is done by first going through the manual steps you learned above to install, patch, and configure an image the way you want it. Once that master image is created, the image is prepared so that it can be used over and over to install the operating system in significantly less time than it takes to do it manually. This is different from other cloning techniques that you may read about on the Internet. Other cloning techniques create an exact copy of the installed image. Microsoft's method ensures that each image deployed is unique, just as if it had been installed manually. This master image is prepared with a utility called sysprep.

Sysprep is a utility that has come with every version of Windows since Windows NT 4.0. Its purpose is to create an image that can be used to clone an operating system configuration in a supportable manner. There are other tools on the market that claim to be able to do the same thing, but this is the only method that is officially supported by Microsoft. Very simply, it prepares the system to be imaged and then installed again and again by removing all the unique identifiers within the base image. All these unique identifiers are re-created when the sysprepped image is used to create a new system, ensuring that each installed instance is unique in the environment.

To create a sysprep image, you first build a host system with all the components you want on it. That means for the first image, you will need to use Server Manager to install Hyper-V and apply all the patches. This is a good time to include other common components, such as antivirus products. I am not going to go into all the details about all the capabilities of sysprep here. For that you can consult TechNet at `http://technet.microsoft.com/en-us/library/cc766514.aspx`. I am just going to tell you how to use sysprep so you can use it to deploy multiple instances of Hyper-V in a quick manner.

The sysprep utility is unique for each release of the operating system, so always use the sysprep utility from the host system that you are preparing. The utility can be found in `%windir%\System32\sysprep\sysprep.exe`. It can be executed either via the command line or in a GUI. Launching it without any parameters on the command line brings up the GUI. Since we want to select only a couple of options, the GUI is the easiest way to do this. Figure 2.1 shows you the sysprep GUI without any selections.

FIGURE 2.1
Sysprep GUI

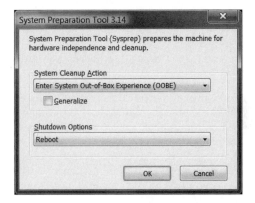

We want to use the Generalize option, so click in the check box. Then, using the drop-down list for the Shutdown Options, select Shutdown. This ensures that we have a generalized image for deployment and we can then capture the image to use for cloning. Figure 2.2 shows you the selections you should make.

FIGURE 2.2
Sysprep GUI with selections

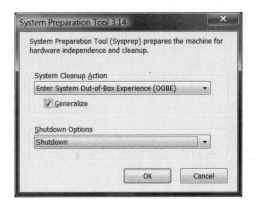

Your on-disk image is now a sysprepped image. That means when it boots, it will step you through a mini-setup procedure for creating a new image, completing the operating system installation. You need to capture the image from your operating system disk and distribute that to the other systems on which you want to deploy Hyper-V. The procedures for doing this vary according to what tools you have available to you. There are many third-party tools as well as a no-cost download from Microsoft called the Windows Automated Installation Kit or the Microsoft Deployment Toolkit. Go to `www.microsoft.com/downloads` and search for ''deployment toolkit.''

After you have used your sysprepped image to create another Hyper-V host, there is still a bit of work that needs to be done. The sysprep process made the image a generic or generalized image. This means that although all the software you had on the original image is still there, you will need to turn some things back on.

The first thing you will find is that Hyper-V is not running. This is because the boot configuration data (BCD) was generalized. BCD is the replacement for the `boot.ini` file that existed in previous releases of Windows. Instead of editing a file as you did previously, you now issue the `bcdedit` command to make changes to the boot process. To start the hypervisor on boot, issue the following command from an elevated command prompt (a command prompt that is started with the Run as Administrator option):

```
bcdedit /set hypervisorlaunchtype auto
```

The next place you need to check is your virtual network switch configuration. If you had defined any of your virtual switches as External, they have been changed to Internal. This is because the physical NIC that Hyper-V saw before the sysprep process is no longer there — it is still on the original system you configured. You need to reconfigure the virtual network to bind to a NIC on this system.

Lastly, you need to check your disk assignment. You should reconfigure your storage to match the server setup. You may have exactly the same storage configuration on the new hardware as you had on the system that you imaged. But it is also possible that you could have a totally different disk configuration.

Unattended Installation

Another way to automate the build process is to use what is known as an unattended installation. During the course of a manual installation and configuration, you answer prompts and select settings to configure the system the way you want it. These responses and selections can be placed into a specially formatted file, which can then be used to automatically build the system.

The unattended installation is another capability that has existed for a long time for installing Windows operating system environments. You can find a complete reference guide for the parameters and the settings to use for an unattended installation at `http://technet.microsoft.com/en-us/library/cc722187.aspx`. I will focus on using the unattended installation procedures for installing an installation of Windows Server 2008 Full configuration with the Hyper-V role.

Over the past few years, Microsoft has been moving from setup files that are simply text files to a format known as XML — Extensible Markup Language — because it is a standard. Windows Server 2008 and Windows Vista now use an unattended installation file called `unattend.xml`. Microsoft has also provided tools that make it easier to manipulate this file. Tools and documentation on the use of them are part of the Microsoft Deployment Toolkit referenced earlier.

In order to keep this explanation as simple as possible, yet still convey the concepts of using an unattended installation for Windows Server 2008 Full, I need to assume a few things. Here are my assumptions:

- You will use the Windows Server 2008 DVD for installing.

- You will use a USB thumb drive to hold your unattend.xml file and the KB950050 patch. If you really wanted to, you could create your own custom DVD or bootable USB drive that contains the Server distribution, the patch, and the unattend.xml file. I plan on keeping the explanation a little simpler.

- You already have an unattend.xml file that you have used for other unattended installations of Windows Server 2008 Full x64. I am not going to attempt to explain all the nuances of what can be put into an unattended answer file because there are simply too many optional variables. http://technet.microsoft.com/en-us/library/cc732280.aspx provides some sample unattend.xml files that you could use.

Given those assumptions, here are the steps.

1. Download the KB950050 patch from www.microsoft.com/downloads/details.aspx? FamilyId=F3AB3D4B-63C8-4424-A738-BADED34D24ED&displaylang=en. Save the .msu file to some temporary directory on your system.

2. The .msu file is a container file containing four files. You will need to expand the files. I will use the example directory of c:\temp as the location I downloaded the .msu file to. Expand the files by issuing the following commands from within a command window:

```
cd c:\temp
expand -F:* Windows6.0-KB950050-x64.msu c:\temp
```

3. Copy the Windows6.0-KB950050-x64.cab file to the root of your USB key, because this is the file that contains the hotfix to bring the Hyper-V role up to released binaries.

4. Open your unattend.xml file with notepad.exe. Insert the following text into your file right after the closing > of the <unattend> tag. It can actually go anywhere in your file as long as it is before the <settings> tag. Notice that the <source> tag specifies that the .cab file will be found in the root of drive E: (in bold below). If your USB thumb drive or the .cab file is in any other location, you will need to edit that tag accordingly.

```
<servicing>
    <package action="configure">
        <assemblyIdentity name="Microsoft-Windows-Foundation-Package"
            version="6.0.6001.18000" processorArchitecture="amd64"
            publicKeyToken="31bf3856ad364e35" language="" />
        <selection name="Microsoft-Hyper-V" state="true" />
        <selection name="Microsoft-Hyper-V-Management-Clients"
            state="true" />
    </package>
```

```
        <package action="install">
            <assemblyIdentity name="Package_for_KB950050"
                version="6.0.1.9" processorArchitecture="amd64"
                publicKeyToken="31bf3856ad364e35" language="neutral" />
            <source location="E:\Windows6.0-KB949219-x64.cab" />
        </package>
    </servicing>
```

5. Save your unattend.xml file as **autounattend.xml** on the root of your USB thumb drive.

You should now be ready to try out your unattended installation. Put your Windows Server 2008 distribution DVD into the DVD reader and insert your USB thumb drive. Boot from the DVD and off you go.

Obviously, if you are not starting with the Windows Server 2008 RTM media that has the beta version of Hyper-V with it, you would modify the above segment to omit the installation of the patch. The purpose of this section is to give you an idea of different ways to automate the installation process.

WINDOWS SERVER 2008 CORE

There are several benefits to installing Windows Server 2008 Core as the parent environment for Hyper-V. The first benefit has to do with maintenance and patching. By installing just the Hyper-V role on a Core installation, there are fewer "moving pieces" that have to be managed. You manage just the base operating system and the Hyper-V role. Along those same lines, this significantly reduces the attack surface — those points in an operating system environment that might be hacked by a nefarious person. Fewer components also mean fewer patches. All of this adds up to why you should consider using Server Core installations with just the Hyper-V role enabled.

I assume that you have already installed Windows Server 2008 Core and are ready to install the Hyper-V role. This includes ensuring that the KB950050 patch has been applied to your server. If you have not installed a Core installation before, a great place to start is the Server Core Installation Getting Started Guide at http://technet.microsoft.com/en-us/library/cc753802(WS.10).aspx. Of course if you have installed Windows Server 2008 R2, you do not have to worry about the KB950050 patch because the latest version of Hyper-V is included in the R2 installation.

If this is your first time working with Windows Server 2008 Core, it may be a little daunting to manage, as there is no graphical user interface. So all the tools and methods you learned to love and depend on in a Full installation are not available. You need to install Hyper-V from the command prompt or issue commands from a remote system. But the commands issued from the remote system are the same commands that would be issued from the local system. Therefore, I will make the assumption that you are logged into the Windows Server 2008 Core system as an administrator, and you are looking at a command window.

There are two commands that are required to see what roles are installed on a Windows Server 2008 Core installation and to install roles: oclist (optional component list) to see what is installed and ocsetup (optional component setup) to install a role.

Enter the command **oclist** without any parameters. You will see a long list indicating which roles and features are or are not installed. Each noninstalled role will be preceded by the string "Not installed:." One of those roles, about halfway through the list, is Microsoft-Hyper-V.

Enter the command **ocsetup** without any parameters. This displays a window that provides the syntax of the ocsetup command. Even though I said there is no management GUI, some programs will still display windows. In fact, with Windows Server 2008 R2, you will see a few more applications providing GUIs, but you will still not have Windows Explorer and Internet Explorer, among other components.

To install the Hyper-V role, execute the following command:

```
ocsetup Microsoft-Hyper-V
```

Note that you must enter the uppercase and lowercase letters as shown. This utility is different from most other utilities in that it is case sensitive.

You may also find some documentation telling you to use the following command:

```
Start /w ocsetup Microsoft-Hyper-V
```

It is the same command except that it starts the installation and then waits (/w) for the installation to complete before returning to the command prompt. Either way works fine.

When the installation is complete, you will get a window telling you the system needs to be restarted. Click Yes to restart the system.

Unlike Windows Server 2008, Server Core installations of Windows Server 2008 R2 use Dism.exe to install and uninstall most server roles. To discover the available server roles (oclist on Windows Server 2008), open a command prompt and type the following:

```
Dism /online /get-features /format:table
```

To install the Hyper-V role (ocsetup Microsoft-Hyper-V on Windows Server 2008), open a command prompt and type the following:

```
Dism /online /enable-feature /featurename:Microsoft-Hyper-V
```

If you remember installing the Hyper-V role on the full installation, you had a couple of configuration steps to complete during the role installation, such as configuring a network interface. In the role installation in Core, you did not have those steps. You have to use your remote management tools to configure Hyper-V when it is installed on Core. These tools will be covered in a subsequent section on configuration. Also, remember that two NICs are recommended, with one dedicated to management. This ensures that you do not temporarily lose connectivity to the Core Hyper-V system when you assign NICs to the hypervisor.

Sysprep and unattended installations also work for Core installations. There is a difference for the unattended installation file that you need to make to the example I gave earlier. Replace the first <package> tag with the following:

```
<package action="configure">
        <assemblyIdentity name="Microsoft-Windows-ServerCore-Package"
            version="6.0.6001.18000" processorArchitecture="amd64"
            publicKeyToken="31bf3856ad364e35" language="" />
        <selection name="Microsoft-Hyper-V" state="true" />
    </package>
```

One thing that happens to everyone sometime when they are working with Server Core is that they inadvertently close the command window in which they are working. If you are sitting there staring at a totally blank screen, remember that there are two ways to get the command window back. Both of them come from starting Task Manager. Pressing Ctrl+Shift+Esc launches Task Manager. Or, you can press Ctrl+Alt+Delete and select Task Manager. From the File menu in Task Manager, select New Task (Run) and enter **cmd** as the command to execute. This gives you your command window back. You can also use this method to open another command window when you want to be running multiple utilities or commands.

Microsoft Hyper-V Server 2008

Installing Microsoft Hyper-V Server 2008 is a snap. Even though it is technically not a version of Windows Server 2008, the installation procedure is almost exactly the same as installing Windows Server 2008 Core. And, because this is a tailored distribution that contains only the Windows kernel and the Hyper-V role, there really is nothing special about the installation.

To download the Hyper-V Server distribution ISO file navigate to www.microsoft.com/downloads and search for "Hyper-V Server." This will find both the RTM and the R2 versions.

The ISO-formatted file that you download is an archive of the distribution contents. You will need to use some utility, such as Nero, to burn the ISO file to DVD. There are freeware programs for this, too, but make sure that you get one that can burn DVDs, as that is different from burning a CD. Simply copying the file to the DVD will give you one large .iso file on the DVD, and you will not be able to boot that to start the installation process. Or, if you have a system running Windows 7, it has an option to burn an ISO file to DVD.

You will notice a difference when you log into the system when compared to logging into the Core installation. You will see two command windows instead of one, like what you see on a regular Core installation. One window is the typical black background of a command window. The other has a blue background. This window is automatically started and runs the sconfig.cmd script to assist with the basics of configuring the host environment. Figure 2.3 shows what this window looks like.

FIGURE 2.3
sconfig command
window

The use of this tool is pretty straightforward. Enter the number shown at the beginning of the line of the option you want to work on. It will then lead you through any options that need to be configured. If you ever need to call this window back up, type **sconfig.cmd** from a command prompt to launch it.

Here is a summary the options:

1. **Domain/Workgroup** This tells you the membership of the machine. The first time you see this, you will see Workgroup: WORKGROUP, as that is the default for any installation. After you join a domain, it will show Domain: *DomainName*, where *DomainName* is the name of the domain to which this system has been joined. If the first thing you do is join a domain, remember that you will need to manually add a domain account to the Local Administrator group in order to manage the machine. Changing from workgroup to domain or domain to workgroup does require a reboot.

2. **Computer Name** This initially shows the default generated name of the computer. Changing the computer name does require a reboot.

3. **Add Local Administrator** Use this selection to add user IDs to the Local Administrator security group. To add a domain user as a member of the Local Administrator group, you need to already be joined to a domain. Adding IDs does not require a reboot.

4. **Configure Remote Management** This brings up another series of options for enabling MMC remote management, enabling PowerShell, and configuring Windows Remote Management (WinRM). It also allows viewing of some pertinent firewall settings. Changes in this selection do not require a reboot.

5. **Windows Update Settings** This selection toggles the use of Windows Update from Manual to Automatic. The Automatic setting uses the default configuration to check for updates every day at 3:00 a.m. Toggling this setting does not require a reboot.

6. **Download and Install Updates** This selection causes an immediate search of Windows Update for available patches. You are presented with a list of available patches and asked if you want to apply them. If you apply them, one or more of them may require the system to be rebooted before they take effect. If you have previously selected an option that requires a reboot, for example, changing the computer name, you will not be able to apply these patches until you have rebooted the system. Any time a system reboot is required, that must be completed before another request that requires rebooting the computer can be executed.

7. **Remote Desktop** Do you want to set up this system so that you can establish a remote desktop connection to it for management purposes? I almost always set this on. Because Hyper-V Server is like a Core installation, it does not have a GUI for local management, but it is very handy to be able to use the Remote Desktop Connection for accessing the console. Toggling this does not require a reboot.

8. **Network Settings** This presents a list of the physical networks connected to the Hyper-V Server. This setting is for configuring the networks of the host and has nothing to do with configuring virtual networks for guests. It allows you to set static or DHCP address, subnet masks, DNS, and gateway servers. Changing network settings does not require a reboot.

9. **Date and Time** This selection displays the Date and Time window, as shown in Figure 2.4. Changes do not require a reboot.

10. **Do not display this menu at login** If you feel you have made all the configurations available from this screen and you no longer want to see this screen each time you log in, select this option. Remember that if you ever want to bring this screen back, you simply have to type **sconfig** at a command prompt and it will display.

FIGURE 2.4
Date and Time

11. **Failover Clustering Feature**   This selection gives you the option of adding the Failover Cluster Feature if it is not enabled and removing it if it is enabled. Adding the feature does not require a reboot, but removing it does.

12. **Log Off User**   This option logs off the current user.

13. **Restart Server**   This option restarts the server. You can accomplish the same thing with the command shutdown -r -t 0.

14. **Shut Down Server**   This shuts down the server. It does the same as the command shutdown -s -t 0.

15. **Exit To Command Line**   This option exits sconfig.cmd and allows you to work in the command window. If you want to restart the script, type **sconfig** from the command line.

As noted in the installation instructions for Windows Server Core, it is very common to inadvertently exit the command window, leaving you with a blank screen. Remember that there are two ways to get the command window back. Both of them come from starting Task Manager. Pressing Ctrl+Shift+Esc launches Task Manager. Or, you can press Ctrl+Alt+Delete and select Task Manager. From the File menu in Task Manager, select New Task (Run) and enter **CMD** as the command to execute. This gives you back your command window.

Configuration

Doing the initial installation of the Hyper-V environment is a pretty simple and straightforward task. Now we need to configure that environment. Every shop I have worked with has different standards and processes in place for this, and they have made those decisions based on their business needs. Whenever I set up a system, I always like to include a few things that simply make my life easier. I am not saying that these are required. You may already do these, or you may have additional settings that you put in place. I am just providing a few suggestions that I have found helpful in my work.

General

When I think of configuring a virtual host environment, many of the things, such as networks and storage, are very similar whether you are running Hyper-V on Windows Server 2008 Full or Core or running Hyper-V Server. In fact, when you use the Remote Server Administrator Toolkit or Hyper-V Manager (covered later in this chapter), you will be configuring things the same way for all environments. But there are some things that I like to do to the host system that make the management of the overall environment easier.

Several of these functions are handled automatically by `sconfig` on Hyper-V Server. You will have to perform these manually on a Core installation, but it is nice to know what `sconfig` is actually doing.

REMOTE ADMINISTRATION

Tasks cannot be performed remotely to a host until the system is set up to be remotely administered. For security reasons, Windows Server 2008 (both Full and Core) and Hyper-V Server are installed without the ability to be remotely managed. You need to turn on those abilities. Even though these might be more commonly used to manage Server Core or Hyper-V Server, they can also be used on full installations of Windows Server 2008.

There are two commands I issue for this. The first command opens the appropriate ports on the firewall to allow for remote administration via MMC. That command is

```
netsh advfirewall firewall set rule group="remote administration" new enable=yes
```

Sometimes you might not want to open up remote management for all MMCs. If that is the case, issue the following command, inserting the appropriate rule group from Table 2.2 that follows. Replace <rulegroup> with the string from the right column of the table, keeping the quotation marks ("") around the string.

```
netsh advfirewall firewall set rule group="<rulegroup>" new enable=yes
```

The second command to enable remote command-line administration is `winrm`. Microsoft introduced Windows Remote Management (WinRM) in Windows Server 2008. WinRM is Microsoft's implementation of the WS-Management Protocol, an industry standard for remotely managing systems. The command to enable remote management by the remote shell is

```
winrm quickconfig
```

This sets up a remote listener that will be able to respond to remote shell commands over a secure channel. You will be prompted with the following message:

```
WinRM is not set up to allow remote access to this machine for management.
The following changes must be made:

Create a WinRM listener on HTTP://* to accept WS-Man requests to any IP on this
```

```
machine.
Enable the WinRM firewall exception.

Make these changes [y/n]?
```

TABLE 2.2:   Rule group table

MMC SNAP-IN	RULE GROUP
Event Viewer	Remote Event Log Management
Services	Remote Services Management
Shared Folders	File and Printer Sharing
Task Scheduler	Remote Scheduled Tasks Management
Reliability and Performance	Performance Logs and Alerts File and Printer Sharing
Windows Firewall with Advanced Security	Windows Firewall Remote Management

Type **y** and press Enter.

WinRM is the first half of a pair of tools. WinRM is the listener that listens for commands to execute. The other half of the pair is a tool to submit the commands to WinRM. The WinRS tool is used from any other Windows Server 2008/Vista or later system to submit any command line on the remote system. There are different ways of specifying commands for the remote system, but the simplest format of the WinRS command is

```
winrs -r:server command
```

In the above command, *server* is the DNS name of the server on which you want to execute the command *command*. The command will be executed on the remote system with the privileges of the user executing the command. It is also possible to send a username and password with the -u: and -p: parameters in order to execute in the context of a different user. To see all the options of this command, type **winrs /?** from a command line. The WinRS command is meant for administrators and not for nonprivileged users.

REMOTE DESKTOP

Another very useful capability to enable is the ability to use the Remote Desktop Connection (RDC) to connect to the host machine's console via terminal services. Microsoft provides two administrative terminal service connections free of charge just for management purposes. Though you can manage Hyper-V with the remote tools mentioned earlier, it is sometimes nice to be able to get to the system console for other management tasks or troubleshooting purposes. This could be to access a GUI management window in a Full installation or to get to the command prompt in a Core or Hyper-V server installation to issue a series of commands directly instead of using WinRS.

Configuring terminal services is an option in Server Manager for a Full installation. The option to enable Remote Desktop is on the first page of Server Manager. See Figure 2.5.

When you select the Enable Remote Desktop option, you will be presented with a System Properties window, as shown in Figure 2.6.

FIGURE 2.5
Enable Remote Desktop in Server Manager

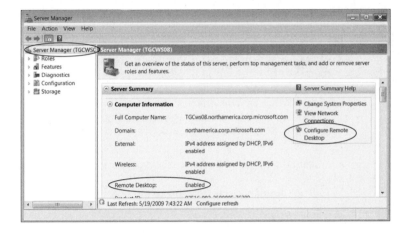

FIGURE 2.6
System Properties

There are three options in the Remote Desktop option of the System Properties window. The first option is self-explanatory — "Don't allow connections to this computer." The second option, "Allow connections from computer running any version of Remote Desktop (less secure)," is needed if you are not using an RDC of version 6.0 or later. So, if you want to use older versions of the operating system, or even connections from Linux (available from a third party) or Macintosh devices, you will need to select this option.

The last option, "Allow connections only from computers running Remote Desktop with Network Level Authentication (more secure)," should be selected only if you can ensure that you will be using RDC version 6.0 or later. As noted, this is the more secure option. Network Level Authentication (NLA) provides network identification between the RDC and the machine being remotely managed, which helps to prevent things like "man in the middle" attacks. If you want to ensure the highest level of security in your environment, this is the recommended setting.

Note that there is also a button labeled Select Users. By default, users who are members of the Local Administrator group are granted access. But if you want someone who is not a member of this group to have access, you will need to add their account through this selection.

It is also possible to set the RDC parameter via the command line on Windows Core and Hyper-V Server. This enables you to set it manually, and it allows you to build a script so you can execute this repeatedly as you build new systems. The command to set this up for NLA access (RDC 6.0 client or later) is

```
cscript c:\windows\system32\scregedit.wsf /ar 0
```

The command to set this up to allow for earlier versions of the RDC client is

```
cscript c:\windows\system32\scregedit.wsf /cs 0
```

This command automatically opens the firewall port to enable Terminal Services access.

Besides giving you access to the console for managing your environment remotely, Terminal Services through the RDC provide some other useful capabilities. See the section "Miscellaneous Tips" in the "Management" section of this chapter to see a couple things that make RDC a handy tool to have enabled.

PING

The next thing I like to do is ensure that the system can be pinged. The ping command is a basic network troubleshooting tool, so it only makes sense to ensure that ping is enabled. With the additional security that Microsoft puts into the environment with its firewall, ping is turned off in any default environment. To enable it, issue this command from an elevated command prompt:

```
netsh firewall set icmpsetting 8 enable
```

Netsh (net shell) is a powerful networking tool. For more information on its use, see http://support.microsoft.com/kb/242468.

When you execute the above command on Windows Server 2008 R2 or Microsoft Hyper-V Server 2008 R2, you will receive an informational message telling you that the netsh firewall command has been deprecated and that you should use the netsh advfirewall command. Here is the format of that command:

```
netsh advfirewall firewall add rule name="ICMP Allow incoming V4 echo request"
protocol=icmpv4:8,any dir=in action=allow
```

You can use the above netsh command to enable ping responses on a Full installation. Or, you can enable it with the Windows Firewall management tool. To enable it through the

Firewall management tools, open Server Manager, select Go To Windows Firewall from the Security Information section on the right-hand side of the Server Manager window. Alternatively, you can click the plus sign (+) in front of Configuration on the left-hand side. See Figure 2.7 for these two options.

FIGURE 2.7
Windows Firewall

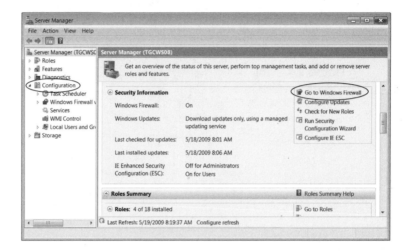

Next, expand Windows Firewall With Advanced Security on the left-hand side and select Inbound Rules. In the middle panel, scroll down until you find the items starting with File And Printer Sharing (Echo Request). These are available for both IPv4 and IPv6. Select either the IPV4 or IPV6 rules or both, whatever you expect to use to enable, by right-clicking and choosing Enable Rule. See Figure 2.8.

FIGURE 2.8
Windows Firewall settings

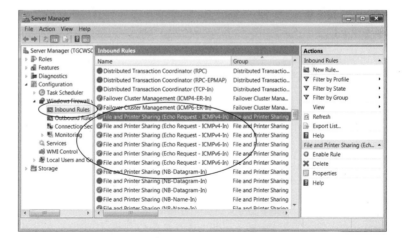

AUTOMATIC UPDATES

It is important for me to ensure that I have my systems fully patched as soon as possible. So, after I have set up some of these basic capabilities listed above, I like to set up the system to automatically check for updates and then download and install all the patches. If you have created an image that you deploy regularly, you should keep this image up to date with all the patches before you run sysprep on it so that you can avoid this step in the future.

In the Server Full installation, you most likely configured your updates as part of the installation procedure in the Initial Tasks Configuration Wizard. If not, you can use Server Manager to set this up. Open Server Manager and scroll down to the Security Information section. There you will see the option Configure Updates. Figure 2.9 shows the appropriate selections within Server Manager.

FIGURE 2.9
Automatic updates

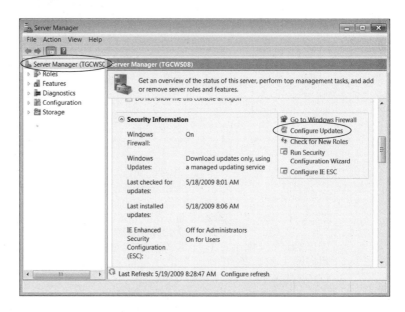

For a Server Core or Hyper-V Server installation, this can be accomplished via the command line. Here are the commands to turn it on, make it take effect, and force a check for updates:

```
cscript c:\windows\system32\scregedit.wsf /au 4
net stop wuauserv
net start wuauserv
wuauclt /detectnow
```

The first command sets the Windows Update service to use the default of 3:00 a.m. as the time to check for updates. Since the Windows Update service was already running without automatic update set, it must be stopped and started to use the new settings. Then, once the setting is enabled, you force the first check to take place.

There is a small problem with the last command. It does exactly what it says it does — it detects missing updates. But it does not download and install them right away; it will download them and schedule them for application at the time set up for scheduled update. Microsoft has published a VBS script that detects, downloads, and installs the patches. Since that is what I really want to do, I use a copy of that VBS script to update my systems right away. You can find that script, WUA_SearchDownloadInstall.vbs at http://msdn.microsoft.com/en-us/library/aa387102(VS.85).aspx.

The WUA_SearchDownloadInstall.vbs script is over 60 lines in length. If you like typing, you can type it in. But it is much easier to use the capabilities of the Remote Desktop Connection to transfer this information to the remote system as a file. See the section "Miscellaneous Tips" in the "Management" portion of this chapter for information on how to transfer a file to a remote system.

If you simply want to check what patches are applied to your Core installation, issue this command:

```
wmic qfe list
```

Alternatively, you can set up your own Windows Server Update Server (WSUS) or manually copy the security patches. WSUS provides the ability to have more control over which patches get applied and when. This is accomplished by setting up a patch server inside the corporate environment that copies the patches from Microsoft's public patch servers. Once patches are copied into the corporate environment, an administrator approves patches for distribution. For information on WSUS, go to http://technet.microsoft.com/en-us/wsus/default.aspx.

Microsoft also maintains a web service, Windows Update Catalog, that provides the ability to search for any patch. This is found at http://catalog.update.microsoft.com/v7/site/home.aspx. Once there, enter a search phrase like "Windows Server 2008 security x64" to find all the security patches that apply to an x64 installation of Windows Server 2008. You can download those manually to your library and apply them offline.

Though it is recommended to fully patch any new installation, you have to determine if you want Windows Update to automatically download, install, and possibly reboot the host system. If the host is running several virtual machines, you might want to schedule a time when you can control any required reboot of the host.

COMMON SETUP COMMANDS

Here is a summary of the above commands that I use when setting up a Core installation. If desired, these commands can easily be put into a command file and executed. There are generally GUI commands for all these in a Full installation, but there is no reason why you cannot also use this command file on Full installations, except for the scregedit.wsf script. It is not found on a Full installation.

```
;
; commands for setting up Server Core
;
; Set up to support WinRS/WinRM - this requires a response
winrm quickconfig
;
; Set up for remote administration
netsh advfirewall firewall set rule group="remote administration" new enable=yes
;
; Enable remote admin mode (Terminal Services)
cscript c:\windows\system32\scregedit.wsf /ar 0
;
; Enable ping
netsh firewall set icmpsetting 8 enable
;
```

```
; Turn on autoupdate
cscript c:\windows\system32\scregedit.wsf /au 4
net stop wuauserv
net start wuauserv
;
; Force update from Windows Automatic Update
wuauclt /detectnow
```

OTHER COMMAND-LINE COMMANDS

Depending on how you are configuring your environment, you may have some other functions that need to be performed. For example, you may want to rename your computer, join it to a workgroup or domain, and/or define some parameters for your NICs. The commands for doing these sorts of functions require the input of parameters that are generally unique for each machine, so they are not as easy to include into a simple command file. Here are some of these other useful commands that I often use when setting up a Core or Hyper-V Server environment. (These commands also work on a Full installation of Windows Server, but there are often management GUIs through which you can make these changes interactively. You can build these into scripts or you can manually use Server Manager or other appropriate MMCs to configure this information.) For Hyper-V Server, these are also built into sconfig.

Computer Rename and Domain Join   If you have not yet joined your computer to a domain, issue the following command to rename the computer to what you want it to be. The commands must be executed from an elevated command prompt by a member of the local administrator group.

```
netdom renamecomputer <oldcomputername> /newname:<new-name>
```

To rename a computer that is a member of a domain requires that a domain user name and password be supplied. That username must have the appropriate rights to allow renaming computer objects in the domain.

```
netdom renamecomputer <oldcomputername> /newname:<new-name>
/userd:<domain\username> /passwordd:<password>
```

Note that the parameters for the user ID and password end with an extra *d*. It is a common mistake to forget the *d*, particularly on the password parameter.

To join a computer to a domain, you can issue this command. The specified username and password must have the right to add computer objects to the domain.

```
netdom join <computername> /domain:<domain> /userd:<domain>\<username>
/passwordd:<password>
```

There are more optional parameters for each of these commands, but these are the basics to get you started.

Networking Parameters   The utility for manipulating networking parameters is netsh. This is a very powerful utility that enables you to set about any parameter in the network. For a complete description of this command, go to http://support.microsoft.com/kb/242468.

By default, Windows assigns default names to network connections as it finds them. This name is not very descriptive — Local Area Connection — with a sequence number if you have more than one NIC defined. I find it helpful to rename the connections to something that is meaningful to me. So, the first command I issue gives me the current information so I can know what values need to be changed.

```
netsh interface ipv4 show interfaces
```

This returns information like this for each NIC in your system:

```
Idx  Met   MTU        State        Name
---  ---   -----      -----------  --------------------
  2   10   1500       connected    Local Area Connection
  1   50 4294967295   connected    Loopback Pseudo-Interface 1
```

There are two important values listed here. The first is the Idx value for the connection you want to work with. That value, in this case a 2, is needed for other commands. The second is the Name value which is the name of the interface. To change the name of the interface to something more meaningful for your environment, enter this command:

```
netsh interface set interface name="Local Area Connection"
newname="PrivateNetwork"
```

Make the string `"PrivateNetwork"` something meaningful for you. Then when you issue commands such as `ipconfig`, the network name will be something you can easily identify. For example, I like to name the NIC I reserve for managing the host environment *Management*.

By default, all NICs are set up for DHCP, with the gateway, mask, and DNS server being provided by the DHCP server. If you want to change an interface to a static IP address with a different DNS server, here are the commands:

```
netsh interface ipv4 set address name="<ID>" source=static address=<StaticIP>
mask=<SubnetMask> gateway=<DefaultGateway>
netsh interface ipv4 add dnsserver name="<ID>" address=<DNSIP>index=1
```

These commands require the Idx value that was obtained from the first `netsh` command. That numeric value is inserted as the `"<ID>"` in the above commands. You would fill in the other values in the above commands with the appropriate values for your particular configuration.

CPU and Memory

No real configuration is required for setting up the host Hyper-V environment. Hyper-V takes care of allocating CPU and memory to the virtual machines. But there are some things you need to be aware of in order to understand how the system works to ensure the best performance.

CPU

The terms *CPU* and *processor* have become confusing in recent years. Not too many years ago, everyone understood these terms were interchangeable because every processor generally had only one central processing unit. With the advent of hyperthreading and multicore processors, the relationship between CPU and processor has changed. Generally speaking, a physical processor is what gets plugged into a socket on the motherboard. That physical processor could be using hyperthreading. *Hyperthreading* is a term for a simultaneous multithreading implementation that can appear to the operating system as two execution units, or CPUs. A multicore processor combines two or more cores (think of them as independent CPUs) into a single processor.

For clarity in this section, I will almost never refer to the physical processor, other than where it is necessary. That is because most of the time we are more interested in how many units of execution are available to either the host or the virtual machines, and a unit of execution is either a CPU or a core. But we need to explain a little about the limits of Windows Server 2008 to help you understand configuring the Hyper-V host.

For licensing purposes, Microsoft counts the number of physical processors for the operating system. That means that no matter how many hyperthreads and/or cores are contained within a single processor, the processor is still counted as a single processor. So a single processor with 1 core, 2 cores, 4 cores, 6 cores, 8 cores, or whatever comes in the future is considered only a single processor to Windows Server. Here are the numbers of processors that are supported by the operating system environments:

Microsoft Hyper-V Server 2008	4 processors
Windows Server 2008 Standard Edition	4 processors
Windows Server 2008 Enterprise Edition	8 processors
Windows Server 2008 Datacenter Edition	64 processors
Microsoft Hyper-V Server 2008 R2	8 processors

A slightly confusing bit of information, though, is that all these environments support a maximum of 64 cores. (Windows Server 2008 in its 32-bit versions supports only 32 cores.) By the time this book is released, I expect the chip technology of Intel and AMD to have each processor supporting up to 8 cores. Using 8-core technology, you can see that it would be possible to configure a 32-bit Datacenter system that would have more cores than 32-bit Windows supports. Since the overwhelming majority of systems sold in the marketplace today have four or fewer processors, meaning a total of 32 cores, there is still headroom.

But there is another limitation existing only for the Hyper-V environment. Even though Windows Server 2008 can support up to 64 cores today, Hyper-V itself is supported only on systems with a maximum of 24 cores. It used to be 16, but Microsoft issued a fix for the Intel 6-core chip that raised it to 24.

Technology is constantly changing. As I write this, Intel's 6-core chip has more cores than any other commercially available chip. But, both Intel and AMD have plans on the board to increase that number. Does that mean that Hyper-V will not be able to take advantage of these technology improvements? No. Windows Server 2008 R2 raised the limit on the operating system to 256 cores and the number of cores supported by Hyper-V R2 to 64. (The majority of servers today have four or fewer processors. With 8 cores coming, Microsoft is ensuring Hyper-V R2 some additional headroom, as four processors multiplied by 8 cores is 32 cores.) You can be assured that Microsoft will continue to increase these numbers as the technology becomes mainstream.

When it comes to actually configuring the host environment for Hyper-V, there really is not much to be concerned about. The Windows kernel, used in both Windows Server 2008 and Microsoft Hyper-V Server, takes care of scheduling access to the cores as needed. Hyper-V allows you to ''oversubscribe'' the cores. What I mean by this is that even on a system with only 2 cores, you can run multiple virtual machines, and when you add up the number of CPUs in all the virtual machines, you have more than 2.

There is a limit, though, but it is pretty generous. Currently, Microsoft has a ratio of 8:1 of running virtual cores to host physical cores. Using a dual-processor, 2-core host as an example, that means I can run virtual machines with a total of 32 cores. If I create single-core virtual machines, I can run 32 virtual machines. If I run 2-core virtual machines, I can run up to 16 virtual machines. .

Notice that I never set a specific number of cores aside for the host operating environment. This is because Hyper-V schedules cores to the host environment in the same manner that it schedules cores to the virtual machines. And, because it is a recommendation that the only role running in a Hyper-V environment is the Hyper-V role, there is very little in the way of processor resources required.

However, remember that Hyper-V supports a maximum of 24 physical cores on the host (64 in R2). Multiplying this by 8, we can have a maximum of 192 logical cores (512 in R2) available to virtual machines in a Hyper-V configuration. Given today's technologies, it is most likely that you will run out of some other resource, such as network, memory, or disk throughput, before you run out of available logical cores, but it is possible to run out of CPU cycles if the virtual machines you are running are heavy users of the CPU.

MEMORY

Memory is often the first limiting factor that people run into when building virtual hosts. Yes, it is possible to saturate a network link or some other resource, but it is often possible to increase that resource by putting another option card into the hardware chassis. You can also increase memory, but the limitation imposed by the host on how much memory it can support is often stricter than the limitations of other resources.

Let's again use the example I used with CPU above. Using a dual-processor, 2-core host, I can run up to 32 single-core guests. If I use just a single gigabyte of memory for each of those virtual machines, that means that I need more than 32 GB of memory in the host. (I will explain some of the memory overhead below.) Here are the maximum amounts of physical memory supported for the different host environments.

Microsoft Hyper-V Server 2008	32 GB
Windows Server 2008 Standard Edition	32 GB
Windows Server 2008 Enterprise Edition	1 TB
Windows Server 2008 Datacenter Edition	1 TB
Microsoft Hyper-V Server 2008 R2	1 TB

Each virtual machine must have enough physical memory on the host to map to the amount of memory the virtual machine is asking for. Plus, there is a little overhead for each virtual machine, and you need to leave some memory for the host operating environment.

The Hyper-V host environment does not need any CPUs or cores set aside for itself, but the host does need some memory reserved for itself. The amount required is a dynamic amount. That is, the kernel will allocate and remove physical memory for the host environment depending on what the host is doing. That is another reason why it is recommended that only the Hyper-V role be installed on the host. The memory requirements for the Hyper-V role itself will be significantly less than if you were also running other roles, thereby freeing some additional memory that would have been used by the other roles.

It is totally valid and supported to run other roles on the host. In fact, there are sometimes very practical reasons for doing so. A good example is in a remote office. You may want to have the host running a domain controller and Hyper-V. The local domain controller provides local login should the network link to corporate be down. Then you can run other virtual machines for things like file and print services.

When I calculate how much memory to leave for the host environment, I generally start with about 2 GB reserved for the parent partition. This is not a fixed amount, nor is there any place to actually lock that amount for exclusive use by the parent partition. It is just an amount that I use for determining how much memory I have available to allocate to my virtual machines. Because this host reserve is a dynamic amount, it can be a more or less — the kernel is in control. In fact, you will find that the parent partition may be running with about 2 GB before you start any virtual machines. The memory manager will trim this 2 GB down as you get close to the maximum memory utilization of the host, but it will not allow virtual machines to "starve" the parent partition of the memory it needs. For example, on a test machine with only 4 GB of memory, I have seen that 2 GB of memory used by the parent partition drop down to about 1 GB. But for planning purposes, particularly for production machines, you should start with 2 GB so that you know how much RAM you have to work with for your virtual machines. Monitor this to see if the system would benefit with more. Using perfmon, you can watch for hard page faults in the parent partition. A low number of hard page faults should not be too noticeable, but if you continually have 10 or more hard page faults per second, that often means that there is not enough memory available for the parent partition to operate efficiently. Adding additional memory to the host, removing a virtual machine, and decrementing the amount of memory allocated to one or more virtual machines are all ways to get more memory for use by the parent partition.

The Hyper-V role itself requires about 300 MB in the parent partition. Then each virtual machine also takes a small amount of overhead. The amount varies according to the amount of memory the virtual machine is set to. For example, a virtual machine allocated 1 GB of memory gets the 1 GB plus about 32 MB more. A virtual machine allocated 2 GB of memory gets 2 GB plus about 41 MB more. This amount increases slightly as more memory is requested by the virtual machine. Certain management functions require this small allocation of memory. For example, virtual processors expose virtual memory and a translation look-aside buffer (TLB), which caches translations from virtual addresses to the guest's physical addresses. Space has to be allocated for this TLB and other control functions. A simple calculator for estimating the amount of memory for the host platform can be found at `http://cid-2095eac3772c41db` `.skydrive.live.com/self.aspx/Public/Hyper-V%20RAM%20Calculator.xls`.

Disk Storage

One of the great benefits of the microkernelized hypervisor and Microsoft's implementation in Hyper-V is that any disk storage that is supported by the Windows Server 2008 kernel can be used as storage for Hyper-V. This is true of both Windows Server 2008 Hyper-V and Microsoft Hyper-V Server 2008 because they both use the same Windows kernel. This means that you can use locally attached disks, USB and FireWire (IEEE 1394) devices, Fibre Channel storage, and iSCSI storage. Windows can boot from any of these devices except for USB and FireWire, as these are considered removable devices and Windows cannot be installed on removable devices.

There are various reasons to select one or another. They all work. They all have reputable vendors. So, I am not going to try to say one is better than another. Some typical uses include using USB and FireWire for desktop development/testing systems, direct attached storage for smaller configurations, and Fibre Channel and iSCSI for enterprise storage. Within any one of these environments, it is common to use different RAID technologies.

Chapter 4 of this book covers some different types of RAID technologies. Different types of RAID deliver different levels of performance. Over the course of the years since RAID was introduced, there have been countless documents on what RAID is and how to determine what is the best RAID for a given situation. If I make suggestions on differing RAIDs, do not take it to mean that is the only way it should be done — it is just a suggestion based on experience.

There are some other factors that you should consider with storage — rotational latency (how long it takes for any point on the disk to come under the read head, typically expressed as RPM), bus speed, and caching. Again, a great deal has been written by the various drive manufacturers about this. What I will say is that the faster the disk spins, the more cache it has, and the faster the bus moves things between the host and the spindle, the better your performance will be.

In my experience, the one item of those three that is the most noticeable is the rotational latency. When you consider that rotational latency is the mechanical aspect of a disk drive, it is typically the slowest component. If cache and bus speed remain the same, and you purchase a disk that rotates faster, you will likely see a visible performance improvement. If you keep the rotational speed the same and increase the bus speed, you may see a difference, but you will need tools to measure that difference. My recommendation for disk drives is to use 10K or 15K RPM drives wherever possible. This becomes very noticeable when running multiple virtual operating system environments from the same physical disk. Just think of all the I/O that is required for the physical host's system disk, and then multiply that by the number of virtual hard drives you have on a single spindle.

Solid State Disks (SSD) are becoming more common in the world today. The prices have been dropping, but they are still quite pricey. They are also relatively small. (I say *relatively* because I remember using 5MB disk drives on the first minicomputers I worked on — and they were asking thousands of dollars for them!) If you have some particularly "hot" virtual hard drives, you can place those onto an SSD and immediately notice a performance improvement. That is because SSDs do not spin, so there is no rotational latency. A couple years ago when they were first introduced, they did not have a very long life cycle — they could only be written to so many times before a bit would no longer be able to store data. The drive manufacturers have made great strides in this area and are now providing warranties of up to five years on their SSDs. If you have a business need for speed, this may be your answer.

Once you have made your decision on the type(s) of drives you are going to use, you should consider how many adapters you will use. Remember, now that you are running multiple operating system environments on a single machine, you are concentrating all the I/O that you had previously spread out over multiple machines with at least a single adapter in each one. As with speed of the disks, more adapters are better for performance. If you can put the system drive on the host on a separate adapter from the drives holding the VHDs, you will benefit.

There are several other storage configuration issues that you should consider. First is how you are going to format the storage volumes. All drives used by Hyper-V will be formatted as NTFS volumes. You should also consider the default blocking factor when you format the disk. The default blocking factor is 4KB blocks. This works well for volumes that are used for many small I/Os. The maximum size is 64KB blocks. This works well for volumes that are used for large, sequential I/Os. You should experiment with different-size blocks to find the size that works best for your particular environment.

Other options to consider include

◆ Multipath I/O for load balancing across multiple adapters

◆ iSCSI

◆ Fibre Channel

MULTIPATH I/O

Windows Server 2008 includes a built-in Multipath I/O (MPIO) capability to enhance connectivity to iSCSI, Fibre Channel, or Serial Attached SCSI (SAS) storage volumes. This provides you with the ability to connect two or more adapters to create a load-balanced and failover connection to your disks. Most of the storage area network (SAN) vendors also provide their own device-specific module (DSM) that is built on top of Microsoft's MPIO. Their DSMs generally have value-added features above and beyond what comes out of the box from Microsoft. You make the decision on which meets your needs — Microsoft's built-in capability or the storage vendor's DSM. Because of the amount of I/O created for a disk that is housing multiple VHDs, load-balancing traffic between two or more adapters can help you achieve greater I/O throughput. And, the failover capability is a great consideration for those environments that are considered mission critical, where downtime would be detrimental to business.

Microsoft's MPIO is installed as a feature from Server Manager. See Figure 2.10 for the feature-selection option. Installing this feature does not require a system reboot. However, for some reason, it does require a reboot when you remove it.

FIGURE 2.10
Multipath I/O

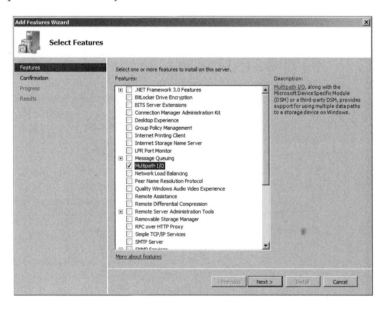

When MPIO is installed, the Microsoft-provided DSM and an MPIO configuration applet are also installed. The configuration applet can be started from either Control Panel or from the Administrative Tools option on the Start menu.

The user guide for Microsoft MPIO can be found at `http://download.microsoft.com/download/a/e/9/ae91dea1-66d9-417c-ade4-92d824b871af/uguide.doc`. This document provides all the examples for setting up MPIO with iSCSI and Fibre Channel, for Microsoft's DSM as well as some information for third-party DSMs.

There is a command-line tool, MPclaim, that can be used to configure MPIO on either Full or Core installs. You can find more information about this command-line tool at `http://technet` `.microsoft.com/en-us/library/cc725907.aspx`.

iSCSI

iSCSI, or Internet SCSI, is a software protocol that carries SCSI commands over IP protocols, but it connects to storage via an IP network instead of the physical parallel SCSI cables directly attached to a server. This is a much more efficient protocol than System Message Block (SMB) used for file shares. iSCSI is a block-oriented protocol for high-speed transfer of data. Network file shares provide record-oriented access to data. Because iSCSI is block oriented, it can be used for accessing and transferring block-oriented data, such as databases and virtual hard drives, for efficient data access.

iSCSI consists of two components: an initiator and a target. The initiator is client software that is included with the Windows Vista and Windows Server 2008 operating systems. It is the software that initiates a connection to a target that is serving up the storage.

iSCSI does work over a standard Ethernet network. Most organizations are running their wired Ethernet networks at 1 Gbps, sometimes known as GigE. Since this is running over IP, the performance is likely not to be as good as what you would see from a 1Gbps connection to a Fibre Channel storage array, due to the fact that Fibre Channel is optimized for storage. 10 Gbps is starting to get installed, particularly in datacenters, as the demand for network bandwidth grows. Windows Server 2008, using 10Gbps network connections, can drive access to iSCSI targets at full network capacity. So if you can put your iSCSI targets and initiators on 10 Gbps networks, you will have great performance. If you do not have a GigE network, iSCSI will still work, but performance will be slower. This will generally work fine in a development and test environment or other workloads that do not demand the higher I/O rates.

The iSCSI initiator is also available for Windows 2000 Server SP4, Windows Server 2003 SP1 or above, and Windows XP SP2 or above. You can download it from `www.microsoft.com/` `downloads/details.aspx?familyid=12CB3C1A-15D6-4585-B385-BEFD1319F825&` `displaylang=en`.

The user guide reference under the MPIO heading above also contains all the information for configuring iSCSI initiators.

iSCSI target software is available from all the major storage vendors, and a variety of software-only vendors can enable you to set up an iSCSI target on a Windows or Linux host with direct-attached storage. Microsoft has an iSCSI target that is part of its OEM product, Windows Unified Data Storage Server. More information on this can be found at `www.microsoft` `.com/windowsserversystem/storage/wudss.mspx`. DoubleTake (`www.doubletake.com/` `english/products/sanFly/Pages/default.aspx`), StarWind (`www.starwindsoftware.com` `/free`), and Nimbus Data Systems (`www.nimbusdata.com/products/mysan.php`) are third parties that have iSCSI target software for the Windows platform.

In order to run the iSCSI initiator, the firewall must be unblocked for outbound iSCSI connections. In an operating system with a GUI, choose Start ➢ Administrative Tools ➢ iSCSI Initiator. If this is the first time you have started this, a window will open telling you that the iSCSI service is not running. Clicking the Yes button will set the service to start automatically and open the appropriate firewall port.

On a Core or Hyper-V Server installation, you issue the following command:

```
netsh advfirewall firewall set rule "iSCSI Service (TCP-Out)" new enable=yes
```

I will be going into more detail on setting up an iSCSI target and initiator in Chapter 5 when I talk about high availability.

Networking

Supported network cards are just like the supported disk devices — any wired network interface card that is supported by Windows Server 2008 is supported for use by Hyper-V. Even though you do not find wireless networks on servers today, it is technically possible to get wireless working on a Windows Server 2008 host by installing the Vista drivers for that NIC. I mention this only because some people use Windows Server 2008 as their desktop or laptop, and they may be using Hyper-V on that laptop. That is where I do most of my experimenting, even though I realize it to be a totally unsupported environment.

Since Hyper-V is considered a datacenter solution and not a mobile solution, Hyper-V itself is prevented from recognizing wireless networks. I know there are blogs that talk of how to install and share wireless networks from the host to the virtual machines, but I am not going to go into that as it is even more unsupported, if that is possible.

Microsoft's recommendation is to have at least two NICs on your Hyper-V host. One NIC should be dedicated to managing the host server, and all the other NICs can then be used by the virtual machines. This ensures continued remote connectivity to the host environment.

As part of the configuration of Hyper-V, when you select a physical NIC for use by Hyper-V, you are telling the host to take down the current physical network interface and hand it over to Hyper-V to use as a virtual network switch. Hyper-V removes all bindings from the NIC and binds the Microsoft Virtual Network Switch Protocol to that NIC, turning that into a virtual network switch. That means there is no IPv4 or IPv6 bound to that NIC anymore, making it impossible to communicate directly through that connection.

When the Virtual Network Switch Protocol is assigned, it creates a new virtual network interface that connects to the virtual network switch, and that is what is connected to the outside world. While the transfer is being made from the physical to the virtual switch, connection to the host is lost on that NIC. If you are trying to manage the system remotely via that NIC, you will lose your connection to the host. Figure 2.11 shows this relationship.

FIGURE 2.11
Network Connections

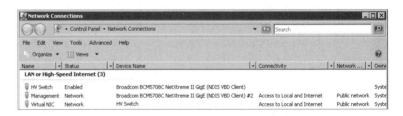

I have renamed my connections from the default of Local Area Connection to something more meaningful. Before I configured Hyper-V, I determined that I would name my management NIC to be *Management*. The NIC I planned on dedicating to virtual machines, thereby changing it into a virtual network switch, I renamed to *HV Switch*. A virtual NIC was automatically created on that external virtual network switch, and I renamed that to *Virtual NIC*. In Figure 2.11 Hyper-V shows that relationship by putting the device name of HV Switch on the Virtual NIC.

If I wanted all communication with the host system to go through my Management NIC, I would simply disable the Virtual NIC in the parent partition. This does not disable anything in any of the other child partitions — they can still fully use that Virtual NIC for access to the outside world. Disabling the Virtual NIC in the parent partition is a way of creating another level of isolation between the parent partition and the child partitions. Remember, this is the Virtual NIC I am disabling — not the NIC that contains the virtual switch. Disabling the NIC that contains the virtual switch would disable that NIC for use by any virtual machine.

This is one of the main reasons I like to rename all the NICs on the Hyper-V host. The relationship between the virtual NICs and the virtual network switches can get lost pretty quickly if you do not put some sort of naming standard in place.

Renaming the NICs in a Full installation is pretty easy through the Network Connections GUI. (This can be called up directly by running `ncpa.cpl` from a command prompt.) Earlier, when I talked about installing networks, I gave you the command:

```
netsh interface set interface name="Local Area Connection"
newname="PrivateNetwork"
```

This comes in very handy for renaming NICs in Core and Hyper-V Server installations.

Management

You need to be able to manage your virtual environment, just like you need to manage your physical environment. The beauty of working in the Hyper-V environment is that many of the same management tools you use for the physical environment work in the virtual environment. In other words, you do not need to purchase and learn a whole new set of tools just to manage your virtual environment. Though there are a few new tools available specifically for managing the virtual configuration, much of the training and education you have had in the physical Windows environment will carry over to the Hyper-V virtual environment.

This is not to say that tools specially developed for the virtual environment should be ignored. In fact, the ability to have a single view of both the physical and virtual environments, and to be able to manage both from a single console, can provide significant management benefits. This book covers only the tools that are built into the operating environments, but if you want to look at all facets of management, you should investigate Microsoft's System Center suite of tools, particularly System Center Virtual Machine Manager.

Remote Server Administration Tools

Microsoft Remote Server Administration Tools (RSAT) enables IT administrators to remotely manage roles and features in Windows Server 2008 from a computer running Windows Vista with Service Pack 1 (SP1) or another Windows Server 2008 system. To manage an R2 environment requires RSAT for Windows Server 2008 R2 or Windows 7; you cannot manage an R2 environment with Vista or Windows Server 2008. You can download the appropriate tools by going to www.microsoft.com/downloads and searching for "remote server windows." Be sure to select the appropriate version of RSAT.

After you have downloaded and installed the appropriate file, you need to configure which remote management tools you want to use. This is done by opening Control Panel and selecting Programs And Features. From the Programs And Features window, select Turn Windows Features On Or Off from the left-hand menu. Expand the entry for Remote Server Administration Tools, and you will see the list shown in Figure 2.12.

Select the tools you want to use for remote administration. When you install tools for the various roles, role services, and features within RSAT, you install only a set of snap-ins and command-line tools for remote management of those roles, role services, and features installed on other computers. Installing RSAT does not install any roles or features on the local computer. To make use of these tools, you will tailor an MMC to include those tools that have MMC snap-ins and select the remote computers you want to manage with those tools, or you will use the command-line tool from a command prompt. There is a link to the RSAT help file in Administrative Tools from the All Programs option on the Start menu to provide you with more detail.

Figure 2.12 shows RSAT for R2. If you do not see an option for Hyper-V Tools, you have installed the RSAT for Vista or 2008, and nothing there is specific to Hyper-V. For that you need to download another remote management tool, the Hyper-V Remote Management Update found at `www.microsoft.com/downloads/details.aspx?familyid=88208468-0AD6-47DE-8580-085CBA42C0C2&displaylang=en`. As above, this URL is for the 64-bit version. There is a link at the bottom of the page for the 32-bit version for use with a 32-bit installation of Windows Vista or Windows Server 2008.

FIGURE 2.12
Remote Server
Administration Tools

Unlike the RSAT, which requires you to build your own MMC console with selected snap-ins, Hyper-V Manager places an entry in Administrative Tools for launching the manager. How to launch the tool also varies. For Windows Server 2008, Windows Server 2008 R2, and Windows 7, choose Start ➤ All Programs ➤ Administrative Tools ➤ Hyper-V Manager. That launches an MMC, as shown in Figure 2.13.

To launch the same program from Windows Vista, choose Start ➤ Control Panel ➤ Administrative Tools. From the list that comes up, double-click Hyper-V Manager. That launches the MMC, shown in Figure 2.13.

To populate the Hyper-V servers you want to manage, click Connect To Server in the Actions pane of the MMC. Enter the name of the server you want to manage. Repeat these steps for as many servers as you want to manage. By pairing the RSAT with the Hyper-V Manager tool, you will be able to remotely manage all your Full, Core, and Hyper-V Server installations from a single workstation. Figure 2.14 shows an example of a single console managing itself plus four other Hyper-V hosts. The small *x* you see on two of those hosts (FRACK and MINIE) indicates there is a problem with those hosts.

FIGURE 2.13
Hyper-V Manager

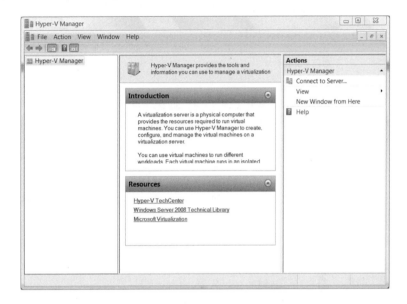

FIGURE 2.14
Hyper-V Manager with multiple hosts

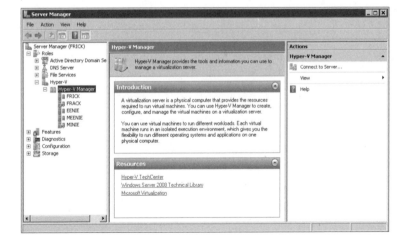

Backup and Restore

Virtualization does not change the need for backup. It just might change the way you back up. For example, in the physical environment, you most likely had procedures in place to run a backup routine on each of your servers. This backup could have been application based or operating system based, depending on the needs you had defined. Now that you will be running multiple virtual machines on a single physical host, you will need to plan accordingly.

The processes and software you are using for your physical environment are likely to work just fine in the virtual environment. But now is a good time to investigate some other options that might save you some money.

Microsoft has provided some built-in capabilities as part of Windows Server 2008. They also have a robust backup package as part of System Center. But there are also a variety of third-party products that support backup of both Windows Server 2008 and virtual machines. If you are using a third-party product, check with them to validate their support for your environment.

VOLUME SHADOW COPY SERVICE

Fortunately, Microsoft introduced some technology in Windows Server 2003 that makes backup much easier than before. This technology is known as Volume Shadow Copy Service (VSS). This service is available for any Microsoft operating system since Windows XP SP1 and Windows Server 2003. See http://technet.microsoft.com/en-us/library/cc785914.aspx for a good description of how VSS works. VSS provides the backup infrastructure for Microsoft operating systems, as well as a mechanism for creating consistent point-in-time copies of data known as shadow copies.

Basically, VSS provides a way to take a backup of a running machine, physical or virtual. This greatly simplifies many backup procedures that sometimes required taking a system down for a full system backup. But VSS does not work by itself. It provides a set of services and APIs that can be used by other software to provide an interface to do the backup. These services and APIs are used by many third-party backup vendors, as well as Microsoft. The major component that needs to be written is a service known as a *writer*. It understands the inner workings of the applications and/or services that need to be backed up and will interact with them to ensure data consistency is maintained.

For example, SQL has a VSS writer. SQL maintains information in memory, known as cache, about the information under its control. If a backup routine simply captured the information that is on the disk, without capturing the information that SQL has in memory, recovery of the disk information captured may have corrupted data. The VSS writer understands this and forces SQL to push all its information to disk to ensure data integrity.

WINDOWS SERVER BACKUP

Part of the Windows Server 2008 operating system is Windows Server Backup (WSB). WSB can be used to perform Hyper-V host- and guest-based backups of your VMs. Because it is written using the VSS API and services, it can perform host-based backups of running Windows VMs that have the integration components installed.

WSB is an optional feature of the operating system. Therefore you need to install this feature before you can use it. Here are the steps required to install the feature:

1. In Server Manager, click Features in the left-hand column.

2. In the right-hand column, click Add Feature.

3. On the Select Features page, expand Windows Server Backup Features and select the check boxes for Windows Server Backup and Command-Line Tools.

Hyper-V does not automatically register its VSS writer for use with WSB. You need to manually edit the Registry. Anytime you are manually editing the Registry, you should take precautions to ensure that you can recover in case you enter some information incorrectly. I have included a step in this process to back up the Registry key you will be modifying.

1. Click Start, click Run, type **regedit**, and then click OK.

2. Locate the following Registry key: HKEY_LOCAL_MACHINE\SOFTWARE\Microsoft\Windows NT\CurrentVersion.

3. Right-click CurrentVersion and select Export. Save the .reg file in a safe location in case you need to go back to it.

4. Right-click CurrentVersion, point to New, and then click Key.

5. Type **WindowsServerBackup**, and then press Enter. This renames the New Key #1 value.

6. Right-click WindowsServerBackup, point to New, and then click Key.

7. Type **Application Support**, and then press Enter. This renames the New Key #1 value.

8. Right-click Application Support, point to New, and then click Key.

9. Type **{66841CD4-6DED-4F4B-8F17-FD23F8DDC3DE}**, and then press Enter. This provides the GUID for the VSS writer.

10. Right-click {66841CD4-6DED-4F4B-8F17-FD23F8DDC3DE}, point to New, and then click String Value.

11. Type **Application Identifier**, and then press Enter.

12. Right-click Application Identifier, and then click Modify.

13. In the Value data box, type **Hyper-V**, and then click OK.

14. On the File menu, click Exit.

If you are going to be doing this with many systems, it can obviously become cumbersome going through the GUI for each machine. Here are the reg commands that you can put into a command file and execute from an elevated command prompt to accomplish the same thing:

```
reg add "HKLM\Software\Microsoft\windows nt\
        currentversion\WindowsServerBackup\Application
        Support\{66841CD4-6DED-4F4B-8F17-FD23F8DDC3DE}"
reg add "HKLM\Software\Microsoft\windows nt\
        currentversion\WindowsServerBackup\Application
        Support\{66841CD4-6DED-4F4B-8F17-FD23F8DDC3DE}" /v
        "Application Identifier" /t REG_SZ /d Hyper-v
```

WSB provides the best integration with those VMs that have the integration components installed. But you can still use WSB to back up a VM that does not have the integration components installed. However, because the VM without integration services is not aware of VSS, it must have a service outage to get backed up. What happens in these cases is that the VM's state will be saved (i.e., written to disk), and then the backup will grab the VM's virtual disks and configuration files. This might not be desirable with an application such as Exchange or SQL because the application will not be aware a backup has run and application logs will not be properly captured. And, because saving the state of a VM requires an outage, and the subsequent backup extends that outage, the outage might be longer than what you would like. You need to determine whether this is acceptable.

To configure WSB for backing up your VMs, follow these steps:

1. Click Start ➢ All Programs ➢ Administrative Tools ➢ Windows Server Backup. (This requires elevated privileges.)

2. If backing up a remote host, choose Connect To Another Computer from the Actions menu on the right-hand side, and type in the name of the remote Hyper-V host.

3. Choose either Backup Once or Backup Schedule from the Actions menu on the right-hand side.

   Note: If you are creating a Backup Schedule, you must use a dedicated local volume that will be formatted and used exclusively by WSB. If you are performing a Backup Once job, you can store the backup on a nondedicated local volume, a removable device, or a network share.

4. Select Backup Configuration — Full Server or Custom. If you choose Custom, ensure that you select all volumes that contain data related to the VM being backed up, including VM configuration data, virtual disks, and snapshots. Otherwise, you will not have a valid backup when you go to restore your VM.

5. Choose the location to store the backup.

6. Choose either VSS Full or Copy Backup. Copy Backup should be used if you are using a different tool to back up content, such as a file or database backup tool. If WSB is the only tool being used, select Full Backup.

7. Once you have confirmed the details, select Backup.

A file created by a successful backup can then be copied to any other Hyper-V host and restored there.

SYSTEM CENTER DATA PROTECTION MANAGER

Though WSB is a free utility that comes with the Windows Server 2008 operating system, it does not provide all the features and capabilities that you might want for a complete enterprise-class backup product. For example, you can run WSB only on the platform on which you have installed it; that is, you cannot use WSB on Host1 to back up Host2.

One of the products in Microsoft's System Center Suite of management tools is Data Protection Manager (DPM). It truly is an enterprise-class backup utility and provides many desirable features:

◆ A single management console for all hosts and guests.

◆ Continuous data protection. VSS snapshots can be scheduled as often as every 15 minutes. Each of these snapshots captures only the data that changed in the host or the VM, meaning that less data is required to be backed up.

◆ Cluster awareness so the backup follows the VM if it moves to different nodes in the cluster.

◆ Flexible backup media. DPM can back up disk to disk, disk to tape, or disk to disk to tape. The last method is really handy if you have a centralized tape library.

◆ Support for Hyper-V guests, Exchange, SQL, SharePoint, and Virtual Server guests.

◆ Ability to insert scripting before and after the actual backup so you can develop custom backup scenarios.

Many third-party backup vendors support VSS for backing up live copies of running VMs. Not all backup tools support VSS, so if you are not using a Microsoft product, check with the vendor to ensure it provides the capabilities you are looking for.

Performance

Managing the performance of a Hyper-V host requires that you consider both the host environment and what is going on in the virtual machines. Most people are surprised the first time they look at perfmon statistics for a Hyper-V server. They expect to see memory and CPU to be much higher, due to the activity of the guests. But remember that when you are logged into the host environment, you are looking at the statistics that are appropriate to the just the parent partition. Each of the guests has its own set of statistics that may not be reflected in the parent partition's statistics. Having separate counters for the parent partition and the guest partitions gives you a more accurate picture of what is really happening in the system. For example, I often run Hyper-V on a single-processor, dual-core laptop. If I have a single virtual machine running, and perfmon within that virtual machine shows that it is running at 100 percent CPU utilization, perfmon in the parent partition may be showing only 20 percent CPU utilization, based on what is happening in the parent partition.

Microsoft has published a detailed performance guide at www.microsoft.com/whdc/system/ sysperf/Perf_tun_srv-R2.mspx. They have included sections on Hyper-V and power management. Why power management? In addition to saving money by having to buy fewer hosts when using server virtualization, it is also possible to save money by controlling the actual electrical power used by the host. There are new capabilities within Windows Server 2008 that enable you to control power levels in the host.

Another great resource is Tony Voellm's blog at http://blogs.msdn.com/tvoellm. Tony is a Microsoft engineer who works on the Windows kernel team, so he really understands what is happening from a performance perspective.

Analyzing disk performance will also be critical to success with Hyper-V. Now instead of having a single workload coming from each host to the storage, you could have 2 or 7 or 20 or more. In the "Installation" section of this chapter, I talked about several considerations on how to use the disks and the types of disks. Here is a brief summary of how to deal with the disks used by the virtual machines. I will be giving more detail about this in the chapter on storage for virtual machines:

◆ Use dynamic virtual hard drives sparingly. Dynamic drives are the slowest performing. These are handy for test and development, because you do not need to know the exact size of the volume, but lack of that knowledge is paid for in performance. Dynamic drives are created with a maximum size, but space is not allocated for the entire drive on creation. As space is needed, it is allocated. Therefore, extra CPU cycles and disk accesses are used to allocate in smaller increments. Some of the performance issues have been mitigated in R2, but there is still some performance overhead due to the nature of how the actual disk space is allocated to dynamic drives.

◆ Use fixed virtual hard drives for production purposes or whenever you want to store either system drives or data drives as files on a storage subsystem. This enables you to carve up a large LUN from your Fibre Channel or iSCSI SAN into multiple, smaller virtual hard drives. They also provide the ability to use the snapshot capability. Fixed drives allocate all the disk space they need on creation. This ensures that there is no extra I/O overhead (as you have with dynamic drives) while data is being written to them.

◆ Use pass-through disks when you want performance and you can dedicate a whole disk to a specific purpose. This is very common in database environments. Also, if you need a drive greater than 2040 MB in size, you need to use pass-through disks. These are not hard-and-fast rules, and there are reasons why you may not want to use pass-through disks, such as their inability to support the snapshot function. More information on the benefits and drawbacks of the different formats is presented in Chapter 4.

Even with these considerations in mind, you still need to monitor disks to ensure they do not become the bottleneck in your virtual machine infrastructure. Many people immediately look at CPU and memory when they have a performance problem, but disk I/O is another one of the core four bottleneck points: CPU, memory, disk I/O, and network I/O. There are few, if any, consistent rules when it comes to managing disks. This is because every application tends to use the disk in a different way. Microsoft has provided a guide to disk performance analysis at `http://download.microsoft.com/download/e/b/a/eba1050f-a31d-436b-9281 -92cdfeae4b45/subsys_perf.doc`. This document is a few years old, but the content is still valid.

One last resource from which you can glean valuable information is the Windows Server Performance Team blog located at `http://blogs.technet.com/winserverperformance/ archive/tags/Performance/default.aspx`. They have many tips and hints for overall Windows Server 2008 performance, but they also have quite a few entries that are related specifically to Hyper-V.

Security

Virtual environments need the same level of security as your physical environment. Some people might even say it takes another level of scrutiny because it is possible to run on the same host two or more environments that are totally unrelated. Microsoft has put a lot of the time and energy of a great number of really talented people into developing the Windows Server 2008 Security Guide. Please start by becoming familiar with this document. It can be found at `http://go.microsoft.com/fwlink/?LinkId=134200`. They have also published a security guide specifically for Hyper-V. Go to `www.microsoft.com/downloads` and search for "Hyper-V security guide" and you will find the guide.

Treat your virtual machines in the same manner as you treat your physical machines. By this I mean that you should evaluate the workload that you have running in the virtual machine and apply the same policies and procedures to it as you did to that workload when it was running on a physical machine. A simple example is that you should run your antivirus program in each of your virtual machines.

I recommend that you also run an antivirus program on your host environment. When you do this, be sure to exclude all the files associated with your virtual machines, such as the .vhd, .avhd, .bin, .vsv, and .xml files. You do not want to have conflicts with a virtual machine trying to access one of its files when the antivirus program is examining it. Besides, I am not aware of any antivirus program that currently can scan a virtual hard drive as anything other than a file. This may change in the future, but today antivirus programs will just see the VHD as a file and cannot look at the files contained in that file.

One of the key tenets of good security is to minimize the potential attack surface. This means that one should install only what is required. Microsoft has provided you with a number of options for this. First, the preferred way to install a host system would be to consider using the Core installation with just the Hyper-V role enabled. Core has only half the potential roles, and there is no Windows Shell or Internet Explorer, two very popular attack vectors. So out of the box you will have a host with a smaller attack surface.

As I mentioned, it is best to install just the Hyper-V role. This can also be done on the Full installations. But, unless you plan to run some other roles or features on the host, there should be little need for a Full installation. The exception I could offer here is that during the time when you are learning the product and developing your management procedures and policies, it is easier to learn on Full than on Core. But you will have an environment with fewer attack vectors by using Core.

By running a Core installation with just the Hyper-V role installed, you also may be able to consider not running your antivirus on the host. Because you are not running any other software, and you are not browsing the network, the possibility of any infected file getting onto the system is slim to none. But, I know that there are many organizations that insist on running antivirus on everything. If it is company policy, there is not much that can be done, other than reviewing why antivirus is required on an installation like this. Obviously, you would still run the antivirus within each of the virtual machines.

The last option is to consider the Microsoft Hyper-V Server platform. Hyper-V Server has pared out all capabilities that are not needed for running virtualization. In the original release it was pretty limited in its capabilities. But with R2, Microsoft has added capacity and the Failover Cluster capability, making this platform on par with a Core installation, except it does not have the ability to add additional roles or features.

Use a dedicated NIC for managing the host. Do not share this NIC with any of the virtual machines. Even though Hyper-V's architecture already isolates traffic between the parent partition and guest partitions, allowing connectivity between those environments only via IP, not sharing the NIC helps ensure another level of isolation between the host and any virtual machine. In some situations this might be very important because of security policies in place in your organization. R2 makes this even easier to implement by including a check box to indicate whether the NIC is to be shared. More on that in Chapter 3.

You may want to take this to the next level by grouping machines with similar or related security policies to the same hosts. As an example, the retail industry has a compliance requirement for something known as Payment Card Industry (PCI) Security Standards. It may make sense to run a system with PCI requirements only on a given host. This is not an absolute requirement, as Hyper-V provides very strong isolation between guests. But some auditors might feel more comfortable with this additional level of isolation. You need to get a final judgment for this from your own auditors.

It should go without saying that you also need to ensure that your virtual machines are fully patched before going into a production environment. This might be a little tricky for those machines that may be turned on only once a month. To assist in this area, Microsoft has a download that can help. It is called the Offline Virtual Machine Servicing Tool. Go to www.microsoft.com/downloads and search for "offline virtual machine." This does not actually service the virtual machine offline as the title implies, in that the machine does have to be running to be patched. But it does automatically bring the machine up in a quarantine environment to apply the patches.

If you are running virtual machines in remote locations, you may want to consider using BitLocker Drive Encryption (BDE) on the host to protect the storage on which the virtual machines are located. Physical security of the host systems should not be too much of an issue in a datacenter environment, because those environments tend to have pretty good physical security. But remote locations often have security that leaves a great deal to be improved upon, as servers may not reside in a secured area, often being deployed in an open office environment. This could lead to potential theft, or temporary "borrowing," of equipment. A drive that is protected with BDE is much more secure than a nonencrypted drive. Should the drive be stolen or borrowed, the content of the drive is fully encrypted with a very strong key. A person trying to read the data from the drive would not find anything readable. For more information on how to configure BDE to help protect your server and the virtual machines running on it, see Windows Server 2008 Hyper-V and BitLocker Drive Encryption at `http://go.microsoft.com/fwlink/?LinkID=123534`.

Many organizations allow business units or departments to have specific management rights for the machines they "own." In the physical world, this was generally accomplished via group policies for many things or giving the department administrative privileges on the physical machine. With virtual machines, role-based management can be accomplished via the Authorization Manager, also known as AzMan. Role-based management is different from the typical access control provided by the operating system. Role-based management involves defining a scope of what you wish to allow and who can perform the functions of those roles. Microsoft has a very complete write-up of this capability at `http://technet.microsoft.com/en-us/library/dd283076.aspx`.

System Center

For the most part, I have included just what is contained within the operating system for managing the Hyper-V environment. I've also included some pointers to some free downloads that make management easier.

However, if you want a complete management solution, you should consider something like what Microsoft offers in its System Center set of products. Other vendors offer solutions in this area, too. The System Center set of products includes these four capabilities:

Configuration Management (SCCM))   Allows you to assess, deploy, and update your servers, clients, and devices across physical, virtual, distributed, and mobile environments. Works across the Windows environment and has wide third-party acceptance for building connections to non-Microsoft environments.

Operations Management (SCOM)   Provides end-to-end service management that is easy to customize and extend for improved service levels across your IT environment. As with SCCM, it works across the Windows environment, with many third parties providing their own management packs to enhance SCOM's ability to work with non-Microsoft products.

Data Protection (SCDPM)   Provides continuous data protection for Microsoft application and file servers to an integrated secondary disk and tape solution on the DPM server. DPM enables rapid and reliable recovery through advanced technology for enterprises of all sizes.

Virtual Machine Management (SCVMM)   This management console ties the SCOM capabilities into a monitoring and management tool for both physical and virtual machines, giving a centralized management experience, even across VMware ESX environments. This is the most complete management interface for any virtualization solution available today.

Microsoft has packaged this solution to be very cost competitive. Obviously, as I am biased toward Microsoft technology, I feel System Center offers the most complete and integrated management solution to consider for the complete management of the virtual environment.

Miscellaneous Tips

In the course of working with virtual machines over the years, I have come across a number of things that make my life easier. These tools and capabilities are not specific to virtualization, but they do help me in my day-to-day work with virtual machines.

REMOTE DESKTOP CONNECTION

The RDC, in addition to providing remote access to your servers, has the ability to share resources from the system on which you are running RDC with the system to which you are connecting. This comes in handy for a number of things. One thing that I use it for fairly often is quickly transferring data from my management system to the remote host. To do so, follow these steps:

1. Open the Remote Desktop Connection. Click Start and select All Programs.

2. Select the Accessories folder and within it select Remote Desktop Connection.

3. Click the Options button from the lower right-hand corner of the RDC (Figure 2.15).

4. Select the Local Resources tab (Figure 2.16).

5. Under Local Devices And Resources, select More (Figure 2.17).

6. Select the local drives you want to share with the remote host. Click Connect.

FIGURE 2.15
Remote desktop options

Now when you open a Windows Explorer window on the remote system, you will be able to access the local drives from your management system. I am sure that as you were stepping through this, you could see that you can also share smart cards and other devices.

OSCDIMG

Oscdimg is a utility that comes with the Windows Automated Installation Kit, which you can download from www.microsoft.com/downloads. Search for "AIK" and select the toolkit for the operating system you are working on. This utility provides a way to quickly build an ISO file of any combination of files that you want to put into it. I build an ISO file containing handy script files, utilities, management agents such as antivirus, and anything else I want to quickly get into a virtual machine.

FIGURE 2.16
Local resources

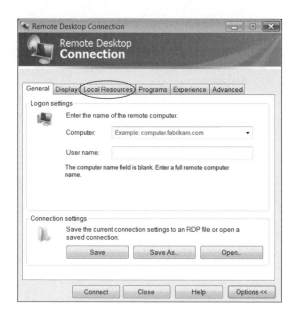

FIGURE 2.17
Local devices

Hyper-V R2 can dynamically add and remove SCSI storage drives. Whereas I often use ISO files for static information that I use on a regular basis and do not change, I will create a VHD for information that is changing on a regular basis. I will then mount that VHD back and forth between my workstation and the virtual machine for the exchange of information.

Core Configurator

Even if you are used to using command-line utilities for configuration of your environment, it is sometimes nice to be able to use a GUI to do some of the common tasks. There is a free download from CodePlex that provides a simplistic GUI for configuring many resources on both Windows Server 2008 Core and Microsoft Hyper-V Server. CodePlex is Microsoft's open-source hosting site.

The download is named Core Configurator, and it can be found at `www.codeplex.com/coreconfig`. You can also download the source files for this utility if you would like to extend it to add additional functions for your particular environment. Figure 2.18 shows what the interface looks like.

FIGURE 2.18

Server Core Configurator

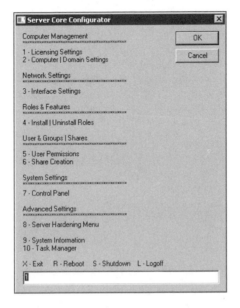

Earlier in this chapter I explained the sconfig tool that comes with the Hyper-V Server product and how it is used for configuring the basic things needed to easily get the system into your environment. Core Configurator does everything that sconfig does, but it adds quite a few more capabilities. Table 2.3 provides a summary of the capabilities of Core Configurator. I have also listed which features are additional over what is available in sconfig.

As you can see, there are quite a few additional functions that you can have with Core Configurator when compared to the sconfig that Microsoft distributes with Microsoft Hyper-V Server, but not with a Core installation of Windows Server 2008. Granted, Core Configurator is not a supported Microsoft product, so you cannot call for help on it. But since it is basically a VB script that calls standard Microsoft utilities, you should not have problems with it. And, since it is provided as open source, and you can download the source, you can modify this to provide additional capabilities you may find useful in your environment.

Hyper-V Remote Management Configuration Utility

John Howard is a senior program manager within Microsoft's Hyper-V product group. He put together a powerful VBScript that is capable of configuring servers for remote management. You can find this free download at `http://code.msdn.microsoft.com/HVRemote`. As with anything that is found on this site, it is to be used as is with no implied support other than through the web page. But, the beauty of this tool is that it can eliminate many of the steps required to set up Hyper-V hosts for remote management and get you up and managing remotely in the matter of a few seconds. It also works in all environments — Full, Core, and Hyper-V Server. For more information see John's blog Configure Hyper-V Remote Management in Seconds at `http://blogs.technet.com/jhoward/archive/2008/11/14/configure-hyper-v-remote-management-in-seconds.aspx`.

TABLE 2.3: Core Configurator

OPTION	DESCRIPTION
Computer Management	
1 - Licensing Settings	This option passes parameters to Microsoft's licensing management utility, slmgr.vbs. You can run slmgr.vbs from a command line and enter various parameters. Core Configurator simplifies the process.
2 - Computer | Domain Settings	This option runs the netdom utility for renaming your computer and joining/removing a computer from a domain. It can also run the dcpromo utility. The ability to run dcpromo is beyond what sconfig does.
Network Settings	
3 - Interface Settings	This option runs the netsh utility to define network settings such as IP addresses, gateways, and DNS servers. It also provides the ability to set up iSCSI. The ability to set up iSCSI is beyond what sconfig does.
Roles & Features	
4 - Install | Uninstall Roles	This option runs the oclist and ocsetup utilities for installing and removing roles and features. sconfig does not have this capability.
Users & Groups | Shares	
5 - User Permissions	This option manipulates membership in the local administrator group. sconfig allows addition of members. Core Configurator provides a couple more options.
6 - Share Creation	This option allows the creation, deletion, and management of file shares. sconfig does not have an equivalent.
System Settings	
7 - Control Panel	This option manages date/time settings, keyboard settings, display settings, and screensaver settings; turns remote desktop on/off; enables WinRM; manages drivers, firewall settings, and Windows Update settings. sconfig manages date/time settings.

TABLE 2.3:   Core Configurator *(CONTINUED)*

OPTION	DESCRIPTION
Advanced Settings	
8 - Server Hardening Menu	This option manages IPV6 network settings and File Server hardening routines. sconfig does not have an equivalent.
9 - System Information	This option runs msinfo32, which displays a window with hardware resources, components, and software environment. sconfig does not have an equivalent.
10- Task Manager	This option starts Task Manager. Hvconfig does not have an equivalent. Of course, pressing Ctrl+Alt+Delete will also allow you to start Task Manager.
Miscellaneous	There are options at the bottom of the list to log off, reboot, shut down, and exit.

The Bottom Line

Installing the Hyper-V role   Windows Server 2008 has been highly modularized when compared to previous versions of Windows Server. The modularization has resulted in the definition of distinct roles that can be separately installed without affecting any other role on the system.

  Master It   Install the Hyper-V role on a Windows Server 2008 Full installation.

Remotely administering Hyper-V Server   Microsoft provides a set of tools that can be installed on a system administrator's workstation for managing Windows Server 2008 hosts and all the roles that can be installed on them.

  Master It   Set up a server for remote administration by using commands instead of the GUI interface. Install the Hyper-V management console on your workstation. Select the remote Hyper-V system to manage.

Backing up Windows Server   Windows Server 2008 comes with a built-in backup utility that can take backups of running virtual machines if the operating system environment running in that virtual machine supports Volume Shadow Copy Services.

  Master It   Set up your Hyper-V Server host to enable the use of Windows Server Backup.

Chapter 3

Creating and Managing Virtual Machines

A wide variety of options are available for managing a Hyper-V virtual environment. Microsoft provides in-box tools for basic management tasks and additional tools for purchase. But, as with any Microsoft product, Hyper-V comes with a full application programming interface (API) to allow partners to complement the product. Thus, besides the Microsoft tools, you will be able to find a variety of other tools, either free downloads or tools for a fee, and more tools are constantly being offered by third parties.

This chapter primarily focuses on the tools that either come with the product or are available as free downloads. I will mention some others in passing, but the idea here is to give you the basics to get started with Hyper-V out of the box without the need to purchase more tools. As you move your Hyper-V environment into larger development and production environments, you will need to evaluate what makes sense for you to use as a corporate management tool.

A key point to remember about managing virtual machines is that they require the same basic tools as physical machines. For example, if you put an Active Directory domain controller on a virtual machine, you will need the same tools to manage that deployment as you would need if you were to deploy it on a physical environment. Therefore, this chapter will not be going into detail on the tools that are common to both environments. It will focus on the components of those toolsets that may have a particular value in the virtual environment.

In this chapter you will learn about:

◆ Managing the Hyper-V parent

◆ Managing the Hyper-V guests or children

◆ Using some common tools for virtual machines

Server Manager

As mentioned in Chapter 2, Microsoft has included a component called Server Manager as an inclusive management view for many of the functions performed by system administrators. When a role is added to the operating system, its corresponding management interface is inserted into Server Manager to give you a single-pane-of-glass view into managing the various roles installed on that server, when it is installed on a Full installation.

This is true with the Hyper-V role. When you install the Hyper-V role on Windows Server 2008 R2, Microsoft inserts the Hyper-V Manager MMC (Microsoft Management Console) into Server Manager. Or, if you prefer, you can call up the Hyper-V Manager MMC by itself without all the other management tools that are in Server Manager. This is done by entering `virtmgmt.msc` at an elevated command prompt or by browsing Administrative Tools from the Start menu. Figure 3.1 shows what the full Server Manager console looks like, and Figure 3.2 shows what the Hyper-V Manager console looks like.

FIGURE 3.1

Server Manager console with Hyper-V

FIGURE 3.2

Hyper-V Manager console

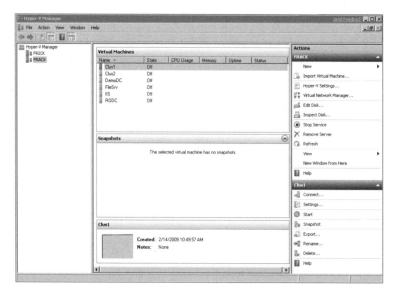

As you can see, they look pretty much the same. Each of these examples shows a console managing two Hyper-V hosts or servers, Frick and Frack. By default, only the local host shows in the console. There are two ways to add another Hyper-V environment installed on Full, Core, or Hyper-V Server to be managed. Because this is a typical MMC, all the rules for working within an MMC environment apply. The first rule of the MMC is that when you select an item, the right-hand column, with the heading Actions, gives you a list of those actions that can be executed on the selected item. So, you can click Hyper-V Manager in the left-hand column and select the Connect To Server action from the Actions column. Similarly, right-clicking Hyper-V Manager will give you a drop-down menu with Connect To Server as an option. This ability to add additional servers to be managed provides you with an out-of-the-box tool that can provide management to a fairly large environment.

Clicking on any server in the left-hand column selects that server as the one to manage. The center column (Virtual Machines) lists all the virtual machines that have been defined on that server. The right-hand column (Actions) shows all the actions that can be performed to manage the virtual environment. Figure 3.3 shows the list of basic actions.

FIGURE 3.3

Basic management actions

You will notice that the Actions menu is divided into two sections. The upper section gives actions that apply to the Hyper-V environment. The lower section lists actions that apply to the currently selected virtual machine. You will also notice the ellipsis (. .) following some entries. This means that there will be more windows to ask you for additional information before the action can be taken.

By selecting a Hyper-V server from the left-hand column and right-clicking it, you will get the list of actions defined below in the "Server Actions" section. By selecting a virtual machine from the center column and right-clicking it, you will get the list of actions defined later in this chapter in the "Virtual Machine Actions" section.

Server Actions

Server actions are those actions that apply to the host or server environment. Note that even though this is listed first in the list of actions, you might want to ensure you have first created virtual networks through the Virtual Network Manager action. There are also global defaults that can be set in the Hyper-V Settings action, but most of those are optional.

NEW

When you click New you are presented with three options:

♦ New Virtual Machine

♦ Hard Disk

♦ Floppy Disk

New Virtual Machine

You select New Virtual Machine when you want to create a new virtual machine. This starts a wizard that leads you through those elements that are required to build a virtual machine, plus a few selections that are optional. The first screen gives a brief explanation of this wizard. After I have read that screen once, I select the option to never show the screen again. Figure 3.4 shows you the second screen of the wizard, the first one that takes inputs for creating a virtual machine.

FIGURE 3.4
Specify Name And
Location

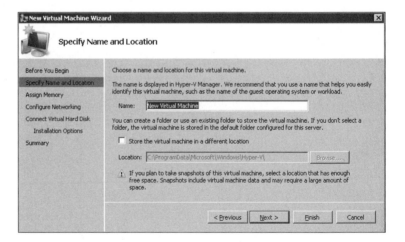

The first entry in this window asks you to enter a new virtual machine name. Naming conventions are totally up to you. By default, the name given here will become the name of the virtual hard drive, but you can override that if you desire. I prefer to keep a fairly straightforward naming convention to make it easier on me.

The second entry asks you where you want Hyper-V to store the information about this virtual machine. The default location is C:\ProgramData\Microsoft\Windows\Hyper-V\. For a simple test environment this might be sufficient, but in a production environment you are likely going to want to isolate information about one virtual machine from that of another virtual machine.

It will be easier to explain if I give you a sample directory structure. Assume that you have defined a specific drive, V:, for storing a collection of virtual machines and that you are creating a virtual machine named SampleVM. In this case, you would enter **V:** as the location to store information about the virtual machines.

Hyper-V creates a V:\SampleVM directory and places the virtual machine's virtual hard drive, SampleVM.vhd, into that directory. It also creates a subdirectory named \Virtual Machines. In the \Virtual Machines subdirectory, it creates an XML file that describes the virtual machine's configuration. It also creates another subdirectory that is named with the GUID of the newly created virtual machine. The name of the XML file is the GUID with an .xml file extension.

If you create a snapshot for this virtual machine (snapshots are explained later), another subdirectory will be created under V:\SampleVM and it will be named \Snapshots. Each new snapshot will create its own subdirectory structure to keep track of information about the snapshot.

The next screen of the wizard asks you how much memory you want to allocate to this virtual machine. This will default to 512 MB, and it can be changed to any amount up to a maximum of 64 GB or the maximum amount of memory on your host system, whichever is smaller. Memory can be assigned in 2MB increments. If the amount of memory assigned to a virtual machine is not available to be allocated when a virtual machine is started, you will receive an error message and the virtual machine will not start. Figure 3.5 shows the Assign Memory window.

FIGURE 3.5
Assign Memory

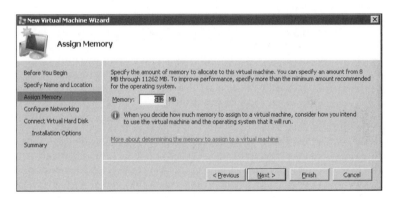

If you remember from discussions in earlier chapters, memory is a critical component in building your virtual machines. There is only so much physical memory on the host, and memory is not shared among virtual machines. Therefore, you should assign only as much memory as you need. One of the interesting features of virtual machines is that they are not locked into the physical constraints of the host environment when it comes to memory assignment. By this I mean that it is just as easy to assign 1016 MB of memory to a virtual machine as it is to assign 1024 MB.

In the physical world, memory generally comes in increments of 512 MB or greater. In the virtual world, there is no such constraint. This comes in handy when you are trying to squeeze the absolute maximum number of virtual machines onto a single server. I often do this in my test environment where I am not as concerned about optimal performance. I will watch the memory usage statistics of my virtual machines and may remove memory in 100 MB increments from machines to see if I can squeeze one more virtual machine into my environment.

This may not be as applicable in a production environment, but if you do have a situation where you want to have certain VMs on the same host, you may be called upon to trim memory. If nothing else, it is worth remembering should the need arise. Currently, changing the amount of memory assigned to a virtual machine requires that the VM be stopped, the memory allocation changed, and the machine restarted.

The next window in the wizard is the Configure Networking window. Figure 3.6 shows you this window.

FIGURE 3.6
Configure Networking

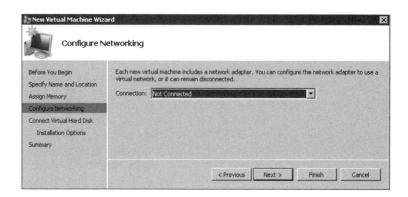

By default, there is no network selected. Clicking the drop-down list will give you a list of all the networks that have been defined for the virtual environment defined on that particular Hyper-V server. The New Virtual Machine Wizard allows you to assign only a single network at this time, even though any given virtual machine can have up to 12. You can use the Settings option of the virtual machine to make changes after you have created the virtual machine.

Connect Virtual Hard Disk is the next window in the wizard. Figure 3.7 shows you the options available in this window.

These are the three options for connecting a virtual hard disk (VHD):

Create A Virtual Hard Disk   This option creates a new VHD in the directory you specify with a name you specify. The VHD is a dynamically expanding disk. The default size is 127 GB, but you can make it any size from 1 to 2040 GB, depending on what you need for your operating system. The dynamically expanding disk does not have the performance of a fixed disk, but it is a handy way to create drives in a test environment. If you want to use a fixed disk as your system disk, you will need to use either the second or third option.

Use An Existing Virtual Hard Disk   This option allows you to assign a disk that you have previously created. This can be either a dynamic or fixed disk of whatever size you have created. It can also be a blank VHD if you plan to install an operating system into this VM, a copy of a VHD that has been prepared by running the sysprep utility against it, or a complete system that was built earlier.

Attach A Virtual Hard Disk Later   This option is used if you are just creating the settings of a virtual machine now and plan to associate a specific VHD with the VM at a later time.

The next chapter goes into greater detail about configuring and using virtual hard drives.

FIGURE 3.7
Connect Virtual Hard
Disk

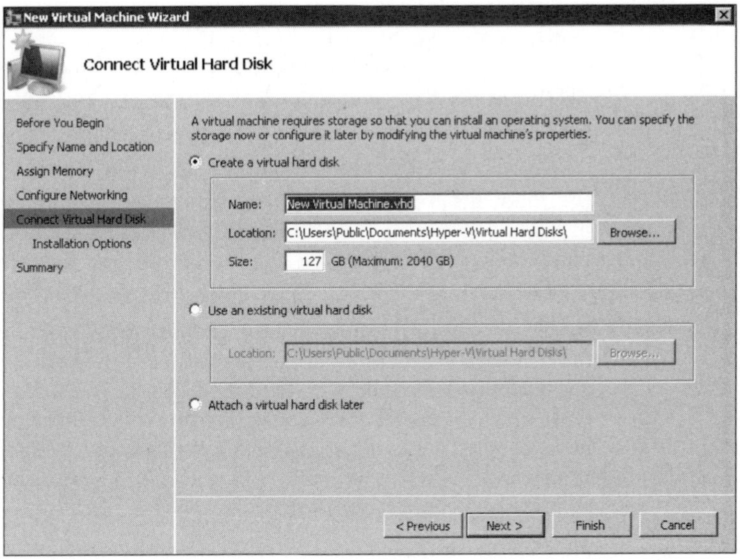

Figure 3.8 shows the various options for installing an operating system into the VM being created.

FIGURE 3.8
Installation Options

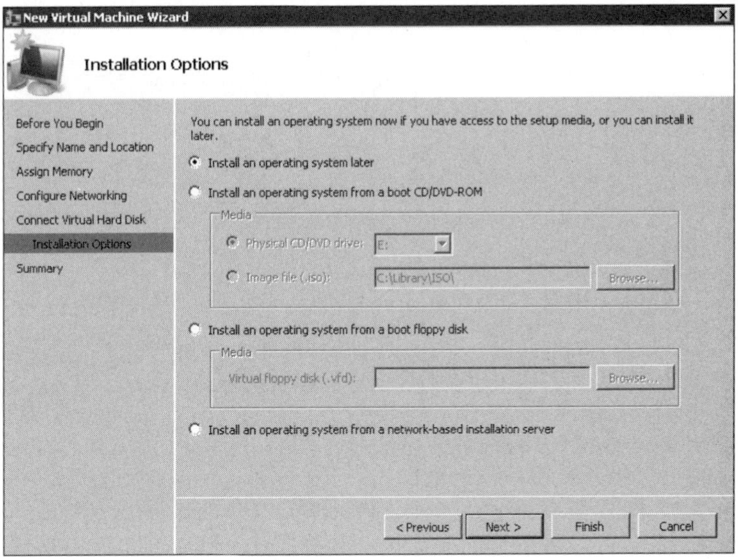

You can select one of the four options:

Install An Operating System Later This option should be used if you are creating a virtual machine with a VHD that already has an operating system installed on it. Or, if you are just setting up virtual machines for later OS installation, you can use this option.

Install An Operating System From A Boot CD/DVD-ROM If you plan to use some form of distribution media for installing the operating system, select this option. The distribution medium must be bootable. This can either be a physical medium that is inserted into the CD/DVD drive of the host system, or it can be a bootable ISO file that resides on a disk on the host system.

Install An Operating System From A Boot Floppy Disk Some legacy operating system environments are installed by booting a small program into memory that, in turn, reads the distribution medium from either CD/DVD, hard disk, or a network location. The boot floppy will often contain something like DOS. This is no longer very common for most modern environments, but it was very common for older environments.

Install An Operating System From A Network-Based Installation Server This option will not be selectable if you did not assign a network from an earlier step. That is because it causes a PXE (Preboot Execution Environment) boot to occur, and a PXE boot requires that a network be available to find the environment from which the operating system can be loaded. If you have installed some sort of PXE environment for loading operating systems, such as Windows Deployment Services, which comes with Windows Server 2008, when this virtual machine is started, it will boot to the network to request that an operating system be loaded.

The last window of the wizard is shown in Figure 3.9. This is the typical summary window with which Microsoft ends its wizards, showing the various options you have selected.

FIGURE 3.9
Completing the New
Virtual Machine Wizard

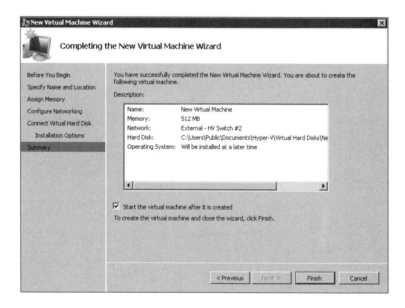

Besides giving you a summary of your options, it also provides the option to start the virtual machine when you click Finish. When you do click Finish, Hyper-V will create the XML file that defines the settings for your virtual machine and will place that file in either the default location or the location you specified. If you asked for the machine to be started, it will make an automatic connection to the virtual machine with the VMconnect utility to provide you with a window to interact directly with the virtual machine. This option to start the virtual machine was removed in Hyper-V R2. VMconnect is a Hyper-V utility that gives you a console window into the virtual machine, just as though you were sitting at the console of a physical machine.

It is necessary to insert a short explanation here to describe some options in creating a Hyper-V virtual machine from an existing VHD from Virtual Server or Virtual PC. One of the options to create a virtual machine is to simply point to an existing VHD. Because the VHD format is a standard, a VHD created by Virtual Server or Virtual PC is fully usable by Hyper-V.

There is an issue in moving VHDs between these environments having to do with the Integration Components (ICs) in Hyper-V and the VM additions in Virtual Server/PC. ICs and additions are unique to both the operating system to which they are deployed and the virtualization management engine. In order to move a Virtual Server/PC VHD to Hyper-V, you should remove the additions before making the move and then add the ICs when the VHD is running on Hyper-V.

When moving from Hyper-V to Virtual Server/PC, the transition is a little more complicated because Hyper-V uses APICs (Advanced Programmable Interrupt Controllers designed by Intel for use in symmetric multi-processor computer systems) for its processors. Virtual Server/PC uses a standard processor. This means different HALs (hardware abstraction layers) are required in the two environments. If you are moving a Windows Server 2008 or Windows Vista virtual machine from Hyper-V to Virtual Server/PC, you must run **msconfig.exe** in the Virtual Server/PC virtual machine, select Boot/Advanced options, select Autodetect HAL, and reboot. If you are working with a virtual machine that is running the Core installation of Windows Server 2008, the command to detect the HAL is **bcdedit /set detecthal true**. If it is an earlier version of Windows that had the ICs installed, you'll need to manually change the HAL from APIC to standard.

New Hard Disk

The New Virtual Hard Disk Wizard is used to create empty virtual hard drives. These drives can be used as the system volume onto which you will install a new instance of an operating system environment, or they can be used for data disks in a virtual machine. Figure 3.10 shows the three options for creating a new hard disk.

- ◆ Fixed Size
- ◆ Dynamically Expanding
- ◆ Differencing

Each of these options leads you through a configuration wizard for that particular type of disk. For details on configuring and using disks, see the next chapter.

New Floppy Disk

Selecting New Floppy Disk simply opens an Explorer window that allows you to browse to the location in which you wish to create a virtual floppy disk (VFD) file. You need to mount this VFD file to another virtual machine to put any information you need onto that disk.

VFDs are useful if you are using legacy deployment technologies, such as a DOS or Windows 95 or Linux boot disk to start your operating system installation. Since most people have moved to using USB drives for newer operating systems, this capability is provided primarily for legacy environments. In the years I have been working with virtualization products in the Windows environment, the only time I created a virtual floppy was just to say that I had done it.

FIGURE 3.10
Choose Disk Type

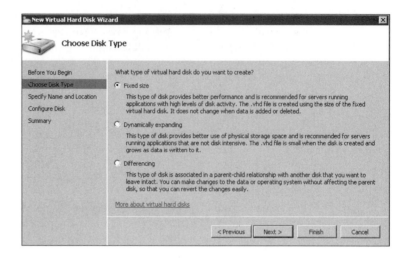

IMPORT VIRTUAL MACHINE

Hyper-V provides the ability to move a virtual machine and its configuration from one host machine to another. This is done by exporting and importing that machine. The Import Virtual Machine action, shown in Figure 3.11, is used to import a machine that has been previously exported. It is important to remember that virtual machines can be imported only if they have previously been exported. Import cannot be used to point to an existing virtual hard drive and its associated XML configuration file and bring it into Hyper-V.

FIGURE 3.11
Import Virtual Machine

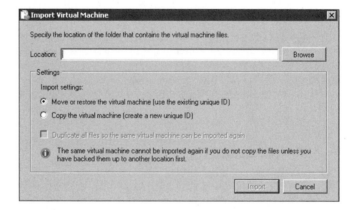

This action is not used for moving a machine from Virtual Server or Virtual PC. It can only be used to import a Hyper-V virtual machine that was previously exported from Hyper-V. Notice the three options:

Move Or Restore The Virtual Machine (Use The Existing Unique ID)   Use this option when you are restoring a virtual machine that is not present anymore on a given server or you are moving it to a different server.

Copy The Virtual Machine (Create A New Unique ID)   Use this option when you want to make a copy of a given virtual machine on the same server from which you exported it. The unique ID is the GUID that Hyper-V creates for new virtual machines.

Duplicate All Files So The Same Virtual Machine Can Be Imported Again   This is a totally new option for Hyper-V R2. If you do not select this option, the same virtual machine can be imported only once. If you do select this option, a copy of the exported virtual machine files is made before creating the new virtual machine.

HYPER-V SETTINGS

Hyper-V Manager is a management console that has some global settings. Selecting Hyper-V Settings from the Actions menu gives you control over these global settings. Figure 3.12 illustrates the various global settings.

FIGURE 3.12

Hyper-V Settings

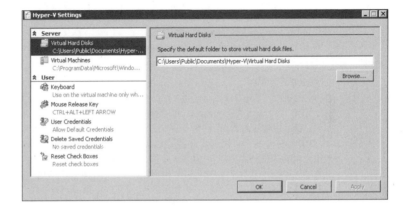

Virtual Hard Disks

This is the default location in which new virtual hard drives are created. This can be any storage location connected to the Hyper-V host system. You have the opportunity when creating new virtual machines to override this location. If you have configured a dedicated storage location for your virtual hard disks, you should specify it here. The value entered here is the default that is displayed in the New Virtual Hard Disk Wizard.

Virtual Machines

This is the default location in which new virtual machine configuration information is stored. It starts out in a public folder on the system drive. If you specify a different location when you are creating a new virtual machine, all this information will be stored in your specified location. If you have configured a dedicated storage location for your virtual machines, you should specify it here. The value entered here is the default that is displayed in the New Virtual Machine Wizard.

Keyboard

Windows provides many shortcut key combinations. For example, Alt+Tab switches the focus from the current window to the window of another running process. When you open a connection to a virtual machine from the Hyper-V host, you are opening a window to another process. By leaving this setting at the default, pressing Alt+Tab will move you off that connection window to the next process running on your desktop on the Hyper-V host.

By default, the shortcut keys work only in the virtual machine if you are running the connection window in full screen. You also have the option to use them only on the physical host or only within the connection window.

Mouse Release Key

Not all operating system environments running under Hyper-V have Integration Components. If you are running a legacy operating system, for example, Windows 98 or MS-DOS, there are no Integration Components for these environments. The Integration Components enable synthetic devices for keyboard, mouse, video, disks, and networking.

If you do not have Integration Components installed, or you are running an environment that does not have Integration Components, when you click the mouse in the connection window, the cursor is captured by the window and you can no longer move the cursor out of the connection window to use in another window on the host. The default key combination for releasing the cursor for use in other windows is Ctrl+Alt+left arrow. You can change this to Ctrl+Alt+right arrow, Ctrl+Alt+spacebar, or Ctrl+Alt+Shift.

User Credentials

By default, when you connect to a virtual machine, the credentials you are currently logged in with are used to access that virtual machine. If you wish to use other credentials, you must clear the check box on this item. Then when you connect to the next virtual machine, you will be prompted with the typical Windows security window asking for credentials. You can either enter an alternate username and password or use a smart card for access. There is also a check box (Remember My Credentials) on this window asking if you want to save your credentials for access to the next virtual machine. These credentials are used only to connect to the console. They do not automatically log you into the virtual machine.

Delete Saved Credentials

If you check the box to remember your credentials at any time, they will become the default credentials used for accessing virtual machines. If you want to go back to the credentials you used to log into the Hyper-V host, you would select this option to delete the credentials you had previously saved.

Reset Check Boxes

Hyper-V is configured with a number of default display options, such as displaying introductory windows at the beginning of a wizard. On each of these introductory windows there is often a check box that, when selected, tells Hyper-V to not bring up that introductory window in the future. If you have checked any of those boxes, click the Reset button and they will appear the next time.

VIRTUAL NETWORK MANAGER

The Virtual Network Manager is used to create virtual network switches to be used by the virtual machines on the Hyper-V host. Figure 3.13 shows an example with two created switches, External and Management. There is no limit to the number of virtual switches that you can configure, even though there is a limit of 12 virtual NICs that can be defined in each virtual machine. However, you are limited to creating a single External switch on each physical network card in the Hyper-V host.

FIGURE 3.13
Virtual Network
Manager

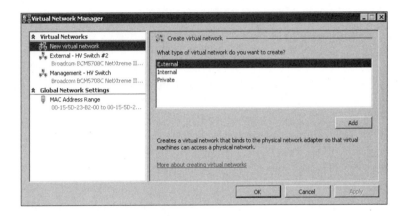

For detailed information about working with networks, see Chapter 4.

EDIT DISK

The Edit Virtual Hard Disk Wizard provides the ability to manipulate virtual hard drives. The virtual hard drives cannot be currently in use by a running virtual machine when you are editing them. Figure 3.14 shows the opening window of the Edit Virtual Hard Disk Wizard.

FIGURE 3.14
Edit Virtual Hard Disk
Wizard

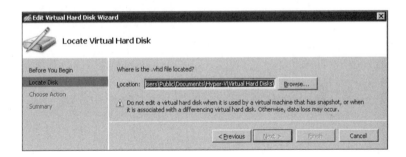

The first thing you need to do is select the VHD on which you want to work by browsing to the location and selecting it. Once you have done that, you are presented with another window with the following options:

Compact This option shrinks the on-disk size of a dynamically expanding VHD by removing blank space that is left behind when data within the VHD is deleted. It does not shrink the defined size of the VHD. For VHDs that are not formatted as NTFS disks, you will first need to find a third-party utility that writes zeros into the deleted space so the compaction routine knows to remove that space. Or you can download a copy of Microsoft Virtual Server or Virtual PC and extract the `precompact.exe` utility that comes with those products. This option does not appear if you select a fixed-size disk because it does not apply.

Convert   This option provides the ability to convert a fixed-size disk to a dynamically expanding disk and to convert a dynamically expanding disk to a fixed-size disk. This option does not allow you to change the size of the disk during the conversion process.

Expand   This option increases the size of either a dynamic or fixed-size VHD. This is useful only if the operating system using this VHD can expand the partition on the disk. Expanding a dynamic disk is almost instantaneous because the actual storage is not allocated to the disk. Expanding a fixed disk may take awhile because all the storage must be physically allocated.

Notice that there is no way to shrink the defined size of a virtual disk. If you want to shrink the defined size of a disk, you'll need to use some other method, such as creating a VHD of the size you want and copying the information to the new VHD.

INSPECT DISK

Inspect Disk asks you for the location of a VHD. It will look at the characteristics of that disk and generate a short report, as shown in Figure 3.15.

FIGURE 3.15
Virtual Hard Disk
Properties

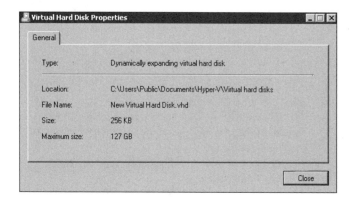

This is a quick way to determine whether you are working with a fixed or dynamic disk and what the actual size is, both on the physical disk as well as what is defined as the virtual limit. In the case of a fixed-size VHD, only the on-disk size will be presented. A dynamic VHD will show how full the drive is. For example, in Figure 3.15 you can see the size listed as 256 MB and the maximum size as 127 GB. This means that the drive has only 256 MB allocated to it on the physical disk, but it has the potential to grow to 127 GB.

Unlike with the Edit Disk option, the VHD can be in use by a running virtual machine. That is because the information about the disk is simply being read and no attempt is made to write to the disk.

STOP SERVICE

Stop Service stops the Virtual Machine Management Service from running. Vmms.exe provides management services for the Virtual Machine Manager. If this service is stopped, the Virtual Machine Manager will be unable to manage this host. This is equivalent to the command-line net stop vmms.

If you have stopped the service, the Actions panel will give you the option to start the service. This is equivalent to the command-line net start vmms. Stopping the service does not stop any running virtual machines. You can still work with the virtual machines through the connect windows.

REMOVE SERVER

Clicking this option removes the selected Hyper-V host from the list of managed hosts. It does not do anything with the virtual machines. This is just to control which Hyper-V hosts you want to manage from this Hyper-V Management console.

REFRESH

Refresh does a new query of what the MMC is looking at to reflect any changes that may have occurred. It is possible to have more than one person running MMCs against the same server — not recommended, but possible. A change on one console will not be instantly reflected in the other console. Clicking Refresh will show the latest status of all information.

VIEW

This option allows you to customize the MMC view. It is common across all MMCs and is not unique to managing Hyper-V. Therefore, there is nothing specific here regarding changing the view for Hyper-V-related displays.

Virtual Machine Actions

The actions that can be executed on a given virtual machine depend on the current status of the virtual machine. A virtual machine can be Off, Running, Saved, or Paused.

CONNECT

Status: Off, Running, Saved, or Paused

The Connect action connects you to the selected virtual machine. This starts a program called VMconnect.exe. If the virtual machine is not running at the time of the connection, you will see a window something like the one shown in Figure 3.16.

FIGURE 3.16
Virtual Machine
Connection

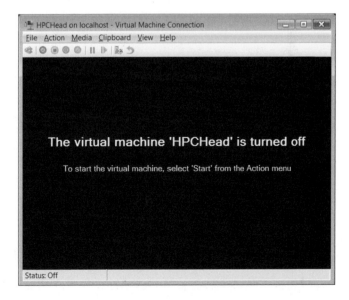

When the virtual machine is running, the window looks very similar to a terminal services connection, presenting you with an image of the console of the running virtual machine. In fact, the VMconnect program is based on the Remote Desktop Protocol (RDP) and the work that has been done by the terminal services team. This is not exactly the same as the Remote Desktop Connection, but it is similar. The size of the window for a running machine is determined by the video settings defined within the virtual machine.

Not only do you have a window to the console of the running virtual machine, but you also have several actions you can perform on or with the virtual machine. These options are selected from the toolbar at the top of the screen or by clicking one of the special icons just below the toolbar. Figure 3.17 shows the icons on a running virtual machine, labeled to show what each icon means.

FIGURE 3.17

Virtual Machine Connection icons

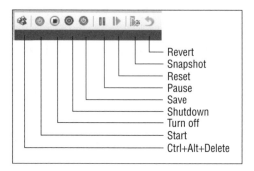

Each of these icons has a corresponding function from the Action menu on the toolbar. VMconnect has five categories:

◆ File

◆ Action

◆ Media

◆ Clipboard

◆ View

There is also a menu selection for Help, but I think that is fairly obvious as to what it does.

The Virtual Machine Connection program is built on top of Microsoft's terminal services technology, using RDP to communicate to the virtual machine. However, all the power of the Remote Desktop Connection is not built into the connection program, but Microsoft is constantly evaluating what may or may not be included. For example, it is possible to share local devices with a remote system by using the RDC. This capability has not been built into the connection program, but the connection program does have a rudimentary capability to pass text information from the Clipboard of the host to the guest machine.

File

The File menu gives you access to two actions:

Settings This brings up a window that allows you to change many of the specific virtual machine settings. I cover this later in this chapter. This action is available on both running and stopped virtual machines, but there are some things that can be changed only on stopped virtual machines.

Exit   This option exits the Virtual Machine Connection program. It does not affect the state of the virtual machine. This action is available on both running and stopped virtual machines.

Action

The Action menu gives you access to nine actions:

Ctrl+Alt+Delete   This option sends a Ctrl+Alt+Delete to the virtual machine. This can also be done by depressing Ctrl+Alt+End on the keyboard. This is necessary to start the login process to the virtual machine. Ctrl+Alt+Delete cannot be used from the keyboard for the virtual machine because that is trapped by the host system. This option is also necessary if you are using a normal Remote Desktop Connection (RDC) to access the virtual machine. RDC interprets Ctrl+Alt+End like Ctrl+Alt+Delete on a physical box, giving you the option to lock the computer, change your password, start Task Manager, and so on. So, if you are using RDC to connect to a Hyper-V host to run VMconnect, you are actually going through two Remote Desktop Protocol connections. You will need this Ctrl+Alt+Delete action to be able to log into your virtual machine.

Turn Off/Start   On a running virtual machine, you will see the Turn Off option to turn off the virtual machine. This is equivalent to pulling the power cord or using the power button on a physical machine to turn it off. The state of the running virtual machine is lost, so any information that may not have been written to disk is lost. A confirmation window is displayed to ensure this is what you really want to do. On a nonrunning virtual machine, you will see the Start option to start the machine.

Shut Down   This option performs an orderly shutdown of the virtual machine. This means that services are shut down and data that may have been cached in file buffers is properly flushed to disk. Once the system is shut down, the system is turned off. This option is grayed out on a nonrunning virtual machine. It is also dependent on Integration Components being installed in the virtual machine. If you have a virtual machine that does not have Integration Components installed, you will not be able to gracefully shut down the virtual machine with this option.

Save   This option saves the current state of the virtual machine. This includes saving the machine's actual memory by writing it to the VHD file, akin to what the Hibernate function is like on a physical machine. Then when this virtual machine is started in the future, the memory and disks are exactly the same as they were when the request was made to save the machine. The status of the machine in Hyper-V Manager is Saved. This option is grayed out on a nonrunning virtual machine.

Pause/Resume   If the virtual machine is running, you will see the Pause action. This puts the machine into a sleep state, similar to what's on a laptop. Information is not flushed from memory, so if the machine is turned off, that information will be lost. If a machine is in a pause state (shown as Paused in Hyper-V Manager), you will see the Resume action. Selecting this resumes the virtual machine from its sleep state to a running state.

Reset   This option is equivalent to doing a hard reset on a physical machine. Memory content is not saved, so changes that have been made may be lost. This is like turning the machine off and then turning it back on immediately.

Snapshot This option takes a snapshot of the currently selected machine. This action can be taken on either running or nonrunning virtual machines. If the virtual machine is running, the snapshot captures the memory image of the virtual machine in addition to taking a snapshot of all the virtual machine's VHDs. If the virtual machine is not running, it takes a snapshot of all the virtual machine's VHDs. Subsequent changes to the virtual machine are saved into .avhd files in the default snapshot location or the location you have specified. The default name given to the snapshot is the name of the virtual machine with a time stamp appended to it. You can rename these to be more meaningful if you so desire. Each time you take a snapshot, a new differencing disk is created to contain all the changes that occur from that point forward. A differencing disk is a separate VHD where any changes that occur within the virtual machine are written to this differencing disk instead of the original. This provides an ability to return to the exact state of the virtual machine at the point in time that the snapshot was taken. A new virtual machine configuration file is also created, giving you the ability to have different configurations for different snapshots.

Revert This option reverts the virtual machine to the previous snapshot. If a snapshot has not been taken, this action is grayed out.

Insert Integration Services Setup Disk This option inserts the vmguest.iso file into the DVD of the virtual machine. If autorun is enabled on the virtual machine, this automatically starts the installation of the Integration Components, which provide the synthetic devices for the supported operating systems. If autorun is not enabled, you may have to select the appropriate setup.exe file from the DVD, either 32-bit or 64-bit. Pressing Ctrl+I from within the running virtual machine accomplishes the same action as selecting this menu option.

Media

The Media menu controls the virtual DVD and floppy drives of the virtual machine. The actions apply to both running and nonrunning virtual machines.

DVD Drive You will see an entry for each DVD drive that you have associated with this virtual machine.

Eject If an ISO file is associated with this DVD, this "ejects" that file so that it is no longer associated. If no file is associated with this drive, the option is grayed out.

Uncapture D: If you have assigned the physical DVD drive of the physical host to this virtual machine, you will see this option instead of the Eject option. Uncapture decouples the physical DVD drive from the virtual machine so that it can be used by another virtual machine. The DVD is not a sharable device, so only a single virtual machine can capture the physical drive at any time.

Insert Disk This option points the virtual DVD to a file with an .iso extension.

Capture D: This option assigns the physical DVD drive of the host system to this virtual machine. The actual drive letter displayed is dependent on the drive letters of the parent partition. You also may see more than one line for this if your parent partition has more than one CD/DVD drive.

Diskette Drive   Though diskette drives, or floppy drives, are not very common any more, the option is available if you are working with some legacy operating systems.

Eject   If a file with a .vfd extension is associated with this virtual machine, this "ejects" that file so that it is no longer associated. If no file is associated with this drive, the option is grayed out.

Insert Disk   This option points the virtual floppy drive to a file with a .vfd extension.

I like using the ability of the DVD to insert ISO files dynamically to pass information into a machine without needing to set up file shares. This is how I may load common utilities and command files if I have not previously loaded them via a virtual machine that I prepared by running the sysprep utility. A variety of utilities can be used for creating ISO files. I use the oscdimg.exe utility that comes with the Microsoft Deployment Toolkit. Go to www.microsoft.com/downloads and search for "MDT."

Clipboard

The Clipboard is operational only on running virtual machines. It has two actions:

Type Clipboard Text   This option provides a way to insert text information you have captured from a copy operation on the Hyper-V host into a text-based application running in the virtual machine. Caution: This is not meant for large volumes of text. I have used it successfully for transferring dozens of characters, but when I have tried transferring hundreds of characters, I have had character losses.

Capture Screen   This option is equivalent to the PrtScrn key on a physical system, except that it works just within the Virtual Machine Connection window. PrtScrn and Alt+PrtScrn from the host console work on the display of the host, so if you wish to capture just what is showing on the console of the virtual machine, without the toolbar and icons of the connection window, use the Capture Screen option. It is possible to change the default action of the Alt+ combinations so that you could use PrtScrn and Alt+PrtScrn within the virtual machine by changing the Keyboard option under Hyper-V Settings, as I described earlier in this chapter.

View

View changes the appearance of the Virtual Machine Connection window. It has only two options:

Full Screen Mode (Ctrl+Alt+Break)   This option displays the connection window on the full screen of the system from which you are running the connection program. This is very similar to what a terminal services connection looks like. If the defined screen size of the virtual machine is smaller than screen size of the machine running the connection program, the virtual machine console will be centered in a black background. The top of the window gives you the option to minimize the window to the taskbar, take the window out of full screen mode, or cancel/exit the Virtual Machine Connection program.

Toolbar   This option lets you display or not display the toolbar. Selecting to not display the toolbar also removes the icons below the toolbar.

SETTINGS

Status: Off, Running, Saved, or Paused

The Settings window, shown in Figure 3.18, is where you manage the virtual machine's "hardware" and some of the management components of that VM. I put *hardware* in quotes because virtual machines use virtual hardware. Even in situations when the virtual machine is in exclusive ownership of a physical device, such as the DVD drive, the hardware is still owned by the physical host, and Hyper-V manages the access to it. The virtual machine is actually accessing either a synthetic or a virtual device, depending on whether the operating system environment running in the virtual machine has Integration Services.

FIGURE 3.18

Settings for
VirtualMachineName

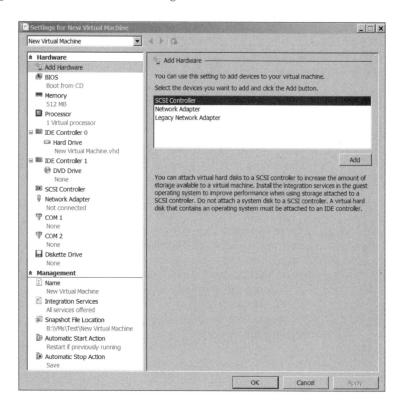

The ability to manipulate the various hardware components of the virtual machine is very similar to manipulating the same components in a physical environment.

Add Hardware

From within the Settings console, you can add or remove both SCSI controllers and network adapters.

The first option is to add additional SCSI controllers to the virtual machine. You can add up to four SCSI controllers, each capable of supporting up to 64 disks, for a total of 256 SCSI drives. With Microsoft Virtual Server, it was recommended to place data drives on SCSI controllers because they had better performance than IDE controllers. With Hyper-V, Microsoft engineers use the same logic for both IDE and SCSI, so there is very little performance difference. However, if you are using more than four drives (the maximum allowed with this IDE configuration), you will need to use SCSI controllers. Hyper-V R2 automatically inserts the first SCSI controller into a newly created virtual machine to ensure that storage can be added or removed from a running virtual machine. This is a new capability that was not available in Hyper-V.

When you select to add a SCSI controller, you are then presented with a window to use for adding a hard drive to the SCSI controller. This window is shown in Figure 3.19.

FIGURE 3.19
Add Hard Drive

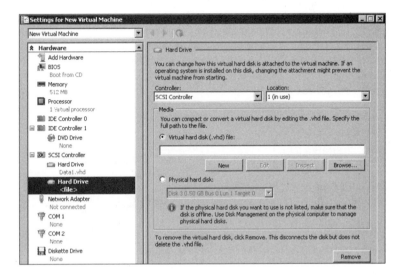

This window can also be reached by clicking a SCSI controller that you have previously added to a virtual machine and clicking the Add button to add a hard drive. Notice that you have two options for the media to be used.

Virtual Hard Disk   This option allows you to point to an existing VHD file to use as the hard disk. The VHD file format is common across Microsoft products, so it makes no difference whether the drive was created by another utility, was created on an IDE bus, or was created by Virtual Server or Virtual PC.

Physical Hard Disk   This option allows you to point to a physical drive connected to the Hyper-V host. This physical drive can be any locally or SAN connected hard disk that is mounted on the host system but is offline. If you do not have any hard drives in this status, this option will be grayed out. Virtual machines will have exclusive access to any physical drive assigned in this manner. So if another running virtual machine has a physical drive assigned to it, that physical drive will also be grayed out. If a non-running virtual machine has it assigned, the virtual machine manager will allow assignment.

Two types of network adapters can be added to your virtual machines:

Network Adapter   This is the synthetic network adapter. It creates a virtual NIC connected to a virtual network switch previously defined through the Virtual Network Manager. This type of adapter is available only if the operating system environment has Integration Components installed. Up to eight synthetic network adapters can be connected to any virtual machine.

Legacy Network Adapter This is the software-emulated network adapter. Similar to assigning a synthetic adapter, selecting a legacy network adapter creates a virtual NIC connected to a virtual network switch previously created. This is the only type of adapter that is available for operating system environments that do not have Integration Components installed. This can also be used for booting into a network installation. Up to four legacy network adapters can be connected to any virtual machine.

Adding or removing SCSI controllers or network adapters requires that the virtual machine not be in a running, saved, or paused state. It must be turned off. However, if you have already configured a SCSI controller, you can add and/or remove hard drives to that SCSI adapter while the virtual machine is running. This is new for Hyper-V R2. Hyper-V required the virtual machine to be in a stopped state for adding or removing any type of storage except for CD/DVD.

BIOS

The BIOS setting turns the Num Lock key on or off and selects the order in which boot devices are checked to start the operating system. Figure 3.20 shows you the options.

FIGURE 3.20
BIOS settings

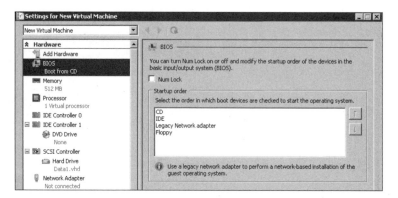

If your plan is to install operating systems to the virtual machines over the network, you should make Legacy Network Adapter the first item in the list by clicking it and then using the arrows on the right side of the box to move it to the top. You need a legacy adapter for this because there are no Integration Components installed in the BIOS to recognize a synthetic adapter.

You should change the boot order to have the IDE controller first in your production machines. This will ensure that the machine starts as quickly as possible since it will not need to check for a bootable device in the CD, which is the default first boot option.

Making changes to the BIOS requires that the virtual machine not be in a running, saved, or paused state. It must be turned off.

Memory

The Memory setting window, as shown in Figure 3.21, is pretty straightforward.

The range of values is any numeric value between 8 MB and the maximum amount of memory available on your host Hyper-V system. However, if you do set the machine to the maximum, you will not be able to start that virtual machine on that host. This is because the parent partition already has memory allocated to itself.

FIGURE 3.21
Memory settings

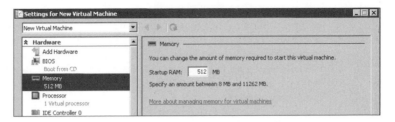

Remember that Hyper-V does not allow the sum of all memory of all virtual machines, and this includes the parent partition in the calculation, to be greater than what is physically available on the host. This is likely to change sometime in the future, but it is not possible today.

Making changes to the memory requires that the virtual machine not be in a running, saved, or paused state. It must be turned off.

Processor

The Processor settings window, as shown in Figure 3.22, provides a number of ways to control the processing power of the virtual machine.

FIGURE 3.22
Processor settings

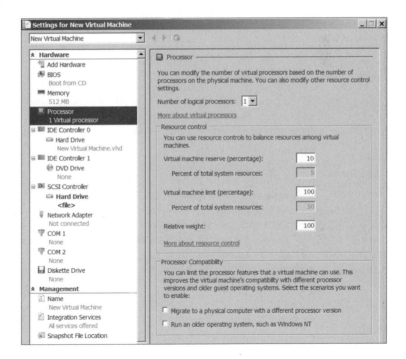

The first option, Number Of Logical Processors, sets the number of virtual processors to be assigned to this virtual machine. If an operating system does not have Integration Components, the maximum value is 1. If the operating system does have Integration Components installed, the value can be 1, 2, or 4, depending on what is supported for that particular operating system. (The latest information on supported number of virtual processors is found at www.microsoft.com/windowsserver2008/en/us/hyperv-supported-guest-os.aspx.)

You may run into a situation where you are working with an operating system, like Windows Server 2008, that supports up to four virtual processors. But when you go to select four processors, you find that your system allows only two. This is because you cannot select more processors than what are available on the Hyper-V host. So if your Hyper-V host has only two processors or two cores, you can create virtual machines with a maximum of two virtual processors. Any Hyper-V host with four or more processors or cores will allow you to specify up to the current maximum of four virtual processors.

Making changes to the number of logical processors requires that the virtual machine not be in a running, saved, or paused state. It must be turned off.

Hyper-V also lets you balance the resources of physical cores in the host across the virtual machines that are running on that host. This is done by allocating a percentage of the total available resources of a single physical core to a specific virtual machine. This is controlled via three settings. I will use the values shown in Figure 3.22 to help explain how the values interact.

Virtual Machine Reserve   This value represents the minimum percentage of resources that you want to guarantee to a specific virtual machine. Notice that I have set the value in Figure 3.22 to 10 percent. That shows the percent of total system resources as 5 percent. This is because I have allocated one processor to the virtual machine on a two-processor host. One processor is one-half of the total available processors. Therefore, 10 percent of one processor is 5 percent of the total processing power. When I change the number of logical processors to 2, the reserve stays at 10 percent, but the total system resources moves to 10 percent because I am now using 10 percent of each of the two processors instead of 10 percent of one processor. By default, this value is set to 0 percent to ensure that each virtual machine gets some resources assigned to it. If you have 10 virtual machines, each with a 10 percent reserve, that would be the maximum number of virtual machines that could be run — you cannot specify more guaranteed resources than are physically available. This is why leaving this at 0 percent ensures every virtual machine some resources.

Virtual Machine Limit   This value represents the maximum percentage of resources that you want a specific virtual machine to be able to use. This is also related to the number of physical cores on the Hyper-V host. In this example, I have set the limit to 100 percent (the default). Since I have also specified a single logical processor from my two-processor host, the total system percentage is 50 percent. When I change the number of logical processors to two for this virtual machine, the total system resource percentage moves to 100 percent because a two-processor virtual machine can now, theoretically, make use of 100 percent of the total system. It is a good idea to leave this at 100 percent if you wish to have the virtual machine make full use of any resources that are made available to it. This is a maximum amount — so if the maximum is not available, it will still run. But the most it can use is the 100 percent that is the default.

Relative Weight   This value is used to determine which virtual machine gets the resources when more than one virtual machine are competing for the resources. By default, the value is 100. That means that if all virtual machines have a relative weight of 100, they compete equally for available resources. If you set one virtual machine to 200 and two to 100, the machine with the relative weight of 200 will be given resources first if all three are competing for the same resources. This is simply a way of categorizing virtual machines. There is no special significance to the difference in the values other than the absolute value — the larger the number, the higher its ranking. You define what the numbers mean in your environment. In order to use Relative Weight rather than Reserved Capacity and Maximum Capacity, set Virtual Machine Reserve to 0 percent and Virtual Machine Limit to 100 percent.

Generally it is best to leave these three values at the defaults. If you do make changes, monitor the performance of all your virtual machines to ensure you are achieving the results you desire.

The Resource Control parameters can be changed on a running virtual machine. It does not have to be in a stopped state. This gives you the ability to monitor how virtual machines are actually running and adjust their utilization on the fly, should the need arise to dynamically adjust what is happening in the data center.

The next box is very useful if you are using Quick or Live Migration (explained in Chapter 5). These migration capabilities can move virtual machines from one host in a cluster to another host. However, you may have hosts in the cluster with different versions of processors. Checking this box ensures that only instructions common to all processors are used by the virtual machine, ensuring that the virtual machine will start without problems on another host in the cluster. This works between processors from the same vendor. That is, this does not enable moving virtual machines between Intel and AMD processors using Quick or Live Migration.

The last check box on this window is used to limit the processor functions available to the guest operating system. Some legacy operating systems, such as Windows NT, do not always run correctly on newer chips with additional hardware instructions. If you are running such a legacy operating system and are experiencing some unexplainable issues, you can try checking this box to see if that corrects the problem.

Making changes to the processor functionality requires that the virtual machine not be in a running, saved, or paused state. It must be turned off.

IDE Controller 0/1

Virtual machines are configured by default with two IDE controllers, and this is the maximum number that can be assigned. One hard disk must be assigned to one of the controllers to provide a boot volume. DVD drives can also be assigned to IDE controllers.

I already discussed how to add drives when I discussed the Add Hardware action above, so see that earlier section for that information. But there are a couple of other things to keep in mind. If you want to, you can assign up to a maximum of three DVD drives. You must reserve one hard drive as the boot volume for your system drive, unless you are doing something strange like running a machine from a bootable DVD, which may be valuable for some debugging situations. On the flip side, you can remove all the DVD drives if you want to use four IDE drives.

Changing an assigned DVD from the physical DVD on the Hyper-V host to an ISO file can be done dynamically; that is, the machine can be running while changes are made to the location of the data coming from DVD.

Making changes to the number of hard disks or DVD drives requires that the virtual machine not be in a running, saved, or paused state. It must be turned off. The ability I mentioned earlier to add or remove storage from a running machine is limited to storage connected to a SCSI controller.

SCSI Controller(s)

As with the IDE controllers, I covered how to add and remove storage from this when I covered the Add Hardware action above. IDE and SCSI use the same underlying logic for disk, so performance in some situations can be fairly similar. But SCSI has some protocol benefits that will improve performance, so SCSI is generally used for the data drives. For example, SCSI can do reads and writes in larger requests than IDE. Another reason for considering using SCSI in production is that you can have up to four SCSI controllers, each with up to 64 hard disks assigned to it. You can use this for load-balancing purposes in the virtual environment, just as you do in a physical environment. For example, if you have more than four physical disks, either pass-through or containing VHDs, you can use SCSI to point to them. IDE limits you to four different disks.

Making changes to the number of hard disks on an IDE controller requires that the virtual machine not be in a running, saved, or paused state. It must be turned off. Hyper-V version 1 had this same requirement for SCSI controllers and disks, but this has changed for Hyper-V R2. You still need to have the machine in a stopped state in order to add a SCSI controller, but once you have a SCSI controller instantiated in a virtual machine, you can add and remove VHDs on that SCSI controller while the virtual machine is running. You can also manipulate the VHDs, such as compressing them or changing them from fixed to dynamic.

Network Adapter(s)

The Network Adapter settings window is used for adding, removing, and modifying the virtual NICs in a virtual machine. Chapter 4 covers the types of networks in more detail, but just so you have an idea of what to select, here are the options:

External An external network has access, through the parent partition, to the physical network interface. This enables virtual machines to talk to other virtual machines and physical machines.

Internal An internal network provides a network link between the guest virtual machines and the Hyper-V host. Network traffic does not go out on any physical wire. Communication is only among virtual machines connected to that internal network and with the host.

Private A private network provides a network link between guests on the Hyper-V host. The parent partition does not see any traffic, nor is any traffic placed on a physical wire.

There is one additional configuration option, MAC Address, that was not available in the "Virtual Network Manager" section. Figure 3.23 shows the MAC address as part of the Network Adapter settings. That is because we are now talking about manipulating the actual virtual NIC instead of the virtual network switch.

Each NIC needs a unique MAC (media access control) address as the physical address to which network traffic is directed. In a physical world, the IEE standards organization provides each NIC vendor a unique vendor ID as the first 3 bytes of the MAC address (shown as 00-15-5D in Figure 3.23). 00-15-5D is the Microsoft IEEE Organizationally Unique Identifier. The next 3 bytes are used to uniquely identify the specific physical device.

Since Hyper-V is creating virtual NICs, it needs to have a method that will minimize the possibility of having MAC address conflicts, not only on a single host but among hosts as well. It does this by creating a pool of addresses for the host on which Hyper-V is running. The 6 bytes of the MAC address are created in three segments. The first segment is the 00-15-5D that is Microsoft's ID. The next 2 bytes (01-66 in Figure 3.23) are pulled from the last 2 bytes of the IP address assigned to the Hyper-V host. This provides a high probability that the first 5 bytes of the MAC address will be unique for each Hyper-V host. The last byte is an incrementing value from 00 to FF (0 to 256).

This is sufficient for most environments. However, this is a pool of 256 numbers that simply starts over from the beginning when the last number is handed out. Most of the time this will not make any difference, but if you have a Hyper-V host on which you have been creating and deleting a lot of virtual machines, it is possible for a MAC address to be duplicated on a new virtual machine if you have an older virtual machine still running. If only one of the virtual machines is running, you will not see any problem, but you may get an error message of "no available MAC address" if you try to start a second machine with the same MAC address.

FIGURE 3.23
Network Adapter settings

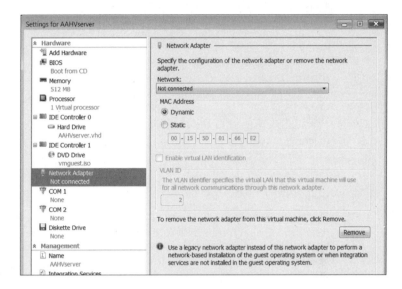

Some shops have management capabilities tied to MAC addresses. Therefore, Microsoft allows static assignment of other addresses instead of the default.

Making changes to the number, assignment, or MAC address requires that the virtual machine not be in a running, saved, or paused state. It must be turned off. However, you can change the VLAN identification on a running virtual machine.

COM 1/2

You can configure up to two COM ports to communication with another computer or virtual machine through a named pipe. This is a software pipe; that is, there is no way to map to the physical COM ports on the host Hyper-V server. See Figure 3.24 to see what this option looks like.

FIGURE 3.24
COM settings

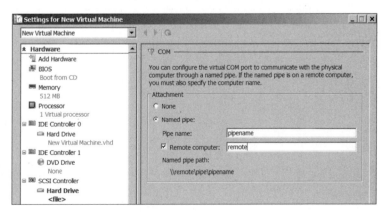

The default for COM assignment is None. I have selected Named Pipe option to demonstrate how the name is constructed. The name contains three pieces: the computer name, the pipe identifier, and the name you provide for the pipe. In Figure 3.24, you can see the name for a pipe on a remote computer. If you were to create this pipe on the local computer, the local computer would be referenced as "\\.", where the period represents the local computer.

Making changes to the COM settings can be accomplished while the virtual machine is running.

Diskette Drive

This setting either disables the diskette drive, which is the default setting, or points to the VFD file you want to use.

Making changes to the Diskette Drive settings can be accomplished while the virtual machine is running.

The next five options deal with management of various components of the virtual machines selected.

Name

The Name setting gives you two options. The first is simply to change the name used to represent the virtual machine. This does not change the name by which the virtual machine is known in the domain/workgroup or network. Nor does it change the name of any files associated with this virtual machine. It merely changes the name used by Hyper-V Manager on this machine.

The second option is to insert notes to the virtual machine. These can be used for any purposes that may make sense to you. When notes are included, the first few characters of the notes appear alongside the thumbnail of the virtual machine shown at the bottom of the center column of Hyper-V Manager.

Integration Services

Integration Services, also known as Integration Components, are software components that run on top of the guest operating system inside a child partition and as part of the virtualization stack in the parent partition to provide some level of integration with the parent partition. They are used to address problems that could possibly arise from the high level of isolation provided by virtual machines.

As a result, Integration Services provide more than just synthetic devices for the guest operating system. There are also some management features that can be turned on and off. The Integration Components must be installed in the virtual machine in order to manipulate these management functions.

Operating System Shutdown   This service allows a virtual machine to be shut down via selecting the Shutdown option from the Action toolbar on Hyper-V Manager or VMconnect or by right-clicking the name of the VM within Hyper-V Manager. This service requires the guest operating system to support a remote shutdown capability. This is different from simply turning off the virtual machine. Using Shutdown allows you to gracefully shut down the virtual machine as if you were logged into the console and issued the shutdown command from there.

Time Synchronization   This service keeps the virtual machine's system clock synchronized with the system clock of the Hyper-V host. Disabling time synchronization is useful if you want to perform tests within a virtual environment where the time is different from the host time. This does *not* override the time synchronization that is done when a virtual machine is started. Remember that a physical machine has a battery-operated clock from which it gets its initial time when it is booted. There is no battery-operated clock in a virtual machine, so when a virtual machine is booted, it always retrieves its initial time from the Hyper-V host, regardless of this setting. Once the virtual machine is running, disabling this service disables further synchronization.

Data Exchange　This service provides a way to exchange small amounts of management data back and forth between the Hyper-V host and a virtual machine running in a child partition. This is accomplished via a process known as key/value pairs, where you have defined keys with the desired value. Some of the more common ones are FullyQualifiedDomainName, OsName, OsVersion, CSDVersion, OsMajorVersion, OsMinorVersion, OsBuildNumber, OsPlatformID, ServicePackMajor, SuiteMask, ProductType, and ProcessorArchitecture. The Windows Management Interface (WMI) can be called to read/write this information, or you can use a scripting language like PowerShell to build management capabilities based on the obtainable results.

Heartbeat　This service reports at regular intervals that a given virtual machine is "alive." This enables management agents to take a desired action should the agent determine that the virtual machine is no longer reporting.

Backup (Volume Snapshot)　This service is used to support backup of running virtual machines by use of backup routines that are dependent on Microsoft's Volume Shadow Copy Service (VSS). Not all operating systems for which there are Integration Components support this service. For example, Windows XP and SUSE Linux do not support VSS at the operating system level. Therefore, even with Integration Components installed, they do not support the ability to be backed up while they are running. If you uncheck this box on a virtual machine that does support VSS, the virtual machine will be taken offline before a shadow copy is taken. This check box makes no difference for those operating systems that do not support VSS. Therefore, operating systems such as Windows XP and SUSE will always be taken offline before a shadow copy is taken.

Snapshot File Location

By default, the location where snapshot files are stored for a virtual machine is in a \Snapshots subdirectory of the location of the VHD file for that VM. This can be moved to a location on any other disk on the Hyper-V host. This gives you the ability to store snapshots on a different spindle for performance or space needs.

Automatic Start Action

This action determines what a virtual machine does when the Hyper-V host system is booted or restarted. One of three options can be selected:

Nothing　Do not manipulate the state of the virtual machine.

Automatically Start If It Was Running When The Service Stopped　If the virtual machine was in a running state when the host system was stopped, start this virtual machine. This can cause both the host and the guest to start more slowly because they are competing for the same hardware resources.

Always Start This Virtual Machine Automatically　Start this virtual machine when the Hyper-V host starts, even if it was not running when the Hyper-V host was turned off. This can cause both the host and the guest to start more slowly because they are competing for the same hardware resources.

It might not always make sense to start all the virtual machines simultaneously on a Hyper-V host because of the amount of resources that may be needed. Or, you may have some virtual machines that are dependent on services that come from another virtual machine. In these cases, you might want to delay the start of a virtual machine to some time after the Hyper-V host is started. That is what the automatic startup delay setting is used for.

For example, you might have a virtual machine that needs to contact network resources to operate. You need to ensure that the host system's physical networks are up and running before you start these machines. Therefore, you might want to wait 5 minutes (300 seconds) after the start of the Hyper-V host before starting the virtual machine.

Automatic Stop Action

When running several virtual machines on a single Hyper-V host, it is not always convenient for an operator to ensure guests are shut down properly before shutting down the host. This setting gives you three options for a virtual machine to perform when the Hyper-V host performs a graceful shutdown. Note that these work only when the Hyper-V host knows it is shutting down; if there is the equivalent of the power switch being pressed, there is no way for the operating system to have enough time to take any action.

Save The Virtual Machine State   This option causes the contents of the memory of the virtual machine to be written to disk so the machine can be restarted from this exact point when the system comes back online.

Turn Off The Virtual Machine   Do not save the state. This is like turning off the power to a physical machine. Any memory state and any uncommitted changes to files or databases are lost.

Shutdown The Guest Operating System   This option performs a graceful shutdown of the operating system. This means that running services go through a normal shutdown, such as SQL writing its memory buffers to disk. This works only if Integration Components are available for the operating system and are installed in the guest.

CHANGE STATUS

A virtual machine can be in one of four states. Table 3.1 shows what those various states are. You can change any virtual machine to another status depending on the status that the machine is currently in. This can be done by using the toolbar icons on the Server Manager toolbar, right-clicking a virtual machine and selecting, or selecting the option from the Action menu.

SNAPSHOT

Status: Off, Running, or Saved

Take a snapshot of the currently selected machine. This action can be taken on either running or nonrunning virtual machines, but not if the machine is paused. If the virtual machine is running, the snapshot captures the memory image of the virtual machine in addition to taking a snapshot of all the virtual machine's VHDs. If the virtual machine is not running, it takes a snapshot of all the virtual machine's VHDs. These files are saved as a file with an .avhd extension in the default snapshot location or the location you have specified. The default name given to the snapshot and presented in Server Manager is the name of the virtual machine with a timestamp appended to it. You can rename these to something more meaningful if you so desire.

TABLE 3.1:   Status table

CURRENT STATUS	POTENTIAL ACTIONS
Off	Start — start the virtual machine.
Running	Turn Off — power off the virtual machine. No information is saved.
	Shut Down — perform a graceful shutdown by telling the operating system and services to have normal exits.
	Save — write the memory state of this virtual machine to disk so it can be started at this exact point sometime in the future. This is similar to the Hibernate option on a laptop or desktop system.
	Pause — put the machine into a paused state. This is similar to the Sleep option on a laptop or desktop system. Because the memory state is not written to disk, as with the Save option, Pause is a nearly instant action.
	Reset — power off and power on the machine in one step. No information is saved.
Paused	Turn Off — power off the virtual machine. No information is saved.
	Save — write the memory state of this virtual machine to disk so it can be started at this exact point sometime in the future. This is similar to the Hibernate option on a laptop or desktop system.
	Resume — bring this virtual machine out of its paused state. Because this is not reading information from disk, it is a nearly instant action.
	Reset — power off and power on the machine in one step. No information is saved.
Saved	Start — restart this virtual machine by reading its previously saved memory state from disk and starting it.
	Delete Saved State — delete the saved state. This deletes any saved memory image from the previous Save command.

The .avhd file is what is known as a *differencing disk*. This means that any changes that occur within the virtual machine are written to this differencing disk instead of the original .vhd file that you defined for the virtual machine. This is how you can revert to an earlier state of the virtual machine. Since changes are not being written to the original .vhd file, when you revert to that earlier point, the machine is in the exact state it was in when the snapshot was taken.

The Snapshot action also captures the virtual machine configuration. This enables you to add processors or memory or other configuration options within different snapshots. When you revert to an earlier snapshot, the exact configuration that was in effect at the time of the snapshot is restored, even if the previously running virtual machine had a different configuration.

EXPORT

Status: Off or Saved

When you want to move a fully configured virtual machine from one Hyper-V host to another Hyper-V host, you first have to export it. When you export a virtual machine, it creates an on-disk structure that is very similar to the structure of the virtual machine you are exporting. Here is a sample of the directory structure created by the export:

```
... TargetDirectory\VirtualMachineName
    ... \Snapshots
    ... \Virtual Hard Disks
    ... \Virtual Machines
config.xml
```

Before importing, you should ensure that the components used by the exported virtual machine are available on the importing Hyper-V host, or you will see some errors in the Hyper-V management event log. Not all errors are fatal. For example, if you have not defined a virtual network switch on the importing Hyper-V host to have the same name as a virtual network switch on the exporting Hyper-V host, you will receive an error. This can easily be fixed by either defining that virtual network switch or by reassigning the NIC of the virtual machine to a virtual switch on the importing machine.

RENAME

Status: Off, Running, Saved, or Paused

This action is used to change the name used to represent the virtual machine. This does not change the name by which the virtual machine is known in the domain/workgroup or network — that name is part of the operating system within the virtual machine. Nor does it change the name of any files associated with this virtual machine. It merely changes the name used by Hyper-V Manager on this machine.

DELETE

Status: Off and Saved

This action is used to remove the pointer to this virtual machine on this Hyper-V host. It does not delete any of the associated files of the virtual machine. This is used to stop managing and forget the configuration for this virtual machine. Generally when you move a virtual machine from one host to another you will use the Export/Import functions. But it is possible to just copy the VHD from one host to another. The difference is that Export/Import saves the configuration information and uses that to build the virtual machine on the new host, so it has the amount of memory, number of processors, defined networks, and so on. If you just copy the VHD across to a new host, you have to re-create the configuration information on the new host.

Other Hyper-V Management Tools

The built-in Hyper-V Manager described above provides all the basic functions for creating and managing a Hyper-V environment. It also provides the ability to have a single console manage several Hyper-V hosts. But a variety of free and for-fee tools can enhance the management capabilities within a Hyper-V environment.

Windows Management Instrumentation

Windows Management Instrumentation (WMI) is a set of extensions to Microsoft's Windows Driver Model. This provides a way for components of the operating system to be enabled to provide information about those components or to send notification of events. This is Microsoft's implementation of an industry initiative called Web-Based Enterprise Management (WBEM) and the Common Information Model (CIM) standards from the Distributed Management Task Force (DMTF). Access to this information can be obtained by using a scripting language like VBScript or PowerShell.

Microsoft provides what are known as WMI providers for nearly every product it produces, including Hyper-V. In fact, Microsoft has an engineering requirement known as its Common Engineering Criteria that defines what must be in a product, and WMI management is one of those criteria. WMI data can be obtained locally or remotely, making it a powerful tool for building management scripts and applications. For more information about the power and implementation of WMI within Microsoft products, see `http://msdn.microsoft.com/en-us/library/aa384642(VS.85).aspx`.

WMI providers implement the functionality described by WMI classes, methods, and properties to manage associated Windows components, such as the operating systems and roles, like Hyper-V. The information can be obtained either via programmatic languages like C++ or via scripting languages like PowerShell or VBScript. You can find sample code for manipulating the various Hyper-V WMI classes at the same reference given above.

Since writing directly in WMI can be challenging, I will concentrate on a couple of downloads that are available from the Internet that provide tools for managing Hyper-V via PowerShell and VBScript.

POWERSHELL

PowerShell is Microsoft's latest scripting language. However, it goes beyond anything Microsoft had done in the form of a scripting language previously. Not only is it a scripting language, but it is also an extensible command-line shell. PowerShell provides many commands (or cmdlets in the language of PowerShell), but the shell itself allows you to create new commands if you don't find exactly what you want. It can be used as a replacement for the venerable CMD window, as all the commands that exist in CMD are duplicated in PowerShell by a feature called *aliasing*, plus you get all the new capabilities provided by PowerShell.

PowerShell was first released as a no-cost download for Windows XP and Windows Server 2003. It is included as an optional feature in Windows Vista and Windows Server 2008. Windows 7 and Windows Server 2008 R2 include version 2 of PowerShell.

With the release of Windows Server 2008 R2, PowerShell V2.0 is installed by default in a Full installation of the operating system. PowerShell is being used as the foundation for building the management interfaces for the various roles and server products. For example, Windows Server 2008 R2 provides a PowerShell module for managing Failover Cluster Services. Previously the capability was handled by a utility program, `cluster.exe`. Another example is that Active Directory has a new management GUI built on PowerShell known as Active Directory Administrative Center. As time progresses, more and more of the operating system roles and server products will be able to be fully managed via PowerShell.

With Windows Server 2008 RTM, PowerShell was not available on Core installations. But Windows Server 2008 R2 Core now includes an option to install PowerShell. And, because PowerShell V2 is fully remotable (that is, you can execute a PowerShell command on a remote computer), this means that it becomes easier yet to manage a Core installation.

If you search the Web for Hyper-V scripts, you are going to find thousands of hits. Many of them provide single-function scripts that are useful, but not many of the hits provide fairly complete management libraries. I have listed three sites that I have found to be very useful.

James O'Neill

James O'Neill is a Microsoft employee who has done a great job on creating a PowerShell management library that makes use of the Hyper-V WMI provider to manage a Hyper-V environment. His blog can be found at `http://blogs.technet.com/jamesone/default.aspx`, where he has fielded a lot of questions and continues to provide additional information not only on his PowerShell library but also on a variety of other Hyper-V topics. His PowerShell library is available from `www.codeplex.com/PSHyperv`. He has classified his library into these major categories, each of which has several functions:

- Finding a VM
- Connecting to a VM
- Discovering and manipulating machine states
- Backing up, exporting, and manipulating snapshots for VMs
- Adding and removing VMs, configuring motherboard settings
- Manipulating disk controllers, drives, and disk images
- Manipulating NICs
- Working with VHD files

PowerGUI

PowerGUI (`www.powergui.org`) is a web-based community of people who have a strong interest in all things related to PowerShell. PowerGUI is also the name of an extensible graphical administrative console and a graphical PowerShell script editor that can be used for managing Windows operating systems. When add-ons are created to extend its capabilities into specific areas of interest, they create a package called a PowerPack. One such PowerPack was created by Kirk Munro, a Canadian software developer, for managing the Hyper-V environment. A good place to learn more about this is `http://poshoholic.com/2008/11/16/use-powerpacks-to-learn-powershell/`. Just like James O'Neill, Kirk has classified his library into these major categories, each of which has several functions:

- Job management
- Server configuration
- Service management
- Physical NIC management
- Virtual NIC management
- Virtual network management
- Virtual machine management

◆ Virtual IDE drive management

◆ Virtual SCSI drive management

◆ Snapshot management

◆ Virtual hard disk management

Taylor Brown

Taylor Brown is a test lead on the Hyper-V engineering team at Microsoft. He has a blog at `http://blogs.msdn.com/taylorb/default.aspx` in which he covers a wide variety of topics. He has a tag for PowerShell on the left-hand side of the page to make it easy to find all his PowerShell entries. Click this link and you will get a variety of useful PowerShell scripts and examples. These are not the full management libraries like James O'Neill's and PowerGUI with the Hyper-V PowerPack, which provide many of the functions to create and manipulate virtual machines, but they provide some very useful capabilities, such as creating and managing disks and networks.

VBSCRIPT

Microsoft Visual Basic Scripting, or VBScript for short, is a powerful and easy-to-learn scripting capability. It is very similar to both the Visual Basic programming language and VBA, Visual Basic for Applications, so many people feel very comfortable in developing scripts in VBScript. I have not found any organized collections of management routines written in VBScript, but John Howard has written a number of VBScripts that can be quite useful.

John Howard is a senior program manager on the Hyper-V team at Microsoft. His blog can be found at `http://blogs.technet.com/jhoward/default.aspx`. He has written a number of VBScripts for various functions. One I mentioned in the previous chapter is his HVremote script for configuring systems for remote management. John has not created a tag on his blog to find the various scripts he has written, but you can search for VBScript and find his useful scripts.

System Center Virtual Machine Manager

Free utilities and libraries can be very helpful. They are often developed based on the real needs experienced by administrators or developers. But when you're looking for a complete management solution that more seamlessly integrates with other management tools, you will generally need to purchase a management package.

Microsoft's first release of System Center Virtual Machine Manager (SCVMM) was made in 2007 to provide enterprise management capabilities for Virtual Server 2005 R2. Since the release of Hyper-V, Microsoft upgraded SCVMM to include support for Hyper-V. In fact, they even took it a step further — they included support for managing VMware's ESX product. That means a single instance of SCVMM can be used to manage installations of Virtual Server 2005 R2 SP1, Windows Server 2008 and 2008 R2 with Hyper-V (Full and Core installations), Hyper-V Server 2008 and 2008 R2, and VMware ESX and ESXi. To visit Microsoft's official website for SCVMM, go to `www.microsoft.com/scvmm`.

To fully explain SCVMM would require either another book or several chapters, and that is not the purpose of this book. So I will just present a quick summary of some of the key features of SCVMM in Table 3.2.

TABLE 3.2: System Center Virtual Machine Manager main features

FEATURE	DESCRIPTION
Host configuration	Host setup and configuration can be automated, including global settings, such as storage, VHD paths, and VM integration services.
Virtual machine creation	Physical-to-virtual (P2V) — a wizard-based user interface to create VMs from physical machines. This can also be used to move virtual machines from other virtualization platforms to a Hyper-V VM.
	Virtual-to-virtual (V2V) — convert Virtual Server 2005 VMs and VMware VMDK-formatted VMs to Hyper-V VMs.
	A wizard for provisioning and deploying VMs, enabling rapid VM creation.
	Ability to save VM definitions as templates to assist in rapid deployment.
Library management	Store and manage offline VMs, templates, and ISO images (files).
	Create, update, delete, and store objects in the library without launching the associated VMs.
Virtual machine placement and deployment	SCVMM can monitor virtualization hosts to provide recommendations for where to place VMs, based on host capacity and utilization. Rules for placement are user configured. Placement can be done when a virtual machine is first created. After it is created and running, SCVMM can optimize the placement of virtual machines by moving them from one host to another via either Quick Migration or Live Migration.
Monitoring and reporting	Provide a centralized view of all hosts and VMs in the environment (Hyper-V, VMware ESX, and Virtual Server) and the status of each VM. View can be customized by user-selected parameters, such as host or VM or operating system.
	Scales to hundreds of hosts (400) and thousands (8,000) of VMs.
	Integrated tools for reporting and health monitoring for both physical hosts and VMs.
Checkpointing	Ability to take VM checkpoints of running virtual machines, allowing for recovery to an earlier point.
Self-service provisioning user interface	User portal to allow users to create, manage, and delete their own VMs within the rules, limits, and permissions set by the administrator of the portal.
Automation	Built on Windows PowerShell for flexibility. Before actions are performed, the PowerShell script created to perform that action is viewable. This enables administrators to develop their own custom scripts for similar functions.

General System Management

Most of what I have covered in this chapter has been about creating the virtual machines and managing those specific aspects of the machines. But management is much broader than that. Things like security, backup, and patch management still need to be done on the virtual machines, just like on your physical machines.

For the most part, the tools and processes you have in place for your physical environment are likely to work on your virtual machines. But there are some nuances. This section will look at those nuances that are specific to the virtual environment. As you look at your overall policies and procedures, take these differences into consideration in order to more fully address your virtual environment.

Security

In the previous chapter on configuring the Hyper-V host environment, I presented some pointers on how to configure the host environment for security. Here are the major points:

◆ Use a Server Core installation of Windows Server 2008 or Microsoft Hyper-V Server 2008.

◆ Do not run any other roles or applications in the parent partition — just run required management agents such as configuration and operation management agents.

◆ Establish a security level for the host and have like virtual machines on the machine — do not mix without justifying why you are mixing.

◆ Do not give virtual machine administrators administrative privileges on the Hyper-V host.

◆ Ensure that virtual machines are fully patched before they are deployed; ensure that they are kept patched.

◆ Ensure that Integration Services are installed on supported operating system environments.

◆ Use a dedicated NIC for managing the host; do not share access to this NIC with the virtual machines.

In the rest of this section we will look at some things that may apply to the host, guest, or both.

BitLocker Drive Encryption

Virtual machines are installed on virtual hard drives. These VHDs exist as files on the host system. This ease of movement of VHDs from one host to another gives a great deal of flexibility to operations to load balance virtual machines. At the same, this ease of moving VHDs makes it easy to make a copy of a virtual machine and remove it from a system. Encryption of the VHDs can provide another level of protection should a VHD end up in the wrong hands.

BitLocker Drive Encryption (BDE) can be used on the physical host to encrypt the contents of physical drives connected to the host. But this is done at the physical level, so you cannot enable BDE in a virtual machine. However, if you wish to encrypt the data on your VHDs, you have two options. The first is to use BDE on the host to encrypt the drives containing VHDs. The other is to use the built-in encrypting file system (EFS) of the Windows operating system within the virtual machine.

When it comes to using BDE on the host, you should consider where it makes sense to do that. If you are talking about your data center environment, you most likely have already evaluated your physical security. With the physical security of a datacenter, there are few cases in which it would make sense to use BDE. If you are talking about remote locations, such as branch offices or manufacturing facilities, where the physical security is not as strong as you would wish it to be, you may want to consider using BDE. If you plan to deploy BDE in your remote locations, read the how-to guide that Microsoft has published, which can be found by searching for hyper-v and bitlocker at `www.microsoft.com/downloads`.

AUTHORIZATION MANAGER

By default, Hyper-V is set up in such a way that only administrators can create and control virtual machines. It is often desired that virtual machines be managed by different people or groups of people than those who manage the Hyper-V hosts. This is similar to an environment where an organization will have separate server management teams and SQL management teams. Or, you may want to simply provide varying levels of access to different groups of users. For example, you may have some people you want to be able to audit the configurations of virtual machines but not have the ability to run anything. Or, you may want to grant some users the right to stop and start virtual machines but not change the configuration. This is often called role-based management.

Windows has historically relied on access control lists (ACLs) to provide a rudimentary level of protection at the file level for some of these types of accesses. For example, Virtual Server relied on ACLs for some simple levels of delegation. But ACLs do not provide the level of granularity of access that we are talking about here. With the introduction of Windows Server 2003, Microsoft included a feature called Authorization Manager, or AzMan for short, as part of the operating system. With AzMan you can define roles and the tasks those roles can perform. You can nest roles to inherit characteristics from other roles, and you can define application groups. Combining AzMan with PowerShell to modify permissions and settings dynamically allows for quick changes to the Hyper-V environment.

It will be helpful for me to explain some of the terms that are used by AzMan and their relevance to the Hyper-V environment.

Operation   Represents an action that a user can perform. Table 3.3 lists the operations that can be assigned to a user within Hyper-V.

Task   A way to group operations. For example, you could create a task to contain the two operations of Start Virtual Machine and Stop Virtual Machine and name it something like Start-Stop. It is a way to simplify and standardize how you assign roles to individuals and groups.

Role   A definition of responsibilities or capabilities that are "owned" by a user or a group. For example, Auditor could be a defined role. One or more people may have the role of Auditor. The operations/tasks that are appropriate for an Auditor would be given to this role.

Scope   Defines which objects (virtual machines) are owned by which roles. It is common to have multiple virtual machines on a single host. But you may want to limit, or *scope*, which of those virtual machines can be controlled on that host by a given role. A default scope simply means you have not defined any scopes.

Table 3.3 gives you an idea about the types of tasks that can be delegated to roles. The list of operations is longer than a single window from the AzMan MMC, so I have transcribed it here for quick reference, and I organized it by the major operations that can be performed.

TABLE 3.3: Authorization Manager operations

OPERATIONS ON HYPER-V SERVICES	DESCRIPTION
Read Service Configuration	Authorizes reading configuration of the Virtual Machine Management Service
Reconfigure Service	Authorizes reconfiguration of Virtual Machine Management Service
View Virtual Switch Management Service	Authorizes viewing the Virtual Switch Management Service

OPERATIONS ON VIRTUAL MACHINES	DESCRIPTION
Create Virtual Machine	Authorizes creating a virtual machine
Delete Virtual Machine	Authorizes deleting a virtual machine
Change Virtual Machine Authorization Scope	Authorizes changing the scope of a virtual machine
Start Virtual Machine	Authorizes starting the virtual machine
Stop Virtual Machine	Authorizes stopping the virtual machine
Pause and Restart Virtual Machine	Authorizes pause and restart of a virtual machine
Reconfigure Virtual Machine	Authorizes reconfiguring a virtual machine
View Virtual Machine Configuration	Authorizes viewing the virtual machine configuration
Allow Input to Virtual Machine	Authorizes user to give input to the virtual machine
Allow Output from Virtual Machine	Authorizes viewing the output from a virtual machine

OPERATIONS ON VIRTUAL NETWORK COMPONENTS	DESCRIPTION
Create Virtual Switch	Authorizes creating a new virtual switch
Delete Virtual Switch	Authorizes deleting a virtual switch
Modify Switch Settings	Authorizes modifying the switch settings
View Switches	Authorizes viewing the available switches
Create Virtual Switch Port	Authorizes creating a new virtual switch port
Delete Virtual Switch Port	Authorizes deleting a virtual switch port

TABLE 3.3: Authorization Manager operations *(CONTINUED)*

OPERATIONS ON VIRTUAL NETWORK COMPONENTS	DESCRIPTION
Connect Virtual Switch Port	Authorizes connecting to a virtual switch port
Disconnect Virtual Switch Port	Authorizes disconnecting from a virtual switch port
Modify Switch Port Settings	Authorizes modifying the switch port settings
View Switch Ports	Authorizes viewing the available switch ports
View LAN Endpoints	Authorizes viewing the LAN endpoints
Change VLAN Configuration on Port	Authorizes modifying VLAN settings
View VLAN Settings	Authorizes viewing the VLAN settings
Create Internal Ethernet Port	Authorizes creating an internal Ethernet port
Delete Internal Ethernet Port	Authorizes deleting an internal Ethernet port
View Internal Ethernet Port	Authorizes viewing the available internal Ethernet ports
Bind External Ethernet Port	Authorizes binding to external Ethernet ports
Unbind External Ethernet Port	Authorizes unbinding from an external Ethernet port
View External Ethernet Port	Authorizes viewing the available external Ethernet ports

Setting up a role-based delegation model with AzMan is not too difficult after you have been through it to define one or two roles. But there are quite a few steps to get there. Two articles on the Internet provide the detailed instructions to set this up. Both of them also have useful code samples.

◆ Use Role-Based Security in Your Middle Tier .NET Apps with Authorization Manager at http://msdn.microsoft.com/en-us/magazine/cc300469.aspx

◆ Dung Hoang's blog post at http://dungkhoang.spaces.live.com/default.aspx?sa= 826879169

There is no predefined AzMan console in Windows Server 2008, so you need to create your own MMC to work with this. Here are the steps to get started:

1. From an elevated command prompt type in **mmc.exe**.

2. Click File. Select Add/Remove Snap-ins from the drop-down menu. Select Authorization Manager from the list of available snap-ins. Then click Add to make it part of the console. Click OK to load the snap-in and get back to the console.

3. (Optional) If you want to save this console for future use, click File and select Save As. Select your save location and give the console a name. It defaults to a file with an .msc extension. If you do not save this, you will have to go through the steps to create the console each subsequent time.

4. In the AzMan console, right-click the node Authorization Manager and select Open Authorization Store.

5. Select XML File. In the Store Name field enter `C:\Programdata\Microsoft\Windows \Hyper-V\InitialStore.xml`, assuming that `C:` is your system drive. `Programdata` is a hidden directory. Depending on how you have configured your Explorer defaults, you might not be able to browse to this location, so you might have to type it in. Figure 3.25 shows what the AzMan console looks like.

FIGURE 3.25
Authorization Manager Console

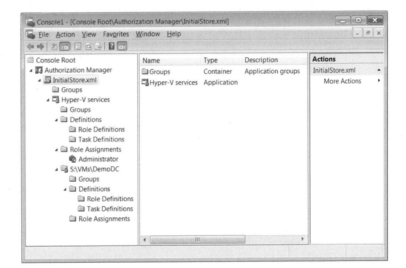

6. If you simply want to give a person or a group of people who are currently not administrators the right to control this instance of Hyper-V, expand `InitialStore.xml` and then choose Hyper-V Services ➢ Role Assignments ➢ Administrator. Go to the Actions part of the console on the right-hand side, click More Actions under Administrators, and select Assign Users And Groups. Select the option From Windows And Active Directory for assigning users from Active Directory or From Authorization Manager if you are selecting users who have accounts only on the local Hyper-V host.

7. If you want to set up different roles, check out my earlier references.

Backup

Backup in a virtual environment gets to be challenging because you now have several operating system environments on a single physical host. It is quite common in data center environments today to perform regularly scheduled backups over the network. But, if you schedule all your virtual machines to back up at the same time, it does not take much to saturate the NIC over which you are performing the backup. Saturating a NIC can cause backups to take longer than the amount of time allotted to perform them. This could then overflow into production windows, which can impact services to clients.

One way to protect against saturating a NIC is to stagger the backups. Another is to put in higher-speed NICs; 10Gbs Ethernet cards are coming onto the market. The problem with the 10Gbs NICs is that you also have to have the rest of your infrastructure upgraded to fully support it. Most organizations are not ready to rip out their current 1Gbs infrastructure just yet.

The problem of backups taking too long was raising its head even in the physical environment. Therefore, with Windows XP and Windows Server 2003, Microsoft introduced a capability into the operating system called Volume Shadow Copy Service (VSS). This enables backup programs to take regularly scheduled differential copies of only what has changed in a file while the file is still in use. By backing up with the file or data store still in use, the application does not have to be shut down to ensure the backed-up data is in a recoverable state. The backup of the open files is accomplished by means of a capability known as a VSS writer.

Let's take a quick look at how the basic file VSS that comes with the operating system works. The goal of the shadow copy, or snapshot, is to ensure that the contents of what is being backed up does not change while it is being backed up. This provides a point for recovery purposes. VSS accomplishes this by creating a read-only copy of the entire volume. During the time the snapshot is being taken, the OS buffers its writes to the open files to ensure the snapshot is consistent. When the snapshot is completed, the OS will continue writing to the file system, but a backup utility can now back up the snapshot from that read-only copy of data that was taken.

The Windows operating system has had this open-file VSS writer since Windows XP and Windows Server 2003. But when it came to applications like SQL and Exchange, those applications needed to have their own VSS writers that specifically address the needs of those applications — which Microsoft has provided.

Now along comes Hyper-V. In a sense, it is an application with a specialized data store known as a virtual hard drive. During execution of a virtual machine, information is regularly being written to the virtual machine's hard drive. Just as with SQL and Exchange, Hyper-V needs to capture the contents of the VHD correctly when a snapshot is requested. Hyper-V has a VSS writer.

But a VSS writer is an *enabler*. It is not the tool that performs the actual backup. It is called by the backup utility. Microsoft has two different backup tools that can be used with VSS for backing up running virtual machines. One, Windows Server Backup (WSB), is a feature of the Windows Server 2008 operating system. The other, System Center Data Protection Manager (SCDPM), is a purchasable product that includes the ability to back up running virtual machines as well as active SQL and Exchange databases.

I covered these two products in the previous chapter on setting up the Hyper-V host environment. See those sections for details on how to set this up for your environment to back up virtual machines from the Hyper-V host.

There are also times when you may want to back up applications that are running within the virtual machines instead of backing up the entire virtual machine. In those cases you would install the WSB feature or the SCDPM product within the virtual machine. This could be a way to ease some of the stress on the NICs because then you are backing up only the data changes instead of all the changes that are occurring within the virtual machines, which includes the data. You will need to follow similar setup steps within the virtual machines as you do to set up application-level backup on the host.

Of course, these are not the only backup tools that are available. Since the introduction of VSS, many third-party backup vendors have written their products to support VSS writers in a similar manner to the way Microsoft has. The SQL and Exchange agents have been around for years. Since Hyper-V is relatively new compared to those products, you should check with your vendor to ensure they support backing up running virtual machines with their products if you want to use them on the host. If you want to run them in the virtual machines, there should be no difference from running the backup agents on the physical machines.

Patch Management

Patch management is just as critical for virtual machines as it is for physical machines. In fact, you might even think a good patch-management process is more important for virtual machines. Here are some things that might happen:

◆ Since it is so easy to create a virtual machine, someone may ignore some of the normal sequence of events during installation and configuration in order to get their machine into use as quickly as possible.

◆ A virtual machine may be offline during a normal patch cycle, meaning that it did not receive the patches when they were normally distributed.

◆ There are desktop products, such as Virtual PC from Microsoft and VMware's Workstation, that provide a way for rogue machines to appear on the network, outside any controls that corporate IT may have in place.

Microsoft has several tools that can assist in controlling the patching of virtual machines.

OFFLINE VIRTUAL MACHINE SERVICING TOOL

Microsoft currently does not have a method to patch a machine that is in an offline state. Some manual methods have been tried, such as opening the VHD file and writing a script to apply patches when the system is booted the next time. But this method has some limitations in that it often requires that a system be rebooted after applying the patch, so the virtual machine is not available for production when it comes online.

Microsoft has released a tool via its Solution Accelerator program known as the Offline Virtual Machine Servicing Tool. Go to www.microsoft.com/downloads and search for "offline virtual machine."

The Offline Virtual Machine Servicing Tool manages the workflow of updating large numbers of offline virtual machines according to their individual needs. The tool employs several different components available from Microsoft:

◆ PowerShell (no additional cost, a feature of Windows Server 2008)

◆ Windows Workflow Foundation (WWF) (no additional cost, part of .NET Framework 3.0 and later)

◆ Windows Task Scheduler (no additional cost, a feature of Windows Server 2008)

◆ System Center Virtual Machine Manager (SCVMM) (additional cost)

◆ Windows Server Update Services (WSUS) (no additional cost, a download from Microsoft)

◆ System Center Configuration Manager (SCCM) (additional cost)

Servicing jobs are created with WWF to manage the workflow of updating offline virtual machines according to their individual needs:

♦ The virtual machines to be updated are managed by SCVMM.

♦ PowerShell scripts are used to build the servicing jobs.

♦ Tasks are created within the Windows Task Scheduler to say when the servicing jobs should start.

♦ The actual update is performed with either WSUS or SCCM.

For each virtual machine selected by the servicing job, the VM is loaded from the SCVMM library and started via PowerShell within a quarantined network. By starting it within a quarantined network, you ensure that you do not impact the production network. Once the machine is running, it is directed to the appropriate update tool, WSUS or SCCM, you are using in your environment. WSUS or SCCM will scan the virtual machine and apply the appropriate patches. Once the patches are fully applied, including any reboots, the VM is shut down and put back into the SCVMM library.

NETWORK ACCESS PROTECTION

Network Access Protection (NAP) is a new capability that comes with Windows Server 2008 as part of the Network Policy and Access Services role. This solution controls access to network resources based on a computer's identity and compliance with company policies. System or network administrators define what the company policies are that indicate a "clean" statement of health. It is common that one of these policies is currency with security patches. This compliancy check can be made before the computer joins the corporate network. The client computer provides a statement of health to the policy server.

If a computer is not compliant — in this case, it does not have the required security patches — NAP can take appropriate action. NAP sends a message to the computer telling it that it is noncompliant and includes instructions on what needs to be done to bring the machine into compliance. At that point, NAP can either grant or deny access to the corporate network.

Or, if there is an automated update infrastructure in place, such as WSUS or SCCM, NAP can automatically direct the computer to be updated by one of those systems, generally on a quarantined network. Once the update is made, the computer again submits a statement of health to the NAP health policy server, and if the client is compliant with all policies, NAP can connect the computer to the corporate network. All decision points are defined by system and network administrators.

See http://technet.microsoft.com/en-us/network/bb545879.aspx for more information on Network Access Protection.

WINDOWS SERVER UPDATE SERVICES

Windows Server Update Services (WSUS) is very much like Microsoft Update, which is available to everyone over the Internet. The difference is that WSUS enables system administrators to build a tailored update environment within the corporate network. Updates are downloaded to the WSUS server, and only the administrator approves which patches will be offered to internal users. When using WSUS, client machines are redirected to the internal location instead of the public Microsoft Update. This ensures that only patches approved within the environment are applied to systems.

WSUS is generally used in conjunction with other tools to ensure patch coverage. It can be used with the Offline Virtual Machine Servicing Tool described above, or administrators can build their own scripts around enforcing patching. See `http://technet.microsoft.com/en-us/wsus/default.aspx` for more information on Windows Server Update Services.

SYSTEM CENTER CONFIGURATION MANAGER

System Center Configuration Manager (SCCM) is part of Microsoft's System Center family of management products. This is a full-fledged, configuration-management product for performing hardware and software inventories, installing and removing software remotely, deploying entire operating systems, ensuring compliance with company policies, and providing robust reporting. Patches are just one of the types of software that SCCM can install.

System administrators create collections of machines based on characteristics they define. They can then create jobs for ensuring machines within those collections meet their defined criteria, such as the patches that they should have.

SCCM is generally used in conjunction with other tools to ensure patch coverage. It can be used with the Offline Virtual Machine Servicing Tool described above, or administrators can build their own scripts around enforcing patching. See `www.microsoft.com/systemcenter/configurationmanager/en/us/default.aspx` for more information on System Center Configuration Manager.

Performance Monitoring

Performance monitoring is still more of an art than a science. So, everything you have learned about monitoring the physical environment will be useful in measuring performance in the virtual environment. There are some good references on the Internet that you should review, as this topic could cover a lot of information:

- Measuring Performance on Hyper-V TechNet article — `http://msdn.microsoft.com/en-us/library/cc768535.aspx`.

- Performance Tuning Guidelines for Windows Server 2008 — `www.microsoft.com/whdc/system/sysperf/Perf_tun_srv.mspx`.

- Tony Voellm is the lead of the Hyper-V Performance Team with Microsoft. He is a regular poster to the All Topics Performance blog — `http://blogs.msdn.com/tvoellm`.

Within the built-in perfmon utility, it is important to note that all the counters you should be viewing for monitoring within this environment are prefixed by "Hyper-V." If you are looking for specific details about things happening within child partitions, and you remember that the root partition contains the controlling operating system, you should generally be concerned only with these Hyper-V counters.

I will give some of the general performance considerations that you should watch for in any situation. Some of these guidelines are applicable just to the host Hyper-V server, and some are applicable just to the guests. Many of these guidelines will have little individual impact on the performance of your environment, but little things have a way of adding up to larger effects. So, if you are trying to get the maximum amount of performance from your environment, try experimenting with some of these.

HOST

What you have running in the parent partition of the host, and how you are managing that, can have an impact on the virtual machines running in the guest partitions.

Hyper-V Role Run only the Hyper-V role in the parent partition. I do not mean that you should not run management agents, as you will need those to effectively manage your environment. But do not run other application roles in the parent partition. You may have very valid business reasons for running other applications in the parent, but you should isolate these configurations to lower-performance environments, such as branch offices. I am not saying that it cannot be done, but if you are looking for optimal performance of your virtual machines, then it is not recommended to run any additional applications in the parent partition.

Windows Server 2008 Core Whenever possible, use just the Core installation or the Hyper-V Server installation. There are fewer services running in these installations, leaving more resources for the virtual machines.

Hyper-V Manager Console The console is constantly requesting resources of the hypervisor. This is true whether the console is running locally or remotely, so this can affect any Hyper-V installation. This is not a major problem, but it does take system resources that could be used by the virtual machines. You can either close the console entirely or just minimize it. When it is minimized, it is idled and does not make requests for more information.

Disks More spindles, faster interfaces, faster rotating speeds, and appropriate RAID technology will all have impact on your performance.

GUEST

Guest virtual machines are where the work gets done. It is important to ensure their best performance.

Integration Services Install the Integration Services for every supported operating system. Besides improving the user interface by capturing the mouse correctly, they also can provide very significant performance improvements. For example, you will definitely notice the improvement in disk and network I/O. The Integration Services install the synthetic drivers for the network and disk adapters, ensuring the high performance from the synthetic devices instead of the emulated devices that are used without the Integration Services. You can use the Hyper-V Manager GUI to load these, or they are found on the host in the `%SYSTEMROOT%\system32\vmguest.iso` file, which you can mount to the guest OS and install manually.

Network Adapter Use the network adapter instead of the legacy network adapter whenever possible. The legacy network adapter is emulated in software; the network adapter is synthetic, so it exploits the hardware-sharing technology of Hyper-V.

SCSI Disks Use SCSI disks whenever possible. Yes, I know I stated earlier that there is basically no performance difference between IDE and SCSI. That is true, in that the engineers used many common routines to ensure top-notch performance of IDE disks. However, the SCSI protocol can do I/O in larger block sizes than the IDE protocol. Therefore, if you are looking to get the maximum performance out of your disks, connect them to a SCSI controller.

VMconnect or Remote Desktop Connection If you are working with a specific VM, you may need to have either VMconnect open or a Remote Desktop Connection open to a virtual machine. But, that takes resources to keep the screen refreshed and to respond to any requests that are coming via the GUI. If you can manage remotely via WMI, you will use fewer resources. And with PowerShell V2 that comes with Windows Server 2008 R2, you will be able to remotely execute PowerShell commands. Yes, there may still be times when you need or want to use VMconnect or RDC, but if you are not using them, close them down so the system does not have to refresh the display.

Disks   I have mentioned this before and I am likely to mention it again. For production, use fixed disks or pass-through disks (more on this in the next chapter). Dynamic disks had a significant performance impact in Windows Server 2008, but the Microsoft engineers improved performance by up to 15 times for R2. There is still a performance difference, but it is not as significant in R2.

iSCSI   This is a great protocol and a very cost-effective way to add storage to an environment. When you access fixed iSCSI disks, you still have to traverse the storage stack, the guest networking stack, and the networking stack on the host. This is somewhat ameliorated with 4Gbs or 10Gbs Ethernet cards, but the network stack still has more overhead. When accessing pass-through disks, you traverse the guest storage stack and disk stack on the host. There is simply less overhead with pass-through access to disks locally attached to the Hyper-V host. You need to balance this with the flexibility difference between iSCSI and pass-through disks. Pass-through disks do not support the Hyper-V snapshot capability or differencing disks. Since both of these use dynamic disks, you will most likely not use this feature in production, but it is something you need to keep in mind.

DVD   Remove the DVD from the guest when it is not in use. If you have either captured the physical drive or just have the virtual DVD pointed to an .iso file, extra time is used while this device is enumerated at boot. But, if you have the physical DVD assigned to a virtual machine and place a CD or DVD into the host drive, the Autoplay action will occur in the guest that owns the physical drive at that time. Since this can be added dynamically, it is best to add it when it is needed and then remove it when you have finished with it.

The Bottom Line

Managing the Hyper-V parent   When Hyper-V is installed on a physical system, you interact with the physical system through the parent partition. Besides providing the host management environment, the parent partition is also used for setting up an environment in which the virtual machines will run.

> **Master It**   What are some of the components that the parent partition manages that affect all virtual machines running on that host and are unique to the virtual environment?

Managing the Hyper-V guests or children   Working with virtual machines, or guests, is very similar to working with physical systems. Most of the software that works on the physical host also works in a virtual machine. But there are a variety of physical functions or actions that you may execute on a physical machine, such as pressing a physical power button, that do not exist on a virtual machine.

> **Master It**   List the actions that you can take on a virtual machine and compare them to actions you might take on a physical machine.

Using some common tools for virtual machines As I have stated many times, managing virtual machines is very much like managing physical machines. In fact, many of the tools you use in a physical environment, like backup and your patch-management tools, will be deployed in much the same way for your virtual environment as for your physical environment.

Master It Some common tools that come with the Windows operating system have been modified to recognize the fact that a virtual machine is another operating system environment on the physical host. What are some of these tools?

Chapter 4

Storage and Networking for Hyper-V

Storage and networking are the two components in a virtualized environment that require more planning and ongoing management than almost any other component. Part of the reason for this is that there are so many different ways to set up storage and networking. Because Hyper-V can use any of the devices that are supported by Windows Server 2008, that translates into all the planning and configurations of the physical world being moved into the virtual world. However, because you now have multiple virtual machines on a single host, the stress put on the storage and networking is multiplied.

In this chapter you will learn about:

◆ Planning storage on your host

◆ Configuring storage for virtual machines

◆ Planning your network configuration for the host

◆ Configuring virtual switches for virtual machines

Storage

In Chapter 1 you learned that Hyper-V can make use of any of the many types of physical storage devices that can be connected to the host. This includes direct-attached storage such as SCSI, IDE, SAS, SATA, IEEE 1394, and USB. Networked storage can be presented as iSCSI or Fibre Channel (FC). Once you have physically connected a disk to the system, you have the option of presenting that storage to the virtual machines in a variety of ways.

Jose Baretto is a storage specialist from Microsoft. He has a blog at `http://blogs.technet`
`.com/josebda/default.aspx` with a lot of good information for all things related to storage. I made a couple changes to his picture of storage options and show that as Figure 4.1.

I will explain the various options by referencing the drive letters in the child partition in Figure 4.1. Often, the figures that I use will show a disk connected to either an IDE controller or a SCSI controller. Any disk can be connected to either type of controller. The only requirement is that your boot disk be connected to the IDE controller. This is a requirement of Hyper-V.

Child Partition Drive C: This is one of the most common ways that disks are used in the virtual machines. Disk 1, drive `J:` on the parent partition, is direct-attached storage (DAS). This can be an IDE, SCSI, SAS, SATA, IEEE 1394, or USB disk drive. A virtual hard drive is created as a file with a `.vhd` extension in an administrator-defined directory on the DAS, and it is associated with a virtual drive in the virtual machine. Figure 4.2 shows how this disk is defined in Hyper-V. Notice the full directory path to the location of the file with the `.vhd` extension.

FIGURE 4.1
Hyper-V storage options

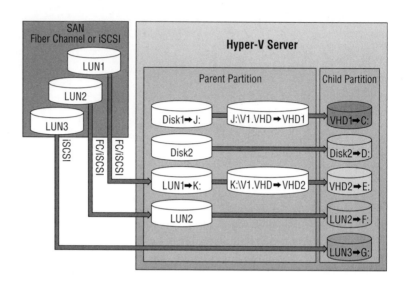

FIGURE 4.2
Virtual hard disk on DAS

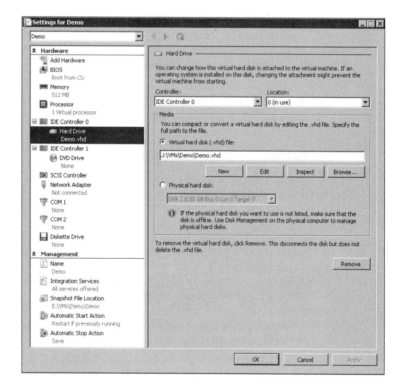

Child Partition Drive D: This method is also using DAS. The difference here is that this is what is known as a pass-through disk. Note that there is no drive letter associated with this disk in the parent partition. Nor is a VHD created on the physical disk on the parent partition. Instead, the disk is physically set to an offline state in the parent partition, and the whole physical drive is assigned to the virtual machine. To assign the disk to the virtual machine, the drive must be set to Offline in Disk Management before you try to assign it. Figure 4.3 shows Disk 2 in an offline state.

FIGURE 4.3
Offline disk

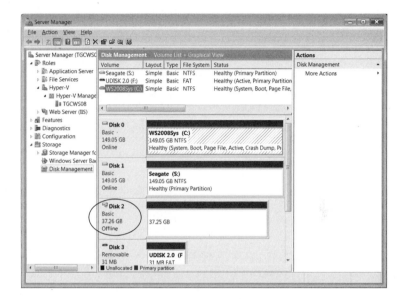

To set a disk in the offline state, right-click in the area that shows a disk in Online status and select the Offline option. This will allow it to be presented to Hyper-V to be assigned as a pass-through disk. Notice the Physical Hard Disk option shown in Figure 4.4. Only offline disks can be presented to Hyper-V as pass-through disks. This is to prevent data corruption that would occur if both the parent partition and a child partition were accessing the same physical disk.

Child Partition Drive E: This drive is a simple variation of Drive C:. The only real difference is that the drive is not directly attached, but it is attached via the Storage Area Network (SAN) to a storage array. The SAN can be either a Fibre Channel or an iSCSI SAN. The LUN is assigned to the parent partition and assigned as drive K:. Once a SAN disk is presented to the parent partition and mounted, the operating system treats it the same as DAS.

Child Partition Drive F: This drive is a simple variation of Drive D:. The only real difference is that the drive is not directly attached, but it is attached via the SAN to a storage array. The SAN can be either a Fibre Channel or an iSCSI SAN. The LUN is assigned to the parent partition, but the parent partition does not bring it online.

Child Partition Drive G: Because iSCSI operates over an IP network, it is possible to connect an iSCSI LUN directly to a child partition via a virtual NIC. In this example, the child partition uses an iSCSI initiator to access an iSCSI Target, bypassing the parent partition storage stack. The iSCSI initiator is part of the Windows Vista and Windows Server 2008 operating systems.

An iSCSI initiator for Windows 2000 SP4, Windows Server 2003 SP1 (and later), and Windows XP SP2 (and later) can be downloaded from www.microsoft.com/downloads by searching for "iSCSI initiator."

FIGURE 4.4
Pass-through disk

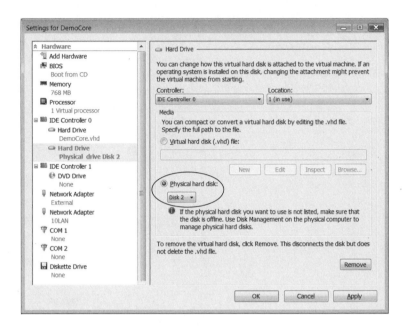

Table 4.1 gives a summary of the various ways a disk can be presented to a virtual machine.

TABLE 4.1: Storage options

VHD FILE	PASS-THROUGH DISK	DIRECT CONNECTION TO VM
Direct-attached storage	Direct-attached storage	
Fibre Channel SAN	Fibre Channel SAN	
iSCSI SAN	iSCSI SAN	iSCSI SAN

Before you even present that storage to the virtual machine, you have some options to choose how you want to manage that storage at the host level.

Physical Disk Considerations

One of the first things you consider is the way to connect the storage to the physical host. As I have mentioned, connections can be made directly via SCSI, IDE, SAS, SATA, IEEE 1394, or USB. Though you will still find systems with SCSI and IDE drives, these are being replaced by some of the newer technologies. The most common direct-attached connections you will find in modern server systems are SAS (Serial Attached SCSI) and SATA (Serial ATA). IEEE 1394 and USB are slower buses and are more often used for removable media. These work as storage devices for Hyper-V, but for the most part you will be dealing with other forms of higher-performing storage.

The next thing to look at is how fast the disks spin. Low-end disks (interpret that to mean low-cost) will spin at 5400 rpm. The default disk sold with most servers will spin at 7200 rpm. For a modest increase in cost, you can get 10K rpm disks. The fastest rotating disks on the market today are 15K rpm, and they cost a premium, but even their prices are becoming quite reasonable. The speed at which a disk rotates is directly related to the disk's ability to perform.

The act of spinning is a mechanical action. Mechanical actions are the slowest component in reading and writing the disk. Information is transferred from/to the disk only when the correct location is under the read/write head. When you compare a 5400 rpm disk to a 15K rpm disk, you can see that the head gets positioned over the proper location nearly three times faster on the high-speed disk. This is referred to as rotational latency — the latency required for a particular block to come under the read head.

A disk is sometimes measured in the number of input/output operations it can perform each second. This is known as IOPS — I/Os per second. A 15K disk can deliver up to about 225 IOPS. A 5400 rpm disk can deliver about 80 IOPS. So, even if these devices are connected to a bus that transfers the data from the disk to the computer at the same speed, you will see a significant performance improvement by using disks that rotate faster.

In the past few years, solid state disks (SSDs) have been appearing on the marketplace. These are just like they sound — solid state, with no moving components. They are basically computer memory connected to a typical I/O bus. This totally eliminates the rotational latency. It does not mean that your access becomes instantaneous, because you still have to deal with the storage protocol, and the memory being used in these devices is low-powered memory, similar to what is used on a USB flash drive, so it does not read/write as fast as the high-speed memory of the computer. SSDs do have performance improvements over even a 15K disk, but the cost is still significant on these compared to what you can purchase the other disks for.

The next thing to consider when putting together your disk environment is the number of disks. As I mentioned, a single 15K rpm disk can handle up to about 225 IOPS. If you put in a single 15K rpm disk with 250 GB of storage, you will get lower performance than if you put in four 15K rpm disks with only 70 GB of storage on each. You have approximately the same amount of storage, but you go from a potential 225 IOPS to a potential 900 IOPS. This is why it is common in RAID arrays (discussed below) to use lots of smaller disks in order to increase overall performance of the system.

One last thing I am going to discuss here is the amount of cache on the drive. Remember that I said rotational latency is the slowest part of reading/writing data to the physical disk. Disk manufacturers have long recognized this and have been placing some solid state cache on their drives for several years. As information is written to disk, it is actually written to the cache for the highest performance, and then it is written to the spinning media in the background. A read first checks for information in the cache. If it is not in the cache, the read causes the information to be read from the disk, and as the information is transferred back to the host, the information is also written into the cache. The amount of cache and the algorithms used by the disk manufacturers can have a noticeable performance impact.

Once you have determined the type of physical disks you are going to use, you need to consider if you are going to use some form of RAID (Redundant Array of Inexpensive — or Independent — Disks), or if you are going to use just a bunch of disks (JBOD). *JBOD* is a term used to describe the disk configuration on a RAID controller when the disks are not assigned to RAID sets. They are used as individual disks.

The various types of storage can be effectively deployed across different environments. For example, I use a laptop for most of my testing and demonstration work. USB and lower-cost disks are fine for this. But I would rarely recommend this sort of solution for a production deployment. For a small production environment, such as a small business or a remote branch location of a larger organization, or for a development and test environment, you might want to move to a local RAID controller for direct-attached storage. Direct-attached storage is easily managed from the host system.

In datacenter environments, I often see storage arrays of some sort, either Fibre Channel or iSCSI. Storage arrays provide the most flexibility in configuration and management, and they often provide additional capabilities, such as full-volume mirroring for business continuance in case of a disaster or shared storage in the case of clustering. It is common for the storage array to be managed by a storage team that is separate from the server team, so the storage team can specialize in performance and backup issues related to storage.

RAID

RAID can be configured with software, through a hardware controller in the host system, or through a storage controller in a SAN (storage area network) that provides either Fibre Channel or iSCSI connections. RAID has two primary purposes. One is to provide a level of data redundancy so that if one disk in a RAID set fails, operations can continue. Not all forms of RAID provide redundancy, which might seem a little strange, as the R in RAID stands for Redundant, but most forms of RAID do provide redundancy.

The other purpose is to provide performance benefits by combining multiple disks into a single volume in order to spread the data transfer over more spindles. A secondary purpose of this is to combine smaller drives into a larger volume. For example, disks that spin at 15K rpm are not as large as those that spin at slower speeds. But if you want to create a single large volume that provides the most performance, you will combine multiple faster, smaller drives into a larger volume. There are trade-offs for each of these that you need to consider as you plan your environment.

Over the years, there have been quite a few different RAID formats. I am going to talk about only the ones that are most prevalent today. Table 4.2 gives a summary of these different types of RAID. The last column gives the minimum number of disks required to form that particular form of RAID. The maximum number of disks that can be configured is dependent on the controller, so you need to check with your supplier for that information.

TABLE 4.2:   Standard RAID Levels

RAID LEVEL	DESCRIPTION	MINIMUM NUMBER OF DISKS
0	Striping. Striping provides performance improvements but at the cost of losing any redundancy or fault tolerance. If you lose any disk in the stripe set, you have lost access to all the data in the stripe set, regardless of the number of disks in the stripe set. This happens because data is written to the stripe set in fragments. The fragments are written in parallel to all members of the stripe set. This is great for performance, but it means that the loss of any disk will put a hole in your data. Adding disks to a stripe set will increase performance, but it also increases the potential for losing a single disk to hardware failure, which will cause the entire stripe set to fail.	2

TABLE 4.2:   Standard RAID Levels *(CONTINUED)*

RAID LEVEL	DESCRIPTION	MINIMUM NUMBER OF DISKS
1	Mirroring. The content of one disk is mirrored to one or more other disks. This provides a high level of fault tolerance because a single drive can fail and I/O continues to the surviving member(s) of the mirror set. It is possible to increase read performance if the controller has the intelligence to split the read requests across all spindles contained in the mirror set. The first disk that responds satisfies the read request. There is a very small overhead on write performance, as the controller will issue the `write` command to all members of the mirror set simultaneously.	2
0+1	Mirrored stripe sets. Mirroring and striping are sometimes combined with other forms of RAID, but 0+1 and 1+0 are the most common. Combining levels increases the complexity, but there are benefits to be obtained. With 0+1, volumes are first striped and then the stripe sets are mirrored. This provides the benefits of striping for performance and mirroring for fault tolerance. If one drive fails, the mirrored drive will handle the I/O. As the number of disks in the RAID set increases, this provides a little better resiliency to multiple disk failures.	4, even number of disks required
1+0	Striped mirror sets. This is the flip side of 0+1. Here the volumes are first mirrored and then those volumes are striped. As with 0+1, it provides the benefits of both striping and mirroring.	4, even number of disks required
5	Stripe set with parity. This provides some of the benefits of striping by creating a single large volume from multiple smaller volumes, but it adds parity as one of the stripe fragments. Parity provides a way to recover the data from a failed disk. Each time data is written to one fragment of the stripe, parity is written to another drive. This way if a drive fails, the parity can be used to re-create the data. Large sequential reads show performance benefits, but writes are slower because the parity information has to be calculated and written to another disk for each write of data. This can recover from a single disk failure, but a double failure will make all the data unreadable, similar to losing a single drive in striping.	3
6	Stripe set with dual parity. This provides another level of fault tolerance over RAID 5 by adding a second parity to the writes. This means that a RAID 6 set can sustain the loss of two drives and continue operations. But the performance hit here is for calculating parity and writing it to two disks instead of one.	4

Reading descriptions of RAID is not always clear. Figure 4.5 shows graphically how data is written across the various RAID levels.

FIGURE 4.5
RAID levels

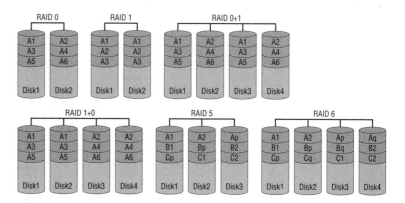

Okay, that describes some of the benefits of RAID and how it is laid out on disk. Now let's look at how RAID volumes are defined. Creating RAID sets can be done within the operating system or it can be done with hardware devices.

SOFTWARE RAID

Windows Server 2008 (and previous versions of Windows) has the ability to create RAID sets in the software. In a Hyper-V environment RAID sets can be created within the parent partition from multiple disks or they can be created within a child partition from multiple VHD files. My first suggestion is to use hardware RAID instead of software RAID if at all possible. Hardware RAID is designed to do RAID. Having the operating system do the RAID uses resources that could better be used for the virtual machines. But, if you do decide to use software RAID, I recommend that you define your RAID sets in the parent partition instead of in a virtual machine. Even though Hyper-V's synthetic disk drivers are very efficient, there is still a slight virtualization impact. Creating RAID sets in the parent partition assesses the performance impact once in the parent partition that would be assessed for each child partition if the RAID set were created in the child partition.

This does not mean that you should never use software RAID in a virtual machine. For example, the maximum size of a VHD is 2040 MB. If you need to have a VHD larger than that, you can create a software RAID set of multiple VHDs that would give you that larger RAID volume.

Software RAID with Windows Server 2008 is managed through the Disk Management console, which is part of Server Manager, or it can be called by executing diskmgmt.msc from a command prompt. Disk Management is a submenu from the Storage section of Server Manager. The disks that you want to use for building your RAID set must be online, but they cannot have any volumes defined on them. If they have volumes, you will need to delete the volumes. In other words, creating a RAID set destroys any data that is already on the disks.

To start the build process, right-click the graphic representation of the disk to get the drop-down menu, as shown in Figure 4.6.

Windows is also limited to three types of RAID sets — RAID 0, RAID 1, and RAID 5. These show as the New Striped Volume, New Mirrored Volume, and New RAID-5 Volume, respectively, in the drop-down menu. Make your selection to start the wizard. The wizard is straightforward, asking you for the disks you want to include in the RAID set and providing a summary to allow you to confirm your selections. When you click the Finish button on the summary window of the wizard, Windows will create the RAID set. RAID 5 requires a minimum of three volumes, so if you select only two volumes, you will not be presented with an option for RAID 5.

FIGURE 4.6
Configure RAID

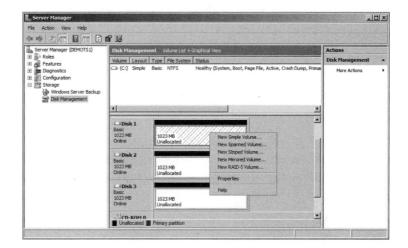

You will also notice a New Spanned Volume option. This is not a form of RAID but a way to concatenate multiple partitions from several volumes into a single volume. As with striped RAID sets, the loss of a single disk in a spanned volume renders the entire spanned volume inaccessible. This technology was popular several years ago when computers came with small disk drives and a larger volume was needed. Now, with drives available in sizes over a terabyte, the use of this capability has dropped off significantly.

ONBOARD RAID CONTROLLER

An onboard RAID controller is an inexpensive way to get into hardware RAID. This is an option card that plugs into an option slot in your server. Most system vendors have embedded cards for their systems, but there are also open-market controllers. Just as with disks, there are all sorts of options in regard to the type of option slot they will fit into, the number and type of disk drives they will support, the number of channels or buses to which disks are connected, and features such as cache and battery backup.

Each vendor has its own configuration program for configuring the RAID. If your system or boot disk is connected to the RAID controller, the configuration program can be launched during the text portion of the system boot. This is because you need to define the RAID before the system software is installed. Sometimes the vendors also have configuration programs that work once the system is up and running. There are so many variables here that the only suggestion I can give you is to read the manual that comes with the controller. There are no standards as to how these applications must look and operate, so no two look the same. In server-class systems that contain embedded RAID controllers, access to the management of the RAID controllers is provided during the boot process of the hardware. Often the boot disk is connected to the embedded controller, so it must be configured before any software can be installed on the system.

Multiple channels on a RAID card give you the option of spreading your disks across multiple I/O channels. Just as spreading your data over multiple disks can help in performance, multiple I/O channels can provide potential performance improvements. When you are creating RAID sets, some controllers allow you to span the disks that compose the RAID set to use more than one channel.

Just as cache on disks can improve performance, cache on RAID controllers can improve performance. Cache on the controller works in a manner similar to cache on the disk. Read requests first check the cache to see if the data being requested is in cache. Information that is written to disk is actually written to cache, and a write-complete message is sent back when the write is done in the cache. Since cache is random access memory, the time to write is nearly instantaneous when compared to writing to the spinning media. Then the controller will move data out of cache to the physical disk, generally within a few milliseconds. This can provide a significant performance boost because the application does not need to wait for rotational latency.

However, there can be issues with this as well. If you have a controller that has cache, any data that is in cache and has not been written out to the disk could be lost if you lose power to the host system or the system crashes or there is any other interruption that does not allow the system to shut down gracefully. If you are writing critical data through this controller, you might want to ensure data is written correctly instead of getting the performance boost.

To mitigate this problem most controller vendors provide the ability to turn on write-through cache. This means that you will still get the use of cache for read operations, but when information is written to the disk, it is not considered a completed write operation until the information is actually written to disk.

Another way this could be handled is with battery backup. Battery backup provides a limited amount of time during which the battery provides power to the cache, thereby saving the contents of the cache until full power is restored. When full power is restored, the controller will finish writing the information to the disk, ensuring data consistency. You need to check with the manufacturer of the RAID controller to determine the amount of time the battery will retain data in the cache.

STORAGE AREA NETWORKS AND RAID

Storage area networks, utilizing either Fibre Channel (FC) or iSCSI networking, are often the highest-performing storage environment used in data centers. SANs can be shared among multiple hosts, providing a centralized point of management for many things related to storage. As with onboard RAID controllers, the management of the different types of RAID is moved from the software into a hardware environment or, more accurately stated, into a hybrid software and hardware environment. Many storage vendors provide numerous configuration and management options in this area. I am just going to cover the basics of their usage, as each one has its own advantages and disadvantages.

The major component of a SAN is the storage array or storage subsystem that serves up the actual storage. In the case of FC storage arrays, there is a specialized controller (or redundant controllers) that manages the disks and serves virtual volumes, or LUNs, to the requesting hosts. These controllers often provide everything from the basic management tools for creating different RAID sets up to utilities that mirror data between storage arrays or automatically back them up or take snapshots of volumes. Because they are often shared among multiple host systems, they often are configured with multiple controllers to provide for redundancy and high availability. Multiple connections can be used to provide multiple paths to the storage for load balancing and failover. Communication to these controllers is done over the Fibre Channel protocol from Host Bus Adapters (HBA) in the host platforms. The initial protocol used a 1 Gbps connection, but 2 Gbps and 4 Gbps are becoming more prevalent.

Some storage array controllers can also have an iSCSI connection to communicate over an Ethernet network. All the capabilities of the controllers mentioned previously remain; the iSCSI connection is just communicating with a different protocol to the host systems. One of the advantages that organizations have found with using iSCSI instead of FC is that iSCSI communicates over the same network infrastructure that is used for connecting all the other computers in the datacenter. It does not require a separate FC network with people trained in that. The downside had been performance, because initially iSCSI was implemented on 100 Mbps Ethernet, which was not really good for high-speed I/O. But it is commonly connected with 1 Gbps Ethernet today, and some companies are even moving to 10 Gbps Ethernet. Microsoft has also optimized its iSCSI initiators that come with the operating system to perform at *wire speed*, or the maximum rate of transfer that is possible on a given connection.

To implement iSCSI, two software components communicate with one another. These are the iSCSI Target and the iSCSI Initiator. As their names imply, the Target, or service, is what is being aimed at, or the actual storage being requested. The Initiator, or client, is the software making a request for data. Microsoft includes an iSCSI Initiator with Windows Server 2008 RTM and R2, Windows Vista, and Windows 7. Downloads are available for Windows Server 2003 and Windows XP.

In addition to the storage solution provided by storage vendors that comes complete with controllers, storage arrays, and management utilities for managing the entire FC or iSCSI environment, the iSCSI Target component can be delivered as a software solution that can be installed on an operating system. For example, Microsoft has a product called Windows Storage Server that is an integrated solution running on top of Windows Server. It provides an iSCSI Target solution on a Windows platform that can be managed with the same tools you are using for managing the rest of your Windows environment.

There are also third-party solutions that run on either Windows or Linux. Some of these solutions are integrated, like Windows Storage Server, and some are software packages that simply install on the host operating system. Packaging an iSCSI solution in this manner will provide a lower cost of entry into the iSCSI storage space because you can use the direct attached storage you have on the server host. But it also means that you might not have all the same capabilities that would be available to you from an integrated controller and storage array solution.

In Chapter 5 you will learn how to use Microsoft's Storage Server solution as a shared storage environment for use with Hyper-V.

As I noted earlier, configuring and managing a vendor's array is unique to each vendor. Microsoft has made life a little easier in this area with a feature of Windows Server 2008 and Windows Server 2003 R2 called the Storage Manager for SANs. You add this as a feature in Server Manager, and the console becomes part of Server Manager. Or you can launch it by issuing the `sanmmc.msc` command. In Windows Storage Server, Storage Manager for SANs is integrated into the console for managing the storage. You will still need the vendor's console for managing advanced features of their SAN, but Storage Manager for SANs does provide an interface to do the most common tasks such as drive and LUN management.

Because of the flexibility in configurations, offloading of management functions, and performance-tuning capabilities of SANs, these will likely be the most common storage option for datacenter deployments of Hyper-V. They are also the only storage solutions that provide the shared storage capabilities required for highly available solutions. SANs can be shared among Hyper-V hosts in a failover cluster environment, ensuring business continuance by moving the workload from one host to another should one host fail. You will learn more about the details of this in Chapter 5.

Types of Storage for Hyper-V

As you remember, you can access storage from a virtual machine in one of two ways. You can either create a virtual hard disk (VHD) or you can access a disk as though it were locally attached to the virtual machine (pass-through).

VIRTUAL HARD DISK

The Microsoft VHD file format specifies a virtual machine hard disk that resides on a native host file system encapsulated within a single file with a .vhd extension. Within a virtual machine, the VHD is represented as a physical disk and is used by the virtual machine as if it were a physical disk. You can store a VHD on any type of disk storage as long as it is recognized by the host system as a local file system; that is, Microsoft does not support VHDs on network-attached storage. Microsoft has released the VHD specification as a royalty-free license to encourage partners and customers to expand its uses. Though the VHD is most often thought of as the format of the virtual hard disk for Microsoft's virtualization products — Hyper-V, Virtual Server, and Virtual PC — Microsoft uses it in other locations as well. For example, System Center Data Protection Manager and the backup utilities in Windows Vista and Windows Server 2008 all use the VHD format.

Microsoft is committed to extending the use of this VHD format. Windows Server 2008 R2 and Windows 7 treat the VHD as a native disk format, up to and including the ability to boot a physical machine from a VHD image. This will enable organizations to define a single image format across their environment whether the machine is physical or virtual. Studies have shown that organizations with fewer images to maintain save money in maintenance and operations. And because Microsoft, in Windows Server 2008 R2, is extending the application of many of its physical disk-manipulation utilities, such as diskpart, to work with VHDs, all that you have learned about working with physical disks will readily transfer over to the VHD.

Microsoft has also ensured that the format of the VHD is compatible across products, because it is built upon this single specification. Therefore, customers who have created virtual machines in Virtual Server or Virtual PC can move those VHDs over to Hyper-V without having to convert them. Data disks can be moved back and forth between the products with no problems. System disks can also be moved from Hyper-V to Virtual Server and Virtual PC, but there are those caveats surrounding Integration Components and HALs that I described in the previous chapter.

Since VHDs are files on the native Windows file system, there is no special formatting of the physical disks of the parent partition in order to provide storage to the virtual machines. This ensures that the same tools you are familiar with using in the physical world work in the virtual environment with no changes. It also means that it is possible to manipulate the VHD as a file when it is not in use by a virtual machine. There are a variety of ways to accomplish this.

Native Consoles

Since Windows Server 2008 R2 and Windows 7 now treat VHD as a native disk format, utilities have been built into the Disk Management console to enable manipulation of VHDs in the same manner as physical disks.

From within the Disk Management portion of the Server Manager console, you can either right-click Disk Management and get a drop-down menu, or you can click More Actions in the

Actions column to bring up the menu to start working with VHDs. See Figure 4.7. (If you want to pull up the old-style Disk Management console, you can also run `diskmgmt.msc` from a command window.)

FIGURE 4.7
Manipulating the VHD through Disk Management

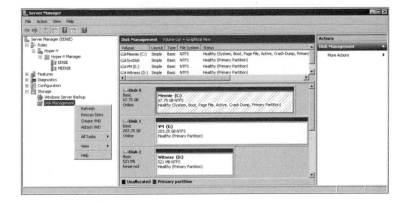

If you select Create VHD, you are presented with the window shown in Figure 4.8. Note that you can create either a dynamically expanding or a fixed-size disk. You should also note that the size of the disk is allocated in MB.

FIGURE 4.8
Create and Attach Virtual Hard Disk

Notice that the title of the window is Create and Attach Virtual Hard Disk. As soon as you create the disk, the disk is presented in Disk Management as an uninitialized disk. See Disk 4 in Figure 4.9.

At this point you would go through the standard steps for initializing the disk with the parameters you desire. This is done in the same manner as if this were a physical disk.

There is a second option available to you. Looking back at Figure 4.7 you see that you can also select Attach VHD. Choosing that option brings up the dialog box shown in Figure 4.10. This option is used to mount an existing VHD file to manipulate its contents. For example, you might have a disk that is used in an automated build process. You can attach to that disk and copy additional configuration files into it without having to spin up a virtual machine to access the disk.

FIGURE 4.9
Uninitialized VHD

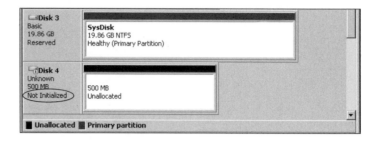

FIGURE 4.10
Attach VHD

Simply click Browse or enter a known path name to select the VHD you wish to manipulate. Notice that you have the option to also attach to the VHD in read-only mode. Once you select the VHD and click OK, your VHD is mounted online and is accessible to your system.

When you view the VHD in the display of the Disk Management console, there is no indication whether the drive is physical or virtual. You will be treating all drives the same way. There is an easy way to see if a disk is actually a VHD. Right-click the disk number, and you will see the option Detach VHD. That option appears only on VHDs.

If you select the Detach VHD option, the window shown in Figure 4.11 will appear.

FIGURE 4.11
Detach Virtual
Hard Disk

Notice that there is an option to delete the actual file that is the VHD. Obviously this is not the default, since you will generally want to keep the VHD for other uses.

Diskpart Utility

Windows Server 2008 R2 also provides the ability to mount and manipulate VHDs as part of the diskpart utility. To mount a VHD to the parent partition on a server hosting Hyper-V, or on a system that is running without Hyper-V enabled, issue the following commands from a command prompt or a PowerShell window:

1. `diskpart`

2. `select vdisk file=<path>\<vhd file>`, where `<path>` is the location (including the drive letter, if needed) and `<vhd file>` is the full name of the VHD file

3. `surface vdisk`

4. `assign letter=<x>` where `<x>` is the letter you want to assign

5. `exit`

Diskpart also contains commands for creating, initializing, formatting, and the like. In other words, anything you can do with a physical disk, you can do with diskpart to a VHD. To detach the VHD, issue the following commands.

1. `diskpart`

2. `select vdisk file=<path>\<vhd file>`, where `<path>` is the location (including the drive letter, if needed) and `<vhd file>` is the full name of the VHD file

3. `detach vdisk`

4. `exit`

PowerShell

Microsoft's previous virtualization product, Virtual Server, contained a utility called `vhdmount.exe` that could be used for mounting VHDs to the host operating system. Hyper-V does not include the `vhdmount.exe` utility, but it does have PowerShell. James O'Neill has written a series of PowerShell cmdlets (`www.codeplex.com/pshyperv`) to exploit the Hyper-V API. One of those cmdlets is `mount-VHD.ps1`, with its associated `unmount-VHD.ps1`. These provide the same capability as the `vhdmount.exe` utility from Virtual Server. These Hyper-V PowerShell cmdlets can be used only on a system on which Hyper-V has been installed because they are making calls to the Hyper-V management components.

To mount a VHD, open PowerShell and enter the command

```
mount-vhd <drive letter>:\<path to .vhd file>
```

where `<drive letter>` is the drive letter on the host system that contains the VHD file and `<path to .vhd file>` is the directory path to where you have the VHD you want to mount. This mounts the VHD to the first available drive letter on the host system. You can now use Windows Explorer or any other file utility to add, delete, or modify files within the VHD. Unlike `vhdmount.exe`, this command does not provide you with an undo capability. Any changes made are permanent.

To unmount the VHD, open PowerShell and enter the command

```
unmount-vhd <drive letter>:\<path to .vhd file>
```

In addition to the mount and unmount capabilities, James has written other PowerShell cmdlets with fairly self-explanatory names: Get-VHDDefaultPath, Get-VHDInfo, New-VHD, Compact-VHD, Test-VHD, Convert-VHD, Merge-VHD.

These cmdlets from James are similar to what can be done from a command line with diskpart, so why have both? The capabilities of diskpart to manipulate a VHD are only in Windows Server 2008 R2, so if you are working on Windows Server 2008 RTM, James's cmdlets will be useful. Second, James's cmdlets bring the ease of developing scripts in PowerShell to Hyper-V, and they can be used to create other PowerShell functions that you may find useful.

vhdmount.exe

If you are working on a Windows XP, Vista, Server 2003, or Server 2008 system and are not using PowerShell, you can use a utility called vhdmount.exe. It originally shipped with Virtual Server. Even though Virtual Server 2005 R2 will install on all these operating systems, if you simply want to manipulate VHD files from one of these operating systems, you can do a custom installation of Virtual Server and select only the vhdmount components.

You do a custom install either through the GUI or through the command line. If you are installing this on a Core installation, you will need to use the following procedure.

1. Download the latest copy of Virtual Server 2005 R2 from www.microsoft.com/downloads and search for "virtual server 2005." This will download a setup.exe file.

2. Extract Virtual Server 2005 Install.msi from setup.exe by typing the following command: **setup.exe /c /t <drive letter>:\<path to the .msi file>**. For example, to extract Virtual Server 2005 Install.msi to C:\SetupFiles, type **setup.exe /c /t c:\SetupFiles**.

3. Start an unattended installation of vhdmount by typing the following command at an elevated command prompt: **msiexec /i "Virtual Server 2005 Install.msi" /qn ADDLOCAL=VHDMount**.

To install using the GUI, simply launch setup.exe and select a custom installation. Deselect all the options but the vhdmount option. Both installation methods install vhdmount.exe into C:\Program Files\Microsoft Virtual Server\.

Once you have installed vhdmount.exe, you can mount a VHD with this command (you must run it from an elevated command prompt):

vhdmount /m vhdfilename driveletter

This mounts the disk to your system so you can now manipulate it with Windows Explorer or any other disk or file commands. You can add, modify, and delete files directly into the VHD. This particular command mounts the drive with an undo disk, so you can discard or commit the changes when you unmount the VHD. If you want to mount it without an undo disk, include the /f switch on the command line.

When you have finished manipulating the VHD, you dismount it with the following command:

vhdmount /u /c vhdfilename

Because I used the example above without the /f switch, I need to either commit (/c) or discard (/d) the changes I made to the VHD. If I had mounted it with the /f switch, it would not have had an undo disk, so all changes would have been committed to the drive.

VhdTool.exe

Creating fixed-sized VHDs requires a fair amount of time because every sector of the allocated file has to be written with zeros to ensure no data is "pirated" from a previously existing file. Chris Eck, a senior development lead on Microsoft's virtualization team, wrote a utility that can create and extend fixed VHDs in much less time than using the native tools that come with the operating system. You can find this utility at `http://code.msdn.microsoft.com/vhdtool`. This tool does not zero out the contents of the file, so it should not be used when security is a concern.

The flexibility of the VHD as both a disk for use in a virtual machine and as a file with content that can be manipulated outside a running virtual machine adds to the ways you can work with virtual machines. The VHD is simply a file. That makes it very transportable. You can create a sysprepped VHD and copy that single file to multiple Hyper-V hosts for rapid deployment of virtual machines. You can mount a VHD and add or remove contents without needing to start the virtual machine. These could be management routines or patches — things you want to ensure get placed into all virtual machines, whether they are running or offline.

The VHD format also provides some other capabilities that are unique to virtual storage when compared to physical storage. With a VHD you can take a snapshot, create a differencing disk, or create a dynamically expanding disk. These features are explained below in the section on working with virtual hard drives. None of these features is available with a pass-through disk. So let's look at how a pass-through disk is different from a VHD.

PASS-THROUGH DISK

A VHD is simply a specially formatted file residing on the storage system of the host, but a pass-through disk can be presented in either of two ways to a virtual machine.

- ◆ direct-attached disk on the parent partition is not mounted but is defined to the virtual machine
- ◆ SAN-attached disk has a LUN assigned to the parent partition, but the LUN is not mounted to the parent partition but is defined to the virtual machine

A primary benefit of the pass-through disk is that it takes an existing disk and simply passes it through to the virtual machine so the virtual machine does not need to read a VHD file. This makes it possible to use a disk on a physical system for awhile and then, without reformatting or changing that disk in any way, mount it to a virtual machine for its use.

A second benefit of the pass-through disk is that you are not limited to the maximum size of the disk enforced on VHDs. A VHD has a maximum size of 2040 GB, or just under 2 TB. Because you are passing the entire disk through to the virtual machine, the entire volume can be presented to the virtual machine. Using the GUID Partition Table (GPT) format instead of the MBR format, you can create a very large disk. The maximum raw partition of a GPT-formatted disk is 16 EB (exabytes, or 1 million times a terabyte), but the Windows volumes currently are limited to 256 TB minus 64 KB (2^{32} clusters minus 1 cluster) each. I do not know about you, but I have not yet found many situations that need a single volume of 256 TB.

Another benefit of the pass-through disk is its performance. A pass-through disk has performance that is slightly better than that of a fixed VHD. In fact, it is very close to the performance of the disk connected to a physical host. QLogic performed an I/O test (`www.qlogic.com/promos/products/hyper-v.aspx`) that proved a pass-through disk performs at about 90 percent to 97 percent of the potential that could be achieved on a physical host. While you might balk at only 90 percent, the results drove about 190,000 I/Os per second to a pass-through disk, which is greater performance than most applications require. So if you need that last 10 percent of performance, that application is most likely not a good candidate for virtualization.

Hyper-V uses the term *pass-through* to define a disk that is accessible as a local disk to the parent to be passed through directly to the client. A third option to directly access the contents of a disk can be added to the two options, direct attached and SAN attached, listed above. That would be iSCSI. It is not considered a pass-through disk by Hyper-V because the disk is accessed directly through the iSCSI protocol. The parent partition does not need to be attached to the iSCSI LUN in order for the child partition to be able to see it. It provides the same sort of limitations or benefits, depending on your perspective, as the pass-through disks.

You already know how to work with physical disks, so you can quickly understand how to manage and manipulate them. There is no difference in working with a physical disk attached to virtual machines than in working with the same physical disk attached to a physical machine. The only thing you really need to remember is that only one machine, physical or virtual, can have access to that disk at any time. That is why you need to have the disk in an offline state on the host in order to select it for use by the virtual machine.

However, since the VHD provides you with additional capabilities beyond what you can do with physical disks, such as snapshots and differencing disks, the tools for exploiting these capabilities are built into the Hyper-V management console and the Hyper-V API for use by programmers and script writers. It is because of these additional capabilities of VHDs that fixed VHDs are commonly recommended as the storage of choice for virtual machines. The next section digs into how to work with VHDs.

Working with Virtual Hard Drives

Within a virtual machine, working with the virtual hard drive is the same as working with hard drives connected to a physical host. There are some differences, though, in setting up the VHD. After all, we are talking about virtualizing the storage in many situations. Therefore some special tools can come into play that may not be used in the same manner in the physical environment.

There are several ways to create a VHD. You can use a PowerShell script or the diskpart utility that I mentioned earlier. But the most common way when working interactively is to use the Server Manager or Hyper-V Management console. Select New in the Actions column and select Hard Disk. This will bring up the window shown in Figure 4.12.

Notice that you can create three different types of disks. The following sections explain each of these.

DYNAMICALLY EXPANDING

A dynamically expanding disk is a VHD that has a maximum size specified when it is created. However, when it is created, only a few megabytes are assigned to it, no matter how large you say the maximum size is. As more data is written to it, it requests additional space from the physical disk on which it is located. It can expand up to the maximum size specified or to the maximum available space on its hosting physical drive. Because it is constantly requesting more storage as it grows, it often becomes quite fragmented. A dynamically expanding disk tends to be the lowest performing of the types of disks you can assign to a virtual machine. Microsoft engineers made some very significant performance improvements (I heard numbers up to 15 times faster in some cases) for Hyper-V R2, but even with that performance improvement, it is still considered the lowest performance option.

FIGURE 4.12
New Virtual Hard Disk
Wizard

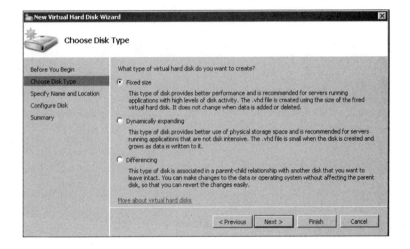

Figure 4.13 shows the options for assigning the name and selecting a location for the storage of the virtual machine.

FIGURE 4.13
Specify Name and
Location

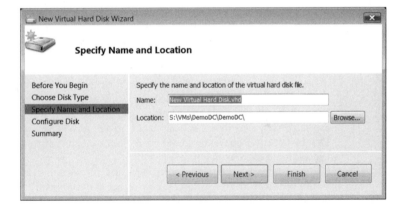

The location can be any storage location connected to the physical host. This means the storage can be USB or IEEE 1394, direct attached, Fibre Channel, or iSCSI.

The next options, as shown in Figure 4.14, give the size and contents of the disk being created.

The first option on this screen allows you to set the maximum size of the VHD, up to the maximum of 2040 GB, or just under 2 TB total. This is the maximum size of a VHD and is the maximum size of a master boot record (MBR) disk in the Windows operating system. If you need disks to be greater in size than this, you will need to use pass-through disks, which I covered earlier.

The second option gives you the ability to copy the contents of one of the physical drives on the host system to the VHD being created. This is a great tool to prepopulate virtual drives.

You can see in Figure 4.14 that the three physical drives I had connected to my test machine are available to be copied. Copying the contents of a physical disk to a VHD during creation is as simple as clicking the option and selecting the drive. Of course, you could copy it afterward, but this makes it a one-step process.

FIGURE 4.14
Configure Disk

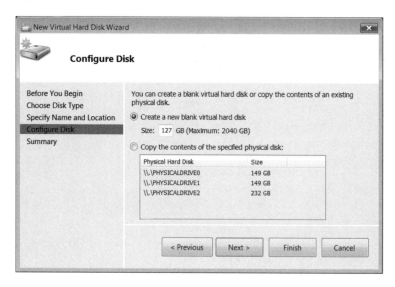

The last window that displays is Microsoft's typical summary window. You can go back and make changes if you do not like the options you chose, you can create the disk, or you can cancel the creation entirely. When you click Finish, Hyper-V creates the VHD with the name and location you specified. Note that it is possible to create a dynamically expanding VHD on a drive that does not have enough space for the entire storage requested because the VHD allocates only a minimal amount when it is created. The created disk is a raw disk — it needs to be partitioned and formatted before use. However, if the disk does expand to the size of the available space on the disk, the virtual machine will go into a Paused-Critical state. Nothing is lost, but you will have to create more space on the physical volume hosting the dynamically expanding disk in order to proceed.

This brings up the need for proper capacity planning. It is possible to oversubscribe the size of the physical drive containing one or more dynamically expanding disks. You need to ensure you have monitoring tools in place in the parent partition to watch for the percentage of storage being used and have procedures documented on how to mitigate this issue should it arise.

FIXED SIZE

A fixed-size disk is created by allocating all the requested size into the VHD at the time of creation. Because the overhead of allocating all the space for the disk is handled at the time of creation, the fixed disk is a good option for production. It performs almost as well as a pass-through disk.

The first window you see in this wizard is the same as the first one for the dynamically expanding disk, as shown previously in Figure 4.13. You enter the name and location you want for the disk.

The next window is also the same, as shown in Figure 4.14, to specify the size and to indicate whether you want to copy the contents of a physical disk to the VHD. Again, the last window is the summary window.

When you click Finish to create the fixed-size disk, Hyper-V attempts to allocate all the storage requested in your entry for maximum size, and then it builds a drive by writing to the VHD. This takes time because Hyper-V is actually writing to the entire contents of the VHD. How long it takes to create the disk depends on how big you are making it and the speed of the storage to which you have assigned the drive. Because it is allocating and writing the entire content of the allocated space, you can create fixed disks only on storage with enough room to contain the entire fixed-size disk. This is different from what happens with the dynamically expanding disk.

DIFFERENCING

The differencing disk is a special-capability disk primarily used in test and development. It creates a parent/child relationship with another disk that you do not want to change. Any changes made to the differencing disk are recorded in the child disk, leaving the parent disk untouched. This provides a quick way to have a base image or data set that is constant and to have a variety of paths off that parent. For example, consider a testing environment. Different testers have responsibility for testing different modules. Rather that create a separate virtual disk for each tester, create a base image. Create a separate differencing disk for each tester. Each tester's changes are recorded in its own copy. This saves space because only the differences for each tester are recorded instead of having to supply a full image for each. It also ensures that the testers are testing from a common base.

It is a good practice to set the parent disk to read-only so someone does not inadvertently make changes to the parent. Changes to the parent are not reflected in the child disks; in fact, changes to the parent make the differencing disks unusable. That is another reason why you should write-protect your parent disks.

The first window of this wizard is the same as the one for the dynamically expanding and fixed disks, as shown in Figure 4.13. However, the information is used in a slightly different manner. This information will be the name and location of the child disk, not of the entire disk. This actually allows you to create a differencing disk on another spindle, which may help with performance.

The second window, as shown in Figure 4.15, is where you specify the location of the parent disk.

The location that appears is the directory of the last-requested VHD. You still need to browse to that directory, or to a new location, to select the specific VHD you want to use as the parent disk. Until you select a specific VHD, you will not have the option to proceed to the next step, which is the summary page.

Notice that you were not presented with the option to select either dynamic/fixed or the size. The differencing disk is a dynamic disk of the same size as the parent disk. Because the differencing disk is a dynamic disk, it should not be used in a production environment.

Windows Server 2008 R2 made significant performance improvements with dynamic disks. They are fully supported, but because of the slower performance, it is generally not recommended to use them in production. While R2 dynamic disks are faster, they are still not as fast as fixed disks.

EDITING VIRTUAL HARD DISKS

Some special actions can be performed on VHDs that cannot be performed on pass-through disks. Some of these functions have equivalents in the physical world, but because the VHD is a file on a hard disk, they need a different utility. The five editing functions are:

◆ Compact

◆ Convert

◆ Expand

◆ Merge

◆ Reconnect

The first thing you need to do in order to edit a VHD is select it. To edit a disk, select the Edit Disk option from the Action menu of Server Manager. Figure 4.16 shows you the selection window.

FIGURE 4.16
Locate Virtual Hard Disk

Edit Virtual Hard Disk Wizard	

Locate Virtual Hard Disk

Before You Begin
Locate Disk
Choose Action
Summary

Where is the .vhd file located?

Location: M:\VMs\DemoNode1\   Browse...

⚠ Do not edit a virtual hard disk when it is used by a virtual machine that has snapshot, or when it is associated with a differencing virtual hard disk. Otherwise, data loss may occur.

< Previous   Next >   Finish   Cancel

This is a common selection window that allows you to either browse to find the disk or to type in the directory and name of the VHD file you want to edit. Notice the warning message in regard to snapshots and differencing disks. You do not want to destroy data you may have on the VHD.

If you accidentally select a disk that is in use by a running virtual machine, you will receive an error message, as shown in Figure 4.17. Windows does not allow for multiple systems to write to the same VHD at the same time. So you must ensure that any disk you wish to edit is not already in use.

FIGURE 4.17
Unable to edit
virtual disk

The type of disk you select will determine the type of action that can be performed. When you select a dynamically expanding disk, you will have the Compact, Convert, and Expand options. When you select a fixed disk, you will have the Convert and Expand options. When you select a differencing disk, you receive the Compact and Merge options. The Reconnect option is a special option that will appear only if you select a differencing disk and the system cannot find the appropriate parent disk. Figure 4.18 shows the selection window that is displayed when you select a dynamically expanding disk.

FIGURE 4.18
Choose Action

If you select another type of disk, you will see a similar window, with the selections listed above. Click the radio button by the option you want to perform, and click Next to continue. Let's examine these options.

Compact

The Compact option applies only to dynamically expanding and differencing disks. Remember that the differencing disk is always created as a dynamic disk, even if the parent is a fixed disk.

During the course of the normal use of any disk, physical or virtual, you will be writing and deleting content on the disk. Over time, you end up with more fragmented space, so performance can be impacted. There are defragmentation capabilities built into Windows, as well as third-party utilities, to lessen the amount of fragmentation by moving segments of files back into contiguous locations. In that manner, sequential reads may be able to bring in more data during a read without needing to move the disk head as much to find all the data.

This works the same in both physical and virtual disks. However, one of the primary purposes of creating a dynamic disk in Hyper-V is to save storage space. As information is written to a dynamic disk, it expands in size. When information is deleted (moving data during a defragmentation process is also considered a deletion), the size of the disk is not changed. The pointers to the actual data are changed, but the data still resides on the disk, even after a delete. It just no longer has a pointer to allow retrieval.

The compact process goes into the disk and finds all the locations that used to have pointers to them but no longer do. It then removes that space from the allocation for the dynamic disk, shrinking it in size to what is really needed to store the data contained on the disk. This process works on NTFS-formatted disks. If the disk is not formatted with NTFS (e.g., FAT, Extended FAT, raw, or Linux), you need to get a utility to zero out this information before you try to compact it. If you do not, you will not see any difference in the size of the disk.

This does not make the maximum size of the VHD any smaller. You have simply freed up unused space so that the amount of space the VHD occupies on the physical disk is less. If you want to have a disk that is smaller in maximum size, you will need to use another tool. You will need to create another VHD of the size you want and copy the contents of the original VHD into the new VHD. If the VHD contains just data, you can use copy utilities such as robocopy to preserve the file protections. If the VHD contains a bootable system image, you will need to use your favorite image-copy tool.

Convert

The Convert option converts a dynamically expanding disk to a fixed-size disk or a fixed-size disk to a dynamically expanding disk. The conversion is not a destructive conversion. The convert wizard asks you for a new location and name for the converted disk.

Note that this action does not change the maximum size of the disk. So be careful if you convert a dynamically expanding disk to a fixed disk. You will need to ensure that you have enough space at the location where you want to store the new disk. Hyper-V will tell you if there is not enough room on the destination location. This can easily happen if you have a dynamically expanding disk that has a maximum size of 50 GB, but when you take a directory of it on the disk, you see it is taking only 10 GB. You might select a destination that has more than 10 GB free, but converting from the dynamically expanding disk to a fixed disk will require the maximum size of 50 GB.

When you convert a fixed disk to a dynamic disk, Convert does read the entire fixed disk, moving only the data content to the dynamic disk. As a result, you will likely end up with a dynamic VHD file on the host's disk that is smaller in allocated size than the fixed VHD file. If the fixed disk was full, you will likely have a dynamic disk that has the same allocation as the fixed disk.

Expand

The Expand option increases the storage capacity of either a dynamically expanding or fixed-size disk. This makes the changes to the VHD file itself, unlike the Convert option, which creates a new VHD file. You will notice that when you increase the size of a dynamically expanding VHD file, a little more space is allocated on the physical file. This is the general overhead that the dynamically expanding disk uses to track its on-disk bounds. Although the Expand option expands the size of the available space in the VHD, the operating system that uses this disk must be able to expand the partition on the disk or create a new partition in order for the additional space to be used.

Merge

The Merge option applies only to a differencing disk. You can select a differencing disk and merge the contents that have been captured with the parent disk. You are given the option to either write back into the parent disk or create an entirely new disk. The new disk can be either a fixed or a dynamic disk.

If you choose to merge back into the parent disk, the contents of the differencing disk are written into the parent and the differencing disk is deleted from the system. You must be very careful when merging back into the parent disk. If you have multiple differencing disks from this single parent disk, you will end up with a single disk that has all the changes of the one differencing disk you are merging. All other differencing disks that are associated with that parent disk will have their relationship with the parent disk broken, and all those changes will be lost.

Reconnect

The Reconnect option applies only to a differencing disk. It is unique when compared to the other options because it does not appear as an option unless the parent disk for the differencing disk cannot be found. When it does appear, it is the only option available to be selected, so it means something has happened, such as you moved or renamed the parent disk. You are presented with the option to browse for the parent disk. Select the correct parent disk and continue.

SNAPSHOTS

Hyper-V has the ability to create virtual machine snapshots. A *snapshot* is a capture of the exact image of a virtual machine at a particular point. The state contains the full memory content, number of processors, disks, machine state, and so on that were assigned to a virtual machine at the time the snapshot was requested. It also contains the configuration of the virtual machine at the time of the snapshot. This includes things like the number and definition of virtual NICs, the number of processors, the amount of memory assigned, and basically any of those items you control from the virtual machine's Settings option. A snapshot can be taken of a running machine or of a machine that is turned off. If the machine is running, there is no downtime — the virtual machine continues running as the snapshot is taken. And it does not make any difference what operating system is running in the virtual machine because this is a feature of Hyper-V, not of the guest operating system. In the previous chapter, I talked about a capability of the later versions of Windows to make use of Volume Shadow Copy Services to take snapshots for backup purposes. This is not related to that feature. This is Hyper-V taking a snapshot of the memory and configuration regardless of the guest operating system.

A virtual machine can have up to 50 snapshots taken of it. Of course, this does require storage to store all these, and I will be talking about that shortly. The ability to take multiple snapshots allows you to recover to various points. This is very useful in a testing and development environment. If a mistake is made in a test, and a snapshot was taken before the test was performed, you can quickly revert to that earlier point to make changes to the test without needing to go through a major restore effort. Taking multiple snapshots also allows you to create different test paths. Figure 4.19 gives a picture of TestVM, a virtual machine of which I took multiple snapshots. Let's refer to that figure as I explain some of the features of snapshots and their uses.

FIGURE 4.19
Hyper-V snapshots

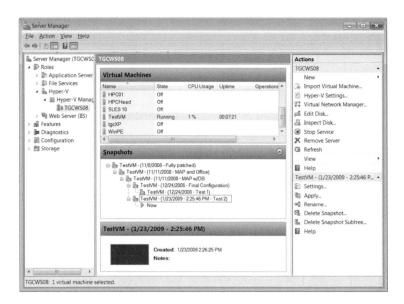

The first thing you notice is that the snapshots, shown in the middle of the console, have a tree structure. Each snapshot is created with a simple time stamp as the description, but within the Hyper-V console I renamed them to show the steps I was following as I was building a system. Most of the snapshots were taken sequentially, but at the bottom of the list you see a slight change. I caused a branch in the structure by reverting to an earlier point, running from that point to do some more work, and then taking a snapshot to capture that work, as shown by the entry with the box around it. You can also tell which is the currently executing snapshot by the little arrow labeled Now.

To take a snapshot, you select a virtual machine from the top part of the console. You can either right-click and select Snapshot, or you can select Snapshot from the Actions menu on the right-hand side. As I said earlier, the action of taking a snapshot captures an exact image of the virtual machine as it is at that exact moment. It stores this information into files in the location you have specified in the Settings window of the virtual machine. Figure 4.20 shows what the directory tree looks like for a virtual machine with snapshots.

I like to store each of my virtual machines in its own directory. Then, by default, the associated snapshots and files are contained within that directory. In this example, you see the Snapshots and Virtual Machines directories that were created when I created the TestVM virtual machine. Those long numbers that are directory names and filenames are known as

GUIDs — globally unique identifiers. Hyper-V does not keep track of its information via the name you call the virtual machine but instead uses GUIDs to ensure that no two files will ever have the same name.

FIGURE 4.20
Snapshots directory structure

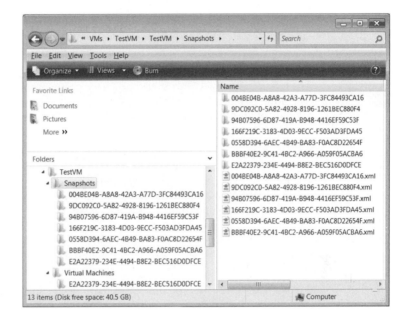

You will find five different types of files in this directory tree:

.vhd file   This is the virtual hard drive of the virtual machine.

.avhd file   If you have taken several snapshots, you will have several .avhd files — these files are the differencing disks, one for each snapshot.

.vsv file   When a virtual machine is saved, all contents of memory are saved to this file.

.bin file   This is a placeholder for the saved state file. It is created to ensure there is enough room to save the state in case the machine is shut down. An example would be a case where there is a power failure and your host machine is connected to a UPS. The UPS may provide only a few minutes of power. When you detect that you are running on the UPS, the safest route is to simply save the state of all running virtual machines so that you can restart from where you left off when power returns. By reserving the storage required to save the state of the machine before it is needed, you ensure that there will be enough space there when a problem occurs.

.xml file   This file contains the configuration information for the virtual machine at the time the snapshot was taken. You see six .xml files in Figure 4.20 because I had taken six snapshots.

These files are used when you perform different actions with the snapshots. That is what we are going to talk about next. When you select a snapshot file in the center of the console, you will see the actions you can perform on the right-hand side of the console.

Apply   To revert to any one of the snapshots that you have taken, select that snapshot and click Apply. You will see a message box pop up, as shown in Figure 4.21.

FIGURE 4.21
Apply Snapshot

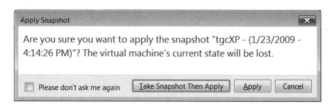

This warning offers you a safeguard should you want to get back to the state where you are right now. If you select Take Snapshot Then Apply, Hyper-V will take a snapshot of the current state of the virtual machine and then apply the selected snapshot. If you select Apply, the current state of the virtual machine will be lost and the state will become the state of the selected snapshot.

There is also a special case for going back, or reverting, to the initial state of the current snapshot. For example, you have taken a series of snapshots during a test. You apply one of those snapshots and start working on that image. You realize you have made a mistake, so you want to go back to the state you were at right after applying the snapshot. If you right-click the virtual machine in the upper part of the Hyper-V Management console, you will have the Revert option. This would be the same as selecting the currently running snapshot and choosing Apply. The difference is that it does not ask if you want to take another snapshot before you revert. It is just a special case that makes it a little quicker to get back to where you were in your testing.

Rename   Rename gives you the option to put a meaningful name on the snapshot. By default, a timestamp is used that contains date and time, accurate to the second. Depending on what I am doing, I leave the date and append a description, or I leave both the date and time and append a description. Believe me, when you come back several days later, you will thank yourself for making a meaningful description.

Delete Snapshot   Delete Snapshot deletes the individual snapshot that you have selected. What this means is that you can no longer go back to that point. For example, you may want to run a series of tests. Before you start your tests, you take a snapshot, which could be considered a base image. Then you run one set of tests. At the end of that test you take another snapshot before running yet a second test. The second test did not turn out the way you wanted it to, and you determine that the cause was a problem in the first test. Therefore you select the first snapshot (the base image) and apply it through the Action menu. Since you know that the contents of the second snapshot (taken at the end of the first test) contain invalid information, you can select it and delete it. You want to delete it because you know that you never want to go back to that particular point for the execution of your program.

Because it is easy to build complicated trees of snapshots, a picture might help you understand how deleting snapshots works. Figure 4.22 shows a tree diagram of a series of snapshots. What happens to the .avhd files differs slightly, and the actual timing differs, depending on where the deleted snapshot file exists in the tree.

In this figure, a base image is created and a snapshot is taken. That first snapshot is labeled Snapshot 1 in the figure. As changes are made, different snapshots are taken to allow returning to a known point. If a snapshot at the end of a branch of the tree is deleted (Snapshot 1.a.a.a and Snapshot 1.b.a), the associated files are deleted immediately.

FIGURE 4.22
Snapshot deletions

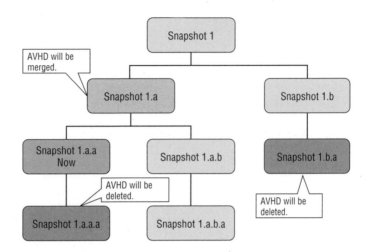

However, if the snapshot has a branch or branches extending from it (Snapshot 1.a), and the currently running image is Snapshot 1.a.a, the files that make up the deleted snapshot (Snapshot 1.a) are not physically deleted on the disk until the virtual machine is shut down. During the shutdown process, the contents of the deleted snapshot (Snapshot 1.a) are merged into its child or branch snapshots. Remember that a snapshot contains changes that occurred to the virtual machine from the point when the snapshot was taken. Since Snapshot 1.a contains changes, and Snapshots 1.a.a and 1.a.b are dependent on those changes, those changes need to be merged into Snapshots 1.a.a and 1.a.b in order for those child snapshots to remain valid.

Delete Snapshot Subtree   Deleting a snapshot subtree is similar to deleting a snapshot, except that it deletes multiple entries with one action instead of multiple actions. In Figure 4.22 you see a series of snapshots. Snapshot 1 has two subtrees, Snapshot 1.a and Snapshot 1.b. Snapshot 1.a has two subtrees, Snapshot 1.a.a and Snapshot 1.a.b.

If I were to select Snapshot 1.b and use the option Delete Snapshot Subtree, both Snapshot 1.b and Snapshot 1.b.a would be deleted in a single step. Since they are at the end of a branch, their associated AVHD files would be deleted immediately.

Snapshots provide a great deal of flexibility in a development and test environment, but I do not recommend them for a production environment. As you can see, each time you create a snapshot, you create another AVHD file. That AVHD file is a dynamically expanding disk with a maximum size equal in size to its parent disk. If you have more than one VHD file associated with the virtual machine, this whole directory structure is created for each VHD file in your virtual machine. Since you generally want to use fixed-size VHD files or pass-through disks for your production environment, using snapshots will transform your environment into one that is using dynamic disks. And you are using additional disk space every time. In addition to the performance difference relative to fixed disks versus dynamically expanding disks, all the VHDs in a snapshot tree need to be read to find the exact state of a virtual machine instead of reading just a single VHD. There are also possible problems at the operating system level. For example, you could revert to an earlier time when a different password was in use on a service. That password may no longer be valid and services might stop running.

Networking

Hyper-V does not change the rules of networking. In other words, once you have the virtual networks defined for your environment, you will be able to use most of the networking tools in your virtual environment you are currently using in your physical environment. I do know of one area that is different. Because Hyper-V implements virtual switches entirely in software, you cannot use an external network sniffer to listen in on VM-to-VM traffic if the VMs are on the same host. But providing the ability to virtualize the network for the virtual machines gives you a lot of flexibility, so much so that you can create some very complex and interesting networks.

If you remember from Chapter 2, when you were setting up the Hyper-V host environment, I recommended that you have at least two physical NICs in your host system. These should be wired NICs. Today, Hyper-V cannot directly make use of a wireless NIC. For the most part, that makes sense because today wireless networks are not common features on datacenter servers, nor are they as fast or reliable as wired NICs. (If you really want to use a wireless NIC on a laptop you are using for testing purposes, you can set up routing on the Hyper-V host and have it route requests from the virtual machines. To see how that is done, read James O'Neill's blog post at http://blogs.technet.com/jamesone/archive/2008/01/09/getting -wireless-access-from-a-hyper-v-vm.aspx.)

There are a couple of reasons for recommending at least two NICs for each Hyper-V host. The first reason is to provide for a management network that is used strictly for managing the physical environment. No application traffic goes over this network. This provides a level of security and isolation. If there is trouble on the application network, such as unavailability of a node or application network saturation, you can still get to the host environment via the management network.

A second reason for recommending two NICs is to provide constant access to the physical server. When a NIC is assigned for use by Hyper-V, Hyper-V binds the Microsoft Virtual Network Switch Protocol to that NIC and removes all other protocols. When all other protocols are removed, you will no longer be able to communicate on that NIC. So if you are managing the Hyper-V host on a NIC, and you select that NIC for use by Hyper-V, you lose your network connection to that Hyper-V host. You will then be unable to manage that machine remotely until you go to the physical system and make the appropriate changes from the physical console.

Two NICs are not a requirement but are recommended. I have only a single wired NIC on my laptop, and I use my laptop for most of my testing. But, because I am sitting at the console of my laptop, I do not have the remote management issues that one would normally have in managing a datacenter.

Types of Networks

Hyper-V does not have the ability to assign a physical NIC directly to a specific virtual machine. Instead, you create one or more virtual network switches through the Hyper-V management console and then you connect your virtual machines to the desired virtual switch, just as you would connect physical machines to physical network switches.

The Virtual Network Manager, located in the Actions menu on the right-hand side of the Hyper-V management console, is used to create virtual network switches to be used by the virtual machines on the Hyper-V host. Figure 4.23 shows an example on a machine that has not created any virtual switches yet. There is no limit to the number of virtual switches that you can configure, even though there is a limit of 12 virtual NICs that can be defined in each virtual machine.

FIGURE 4.23
Virtual Network
Manager

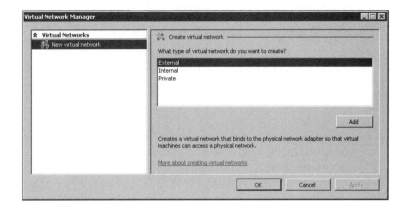

You can define three types of virtual network switches, and each serves a different purpose:

External   An external switch is created to bind virtual NICs to a physical NIC on the host. By assigning this virtual switch to a physical host NIC, virtual machines can also gain access to the external network. Only a single external switch can be configured for each physical NIC.

Internal   An internal switch is created to provide a line of communication between the Hyper-V host and any virtual machine running on that host. It also provides a means of communication among virtual machines running on the Hyper-V host. An unlimited number of internal switches can be created.

Private   A private switch is created to provide communications among the virtual machines running on a single Hyper-V host. The host cannot use this switch to communicate with any virtual machine. An unlimited number of private switches can be created.

You will notice in the following descriptions of the various virtual network switches that I never talk about defining the IP parameters for each switch. When you stop to think about it, this makes perfect sense. This process is defining virtual network switches, and switches do not have IP addresses. (Well, sort of. Yes, you can assign management IP addresses to physical networking devices. But you can get to the virtual switches by connecting to the Hyper-V host system.) You define the IP parameters on the virtual NICs that are created in the virtual machines, just as you would define the IP parameters on a physical NIC on a physical host.

EXTERNAL

Creating an external network requires that you select one of the host NICs to associate with this switch. Figure 4.24 shows the Virtual Network Manager when creating your first external virtual network switch.

As noted earlier, you can create only a single external switch per host NIC. The drop-down list shows all NICs that are on your host system, whether or not a switch has already been defined on them. Therefore, if you inadvertently select a NIC that already has a switch defined, you will receive an error when you click the OK or Apply button, signifying you have completed defining the switch.

In this example, there are two potential physical NICs from which to select. You can choose either one, but I suggest that if you have multiple Hyper-V servers, it would make sense to establish some sort of standard. In my case, I generally always leave the first adapter for management and select other adapters for use by virtual switches.

FIGURE 4.24
External switch

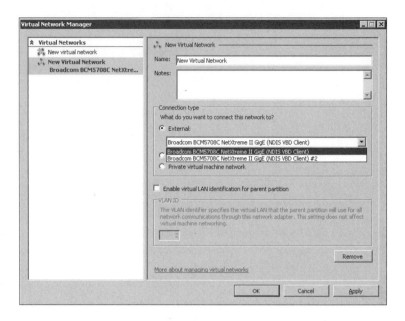

When you verify that you want to create an external virtual switch, Hyper-V displays the warning shown in Figure 4.25. Hyper-V is stressing what I have said about the possibility of losing network connectivity if you select the wrong NIC for an external switch.

FIGURE 4.25
Change warning

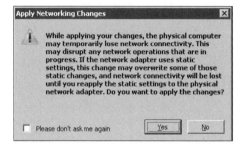

If the external NIC is connected to a physical network switch that supports VLAN tagging, you can make use of that capability on this virtual network switch. This gives you the ability to be connected to any VLANs to which the physical NIC is connected by simply entering the VLAN ID. Until you choose to enable VLAN identification, the VLAN ID box will be grayed out.

When dealing with VLAN IDs, you need to realize that you can manage them at two different points for the virtual machine. First, you must have a physical switch that supports VLANs. This switch can be defined to have one or more VLANs on any or all ports. Each physical NIC that is connected to this switch has the ability to communicate over any of the VLANs defined on the port of the NIC to which it is connected. Therefore, if you set the VLAN ID on the NIC from the Hyper-V host, that will connect all virtual machines using the virtual network switch connected to that NIC to the VLAN ID of the host.

If you do not set the VLAN ID at the host level, you can give the virtual NICs connected to the virtual network switch the ability to set their own VLAN IDs. This means that multiple virtual machines on the same virtual switch can be communicating over different VLANs. Be sure in your planning that you determine which way you want to manage your VLANs.

One last thought: The VLAN ID is a dynamic value. By that I mean that you can actually change the VLAN ID on a virtual machine that is running without shutting it down.

As you can see in Figure 4.24, a default name of New Virtual Network is assigned to any new virtual switch created. I like to change that to something meaningful to me. And if I am creating a virtual switch on other Hyper-V hosts that have the same purpose, I use the same name across this environment. This will be particularly important when we start setting up a clustered environment, which will be covered in Chapter 5. Therefore, I strongly recommend using a naming standard.

To make this naming a little more confusing, Windows actually assigns a default name to each new NIC it finds. By default, every external virtual switch you define in Hyper-V is automatically added to the parent partition as a network connection. Figure 4.26 shows the external switch I just created as Local Area Connection.

FIGURE 4.26
Network Connections

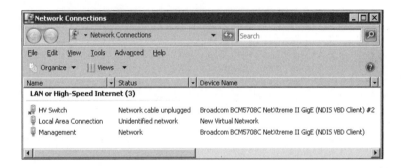

If I had created more than one switch, Windows would simply have added a sequence number to that string. This is not very helpful when trying to debug an environment, so I always rename the newly created NIC in the parent partition to be the same as I named the switch. For example, if I had named the first external switch External instead of New Virtual Network, I would have named the NIC in the parent partition External instead of Local Area Connection. I do the same thing in any virtual machine that connects to this virtual switch by renaming the virtual NIC in the VM to match what I named the virtual switch to which it is connected. As you can see in Figure 4.26, I have already renamed the physical NIC I use for management to Management. Any virtual NIC that connects to the same virtual switch in a virtual machine would also be named Management.

As you can see in Figure 4.26, I now have three entries — HV Switch, Local Area Connection, and Management. I have explained the Local Area Connection and Management switches, but what is that HV Switch? Remember from earlier in this section, during the installation of the Hyper-V role, the wizard asked which physical NICs I wanted to use with Hyper-V. The NIC that I selected for this role is what I have renamed HV Switch. You can tell this by the fact that the Device Name column identifies HV Switch and Management as associated with physical NICs. Figure 4.27 shows you the difference in the properties of these two physical NICs in the parent partition.

Looking at Figure 4.27 you can see that HV Switch Properties shows only the Microsoft Virtual Network Switch Protocol assigned to it. This is what enables the ability to create the external virtual switch on this NIC. Do *not* try to alter the properties of this NIC. It is almost a guarantee that you will have problems if you do.

FIGURE 4.27
NIC properties

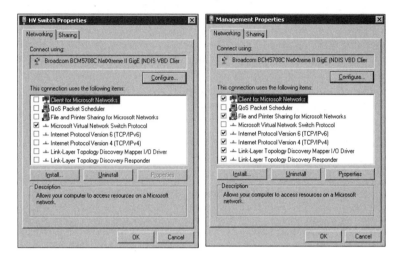

Sometimes you may want to provide a level of isolation between the parent partition and any virtual machines that are using an external switch. In the RTM code, the default is to share the external NIC between the parent and the guest. In R2 the default is to set up this isolation. See Figure 4.28.

FIGURE 4.28
Allow management

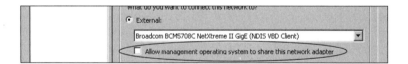

By default, the R2 parent partition does not have access to the use of an external virtual switch. If you want to share the use of the external virtual switch between the virtual machines and the parent partition, check this box while creating the switch, or come back later and select it. But if you leave it blank, the parent partition will not be able to use this virtual switch, providing an added level of security between the host platform and the virtual machines running on that system.

For the earlier release of Hyper-V, simply disable the virtual NIC created on the external switch. Do *not* disable the physical NIC, in this case the one I have labeled HV Switch. If you disable HV Switch, all virtual machines that are using an external switch bound to that NIC will stop operating.

INTERNAL

Creating an internal switch provides communication between the Hyper-V host and any virtual machines running on that host, as well as among all virtual machines on that host, as long as they assign a virtual NIC to this switch. This switch is completely virtual since it is not assigned to a physical NIC. You can also create VLANs on this switch. This is handy for testing a VLAN environment before deploying into a physical environment with VLANs.

As with the external virtual switch, Hyper-V automatically creates a virtual NIC in the parent partition that is attached to this internal switch. If you want to isolate the parent partition from the guests, disable the virtual NIC in the parent partition. But if you want to use the parent partition as a bridge to a physical network, using the internal switch allows for network communication between the virtual machines using this switch and the parent. In general, all the things I said about naming and disabling the external switch apply to the internal switch. It is less complex than the external switch, though, because it is not associated with any physical device.

PRIVATE

The private switch is very similar to the internal switch because it is set up for local communications, except the private switch permits communications only among the virtual machines that reside on this given Hyper-V host. Since it cannot be used to communicate with the parent partition, it does not create a NIC in the parent partition. It is not associated with any physical NIC, and it is not possible to make use of VLAN IDs. I still highly recommend using a standard naming convention on these switches, in case you move the machines from one Hyper-V host to another. This will allow virtual machines looking for a private network to locate it immediately.

A benefit of both the internal and private switches is that the network traffic never goes onto a physical wire. All information traveling over these switches is handled 100 percent within the Hyper-V environment. This gives memory-to-memory network performance, unrestricted by the limits of physical cables. When you look at the switches from within the virtual machines, you will see them listed as 10 gigabit networks, but that is only to provide a description — they really are not limited to that.

Working with Virtual Networks

Once you have created your virtual switches, you can start using them within your virtual machines. There is no physical limit to the number of virtual switches you can create, but each virtual machine can access a maximum of 12 virtual switches at any time. Assigning virtual switches is done via the Settings action for a given virtual machine. Figure 4.29 shows the Settings window.

In this example, I have a virtual machine that already has two virtual NICs assigned — one to External and one to 10LAN. To add another virtual NIC, select either Network Adapter or Legacy Network Adapter. You can use the network adapter only for an operating system that has Integration Components available and installed. You may be able to actually assign it to an operating system that does not have Integration Components, but it cannot be used.

Always check www.microsoft.com/windowsserver2008/en/us/hyperv-supported-guest-os.aspx for the latest list of operating systems supporting Integration Components. This list will change as more operating system environments are tested and added.

It is preferable to use the network adapter whenever possible because that is the synthetic adapter to provide the best performance. See Chapter 1 for more information on the synthetic drivers used in Hyper-V. The legacy network adapter can be used in virtually any operating system because it emulates a very well-known NIC that has been around for years. Nearly every x86 operating system has drivers for this NIC, the DEC21140 or Intel 21140. But because it is emulated, the performance of this NIC is not nearly as good as the network adapter, and it puts more of a load on the overall system to run the emulation.

Many companies use WinPE (Windows Pre-installation Environment) for automated build processes. It is built using the technology of Windows Vista and Windows Server 2008. But even though it is built on technologies that do have Integration Components available, WinPE itself cannot make use of the Integration Components. Therefore, you need to use the legacy network adapter with WinPE. There is an unsupported way to inject the necessary drivers into WinPE, and you can find those instructions in Mike Sterling's blog at `http://blogs.msdn .com/mikester/archive/2008/05/30/using-the-hyper-v-integration-components-in -winpe.aspx`. Mike is a program manager in Microsoft's Virtualization Product Group.

FIGURE 4.29
Settings

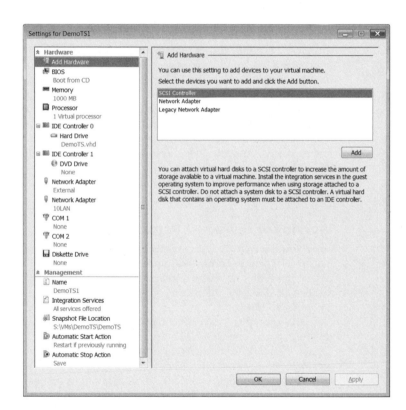

Once you have selected which network adapter you want to add, you are presented with a window like that shown in Figure 4.30.

FIGURE 4.30
Network settings

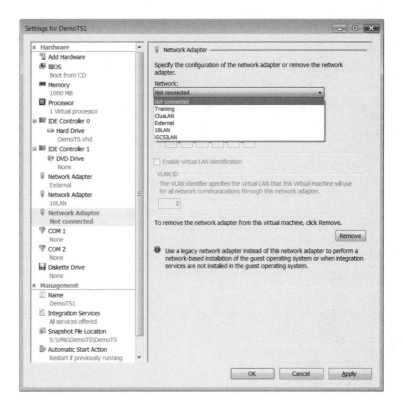

On the left-hand side, you can see that I have selected to add a network adapter, but it is not connected to any specific switch. On the right-hand side is a drop-down list that provides a list of switches from which to select.

Here is where you would also select the VLAN tag. If you have a physical switch that supports VLANs, it is possible to define multiple IP subnets on the same port on the switch. This lets you have multiple network connections to multiple networks, or VLANs, through a single cable to the switch, simply by creating multiple virtual NICs, with each one defined on a different VLAN.

After you make your selection, you will see an option to set up a MAC address, as shown in Figure 4.31.

FIGURE 4.31
MAC address

A MAC (Media Access Control) address is a physical address assigned to every NIC connected to the network. MAC addressing is a standard of IEEE. A MAC address is 6 bytes in length, with the first 3 bytes being known as the Organizationally Unique Identifier. Each manufacturer is assigned one or more 3-byte identifiers, and these are generally stored on the NIC. The last 3 bytes are sort of like a sequence number — a way to ensure unique addresses within a manufacture's ID. In a physical world, you generally do not need to worry about having any MAC collisions on the network because of the way NIC vendors try to keep each MAC address unique.

But when you are dealing in the virtual world, and the virtual machine is using the physical MAC address on the host system, Hyper-V needs to ensure that each MAC address is unique. As you can see in Figure 4.31, you are given two options — Dynamic or Static. By default, a dynamic address is used. Hyper-V will keep track of the MAC addresses it has handed out, but it has a range of only 256 possible MAC addresses. That is generally enough to ensure uniqueness on each Hyper-V server. If this is sufficient for your needs, just leave the selection as Dynamic. In the case of multiple Hyper-V hosts on the same network, the MAC address is further differentiated by using the last two octets of the Hyper-V host's IP address as the part of the MAC address before the number it increments from 1 to 256. This pretty much ensures, though does not guarantee, that you will not have MAC address conflicts between two hosts on the same network.

Some organizations use the MAC address as a way of identifying systems for specific purposes. If you use that capability, Hyper-V allows you to put in a specific MAC address, just as you would in your physical environment.

NIC Teaming

NIC teaming is a term that describes using two or more network ports in parallel for additional capabilities like load balancing (link aggregation) and failover. With Hyper-V or Windows Server 2008 today, NIC teaming is always provided either by the vendors of the NICs or by the vendors of the systems into which the NICs are placed.

Teaming NICs is common practice in datacenters to provide failover in case of a hardware malfunction or to provide greater throughput by balancing the traffic over two or more NICs that are bound together. Sometimes companies combine these functions to provide both protection against hardware malfunction and greater throughput. When you consider that you are going to be putting multiple virtual machines on a single physical host, the benefit of teaming becomes obvious. So, how is this handled in Hyper-V since the NICs are virtual and the teaming is done at the physical NIC level?

Microsoft relies on its partners for NIC teaming software. Even though Windows contains thousands of device drivers, those device drivers are generally written by the hardware vendors and not by Microsoft. Therefore, any NIC teaming that is done in the environment is done at the physical level and not within the virtual machines.

But that puts a fly into the ointment. Microsoft's support statement is defined in `http://support.microsoft.com/kb/254101`. Because Microsoft has not written the teaming software, it cannot provide support for it. And, though it works most of the time, and works quite well most of the time, Microsoft has had multiple support calls where something in the teamed network is not working, but when the teaming is removed, the network works fine. Therefore, Microsoft relies on the NIC vendors to provide and support their teaming.

Microsoft understands the need and value for NIC teaming, particularly in the virtualization environment. Though Microsoft cannot make recommendations for a particular vendor's offerings, and their support statement remains that as defined in the above-referenced KB article, they have found that Broadcom and Intel teaming products work. In fact, HP has published a how-to article on setting up ProLiant servers with NIC teaming. You can find this article at `http://h20000.www2.hp.com/bc/docs/support/SupportManual/c01663264/c01663264.pdf`.

The Bottom Line

Planning storage on your host   The Hyper-V host platform supports all the storage options that are supported by the Windows Server 2008 platform. This means that USB, IDE, SATA, SAS, Fibre Channel, and iSCSI disks are all available for use by the host. This provides a significant amount of flexibility in storage options for your host environment.

Master It   List the various storage options that you would consider to fall into the low-end, midrange, and datacenter-class solutions. Explain why you think they belong where you placed them and what you would consider a typical usage for that solution.

Configuring storage for virtual machines   Hyper-V virtual machines can utilize either physical disks (pass-through) or virtual hard disks, and the virtual hard disks can be created in different ways. Each selection has various advantages and disadvantages from both management and performance aspects.

Master It   List some advantages and disadvantages of each type of disk that a virtual machine can use.

Planning your network configuration for the host   The Hyper-V host systems provide access for the virtual machines to the physical network resources you have in your organization. Because you will most likely now have more than one system communicating over each physical NIC, you will need to plan accordingly.

Master It   Describe some considerations about the number of NICs you should have on a host machine.

Configuring virtual switches for virtual machines   Hyper-V can operate in a complex networking environment. It accomplishes this by creating virtual switches that are used for connecting into either the physical or the virtual environment.

Master It   There are three types of virtual switches that can be defined and used. List the three types and what their normal usage is.

Chapter 5

High Availability and Hyper-V

Server virtualization is making a significant impact on datacenters. The consolidation of servers onto fewer physical machines provides very measurable advantages in resource and cost savings. But when many physical machines are consolidated into virtual machines on fewer physical servers, the need for those physical machines hosting the virtual machines to be up all the time becomes critical. Problems or failures on physical servers can have a significantly greater impact on operations. Windows Server 2008 and Hyper-V provide solutions that can be implemented to provide High Availability (HA) of virtual machines as well as the workloads being hosted inside those virtual machines.

In addition to the need for HA, the flexibility to move these virtual machines from one environment to another has also given rise to the desire to use the virtualization infrastructure to plan for business continuity in the case of a disaster in a site. Since the entire virtual machine can be easily transported to another server, customers are starting to see how virtualization can be used to lower costs for maintaining a disaster recovery site.

In this chapter you will learn about:

◆ Setting up a highly available environment on physical machines hosting virtual machines

◆ Setting up an environment with the ability to move running virtual machines from one server to another with no downtime

◆ Setting up a highly available environment on virtual machines

Failover Clusters

A failover cluster, also known as a High Availability cluster, is a group of two or more loosely coupled machines working together to appear as though it is a single system. A failure of a single component, which would bring down a stand-alone system, may cause only a slight outage of a service, which may or may not be noticeable, in a cluster. In order to ensure that there is no single point of failure in a cluster, clusters generally have multiple instances of the individual components that can automatically take over the function of the failed component.

Failover clusters, as we know them today, had their first commercial success starting in 1984 when Digital Equipment Corporation (DEC) released products for its TOPS-20 and VMS operating systems. DEC continued to lead the market in failover clusters and released Digital Clusters for Windows NT in 1997 shortly before DEC's demise. The next year, 1998, Microsoft released its first product, Microsoft Cluster Server. This was an add-on product to Windows NT Server

4.0, Enterprise Edition. These initial releases of clustering software for NT comprised two identical servers, or nodes, connected to some sort of shared SCSI storage.

In 2000, Microsoft released Windows 2000 Server, which included an improved Cluster Services as an optional install for the Advanced version of the operating system. Further improvements came with the release of Windows Server 2003, again as part of the Enterprise and Datacenter Editions of the operating system. Each release made improvements in the applications supported, stability, management, and scalability. As a result, clusters built on Windows Server products are used by millions of customers around the world.

With the growth of virtualization and the desire to ensure high levels of availability for virtual machines, Microsoft released scripts to support clustering of virtual machines running under Virtual Server on Windows Server 2003. But, just as Virtual Server was not the product that the industry was looking for, neither was this fix to make them highly available. They both worked, and many customers implemented them as a solution, but Microsoft was already working on Hyper-V and a totally new form of clustering for Windows Server 2008.

When dealing with virtual machines, there are two different ways to implement failover clusters. The first way they can be implemented is at the host level, so that any virtual machines running on a physical node configured in a cluster can be failed over to another node in the cluster. This is exactly what is done today in the physical world with things like SQL Server and file services. The other way is to cluster the actual virtual machines that are running different applications such as SQL and file services. What makes the Microsoft environment so easy to understand is that the failover clustering technology is pretty much the same for the host environment as it is for the guest environment. That means you need to learn the mechanics of only one clustering environment to manage both the physical and the virtual clusters.

Before I explain how to set up Failover Clusters, let's look at the specific features that are important for Hyper-V configurations.

Failover Clusters with Hyper-V

Clusters have been used for many years to provide highly available environments for file and print services, applications, SQL Server databases, and other services. With Windows Server 2008, Microsoft added Hyper-V to the list of supported services in a highly available cluster environment. With Windows Server 2008 R2, Microsoft enhanced the capabilities of Hyper-V and Failover Clusters even further. The added features specific to Hyper-V are Quick Migration, Live Migration, and Cluster Shared Volumes, which are explained below. But before I explain what these Hyper-V-specific features are, let's see how Failover Clusters provide High Availability to Hyper-V.

HIGH AVAILABILITY AND HYPER-V

High Availability, often referred to as HA, provides the ability for a service running on one node, or server, in a cluster to automatically restart on another node in the cluster should something happen to the first node that prevents the service from running. When a failure occurs on one server, another server will detect the failure and take over the resources associated with the service — these could include server names, IP addresses, disks, or other resources. This capability protects the service from unplanned downtime, such as the failure of a power supply in a host system. Microsoft provides this capability for many different services, including Hyper-V. With Failover Cluster Services in Windows Server 2008, a cluster can contain from 2 to 16 nodes, and a service can be set to restart on any other node in the cluster. This feature is included as part of the Enterprise and Datacenter Editions of Windows Server 2008.

This is a very simplistic explanation, but in a Hyper-V cluster, when a node failure occurs, the ownership of the disk(s) containing the VHDs and the virtual machine configuration is taken over by a surviving node. The surviving node takes ownership of all the virtual machines that were defined on those disks and starts them. The start of the virtual machine is a boot of the operating system in the virtual machine. This unplanned stop and restart on another node is similar to walking up to a physical server, unplugging it, and then plugging it back in and booting it. The unexpected stoppage does not give any applications or services running on the host time to gracefully shut down, doing such things as clearing memory buffers to disk. So, just as there is the possibility of data loss when a physical machine is powered off, if the host machine fails, causing the virtual machine to stop unexpectedly, there is a possibility of data loss in a virtual environment. This is typical of any HA solution for virtual environments.

HA is available to physical servers hosting the Hyper-V role or among virtual machines running under the hypervisor, but there is a difference in how they work. When two or more Hyper-V hosts are built into a Failover Cluster, it makes the entire virtual machine into a highly available resource. When two or more virtual machines are built into a Failover Cluster, it makes the application workloads running within the virtual machines highly available. One big difference between host clusters and application clusters is the time required to restart. In a host cluster, when a host fails, the virtual machines running on that host are restarted (rebooted) on a surviving node. Then the application or service running within that virtual machine needs to initialize. In an application cluster, when a node fails, only the service needs to be started on the surviving node because the surviving node still has the operating system running. Though either way may provide the same end results, an application cluster will generally put a service or application back into production in a shorter period of time.

As I mentioned earlier, there are three features of Failover Clusters that provide unique capabilities to Hyper-V. Two of these features, Quick Migration and Live Migration, provide ways to move virtual machines from one node to another without losing the state of the virtual machine. The third feature, Cluster Shared Volumes, allows management of the cluster storage used by the virtual machine to be more flexible. Live Migration and Cluster Shared Volumes are available only on Hyper-V R2.

Quick Migration

Whereas HA handles unplanned downtime (nobody knew the node was going to fail) and automatically starts the virtual machines on another node, Quick Migration is used for planned migration. For example, let's say you have to patch the parent partition. You can select the virtual machines running on one node and then use the Quick Migration feature to move those machines to another node in the cluster. Quick Migration is a three-step process, and it ensures that no data is lost, nor is the state of the running virtual machine lost.

1. The operator (or a script) instructs the cluster to move a virtual machine (or several virtual machines) from one node to another. This causes Hyper-V to save the running state of the virtual machine to its save file (.vsv) on the shared storage of the cluster.

2. When the process of saving the state of the virtual machine is completed, the ownership of the LUN on which the virtual machine resides is transferred from the currently owning node to the node to which the virtual machine was directed, and the virtual machine is deregistered from the original Hyper-V host.

3. The node now owning the LUN reads the saved state of the virtual machine into its memory, registers the virtual machine on Hyper-V, and starts the machine.

Even though the state of the machine is saved, and the machine resumes execution at the exact point it was at when the process started, access to the virtual machine is unavailable during this entire process. Therefore, if there were other systems accessing the virtual machine's services, those other systems would need to reestablish their connections to this virtual machine to continue processing. The outage can last from a few seconds to a couple minutes. The time is totally dependent on the amount of memory that has to be written to disk to save the state of the virtual machine and the speed of the data transfer to and from the LUN. If services can be interrupted for short periods of time, typically in development and test environment, but even in some production environments, Quick Migration works fine.

Quick Migration is available only on physical hosts to quickly migrate virtual machines from one Hyper-V host to another. It is not possible to run a virtual machine with Hyper-V installed within another Hyper-V virtual machine, so you cannot set up Quick Migration within a virtual environment.

Live Migration

Live Migration is a new feature of Windows Server 2008 R2 and Microsoft Hyper-V Server 2008 R2. There are some situations where the outage required for Quick Migration is unacceptable. There may be applications that require round-the-clock access, and any interruption in service is considered bad. Or the application may have been written poorly so that it does not recover from short network outages. For those situations, Live Migration is the answer. Live Migration works at the memory level to move a running virtual machine from one node in a Failover Cluster to another node with no interruption of services provided by the virtual machine.

As with Quick Migration, Live Migration is a planned move that is built on top of the Failover Cluster Services running in the parent partition. And, similar to Quick Migration, the movement of a virtual machine from one node in a cluster to another node is a multistep process. I say *multistep*, because it could be argued that the steps I list below could be broken down to finer increments, but they happen so quickly that they are easier to explain this way.

1. The operator (or a script) instructs the cluster to move a virtual machine from one node to another. This starts a process that does an iterative copy over the network of the running virtual machine's memory from one node to another. The process is iterative to ensure the actual running state of the virtual machine is preserved. The first copy copies all memory. While the copy is being performed, the virtual machine continues to execute and will make changes to memory locations. A change to a page of memory becomes known as a "dirty" page because the page changed. The dirty pages are tracked so the copy process will know to just copy those changed pages during the next copy iteration. The iterative nature ensures that each time through, the number of dirty pages gets smaller and smaller. As the pages are copied from the first node's memory, they are loaded into the second node's memory.

2. When the number of dirty pages gets small enough, the running virtual machine is paused, the last dirty pages are copied, and the virtual machine is unpaused on the second node. The time of the pause is under half a second, which is well within the timeout of a typical TCP request. Therefore, any service being accessed via TCP will either not notice the very brief outage or simply retry and find the virtual machine running on a different node. There are additional steps performed on the network to ensure the virtual machine is found on the new host, but all these things take place so quickly that TCP, in essence, does not see an outage.

Live Migration is available only on physical hosts to migrate virtual machines from one Hyper-V host to another with no network timeouts.

Cluster Shared Volumes

Prior to R2, clusters from Microsoft provided shared physical access to the disk resources of the cluster but limited full read/write access to a single node of the cluster at a time. In other words, even though there was a physical connection that enabled all nodes physical access to a LUN, the cluster software allowed only one node to read and write to that LUN. When a failure required a service to be moved to another node, the LUN was one of the resources that was transferred to enable the service to start on another node.

R2 introduced a significant change in the way storage volumes can be accessed for virtual machines, and this feature is available only for Hyper-V R2 virtual machines. This is known as Cluster Shared Volumes (CSV). CSV functions as a distributed-access file system for access to virtual hard drives. Other cluster technologies from other vendors have accomplished a similar function by creating proprietary cluster file systems. These cluster file systems provide a locking mechanism shared among all the hosts in the cluster that limits access to the disk to a single node at a time, but all nodes have read/write access. CSV does not use any proprietary volume format; it uses the standard NTFS that Windows has used for years. And CSV enables all Hyper-V hosts to have full read/write access to the VHDs of the virtual machines they are hosting.

CSV is an option that is turned on in a Failover Cluster that is built with Hyper-V R2 hosts. It is implemented by creating a directory on the C: volume of each node in the cluster. See the following example of a directory with two Cluster Shared Volumes.

```
C:\ClusterStorage
C:\ClusterStorage\Volume1
C:\ClusterStorage\Volume1\VM1
C:\ClusterStorage\Volume1\VM2
C:\ClusterStorage\Volume2
C:\ClusterStorage\Volume2\VM3
C:\ClusterStorage\Volume2\VM4
C:\ClusterStorage\Volume2\VM5
```

In this case, two shared disks in the cluster are assigned to CSV. The first volume has two virtual machines stored on it. The second volume has three virtual machines stored on it. Only one node of the cluster will own the physical LUN of the shared volume, but each volume can be owned by different nodes of the cluster. CSV provides the ability for each node to have full read/write access to the individual VHDs that are used by different virtual machines.

CSV addresses a management issue that existed in using Hyper-V in a Failover Cluster in the original release of Windows Server 2008. In the original release, a disk resource was the unit of failover. By this I mean that all virtual machines stored on a given LUN had to be moved or failed over together, because only one host could own the LUN. This worked fine for unplanned downtime, where all the virtual machines would be restarted on the host that took ownership of the LUN. But if you had configured two virtual machines with two totally different applications onto a single LUN, this forced both virtual machines to be migrated, creating that short period of outage that Quick Migration required. It was not possible to move just a single virtual machine unless it was the only virtual machine on the LUN. This made for a complex environment to manage to try to ensure which machines could or could not share storage with other virtual machines. Or, it was necessary to create a separate LUN for each virtual machine to ensure no downtime except for the virtual machine being moved.

CSV changes that by allowing the individual virtual machines to move or migrate independently of which node has ownership of the LUN. Since the ownership of the LUN does not have to change from one node in the cluster to another node in the cluster, there is virtually no outage of the virtual machine's services. It also enables multiple virtual machines to reside on a single LUN and still have HA for each virtual machine.

There is a lot more detail behind how these are implemented, but I think this gives enough information to help you understand the concepts of what is happening. It is still possible to use both CSV and non-CSV volumes in a cluster. The differences will be explained in the steps for setting up a Windows Server 2008 Full installation Failover Cluster. For now, let's look at how the host Failover Clusters are set up to provide High Availability for virtual machines. Once you have learned how it is done in the physical world, it will be pretty simple to understand how it works in the virtual world.

Host-Based Failover Clusters

Host-based Failover Clusters provide you with HA and are the foundation upon which both Quick Migration (original and R2) and Live Migration (R2 only) are built. Failover Cluster is a feature of Windows Server 2008 Enterprise and Datacenter Editions and can be installed on both the Full and the Core installations. With the release of R2, Microsoft Hyper-V Server also has the Failover Cluster feature.

To keep the explanation of how to build a cluster easier to understand, I will explain how to set up and run a two-node cluster. The simplicity of Microsoft's model makes it easy to add a third or fourth node, or up to 16 nodes in the cluster. To start with, what does a two-node cluster look like? Figure 5.1 depicts a basic two-node cluster.

FIGURE 5.1
Two-node failover cluster

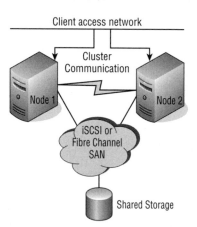

The basic components of a cluster include host systems (2 to 16), shared storage, and two or more network connections on each host. Using Figure 5.1 as a reference, let's look at the hardware requirements for a cluster.

HARDWARE REQUIREMENTS

One of the first things I like to state when talking about putting clusters together is that the purpose of clustering is to ensure highly available applications. Generally speaking, when you want to have an application highly available, there is a business reason that justifies the added expense of clustering. This is no time to try to cut corners by using cheaper and possibly less-reliable components. Yes, a cluster is designed to be able to survive the failure of any single component, but that does not give you a reason to build in a potential point of failure. I have had too many customers try to save a few dollars in their configuration, just to have it come back and bite them at the worst possible time. I believe the "pay me now or pay me later" phrase became popular from an STP commercial talking about protecting your investment in your car with a low-cost oil additive now rather than paying high repair bills in the future. This is also very true of configuring clusters. You will be able to put together many configurations that pass the validation wizard, but you may not have the most reliable configuration if you are cutting corners to get there.

The validation wizard is one of the new features provided in Windows Server 2008 that makes configuring a cluster so much easier than it was in earlier versions. In order to have a supported cluster configuration prior to Windows Server 2008, you had to find a complete cluster solution that included specific host systems, specific host bus adapters (HBA) at a specific revision, specific storage arrays, and specific versions of the firmware on the storage controllers (if present). It was an onerous task, and any change, such as an updated driver for an HBA, could create an environment that was no longer supported.

The release of Windows Server 2008 brought in two major changes to make it easier to specify the components of a cluster and then actually configure it. The first change concerns how to determine what components can be used. Microsoft describes this on their website at www.windowsservercatalog.com/results.aspx?bCatID=1291&cpID=0&avc=10&OR=1:

> With the debut of Windows Server 2008 Microsoft is pleased to announce the release of the Failover Cluster Configuration Program (FCCP). The new program is a change in the way customers procure hardware for high availability clustering infrastructure. Windows Server 2008 program partners will be listing complete cluster configurations on their own websites that they have tested and validated to work for Windows Server 2008 Failover Clustering rather than listing configurations on the Windows Server Catalog. All hardware components that comprise a cluster configuration need to earn "Certified for" or "Supported" on Windows Server 2008 designations and will be listed in the Windows Server Catalog.

Once they made it easier to find and mix and match components instead of making a customer purchase a specific configuration, Microsoft created a validation wizard to ensure the selected components would be a supported configuration. The validation wizard runs hundreds of tests against a configuration to ensure that all the components work together as they should and that resources can fail over from one node to another.

Servers or Hosts

Because you are going to be running Hyper-V as the highly available application, you will need to have x64-based processors that conform to the requirements listed in Chapter 2. Briefly, this requirement is that the processors support hardware virtualization (Intel VT or AMD-V) and data execution prevention. The recommendation is to use host systems that are fairly equal in capability, but it is not a strict requirement. The only other thing to remember is to ensure that all nodes are either Intel or AMD; you cannot mix those two architectures.

This is different from clustering other services where the different chip architectures can work together. When I describe the Quick Migration and Live Migration features of Hyper-V later in this chapter, you will see that we are moving actual memory locations containing executing instructions from one node of the cluster to another. All processors in a Hyper-V cluster must have the same hardware instruction set for this to work.

Networks

Network cards must be compatible with Windows Server 2008, and it is recommended that the NICs be of similar speeds when talking to the same network. You do not have to have the exact same network cards in each host, but for reliability reasons, you may want to ensure that you do. You should also make all the settings on the cards the same for things like speed, duplex mode, flow control, and the like.

In Figure 5.1, there is a possibility of three distinct networks. The first network is the client access network. This is the network that clients use to access the applications and services of the cluster. By default, cluster communications, sometimes referred to as a heartbeat, also travel over this link in order to provide a level of redundancy for this important communication. It is not uncommon to use network aggregation or NIC teaming on the client network. Although Microsoft does not provide support for the teaming software, since it is written by the NIC or system vendors, Microsoft does support clusters that have their client access network teamed.

The second network is used for cluster communication. This is often set up as totally separate from the client access network. This is one of those areas where I have seen a lot of customers try to cut corners. They will connect both the client access and cluster communication networks to the same network switch. They figure they have isolated the traffic to different IP subnets, but they are going into the same network switch, providing a single point of failure. So if you really want to have a truly highly available configuration, ensure that this network has its own separate components. It will work in the cost-cutting method, and it creates a supported configuration, but it is just a problem waiting to happen. I have seen it happen.

The third possible network would be the network to the shared storage. I will talk more about shared storage in a little bit, but if you are using iSCSI as your shared storage, you are really using an IP network to talk to your shared storage. When you have this sort of configuration, you need to ensure that the iSCSI network is not shared with other network communication. Cluster communication and client access communication can share (not recommended) the same networks, but you should not share your iSCSI traffic with other network communication.

Figure 5.1 is a simple picture without all the network switches drawn in that would be part of a corporate deployment. Remember when configuring a cluster, even though network switches are not technically part of the cluster, it is easy to overlook them as a possible single point of failure. Carefully plan the use and placement of switches in your environment to ensure that losing a single network switch does not cause the cluster to fail.

Storage Device Controllers

Three different types of storage devices are supported as shared storage for failover clusters — serial attached SCSI (SAS), Fibre Channel (FC), and iSCSI. If you are using SAS or FC, you must have identical controllers in every node that is accessing the shared storage in the cluster. You must also ensure that every controller is at the same firmware version and the same device drivers are used in each node accessing the shared storage.

Shared storage is sort of a tricky term. Storage is shared at the physical level in that all system nodes in the cluster have a physical connection to the storage. But at the software level, only one node at a time owns and has the ability to read/write to a given device. This means there has to be very precise communication among the storage controllers to ensure that data does not get corrupted because of miscommunication among the storage controllers. The only way to guarantee that is to ensure that all controllers are identical down to the firmware.

If you are using iSCSI, you use network adapters to connect to the SAN. The network you use should be used only for communicating to the SAN. As with the SAS or FC storage controllers, you should use identical network cards. If you are using iSCSI storage controllers, they must be identical down to the firmware. (An iSCSI storage controller is a specialized NIC that has firmware on the NIC to offload the iSCSI protocol to the NIC. It is very similar to a host bus adapter used for accessing Fibre Channel or SAS.) The speed of the network adapter should be at least 1 Gbps. For better performance, you can move to higher-speed links.

Storage

There are various options to consider when configuring storage for a failover cluster. Hyper-V requires a shared storage solution, so what I show in Figure 5.1 is a common way to configure shared storage. I'll focus on shared storage solutions in this explanation.

Windows Server 2003 R2 introduced a concept called *majority node set* clusters that did not require shared storage, and that same capability has been brought into Windows Server 2008, renamed slightly as *node majority*. This method of clustering does not require the use of any form of shared storage, so it relies on either software or hardware to replicate the contents of one storage device to another so the contents of that device will be available when the service fails over to another node. Microsoft does not provide any replication software that enables this capability, so I will go into more detail later in this chapter when I talk about third-party solutions that provide replication capabilities.

For a two-node failover cluster, it is recommended to have at least two LUNs presented from the storage array to the cluster. One of the LUNs will contain the *witness disk*. The witness disk is used by the cluster to ensure continued operation if there is a failure in the compute nodes such that exactly half of the nodes of the original cluster remain. The other LUNs will each contain one or more virtual machines that are being run by Hyper-V.

It is possible to have more than one virtual machine stored on a single LUN. But that may not provide the level of High Availability that you are looking for. Within Windows Server 2008 Failover Clusters, a LUN is a unit of failover. In other words, everything that is contained on a single LUN will fail over should anything on that LUN fail over. The proactive migration of a virtual machine from one node to another by using Quick Migration also makes use of the transfer of the ownership of the LUN. If you have two unrelated virtual machines, and you want to move one of them to another host in the cluster, the second one has to move at the same time, incurring downtime for both virtual machines. This changed in Windows Server 2008 R2 with the addition of Cluster Shared Volumes.

It is also possible to have disks, either locally attached or coming from the SAN, that are not exposed to the cluster. You are in control of which disks get assigned to the cluster. Do not expose disks to the cluster if you do not wish to use them for shared storage.

Disks used for shared storage in a cluster must be basic disks, not dynamic disks. This is *basic* in the sense that the Windows operating system recognizes two types of storage, those being either basic disks, sometimes referred to as simple volumes, or dynamic disks, which can be used to create software RAID sets. This does not refer to the type of virtual hard drive that can be either fixed or dynamic. The VHDs reside on the physical disks that are defined as basic disks to the parent partition.

Dynamic disks provided two features that people would sometimes want to use in a cluster. The first was the ability to expand the size of a volume without the need to bring down the system. Dynamic disks let you expand volumes. With Windows Server 2003 SP1, Microsoft enabled its diskpart utility to expand a basic volume as long as the underlying LUN on which it was defined could be expanded. That eliminated that need. In fact, in Windows Server 2008,

Microsoft also includes the ability to shrink the size of a partition on the volume without bringing it offline.

The second feature provided by dynamic disks is the ability to create software RAID volumes. Because of the performance overhead of performing RAID in software, it is always recommended to use hardware RAID in production environments. So, the two desires for using dynamic disks are not required.

It is also required that you use volumes that are formatted with the NT File System (NTFS). Lastly, I like to recommend that you use GUID Partition Table (GPT) partitions instead of Master Boot Record (MBR) volumes. Both of them work, but there are a couple benefits to GPT that are not available in MBR. The first is the size of the partition. For LUNs containing individual virtual machines, this is not likely to be of concern, but an MBR partition has a maximum size of 2 TB. You are more likely to go over this size with a data disk than with a disk storing individual VHDs. If you are using Cluster Shared Volumes, you may also exceed that size when storing many virtual machines on a single LUN.

There are a couple other differences between MBR and GPT partitions, but the second point that I think is more important is the replication of the partition table information. On an MBR disk, you have a single partition table. On a GPT disk, the partition information is replicated to another part of the disk. This means that a disk error in the partition table is less likely to cause a problem with a GPT disk because it can read information from two locations on the disk. Since Failover Clustering is all about doing whatever you can to ensure High Availability, this is just another way to build in some fault tolerance.

Storage Planning

In Hyper-V V1, only Quick Migration was supported, so you would create a volume and store all VHDs associated with a single virtual machine on one volume or LUN. Quick Migration saves the state of a virtual machine, transfers ownership of the LUN to another node, and restores the state of the virtual machine on another node. This ensures that a machine is highly available, as every VHD on that LUN would fail over as a unit. If you are setting up your cluster for V1, you should create a separate LUN for each virtual machine. Technically it is possible to put more than one virtual machine on a single LUN. But that does not provide the highest level of availability for all the virtual machines. Since the goal of a cluster is to provide the best level of availability, multiple virtual machines on a single LUN work contrary to that.

In Hyper-V R2, Live Migration and Cluster Shared Volumes are supported. This provides the ability to store multiple virtual machines on a single LUN and have them fail over independently of one another. You can create a large volume and store multiple virtual machines on that single volume. In general storage managers would rather manage fewer LUNs, so it is recommended to use CSV when working with Hyper-V R2.

STORAGE AREA NETWORKS

Storage area networks (SANs) used to be considered very expensive storage options that required special expertise to manage. Over the years, with storage vendors introducing lower-cost SANs meant for smaller shops, the acceptance of iSCSI SANs, and Microsoft's introduction of its Storage Manager for SANs in Windows Server 2003 R2, SANs have become less imposing. Yes, the large multiterabyte and even multipetabyte SANs will still most likely be managed by dedicated storage specialists. But SANs have become much more common and are the recommended way to provide shared storage for a Failover Cluster.

As the SANs have improved, the improvement has come with some changes. When you use a SAN with Windows Server 2008 Failover Clusters, you need to keep a few things in mind:

Compatibility

Windows Server 2008 has made a number of changes in how it deals with storage. One of the most important is the SCSI commands it uses to access shared storage devices in a Failover Cluster. The easiest way to ensure compatibility is to check with the storage vendor to ensure that they have tested their products and support their products in a Windows Server 2008 Failover Cluster.

Just because the storage system worked with Windows Server 2003 does not mean that it will work with Windows Server 2008. Windows Server 2003 used the SCSI-2 standard for communicating with devices. There were some areas of the standard that allowed for interpretation on the part of the implementers. This resulted in different interpretations of the same command, or assumption of a command if it did not recognize a command, at different levels in the storage stack. Windows Server 2008 switched to the SCSI-3 standard, which is much better defined through the storage stack. But there are older storage devices that understand only SCSI-2. Parallel SCSI is an example of this. Parallel SCSI was supported from the first Windows clusters through Windows Server 2003, but because it does not support SCSI-3 commands, it is no longer supported. The moral of this story is to check with your vendor or to check www.windowsservercatalog.com for storage that has been certified for use in a Windows Server 2008 Failover Cluster.

Single Cluster Use

This is no different from what was required in any earlier version of Windows Failover Clustering. You cannot share a single volume between two or more clusters. The storage is shared among nodes of a single Failover Cluster. This does not mean that you cannot have multiple clusters on a single SAN. What it means is that you must ensure that any LUN you create in the SAN is exposed to only a single cluster.

Multipath I/O

The primary goal behind failover clustering is to ensure High Availability. The more places you can build redundancy into the cluster, the more likely you are to be able to ride through individual component failures without affecting the operation of the applications you want to be highly available. Multipath I/O, or providing multiple I/O paths to your storage, is a great way to enhance High Availability.

Creating a multipath environment means that you place two or more storage controllers (or NICs for iSCSI) with multipath software controlling access to the multiple paths. The default way to set up the multiple paths is to set them up for failover; if one path fails, all traffic is transferred to the other path. They can also be set up to provide load balancing to improve throughput. This sort of configuration provides both High Availability and high performance.

Windows Server 2008 has multipath software built into the operating system. You can use this software with any SAN to which you have connected via two or more network connections. These network connections can be over Fibre Channel or iSCSI. SAN vendors usually provide additional capabilities for their storage environments via a device-specific module (DSM). SAN vendors build on top of Microsoft's capabilities, so you need to see if what Microsoft provides is sufficient for your needs or if you would benefit from the vendor's DSM.

SOFTWARE REQUIREMENTS

Failover Clustering is a feature of Windows Server 2008 Enterprise and Datacenter Editions. It is not available in Standard or Web Editions. All systems in a cluster must be running the same version. In other words, you should keep them at the same patch level. It is possible to perform a rolling upgrade from one patch level to another by moving all the failover groups off one node, upgrading it to the next patch level, moving the failover groups back, and upgrading the next node. You may have a period of time when you want to test to see that everything continues to work in the updated patch level but you should not run for extended periods of time with different patch levels. This does not apply to upgrading from one release of the operating system to the next release. There is no such upgrade path; you have to build a new cluster and migrate the services you are clustering.

You also must have the same type of Windows Server installation on all nodes in the cluster. You cannot mix Full installations with Core installations. This is primarily to ensure that no applications can fail over to a Core installation when the application requires features of the operating system that do not exist in the Core installation. Enterprise and Datacenter Edition mixes work, but because of the licensing considerations, that is, the number of allowed virtual machines, that could put you in an environment whereby you might break the terms of your licensing agreement. So, although it works fine, it is not recommended.

If you are using Datacenter Edition as the host environment, the product use rights provided by that edition allow you to install Datacenter or any down-level edition, such as Enterprise, Standard, or Web, in any of the virtual machines. Datacenter Edition also allows you to run an unlimited number of instances of Windows Server virtual machines on the physical system to which the license is assigned. If you are using Enterprise Edition as the host environment, the product use rights provided by that edition allows you to install Enterprise or any down-level edition. Enterprise Edition allows you run up to four instances of Windows Server virtual machines for each license assigned to the physical host. In addition, the product use rights provide for installing previous versions, such as Windows Server 2003 or Windows Server 2000. The licensing rights pertain to server versions of the operating systems, not to desktop versions.

DOMAIN REQUIREMENTS

Systems running Windows Server 2008 Failover Cluster Services must be members of a domain. This ensures a common authorization framework for services as they fail over from one node to another. It also means that the clients accessing the services of the Failover Cluster can participate in this same authorization framework.

It is recommended that the cluster nodes be member servers and not domain controllers. There might be certain situations that make sense for making the servers domain controllers, but in general, it is best to have them as member servers. The Active Directory domain architecture is already highly available in its design and does not need something like Failover Cluster to make it highly available. In fact, if you do make the servers domain controllers, no aspect of the Active Directory can be placed into a failover group. It will not work and is not supported. For test environments, I have regularly created clusters with both servers as domain controllers, but I do not recommend that configuration for a production environment.

If you are familiar with earlier versions of Failover Clustering, a specified domain account, known as the cluster service account, was granted rights necessary for the cluster service to perform correctly. This changed in Windows Server 2008 by removing the need for a specific cluster service account. The cluster service now uses the local system. Now you will just need a domain account that is a member of the local Administrators group on each server in the failover cluster. The only other permission required is the Create Computer Object permission. When you create a failover cluster, a Cluster Name Object is created in Active Directory. A Domain Administrator account has both of these requirements, so there are no special requirements if you are running under the Domain Administrator account. Of course, in any production environment, use of the Domain Administrator account is typically sharply curtailed to only those functions that should be performed by those individuals designated as domain administrators.

NETWORK REQUIREMENTS

Earlier I stated that you should try to match the NICs in the servers to have the same settings, and also that it is preferable to use the same manufacturer's NIC in all nodes. You also need to check the switches to which the networks are connected to ensure that the settings on the switches are not different from what you have set on the NICs, such as line speed, duplex, and flow control.

Each different network that you use needs to be on a unique IP subnet. In other words, the client communication network is on one subnet and the cluster communication network is on another subnet. If you are using iSCSI storage, that should be on another subnet. This is because the cluster service is not capable of detecting more than one network adapter per node in a given network. For example, if you use 192.168.1.0/24 subnets for two distinct physical networks, say iSCSI and client access, even though you are using different unique IP addresses, the cluster software will ignore one of those addresses on that subnet. If you are concerned about things like overloading the capacity of a given network connection, that is where you should consider link aggregation for the public-facing network and multiport I/O for iSCSI traffic.

All servers in the cluster must be able to talk to the DNS server for name resolution. In previous versions of Failover Clustering, it was required that you use fixed IP addresses. Windows Server 2008 works fine with DHCP for IP assignment. This means that the DNS dynamic update protocol is also supported. You will need to check with your network management team to see how they would prefer you set things up in your environment.

Guest Failover Clusters

Almost everything that I just covered in the previous section on host-based Failover Clusters applies to guest Failover Clusters, or clusters comprising virtual machines. There are some slight changes because we are working in a virtual environment. Most notable is that you cannot install and run the Hyper-V role within a virtual machine.

HARDWARE REQUIREMENTS

There are no specific hardware requirements in the guest Failover Cluster because all the hardware is virtualized for you. You create virtual servers on virtual processors using virtual networks.

There is a slight difference in accessing the storage. Hyper-V has virtual storage controllers for IDE and SCSI. IDE has never been a shared-bus protocol, so, just as you could not use IDE to share storage in the physical environment, you cannot use IDE to share storage in the virtual environment. The SCSI implementation in Hyper-V shares many of the internal components of the IDE implementation, so there is no shared SCSI support. There is no virtual HBA provided in Hyper-V for accessing Fibre Channel or SAS SANs.

That leaves iSCSI as the only supported way to access shared storage between virtual servers in a Failover Cluster. If you want to set up a cluster between two or more virtual machines, you will need to set up an iSCSI Target to serve up storage. Because iSCSI is accessed via the network, the iSCSI Target can be a physical server or a virtual server; it does not make any difference to the virtual machine trying to access it.

If you do not have access to a physical iSCSI SAN, here are some locations of trial copies that you can use for your testing purposes. I will be using Microsoft's Windows Storage Server 2008 (WSS) for the examples I give.

Windows Storage Server 2008 `http://microsoft.download-ss.com/default.aspx`. Be sure to download the Microsoft iSCSI Target software from the same site. It is an optional install for WSS. The download for Windows Storage Server 2008 contains the instructions for installing the operating system, the Administrator password, and installing the iSCSI Target software. Be sure to read and follow the directions for getting your system operational.

Double-Take sanFly `www.doubletake.com/english/products/product-evaluation/Pages/default.aspx`.

StarWind Free iSCSI Target `www.starwindsoftware.com/free`.

Nimbus MySAN iSCSI Server Software `www.nimbusdata.com/products/mysan.php`.

Since I just covered the storage requirements above, and the software requirements in a guest cluster are exactly the same as those in the host cluster, the last thing to look at is the network requirements.

NETWORK REQUIREMENTS

From a pure networking standpoint, the network requirements of the guest machines are the same as for the host machines. The requirement for maintaining separate subnets for different functions is the same.

The only real difference comes with either link aggregation or multiport I/O. Since Microsoft does not provide any link-aggregation software, and I am not aware of any vendor that is writing link aggregation software for virtual machines, it is not possible to use link aggregation at the virtual machine level.

Virtual NICs do not really need link aggregation or failover because the NICs have a default line speed of 10 Gbps and the virtual NIC will never fail. But when they are connected to physical NICs on the host, then you may need to aggregate NICs for load balancing or for failover. This is done at the host level, though, and not within the virtual machine, and I already talked about this.

It is a similar situation with the DSMs from the different storage vendors. Generally speaking, they write DSMs for their particular host bus adaptor and storage configuration. Because these are not exposed directly to the guest machines, you will generally only be able to use Microsoft's built-in MPIO capabilities. I am not aware of it, but maybe one of the iSCSI SAN vendors has written their own DPM for iSCSI that is not dependent on an iSCSI host-based adaptor and only uses NICs.

SOFTWARE REQUIREMENTS

There is no difference in the software required in a virtual machine from what is required in a physical machine. You can install either Windows Server 2008 Enterprise or Datacenter Edition in order to create the cluster of virtual machines. There is no need to install Datacenter, though. Enterprise Edition supports up to eight processors, while Datacenter supports up to 64. Since Hyper-V currently supports a maximum of four virtual processors, Enterprise Edition will suffice.

As to the various server applications from Microsoft, they will have the same or very similar rules for installing in a cluster of virtual machines as in a cluster of physical machines. The best place to go to check for any variances would be http://support.microsoft.com/kb/957006. This provides a list of all Microsoft Server software that is fully supported in a virtual environment. If there are any exceptions for a given product, there will be a link to a more detailed article detailing what those variances may be.

Windows Server 2008 Full Installation

It is easier to learn to set up a host-based cluster when using the Full installation of Windows Server 2008. My recommendation is to first get comfortable working with building and managing clusters with a Full installation before moving on to working with a Core installation. Besides, you will want to learn to use the Cluster Management MMC, which works with both Full and Core installations.

These instructions cover how to install on both Windows Server 2008 and Windows Server 2008 R2 environments. For the most part, the procedures are exactly the same for the R2 environment, but there are additional capabilities that I will call out as I go through them.

INITIAL CONFIGURATION

Since earlier chapters taught you how to install Hyper-V and how to get your management environment set up, I am going to assume that you now have two servers that meet the requirements explained at the beginning of this chapter.

◆ Two similar servers running Windows Server 2008 with the Hyper-V role installed and updated with all current patches. It is recommended that you use an existing domain controller that is separate from the Hyper-V servers. Both nodes need to be joined as member servers in that domain.

◆ At least two physical NICs connected to two different subnets. Your particular needs may vary depending on your networking requirements. For example, you may want to have at least four different NICs — one for host management, one for client access, one for cluster communication, and one for iSCSI (if using iSCSI for SAN). This is optimal, but I will show you how to configure with only two NICs. It is possible to even use crossover network cables between the two hosts, at least for the cluster communication network. I do not recommend this, though, as you will need to change that as soon as you grow the cluster beyond two nodes.

   ◆ The first NIC is the NIC that I use for domain and client communication. I configured it with a fixed IP address that has its DNS server as the Active Directory domain controller. I have also pointed at my domain controller as the gateway address because it is also set up to perform the task of a network router. If you have a router in your network, you would specify that as your gateway address. This is also known as a routable address, and the cluster needs at least one routable network.

   ◆ The second NIC is dedicated to iSCSI traffic. Only the iSCSI Targets and iSCSI Initiators will be communicating on this network. Therefore, it is also given a fixed IP address. But, since I am using this only for iSCSI traffic, which means that no traffic will ever need to access anything off this network, I have not defined any gateway address, making this a nonroutable network.

   ◆ If your company has specific ways they require networking to be set up, check with them for the best way to set this up in your environment.

- ◆ Matching, supported, host bus adapters if using Fibre Channel SAN.

- ◆ LUNs defined on the SAN for use by the cluster. I will be showing you how this works with iSCSI.

I will show you how to set up iSCSI storage using the Microsoft Windows Storage Server (WSS). If you already have an iSCSI solution, you can move to the step on installing Failover Clustering. If you are using Fibre Channel for shared storage, you may still want to learn how this is done with iSCSI because that is the only way to set up shared storage for Failover Clusters between virtual machines instead of between Hyper-V hosts.

The environment that I will be working in is illustrated in Figure 5.2.

FIGURE 5.2
iSCSI Failover Cluster

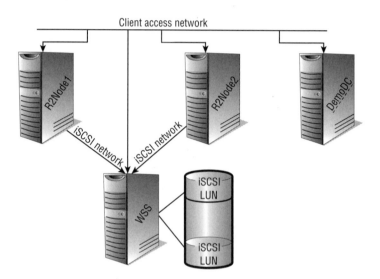

Though you will notice the similarity to the cluster shown in Figure 5.1, there are also a couple of slight differences. First you will see that I have included a separate domain controller, DemoDC, and a system that is running the WSS software to be able to present iSCSI targets. I named that system WSS to keep it easier to understand. The two cluster nodes are R2Node1 and R2Node2, because we are building a cluster with Windows Server 2008 R2. As I said earlier, the procedures will be pretty much the same for both releases, and I will ensure that you know when there is a difference. You will also notice that I have defined only two networks instead of the three I defined for Figure 5.1. I have done this because the machines I have contain only two physical NICs. This is not optimal, but it will work for learning purposes. I will reference these names in the following instructions, but it is obvious that you can name these machines how you want to. All these machines are joined to the same domain.

To get things started, you will need to make sure that the iSCSI Initiators (R2Node1 and R2Node2) can communicate with the iSCSI server. By default, Windows Server 2008 has this blocked at the firewall level. You need to open up the firewall on both the WSS iSCSI Target and iSCSI Initiators.

1. On the WSS server, start the Windows firewall. Click Start, select Control Panel, and select Windows Firewall.

2. On the left-hand side of the Windows Firewall window, click Allow A Program Through Windows Firewall. See Figure 5.3.

FIGURE 5.3
Windows Firewall

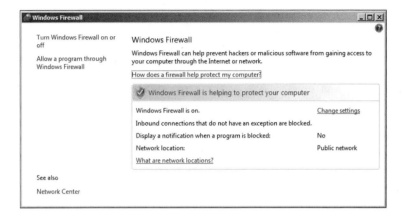

3. Click the Exceptions tab. The window that displays presents you with a list of predefined services and applications that you can select. Select the iSCSI Service. See Figure 5.4.

FIGURE 5.4
Windows Firewall
Settings

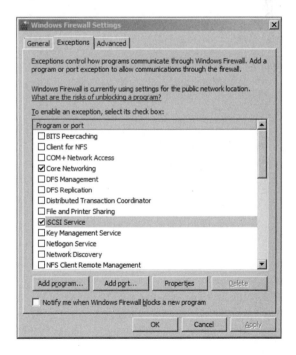

4. You will also need to create a new exception specifically for the iSCSI Target executable. Click the Add Program button in the lower left-hand corner of the Windows Firewall Settings window.

5. Click the Browse button on the Add A Program window. See Figure 5.5. Browse to %windir%\system32\Wintarget.exe, select it, and click OK. Then click OK to exit the Windows Firewall Settings window.

FIGURE 5.5
Add a Program

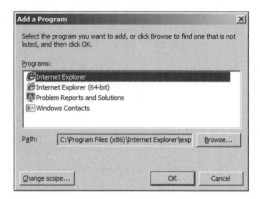

That takes care of the iSCSI Target system. If you are using a different iSCSI Target, the configuration may be different. Table 5.1 shows you the ports that need to be open on the firewall.

TABLE 5.1:   Firewall ports for iSCSI Target

COMPONENT	PORT	NOTES
NetBIOS Datagram Service	UDP 138	This entry should already exist in Windows Firewall for the File and Printer Sharing exception.
Remote Procedure Call (RPC)	TCP 135	Required by DCOM.
iSCSI Software Target	TCP 3260	This is the default iSCSI port that iSCSI Software Target uses to service requests.
Microsoft iSCSI Software Target Service	N/A	On the iSCSI Target server firewall settings, enable %windir%\system32\Wintarget.exe as an application exception.

Now let's turn our attention to the iSCSI Initiator's firewall. You need to follow these steps for both R2Node1 and R2Node2. There is only one step required for the Initiators — selecting the iSCSI Service as shown in steps 1–3 for the target. If you are using Windows Server 2008, you will be seeing the exact same screens as shown in Figure 5.3 and 5.4. If you are using Windows Server 2008 R2, the screens will appear slightly different. Instead of the first Windows Firewall screen appearing as it does in Figure 5.3, it will look like Figure 5.6.

Windows Server 2008 presents the various network types that a machine can be connected to, Domain, Private, or Public, in this window. This is a new feature in R2. Notice that in my example, I am connected only to the domain network. That is because this R2Node1 and R2Node2 are both connected only to the domain network. To get to the list of exceptions, click Allow A Program Or Feature Through Windows Firewall. This brings up a window that looks like Figure 5.7.

FIGURE 5.6
Windows Firewall for R2

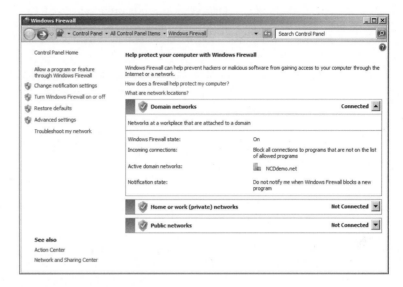

FIGURE 5.7
Allowed Programs

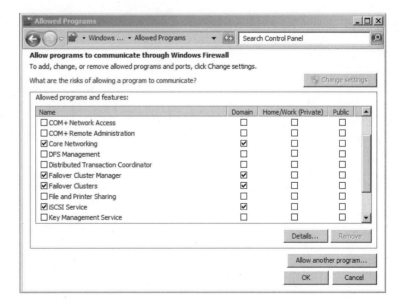

This window, though similar to the one in Windows Server 2008, gives you the option to open ports on different networks. In this case, we are interested in only the Domain network, so click the check box in the Domain column for the iSCSI Service. Click OK to exit. You should now be able to proceed with setting up the iSCSI Target and associate that target with the servers that will be cluster nodes.

iSCSI Setup

After you have installed WSS (or your preferred iSCSI Target) and set the correct firewall exceptions, you need to make the connection between the iSCSI Initiators running on R2Node1 and R2Node2 and the iSCSI Target portal, WSS. From both R2Node1 and R2Node2, complete these steps:

1. Click Start, and select Administrative Tools. From the menu of tools, select iSCSI Initiator. (The iSCSI Initiator is part of the operating system. You do not need to do anything to get it on the system.)

2. If you have not previously set up iSCSI Initiators on the systems, you will get a warning message asking you to start the iSCSI Service. Click the Yes button to accept starting the service.

3. Click the Discovery tab, and then click the Discover Portal button. See Figure 5.8.

4. In the Discover Target Portal window, enter either the name of your iSCSI Target portal or its IP address. See Figure 5.9. Click OK twice to exit the iSCSI Initiator.

FIGURE 5.8
iSCSI Initiator Properties

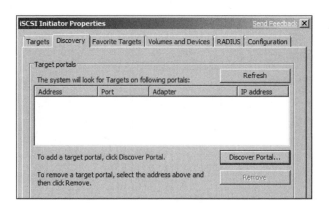

FIGURE 5.9
Discover Target Portal

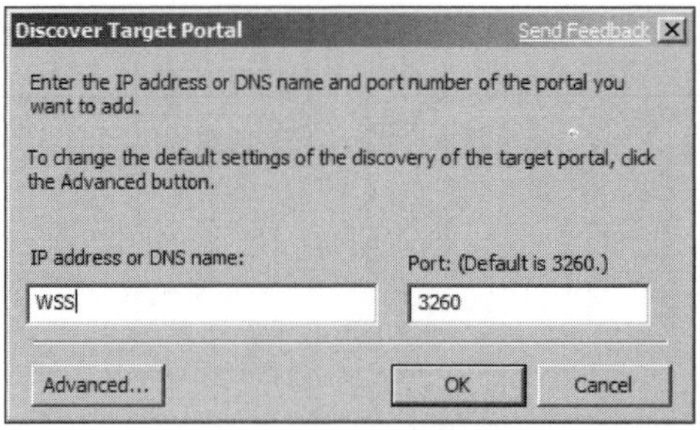

If you get a connection error, you might still be having a problem with your firewall settings. Ensure that you have opened the iSCSI Service in your firewall as detailed above. If you have further restrictions on your corporate network, you will need to work with your network security team to get this to work.

5. Log onto WSS (iSCSI Target Portal). Click Start, select Administrative Tools, and select Microsoft iSCSI Software Target from the drop-down menu. It is also available in the Server Manager console under the Storage icon on the left-hand side.

6. Right-click the iSCSI Target line, and select Create iSCSI Target from the drop-down menu. See Figure 5.10. This will launch a wizard to step through the process of creating iSCSI targets.

FIGURE 5.10
iSCSI Target

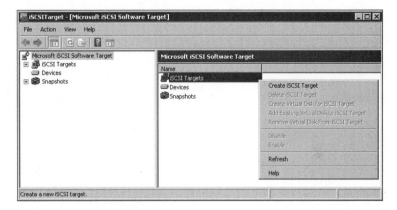

7. Enter a name for your iSCSI Target. In my example I am naming it R2Cluster. You can enter any string here that you want. A single iSCSI SAN can present multiple LUNs. This identifies a single target that may present one or more LUNs. In subsequent steps you will grant permission to specific iSCSI Initiators to have access to this target and the LUNs defined within this target. If you want to use this same iSCSI Target portal for another cluster, you would create another target with different LUNs. I have also entered an optional description. See Figure 5.11. Click Next to proceed to the next step.

8. In the iSCSI Initiators Identifiers window, click the Advanced button. This opens the Advanced Identifiers window. Click the Add button to open the Add/Edit Identifier window, as shown in Figure 5.12.

9. Ensure that IQN is selected as the identifier type. Click Browse to bring up the Add iSCSI Initiator window, which allows you to select the initiators that will have access to the target you are creating. See Figure 5.13.

10. Notice that both R2Node1 and R2Node2 are listed. The string in front of the node name is a unique identifier identifying the type of initiator. Click the first line to select it, and then click OK. Click OK in the Add/Edit Identifier window, which returns you to the Advanced Identifiers window, now showing that the first selection is made. Repeat the steps to add the second node.

FIGURE 5.11
Create iSCSI Target
Wizard

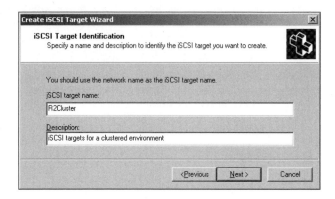

FIGURE 5.12
Add/Edit Identifier

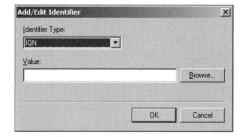

FIGURE 5.13
Add iSCSI Initiator

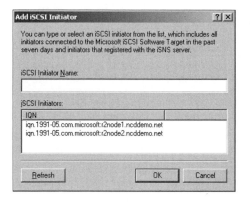

11. You should now see an Advanced Identifiers window that looks something like Figure 5.14. Both of the selected initiators should be showing. Click Next to return to the Create iSCSI Target Wizard window.

12. Click Next in the window, and then click Finish to exit the wizard. You now have granted permission to the nodes of the cluster to access the shared storage defined as the LUNs within the target.

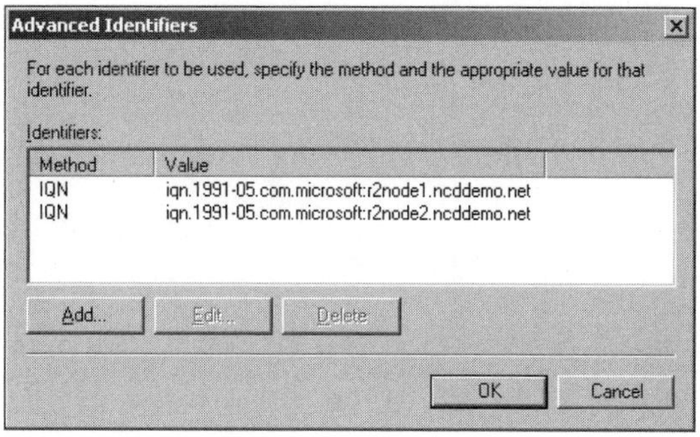

FIGURE 5.14
Advanced Identifiers

Advanced Identifiers dialog box

For each identifier to be used, specify the method and the appropriate value for that identifier.

Identifiers:

Method	Value
IQN	iqn.1991-05.com.microsoft:r2node1.ncddemo.net
IQN	iqn.1991-05.com.microsoft:r2node2.ncddemo.net

Add...   Edit...   Delete

OK   Cancel

Create iSCSI Volumes

Now that you have established the relationship, you need to create the actual iSCSI volumes, or LUNs, that will be the disks that are shared among the nodes of the cluster. Before I take you through the steps to do that, I need to explain just a little bit about how the iSCSI Targets work.

In my configuration, WSS has a single physical data disk that I have assigned the letter E:. I will be creating the iSCSI Targets on this drive. Microsoft's iSCSI Target software creates the iSCSI volumes. I can create many virtual disks on the single storage volume, thereby presenting many logical volumes to the iSCSI Initiators.

This is similar to the way a Fibre Channel storage array can carve its large RAID sets into multiple LUNs. The iSCSI target software does the same sort of thing. It masks the actual physical storage configuration and creates a fixed VHD file, which is presented to the network as a LUN. An iSCSI Initiator from either a physical or a virtual machine connects to that LUN and can manipulate it as though it were local storage. Because you can give permission to multiple servers over the network, you have created a shared storage environment for use by the cluster.

The following steps show how this is set up:

1. In the iSCSI Target window, right-click Devices and select Create Virtual Disk from the drop-down menu. See Figure 5.15. This will start the Create Virtual Disk Wizard.

2. The Create Virtual Disk Wizard opens with a welcome window. Click Next to get to the File window. See Figure 5.16. This window permits you to browse the file system to specify the location to create the virtual hard disk, or you can simply enter the information if you know where you want the VHD to be stored. I have simply entered the information. Click Next to continue.

3. Enter the size you want the VHD to be. See Figure 5.17. Notice that the size is listed in MB. I recommend that the first disk you create be only 512 MB in size. The simplest cluster to build makes use of a witness disk. The witness disk needs to be only 512 MB in size, so this will be that disk. Click Next to continue with the wizard.

4. The next step in the wizard is to optionally provide a description of the VHD you are creating. Click Next to continue with the wizard. The window that appears is shown in Figure 5.18. This window makes an association between the iSCSI target that you created earlier and the VHD. In this case I have created only the single target. Click Next and then Finish, and you have created your virtual hard drive for your iSCSI Target.

FIGURE 5.15
iSCSI Target

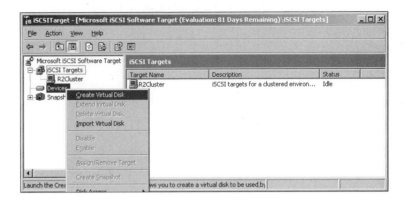

FIGURE 5.16
Create Virtual Disk
Wizard — File

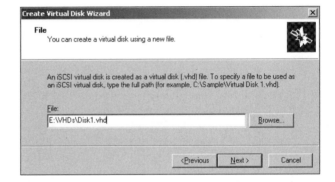

FIGURE 5.17
Create Virtual Disk
Wizard — Size

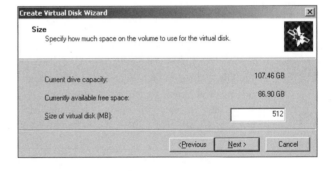

5. Repeat steps 1 through 4 for additional VHDs. Subsequent VHDs will serve as data disks for this cluster. These will be seen as physical disks by the cluster nodes where the virtual hard drives for the operating systems and applications of the virtual machines will be stored. Make sure you make them large enough to contain all that information. If you are using Windows Server 2008 software, you will need to create separate LUNs for each virtual machine you wish to make highly available. With Hyper-V R2 you can create a single large LUN and make use of CSV and many virtual machines on a single LUN.

FIGURE 5.18
Create Virtual Disk
Wizard — Access

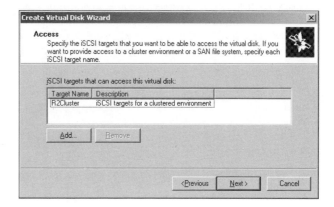

Connecting to iSCSI Storage

That takes care of creating one or more iSCSI Targets (virtual hard drives) that can be used for the shared storage in a failover cluster. The last thing that needs to be done is to prepare the targets for use by the cluster nodes. Here are the steps to accomplish that.

1. Log into one of the cluster nodes. Click Start, select Administrative Tools, and select iSCSI Initiator from the menu.

2. See Figure 5.19 for the next steps. On the Targets tab, click the Refresh button to refresh the display of the discovered targets. Select the target on which the VHDs were defined, and click the Connect button.

FIGURE 5.19
iSCSI Initiator Properties

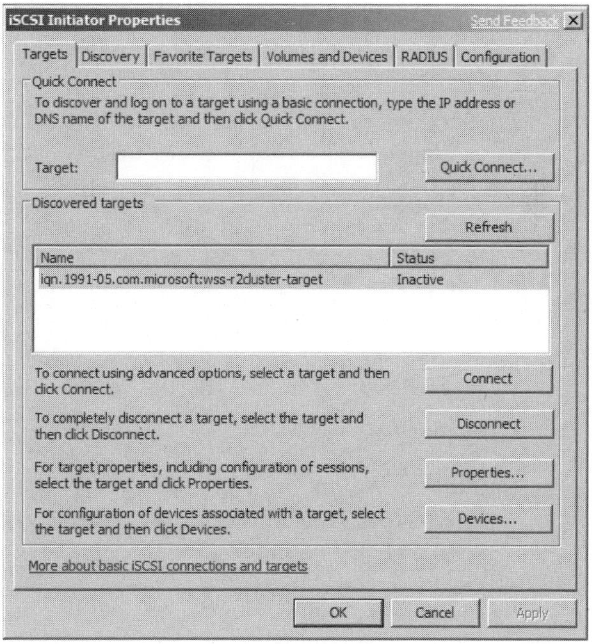

3. Clicking the Connect button brings up the Connect To Target window, as shown in Figure 5.20. Make sure that the first box is checked. This ensures that you are automatically connected to the target whenever the machine is started. Click OK to continue. You will see that your status has changed to Connected. You can click OK to exit the iSCSI Initiator.

4. Repeat steps 1 through 3 for the other node in the cluster.

FIGURE 5.20
Connect To Target

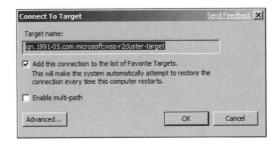

Prepare iSCSI Disk for Use

There is one last thing that needs to be done to prepare the shared storage for use in the cluster. You need to initialize and format the disks presented by the iSCSI Target from one of the nodes in the cluster. You do this on only one node in the cluster. Remember that in the shared storage environment of the Failover Cluster, only a single node at a time actually owns a drive. If you try to have two nodes accessing the storage simultaneously, you will end up with corrupted disks. When the clustering software is installed, it will protect against two nodes writing to the same storage, but until the cluster software is installed, you need to be careful. It is also a requirement that the disks be NTFS disks. This ensures that one set of Disk Management tools can be used to manage your storage across the entire environment.

From one of the nodes that will form the Failover Cluster, perform the following steps:

1. In Server Manager, open Storage and select Disk Management. See Figure 5.21 for my configuration on R2Node1. It shows the system and boot partitions on one disk and two other disks that are offline.

2. Right-click each of the drives and select the Online option to bring the disk online. Then right-click one of the disks and select Initialize Disk. The Initialize Disk window that opens has automatically selected all the disks that are not initialized. Click OK to start the initialization.

3. When the initialization completes, right-click the unallocated space on a disk and select Create Simple Volume. Make the selections in the wizard to format the disk in the manner you want it formatted. Disks must be formatted as NTFS for use in a cluster. You will not need to assign drive letters. Repeat for any other disks you have created for use by the cluster.

4. Right-click each of the newly created disks and select Offline. Your Disk Management display should now look something like what you see in Figure 5.22.

FIGURE 5.21
Disk Management

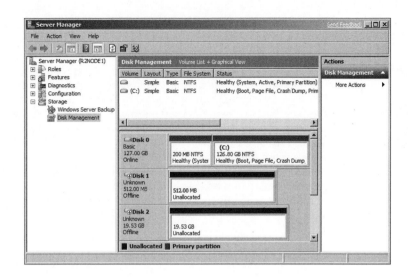

FIGURE 5.22
Disk Management with basic disks

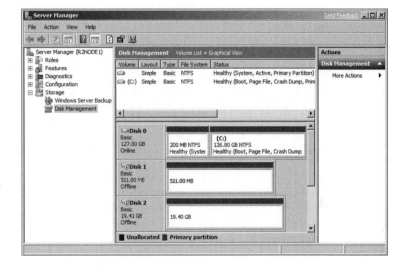

Congratulations! You have now provisioned some iSCSI storage to be shared among the nodes of a cluster. The beauty of iSCSI LUNs is that they can be accessed directly by the host or by a virtual machine. The explanation I have just gone through is geared toward getting a physical cluster set up; you would follow very similar steps to prepare iSCSI LUNs for direct access by virtual machines or for a guest cluster.

Cluster Networking

Earlier chapters taught you how to configure network adapters for use by Hyper-V hosts. Generally speaking, when naming networks on the Hyper-V hosts, it is not necessary to maintain any sort of naming convention. However, it is always a good practice to do so, as it makes your system easier to manage if you have common names representing the same entity.

Laxness in naming conventions is not abided in Failover Clusters for Hyper-V. You must have your NICs named exactly the same, including upper- and lowercase, on all nodes that participate in a cluster. This is because a virtual machine moving from one host to another host will need to have the same NIC name referencing the correct network on the next host. If the names are not the same, there is no way for the software to know which NIC talks to which network. Therefore, this is a good time to double-check your NIC naming to ensure you have used the same names on the same networks.

Let's take another look at the diagram of the configuration we are building here. Figure 5.23 shows the basic configuration.

FIGURE 5.23
Hyper-V Cluster with
iSCSI Targets

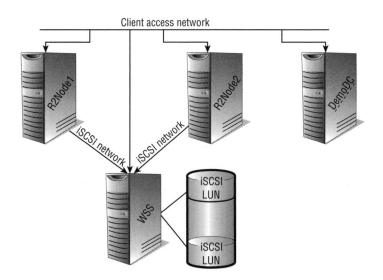

In a Hyper-V Failover Cluster that is using iSCSI for its shared storage, the optimal configuration would have at least four NICs:

Management This NIC would be used only for management functions. It would ensure that any management functions do not impact the production use of any other network.

Cluster Communication This NIC would be used for the cluster nodes to communicate information about the configuration and status of the cluster. It is recommended that there be at least two NICs carrying this traffic. This is also sometimes called the "heartbeat" network.

Client Access This NIC would be used for client machines to access the services being provided by the Failover Cluster. This NIC should also allow Cluster Communications.

iSCSI Communication This NIC would be used only for access to the iSCSI targets, ensuring optimal performance.

Cluster communication uses very little bandwidth, and running it on multiple NICs is a way to protect against single points of failure. In this optimal configuration I have inserted a fourth NIC just for client communication. You could configure this cluster without a dedicated cluster communication network, but to ensure cluster communication is not a single point of failure with three networks, you should run cluster communication on both the management and the client communication NICs.

Notice in Figure 5.23 that I have only two networks, labeled Client access network and iSCSI network. I am setting up this test or lab environment to perform three different functions on the Client access network and two functions on the iSCSI network. The Client access network is my management, client access, and cluster communication network. The iSCSI network is my iSCSI traffic and cluster communication network. I am doing this for the test environment only. I would *never* recommend this sort of configuration for a production cluster. But since many people may be testing with hardware that might not be recommended for production deployment, I am showing you how to do this for those limited environments.

Technically, this configuration could be built with a single NIC in each server; the iSCSI Target (WSS) could be connected to the Client access network. Doing that would create a single point of failure in the environment, and the validation wizard would flag this as a warning. If anything happens to the network, the entire cluster would become unavailable. Since one of the primary goals of clustering is to ensure High Availability, that would not make sense. Therefore, when you run the validation wizard on a configuration with only a single NIC, it will give you a warning about a single point of failure. I note this here in case your hardware does not have two NICs; you should still be able to build this cluster.

Windows Server 2008 Failover Clusters can work with either fixed or DHCP-assigned IP addresses. Earlier versions of Windows clustering required that each node and the cluster be assigned fixed IP addresses, but the Windows Server 2008 cluster works fine with DHCP. For this exercise I would recommend that you use fixed IP addresses, if possible, just to keep things easier to follow.

You will also notice that with Windows Server 2008, Internet Protocol version 6 is also bound to each NIC. *Do not turn it off.* Yes, technically everything will still work with it off, but all of Windows Server 2008 and Windows Vista and Windows 7 are written to support IPv6. Microsoft is not testing its products with just IPv4 enabled, so if you do turn it off, you are running in an environment that has not been fully tested. The change is coming, and some products from Microsoft will require it. It does not add any additional overhead to the system, so it is a good idea to start getting used to working with it.

INSTALL FAILOVER CLUSTERING

Once you have configured your storage and networking and ensured that it is accessible by both nodes in your cluster, you can install Failover Clustering. This needs to be done on both nodes. Failover Clustering is a feature of the operating system. In addition to installing Failover Clustering, you will also want to install the Failover Cluster Manager console somewhere within your environment. First, let's install the Failover Clustering feature:

1. Start Server Manager and select Features in the left-hand column. In the Features pane, select Add Features. See Figure 5.24.

2. From the selection list of features, select Failover Clustering. Click Next, and then click Install. See Figure 5.25.

3. Repeat this process for the second server you are putting into the cluster.

FIGURE 5.24
Feature selection

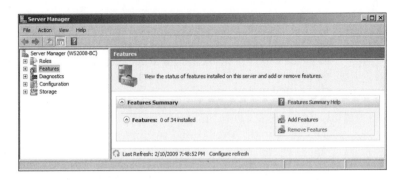

FIGURE 5.25
Failover Clustering
feature

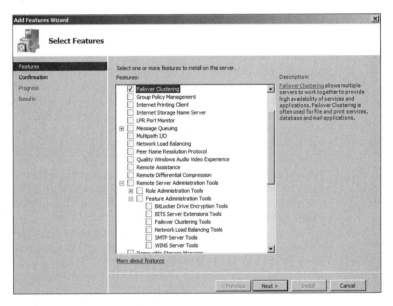

By default, the Failover Clustering Tools, which includes the Failover Cluster Manager console, are installed when you install the Failover Clustering feature. In Windows Server 2008, you have to launch the management console separately. You go to Administrative Tools in the Start menu and select the Failover Cluster Manager. In R2, the Failover Cluster Manager console is automatically added to Features section of Server Manager. Remember we are working on a Full installation of the operating system. Since the management console is a graphical tool, it will not be installed when you install the Failover Clustering feature on a Core installation.

Though it is handy to have the management console on the nodes of the cluster for debugging purposes, you will generally want to have it installed on another system in your environment. This can be on another server, or you can install the Remote System Administrative Toolkit and install that on a Vista or Windows 7 workstation. I covered how to download and install this toolkit in Chapter 3.

Installing the Failover Clustering Tools on another Windows Server 2008 system is just like installing any Failover Clustering feature. The difference is that you select Remote Server Administration Tools, expand Feature Administration Tools, and select Failover Clustering Tools. See Figure 5.25.

One thing that is important to remember when using the Failover Cluster Manager console is that the 2008 console can create and manage only clusters formed by Windows Server 2008 servers. The R2 console can create and manage clusters formed by both 2008 and R2 servers.

VALIDATE A CLUSTER CONFIGURATION

Now that you have defined the shared storage that will be used by the failover cluster and the networks that will be used for communication to clients and between nodes, and you have installed the Failover Clustering feature, it is time to validate that your cluster is ready to go. The Validate a Configuration Wizard, generally referred to as the Cluster Validation Wizard, is a significant addition to Windows Server 2008. It runs hundreds of tests against the components that you have used to build the cluster to ensure that they will all work together correctly to provide a supported failover cluster configuration.

CLUSTER VALIDATION WIZARD

The Cluster Validation Wizard is more than just a quick way to determine if you have a supported cluster configuration. During the initial configuration of a cluster, you may have configured something incorrectly. The wizard will give you a detailed listing of the errors it finds, making it much easier for you to find the problem. Then, after you have fixed the error, you can run a selective test to see if you actually did resolve the error.

The wizard can also be used after the cluster is in production. If you are having a problem, you can run the wizard to see what sort of errors it finds. It is a good idea to keep a copy of the successful validation report to provide to Microsoft Support if you do have a problem. It helps them see the starting configuration, and subsequent executions of the validation wizard requesting specific tests can be compared to the original, successful report.

To run the Cluster Validation Wizard, you need to the run the Failover Cluster Manager console that you installed earlier. You may have installed it on another system or on one or both nodes of the cluster. From whichever system you installed the console on, launch and run the wizard.

1. From Start, select Administrative Tools, and select Failover Cluster Manager. Figure 5.26 shows you the opening window of the console.

2. Notice that in the central portion of the screen you have access to several links to information and documentation on clusters. This is also where you select Validate a Configuration to validate your cluster components. Click on Validate a Configuration, then click Next on the opening informational screen. If you desire, you can click the check box to prevent this page from showing again.

3. The next window is for selecting the nodes that you will include in your cluster. You can either browse your Active Directory for the node to enter, or you can type in the name, as illustrated in Figure 5.27. (The validation wizard can also be used for diagnostic purposes after a cluster is running, so it also has the option to select an existing cluster. We are just interested now in building the cluster.) Type in the name, click Add to add it to the list of nodes, and click Next to continue.

FIGURE 5.26
Failover Cluster
Manager

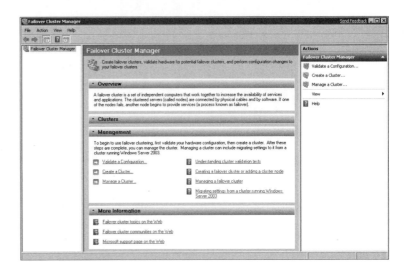

FIGURE 5.27
Select Servers or
a Cluster

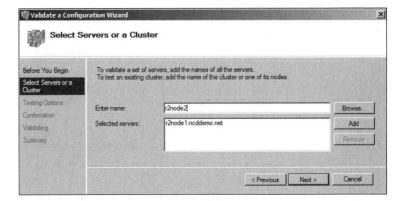

4. The next window gives you the option of selecting to run all tests or to run selected tests. It is recommended to always run all the tests before you build any new cluster. It is a lot easier to determine and fix errors before you build a cluster than after you build the cluster. Therefore, leave the default selection for all tests, and click Next to continue.

5. The next window is a confirmation window that shows you all the types of tests that are to be run. Since we are selecting all tests, there really is no need to check what has been selected. Click Next to continue.

6. The Cluster Validation Wizard starts performing hundreds of tests against all the components of your cluster. It validates network connects, software versions, disk connections, and the ability to fail over resources among all nodes in the cluster. The window is constantly updating status as the wizard runs. In a small cluster with two nodes and two disks, the wizard takes only a few minutes to run all the tests. As the configuration of the cluster gets larger, that is, more host nodes and shared storage, the number of tests increases exponentially because all combinations of networks, disks, and failovers must be tested. This is a good thing to remember when you are building large clusters in production. If you are using many similar components, such as servers, NICs, and storage, you may want to run the Cluster Validation Wizard only on a representative subset of what you plan to put into the cluster. If you include all unique items in your validation, you can then add the full complement when you actually build the cluster without fear of it not working. For detailed information about what happens during the cluster validation, see http://technet.microsoft.com/en-us/library/cc732035.aspx.

7. When the validation report completes, it display a Failover Cluster Validation Report window, as shown in Figure 5.28. This gives a summary of the results on the various categories of tests run. Scroll through this summary report to see if any warnings or errors were found. If a warning or error is flagged, click the View Report button to see the entire report. Any warnings or errors show the reasons in the detailed report. Click Finish if there are no warnings or errors.

FIGURE 5.28
Failover Cluster Validation Report

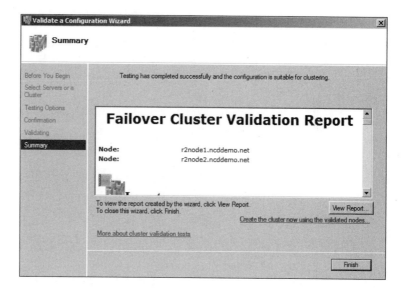

8. After successfully validating your configuration, you can move on to creating the cluster. If you do find warnings or errors, correct them and rerun the validation wizard. You really want to have a completely approved configuration before you start.

CREATE THE CLUSTER

Creating a cluster starts out similar to validating a cluster. You can start with the Failover Cluster Manager console, just like step 1 in the previous section. Or, as you can see in Figure 5.28, there is an option right below the View Report button to create the cluster from the configuration just validated, which will take you to step 2 below. If you start as you did in step 1, select the Create a Cluster option from the middle pane.

1. You will be presented with the Select Server window, similar to step 3 in the previous section. The only difference is that since you are creating a cluster, there is no option to select an existing cluster. Therefore you simply enter the names of host servers you want to

join into a Failover Cluster. Click Next to continue after selecting your host systems to be clustered.

2. Figure 5.29 shows the Access Point for Administering the Cluster window. The first required field is Cluster Name. This is a virtual name that can be used for accessing and managing the cluster. Enter a name that abides by your computer naming conventions; a computer name entry will be made in Active Directory for the cluster with this name. The rest of the window will vary depending on your network configuration. In this case, as recommended, I have used fixed IP addresses on my two networks. Because I used fixed IP addresses, the cluster manager is asking me which fixed IP address I should use for cluster communication on those networks. Remember that I have opted to have cluster communication on both networks to provide a level of redundancy in my configuration.

FIGURE 5.29
Access Point for Administering the Cluster

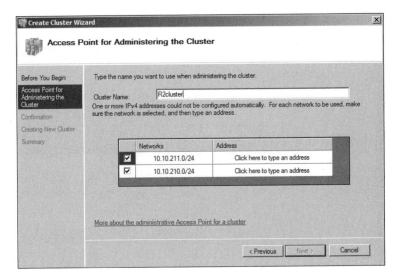

If your display does not look like Figure 5.29, but instead it has a line stating that you have a DHCP network, it means that the cluster will use a DHCP-assigned address for the cluster name. This will work fine, and if your company has a policy of using DHCP-assigned addresses as much as possible, you can configure it this way.

3. Click Next to advance to the summary page that shows the settings you have selected. Click Next to build the cluster. It will take a few minutes for the cluster software to check things out and put things together. When it completes, it gives you the status of the build. Click Finish, and the system connects the Failover Cluster Manager console to the cluster you have just created.

4. Expand all the elements in the left-hand column, and click the cluster name. You should have a display similar to what is shown in Figure 5.30.

5. Notice that the network names are generically named Cluster Network 1 and Cluster Network 2. I recommend that you rename these to reflect the actual names you named your networks on the nodes of the cluster. It is not necessary, but it does make it easier to keep track of things when managing the environment. Remember that for Hyper-V failover to work properly, you must have the same network names on every node in the

cluster specified exactly the same. Although it is not required for the names to be the same on the management console of the cluster, I think it is easier to keep track of things when they are.

FIGURE 5.30
Failover Cluster Manager with cluster

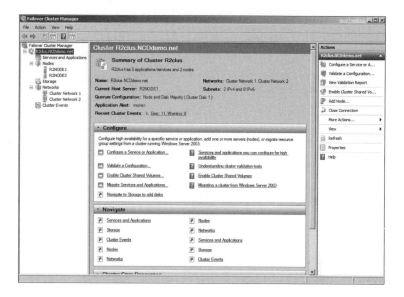

At this time you have created a cluster but have not made any resources highly available. If you created two disk volumes to be used by the cluster, when you look at the Storage option of the Failover Cluster Manager, you will see something similar to what is shown in Figure 5.31. This shows the disks recognized by the cluster, the status of the each disk (online or offline), and the name of the node that currently owns the disk resource.

FIGURE 5.31
Cluster Storage

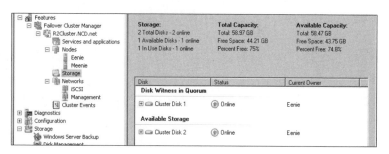

First, you will notice that I renamed my networks to iSCSI and Management, just to make it easier for me to see what I am working on. You will also notice two disks. The first disk discovered by the cluster is automatically assigned as the witness disk. As mentioned earlier, in a cluster with an even number of nodes and a quorum configuration that includes a witness, when the witness remains online, the cluster can sustain failures of half the nodes. If the witness goes offline, the same cluster can sustain failures of half the nodes minus one. You do not store anything on this disk; therefore, the cluster does not assign it a drive letter or show it as available storage.

You want to ensure that the witness disk is the 512MB disk. Click the Storage icon to see the assignment. If the 512MB disk is not your witness disk, you will need to change that.

1. Right-click the cluster name. From the drop-down menu, hover your cursor on More Actions and then select Configure Cluster Quorum Settings from that drop-down menu. See Figure 5.32.

FIGURE 5.32
Configure Cluster
Quorum Settings

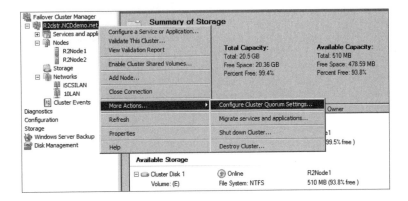

2. Click Next to move past the introductory window. On the Select Quorum Configuration window, click the radio button by Node Majority. See Figure 5.33.

FIGURE 5.33
Select Quorum
Configuration

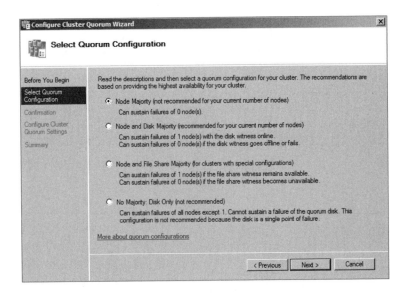

3. Click Next, Next, and Finish to change the configuration. This is not the recommended way to configure a two-node cluster, so you will see a warning in the center part of the Failover Cluster Manager console, but this sets both disks as just shared disks.

4. Now you start over to change it back to a disk majority cluster. Follow step 1, above, to bring up the Configure Cluster Quorum Wizard. This time, select the radio button by Node And Disk Majority. Click Next.

5. This will bring up the Configure Storage Witness window. See Figure 5.34. Select the 512MB disk. Click Next, Next, and Finish to complete the reassignment.

FIGURE 5.34
Configure Storage Witness

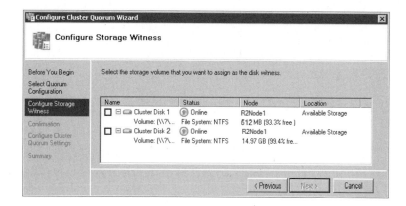

The second disk (and any others if you defined more than two) is listed as available storage. If you are on the node that owns the available disk (look in the third column for the node name of the owner), open Windows Explorer. You will see that the cluster disk appears the same as a locally attached disk. You can create directories, copy files to it, and perform any other operation you can do on a locally attached disk. If you go to the node that does not own the disk, you will not see it in Windows Explorer.

Since this chapter is about highly available Hyper-V, we will show you how to make virtual machines highly available.

CREATE A HIGHLY AVAILABLE VIRTUAL MACHINE

Creating a highly available virtual machine is dependent on the Failover Cluster Services feature of Windows Server 2008 Enterprise and Datacenter Editions. With Windows Server 2008 R2, Microsoft enhanced its abilities and also added this enhanced ability to the stand-alone product, Microsoft Hyper-V Server 2008 R2.

At the beginning of this chapter, in the section "Failover Clusters with Hyper-V," I explained what is meant by High Availability (HA), Quick Migration (QM), and Live Migration (LM). Since HA is part of the host environment, and was included with the R2 release of Hyper-V Server, the only cost to implement HA for Hyper-V is the cost of shared storage and additional networking. And, since QM and LM are both built on top of HA, there is no additional cost for these capabilities, either. These are integral components of planning for your disaster recovery or business continuance environment.

When setting up highly available virtual machines, you have two options for presenting the storage for use by the Failover Cluster software. If you followed the earlier instructions and created two volumes and built the cluster, by default you have created an environment that would use storage without the Cluster Shared Volumes (CSV) capability. You have to go through a couple more steps to make use of the CSV. I will first explain how to use non-CSV with virtual machines, and then I will explain the use of CSV. With the initial release of Hyper-V, you could only use non-CSV disks and Quick Migrate virtual machines from one host to another. R2 introduced both CSV and Live Migration. A logical conclusion would be that CSV is a prerequisite of LM. However, that is not true. It is possible to use LM with non-CSV storage. The main difference to remember is that CSV enables multiple virtual machines to reside on the same storage LUN and these machines can migrate independently of one another. If you are using non-CSV storage and you want to use LM, you can have only a single VM on that volume. If you put multiple VMs on a non-CSV volume, you are limited to the Quick Migration capability.

VMs on Non-Cluster Shared Volumes

As you saw back in Figure 5.31, when you create a new cluster, it will automatically assign any disk that is accessible to all nodes to the cluster. The first disk is the witness disk, and the second disk is available for use by a service that will be made highly available. In this case, we will be creating a highly available virtual machine.

There are two ways to get a virtual machine built on the cluster. You can make use of virtual hard drives that are already created on the cluster disk, or you can create a new virtual machine on the cluster disk. Let's start by creating an entirely new virtual machine.

The first thing you need to do is determine which node in the cluster is the current owner of the shared storage volume. Click Storage in Failover Cluster Manager. In the center column you will see which node is the owner of storage device. From Figure 5.31, you can see that the node Eenie owns both disks — Disk Witness and Available Storage. This means you can create a highly available virtual machine on Eenie. Since Eenie is the current owner of the volume, Meenie does not have write access to that shared storage.

You can create the virtual machine either from Hyper-V Manager or from Failover Cluster Manager. Both of these consoles are available as part of Server Manager, either by installing the remote management tools on another server or by using them from the nodes of the cluster. Chapter 3 explained how to create virtual machines from Hyper-V Manager console. Even though you are now working within a clustered environment, you can create the virtual machine in exactly the same way. Just make sure that you select the shared storage for storing the virtual machine in order to make it highly available. Do not start this virtual machine once you have created it.

You will notice that the virtual machine is defined in Hyper-V Manager, just as though you had created a virtual machine on a stand-alone server. However, you do not yet have a virtual machine that is highly available. That takes one more step. In Failover Cluster Manager, right-click Services and Applications and select Configure a Service or Application from the drop-down menu. This starts the High Availability Wizard. The wizard starts with an informational page, so simply click Next. Scroll to the bottom of the list of services and applications that can be made highly available and select Virtual Machine. Click Next. You are presented with a list of virtual machines that are in the off or saved state. See Figure 5.35.

Any virtual machines that are running will not show up in this list. Select the virtual machine you created and click Next. Click Next again, and Failover Cluster Manager will finish the wizard and present you with a report. View the report to see if there was an error of any sort, and use the information in the error report to correct the problem. Click Finish to close the report. You will see in Failover Cluster Manager that you have a virtual machine that is highly available. See Figure 5.36.

As you can see, creating a new virtual machine is a two-step process. A virtual machine can be created in a single step if you start with Failover Cluster Manager. To create a virtual machine from Failover Cluster Manager, right-click Services and Applications, select Virtual

Machines from the drop-down menu, select New Virtual Machine, and then select your node that owns the shared storage. See Figure 5.37.

FIGURE 5.35
Select Virtual Machine

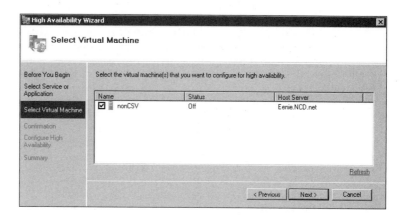

FIGURE 5.36
Highly available virtual machine

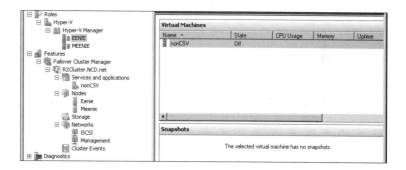

FIGURE 5.37
New virtual machine

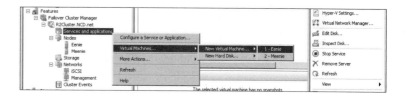

This opens the same New Virtual Machine Wizard that you used from Server Manager. Create your virtual machine, but do not start it upon completion. You will notice a difference between the results of this creation and the creation when using the Hyper-V Manager.

When you create a new virtual machine through Failover Cluster Manager, it will not only create that machine and show it within the Hyper-V Manager, but it also will create it as a highly available resource. This is shown by the fact that the machine appears in Failover Cluster Manager under Services and Applications. Figure 5.36 would look the same no matter which of these two ways you used to create the virtual machine.

This works well if you are creating new machines, but maybe you already created some machines on stand-alone Hyper-V servers and you now want to make them highly available. Does this mean that you need to re-create those machines from scratch? Not at all. Since the shared storage is available to the cluster, you can copy VHD files or even exported virtual machine files to the shared storage. If you copy just the VHD files, you will need to follow the steps in the first example to build new virtual machines, but when you build the virtual machines you will specify to use an existing VHD instead of creating a new one. In the case of a previously exported machine, you can use the virtual machine Import option. In either case, once you have defined the virtual machines through Hyper-V Manager, you would then use Failover Cluster Manager to make them highly available.

Now start the virtual machine you just created. There are several ways of doing this. You can use Hyper-V Manager using any of the methods described in earlier chapters. Or, because your virtual machine is now a resource within the cluster, you can use Failover Cluster Manager. You can right-click the virtual machine in Failover Cluster Manager and select Start Virtual Machines. Or simply click the virtual machine and then select Start Virtual Machines from the Actions menu in the right-hand column. Or you can click the virtual machine in the left-hand column, then right-click the virtual machine in the center column, and select Start. This demonstrates how well integrated the Hyper-V service is with Failover Clusters.

Once the virtual machine is running, you can see how both Quick Migration and Live Migration work. Select your virtual machine by right-clicking it in the left-hand column, and select Quick Migrate Virtual Machine(s) to Another Node. Since you have only a dual-node cluster, you will see only the name of the node on which the virtual machine is not running. Select that machine. You will now be able to see the exact steps that are happening. In fairly rapid succession you will see the following occur:

1. A window will display saying that it is detecting your virtual machine. If the virtual machine is running, it will have to save its state. If it is in a saved state, it does not have to save the state. The cluster is simply checking the state to determine what the next steps are. The rest of this description assumes that your machine is running.

2. You will see your storage volume change its status to Offline Pending. Remember that with Quick Migration, the ownership of the disk changes nodes, so the volume will go offline.

3. If your virtual machine is running, you will see its status change to Saving and a changing message about how far it is in the saving process. The state of your virtual machine is being written to disk.

4. The status of the virtual machine will quickly change to Saved.

5. When the status of the virtual machine changes to Saved, the status of the disk drive will change to Online Pending. This means the ownership of the disk has changed and the new node is trying to bring it online.

6. When the status of the disk drive changes to Online, you will see the status of your virtual machine change to Starting. There is also a constantly updating message telling you how far it is in the restoration process. This is the new system reading in the contents of the saved state.

7. When the entire contents of the saved state are loaded into memory, the virtual machine is started and its status changes to Running.

Live Migration, which is available only on the R2 release, is initiated in the same way that Quick Migration is. The obvious difference is that you select the Live Migrate option instead of the Quick Migrate option. However, as you watch what happens, you will notice a difference:

1. As with the Quick Migration, the first thing that happens is that the cluster determines the state of the virtual machine.

2. You will see the status of the virtual machine change from Running to Running (Migrating). The memory of the running virtual machine is being copied from the node currently owning the virtual machine to the machine to which you have directed it.

3. The status of the disk will quickly change from Offline Pending to Online Pending as the ownership of the disk is quickly changed.

4. When the disk status changes to Online, the virtual machine status quickly changes from Starting to Running. That brief flash of time is when the virtual machine stops as the last bit of the machine's state is placed into the memory of the new node and started.

Note that the Live Migration function will work only if you have a single virtual machine on the LUN. If you have multiple virtual machines, you will receive an error because this virtual machine is not on a cluster-shared volume.

Before we talk about virtual machines on Cluster Shared Volumes, let's look at a couple of things when you place multiple virtual machines onto a single shared storage, not a CSV. In Figure 5.38, by viewing the configuration from Hyper-V Manager, you can see that I have multiple virtual machines running on node Eenie: CL-Srv1, CL-Srv3, and CL-Srv4.

FIGURE 5.38
Multiple running VMs

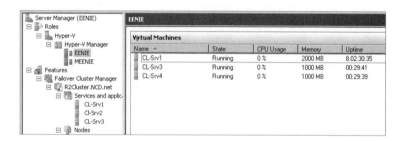

But looking at what shows in Failover Cluster Manager, under Services And Applications, you see a slightly different view. It looks like I have three virtual machines: CL-Srv1, CL-Srv2, and CL-Srv3. What is CL-Srv2? And where did CL-Srv4 go? If I had clicked on node Meenie in the Hyper-V Manager console, you would have seen that CL-Srv2 is running there. But that still leaves the question about what happened to CL-Srv4 that we see running on Eenie. In this case, I created CL-Srv3 as a highly available virtual machine and placed it on shared storage and not on a CSV. I then created CL-Srv4 and also placed it on the same shared storage. The cluster software automatically created a resource group that contains both the virtual machines and the shared disk. All components of a virtual machine resource group will fail over or be moved with Quick Migration. You can see this by looking at a dependency report (right-click CL-Srv3 and select Show Dependency Report). Figure 5.39 shows you the dependency report for this resource group.

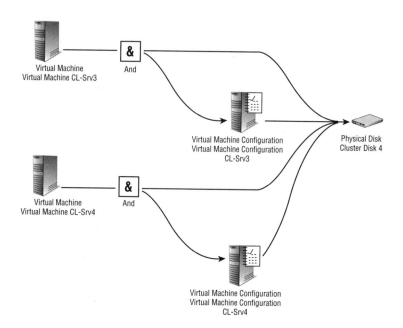

FIGURE 5.39
Dependency report

When managing multiple virtual machines on a shared storage volume, you may want to rename the label that appears in the Services And Applications section of the Failover Cluster Management console. It will help prevent some confusion that may occur if you leave the names at the defaults supplied by the cluster software.

VMs on Cluster Shared Volumes

Cluster Shared Volumes are a new feature introduced in Windows Server 2008 R2. They operate a little differently from anything you may have worked with before on Windows.

The first thing we need to do here is determine what storage is available for you to use. If you are following these steps sequentially, you most likely now have the single shared volume used by the non-CSV volume and you have a virtual machine stored on that volume. If you skipped the previous steps, you have a cluster with a witness disk and a disk available for use by the cluster. In either of these cases, you need to get the storage available for use by the CSV feature. A storage volume that is hosting virtual machines must be used either as a regular storage resource or as a Cluster Shared Volume. If you are willing to "lose" the current virtual machine, follow the steps listed here. This does not delete the virtual machine files from the storage, so you will be able to reinstantiate this virtual machine on the CSV. Another option would be to export and import the virtual machine, but in these instructions I will cover just deleting and re-creating the existing virtual machine.

Remove VM from Shared Storage

You have a virtual machine defined and running on the current shared storage volume. If you want to save this machine setup, jump to the next section that teaches you how to add additional storage to the cluster. You can use the same virtual machine, but change it to be used with CSV.

1. In the right-hand column of Failover Cluster Manager, under the Services and Applications section, right-click the virtual machine. Select Shutdown Virtual Machines.

2. Confirm Action window asks you if you really want to shut down the virtual machine. Confirm your action.

3. In the right-hand column of Failover Cluster Manager, right-click the same virtual machine and select Delete.

4. A Confirm Action window asks you if you really want to delete the virtual machine. Confirm your action.

You are back at the point shown in Figure 5.31. You have a Node and Disk Majority cluster with two disks. The first disk is the Disk Witness and the second disk is shown as Available Storage. The next thing you want to do is configure the Available Storage for use as a Cluster Shared Volume. To enable CSV on the cluster, right-click the name of the cluster in Failover Cluster Manager and select Enable Cluster Shared Volumes. See Figure 5.40.

FIGURE 5.40
Enable Cluster Shared Volumes

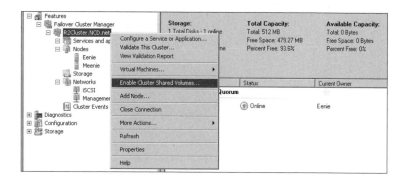

Enabling CSV is supported only for use with Hyper-V R2 virtual machines. This is not a general feature that can be used by SQL or File and Print Services. Thus, when you select to enable it, Failover Cluster Manager displays a warning window to ensure that you are provided that information and you do not try to use it for other highly available services. See Figure 5.41. You need to click the check box to indicate that you have read this.

FIGURE 5.41
CSV warning

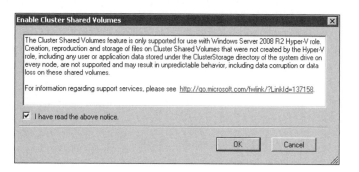

You have now enabled the CSV feature. The next step is to assign storage to the CSV. Right-click Cluster Shared Volumes in Failover Cluster Manager and select Add Storage. This will display all storage that is available for use by the cluster. If you have been following the steps I have been outlining, you will see a display similar to what is shown in Figure 5.42.

FIGURE 5.42
Add Storage

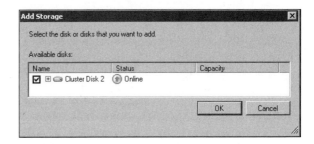

Click OK to accept adding that volume to your cluster as CSV. A status window displays. When complete, your new storage configuration looks very similar to what it was before, only now the storage is listed as Cluster Shared Volumes instead of Available Storage.

At this point, go to any host in the cluster and open a Windows Explorer window. Open the C: volume. There you will notice a directory named \ClusterStorage. This is where every node in the cluster maintains its information about all CSVs in the cluster. If you have added just a single volume to CSV, you will find a single subdirectory, \Volume1. If you open that subdirectory, you will find any information that was on that disk, such as the virtual machine files for the previously created virtual machines. Every time you add a new storage volume to CSV, you will get another \Volumex subdirectory, where x is just a sequential number. You can rename the \Volumex subdirectory to be anything you want it to be. But *never* rename the \ClusterStorage directory, or CSV will stop working.

You will also notice in Windows Explorer that there is no new volume that the host sees. In fact, whereas when you were using the shared storage, Windows Explorer showed a drive letter on the cluster node that owned the volume. CSV does not use drive letters, so you will have "lost" that drive letter. In other words, even though you can see in Failover Cluster Manager that the CSV is owned by a particular node of the cluster, it does not show up in Windows Explorer. The \ClusterStorage directory structure is creating a link to the actual storage that is assigned by means of the reparse point capability that has long been part of the Windows file system. This means that when you create a virtual machine or virtual hard disk to reside on the CSV, you will define it in the C:\ClusterStorage\Volume1 hierarchy. This will not use any storage space on the C: drive (well, a little bit for the reparse points), as it is pointing to the CSV volume and allocating the storage from there.

To create virtual machines in this environment, simply follow all the things you have learned earlier in this chapter. You need only remember that when you define storage locations in the Hyper-V Manager console, you will point to C:\ClusterStorage\Volumex for storage. By default, Hyper-V will then create the virtual machine VHD and configuration file in a subdirectory with the same name as the virtual machine.

Managing HA Virtual Machines

As you can see from creating virtual machines, building them in a Failover Cluster Services environment is pretty much the same as building them on a stand-alone server. Yes, setting up the storage is a little different, but once you start the process of building a machine, it is the same.

There is a slight difference in making changes to a virtual machine that is configured in a cluster. Because the virtual machine is now a resource that can be run on any node in the cluster, changes to the virtual machine must be known to the entire cluster. Therefore, when you want to make any changes to the virtual machine, you should use the Manage virtual machine option in the Failover Cluster Manager console. See Figure 5.43. Although we have not talked much about System Center Virtual Machine Manager, it also has this full integration with Hyper-V and clustering. That is, if you make a change to the configuration of a virtual machine that is under the management of SCVMM, the configuration does not need to be refreshed to the cluster.

FIGURE 5.43

Manage virtual machine

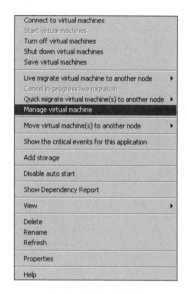

If you do not use the Manage Virtual Machine option from within the Failover Cluster Manager console but instead use the Hyper-V Manager console to make changes to a virtual machine, then you will need to make all nodes of the cluster aware of those changes. This is done by refreshing the virtual machine configuration within the Failover Cluster Manager console. See Figure 5.44.

If you are running an earlier version of Hyper-V or Windows Server 2008 that is pre-R2, you will need to refresh the configuration any time you make a change because pre-R2 did not have the same level of integration.

TESTING FAILOVER

In the steps above, you created virtual machines and performed controlled, or planned, failovers. That function is very useful in the management of the environment, but the real strength in Failover Clusters is their ability to automatically restart a virtual machine on another node in the cluster if something happens to the node on which the virtual machine is currently running.

In addition to Quick Migration and Live Migration, you also have the ability to move the virtual machine from one node to another. The ability to move a running service from one node to another node in a Failover Cluster is something that is common to all services running as clustered services. The fact that a Hyper-V virtual machine can also be moved, as can other services, simply proves the complete integration of Hyper-V with Failover Clusters. In fact, a Move works exactly the same as Quick Migration. It saves the state of the machine, transfers ownership of the LUN on which the virtual machine exists, and restores the virtual machine on the selected node. Of course, if there are multiple virtual machines on the LUN, they will all be saved and restarted.

FIGURE 5.44
Refresh virtual machine configuration

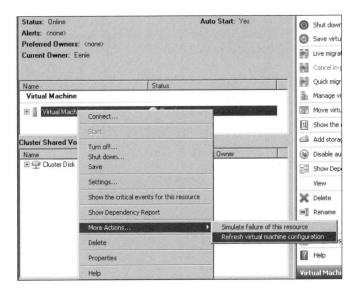

To execute a planned failover of a virtual machine by using the Move function of the cluster, do the following:

1. In the Failover Cluster Manager console, under Services and Applications, right-click the virtual machine you want to move.

2. From the list of options, select Move Virtual Machine(s) to Another Node. Then select the node you want to move it to.

3. With an R2 cluster, you will see in the center column the status of the virtual machine as it is saved, moved to the other node, and restored — just as though you had selected Quick Migration. In pre-R2 clusters there was no Quick Migration, so the virtual machines were shut down, moved to the other node, and restarted.

Now that you know that the failover mechanism is working in a controlled environment, it is time to create a critical error that will simulate a major problem to create an unplanned failover from one node to another.

1. In the Failover Cluster Manager console, determine the node that is currently running the virtual machine. You are going to be stopping a service. Make sure you initiate this either from a host that is running just the Failover Cluster Manager console or from the cluster node on which you will not be stopping the service.

2. Right-click the node running the virtual machine, select the More Actions option, and then select Stop Cluster Service. This will simulate a software problem on this node as the cluster service stops. See Figure 5.45 for these selection options.

FIGURE 5.45
Stop Cluster Service

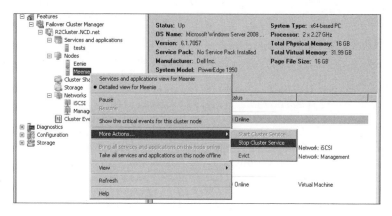

3. Click the virtual machine to watch what happens. In this case, because the host machine continues to operate and the cluster service is shut down gracefully, the virtual machine gets saved, LUN ownership is changed, and the virtual machine is restarted. Failover Cluster software tries to cause as little damage as possible. Because this was not a catastrophic failure, it was able to gracefully recover from a possible operator error.

4. Repeat the steps from above, but start the cluster service to bring the node back into the cluster. This will take a few moments.

If you were to go to the console of the host that is running the virtual machine and perform a controlled shutdown or restart of that host, again the Failover Cluster Service would gracefully move the virtual machines to another node in the cluster. The cluster service is very robust and tries very hard to protect against all the possible combinations of issues and failures that could occur in as elegant a manner as is possible.

Creating a truly catastrophic condition requires that you do something that does not give the cluster service a chance to do anything from the failing node. Pulling the plug or turning off the power on the host running a virtual machine is the easiest way to create that catastrophe.

You should monitor the progress of the catastrophic error from the Failover Cluster Manager console. When you turn off the power, you will notice that the process of restarting the virtual machine on another node in the cluster does not happen immediately. The remaining node(s) in the cluster need to ensure that there simply was not a temporary disconnection to the node running the virtual machine. So another node in the cluster waits a set period of time before it will take ownership of the LUN containing the virtual machine(s). Once that node has ownership of the LUN, it will start the virtual machines that have been defined to the cluster. Since the virtual machines were not gracefully shut down on the original node, the virtual machines have no saved memory state, so they will boot from their image on their associated VHD. This is the same sort of start you would have when you turn off a physical machine without shutting it down gracefully. In other words, you have lost the state of whatever was running in the virtual machines because there was no time to save it to disk, as in the other examples given previously. But since there is no intervention on the part of an operator to get the virtual machine up and running, the applications are operational in the shortest time possible.

ADDING STORAGE

Everything you have learned so far in this chapter has dealt with a single storage volume on which you can place your virtual machines. The next task is to learn how to add more storage

volumes to the cluster. This can typically be done while the cluster is running, so your operations will not be interrupted by the addition of storage. You will have to check with your SAN
vendor to determine whether they can add or increase storage without bringing down the SAN.
After all, the goal of the High Availability provided by Failover Cluster Services is that the
system continues running, and if something fails, the services pick up running on another node
in the cluster.

Depending on how you are presenting storage to the cluster, you will have to create new
LUNs on your SAN. If you are using Fibre Channel, you will have to follow the procedures
for your environment. As mentioned earlier, there are many variations from vendor to vendor
on this, so I have not included any instructions for Fibre Channel LUNs. The same can be said
about the various iSCSI SAN vendors.

If you are using the Windows Storage Server 2008 that I explained earlier, go back to the
steps provided there and create another LUN on the iSCSI target. Then follow the steps for
connecting to that with the iSCSI Initiator on each node of the cluster. You will find this information in Figures 5.15 through 5.22. If you create more than one LUN, when you come back to
Failover Cluster Manager, you will see all those new storage volumes available to be added as
either shared storage or as Cluster Shared Volumes.

To add a LUN to the CSV, you would right-click Cluster Shared Volumes in Failover Cluster
Manager and select Add Storage. To add a LUN to the shared storage, you would right-click
Storage in Failover Cluster Manager and select Add Disk. It really is that easy to add storage to
a running cluster.

Windows Server 2008 Core Installation

As I said at the beginning of the previous section, it is easier to learn to set up a host-based
cluster when using the Full installation of Windows Server 2008. My recommendation is to first
get comfortable working with building and managing clusters with a Full installation before
moving on to working with a Core installation. Besides, once you get all the infrastructure
in place for the Full installation, it is really easy to build on that infrastructure for the Core
installation.

Chapter 2 explained how to install and configure a Core installation for remote management. If you have not yet created a pair of Core installations, go back to Chapter 2 and follow
the instructions. Remember that you should build both nodes with the same version of the
operating system.

Once you have your Core installations correctly configured for remote management, you
can install the Failover Cluster feature. This is accomplished through the command window.
Log into each of the nodes you plan to cluster and issue one of the following commands:

```
ocsetup FailoverCluster-Core
```

or

```
start /w ocsetup FailoverCluster-Core
```

Either command works, and you will see either variation in different documentation. Do not
forget that the keyword FailoverCluster-Core is case sensitive. If you misspell or do not use
proper case, the ocsetup command will not be able to find the feature to install.

The next thing you need to do is configure iSCSI to access the targets you have set up. You
can follow the instructions given earlier for setting up a target for a Full installation, but define

a new target just for the Core cluster. To start the iSCSI Initiator on the Core installation, issue the following command from the command prompt:

```
iscsicpl
```

This brings up a windowed interface. Just like in the Full installation, by default the iSCSI service will not be running on the operating system. You will get an informational window that tells you this and asks if you want to start it. Click Yes, and you will see a window like what is shown in Figure 5.46. This is a new addition in R2. In the original release, configuring iSCSI on Core installations required using the `iscsicli.exe` command-line utility.

FIGURE 5.46
iSCSI Initiator Properties

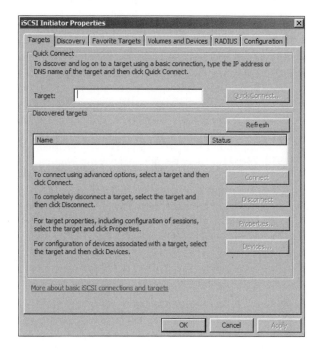

You will recall from working with the Full installation that this is the same window you worked with there. Follow the same instructions for connecting to the iSCSI Target and preparing the disks for use in the cluster.

There is also a command-line interface, `iscsicli`, that can be used for configuring the iSCSI Target. Here are the commands:

```
sc config MSiSCSI start= auto
net start MSiSCSI
iscsicli QAddTargetPortal wss.ncddemo.net
iscsicli Qlogintarget iqn.1991-05.com.microsoft:WSS-R2CoreClus-target
iscsicli PersistentLoginTarget iqn.1991-05.com.microsoft:WSS-R2CoreClus-↵
target T * * * * * * * * * * * * * * * 0
```

The first line calls the command-line interface to the Service Control Manager to configure the iSCSI service to start automatically on system startup. Note that there is a space character in front of the word auto.

The second line starts the iSCSI service.

There are both long and quick formats of various iscsicli commands. I am teaching you the quick formats because those are all you will need. For help on the commands, type **iscsicli ?** at a command prompt.

The first iscsicli command is pointing to the iSCSI Target. You can use either the fully-qualified domain name, as in the example, or the IP address or NetBIOS name.

The second iscsicli command logs into the iSCSI Target to enable access to the LUNs being offered. The string starting with iqn is the way the server and the target are identified. The string iqn.1991-05.com.microsoft says that this is a Microsoft implementation of the iSCSI Target. The WSS string identifies the host system. The R2CoreClus string identifies the actual iSCSI Target on the host system. This same string can be found on the iSCSI Target host in the iSCSI Target Manager console when you look at the properties of the target.

The last iscsicli command establishes a permanent, or persistent, login to the target. That is, when the node starts up, it will automatically make the connection to the target specified in the iqn string. The string starting with T and ending with 0 defines required parameters to establish this persistent connection. There is a full explanation of all these parameters in the Software Initiator Version 2.X Users Guide found at http://download.microsoft.com/download/a/e/9/ae91dea1-66d9-417c-ade4-92d824b871af/uguide.doc. The string entered is the minimum you need.

You remember from the instructions on the Full installation that when the iSCSI Target LUNs are presented to the iSCSI Initiator, the disk has not been formatted. A disk has to be formatted as an NTFS volume for use by a cluster. It was pretty easy to use the Disk Management GUI on a Full installation to format the disk. But you do not have that option on a Core installation, so you need to use the diskpart utility. Start by entering **diskpart** at a command prompt to start the utility. You could also put these commands into a command file and execute them with the command **diskpart /s script.txt**. If you do build them into a command file, you will most likely want to add some error processing. For a full description of the diskpart commands see http://technet.microsoft.com/en-us/library/cc766465.aspx. Here are the diskpart commands you will need:

```
List disk
Select disk 1
Online disk
Attributes disk clear readonly
Create partition primary
Format FS=NTFS Label="name1" Quick
Offline disk
Select disk 2
Online disk
Attributes disk clear readonly
Create partition primary
Format FS=NTFS Label="name2" Quick
Offline disk
Exit
```

The `List disk` command gives you a list of the available disks on this system. It will show something like the following if you created two iSCSI LUNs and have them connected:

```
DISKPART> list disk
  Disk ###  Status          Size     Free    Dyn  Gpt
  --------  -------------   -------  -------  ---  ---
  Disk 0    Online          126 GB      0 B
  Disk 1    Offline         512 MB   512 MB
  Disk 2    Offline          20 GB    20 GB
```

The sizes may vary depending on the size of the disks you created. The important part here is to see the number of the disks you are going to be manipulating. If you had more than one physical disk attached to your host system, you will see different disk numbers and those will have to be reflected in the commands listed above.

The rest of the commands are pretty straightforward. You need to select the disk you want to work on and bring it online. By default, the disks are set up to be read-only, so you need to turn that off. Then you create the partition, format the volume, and set the disk offline again so that the cluster can use it.

You have now prepared your hardware for setting up a cluster. The steps for validating and building the cluster are exactly the same at this point as those steps you followed for creating a cluster with the Full installation of Windows Server 2008 except that you need to run the Failover Cluster Manager console from a Full installation machine. You cannot install the console on a Core installation. Use Failover Cluster Manager to build the cluster and build your virtual machines.

Guest Cluster Installation

Creating a cluster between two or more virtual machines builds off everything you have learned so far. The only shared storage that a guest cluster can use is iSCSI, so if you have been using iSCSI throughout the earlier exercises, you already have everything you need to know to configure guest clusters. If you were using SAS or Fibre Channel shared volumes, you will need to go through the instructions given above for setting up an iSCSI Target and connecting iSCSI Initiators to those targets.

The primary difference between building a physical cluster and building a guest cluster is that you cannot install Hyper-V to create and run virtual machines from within another virtual machine. Otherwise, you follow all the same instructions given above for building a physical cluster when you build a guest cluster.

If clustering the Hyper-V hosts provides High Availability to the virtual machines running on those hosts, why would you want to build guest clusters? This boils down to a personal preference, but there are sometimes reasons why you may want to consider guest clusters. Let's use a simple example of a two-node SQL Server cluster. When SQL Server is installed in a Failover Cluster, the SQL Server service is installed on both nodes of the cluster. If one of the nodes fails, the surviving SQL Server service will relatively quickly take over the processing that was being done on the failed node. This contrasts with the situation where you have a single SQL Server virtual machine running on one node in a cluster. When the node that is hosting the SQL Server virtual machine fails, SQL Server will restart on another node in the cluster. But, before SQL Server can continue responding to client requests, the SQL Server virtual machine must reboot and the SQL Server service must be started. Only after these time-consuming tasks have completed will SQL Server be available to service client requests. So it depends on how quickly you want a failed resource to come back online.

Disaster Recovery

There are quite a few ways to re-create an operating environment after a disaster has occurred. They span the gamut from very manual to very automatic solutions. As you can imagine, the costs also vary from relatively inexpensive to maintain and build to more expensive. You need to determine what is best for your business. I want to concentrate on a singular capability that exists within the Microsoft virtualization solution — that being what is sometimes known as a stretch or multisite cluster.

Through these first few chapters you have learned how to build the infrastructure necessary to operate a virtual machine environment. You have learned how to build and manage systems via the built-in tools that come with Windows Server 2008 and Hyper-V. All those earlier components come together to enable you to build a highly available environment in your datacenter for your virtual machines.

The High Availability basics provided by Failover Clusters in Windows Server 2008, and with Microsoft Hyper-V Server 2008 R2, establish a foundation on which to build an even more enhanced solution. The enhanced solution can provide automatic failover between two geographically dispersed sites or a disaster recovery site in which manual intervention is used to restore business services. Figure 5.47 gives a very simplistic diagram of a typical configuration used for disaster recovery.

FIGURE 5.47
Disaster recovery configuration

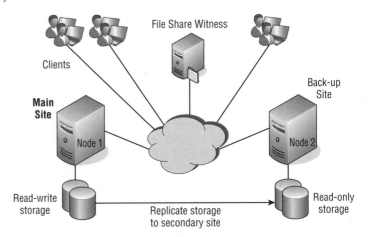

There is always a main or primary site at which the regular day-to-day processing and operations occur. But if a disaster of some sort occurs, operations can continue at the backup or secondary site. A typical configuration will have one or more cluster nodes in the primary site and one or more cluster nodes in the secondary site. A third site will have what is known as a file share witness. This can ensure a majority configuration in the surviving site if a whole site goes down and you want to enable automatic restart in the backup site.

Stretch Cluster

A stretch cluster is known by other names, such as multisite cluster or geographically dispersed cluster. This provides the highest level of availability in that if there is a disaster at the main site, all operations can continue automatically within a very short period of time at the backup site. This capability is provided by a combination of Microsoft Failover Cluster software and volume replication software from a third party. This design has been proven over many years with other application services such as SQL and File and Print Services. Microsoft has simply added Hyper-V as a service to this environment.

A stretch cluster depends on a third-party storage replication solution to ensure that the contents of the disks containing the virtual machines and their data are replicated to the other site. Microsoft does not provide any replication solution for this and has always relied on the storage vendors or independent software vendors (ISVs) to provide it, so you will need to work with your storage vendor or ISV to help you get this in place. In this configuration, operations are generally run at the primary site, with the storage replication continuously replicating the changed contents of the disks across the network to the backup location. While the content is being replicated from the primary site to the backup site, the backup site does not have full access to the drives to which the data is being replicated. This ensures that the drives are not inadvertently written to, thereby invalidating the data that has been replicated.

When a disaster occurs (or the failover process is tested), the storage vendor or ISV has routines that it runs in Microsoft's Failover Cluster service to remap the SAN LUNs or storage volumes to be fully exposed as read/write LUNs or volumes in the backup site to the nodes in the backup site. The standard process of failing over a virtual machine from one node in a cluster to another is performed, and the virtual machine is restarted in the backup site. As of this writing, this method only works with non-CSV volumes, as everything is managed at the LUN level. So if you have highly critical applications that need the ability to recover in one site and then fail back to the primary site when the primary site comes back online, you should use the non-CSV solution.

Microsoft has worked with a number of storage vendors and ISVs to provide this stretch cluster capability. Because the stretch cluster solution is very dependent on the storage solution, it is critical to work with the storage vendor or ISV to ensure a successful implementation. Here are a couple examples.

DOUBLE-TAKE SOFTWARE: DOUBLE-TAKE FOR HYPER-V

Double-Take has long been a partner with Microsoft for disaster recovery solutions. They provide a slightly different approach in their solution in that it does not require shared storage or have geographic restrictions, and it can be deployed using components of the existing infrastructure. Based on Double-Take GeoCluster replication, cluster nodes can be located anywhere and are kept current asynchronously. This solution is based completely on software data replication and can be used with heterogeneous storage environments. Failover to the remote site can be automatic or administrator initiated. In fact, there can even be multiple failover sites for different components of the primary site. For a more complete explanation of Double-Take's capabilities, see www.doubletake.com/english/products/double-take-virtualization/pages/double-take-for-hyper-v.aspx.

HITACHI: TRUECOPY OR UNIVERSAL REPLICATION

Hitachi's configuration requires the use of the Hitachi Universal Storage Platform V. Hitachi Storage Cluster integrates Microsoft's virtual machine Quick Migration capabilities with Hitachi storage system replication to enable reliable, remote replication with automated or IT administrator–initiated failover. The solution provides resynchronization of disk resources for simplified failback. Hitachi Storage Cluster manages the direction of replication and storage resource ownership within the Hyper-V clustered environment. The solution can be configured for synchronous replication using Hitachi TrueCopy replication and for asynchronous replication using Hitachi Universal Replicator. For a more complete explanation of Hitachi's capabilities, see `www.hds.com/assets/pdf/hitachi-universal-storage-platform-family -best-practices-with-hyper-v.pdf`.

DIFFERENT IP SUBNETS

Prior to Windows Server 2008, in order to build a stretch cluster, the networks handling cluster communication had to be in the same IP subnet, and the maximum round-trip time of these network connections could be a maximum of only half a second. This generally meant that stretched clusters required a VLAN between the two sites, something LAN administrators did not like to set up, and the two sites could not be very far apart, often less than 10 miles. One of the new features in Failover Clusters is the ability to have the different sites of a stretch cluster located in different IP subnets and without the maximum round-trip time requirement. This is something that customers have been requesting for many years, but it presents a challenge for applications to automatically fail over to a backup site. The applications, such as the virtual machines, will have no problem failing over — that works just fine. But, since those virtual machines are coming up in a different IP subnet, something has to be done to make them accessible.

If you are using DHCP for your cluster nodes, your virtual machines will automatically obtain a new IP address as they come up. But, if clients were accessing them via the old IP addresses, you will need to force an update to all the DNS servers to contain the new address, as well as force the client to query DNS again to obtain the new address. TCP/IP does not have anything built in to handle this, so it is something that you will need to work with your networking people on to implement a solution. You will need to use some sort of monitoring utility, such as System Center Operations Manager, to watch for a change in the host on which the virtual machine is running, and then the virtual machine could execute the `ipconfig /registerdns` command to quickly get DNS updated with its new IP address.

If you are using fixed IP addresses for your cluster nodes, you may end up with IP addresses that are simply not available in that particular area. This is even more difficult to resolve than the DHCP environment. But it can also be handled by scripts and commands to update DNS and flush routers. Fully addressing how to resolve these issues is beyond the scope of this book, as they are networking issues that have nothing to do with virtualization or Hyper-V. But the increase in the use of virtualization is going to force more organizations to look at how they will address these issues, so you may as well start the conversation with your networking team today.

The Bottom Line

Setting up a highly available environment on physical machines hosting virtual machines

> **Master It**   In Windows Server 2008 pre-R2 and R2 and in Microsoft Hyper-V Server 2008 R2, it is possible to set up Hyper-V as a highly available service in a Microsoft Failover Cluster. This ensures that if a Hyper-V server hosting virtual machines fails for whatever reason, the virtual machines on that failed host are failed over, or restarted, on a surviving node

of the Failover Cluster. The hardware configuration has several requirements in order to create a Failover Cluster that is fully supported by Microsoft. List the requirements of the configuration.

Setting up an environment with the ability to move running virtual machines from one server to another with no downtime

Master It   A new capability provided in Windows Server 2008 Hyper-V R2 and Microsoft Hyper-V Server 2008 R2 is the ability to move a running virtual machine from one node in a Failover Cluster to another node with no loss of machine state and no loss of network connections to the virtual machine as it is moved. This capability is known as Live Migration. It is built on top of the Failover Cluster feature. Since the previous question defined the base configuration for a Failover Cluster, list the recommended new components that are required to upgrade the configuration to support Live Migration.

Setting up a highly available environment on virtual machines

Master It   Not only is it possible to create highly available host environments with Failover Clusters, but it is also possible to create highly available virtual machines, regardless of whether the virtual machines hosts are members of a Failover Cluster. Describe the recommendations to create a Failover Cluster between two virtual machines.

Chapter 6

Planning a Virtual Infrastructure with Hyper-V

Companies are evaluating virtualization as a way to save money in a number of different ways. The plan could be something as simple as server consolidation to lower the number of physical servers they need to buy, which could also translate into lower heating and cooling costs. Or, they could be at the other end of the spectrum, trying to create a more dynamic environment that can adapt to changing business needs based on business rules they implement. Whatever your reason is for considering virtualization, planning is the most important step in implementing a virtualization strategy. In order to hit a target, you must have one. Planning helps you define that target.

The process of planning for a virtual infrastructure is very similar to planning for any other infrastructure project. If your company already has an established project methodology, that can be adapted. There are many books and seminars on the topic of project management. Microsoft has published a general project methodology called the Microsoft Solution Framework and published it on TechNet. Microsoft even offers a consulting engagement, Server Virtualization with Advanced Management (SVAM), to cover not only the planning but all the steps through the implementation and operation of a virtual infrastructure.

This chapter is about planning for the infrastructure. Implementation and operations details will vary considerably from company to company.

In this chapter, you will learn about:

◆ Defining the scope of your project

◆ Discovering what you have to work with

◆ Assessing what you can accomplish with your resources

◆ Financially justifying a virtualization project

Envisioning

Envisioning is the earliest phase of an entire project. This process could start with a single person or with a group of people who have observed a problem that needs a solution. Coming to a clear, nontechnical definition of the observed problem and a nontechnical solution to that problem is the ultimate goal of the envisioning process. Note that the goal is not to develop the solution but to define what will be required in order to develop that solution.

During the envisioning stage of a project, you will need to define the team that will have to be assembled in order to provide a complete definition of the problem as well as what the end goal will be. The team members will have various areas of expertise to cover all areas the solution will touch. That often means that some of the team will be businesspeople, not just technical people, which may create some friction. That is, there may be conflicting ideas about what needs to be done. The team needs to come to agreement about what the project will entail.

Some of the things that you should expect to deliver from the envisioning stage include:

◆ A clear nontechnical definition of the problem

◆ A consensus of what the end goal should provide

◆ A team that is able to address all phases of the solution

◆ What is part of the project and what is not

◆ Risks to success and how might they be mitigated

◆ An estimated cost to complete the project

◆ A nontechnical document that contains all this information

Notice that I use the term *nontechnical* a couple of times. This is very important during this phase of the project. The purpose of envisioning is not to come up with all the technical steps required to deliver the solution. The purpose is to define the path that will be used to get there. If you try to start by defining the technical solution, you are almost guaranteed to fail. There is a long history of project failures due to too much effort going into technical details too early in the project cycle.

Problem Definition

Sometimes it is easy to see that a problem exists, but saying there is a problem generally does not get you the budget needed to solve it. Often the problem has both technical and business components. The best way to define the problem is to break it down into both technical and business components. Try to make these problem statements quantitative, based on known quantities from your particular environment. Then, for each problem statement, associate a quantitative goal. Some of these you may already know, but some of them may require more investigation.

For example, it is not uncommon for companies to monitor their computer environment for performance and utilization statistics. If you work for one of those companies that regularly monitors system utilization, it is a pretty simple task to come up with a technical problem statement like, ''The average system utilization on our servers is 11.3 percent.'' If somebody questions that statement, you will have data to back it up. Then you turn around and state what you would like to see improved. For example, ''Increase average system utilization on our servers to 60 percent.''

Using specific statements like these will help the business decision makers, those to whom you must go to get money to implement the solution, understand the benefits you plan to achieve. In this case, you are saying that with virtualization you expect to be able to deliver more than a fivefold improvement in the utilization of the system resources and similarly improve the value received from those resources.

Business problem statements should be quantifiable, too. In companies I have worked with over the years, I regularly hear that it takes anywhere from four weeks to three months to satisfy a business unit's request for a new physical server. Change that into a quantitative business problem statement such as, "The average time it takes to set up a server for a business unit is six weeks. That translates into a six-week lag time to achieve the benefit expected from the application to run on it." Base this statement on the statistics you have for your business. Looking at a quantitative solution, you could say something like, "Reduce the time to deploy a new operating system environment to 48 hours." Forty-eight hours might seem like a pipe dream with physical hardware, but with proper planning and execution, that turnaround time is common for a virtual environment. That means you have just reduced time to deliver by a factor of 21:1.

Table 6.1 provides some more examples of technical problem statements.

TABLE 6.1:   Technical problem statements

PROBLEM STATEMENT	GOAL
Power consumption per individual server is 750 watts.	Reduce average power draw of the total of all servers to 25 percent of current.
Network cabling for each individual server takes four ports on a network switch.	Reduce required network switches to 25 percent of current.
Legacy applications cost $X per year to maintain older hardware.	Eliminate older hardware and associated maintenance costs, saving $X per year.
Datacenter is operating at 85 percent of physical space.	Datacenter will operate at 50 percent of physical space.

Table 6.2 provides some examples of business problem statements.

TABLE 6.2:   Business problem statements

PROBLEM STATEMENT	GOAL
Our quarterly test of our disaster recovery plan requires five days of our IT staff's time.	Reduce disaster recovery plan testing to one day.
Business continuity requires doubling hardware costs in order to have the same, nonutilized hardware in a backup site.	Reduce the amount of hardware for business continuity to 25 percent of current by use of virtualization.
Peak demands require one extra server for each workload to support maximum loads.	Make use of virtual machines to temporarily increase available machines dynamically. Eliminate 90 percent of excess hardware.

As you can see, each problem statement is balanced with a quantifiable goal. Each environment is different. That is why the project team needs to comprise both technical people and businesspeople in order to identify all the various benefits that an organization might want to achieve.

Use a variety of techniques to obtain this information from different parts of the organization that might be impacted. You might be able to gather some of the information by soliciting input via e-mail. Team meetings are great places to discuss ideas and capture input, particularly if your management asks for areas of improvement. Or you might set up surveys. The idea is to gather enough information to help you make a business case for proceeding. After all, it always comes back to helping your organization become more profitable. If infrastructure virtualization will not provide a meaningful business value, there are most likely other areas in the organization that do have projects that will help make the company more profitable.

Once you open the faucet of trying to find all the problems out there, you will end up with way too much to address in any one project. That is why it is very important for you to come up with a method to prioritize the information once it is collected. For this reason, it is important to form a team of both technical people and businesspeople. Something the technical side sees as a low-priority issue the business side may see as critical. The opposite can also occur. Try not to create too many priority levels. It is best to stick with about three levels. This gives you an easy way to define the scope of the project. You may decide to execute only the top-priority problem statements, or you may decide to break the project into three phases, with each phase addressing a different priority level. Do whatever makes the most sense for your environment.

This leads into the next phase of this envisioning process — consensus on the end goal.

Clear Goal Statement

A clear goal implies a clear statement. Be concise. If you can get this down to a single sentence, that is best. But if you need more detail, you should still try to keep it to only one or two short paragraphs. This is a team effort, so ensure that all members of your team are in agreement and understand exactly what the goal statement means. Conciseness also helps executives get on board. It is a lot easier to envision an end result from a well-formed single statement than from a wandering paragraph.

Also, know what is top of mind with your executives. For example, if they are more concerned about the cost of IT, bring the idea of reducing costs while better utilizing resources into the statement. If executives are more concerned with quickly responding to the changing business environment, introduce the idea of virtualization providing agility.

Project Team

Putting together a virtualization strategy is a team effort. As with any team, you must have the right people for the right positions. You also need to ensure you are all working from the same playbook. That is one of the reasons why everyone on the team must agree with the problem statements and the goal statement. Agreement helps ensure everyone has the same focus.

As noted earlier, both technical people and businesspeople are needed on the team. Neither of these groups operates in a vacuum. The technical people are there to provide solutions to technical problems. The business people are there to drive a profitable business. Profitable businesses need solutions to problems.

Any successful project also has well-defined roles within the team. Some of these roles will exist throughout the life of the project. But there will also be special team roles — individuals who may come in for a specific job only. For example, a project needs a project manager from the beginning to end to ensure success. But architects may be needed only early on in the project to define the architecture to be followed.

Each virtualization project is different, but there are some fairly common roles. In smaller projects, each role may be a single individual, or one person may take on multiple roles. In larger projects, each role may be split among multiple individuals:

◆ Project sponsor/steering committee

◆ Project manager/project management team

◆ Architect/architecture design team

◆ Technical experts

◆ Operations expert/operations management team

PROJECT SPONSOR

In a small project, the sponsor is most likely a single person. In a large project, it may grow into a whole committee. This person is either the one who came up with the initial idea about how virtualization may be beneficial to the company or one who had to be convinced that the end goal is worthwhile.

In either case, the project sponsor acts as a mediator between the project team members and the people who are funding the project. This person will provide the initial direction of the project and then provide guidance to help keep the project on track once it is under way.

PROJECT MANAGER

The project manager is the person accountable for accomplishing the stated project objectives. Key project management responsibilities include creating clear and attainable project objectives, building the project requirements, and managing the three legs of the project "stool": cost, time, and scope. All changes are tracked in a project report maintained by the project manager and shared with all team members.

It is important that this person be either a professional project manager or someone who has had experience in running projects. This is more important than the person having in-depth knowledge of virtualization technologies. I have seen many projects fail from the lack of a good project manager. But I have also seen many successful projects led by a person who, at the beginning of the project, did not have a deep understanding of the technology of the project.

Depending on the size of the project, this could be a single individual, or it might be a team. In either case, there are subroles:

◆ Project scheduler

  ◆ Maintains/tracks progress against project milestones

  ◆ Manages resource scheduling

  ◆ Modifies project plan for approved changes

◆ Budget manager

  ◆ Manages/tracks project budget

  ◆ Manages requests for hardware and software

◆ Communications manager

  ◆ Single point of communication for status

  ◆ Maintains overall project report

ARCHITECT

The architect is a special subject matter expert. This individual is well versed on the capabilities of virtualization and other technologies that may intersect with virtualization, which enables the architect to draw up functional specifications of what needs to be done and to identify risks. If this is a large project, it may make sense to assign a lead architect who will be part of the project from beginning to end. The lead architect will have responsibility for the overall design of the solution but can also rely on other architects who specialize in certain functional areas. For example, if highly available systems will be part of the solution, a functional architect may be called in to write the functional specification to support them.

TECHNICAL EXPERTS

Very rarely is this role filled by a single individual because there are always two facets to a virtualization project. One side deals with the technologies that will be deployed to achieve the goal, and the other side deals with how this technology will fit into the business. As with all other roles, this might be a single technician and a single businessperson, but it also may be a team of technical and business experts.

The technical experts have the detailed knowledge required to take the functional specifications provided by the architects and apply the right technology to them to deliver on the stated end goals. They will also define the specific technical requirements (servers, storage, networking) required to implement the solution from a technical side. And from the business side, they will define which procedures may have to be modified, added, or deleted in order to achieve the end goal.

The technical experts are also responsible for testing the components of the solution to see that everything works as defined. This includes writing up test procedures to ensure complete testing of the solution. If this is a large project, the technical experts may pass off these test procedures to a test team that will do the actual testing.

OPERATIONS EXPERT

Virtualization will change operations. There is no question on that. Now, instead of having a single application running on a server, a server may have two, four, eight, or more workloads running. So it is important that before the solution is delivered to production, an operations expert be involved in determining how the solution will change current operational procedures. In fact, there may even be operational considerations that could alter the overall architecture of the solution. It is important that operations be involved from the beginning of the project.

Depending on the scope of the changes, there may be a need to define some new training. The last thing one wants to do is throw the new solution over the wall to operations without getting their input and approval ahead of time. No matter how well designed and executed all the other steps are, not getting proper training in new methods and technologies will almost guarantee the failure of the project.

OTHER TEAM ROLES

This list of roles is not exhaustive. If the infrastructure virtualization project is large enough, it may be necessary to define additional team members. You may need to have technical writers to assist in writing test procedures and product documentation. You may need trainers to write and develop training procedures to ensure a smooth introduction of the new technology. You may have a separate test team to execute the tests defined by the technical and operations experts. Sometimes these roles can be combined with other roles. You need to make the determination of the best organization required for your particular project.

Scope — What's In and What's Not

If I had to guess, I would say that poorly defined project scopes have caused more projects to fail than any other single item. It is impossible at the beginning of a project to know all the possibilities and benefits. For example, even though virtualization has been around for a very long time, most of the people working in the Windows environment have had little to no experience working with those earlier technologies. As a result, many of us are still learning about different ways to apply this technology to different business problems.

Simply put, the scope of the project defines what will be done. Having a clear goal statement helps you determine whether different tasks are in scope, or required to attain the goal. If a task or feature is not required to attain the goal, then that item should likely be considered out of scope.

Making a change to what is in scope, either adding a new feature or capability or removing an earlier design component, has a cascading effect on a project. It affects the amount of budget needed. It affects the schedule. It may require additional people to get a task done on time.

By the same token, it may be necessary to redefine some of these project elements as new knowledge comes in. So, you must have a way to add or remove elements from the scope.

When you prioritized your problem statements, you started to define the scope of your project. At that point you were deciding which of those problem statements should stay as part of the project and which should be delayed or dropped. But, it might also be necessary to add detail to some of the problem statements. Even though you made quantitative problem statements, it may still be necessary to specify to what area that statement applies. For example, take the earlier example statement about average system utilization moving from 11 percent to 60 percent. You may decide for this project that only certain types of server platforms, say those averaging less than 10 percent utilization, will be included.

You may also want to break the project into phases, with only certain things in certain phases. The 10 percent utilization limit is an example of going for those systems that may be seen as returning the most benefit in the shortest period of time. Or, it may be easier to work on local systems before implementing solutions in branch offices. Get all these constraints defined as being explicitly in scope or explicitly out of scope. The project manager's job is much easier when everyone is working from the same set of directions.

Managing Risks

Risks are anything that can impact the delivery of the project on time and within budget with the resources provided. Risks are a fact in any project. It is best to spend time at the beginning of the project trying to identify potential risks. Some of them are totally unpredictable and have such a small chance of actually happening that it makes no sense to spend time trying to plan for them. For example, you might consider an earthquake that disrupts datacenter operations. For those who live on the West Coast, that might be something that needs to be put in the plan. But if you are in the Midwest, there is such a slight risk of an earthquake that planning for it is most likely a waste of time. On the other end of the spectrum, virtualization software for the Windows platform is changing right now. How will this constant change affect your deliverables? Will you use only currently released products, or will you plan to use some beta or early-release software during the evaluation phase, knowing that the new features may or may not be in the product when you go to implement them?

As the project proceeds, you will uncover more risks. Risks in and of themselves are not a problem. Ignoring risks is a problem. Therefore, you must develop a risk document that includes an associated mitigation. Review the risk document during every status report.

Your risk document should contain at least this information:

Risk Identifier A unique identifier.

Date Identified The date the risk was determined.

Status Can be open, mitigation in process, or closed (with date).

Description As much information about the risk as you have.

Consequence What happens when this event occurs. This should include information about financial impact, schedule impact, resource impact, and the like.

Probability A percentage probability of the event happening, with 1 percent being a very low probability and 100 percent being sure it will happen.

Severity What effect this will have. This is different from the consequence. This could be a simple scale of 1 to 5, with 5 being the highest. The product of probability times severity will give you a good sense of those risks that need to be addressed soonest.

Owner The person or team responsible for managing or mitigating this risk.

Budget

When all is said and done, it always comes down to this: You have to accomplish the end goal with resources available. Obviously, at this early stage in the overall project, all you can provide is a preliminary estimate of what you think the project will cost. The project sponsor and executives will make the decision, based on this input, whether or not the project should be funded. A final budget number can be produced after the discovery, analysis, and financial justification documents are complete.

Items that affect the budget number are the time to complete, any software and hardware that may need to be purchased, and the number of people expected to work on the project. Try to be fairly detailed in assigning these values so that if the project sponsor wants to make changes to the various resources, you can come up with a new estimate in a short time.

Documentation

All the information gathered during this envisioning phase needs to be summarized and presented to the people who will be making the decision on whether or not to pursue the project. As I stated previously, try to be concise. Keep the technical jargon to minimum. Be honest and accurate. The more quantifiable statements you make, the more likely it is that you will be able to get the project approved. Try to keep the documentation of this initial phase under a couple dozen pages. If you produce a tome, the executives are less likely to take the time to read it. Most companies have a certain process that needs to be followed to gain approval for expenditures. It is sometimes called a request for expenditure, or RFE. If you do not have experience in writing an RFE, get help from someone who has successfully written them in the past.

After you are successful in obtaining the approval, the fun work begins. Now you will move into the discovery phase of the project.

Discovery

It is very important to complete the vision/scope document because it provides organization to the process. But discovery is the phase where you start to find the size of the project. Before you can determine what can be virtualized, you need to collect, or discover, the data about your environment. Once you have that data, you move to the analysis phase.

There is a lot of information to gather. You need to collect information about hardware, software, and performance on every server that is a potential candidate for virtualization. Fortunately, you defined what was in scope in the earlier phase, so you may not need to collect information on every single system in your environment. If you know up front which servers definitely fall outside the constraints of what you are looking at, you do not need to collect information from them. Of course, you may want to collect the information anyway as a baseline should you wish to expand the project after your initial success. You also want to know the physical size, power rating, and heat output of every server. All this information helps to establish costs today versus costs you expect to see after virtualization.

You can use manual methods to gather information, or you may be able to extract information from your configuration management database if you have one. There are also many free scripts available on the Web. Windows also has a couple of built-in tools that can capture some valuable performance data. Perfmon is a monitoring tool that can capture information over long periods of time, but because it is run through a GUI, it has some limitations. Logman (http://technet.microsoft.com/en-us/library/cc755366.aspx) is a command-line tool that can also be used to capture statistics over a longer period of time. By being a command-line tool, it lets you also create and schedule jobs to collect information for specific periods.

However, Microsoft has a free tool that collects most of this information for you: the Microsoft Assessment and Planning (MAP) Toolkit, available at www.microsoft.com/map. It has many of the features needed to analyze an environment for virtualization.

MAP performs three major functions:

◆ Inventory

◆ Analysis

◆ Reporting

MAP can generate both detailed inventory reports in Microsoft Excel spreadsheets and assessment reports in Microsoft Word documents. The outputs include the following:

Windows Vista Hardware Assessment identifies Windows clients and determines whether they can support running Vista.

2007 Microsoft Office Assessment identifies the current Office installation and determines whether client systems can support running Office 2007.

Windows Server 2008 Readiness and Role Migration identifies Windows servers and determines whether they meet minimum requirements for running Windows Server 2008.

Server Consolidation and Virtualization identifies candidates for consolidation or virtualization by analyzing performance metrics.

Application Virtualization Assessment identifies clients capable of running Microsoft Enterprise Desktop Virtualization.

SNMP Devices Report lists all computers and devices found via SNMP.

Security Assessment identifies physical and virtual machines that are not running the basic security functions of antivirus, antimalware, or firewall.

SQL Server Assessment identifies systems running SQL Server and determines whether they can support running SQL Server 2008.

Power Savings Assessment identifies systems in your environment that have available power management capabilities and projects potential savings if these capabilities are exploited.

Notice that MAP includes more than just reports for virtualization. But you need to determine whether virtualization is the solution for everything. You might receive better financial benefits by consolidating workloads onto physical hardware instead of virtualizing everything. For example, it is often very effective to consolidate multiple SQL Server hosts onto a single host running either multiple databases or multiple instances of SQL. Another report helps you understand your security environment better, and planning the security aspects of the virtual environment is also important. Obviously, we will be quite interested in the candidate assessment report for server virtualization. However, you will be able to gain some significant information to include in your cost justifications from the power savings report. Remember, though, everything you are looking at must be considered in scope according to the work you did during the envisioning phase.

As I said earlier, this is not the only tool you can use, but it is very complete and Microsoft regularly adds more components to it. For example, MAP has components for Vista, SQL, and Office. Microsoft has several other tools from their System Center family of tools that can provide much information you can use to discover and analyze your environment, but they are licensed software. They were not designed as an integrated tool like MAP, but they can provide additional information that you can inject manually into your analysis.

System Center Configuration Manager (SCCM), as its name implies, is a configuration management tool. As such, it has the ability to perform inventory collection and reporting. It requires an agent to be installed on each client and can be more selective and interactive for finding specific information. It is not designed for collecting information specifically for virtualization, but you can create queries against the Configuration Management database to find potential candidates for virtualization based specifically on hardware configuration.

System Center Operations Manager (SCOM) is a monitoring and alerting tool that can gather performance statistics that can be used for determining possible virtualization candidates. SCOM has components known as Management Packs that can collect information about specific characteristics of individual applications or the operating system as a whole.

System Center Virtual Machine Manager (SCVMM) seems like a strange tool to bring in during the analysis phase. However, Microsoft has built a SCVMM Management Pack for SCOM that can collect performance information and create a Virtualization Candidate Report based on criteria you enter into the system. Then you can use SCVMM to perform a physical-to-virtual conversion of target machines.

Though the System Center family of products is very powerful in each of the tasks it performs, MAP was designed to help in consolidation projects. And, as a free download, you cannot beat the price, particularly for all the capabilities built into this one tool. Microsoft also provides a Return on Investment calculation tool (`www.microsoft.com/virtualization/why/roi/default.mspx`) to help you put together your cost justification. Data collected by MAP can be exported into an XML file. This ROI tool can then import that XML file. It is a great time saver. Though you can link to this tool from the Microsoft site, it is actually maintained by a third party, Alinean, which provides a similar ROI tool for other virtualization vendors.

Inventory

MAP is an agent-less tool. In other words, you do not need to install any software on any of the systems for which you are taking an inventory. It uses Windows Management Instrumentation (WMI) to query every machine for hardware, software, and performance data. You do need to have administrative access to every machine that you want to inventory, and you have to open the appropriate ports on your firewalls to manage a server with WMI. MAP lets you use multiple accounts if you do not have a common account with administrative privileges across all your systems. The Getting Started Guide that comes with MAP provides detailed instructions for configuring MAP in your environment.

MAP allows you to select the machines to be inventoried in a number of ways. Figure 6.1 shows the Inventory and Assessment Wizard with all the options.

FIGURE 6.1
Inventory and
Assessment Wizard

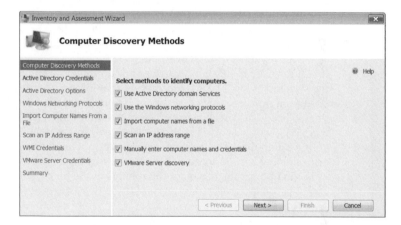

As you can see, I have selected all the options in order for you to see what is available. You can select as many or as few as you wish. The wizard will step through the detailed selection entries that you want to use. Once you complete the selection criteria, you can run the inventory collection at any time. You can also enter different selection criteria to create different reports.

Hardware inventory includes the configuration information for the processor (clock speed, number of physical and logical processors, BIOS, make, model), the amount of memory, network (number of NICs, speed, MAC, IP, make, model), and disk systems (number of disks, size, type).

Software inventory includes the installed operating system and version, domain membership, installed applications and version, and update information.

In addition to performing the inventory, MAP can also collect performance information. You need to specify the exact computer names from which you want to collect performance information. If you have run the Inventory and Assessment Wizard, you can extract computer name information from an appropriate spreadsheet, because MAP will output its findings into a Microsoft Excel spreadsheet. Or you can create a simple text file with Notepad to contain the specific systems from which you want to gather information. Figure 6.2 shows you the Gather Performance Metrics Wizard.

FIGURE 6.2
Gather Performance
Metrics

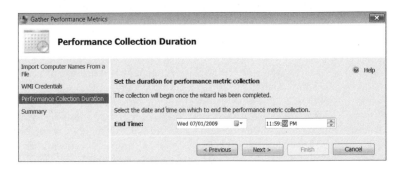

As with the Inventory and Assessment Wizard, you will need to enter credentials to gain access to the systems being monitored in order to collect the performance information. You specify only a stop date and time because this wizard starts the collection process as soon as you exit it.

Performance statistics include average CPU utilization, average storage usage, average disk I/Os per second, and average network bandwidth usage for the period of time the test was run. You should run MAP over a long enough period to capture meaningful data. For example, if you have an application that does not do much during the month but at month end spikes the system, it would be wise to capture that information at the end of the month. MAP can also produce a power savings assessment report. This report is based on many assumptions about things, like your cost of power. The method and formula it uses are explained in the Getting Started Guide that comes with the MAP tool, so you will have the ability to tailor the output to your assumptions. The assessment provides potential energy savings that may be possible by consolidating servers through virtualization as well as through operating system migration and exploiting power management capabilities in the hardware.

Analysis

After MAP collects the inventory of your targeted systems, it can do some analysis of the data, but it is fairly generic. After all, everybody's environment is different, and the business reasons, desired benefits, and physical environments vary from one customer to the next. Therefore, you will need to compile the data in a manner such that it can be used as a basis for your more in-depth analysis.

For example, the hardware inventory report provides a list of your machines and their specific hardware configurations. If, during the envisioning stage, you decided that you were going to try to virtualize only physical systems that were using 2 GB of memory or less, you could use the Excel inventory report to filter on memory to get a list of those servers. You would then use that list to feed the Server Consolidation Wizard.

This Server Consolidation Wizard generates reports that show how many Hyper-V host computers you will need in order to consolidate your physical servers using virtualization. It can also recommend the placement of current physical machines, converted to virtual machines, on the Hyper-V hosts. The wizard requires you to define the virtualization computers you wish to run as virtual machines and a target configuration of a Hyper-V host server that will run your virtual machines.

The Server Virtualization Wizard is one of the reasons why MAP is such a good tool for assisting in your analysis. MAP uses the observed utilization values for resources such as CPU and memory it found on the physical systems. This includes estimating high average CPU utilization and maximum observed disk and network input/output (I/O). It then makes projections on how a workload might scale from observed physical processor to Hyper-V host processor. Placement of the servers in the virtualized environment is based on peak utilization calculations.

Before MAP can generate the assessment of how many virtual machines you can get onto a Hyper-V server, you have to provide MAP with some information. The basic analysis performed by MAP is driven by two factors. The first factor is data you provide as to the configuration of the physical servers onto which you plan to consolidate your virtual machines. Figure 6.3 shows you the Summary page of the Server Consolidation Wizard.

FIGURE 6.3
Server Consolidation
Wizard

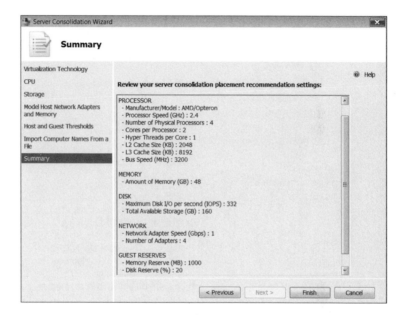

As with any of the Microsoft wizard summary screens, this screen summarizes the information you have entered. The left-hand column allows you to go to the individual windows where you define the processor, memory, disk, and network configuration of a sample Hyper-V host system. In this case I have defined my Hyper-V host system to have four dual-core processors, 48 GB of memory, and four NICs, and I set the amount and speed of my storage. You also specify either the maximum number of VMs you want to put on each host or, as I did in this example, the amount of memory and disk to reserve for each virtual machine. When you specify the guest reserves, MAP will automatically try to place as many virtual machines on that Hyper-V host as these reserves will allow.

If you plan to use more than one type of physical configuration for your Hyper-V hosts, you will need to configure it and run the report another time. MAP plans for this by also asking for a list of the discovered machines that you want to place. This enables you to tailor your results according to different selection criteria.

This is what I mean when I say the analysis is pretty generic. Later in this chapter you will learn how you can take the raw data output from MAP and analyze it for your specific environment.

Depending on what your end goals are, it may be worthwhile to look at some of the data for other than the Windows Server environment. For example, if you are considering other virtualization technologies such as application virtualization or Remote Desktop Services, or if you are considering implementing a virtual desktop infrastructure, you may want to look at some of the reports that provide the inventory information of those technologies.

The second factor in MAP determining the resultant Hyper-V server configuration is a collection of machine names that you want to try to place. The inventory step provided you with information about the machines in your environment. During your envisioning stage you should have defined some of the limits you were placing on the potential physical machines you wanted to migrate to virtual. You can use the Excel spreadsheet that MAP creates from the Inventory and Assessment Wizard, filter that to contain only machines that fit your predetermined criteria, and then feed that list into Server Consolidation Wizard.

Reporting

MAP produces generic reports for the various assessments that you asked to be performed. It does not do any combining of multiple assessments into a single assessment. But the generic reports produced provide a good framework for you to develop some collateral for your reports and justifications to management. Figure 6.4 illustrates a sample table of contents from the Windows Server 2008 assessment report.

FIGURE 6.4
Assessment Table of Contents

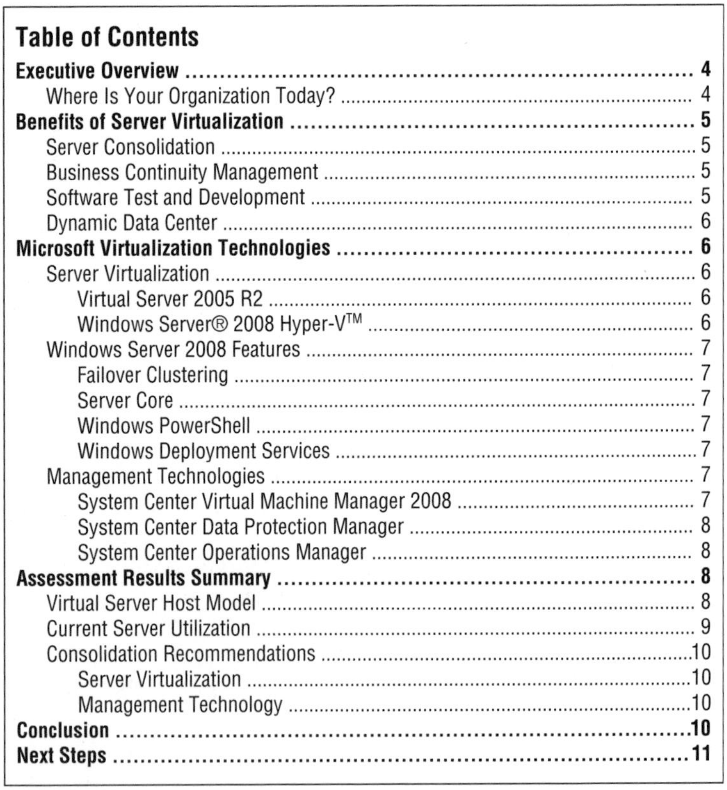

Table of Contents

Executive Overview **4**
Where Is Your Organization Today? 4
Benefits of Server Virtualization **5**
Server Consolidation 5
Business Continuity Management 5
Software Test and Development 5
Dynamic Data Center 6
Microsoft Virtualization Technologies **6**
Server Virtualization 6
Virtual Server 2005 R2 6
Windows Server® 2008 Hyper-V™ 6
Windows Server 2008 Features 7
Failover Clustering 7
Server Core 7
Windows PowerShell 7
Windows Deployment Services 7
Management Technologies 7
System Center Virtual Machine Manager 2008 7
System Center Data Protection Manager 8
System Center Operations Manager 8
Assessment Results Summary **8**
Virtual Server Host Model 8
Current Server Utilization 9
Consolidation Recommendations 10
Server Virtualization 10
Management Technology 10
Conclusion **10**
Next Steps **11**

The information in this report is quite generic, including even some marketing information from Microsoft. But the format does work as the basis of creating an executive-level report to present your findings. Remove the standard text that comes with this report and replace it with the information that you came up with during your envisioning process. A nice feature of these reports is that they provide pie charts of the status of your environment. That makes the report more impactful going back to your business decision makers.

In addition to the above types of reports, MAP will also provide you with the details of everything it finds. The information is formatted into Microsoft Excel spreadsheets to give you an easy way to categorize and summarize the details. These Excel spreadsheets can also be used during the subsequent proof of concept or migration. You can filter the data according to the criteria you defined in your planning process.

Summary

MAP is a reasonable tool for gathering a fair amount of information about what you have in your environment. But as I said earlier, there are other tools available to assist. Or you may even have some homegrown tools that you already use and that can be used to generate some of these reports. PlateSpin, Ltd. (`www.platespin.com`) has a tool called PowerRecon. Different versions of that tool provide inventory and performance data. I already mentioned Microsoft SCCM and SCOM. If you already have or are considering purchasing the System Center family of products, the combination of SCVMM and SCOM is a very powerful tool to assist you in migration, providing you with a virtualization candidate report. MSDN also contains a variety of scripts for collecting data from systems (`http://msdn2.microsoft.com/en-us/library/aa394585.aspx`).

Whatever tools you use to gather all this data, you will need to analyze what it means. That moves you into the next phase of preparing for virtualizing your environment: analysis.

Analysis

You limited the scope of what systems you were going to look at in the envisioning phase. You collected lots of information about those systems in the discovery phase. Now you want to analyze that information to find candidates for virtualization and the potential savings to be expected by virtualizing. Not every server is a good candidate for virtualization. Financial benefits may not be obtainable from every movement to virtualization. There may be a special hardware configuration that cannot be handled by a virtual machine.

So what makes a good candidate for virtualization? Some of that you should have defined in your vision/scope document. But there is not really a single factor that tells you that a machine should be virtualized. You have to look at the data that you collected in the discovery phase and then, based on hardware, software, and performance data for each server, compare that information to your decision criteria.

It is generally easier to start by eliminating those physical servers that do not look like good virtualization candidates based on your criteria. For example, if you have an application that is running on a quad-processor, quad-core machine with 64 GB of physical memory connected up to a couple terabytes of storage, and the machine averages 50 percent utilization, that would be an obvious machine to put on the list to consider at a later time. Such a physical machine using 16 logical processors is larger than what could be created as a virtual machine with 4 logical processors.

Several criteria can help refine the massive amounts of discovery data into a usable list of candidates. Set your thresholds for these criteria:

♦ CPU

♦ Memory

◆ Disk

◆ Network

◆ Age of hardware

Except for that last item, those items are pretty typical for any analysis work. What is the upper threshold that you would consider for each of these before you would say that the physical machine is not a good candidate for virtualization? One way to start is to look at what Hyper-V supports. Hyper-V has some pretty large bounds, so this will not be totally definitive, but it does help to wean the list. Table 6.3 shows the maximum values that can run in Windows Server Hyper-V and Hyper-V Server for the first four items in the list above.

TABLE 6.3:   Hyper-V upper limits

VM MAXIMUMS	WINDOWS SERVER HYPER-V	MICROSOFT HYPER-V SERVER
Number of virtual processors	4	4
VM memory	64 GB per VM	31 GB total per host (64 GB per VM for R2)
Disk	2 IDE controllers w 2 disks per	2 IDE controllers w 2 disks per
	4 SCSI controllers w 64 LUNs	4 SCSI controllers w 64 LUNs
Network	12 NICs	12 NICs

For all but one of these maximums, both Windows Server Hyper-V and Microsoft Hyper-V Server have the same limits. The one difference is the amount of memory available to virtual machines in the original 2008 versions. Windows Server 2008 Hyper-V can provide up to a maximum of 64 GB of memory for a virtual machine. Microsoft Hyper-V Server 2008 supports a maximum of only 32 GB in the physical system, so it is limited to providing a maximum of 31 GB of memory to a virtual machine. Microsoft Hyper-V Server 2008 R2 increases the memory limits to be equal between the two products. This memory difference has more to do with the scalability of the host solution than with determining candidates for virtualization, but it is something you should keep in mind if you are planning to deploy the original release of Microsoft Hyper-V Server.

The next thing you notice in Table 6.3 is that the limits are pretty generous. Not many systems require 12 NICs or 256 disks or even 32 GB of memory. So you need to establish some upper limits or thresholds that will help you refine your list quickly. For example, I have talked with a number of customers who started virtualizing only those physical machines that had one or two processors (one or two cores) and no more than 4 GB of RAM. They had enough of those in their environment to ensure a good start on their virtualization project. Based on what they learned from virtualizing these smaller machines, they went on to develop plans for virtualizing large physical machines.

Eliminating systems is an iterative process. If you want to start by working on the low-hanging fruit, you can define your thresholds to what may have been considered a reasonable system a few years ago. For example, you could say that any physical machine that has more than four logical processors, has more than 4 GB of memory, and more than four NICs is immediately put on the exclusion list.

This is not to say that a system that exceeds any of these thresholds is a poor candidate for virtualization. On an iterative pass through the exclusion list, you may find that a system exceeds these thresholds, but the performance never exceeds 10 percent utilization. That implies that the system may not have been configured appropriately and could easily run on a smaller configuration. This actually may point to a better virtualization candidate because the configuration being used to host the application is more expensive than what is really needed.

The Microsoft Excel spreadsheets generated by MAP can assist you in looking at some of this data. You can filter or create pivot tables on different values in the spreadsheet, enabling you to quickly consider different values and criteria.

Number of Processors

When talking about processors, we need to discuss processors in the physical host and processors in the virtual machine. In the physical host, I will use the term *logical processor* to denote the ability to execute a hardware instruction. For example, a two-processor, dual-core system has four (2 x 2) logical processors. If you have a four-processor, single-core system, it also has four (4 x 1) logical processors. There are also hyperthreaded processors that generally provide two execution threads for each processor or core. Therefore, a two-processor, dual-core, hyperthreaded system has eight (2 x 2 x 2) logical processors.

When we move into the virtual machine, counting processors becomes much easier. Each logical processor in the host can be used as a virtual processor in the virtual machine. But the number of virtual processors in a virtual machine is the most restrictive component in selecting which physical machines may make good candidates for virtualization. Today, the limit on the number of virtual processors that can be used by a virtual machine running under Hyper-V is four. If you have set the number of processors as a limiting criterion, any physical system that is effectively using more than four logical processors can most likely be excluded from the list of virtualization candidates.

The number of logical processors on the host should not be the exclusive determining factor when considering the number of processors. Just as important is the utilization of those processors. You really need to combine the number of processors with the utilization of those processors. If we assume that a virtual machine can have a theoretical maximum of 400 percent processor utilization (four virtual processors, each at 100 percent utilization), you may want to define the number of processors threshold as 200 percent. This could be a physical machine with four logical processors operating at 50 percent utilization each or 16 logical processors operating at 12.5 percent utilization each. Virtualizing either of these physical workloads would utilize about the same amount of processor power in a virtual machine. But if some of those logical processors on the host are hyperthreaded processors, you will need to determine exactly how much power is available from the hyperthreaded processor. Generally, hyperthreaded processors run at just a fraction of the physical processor, and it varies greatly depending on the type of workload being applied to the hyperthreaded processor. It could be that the hyperthreaded processor is only providing 10–15 percent more processor power in the physical machine, so that would have to be included in your true utilization.

You do need to throw one more consideration into this equation. That is the processor speed, generally measured in megahertz (MHz) or gigahertz (GHz); 1000 MHz is equal to 1 GHz. MHz is not a linear indicator of system performance, as things like cache, internal bus speeds, memory speeds, amount of disk I/O, and network I/O all factor into determining the overall performance of the system. But for doing rough calculations to try to equate physical to virtual utilization, it is accurate enough. You will be able to refine your initial assumptions in the lab as you start moving machines into the virtual environment. In this case, you need to see what percentage of utilization is being used on what speed processor. If you will be deploying the virtual machines onto a system with a fast processor speed, you can expect to get more performance, or a lower processor utilization, out of it. But some of your older, single-core processors actually ran at higher clock rates than newer, multicore processors. You need to factor in a possible lower-speed processor in those situations. Again, this is a rough calculation, but if you are running an application on a 2000MHz (2 GHz) physical system, but plan on moving it to a host with 3GHz processors, you can very roughly assume that the application is going to run 50 percent faster on the new system. This equation totally ignores wait time for disk and network I/O and some other factors, so you may want to adjust it to suit your preferences.

Lastly, remember that logical processors in the physical host can be utilized by more than one virtual processor in the virtual machines. For example, if you have a two-processor, dual-core host system, you have a total of four logical processors, and you want that to be your virtualization host machine. You also have four physical machines that each have two processors, and each of those physical machines is running at only 10 percent utilization, making them good candidates for virtualization. You can create four virtual machines, each with two virtual processors, and run all of them simultaneously on the virtualization host, even though it only has four logical processors. In fact, with Hyper-V, the maximum ratio is eight virtual processors to each logical processor. In my experience, I have yet to find any organization that has even come close to that sort of density in a production environment.

Memory

Memory is the next most restraining factor in the virtualization space. Not because 31 GB or 64 GB is constraining for most applications, but because the typical host that is used for virtualization has a finite amount of physical memory that can be placed in it. System vendors are constantly changing the amount of maximum memory they will support in different models, but the most common platforms I see being used today for virtualization have between 16 and 64 GB of physical memory. Hyper-V allocates memory to virtual machines by allocating all the memory needed for each virtual machine for its exclusive use. There is no sharing of the memory space between virtual machines or overcommitment of memory. Memory overcommitment means that the sum of the memory allocated to all the running virtual machines is more than the physical memory on the host.

Let's look at a sample environment from what I have regularly seen. Let's assume that you have decided that your Hyper-V host will have a maximum of 64 GB of physical memory.

What I often see is that people first look at virtualizing physical machines with less than 4 GB of memory. This allows up to 15 virtual machines each with 4 GB of memory on a host, leaving 1 or 2 GB for the parent partition. If the virtual machines are using only 2 GB, then that allows for up to 31 virtual machines per host. Though it is possible, I am not seeing many customers putting 30 servers onto a single Hyper-V host. There are generally some considerations for "putting all your eggs in one basket." Yes, you can put these in a Failover Cluster, but when a node in the cluster fails, all the virtual machines need to start on another node. The time required to start all those virtual machines might not meet service-level agreements with the business units.

As with processor decisions, you also should look at memory utilization in the virtual machines. Often a physical machine is running a corporate standard. That standard may be a machine with 4 GB of memory. Looking at the MAP reports, you may find that the machine is using only 30–40 percent of the total amount of memory. When you convert that physical machine to a virtual machine, you would be wasting memory to create the virtual machine with all 4 GB. Instead, once you have created the virtual machine, you should change the settings to more correctly address the actual memory used.

This is also where some of Hyper-V's memory flexibility comes into play. Physical memory is often purchased in 1GB, 2GB, 4GB, or even 8GB increments, as that is how the memory is manufactured. Hyper-V is not limited to those physical constraints. You can allocate memory to virtual machines in 2MB increments. If you convert a physical machine that has 2 GB of physical memory, but your analysis shows that it needs only 43 percent of that memory, you can allocate 902 MB of virtual memory to the virtual machine. Being diligent in monitoring the memory could possibly get you one or two more virtual machines per Hyper-V host, giving you a better return on your investment. In fact, if you are using System Center Operations Manager to monitor your virtual machines after you have deployed them, you can get reports telling you exactly what the actual memory utilization is. You can then adjust according to the actual reported usage in the virtual machine.

For Hyper-V, you also need to plan for the memory overhead in the parent partition that Hyper-V requires for each virtual machine. In order to manage the translation between the virtual memory address of the virtual machine and the physical memory address of the host machine, Hyper-V requires some additional memory space in the parent partition (called the Translation Lookaside Buffer, or TLB) for each virtual machine. This amounts to an additional 32 MB for the first 1 GB of memory in the virtual machine. The requirement increases as the size of the virtual machine grows. Table 6.4 gives you an idea of the amount of overhead that needs to be added to the memory requirements you determined from your analysis. The final column is always rounded up to ensure an even number of MB for this additional memory allocation.

TABLE 6.4:   RAM overhead

VM MEMORY ANALYSIS	FIRST GB PARENT OVERHEAD	REMAINING PARENT OVERHEAD	TOTAL MEMORY REQUIREMENT
Up to 1024 MB	32 MB	0 MB	Up to 1056 MB
1024–2048 MB	33 MB	8 MB	Up to 2080 MB
2048–4096 MB	34 MB	24 MB	Up to 4156 MB
4096–8192 MB	35 MB	56 MB	Up to 8284 MB

Hyper-V R2 supports Second Level Address Translation (SLAT), which uses features on new CPUs. On Intel-based processors, this is called Extended Page Tables (EPT), and on AMD-based processors, it is called Nested Page Tables (NPT). SLAT provides an indirection layer from virtual machine memory access to the physical memory access of the host system. In other words, it supports in hardware what the TLB does in software. In virtualization scenarios, hardware-based SLAT support improves performance because it eliminates the TLB.

If you find that memory is the factor that constrains the number of virtual machines you get on a host (that is, the other resources of available CPU, disk, and network all have more room for expansion), you may want to consider a different configuration for your Hyper-V host. There are two ways to upgrade the memory.

The first option is to consider putting higher-density memory chips into your current model. I know that some organizations have hesitated on upgrading to the higher-density memory chips because of their premium pricing. However, the more expensive memory may actually be cheaper if you consider the total cost of the system. Assume that you upgrade to memory chips that double the current physical memory on your host, allowing you to put twice as many virtual machines on a Hyper-V host. If that cost is less than the cost to purchase another physical system, provide the power and cooling, provide for the rack space, and pay for all the software licenses for another system, then it might make sense to double the memory rather than purchase a second system.

The second way would be to change the model of the system you currently use to a model that supports more memory. This can sometimes conflict with corporate standards and maintenance issues, so it might not be an option.

Disk

It is pretty hard to say that there are practical limits on the number of disks that a virtual machine running under Hyper-V can support. With two IDE buses, each capable of two disks, and four SCSI buses, each capable of 64 disks, and each disk capable of being nearly two terabytes in size, that means we can have up to 512 TB of storage connected to the virtual machine via virtual hard drives. If you use pass-through disks instead of VHDs, you are not limited to 2TB volumes. Pass-through disks can use GPT (GUID Partition Table) volumes. They have a theoretical limit of 18 exabytes in size, though Windows currently has a volume size limit of 256 TB. Just for a fun exercise in math, fully load all the SCSI connections with 256 TB pass-through disks. Without even factoring any storage that may be also connected via iSCSI, that would be more than 65 petabytes (10^{15} bytes) of storage. That does not appear to be much of a limit.

Well, if we do not have a practical constraint on the amount of storage we can put into a virtual machine, what do we look at? The next thing would be the actual rate of I/O to the disks. Here we run into a similar situation. Performance to disks in a virtual environment is only slightly lower than in a physical environment. QLogic Corporation performed a benchmark of Windows Server 2008 running as a physical host against a Windows Server 2008 virtual machine (www.qlogic.com/promos/products/hyper-v.aspx). They stressed both the physical and the virtual machines to the maximum. The end result was that at the upper limit, the physical outperformed the virtual by only 10 percent — 200,000 input/output operations per second (IOPS) to 180,000 IOPS. There are very few applications that can even come close to using 180,000 IOPS. Other benchmarks have shown smaller differences at lower IOPS rates. And Windows Server 2008 R2 has improved the performance of access to virtual hard drives. Of course, this test was done against a system that was capable of performing that level of IOPS. If you are unable to configure a storage system capable of handling your IOPS rate, then it would be possible for disk be a limiting factor.

Seeing that there is no practical limit on the number of disks or on the disk performance, you will have to come up with some other threshold for selecting machines based on disk. If you are looking for ease of management, you may want to set your threshold at a maximum of four disks. Four is an easy number to work with. And, when you consider that you may consolidate 8 to 10 (or more) physical machines to a single physical machine hosting them as virtual machines, that could be up to 40 disks you would need to manage in that environment.

In addition to the number of disks you plan to virtualize, you will also need to consider the potential performance difference between the disks on the original system and the system to which you are consolidating. Again, MAP provides the raw details for you, giving you the average I/O load of each virtual machine. But there is no easy tool for taking the I/O requirements from several virtual machines and spreading the load over a different disk configuration. You will need to look at the information from MAP and make individual determinations of the best placement for each disk workload.

You may also want to look at data usage patterns. MAP is not going to give you this information, but you will be able to obtain that from Perfmon, Logman, or System Center Operations Manager data. When are the peaks in I/O requirements? You may want to try to balance virtual machines across the host environment to ensure that several peaks do not occur at the same time or occur on different hosts.

Lastly, you also need to consider what your host configuration is going to be. How many host bus adapters do you plan on having on your host if you are deploying Fibre Channel disks? How many NICs will you use if you are deploying with iSCSI storage? Are you going to load-balance the adapters for better performance? What are the speeds of the adapters? How many adapters will you have? How many spindles will you spread the load over? Which virtual machines will use virtual hard drives? Which virtual machines will use pass-through disks? You learned the pros and cons of these variables on the host system in Chapter 4.

So for disks, it boils down to what your team wants to tackle. There is no real technical limitation. The limitation will come in what the host system is able to provide and what makes sense from a management standpoint. Do not underestimate the importance of analyzing the disk requirements of the virtualized environment.

Network Cards

We have a situation similar to the disks when we look at the limits imposed by virtualizing. A virtual machine under Hyper-V can have up to 12 NICs. I have run into just one situation where a customer was looking for more than 12 networks in a single machine. But even in that environment, the customer was not using 12 physical NICs, but rather they were using virtual LANs (VLANs) to segment their physical networks into multiple virtual networks running on each physical connection. So each physical NIC was communicating over multiple VLANs.

Up to eight of the NICs assigned to a virtual machine can be synthetic, and up to four can be legacy. For practical purposes, legacy NICs, since they are emulated in software, should not be considered for production use. However, if you are going to be virtualizing operating system environments that do not have Integration Components available, you will have to use just the legacy network adaptors.

As with disks and CPU, MAP will report the average network utilization. You will need other tools to capture the peaks, and you will need to plan for the peaks. For your analysis, you can use the MAP data as a starting point, and then you can add in the peaks to determine the optimal placement to ensure you are not overloading any physical network.

We first need to look at the constraints on the host when determining how to place virtual machines. Many system vendors have a limited number of NICs that can be inserted. I have worked with many customers that have a limit of four to six NICs in their host. When they're running in a physical environment, this has worked well for them, but as they move to a virtual environment, and they are placing multiple virtual machines on a single physical host, they find they are running into bandwidth constraints. For example, if each virtual machine is using 10 percent of the available bandwidth, putting 10 virtual machines onto a NIC will saturate the link, causing potential performance problems.

Once you know the limit of physical NICs, you need to look at the purpose for each NIC. Microsoft recommends that a NIC be reserved in the physical host for management purposes. This is to ensure a network path to a host system should access via application networks become unstable or impossible. This management NIC is not exposed to the virtual machines.

If you are using iSCSI storage, you should dedicate a NIC to that role. You may be able to share this NIC with the guests, particularly if they are accessing the same iSCSI storage array. In this case, you will be combining your analysis of the network traffic on this NIC with the disk traffic to the iSCSI target for determining best placement of virtual machines.

You will most likely have a separate NIC assigned to the virtual machines for access to the resources they are providing. For example, you might be virtualizing a web application, and you need to provide clients access from the intranet or Internet to the application.

One of the new features introduced in Hyper-V R2 is the ability to Live Migrate a virtual machine from one Hyper-V host to another. This transfer of the memory contents of the virtual machine is done over the network. When it is done, it requires a lot of bandwidth for a short period of time as it is transferring the entire contents of the memory of a virtual machine across the network. Though it is not an absolute requirement, you may want to dedicate a NIC to that function.

In addition to these various functions that you might want to dedicate to a specific NIC, you may also be using network teaming software to provide failover or load-balancing capabilities. Looking at all these requirements, you can see how the number of NICs that can be placed in a physical host can impact your planning for deploying virtual machines.

Some of this can be mitigated by making use of VLANs to isolate traffic to different networks, if your physical switches support this capability. This will enable you to use a single physical NIC to connect to two or more virtual networks. Of course, that does not mitigate the actual amount of traffic that is passing over each NIC. You are still limited by the capabilities of the physical NIC and the switch to which it is connected for how much traffic can be moved across the wire that connects the two.

Most customers I have worked with in this space currently have a gigabit Ethernet (GigE) infrastructure. This will generally be sufficient for smaller datacenters and branch office environments, but when you start looking to deploy this into a datacenter environment, your analysis may tell you that you would be better served by implementing a 10GigE network segment specifically for handling the consolidated requirements of virtualizing your workloads. If this is the case with you, you will need to include this additional cost in your financial justification for the virtualization project. Some of my larger customers are moving to the 10GigE infrastructure to ease the cabling issues. After all, it takes ten GigE connections to equal a single 10GigE connection. So the cost of upgrading could possibly be offset by management cost savings. You will need to factor that in.

Age of Hardware

MAP provides an easy way to capture statistics on CPU, memory, disk, and network utilization. But gaining better utilization numbers is not the only justification for virtualization. Many organizations are looking at the age of their infrastructure. They may have fully capitalized server systems that are four or five or more years old. If these servers are not utilizing any special hardware devices that cannot be virtualized (e.g., real-time device drivers, fax cards), these are often some of the best candidates for virtualization. Even if they are running under high-utilization workloads, those workloads are generally running on older (slower) processors, slower memory, slower disk drives, and slower NICs. It is not uncommon to move an older physical server to a virtual machine and see it run faster than before because the host server is much more capable than the older server.

It is also not uncommon for these older systems to be quite inefficient in their power utilization and cooling requirements. In fact, it is possible that their operational costs alone could be high enough to justify replacing them with newer, more efficient hardware, and virtualizing the workloads running on these older servers may provide you with a larger return on your investment.

Unfortunately, there is no easy way to determine the current power and cooling requirements of your servers. The only really accurate way to determine this is to put an electrical line monitor on each server to determine its actual electronic draw. Then you can use that value to determine what the cooling requirements are. Combine those two to get the actual operational cost. If you are looking at a large number of servers, this is not very practical.

MAP can give you an idea of which machines are older machines, because it reports the model of the CPU running in each system. You can filter the Excel report to group the older models for individual analysis. When you have that information, you can either place an electrical line monitor on sample systems to determine their actual draw or use the numbers provided by the manufacturer of the system. Once you have the power draw, you can use that information to calculate the cost in your area. For example, assume that you have a system that is drawing 650 watts of power. That system will consume about 5,694 kilowatt hours per year. At a cost of $.10/kWh, that comes to almost $570 per year just to keep the machine running. Then there is the associated cost to cool that system. It is easy to see that a single machine may be costing you $600–700 per year.

Many of the older systems did not have much, if any, power management capabilities built in. New systems can often be managed to provide different electrical power draws depending on the actual work being done by the system. This means that most recent server systems can be run much more efficiently than those systems deployed four to five years ago. But even if we assume a modern system is going to have the same power and cooling requirements, you can easily see that putting 10 of these older systems onto a new Hyper-V host could save you $5,400–6,300 per year.

It may take more manual effort to analyze the benefit of virtualizing the older hardware based on power needs, but the dollar figures that result can help you financially justify moving forward with a virtualization strategy.

Applications

The applications being run on the servers could be the most limiting of the parameters to look at. Microsoft provides the same level of support on its operating system environments in the virtual world as it does in the physical world. It has also published its support policy for its server products such as Exchange and SharePoint at http://support.microsoft.com/kb/957006.

But everybody is not as comfortable with supporting in the virtual and the physical. Therefore, based on your analysis of what is running on the physical servers, you will need to determine which applications are supported. In the case of internally developed applications, if your company is making the move to virtualization, that seems like a given. Start with Microsoft server applications and your own company-written applications.

Independent software vendors (ISVs) may have a different support policy. After all, they have to test it in a virtual environment before they feel comfortable. Since virtualization is becoming more mainstream in the industry, this is not as limiting as it was during virtualization's early days. More and more ISVs are providing support statements for their applications, so check with them about those applications you are running.

There are some situations that require some mitigation. Sometimes an application makes use of specialized hardware. If that hardware requires special interface cards in the server, those will not be good candidates for virtualization. Remember that virtualization does not provide direct access to the physical server — the virtual machines talk through the parent partition to gain access. There is nothing in the virtual environment that provides support for this specialized hardware, so those applications will need to be excluded.

If those hardware devices are connected via a COM port, it will most likely not be possible for that application to be run in a virtual machine. Yes, there is the ability to assign a COM port to a virtual machine. But the COM ports assigned are not assigned to the host's physical COM ports — they enable a virtual machine to communicate via a named pipe to another software application.

USB devices may also present issues. USB devices on servers are generally special-purpose devices required for a specific application to run. This may be a license dongle or something similar. Virtual machines cannot directly attach to a physical USB device on the host (other than a physical disk drive). Some vendors provide network-based USB solutions. I have not used them myself, but some of my peers have had success using products from FabulaTech (www.fabulatech.com) and KernelPro (www.kernelpro.com). These solutions will require thorough testing before being put into production.

Financial Justification

Once you have compiled the list of servers that you plan to virtualize, you can start putting together the data on how much you are going to save by moving to a more virtual environment. Every company charges different rates for different components. During your planning, you will need to decide how you are going to determine the costs and savings.

I will mention it again that MAP has the ability to output some of its findings into an XML file that can be imported into an ROI tool found at www.microsoft.com/virtualization/why/roi/default.mspx. Even if this tool does not calculate exactly the same way as your organization requires, it can possibly save you a lot of time building your cost model.

Server Costs

Virtualization has both costs and savings. Unless you plan to repurpose some of your existing servers as virtualization hosts, you will have to expend some capital in order to set up your virtualization host environment. These are sometimes larger servers containing more storage, memory, and networking than your current standard servers. If you have servers that can be upgraded, you will need to purchase the additional processors, memory, storage, and networking to turn them into suitable virtualization hosts.

When you look at saving on the cost of the physical server, you have to consider how your company is currently paying for those servers you have. If your company has already purchased the servers, no capital will be saved on virtualizing one of those servers because the money has already been spent. If the servers are being leased, you need to evaluate what the cost will be to get out of the lease and then calculate how much less you will spend as a result of making the lease term shorter.

Where you really start to see the savings is when you purchase new servers. Maybe the server you plan to virtualize is due to be refreshed. Now you can calculate what the cost of the new server would have been and remove that expense. The same holds true if the plan for virtualization is to include new applications. You can capture what would have been spent to provision for that server and storage and record that as a potential saving.

Lastly, if there is any residual value in the servers that will be retired, you can include that value into the calculation of how much you will save on your servers.

Another area that can provide significant cost savings is your disaster recovery model. Disaster recovery sites often contain a significant amount of underutilized or unused hardware. This hardware is there in case a disaster occurs and it is necessary to move operations from the primary site to the backup site. If one of the goals of your virtualization project is to virtualize the disaster recovery site, you can almost double the savings of your primary site simply by replicating the figures to your disaster recovery site.

This can even be a cost benefit. It is not uncommon for companies experiencing a disaster to bring up just the core components they need to continue basic operations. By expanding this list to include many of the other components that support field operations, you may be able to ensure less disruption to your business, with a positive impact on your bottom line.

When you start looking at server costs, you realize that the initial cost of obtaining a server is but a single component of the overall cost of the server. In fact, I have heard from some customers that the initial cost of the server is equal to the sum of the other operational costs over about three years.

POWER AND COOLING

With the cost of energy only going up, you should not overlook calculating the amount of energy savings provided by virtualization. Depending on the tools used during the discovery phase, you most likely received some very generic, if any, information about the power of the servers in your environment. For example, MAP will provide you with the CPU model used in the systems surveyed. The only real way to determine power utilization is to actually put an electrical line meter on the plug where it goes into the wall for each server. This is not really practical for large environments, so determining the savings for power and cooling is going to take a bit of work. How much work you want to put into this will determine the accuracy of the results, but there is a law of diminishing returns. Trying to determine if an option card draws 5 watts or 4 watts is not going to make a significant difference in your overall calculations, even if that goes across all your servers. After all, 1 watt across 1,000 servers is only 1 kilowatt. That will be but a rounding error in these calculations.

When your vendor provided the server to you, they may have included documentation about its power draw. If so, you can use that information. If not, it might be easiest just to use very macro numbers of the maximum electrical draw of the power supplies that are in the servers. Using this information, you can provide a rough estimate of the amount of power that the target servers currently use. Subtract that from the power the new virtualization hosts will be drawing, and you get an estimate of the amount of power that will be saved. You could also put an electrical line meter on a sample server and then use the information from that across all similarly configured servers.

For these calculations, just concern yourself with what is actually in the physical server. I'll cover costs of other components such as external disk and network equipment shortly in the "Other Infrastructure" section.

Using that estimate of how much less power will be used, you can then calculate how much less cooling will be required.

RACK SPACE

The amount of space saved in a rack may or may not be of concern to you. I have been at the sites of a number of customers where this is very critical. The cost of a new datacenter can run into the tens of millions of dollars. If companies can delay building a new datacenter based on the ability to put more into the same physical space, that can be a very compelling reason to virtualize.

Before you start calculating the amount of rack space that can be eliminated, you need to determine how many virtualization hosts can be placed into a rack. Newer servers often produce more heat from the same amount of rack space than older servers. Depending on your current cooling environment, it may be necessary to leave air space in a rack of newer servers to ensure proper cooling. Of course, the older machines may take up more space than the newer, higher-performing servers, so there may be no difference in the amount of rack space required for the server.

Or, you may even determine that it makes financial and operational sense to switch to a server blade environment. They are designed to provide a denser rack configuration — that is, they can place more resources in less space. They have special designs for sharing things like NICs and host bus adapters.

There is no automated tool to collect all this information, since you also may have other components in the rack, such as network switches or power distribution units. So this step will require some manual work of mapping out what you currently have and estimating what the new configuration will be. This is also where it is beneficial to have differing sets of expertise on your team because operations will likely have some things to say about the best way to configure a rack to make operations most efficient. You may want to work with your system vendor. I have worked with some vendors that provide tools for building rack configurations, and they often provide some of these outputs.

OTHER INFRASTRUCTURE

There are quite a few other components that you might want to consider in your financial jus-tification model. Depending on your particular environment, these may or may not be of a concern to you. You will need to determine which will provide either hard or soft savings. Some of the other infrastructure to consider would be networking components, external disk storage, cable management systems, or power distribution units.

You may be able to realize savings in networking components. In the physical world, you had to size for every physical connection in all your hosts. With virtualization, you will be sharing network connections among virtual machines on a physical host. As with the server count, you may have already spent the money on these components, so you will need to calcu-late the savings of future purchases. After you consolidate to virtual machines, you will most likely have excess capacity in the number of switch connections available in your networking infrastructure. For example, maybe you currently place a single 32-port switch in each rack to connect eight servers with four NICs each. If those eight servers could be consolidated to a single Hyper-V host with four NICs, you would have 28 switch ports available for other con-nections. Instead of placing a single switch in each rack, you might be able to get by with one switch for two racks, assuming you get more than one Hyper-V host in each rack. Of course, you still need to use the network analysis you did earlier to determine if that bandwidth capac-ity will work for you.

The same holds true for disks. Sometimes virtualization may even temporarily increase costs of storage. Maybe you have all your current servers using direct attached or internal storage. You may still use direct-attached storage in the virtual environment, but if you are expecting to provide a highly available environment for your virtual machines, you will need to invest in some sort of shared storage, such as iSCSI or Fibre Channel storage arrays. A smaller envi-ronment may find a shared SAS storage enclosure sufficient. These shared storage systems may be able to save you money and provide more efficient storage utilization, but if you currently do not have them, there will be an additional cost to get them installed. Remember to include training dollars for any new acquisitions to ensure that the utilization of new technologies is not impeded by the lack of operational knowledge.

But even if you continue to use direct-attached storage, you have the potential of saving money on storage. By putting multiple virtual hard drives (VHDs) onto a single disk, you will have a higher utilization ratio on the direct-attached storage than by having just a single machine on that disk.

Another factor you should consider is the number of keyboard-video-mouse (KVM) devices you will need. Because you will be reducing the number of host systems, you may be able to save some money on future purchases. Because your environment is most likely provisioned with what you need today, you will have more than enough for an environment where you have reduced the number of physical hosts. The same consideration should be made for power distribution units.

Some of these items might not be worth your time to consider. But if your company requires detailed analysis of all potential cost savings and capital outlays for any new project, you will need to take everything into consideration.

Software Costs

One of the major expectations with any virtualization project is that you will end up with fewer servers than when you started. Depending on the way your software is licensed, you have the potential to save a fair amount of money in licensing costs. For example, Microsoft changed the way they license the operating system in a virtual environment. Until Windows Server 2003 R2, Microsoft did not even have a provision for licensing their operating systems (or other software) in a virtual environment. When you purchase a copy of Windows Server 2008 (or R2) Enterprise Edition, the license grants you the right to install a copy of the operating system on the host and to run up to four virtual instances of Windows Server. Enterprise Edition supports running on systems with up to 8 processors and is licensed by system. This means that one Enterprise Edition can support anywhere from 1 to 8 single-core or multicore processors.

With Windows Server 2008 (or R2) Datacenter Edition, the license grants you the right to install a copy of the operating system on the host and run an unlimited number of virtual instances of Windows Server. Datacenter Edition supports running on systems with anywhere from 2 to 64 single-core or multicore processors and is licensed by processor, with a minimum purchase of two processors.

So, let's take a look at the potential savings with these changes. If you plan to consolidate 4 physical machines onto a single Enterprise Edition of Windows Server 2008, you now will have to pay for only a single copy of Windows Server Enterprise Edition instead of five copies — one for the host and four for virtual instances. If you plan to consolidate 16 physical machines, you could either purchase four copies of Enterprise Edition or two or four processors of Datacenter Edition, depending on how many physical CPUs are in the host. Microsoft has created an easy-to-use calculator (www.microsoft.com/Windowsserver2008/en/us/hyperv-calculators.aspx) to help you determine the most cost-efficient way for you to license your environment. Make sure to include your licensing specialist and Microsoft representative in any discussions about potential cost savings to ensure that you are applying the licensing requirements correctly. I have significantly simplified what Microsoft has done, and there are many variables you need to consider.

You are not limited to saving money on your operating system licensing costs. Microsoft has also changed many of their other products to be system based instead of instance based.

For example, Microsoft has packaged its System Center suite of management products (Configuration Manager, Operations Manager, Data Protection Manager, and Virtual Machine Manager) into a single bundle that applies at the host level instead of at each system. I have heard of customers that have saved well over a million dollars by purchasing this packaged suite for their virtual environment compared to what purchasing the individual licenses for the physical machines would have cost.

During the discovery phase, MAP provides you with a list of all the software that is running on each server surveyed. You can filter the contents of this Excel spreadsheet to help you determine which software you are using and where. Use the contents of this list to approach your software vendors to determine how they charge for their software in a virtualized environment. There is no way to make a blanket statement about how this might change your software costs, as each vendor has their own policies. Some software vendors will continue to charge per running instance. Some are continuing to charge per number of cores utilized. Some, like Microsoft, might have begun charging for the host and all virtual instances running on that host.

Soft Costs

Soft costs are those costs that are often not attributable to things that you can put on an inventory list with vendor part numbers. In other words, soft costs are generally thought of as those items that are considered improvements in productivity. Whether or not you include soft costs depends on whether or not your company allows it. I have seen some companies that do not allow consideration of soft costs and others that will put a ranking on them in order to show some value from improved efficiencies.

Some soft costs translate directly into real savings, though. For example, to unpack and configure a physical server takes a measureable amount of an employee's time. This can be measured in hours, and employees have an hourly cost associated with their time. Setting up a virtual machine from a library of virtual images can be measured in minutes. In this age of trying to do more with less, this savings can readily turn into a very significant number.

Another component of the speed of deployment can be important to companies that are trying to be more agile in responding to changes in their business needs. Deploying a virtual machine is much more responsive than ordering a physical machine, waiting for it to come in, and then unpacking and configuring it. You may be able to define a lost opportunity cost for the amount of time currently spent waiting for the physical setup of a server.

The flexibility of virtual machines is also very important for recovery purposes. Even in companies that have optimized their procedures for building a physical machine, it takes time to rebuild an operating system environment after a disaster to a physical machine. In the case of a virtual machine, it can be as simple as copying a file to create a new virtual machine and then spending a couple minutes configuring it.

Summary

As you can see, there are quite a few ways that virtualization can save money. Maybe not all of them are acceptable to your company, and that is the purpose of this planning. Determine what is in scope and what is out of scope before you present your proposal to management. Get buy-in as to what they will consider and what they will not consider. No two companies are going to come up with the same components, and they will cost them differently.

Proof of Concept

Once you have put together your financial justification and received approval from the proper people, you should set up a proof of concept to prove the technology works as expected. A key factor in the success of your Hyper-V project is thorough testing based on realistic scenarios, hence the term *proof of concept* (POC). Realistic scenarios require a test environment that simulates your production environment as closely as possible. In the POC, members of the planning teams can verify their assumptions, uncover deployment problems, and optimize the deployment design, as well as improve their understanding of the technology. Such activities reduce the risk of errors and minimize downtime in the production environment during and after deployment.

You can really view the POC as a smaller project of the overall virtualization project. The difference is that you will be working with a smaller subset of goals, and it will address samples of the target base instead of trying to accomplish everything all at once. Thus, you will do well to define a simple format to follow. Here is a sample outline of what you may place in your POC document:

◆ Scope

◆ Method

◆ Requirements

Each entry will be explained in more detail below.

Scope

Just as you set up a scope to define the limits of your infrastructure virtualization project, you should set up a scope to more narrowly define exactly what you need to know in order to proceed with the entire project. Whereas the scope of the overall project was designed to define the financial benefits to the company by a wide implementation, the scope of the POC should be defined to prove the technology and testing assumptions.

Your planning and vision statements from your overall project document should be carried forward into the POC document. This helps the team focus on the overall goal of the virtualization project. But from the individual technical and business problem statements, select those that are critical to the success of the overall project. Some of this intelligence will come from understanding what your executive sponsors thought were most important for the financial justification. For example, if one of the problem statements was about the amount of money to be saved on power and cooling, plan your POC to demonstrate a clearly measurable result in this area.

As you define these specific items to be attained, you will be able to define what groups of people should be involved in the testing and what sort of testing environment will be required to accomplish the goals. Document all these requirements and ensure the interested parties agree that what you are planning to do is what they are expecting.

Method

You might already have a lab environment that you plan to use for your Hyper-V POC, or maybe you need to obtain new hardware based on different hardware architecture. For example, your long-term plan may be to deploy on your standard server environment in order to obtain better utilization of that configuration. Or, you may want to use your Hyper-V hosts as larger servers in order to consolidate more virtual machines onto a single host. Regardless of your selection, it is valuable to think through your goals for the lab and its long-term purpose.

You should define your approach to set up, run, and measure the results of each proof point. This can be simple lists, but you need to ensure that all are in agreement that this is the best way to proceed. I'll provide more detail on how to measure in the next section.

What is very important is that you test on a configuration in an environment that is as close as possible to what you will have in production. This ensures that results can be easily mapped to the financial justifications you developed earlier.

Requirements

The requirements section of your POC document drives the activities of the people involved in this project. You will need to define, in detail, what you want to accomplish, how you propose to accomplish it, how it is to be measured to declare success, and who is responsible. A sample worksheet for each proof point may look something like Table 6.5.

TABLE 6.5: Proof requirements

ENTRY	DESCRIPTION
Proof title	Insert a brief title to be used for tracking purposes.
Description	Add a description of the requirement to be proven. Make it understandable to both technical people and businesspeople.
Objective	Relate the objective to specific goals and problem statements made in the overall document. If you cannot relate it to specific goals or problem statements, it does not belong in the proof of concept.
Author	Provide the name of the person who wrote this proof requirement. This person may need to be consulted by the tester if there are questions on the objective or how it is to be attained.
Method of proof	Describe how this proof will be accomplished. This often is a demonstration of the capability, but it could be the output of a report, a nonteam member performing the activity, or any other method.
Acceptance criteria	Define the exact steps that need to be performed to prove this requirement. This could also define a specific output that is expected.
Definition of success	Define how the success will be objectively measured. For example, if you stated you would reduce power consumption, record the specific before and after results.
Status	Keep track of the status by using a simple red, yellow, or green measurement for the proof. Red — not started or is having an undefined problem. Yellow — in process, no critical issues. Green — completed.
Blockers	Whenever a proof requirement is in a Red or Yellow state, document the reason why. This should contain a history of what has occurred for the team to carry out the full project.

TABLE 6.5: Proof requirements *(CONTINUED)*

ENTRY	DESCRIPTION
Completion date	Enter the expected date of completing this proof requirement.
Owner	Name the person who is responsible for seeing that this proof requirement is successful. Achieving the proof may require working with others, but this is the person who will see that it gets done.

One of these proof requirements entries should be completed for each proof point. At least on a weekly basis, the project team should review the status of all proof requirements to ensure the project is tracking according to plan.

The Bottom Line

Defining the scope of your project   Projects often tend to take on a larger number of require- ments if the end goals are not carefully defined. One of best ways to protect against project creep is to define the specific problems that are to be solved.

Master It   Define two classes of specific problems to be addressed by a project. Give an example of each.

Discovering what you have to work with   Before you can start a successful project, you need to know what you have to work with. For an infrastructure virtualization project, you need to be able to identify which physical machines are good candidates for virtualization.

Master It   List some of the capabilities of the Microsoft Assessment and Planning Toolkit that make it a key tool for taking an inventory of your environment to determine virtualiza- tion candidates.

Assessing what you can accomplish with your resources   Once you have discovered what you have in your environment, you can make better judgment calls about which physical machines should be moved first into a virtual environment. This requires an understanding of your specific business goals defined in the envisioning phase.

Master It   List some of the ways you could decide which physical machines to select for virtualization and why you might use each method.

Financially justifying a virtualization project   If you cannot prove that your project saves the company money or brings in significantly more money than it costs to implement, it generally does not make sense to proceed. Virtualizing an infrastructure is one method that often proves a return on the investment in a very short period of time.

Master It   List some ways that virtualization can save expenditures now or in the future.

Part 2

Microsoft Application Virtualization

Chapter 7

Understanding Microsoft Application Virtualization and Streaming

Businesses run on applications. Networks, servers, laptops, and desktops all exist to bring applications to users, which ultimately make users more productive. Independent of the computing model, whether server-based or client-based, if businesses can find a centralized way to make applications simpler, accessible, and stable, they can add much value to their bottom line. Microsoft Application Virtualization (App-V) is a way to realize these benefits.

In this chapter you will learn to:

◆ Understand and apply App-V terminology

◆ Learn the core benefits of App-V

◆ Set up an App-V environment where applications will be provisioned to users based on Active Directory group membership

Microsoft Application Virtualization Terminology

App-V is a relatively new technological paradigm, and new language is needed to describe its components and features. Here are some of the important components discussed in this chapter:

App-V ADM Template   A Group Policy template with which an administrator can control the permissions, interface, and communication settings of client machines.

Active Upgrade   The process whereby a user has the ability to shut down an application and, upon next launch, the application is updated by streaming the block-level differences between the updated application package and the older version of the package. This assists in ensuring a homogenous and predictable application environment.

Application Source Root   A Registry setting that controls from where the App-V client should stream the application package. You can set this via the App-V ADM template. The Application Source Root (ASR) overrides any settings in the .osd file, which is defined below.

App-V Client   The client component of App-V that is locally installed on the desktop that translates the SFT file into a locally executed application. The client also handles publishing refresh requests, which are defined below.

Content Share A location in a streaming scenario where the various application packages are stored.

Dynamic Suite Composition At times two virtual applications may require a direct method of communication to each other. In this scenario a new feature called Dynamic Suite Composition (DSC) will dynamically compose a single virtual environment for two separate applications.

App-V Management Console A console typically residing on the Management Server with which an administrator can perform functions such as creating new application records, determining application permissions, performing active upgrade tasks, reporting, and licensing. The App-V Management Console connects to the Management Server over HTTP or HTTPS.

Management Server A server that performs administrative functions such as publishing, inventorying, and controlling access to virtual applications. The Management Server acts as an intermediary between the App-V clients and the SQL database, which houses all administrative settings.

Mount Point Drive A drive letter created by the App-V client installer that acts as a redirector to a local virtual application cache file. The default drive assignment is Q. If a Q drive already exists on the client machine, then the next alphabetically available letter will be chosen. Note that this is not a true partition and the users have no access. The requirement is a byproduct of the process in which App-V virtualizes applications.

Microsoft Application Virtualization for Remote Desktop Services App-V for RDS can offer the same benefits realized in an App-V desktop environment in a server-based computing model. App-V for RDS can help consolidate Remote Desktop Services servers or Citrix servers that are currently being siloed for application coexistence issues.

Minimum Launch Threshold When sequencing an application, the Sequencer watches the launch and use of an application. The files, Registry keys, and other application components that are touched during that launch are marked as more important to the application launch and are defined as the minimum launch threshold. In a streaming scenario this allows the user to become productive much faster because the application will launch with this minimum launch threshold. Applications that are 2 gigabytes in size may require only 80–100 megabytes on initial stream for the application to launch.

OSD File An XML-based file that defines how to access the virtual application package and how it will behave. A detailed explanation of the Open Software Description (OSD) contents and customizations is provided in Chapter 9.

Publishing Refresh Request A process whereby the App-V client requests a list of applications to which the user is entitled from the Management Server. Once the client receives this entitlement information, the corresponding application icons are downloaded and displayed on the user's computer.

Sequencer A packaging utility with which virtual applications are created. Sequencer works by actively watching and capturing install and post-install configurations of an application and creates a virtual application from that information.

SFT File A file which stores all virtual application assets such as virtual files and virtual Registry settings. SFT is an abbreviation of Softricity, the company acquired by Microsoft which developed App-V's underlying technology.

Benefits of Application Virtualization

App-V technology is based on an acquisition in July of 2006 of Softricity, Inc. Softricity was a pioneer of virtualization at the application level and had been developing the software since 2001. Since the acquisition, Microsoft has greatly matured the product in many areas such as globalization/localization, security, and scalability.

At its core, application virtualization is a way of decoupling an application from an operating system, which enables it to run locally on a device without being installed. During the decoupling process all application assets such as files, Registry information, and COM/DCOM namespaces are monitored, translated, and copied into the SFT file. During this monitoring, the application dependencies, such as a specific version of the Java Runtime Environment or Oracle client, are also monitored. Since the application now has all it needs, it can run across your environment more reliably because correctly configured and installed dependencies are no longer a requirement.

Simplifying Your Applications

Many help desk incidents are caused not by applications not running well on a particular piece of hardware but often by software installs overwriting and contending for files and settings. You can verify this by taking an application that is not running well and installing it on a fresh copy of an operating system. It will usually work fine when the variables are reduced. Knowing this, many organizations undergo rigorous application regression testing processes to ensure a stable deployment.

Application regression testing is the process of testing software installations against other software installations to ensure that all combinations work well together. Application X can work fine until application Y is installed. Worse is that X and Y can work fine when remediated until Z is installed. When an organization has hundreds of applications, the complexity of this process can increase by orders of magnitude very quickly.

App-V addresses these issues by isolating applications from each other. Each virtual application has the resources it needs contained in its virtual environment. Figure 7.1 shows a scenario where two normally conflicting applications can run without problems at the same time when each has its own resources. Application X can write a Registry value it requires in its virtual Registry and Y can write a different value, and each will see only its own. The same holds true with files and directories. Application X can copy a file named foo.dll to C:\windows\system32\ in its virtual filesystem, and application Y can copy a different version of foo.dll to its C:\windows\system32\ without stomping on application X's version.

FIGURE 7.1
Application isolation

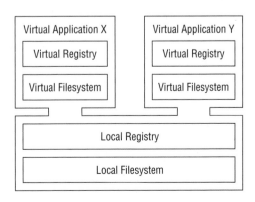

The reduction or elimination of regression testing is a great motivator to explore application virtualization. When an application has all it needs within its virtual environment, it becomes resilient to changes in the local operating system and in software installed on the same device. This removes many of the challenges of installing applications in modern operating systems, which are designed as a canvas to allow applications to interact with each other but lack prescriptive rules defining an acceptable way to interact. For instance, creating a single global Registry creates an easy way for developers to access an operating system model. What traditionally has been a sticking point is that operating systems don't have an *application model*. Since operating systems don't have enforced application models (some mobile OSes come close), developers have the freedom to place user-state information in nonstandard places. Line of business (LOB) applications have a much greater tendency not to code to best practices, because they are sometimes written internally in an organization or by a highly specialized independent software vendor. These LOB applications are the lifeblood of most of today's organizations. When a user undocks a toolbar to a new location and exits the application, for example, that setting should be written to the user's profile, if the developer is following Microsoft's best practices. What is common, however, is that this setting is written to an `.ini` file that is placed parallel to the executable in `%programfiles%\<appname>`. This seemingly insignificant development choice has several repercussions:

◆ When the next user logs in and launches the application, they will see the previous user's settings. This mixing of user states is particularly an issue in a multiuser environment such as one based on a Microsoft Remote Desktop Services server or Citrix XenApp server.

◆ This application would require the user to have local administrator privileges because it writes to a folder that is protected from a standard user.

◆ Backing up or migrating this user state will require specific steps for this application. Simply backing up this user's profile and restoring it will not migrate this setting to another OS instance because it is now effectively glued to this OS.

Microsoft Application Virtualization (App-V) works to alleviate this type of issue by creating a hard delineation between the user state and an immutable application state, which forces any application into an application model. When a user undocks a toolbar and the application attempts to write that setting to a nonstandard location, App-V intercepts that write and forces it into that application's virtual Registry in the user's Windows profile.

Figure 7.2 illustrates how App-V can often solve a problem many application deployment administrators contend with daily — making legacy coded applications run in a Least-privileged User Account (LUA) environment.

Since the `.ini` file is written to `%programfiles%\<appname>` at runtime, a standard user would have no access, and this application would need to be remediated to run properly. The typical outcome is a script or policy that loosens the local security in either the Registry or the filesystem to accommodate the misbehaving application. With Microsoft App-V the user needs no such access to the actual filesystem location because the `.ini` writes are abstracted and forced into the user's profile, giving that user a unique view into the application. The packaging administrator needs no special knowledge of the application to make this happen because it is a result of the packaging process of App-V.

FIGURE 7.2
Virtual apps can often run without local admin rights.

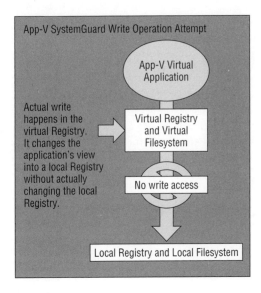

Stabilizing Applications

A large part of an organization's IT spend is in managing application life cycles. Whether the life cycles are explicitly defined or not, all organizations deploy, update, support, and terminate applications. Virtualizing your applications can help stabilize and minimize effort at every stage. Figure 7.3 shows the life cycle of a typical application.

FIGURE 7.3
Application life cycle

DEPLOYING VIRTUAL APPLICATIONS

When deploying a virtual application, your considerations are minimized in that the virtual application package contains all of the assets it requires to run, such as middleware, ODBC driver settings, and other dependencies. It is not necessary for the administrator to check the target machine for the correct version of the Java Runtime Environment because it can be embedded with the application itself. This essentially creates fewer "moving parts" with which issues can arise. If you're using a streaming deployment method, a virtual application can be tied to users via Active Directory, enabling a dynamic deployment where applications are turned effectively into network services and users can access their applications from any computer. These types of scenarios with instant provisioning are now possible since with virtual applications there is no danger of contaminating a machine with an application that will break an incompatible application.

UPDATING VIRTUAL APPLICATIONS

Updating virtual applications can happen in several ways depending on the deployment method chosen. A discussion of deployment and architectural considerations is the focus of Chapter 8. If you're using streaming with App-V, applications can be updated seamlessly across an organization. When a user launches an application, the App-V client checks the server for an updated package. If it finds an update, it will stream down the block-level changes and update the application. Nonvirtualized application updates often require reboots, which could require scheduling with end users, which in turn would require extra reporting on which devices were updated for compliancy. In an App-V scenario, those reboots are preprocessed into the streaming package, thus obviating the need to schedule reboots. It is possible to apply important updates during work hours instead of leaving a security hotfix for an application until the evening, when most updating typically occurs.

SUPPORTING VIRTUAL APPLICATIONS

The support phase of an application's life cycle is typically the most costly for an enterprise for several reasons, the foremost being the downtime for the end user. An unproductive end user calls the help desk, which then may have to dispatch a deskside technician. This costs the enterprise three employees to resolve the issue. The deskside technician can spend much time poring through the user's setting and application state to determine the cause of failure. When the application is virtual, the application is much more resilient to previous and subsequent installs of incompatible software on that computer. What is very likely is that the duration of the support calls will be much shorter in length, and the first tier of the help desk can usually solve most application issues.

For instance, the user of an App-V application can change the look and feel of their application at will and can possibly create a situation where the application is nonfunctional just as easily as can a user with a locally installed application. The remediation path from a help desk perspective is much different than with a local installation. In the user's context a help desk technician can execute the following command line:

```
SFTMIME REPAIR APP:<appname>
```

This command will delete this user's state for this particular application and revert to the original known-good state in the same manner as reverting to an earlier snapshot of a virtual machine. It may be desirable to allow users to self-repair their application by either giving them access to an App-V client console or creating a script to allow them to reset their application state at will. However, giving users access to do this without proper training can lead to inadvertent loss of their application settings.

From a supportability standpoint, a limitation of App-V is the complexity of troubleshooting an application when it does not work on a particular group of computers in an environment. When packaging a virtual application the engineer can make assumptions about the environment to which the virtual application will be deployed. For example, if the engineer assumes that all machines in a specific domain have a certain ODBC driver configured locally, then it is not necessary to include this ODBC driver in the virtual package. However, if there is a case where a machine does not contain this driver, the application may fail to connect to its backend database. A power user not familiar with App-V may look for the application in the filesystem and Registry and will not find the files and keys because they are in a cache in the Windows All Users profile. Even more puzzling will be that tools such as Sysinternals's Process Monitor will not natively have a view into the virtual filesystem or virtual Registry to discover that the ODBC connection is not configured on the power user's PC.

APP-V WITH SYSINTERNALS PROCESS MONITOR

The latest version of Sysinternals Process Monitor can have a view into the virtual Registry on Vista 32-bit and Server 2008 32-bit if started with the command-line option /HookRegistry.

Chapter 9 covers advanced troubleshooting and remediation techniques.

TERMINATING VIRTUAL APPLICATIONS

Many organizations terminate application X at the end of its life only through the attrition of hardware. Removing applications that are no longer used can be a large task, and it usually needs to be coordinated with the help desk to field the calls for the applications that are left nonfunctional. The issue is that a natively installed application Y may use shared resources such as a DLL or COM object that was a casualty of the removal process. This reluctance to terminate applications can lead to costly over-licensing and bloated Registries and filesystems. In an App-V scenario, an administrator has two choices to decommission an application: either clear a check box on the Application Virtualization server to disable the application enterprisewide for everyone or remove a particular user from an Active Directory group that gives them access to the virtual application. That user's access to the application is removed the next time the App-V client completes a publishing refresh request, which is when the client contacts the server to verify entitlement to a particular application. Essentially with a check box or AD group membership change, you remove the application enterprisewide from all desktops but do not touch any files or Registry entries that could impact other applications.

APPLICATION AGILITY

Disabling an application enterprisewide that has a security vulnerability is quick and painless with virtual applications.

Application Accessibility

One of the greatest advantages of the Internet is the ability to access websites and online profiles from anywhere and at any time. Mobile knowledge workers expect their applications, data, and user state to always be accessible. If a user's machine malfunctions, the user can go to a neighboring machine and expect access to the same web applications and online profiles. This paradigm is possible for any application once it is sequenced with App-V but with the added benefit that App-V applications can be made available offline. If the user is connecting to a Remote Desktop Services server, the user's applications will be streamed to that server in real time.

In version 4.5 of App-V, Microsoft introduced support for Internet-facing scenarios. This means that both client and server are hardened from a security perspective to the level where they may exist on untrusted networks and securely communicate, providing an organization with an infrastructure where on-demand applications over the Internet are possible. A Public Key Infrastructure (PKI) is required for this level of functionality.

In versions prior to 4.5 the roles of the Management Server and Streaming Server were intertwined and had to be installed on the same server. This led to scalability issues where either users at remote offices would need to stream applications across the WAN or the administrator would need to place another independently managed App-V server at each location. These two roles have been separated in versions 4.5 and later to enable streaming from a content source local to each branch office, while still having the benefit of centrally managing access and policy. End users at remote offices can now stream their applications from many local client transport types such as UNC/SMB, HTTP/S, and RTSP/S.

Microsoft Application Virtualization Components

The Microsoft App-V solution consists of several major components:

- Application Virtualization Client
- Application Virtualization Management Server
- Application Virtualization Management Console
- Application Virtualization Data Store
- Application Virtualization Management Web Service
- Application Virtualization Streaming Server
- Application Virtualization Sequencer

To obtain the installers for App-V you may download them via MSDN, Microsoft Volume Licensing Services (MVLS), or TechNet by locating Microsoft Desktop Optimization Pack 2009 (x86 and x64) — DVD (English).

Application Virtualization Client Details and Installation

The App-V client can be configured in many ways depending on the chosen architecture. Microsoft has released an ADM template that lets an administrator centrally control the behavior of the App-V client via a Group Policy Object (GPO). Two of the basic ways of configuring the client are the default online mode and standalone mode. In the default mode, applications are dynamically provisioned to end users via a Management Server. In standalone mode, a virtual application still runs in a virtual environment, but it is deployed via an Windows Installer file (MSI). Standalone mode is useful when the device is never or rarely connected to the corporate network or in very-low-bandwidth situations where delivering the application via DVD or USB drive is desirable. To install the client in standalone mode use the following command line:

```
setup.exe /v"MSIDEPLOYMENT=TRUE"
```

The App-V client creates a virtual environment for the application. This environment can consist of the following components:

Virtual COM/DCOM   This keeps COM and DCOM calls from conflicting. If you require interaction with the local operating system, you may use the `ALLOW_LOCAL_INTERACTION` tag in the `.osd` file. This will create a COM object in the global namespace.

Global Virtual Filesystem   This filesystem is physically located in a shared cache file on the local machine's public-user profile to which the client redirects application calls from a virtual application process to mimic the file actually existing in the local filesystem.

User-Specific Virtual Filesystem   This is where the user's personalizations to the application are stored. By default these are stored per user and per application in the user's Windows profile.

Virtual Services   Some client applications, such as a record-locking service, install and require services to run. Some services cannot be virtualized in App-V, such as those that rely on 16-bit COM processing and those that rely on environmental variables during the install.

Virtual Registry   This is the skeletal hierarchy of the Registry that was created or touched during the sequencing of the application. The application will look here first for keys. If the keys are not found, the application will fall through to the local Registry to look for the key.

All of these components of the virtual environment act as a translator that can translate the contents of the `.sft` file into a usable application.

Several manageability features are included with the client, which enable virtual applications to be inventoried and monitored. When a virtual application runs on a local machine, the application does not leave a footprint in the local Registry, nor does it register itself with Programs and Features or Add/Remove Programs, so alternate methods of inventorying are required. With App-V 4.5 Microsoft introduced a WMI provider that can query inventory and metering information targeting virtual applications. The classes are located in the WMI `root\microsoft\appvirt\client` namespace and can be queried using PowerShell, VBScript, or directly using `WBEMTest` from a command prompt. In addition, the App-V client has Watson and event log support.

In the following scenario we will simulate a proof of concept to illustrate the steps of installing a streaming environment where we will install and configure common components and stream and launch the application on a client computer. Completing this scenario entirely on virtual machines is encouraged because it will make things easier since two machines are required (three if you want to package your own application in Chapter 8) and also allow you to revert to an earlier state when necessary. Both machines should be configured with IP addresses on the same subnet.

◆   The first machine (with a hostname of App-V) will contain the server components and should be either Microsoft Windows Server 2003/R2 or Microsoft Windows Server 2008/R2 with 1.5 GB of RAM and 20 GB of free hard disk space with all the latest patches installed. Active Directory services should be available.

◆ The second machine will act as a client and should be Windows XP 32-bit, Vista 32-bit, or Windows 7 32-bit with 1–2 GB of RAM and 10 GB of free hard disk space with all the latest patches installed.

Chapter 8 includes detailed instructions on packaging techniques, including packaging your own application and streaming using the infrastructure installed in this chapter. In Chapter 8 another machine will be required to package your own application. The following are required specifications for your Sequencer (packaging) machine.

◆ The Sequencer machine should use the same operating system as your client machine with 1–2 GB of RAM and 10 GB of free hard disk space patched to current with a separate 5GB partition designated as Q:.

You should be familiar with Microsoft Windows (XP, Vista, or Windows 7), Microsoft Active Directory, Microsoft Internet Information Server 7 (IIS), and Microsoft Windows Server 2008.

INSTALLING THE APP-V CLIENT

Install the App-V client on the Windows client machine as follows:

1. Copy the setup files for the App-V client locally and run `setup.exe`.

2. On the Welcome screen click Next.

3. Read and accept the license agreement and click Next.

4. On the Microsoft Update Opt In dialog box, select Use Microsoft Update When I Check For Updates.

5. On the Setup Type dialog box, click Custom and then Next.

6. On the Destination Folder dialog box, click Next.

7. On the Application Virtualization Data Location screen, you are presented with several options (see Figure 7.4).

FIGURE 7.4
Data location

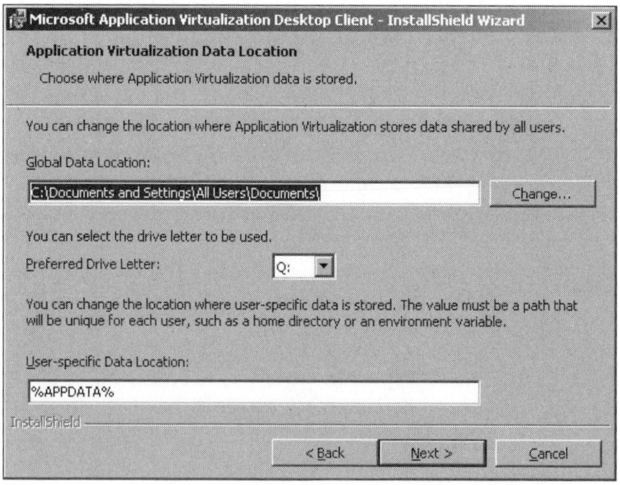

The Global Data Location is a single location where all virtual applications on a computer are stored in an immutable state. This folder must be on a local drive and accessible to all users who will log in to this machine. The preferred drive letter is a logical mount point on the client and is a pointer to a local cache in the Global Data Location. The User-Specific Data Location is where the user's application state is located. This can be a network share to allow the user state to roam with the user. You should test to determine the size because the size of user states can vary widely across applications, and it could become too large to roam and lead to decreased user satisfaction.

On the Application Virtualization Data Location screen, click Next.

8. On the Cache Size Settings screen, two options are available (see Figure 7.5).

FIGURE 7.5
Cache Size Settings

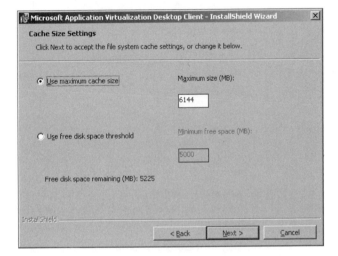

If you choose Use Maximum Cache Size, the cache size will be allowed to grow only to that amount. If it reaches that amount, an algorithm based on least recently used will flush out the application used the least to create more space for the newly streamed application. Sizing your cache really depends on the applications expected to run on this machine. If this is a heavy CAD or multimedia machine, size this cache accordingly. Keep in mind that App-V handles cache in such a way that if the application streams only the minimum launch threshold (which can be as little as 5 percent of the app), the total amount of space (100 percent) is allocated in cache. If you choose Use Free Disk Space Threshold, the cache will grow until the disk is nearly full except for the amount of space selected in this box. If the cache size is set small, applications will be flushed from the cache more frequently. Make your selection and click Next.

9. In the Runtime Package Policy Configuration screen, there are several options controlling the behavior of the client (see Figure 7.6). These can also be controlled via a Microsoft-provided ADM Group Policy template.

◆ The first setting defines the Application Source Root (ASR). The ASR is a Registry setting indicating from where the App-V client should stream the package. The ASR overrides any settings in the `.osd` file. The Require User Authorization Even When

Cached setting should be disabled in standalone mode when it is not desirable to authenticate the user when the MSI has precached the application.

♦ Allow Streaming From File permits the user to stream from a local `.sft` file, perhaps on the desktop, to populate the App-V application cache. This can be useful in low-bandwidth situations where users may be mailed a DVD containing an `.sft` file.

♦ The Auto Load functions define if and how background streaming will take place. Background streaming streams 100 percent of the application in the background after the minimum launch threshold has streamed, even if the user never uses those functions. Auto loading is ideal for mobile devices such as laptops. If a laptop were to stream only the minimum launch threshold and subsequently go offline, the application would be in an unpredictable state if it is only partially cached. For mobile devices a best practice is to auto load all applications to 100 percent. On Launch waits for the user to launch the application and at that point streams 100 percent of the application.

♦ On Login will auto load all of an application upon user login.

♦ On Publishing Refresh will auto load all of an application when a publishing refresh request takes place.

♦ Selecting Do Not Automatically Load Applications will only stream the minimum launch threshold upon the user launching an application. This setting is good for highly connected devices because they may never need 100 percent of the application local since they can stream anytime they need a new block. This can prevent unnecessary network traffic.

♦ Automatically Load Previously Used Applications auto loads only the applications that the user has actually used. This can save bandwidth because the user may not need the whole application if they have never used it.

♦ The most common setting for mobile devices is the Automatically Load All Applications.

Make your selection and click Next.

FIGURE 7.6
Runtime Package Policy
Configuration

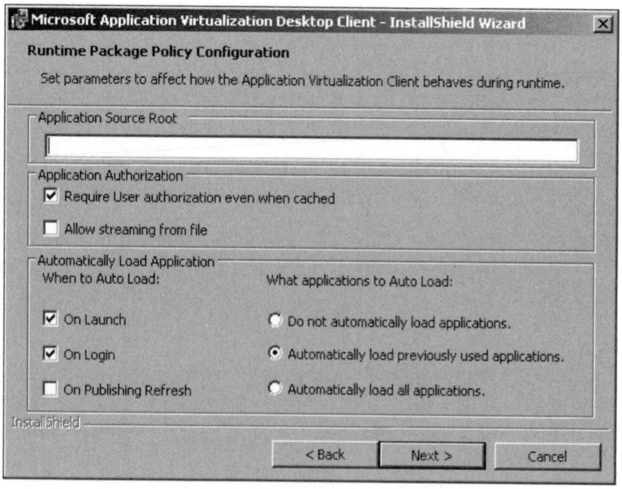

10. The Publishing Server dialog box is where we instruct this client as to which Management Server will perform its publishing refresh request. See Figure 7.7.

Check the Set Up A Publishing Server Now check box. Type in **My App-V Server** or any friendly but useful name in the Display Name field. From the Type combo box select Application Virtualization Server. In the Host Name field type **app-v**. Leave the port at 554. Leave the Automatically Contact This Server To Update Settings When A User Logs In check box checked. This will perform a publishing refresh request at every user login. Click Next.

FIGURE 7.7
Publishing Server
dialog box

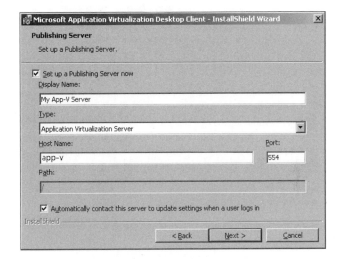

11. On the Ready To Install The Program dialog box, click Install.

12. On the InstallShield Wizard Completed dialog box, click Finish.

13. Reboot the machine even if not prompted to do so.

This concludes the installation and configuration of the client.

Application Virtualization Server Components, Details, and Installation

One of the most useful features of an App-V environment is the ability of an application to be tied to a person rather than to a device. With an App-V Management Server, applications can be available immediately, without an install, on any networked machine in an enterprise based on a user's Active Directory group membership. An App-V Management Server is the quickest way to enable this function. The capabilities to make such a solution possible include responding to publishing refresh requests, license tracking, active upgrade, application policies, and a reporting engine.

PUBLISH REFRESH REQUEST

Central to the end-user experience is the concept of a publishing refresh request. The following is a common scenario: A user logs on or a preset time interval passes on a workstation, application shortcuts appear on the desktop, the user clicks the icon, the minimum launch threshold is streamed, and the application is launched. Depending on network speed, this process can take only seconds. Figure 7.8 is a look into what is actually happening behind the scenes.

FIGURE 7.8
Publishing refresh request process

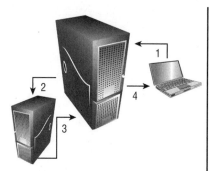

1. **Client**—User logs in and initiates a publishing refresh request.
2. **Management Server**—Requests XML cache, policies, and allowed application IDs from database.
3. **SQL**—Returns XML cache, policies, and application IDs.
4. **Management Server**—An XML file containing a list of allowed applications is returned to the user.

The client initiates a refresh either by user login or by a preset time period. You can set this time either manually in the App-V client console, by the App-V Group Policy admin template, or by modifying the Registry key `Period` in `HKLM\SOFTWARE\Microsoft\SoftGrid\4.5\Client\DC Servers\<servername>` to an integer decimal value mapping to the number of minutes between requests. A publishing request carries a Kerberos service ticket, which includes the SID of the security groups of which this user is a member. App-V compares this list against the application records configured in the database to determine which apps this user is entitled to run.

Once the request has been made to the Management Server, the server will check to see if there is an existing copy of an App-V XML cache. The XML cache contains a list of all App-V applications, file type associations, and policies. If the local copy of the cache has timed out, the Management Server will refresh its data from the SQL database and query using the SIDs from the Kerberos service ticket to get the specific user's application list. The Management Server uses all this information to create a user-specific XML document and sends this document back to the user who initiated the publishing request. The client then uses this document to download and place icons, `.osd` files, and file type associations, readying the user for launch. Then, when the user launches an application, the minimum launch threshold of the application (5–40 percent of an application's total package size) is downloaded, and the user can begin using the application. At this point the auto loading settings take over and background streaming can begin.

INSTALL THE APP-V MANAGEMENT SERVER

Before installing the server it is important to understand a basic App-V architecture. We will be installing all backend components on a single server, and a client machine with the App-V client will be installed and configured for streaming, as shown in Figure 7.9.

Advanced configuration options are discussed in depth in Chapter 9. For this scenario you will need the following:

◆ A Microsoft Windows Server 2008 with all current patches and with access to Active Directory services. Name this machine **app-v**. Server 2003 will work, but the instructions for IIS 6 will vary.

◆ An available SQL Server and an account with sysadmin rights. In this chapter we assume that no SQL Server is available on your network, so we will need to install SQL Express 2005 as one of the first steps.

FIGURE 7.9
A basic App-V streaming
environment

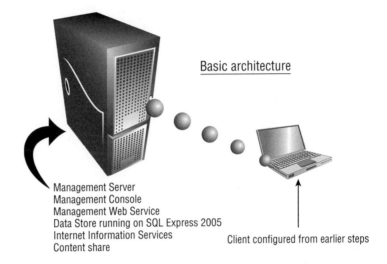

On the server we'll install the Management Service, Management Console, Management Web Service, IIS, SQL Express 2005, and the content share. Download the App-V installers from MSDN, TechNet, or Microsoft Volume Licensing Services (MVLS) by searching for Microsoft Desktop Optimization Pack 2009. Extract or mount the .iso image in Windows, and copy the entire folder <root>\App-V\Installers\Server\Management to the desktop of the server.

CONFIGURE THE SERVER OPERATING SYSTEM

In this section we'll prepare the environment to install the App-V server. In Active Directory Users and Computers, perform the following steps (see Figure 7.10):

FIGURE 7.10
Active Directory objects

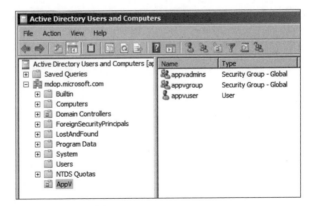

1. Create a new organizational unit called AppV, and inside this OU create the following three objects.

2. Create a user named appvuser. This will be the test user who will run the virtual applications.

3. Create a global security group named appvgroup; place the appvuser user account created in the previous step into this group. This will be the group in the provider policy that will

be allowed to run virtual applications if any are assigned. Typically organizations use the Domain Users group here because they want all domain users to have the ability to receive a virtual application should an administrator choose to deploy an application to the user.

4. Create a global security group named appvadmins, and place appvuser in this group also. This group will be allowed to connect to the database through the Management console for administrative purposes.

5. Create a folder named `c:\content`; then share it with the name content and give appvuser owner or co-owner permissions. This is where we will place our virtual applications once sequenced.

In this section we will install and configure Internet Information Services 7 (IIS7):

1. Open Server Manager (Start ➤ All Programs ➤ Administrative Tools ➤ Server Manager).

2. Right-click the Roles node and click Add Roles.

3. In the Add Roles Wizard click Next.

4. In the Select Server Roles screen check the Web Server (IIS) box. Click Install. During the install a dialog box may appear asking if you want to add features required for Web Server (IIS). Click Add Required Features.

5. In the Web Server (IIS) screen click Next.

6. In the Select Role Services screen, select the following (see Figure 7.11).

FIGURE 7.11
IIS role services

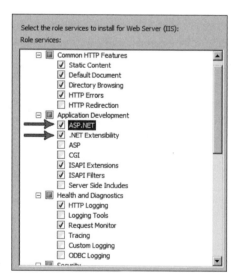

- ◆ ASP.NET
- ◆ If an Add Roles Wizard appears, click Add Required Role Services.
- ◆ NET Extensibility (Do not click Install yet.)

7. Configure IIS by selecting the following options in addition to the defaults (see Figure 7.12).

◆ Windows Authentication

◆ IIS Management Scripts and Tools

FIGURE 7.12
IIS role services
continued

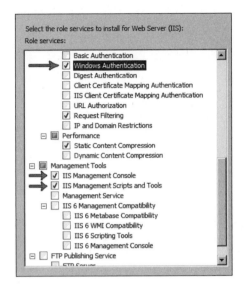

8. Check IIS Management Console if it is not already checked.

9. Click Install to complete the install of IIS.

10. On the Confirm Installation Selections screen, confirm that all changes above are reflected in the list. Click Install.

IIS is now configured for App-V.

INSTALL AND CONFIGURE SQL EXPRESS 2005

In this section we will install and configure SQL Express 2005. Follow the steps closely because it can be difficult to later troubleshoot a mistake made here.

1. Download SQL Server 2005 Express Edition SP2 (named SQLEXPR32.exe) from Microsoft and launch the installer from the server. Follow these steps closely.

2. Accept the EULA and click Next.

3. Install any prerequisites and click Next.

4. On the welcome screen click Next.

5. On the System Configuration Check screen, resolve any errors found on the server and restart the installation if needed. Click Next.

6. Enter a name and company, leaving the Hide Advanced Configuration options checked.

7. On the Feature Selection screen, leave the default settings and click Next.

8. On the Authentication Mode screen, be sure Windows Authentication Mode is selected. Click Next.

9. On the Configuration Options screen, check the Enable User Instances box and also the Add User To The SQL Server Administrator role. Click Next.

10. On the Error And Usage Report Settings screen, click Next.

11. On the Ready To Install screen, click Install.

12. On the Setup Progress screen, be sure all products installed successfully, and click Next.

13. On the Completing Microsoft SQL Server 2005 Setup screen, click Finish.

14. To configure SQL Server to work with App-V, open SQL Server Configuration Manager (Start ➢ All Programs ➢ Microsoft SQL Server 2005) and expand the SQL Server 2005 Network Configuration node. Highlight Protocols For SQLEXPRESS, and enable all protocols listed. Under the SQL Native Client Configuration node, highlight Protocols and again enable all that are listed. Highlight the SQL Server 2005 Services node, and in the right-side pane right-click SQL Server (SQLEXPRESS) and click Restart. Once the restart is complete, close SQL Server Configuration Manager.

15. Launch SQL Server Surface Area Configuration (Start ➢ All Programs ➢ Microsoft SQL Server 2005), and select Surface Area Configuration For Services And Connections. Expand SQLEXPRESS ➢ Database Engine ➢ Remote Connections and ensure that both Local And Remote Connections and Using Both TCP/IP And Named Pipes are selected. Click OK on the Connection Settings Change Alert message box.

16. Back on the opening screen of Surface Area Configuration, click the Surface Area Configuration For Features link.

17. Expand SQLEXPRESS ➢ Database Engine and enable CLR Integration, OLE Automation, and xp_cmdshell. Reboot the server, and be sure that the SQL Server (SQLEXPRESS) service starts after the reboot.

WARNING

The Management Service is dependent on SQL being fully started. When both are installed on the same box, SQL can take longer to load than the Management Service, so the Management Service must be manually started after a minute or two.

INSTALL AN APPLICATION VIRTUALIZATION MANAGEMENT SERVER

In this section we'll begin installing the App-V server components.

1. Launch App-V\Installers\Server\Management\setup.exe with administrative credentials by right-clicking it and selecting Run As Administrator.

2. On the Welcome screen, click Next.

3. Read the license agreement, and select the I Accept The License Terms And Conditions check box.

4. On the Microsoft Update screen, click Next.

5. On the Registering Information screen, enter registration information and click Next.

6. On the Setup Type screen, select Custom and click Next.

7. On the Custom Setup screen, note that it is possible to install only select features (see Figure 7.13). A common use is to install the Management Console on an administrator's personal workstation. The administrator can then remotely manage an App-V system. Be sure that all features are selected, and click Next.

FIGURE 7.13
Installation options

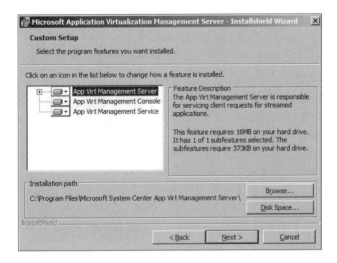

8. In the Configuration Database screen, select the APP-V\SQLEXPRESS entry and click Next (see Figure 7.14).

FIGURE 7.14
Select a database server.

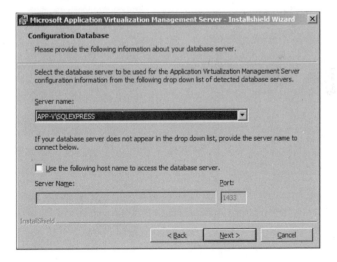

9. In the next Configuration Database screen, click the Create A New Database radio button (see Figure 7.15). If you're upgrading from a previous version of App-V, click the Use An Existing Database radio button to upgrade the older database. Click Next.

FIGURE 7.15
Create a new database.

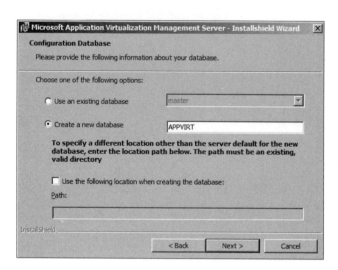

10. On the Connection Security Mode screen, click Next. In an Internet-facing scenario, you would deploy certificates using a Public Key Infrastructure (PKI). This scenario will not use Internet-facing servers or clients.

11. On the TCP Port Configuration screen, select the Use Default Port (554) radio button and click Next.

12. On the Administrator Group screen, enter the group created in an earlier step, **appvadmins** (see Figure 7.16). This group has permission to administer the App-V Management Server. Click Next.

FIGURE 7.16
Set the App-V administrator group.

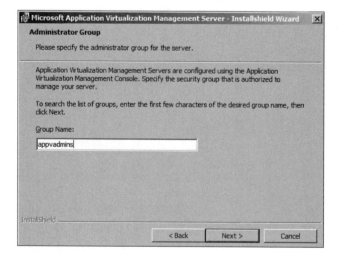

13. On the Default Provider Group screen in the Group Name text box, enter **appvgroup** (see Figure 7.17). This group has access to the App-V environment but not necessarily access to any applications. Click Next.

FIGURE 7.17

Set the App-V default provider group.

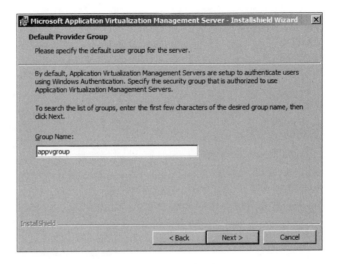

14. On the Content Path screen type **c:\content** in the Folder Name text box. This folder is where we will place our virtual application once it is sequenced and from which the IIS Server will stream the virtual apps. Click Next.

15. On the Ready To Install The Program screen, click Install.

16. On the InstallShield Wizard Completed screen, click Finish.

17. If you're prompted to restart the system, click Yes. If there is no prompt, restart the system anyway. When the system has rebooted, be sure the Application Virtualization Management Service has started.

Your Application Virtualization Management Server is now installed. Next we'll need to configure the server to manage the virtual environment.

CONFIGURE AN APPLICATION VIRTUALIZATION MANAGEMENT SERVER

Now that the server is installed, you must complete initial configuration steps.

1. Launch the Application Virtualization Management Console from Start ➤ Administrative Tools.

2. In the Web Service Host Name text box, enter **app-v**. It may be necessary to enter the fully qualified domain name (FQDN), depending on the machine's network settings. If you are connecting the Management Service via HTTPS, select the Use Secure Connection check box. Under Login Credentials click the Specify Windows Account radio button and enter the user <**domain**>**appvuser** we added to the appvadmins security group created earlier in this scenario. Click OK.

3. When the Management Console loads, right-click the top-level app-v node and click System Options. For the Default Content Path enter the UNC path **\\app-v\content**. Do not point to C:\content because that would break all imported applications.

4. Microsoft has included a default application to test the App-V install. To configure this application for initial streaming, highlight the Applications node and double-click the

Default Application record. This is where the policies can be set per application. In the OSD Path text box, enter **\\app-v\content\DefaultApp.osd** and for the Icon Path enter **\\app-v\content\DefaultApp.ico** (see Figure 7.18). These are the locations from which the clients will be instructed to download the icons and **.osd** files for this application.

FIGURE 7.18
Set the OSD and
icon paths.

5. Still in the Default Application Properties screen, switch to the Shortcuts tab and select Publish To A User's Desktop.

6. Click the File Associations tab. This is where an administrator can create or delete File Type Associations (FTAs), such as **.docx** for Microsoft Office Word 2007. By default when sequencing an application, the Sequencer software automatically detects the FTAs and will populate this list.

7. Switch to the Access Permissions tab. Be sure that appvgroup is listed. Any user in a group in this list will be entitled to use this application. Click OK.

8. Microsoft shipped App-V defaulting to secure protocols, and thus the default test application package is set to stream via secure protocols. For this scenario we will not use secure protocols, so we'll need to modify the **.osd** file for the default application to complete the streaming test. Open Windows Notepad, and open c:\content\DefaultApp.osd. Edit the CODEBASE XML tag by removing the trailing S in RTSPS and changing the port from 322 to 554, as shown in Figure 7.19. Save and close this **.osd** file.

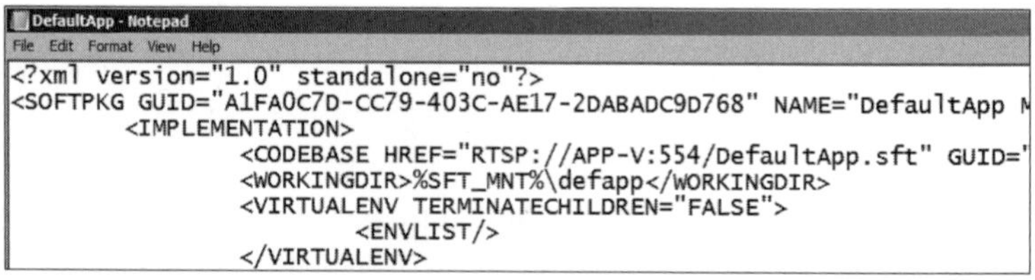

FIGURE 7.19
Modify the OSD.

```
DefaultApp - Notepad
File  Edit  Format  View  Help
<?xml version="1.0" standalone="no"?>
<SOFTPKG GUID="A1FA0C7D-CC79-403C-AE17-2DABADC9D768" NAME="DefaultApp N
        <IMPLEMENTATION>
                <CODEBASE HREF="RTSP://APP-V:554/DefaultApp.sft" GUID='
                <WORKINGDIR>%SFT_MNT%\defapp</WORKINGDIR>
                <VIRTUALENV TERMINATECHILDREN="FALSE">
                        <ENVLIST/>
                </VIRTUALENV>
```

App-V streaming over RTSP from a firewalled server requires that an inbound rule be configured on the server's host-based firewall. App-V streaming works by the client initiating contact over port 554, negotiating a high port (any port higher than 49152) for each application launched, connecting using the high port, and finally streaming the application. Perform the following to create two program rules in the Windows firewall for App-V RTSP streaming:

1. Click Start ≻ Run and enter **wf.msc**.

2. In the Actions pane, click New Rule to start the New Inbound Rule Wizard.

3. In the Rule Type screen, ensure that the Program radio button is selected, and click Next.

4. In the Program screen, select the This Program Path radio button, and browse to %ProgramFiles%\Microsoft System Center App Virt Management Server\App Virt Management Server\bin\sghwdsptr.exe. Click Next.

5. In the Action screen, select Allow The Connection and click Next.

6. In the Profile screen, be sure that all options are selected and click Next.

7. In the Name screen in the Name field, type **App-V Dispatcher Exception**, and click Finish to create the rule.

8. Create a second rule, but on the Program screen point to %ProgramFiles%\Microsoft System Center App Virt Management Server\App Virt Management Server\bin\sghwsvr.exe and name it **App-V Heavyweight Server Exception**.

Note that if streaming over high ports is undesirable for security reasons (it requires many open ports), streaming over RTSPS forces all traffic through port 322. The tradeoff is that RTSPS requires that an X.509 V3 certificate be provisioned to the App-V server and that the client trust the certificate authority (CA).

TEST THE APPLICATION VIRTUALIZATION ENVIRONMENT

Now we'll stream an application to test our environment. The following steps take place on the App-V client machine.

1. In the system tray right-click the App-V icon and click Refresh Applications (see Figure 7.20). This will initiate a publishing refresh request.

FIGURE 7.20
Initiating a publishing
refresh request

2. Look for a new icon on the desktop named Default Application (see Figure 7.21). Launch the application and notice the streaming progress indicator above the system tray. When

this reaches 100 percent it does not indicate that all of the application has streamed but indicates that 100 percent of the minimum launch threshold has streamed.

If everything is working right, you should see the splash screen in Figure 7.21.

FIGURE 7.21
Launch the Default Application.

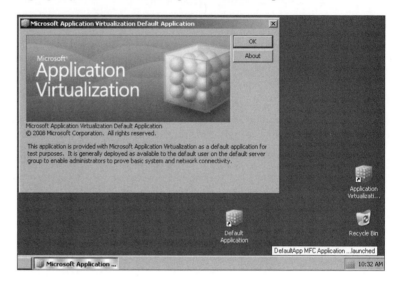

Summary

With the installation of an App-V infrastructure with streaming, many benefits are realized. Application life cycle management, quicker deployment of new applications (less regression testing), and on-demand application delivery tied to users are some of the paradigm-shifting technologies that administrators are finding attractive. Some complexity is involved in designing a great architecture, packaging the applications, and troubleshooting common application issues. This is covered in the following two chapters.

The Bottom Line

Understand and apply App-V terminology.   App-V introduces many new concepts to traditional application deployment and requires new language.

Master It   A key concept in understanding App-V streaming is the minimum launch threshold. Describe the minimum launch threshold and how this is important in a free-seating scenario.

Learn the core benefits of App-V.   App-V offers many benefits with regard to an enterprise's application life cycle. These benefits include simplifying and stabilizing your applications and at the same time making your applications more accessible.

Master It   An old version of an Oracle client needs to be deployed alongside a locally installed newer version. The user still needs the newer version for production testing purposes. How can App-V help in this scenario?

Set up an App-V environment where applications will be provisioned to users based on Active Directory group membership.   Tying applications to users rather than to computers can make sense in many situations. The simplicity of changing group membership in Active Directory and the applications appearing on users' desktops without the possibility of interfering with other applications is driving a revolution in the way modern enterprises view application deployment.

Master It   You've just provisioned both Visual Studio 2008 and AutoCAD 2009 to a user, and the user has called the help desk and complained of not yet receiving the applications. What is a likely reason the user does not have the applications?

Chapter 8

Creating Virtual Applications

To enable the isolation and on-demand streaming of applications in an App-V environment, the application must be repackaged in a process called *sequencing*. App-V includes an aptly named wizard-driven utility called App-V Sequencer. App-V Sequencer is essentially a piece of software that will actively watch an application install and detect the changes to the operating system. A virtual application package, or sequence, is different from a traditional installer, such as a setup.msi or setup.exe, in that the application will be delivered to end users in a pre-configured state ready to be used once the bits are delivered — a deafening lack of an install. Applications that require reboots no longer have to be scheduled during off hours because applications can be updated live, applications can easily be restored to the known good state originally deployed, and post-install configuration scripts or settings are greatly reduced or eliminated.

In this chapter you will learn to:

- ◆ Understand sequencing concepts
- ◆ Install and configure a Sequencer workstation
- ◆ Sequence an application with middleware
- ◆ Publish an application to users

Sequencing Concepts

Sequencing a basic application requires little or no knowledge of Windows internals. Some enterprises actually have application owners or application subject matter experts do the application configuration during the sequencing phase. That said, the most successful sequencing engineers possess the following skills:

- ◆ Knowledge of the Windows Registry, .ini files, and user profiles
- ◆ Fluency in command prompt use and working with environmental variables
- ◆ Experience troubleshooting application failures and anomalies using tools such as Microsoft/Sysinternal Procmon
- ◆ Batch file creation and VB scripting

Understanding how the virtual application operates and interacts with the operating system is critical when an application needs troubleshooting. For instance, if an application throws an error indicating it can't find the correct version of a DLL, it is helpful to know whether it is looking first in the virtual Registry or in the local Registry.

SystemGuard™

SystemGuard is a virtual environment or sandbox running on the local PC in which the virtual application or a suite of virtual applications execute. SystemGuard's function is to isolate the application from the operating system, locally installed applications, and other virtual applications where it makes sense to do so. For example, virtual applications need to be able to write to the Windows printer subsystem so a user of a virtual version of Microsoft Word can print, but the same virtual application would not have access to change a local Registry key or a local .ini file, as illustrated in Figure 8.1.

FIGURE 8.1
SystemGuard
environment

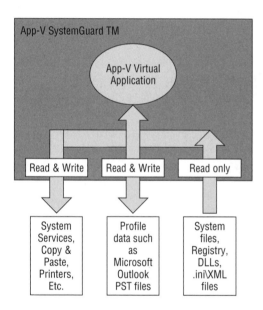

When a user makes a change within the virtual application that writes the setting to the Registry, including parts of the Registry that require elevated privileges to write to such as HKEY_LOCAL_MACHINE, SystemGuard will prevent the write to the local Registry and abstract the write to the virtual Registry located in a per-application PKG file in the user's Windows profile. The next time this virtual application requests this setting, SystemGuard will present the virtual Registry first to the virtual application. If this setting is not found in the virtual Registry, SystemGuard will allow the virtual application read-only access to the local Registry. This keeps the local Registry untouched and allows multiple virtual applications to run simultaneously by eliminating Registry conflicts.

Another benefit of this approach is in helping applications that require elevated rights at runtime to run in a Least-privileged User Account (LUA) environment. In a typical LUA environment, a packaging engineer would need to loosen file and Registry permissions to allow certain applications to run. With App-V, such loosening can often be avoided. Figure 8.2 shows how SystemGuard handles an application's attempt to write a local Registry setting to which the current user has no privileges.

FIGURE 8.2
Write operation attempt

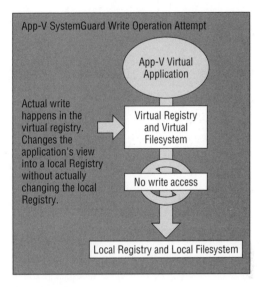

App-V SystemGuard Write Operation Attempt

App-V Virtual Application

Actual write happens in the virtual registry. Changes the application's view into a local Registry without actually changing the local Registry.

Virtual Registry and Virtual Filesystem

No write access

Local Registry and Local Filesystem

DOESN'T WINDOWS 7 HAVE VIRTUAL REGISTRY TECHNOLOGY?

Windows 7 and Vista have a form of virtual Registry capability, but it is a single virtual Registry per user for all applications. It works essentially by redirecting write attempts from HKEY_LOCAL_MACHINE\Software\<appname> to HKEY_USERS\<UserSID>_Classes\ VirtualStore\Machine\Software\<appname>. App-V virtual Registries and filesystems are unique not only per user but also per application.

Typically, virtual applications can access only operating system resources and locally installed applications. A new feature was introduced in App-V 4.5 called Dynamic Suite Composition (DSC) to address situations where you want one virtual application to be able to mutually access the virtual Registries and filesystems from another virtual application. This is accomplished by dynamically merging two SystemGuard environments, which allows two separately sequenced virtual applications to "see" each other's virtual Registries and filesystems. For example, if several virtual applications require the same middleware application such as the Java Runtime Environment, it is possible to create a parent-child relationship between virtual applications. This can benefit the sequence update process in that only one Java sequence needs to be updated, and all those sequences to which Java served as a child package would now use the updated package as opposed to putting Java in each package and updating all packages. In this scenario DSC will place both packages in the same SystemGuard environment at the application runtime. Microsoft has released a free downloadable tool for establishing these relationships called the Application Virtualization Dynamic Suite Composition Tool.

The Sequencing Life Cycle

Figure 8.3 illustrates a typical scenario for creating a virtual application for streaming.

1. The installation source directory, typically containing a Microsoft Installer file (MSI) or Setup.exe, is copied to the sequencing workstation.

2. The application installer is launched while the Sequencer software is monitoring.

3. Once the install is complete, the sequence files are created. Those file artifacts including the .SFT, .OSD, and .SPRJ files.

4. The sequenced files are then copied up to a content share.

5. From that content share virtual applications are imported into the Management Server and assigned to Active Directory global security groups.

6. Users in this group who have the App-V clients installed and configured on their PCs will then receive access to the virtual application at the next publishing refresh request and can stream the application.

FIGURE 8.3
The sequencing life cycle

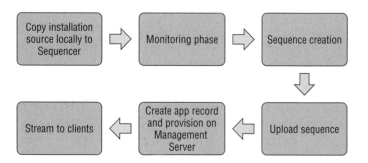

Installing and Configuring a Sequencer Workstation

Configuring a Sequencer workstation correctly is critical in creating a sequenced application correctly. A small amount of prep work during this phase can save much time later when a virtual application misbehaves.

A CLEAN WORKSTATION IMAGE

It is vitally important when sequencing to start with a machine that is very close to "vanilla." Many times sequencing engineers will attempt to use their standard corporate image, which has had many applications installed and uninstalled over time. This uninstalling of applications usually leaves the Registry and filesystem in a less than pristine state. This can be problematic during the capture process because the Sequencer software may not recognize certain changes to the system and may not add required Registry keys to the sequence. This requirement to have a clean install reinforces the benefit of using machine virtualization because rolling back changes between sequencing applications is quick and simple. If multiple sequencing engineers are working in an environment, it is very helpful to use the same image to reduce variables and troubleshooting in later phases.

SECOND PARTITION (Q: DRIVE)

On a client computer configured to run virtual applications with App-V, a virtual mount point is created when the client software is installed. This mount point is used to achieve a very high application compatibility rate. Applications installed physically have their file location paths configured by their installers to account for systems that may not have a C: drive or may resolve %programfiles% to nonstandard locations such as z:\progfiles\. When applications are delivered with no installer, as with App-V, it becomes imperative that the locations of file resources are correct. This is why a Q: drive is created — so App-V can be sure it is there. When the App-V client is installed, the mount point will default to a Q: drive. If Q: is not available, it will take the next available drive, possibly R:. Because this is in fact not a true disk partition but a pointer to a local cache located in %allusersprofile%\Documents\SoftGrid Client, users will get an access-denied message if they click the drive from Windows Explorer. To hide the App-V drive from users, see the Microsoft Knowledge Base article KB231289.

While having a mount point solves the application pathing issue, it does create an extra step during the sequencing phase. On the Sequencer machine, the Q: drive needs to be an *actual partition* because this will serve as the target drive of our application install during the capture phase.

```
Default installation path c:\program files\foo\
App-V sequencer best practice path Q:\foo.v01\foo\
```

When sequencing an application the installer usually will prompt for the installation directory. At this point you define the installation directory as one on the Q: drive.

Any .ini files or hardcoded references that the installer makes to the software install will then be directed to this mount point. For example, an installer would create a line in an .ini file that would point to Q:\foo.v01\foo\toolbarlocation.xml rather than C:\program files\app1.v01\toolbarlocation.xml. The Sequencer creates a variable called %SFT_MNT%. SystemGuard now can make calls to %SFT_MNT% regardless of the drive letter assigned by the App-V client installer. The Sequencer defines and uses %SFT_MNT%. The App-V client installer defines the %SFT_MNT% variable as Q: or whichever is the next available drive. Then the virtual application references %SFT_MNT% and gets redirected.

MACHINE RESOURCES

Sequencing is a hardware-intensive process. Many sequencing engineers prefer to use a virtual machine for this process, which has the great advantage of being able to restore to a clean machine state quickly but creates the additional overhead of an extra operating system. The Sequencer is a single-threaded application, meaning that using the latest multicore processor will not give much improvement in performance. Being an I/O-intensive application, sequencing gets its greatest boost in performance from having at least two physical disks. If two physical disks are available, relocate the %tmp%, %temp%, and the scratch directory option located in the Sequencer software in Tools ➤ Options.

GOTCHAS

One of the most important parts of sequencing is documenting the process. When it comes time to update your application, it is very helpful to know the steps taken previously because you may need to take them again. For extra points use a screen-capture utility and place the video or content in the same folder as the corresponding sequence in the content share.

If possible, not only disable but uninstall antivirus software on the sequencing machine because there is a good chance it will interfere with the capture process.

Disable disk-defragmentation software.

Add a dummy ODBC DSN on your sequencing image. If there is no dummy ODBC DSN on your sequencing image, applications that require one will not function when deployed to workstations. For more information on creating a dummy DSN, see the Microsoft Application Virtualization 4.5 Sequencing Guide located at `http://technet.microsoft.com/en-us/appvirtualization/cc843994.aspx`.

Add a dummy printer as well. Create a LaserJet 4 printer on an LPT port.

When sequencing on Vista, leave User Account Control on if you are deploying to Vista machines with UAC turned on.

INSTALLING THE SEQUENCER SOFTWARE

Now that we have the Sequencer workstation configured correctly, we can begin sequencing our first application. Though the application is simple, the process we will go through is very similar regardless of the complexity of the application. If you can sequence XML Notepad as we will now, then you should be able to sequence 80 percent or more of all applications that can be virtualized by following this process.

Here are the requirements for this scenario:

♦ A Windows XP or higher machine patched to current (if Vista or higher, leave UAC turned on if you plan to deploy to UAC-enabled clients).

♦ XP installed on the C: drive of 20 GB minimum (10 GB free) and a Q: partition of an additional 20 GB minimum (10 GB free). Minimum of 256 MB of RAM and 3 GB of RAM recommended.

♦ The installer for XML Notepad. Search Microsoft.com for the XML Notepad 2007 `.msi` download.

♦ The installer for .NET Framework 2.0 if you elect to add it to the sequence. You can find this by searching Microsoft.com for .NET Framework Version 2.0 Redistributable Package. The file name will be `dotnetfx.exe`.

♦ The `setup.exe` and `setup.msi` for the App-V Sequencer. Download the latest through TechNet, Microsoft Volume Licensing Services, or MSDN by searching from Microsoft Desktop Optimization Pack. Extract or burn the ISO file, and App-V Sequencer installers will be in `\App-V\Installers\Sequencer\`.

Here are the instructions for installing App-V Sequencer software:

1. Launch `setup.exe` from the App-V Sequencer installer folder.

2. On the Welcome To The InstallShield Wizard For Microsoft Application Virtualization Sequencer dialog box, click Next.

3. On the License Agreement dialog box, click the I Accept The Terms On The License Agreement radio button, and click Next.

4. On the destination folder dialog box, accept the default and click Next.

5. On the Ready To Install The Program dialog box, click Install.

6. On the InstallShield Wizard Completed dialog box, clear the Launch The Program check box, and click Finish.

7. Reboot the computer and log in.

Sequencing an Application

Before sequencing an application, always install the application locally without the App-V Sequencer software monitoring. This will familiarize you with the application, document any unexpected behavior, and determine whether a problem is an App-V issue or an application issue. Sequencing engineers can spend too much time troubleshooting virtual Registries when a problem exists, even when the application is locally installed.

This would be a great time to create an application install guide if one does not exist for this application.

This is also the time to make sure that any network drives are mapped. Close all other applications including Explorer windows, and under Folder And Search Options in Windows Explorer, click the View tab and check the Launch folder windows in a separate process.

If there is any middleware software that you can assume is on every client target machine already, .NET Framework 2.0, for example, you may also install that locally on the Sequencer machine. You won't want to add that to a package because the virtual application will use the locally installed .NET Framework 2.0 when it is streamed to your users. This can reduce the size of the sequence considerably.

1. Since the Sequencer machine is now configured correctly, take a snapshot or image of the machine at this time. You will be reverting to this state every time you begin sequencing a new application. We'll call this the clean state.

2. Copy XmlNotepad.msi to the desktop of your local machine.

3. Install XML Notepad 2007 locally and launch it. Watch for any anomalous behavior. If you don't have .NET Framework 2.0 installed, you'll receive an application error.

4. Revert the machine to the clean state before .NET Framework and XML Notepad 2007 were installed.

5. Copy the installer files for XML Notepad 2007 and .NET Framework 2.0 to the desktop of your Sequencer machine.

6. Create the package root folder at Q:\XMLnotpd.v01. At this step you must follow an 8.3 naming convention — meaning that before the period there are at most eight characters and after the period there are at most three characters. In our example, making this package root q:\XML Notepad 2007\ may not sequence it correctly.

7. Launch the Sequencer software by choosing Start ➤ Programs ➤ Microsoft Application Virtualization ➤ Microsoft Application Virtualization Sequencer.

8. Choose File ➤ New Package. The Sequencing Wizard opens.

Next, we'll complete the Sequencing Wizard.

1. In step 1 of 7 of the Sequencing Wizard, enter **XML_Notepad_2007** in the Package Name field, and put relevant information in the Comments section, as shown in Figure 8.4. Typical entries there are OS version and service pack level, Sequencer name, and system requirements that the virtual application needs to run on target machines. Click the Show Advanced Monitoring Options check box, and click Next.

FIGURE 8.4
Package
Information screen

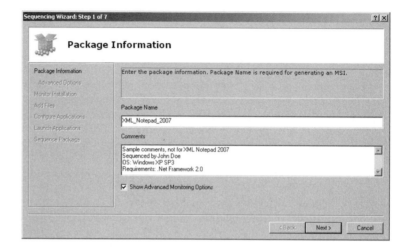

2. On step 2 of 7 of the Sequencing Wizard, leave the block size at 32 KB. Also leave both check boxes clear.

   ◆ The 4.5 App-V sequencer allows you to choose the size of the blocks that the SFT file will be divided into when streamed (see Figure 8.5).

FIGURE 8.5
Advanced Options
screen

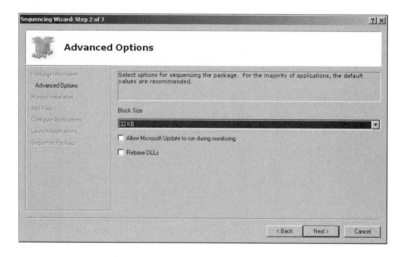

The larger the block size, the more information is passed per block; the downside is whether the client requests all of that data or not, the whole block will come down, which can lead to inefficiency in low-bandwidth situations. If the block size is reduced to 4 KB, only the very specific parts of the SFT file will stream down, the downside being extra header information, because there will be more total blocks streamed, which can lead to inefficiency in high-bandwidth situations. Unless Microsoft support indicates otherwise, 32 KB is a good balance.

◆ The Allow Microsoft Update To Run During Monitoring option will ensure you're sequencing the latest version of Microsoft software available. For example, if you are sequencing Visio 2007, this option allows Windows Update to run, so all the latest patches are included in the sequence.

◆ The Rebase DLLs option can optimize memory usage and possibly launch times of the application on a multiuser device, such as a Microsoft Remote Desktop Services device.

3. On step 3 of 7 of the Sequencing Wizard, click Begin Monitoring.

4. In the Browse For Folder screen, always select the package root. In this case, browse to q:\XMLnotpd.v01. Be sure the Folder field reads XMLnotpd.v01. If not, deselect q:\XMLnotpd.v01 and reselect it. Click OK.

   At this point the Sequencer will load the virtual environment and begin monitoring everything you and the application are doing. Depending on the operating system, the previous dialog box may or may not minimize itself. If the Sequencer software does not minimize itself, be sure to wait for the virtual environment to load. You'll know it is ready when the screen reads, "Monitoring started. Please begin installation."

5. If you want to add the .NET Framework 2.0 middleware for XML Notepad 2007, install it now by launching dotnetfx.exe on the desktop. If after the .NET installer completes, Windows asks for a reboot, click Yes to reboot. The computer will not actually reboot because the Sequencer will intercept the request and process the reboot actions such as the dll-registration and runonce keys in the Registry. Once this process is complete, the Sequencer will prompt you to begin monitoring once again. Some applications require two or three reboots, in which case you need to repeat the previous steps until all middleware is installed. Click Begin Monitoring to start the next phase of the install.

Now we'll install Notepad 2007:

1. Launch XmlNotepad.exe on your desktop (see Figure 8.6).

FIGURE 8.6
Notepad 2007 installer

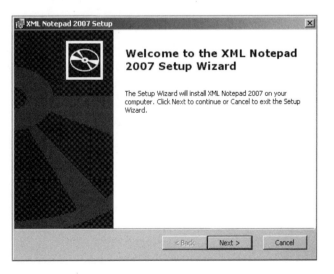

2. On the Custom Setup dialog box, notice that the default install location is set to `c:\program files\XML Notepad 2007\`. Following sequencing best practices, we'll redirect this to a sub-folder of the package root.

3. Click the Browse button. In the Look In drop-down menu select Q: and then `XMLnotpd.v01`. Click the Create New Folder button.

4. Create a folder called `XML Notepad 2007` under `XMLnotpd.v01`. The result in the Folder Name field should be `Q:\XMLnotpd.v01\XML Notepad 2007\`, as shown in Figure 8.7. Click OK.

FIGURE 8.7
Redirected
installation directory

5. Back on the Custom Setup dialog box, verify that the Location value has reflected the changes, and click Next.

6. On the Ready To Install dialog box, click Install.

7. On the Competed Setup Of XML Notepad 2007 dialog box, click Finish.

8. If a browser window opens, close it.

This is a good time to make any changes to the Registry or file system should your application require any customizations. To make changes to the Registry, launch `REGEDT32.EXE` and make your configuration changes. To add files, use Windows Explorer to make any changes. Add any system variables at this time also. All changes will be captured by the Sequencer. For this example, no post-install changes are required.

1. Restore the minimized Sequencer software, and click Stop Monitoring.

2. Once monitoring has finished, click Next.

3. On step 4 of the Sequencing Wizard, you can manually add any files you forgot on the previous step. This is rarely used. Click Next.

On the following step you would typically want to keep all shortcuts unless you are absolutely sure that you will never need them. Later in the provisioning process on the server, you can choose who will receive each icon.

4. On step 5 of the Sequencing Wizard, the shortcuts that the application tried to create are represented. Remove all but the one for XML Notepad 2007 by right-clicking the application shortcut and clicking Remove. Click OK when asked if you are sure you want to remove the selected items.

5. Click Next.

6. On step 6 of the Sequencing Wizard, select XML Notepad 2007 and click Launch.

Once you launch this application, the Sequencer software will begin creating the minimum launch threshold. Every file, folder, Registry key, or other application asset is being tagged with a higher priority in relation to other parts of the application. The more you use the application during this phase, the larger the minimum launch threshold, but also the more functional the app will be at initial launch. In a streaming scenario, a larger minimum launch threshold means it will take users more time to launch the application the first time it is used on a particular device, the tradeoff being they'll have more of the application and less subsequent streaming is necessary. A good rule of thumb for creating a right-size launch threshold is by using the application in the top five ways a user would. Normally this is by logging into the application, opening and closing a sample document, and going into all of the preferences or options windows. In this case we'll open a dialog box and change a setting.

1. Once XML Notepad has launched, click File ➤ Open. Click Cancel.

2. Click View ➤ Options. Change the background color to your favorite.

   This is the time to make any user state changes. You can set toolbar locations, alter the look and feel, edit any custom .ini entries, and customize Registry settings now. All these changes you make to the application from within the application itself will be mirrored to your users.

3. Close XML Notepad.

4. Step 6 of 7 should reappear once the Sequencer has detected that the XML Notepad process has ended.

5. Click Next.

6. On step 7 of 7 click Finish.

The sequencing phase is completed. The Sequencer now shows the properties of the package, as shown in Figure 8.8.

On the Properties tab you can inspect such items as the minimum launch threshold size (Launch Size).

1. Highlight the Package Name entry and press Ctrl-C to copy it to the Clipboard. We'll use this later.

2. Click the Deployment tab.

3. Change the protocol to RTSP, the hostname to the streaming server, in this case **app-v**, and paste the Clipboard entry into the Path field, as shown in Figure 8.9.

FIGURE 8.8
Sequence properties

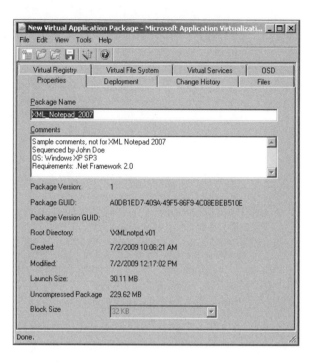

FIGURE 8.9
Deployment tab

- ◆ The Operating Systems selection on this tab does not port the application to various operating systems. When you select an operating system here, it means that if a user logs in to the network using this operating system, this application will be available. For example, if XML Notepad 2007 worked only with Windows XP, you would add only XP as a selected operating system. Then only when a user logged in to a Windows XP machine would this application be available.

- ◆ The Enforce Security Descriptors option will copy and enforce NTFS permissions from the files sequenced to those inside the package. For example, if you want to restrict who has access to an Access 2007 .mdb file, you can set the permissions on the files on the Sequencer workstation while monitoring, and those will be respected after streaming. Note that as of App-V 4.5, Registry security settings are not enforced in this same manner.

- ◆ The Generate Microsoft Windows Installer (MSI) Package option creates an MSI file, which can be used to distribute this virtual application to a stand-alone machine with no need for a streaming server. This is helpful for contract or home workers who need access to an application but don't have Active Directory domain access.

4. Clear the Enforce Security Descriptors check box.

5. Check the Generate Microsoft Windows Installer (MSI) Package check box.

6. Change the Compression Algorithm setting to Compressed (ZLIB).

7. Choose File ➢ Save As and create a folder on your desktop called XML_Notepad_2007 (Ctrl-V if you still have it copied to your Clipboard).

8. Inside this folder change the filename to **XML_Notepad_2007** and click Save.

9. Copy the XML_Notepad_2007 folder from the Sequencer machine's desktop to the \\app-v\content share.

At this point, the Sequencer can be reverted. Any updates to the application will work as follows:

1. Copy the application folder back down to the Sequencer workstation.

2. Open the package for a package upgrade.

3. Run the Sequencing Wizard again, apply the update, and save.

4. Copy the new SFT and SPRJ files back to the folder on the content share.

Publishing an Application to Users

Now that we have a new virtual application in our content directory, we need to create an application record that will control its behavior.

1. Back on the Management Server, log in and open the Application Virtualization Management Console located in Administrative Tools.

2. Expand the tree until you see the Applications node. Right-click the Applications node and select New Application Group.

3. In the Application Group dialog box, enter **Developer Tools** in the Application Group Name field. Click Finish.

4. Expand the Applications node, right-click the Developer Tools node, and select Import Applications, as shown in Figure 8.10.

FIGURE 8.10
Import Applications

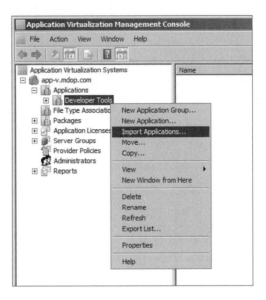

5. Browse to \\app-v\content\XML_Notepad_2007\ and select the .sprj file.

6. On the General Information dialog box, click Next.

7. On the Published Shortcuts dialog box, be sure at least Publish To User's Desktop is checked, but you may also want to check the Start menu because that is more common. Click Next.

File type associations (FTAs) can be centrally managed for App-V applications. For instance, we can associate XML files to be opened with XML Notepad 2007. The Sequencer will pick up the default FTAs that the application required during the monitoring phase on the Sequencer. A caveat here is that every time the client machine initiates a publishing refresh request, these FTAs from the virtual application will overwrite any existing changes to the FTA assignments. For instance, if a user has Adobe Acrobat installed locally associated with the PDF type, and that user has provisioned a virtual Adobe Reader 9, the virtual Adobe Reader 9 will associate itself with PDF no matter how many times the user tries to manually override it.

1. In the File Associations dialog box, click Add.

2. In the New File Type Association dialog box, type **XML** in the Extension field.

3. In the File Type section, click the Create A New File Type With This Description radio button, and type **XML Notepad 2007 file**, as shown in Figure 8.11, and click OK.

FIGURE 8.11
FTA setting

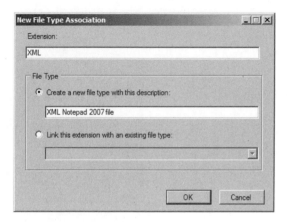

4. On the File Associations tab, be sure that the XML FTA is showing and click Next.

5. On the Access Permissions tab, click Add, type **appvgroup**, and click Check Names To Resolve. Click OK.

6. On the Access Permissions tab, click Next. On the Summary dialog box, click Finish.

Now that we've sequenced and provisioned the application, it is time to test it with a client. The following steps take place on the App-V client machine.

1. On the client machine go to Control Panel ➤ Administrative Tools ➤ Application Virtualization Client.

2. Highlight the Publishing Servers node, and in the Name pane right-click the listed server and click Refresh Server (see Figure 8.12) to check for the newly provisioned application.

FIGURE 8.12
Publishing refresh request

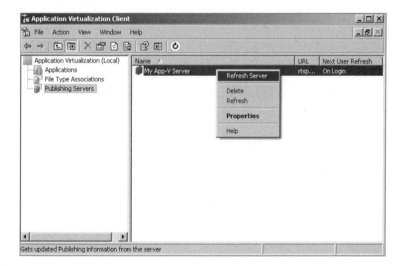

3. Look for the XML Notepad 2007 icon on the desktop (see Figure 8.13).

FIGURE 8.13
XML Notepad icon

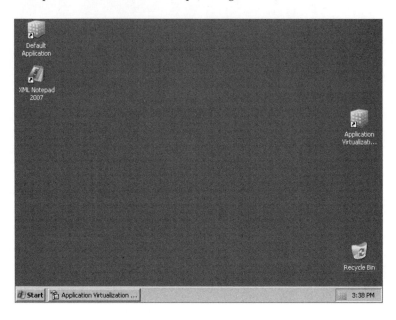

4. Double-click the XML Notepad 2007 icon on the desktop to stream the application.

The Bottom Line

Understand sequencing concepts. Sequencing and provisioning applications can take a few times to get the process down completely. The great thing is that once you are familiar with the process, packaging is nearly identical for both easy applications and those that are normally difficult to package using traditional technologies. In the previous example, the application was delivered instantly and on demand surrounded by policy and control.

Master It Which two of the following is correct syntax for an 8.3 package root directory?

1. C:\fooapp.v01

2. Q:\fooapp.v01

3. Q:\foo_app_2009\

4. Q:\fooapp

Install and configure a Sequencer workstation. Properly configuring your Sequencer workstation can lead to much more reliable and predictable sequences. A few minutes spent up front can save many hours of troubleshooting when the applications are streamed enterprisewide to clients.

Master It   Your packaging team has reported that sequencing applications takes too much time to process. What is the best way to speed up the process?

Sequence an application with middleware.   One of the benefits of virtual applications is the ability to bundle middleware with the application that requires it. This can lead to efficiencies in deployment because you no longer have to check whether the dependency is deployed to your target machine because the application has all it needs in its virtual environment.

Master It   Part of your App-V deployment is a requirement to deploy to contract workers who have PCs that are not domain joined. Realizing that you can deploy a virtual application by MSI, you look in the virtual application folder in \\App-V\content\<appname> and don't see any MSI files. Think of a way in which you might be able to create these MSIs.

Publish an application to users.   Publishing applications to users is a powerful feature of App-V. Simply changing a group membership in Active Directory can entitle users to a range of applications.

Master It   Many users have complained that icons for virtual applications placed on their desktops keep reappearing even after they delete them. How can you centrally prevent this from happening?

Chapter 9

Deploying Virtual Applications

In the early days of application virtualization, features were tied together, creating problems when deploying to large organizations. For example, if your company had coexistence issues with a couple of web apps on two computers in a remote location, all of the App-V backend components, including the management and SQL servers, would need to be installed at that remote location. The separation of product features sets allows much greater flexibility in right-sizing solutions such that overengineering is not required. Scalability has also been addressed by allowing virtual applications to be either streamed or copied from nearly any source.

Another step in the right direction is a greater focus and simplification of the ability to customize complex applications for security or functionality. This can be a requirement when deploying either physical or virtual applications. For example, some virtual apps require the environment on the workstation to be configured before the application is run. In one exercise we will create a script that will map a network drive, launch a virtual application, and delete the network drive once we close the application.

In this chapter, you will learn to:

♦ Customize package behavior with OSD file scripting

♦ Deploy a stand-alone MSI architecture

♦ Deploy a hybrid architecture

♦ Scale the full infrastructure model

Customizing Package Behavior with OSD Scripting

Being able to modify the behavior of a virtual application or the workstation on which it is run can be a valuable tool to the experienced sequencing engineer. Often it may save time by not having to resequence an application for accounting because that department has a different executable parameter than human resources. That being said, editing OSD files is not usually a hard requirement for success in deploying virtual applications but will definitely make things much smoother and quicker.

OSD files are essentially XML files, meaning that you can and should use an XML editor (such as XML Notepad 2007, sequenced in chapter 8) to mitigate syntax errors. The OSD is composed of elements, parameters, and values. Let's take a closer look at the administrator-relevant sections of the XML Notepad 2007 OSD, which, if you followed along with the Chapter 8 sequencing exercise, should be located in the content share of the App-V Management server. Right-click the OSD file, and open it with notepad.exe. The following is an excerpt from the OSD file:

```
<SOFTPKG GUID="4F327184-FACB-4A8E-A3C6-420F02AD4C81" NAME="XML Notepad 2007" VERSION
="2.5.0.0">
```

The GUID, or globally unique identifier, is created by the sequencer for this particular application within the package to which this OSD file points. When upgrading a virtual application in an active upgrade scenario, the sequencer does not create a new GUID but simply streams the newly updated blocks. If desired, create a test package that will run alongside the original; then at the completion of sequencing, click Save As in the sequencer, and it will create a new GUID. As far as App-V is concerned, a new GUID is a new application. In this scenario be sure to change the 8.3 asset directory name in the sequencer before saving because that will also need to be globally unique.

```
<IMPLEMENTATION>
        <CODEBASE HREF="RTSP://app-v:554/XML_Notepad_2007/XML_Notepad.sft"
        GUID="A0DB1ED7-409A-49F5-86F9-4C08EBEB510E" PARAMETERS=""
        FILENAME="XMLnotpd.v01\XML Notepad 2007\XmlNotepad.exe"
        SYSGUARDFILE="XMLnotpd.v01\osguard.cp" SIZE="247692466"/>
        <WORKINGDIR/>
        <VIRTUALENV TERMINATECHILDREN="FALSE">
                <ENVLIST/>
        </VIRTUALENV>
        <VM VALUE="Win32">
                <SUBSYSTEM VALUE="windows"/>
        </VM>
        <OS VALUE="WinXP"/>
</IMPLEMENTATION>
```

The IMPLEMENTATION element of the OSD is what ties this OSD to a particular package. The URL in CODEBASE is the reference to the package. The GUID here is the GUID for the entire package, not the application. For example, if you're sequencing Office 2007, this GUID would refer and be unique to the Office 2007 package, whereas the GUID in the SOFTPKG element may refer to the Word 2007 application. The PARAMETERS parameter is how you would pass a parameter to the executable. For example, if every time you launch XML Notepad 2007 you want a default file to open, you could change the XML to PARAMETERS="FOO.XML". The FILENAME parameter refers to the file that will be launched in the package. You'll notice that our 8.3 asset directory is listed in the path XMLnotpd.v01\XML Notepad 2007\XmlNotepad.exe, but the drive is not enumerated. The mount point defaults to Q:, so there is no need to add Q:\ to the path. The SIZE parameter refers not to the size of the package but to the size of the minimum launch threshold given in bytes. The WORKINGDIR element sets the working directory for the virtual application. When the TERMINATECHILDREN element is set to "TRUE", all child processes spawned from the virtual application are forcibly shut down when the parent process is terminated. Normally the parent process will terminate the child process, but there are exceptions, most commonly in middleware applications that are sequenced in the same virtual environment. The SUBSYSTEM element's VALUE parameter refers to the type of display Windows will draw for the virtual application needs. For instance, if you were sequencing a DOS application, you'd set the VALUE value to CONSOLE in order for Windows to draw the DOS box correctly. The OS element designates on which operating systems this virtual application will be available. If a user logs in to a Vista machine and WinVista is not enumerated in this OS element, the icon will not show up on the desktop. If this application works well on Vista, you could copy the whole WinXP line, paste it directly below, and change the value to WinVista.

Creating Scripts

Many times the built-in XML elements will not be enough to set up the environment for the application. App-V supports most any scripting engine that the client can interpret. The most commonly used are SCRIPTBODY, HREF, batch files, and VBS scripts, all of which must be children of the <DEPENDENCY> tag. When designing a script, it is important to think about when, during the application launch cycle, the script will need to run, as shown in Figure 9.1.

FIGURE 9.1
Script launch timing

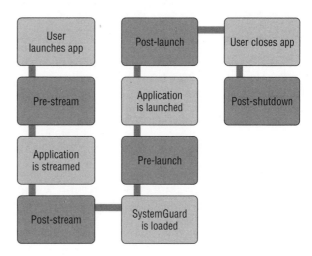

We'll now create a script that will map a network drive only for the duration that the application is launched. Open the XML Notepad 2007 OSD file or any other OSD file you've created to follow along.

For our example we'll need to create a script that launches at PRE LAUNCH.

```
<DEPENDENCY>
        <SCRIPT TIMING="PRE" EVENT="LAUNCH" WAIT="TRUE" PROTECT="FALSE">
</DEPENDENCY>
```

In an App-V context, the DEPENDENCY tag refers to any prerequisites the package requires, whether a script or a Dynamic Suite Composition child application. Above, SCRIPT is the name of the tag, and the TIMING parameter indicates when the script executes in relation to the value specified in the EVENT parameter. WAIT indicates whether the App-V client should wait for the script to complete before moving on to the next step. PROTECT indicates whether the script should run within the virtual environment; in this case we want to map a network drive on the local machine outside the virtual environment, so we'll set the parameter to FALSE. Two common mistakes are not putting the SCRIPT tag as a child of the DEPENDENCY tag and forgetting the closing tag </DEPENDENCY>.

The two script types available directly in the OSD (others can be launched from the OSD) to App-V are HREF and SCRIPTBODY. Table 9.1 describes some of the important differences.

TABLE 9.1: Scripting methods

<HREF>	<SCRIPTBODY>
Does not require doubling your backslashes, which makes HREF less likely to have syntax errors.	Requires doubling your backslashes because the backslash is an escape character.
Cannot be used with nonexecutable commands, such as the DOS RD command, which execute in command.com.	Can use nonexecutable commands.
Does not create a temporary batch file to execute commands.	Creates a temporary batch file to execute commands.
Does not create a DOS window when launched unless the HREF calls a DOS command.	A DOS window appears during execution, which may disturb users when launched.
	Requires a /n at the end of each line.

We'll choose HREF here for the simplicity of pathing syntax.

```
<DEPENDENCY>
        <SCRIPT TIMING="PRE" EVENT="LAUNCH" WAIT="TRUE" PROTECT="FALSE">
                <HREF>NET USE Z: \\APP-V\CONTENT</HREF>
        </SCRIPT>
</DEPENDENCY>
```

Notice that the HREF script uses DOS syntax and pathing. We need to create another script to delete the network drive once the user has closed the application. Referring to Figure 9.1, we'll choose the POST SHUTDOWN event timing.

```
<DEPENDENCY>
        <SCRIPT TIMING="PRE" EVENT="LAUNCH" WAIT="TRUE" PROTECT="FALSE">
                <HREF>NET USE Z: \\APP-V\CONTENT</HREF>
        </SCRIPT>
        <SCRIPT TIMING="POST" EVENT="SHUTDOWN" WAIT="TRUE" PROTECT="FALSE">
                <HREF>NET USE Z: /DELETE</HREF>
        </SCRIPT>
</DEPENDENCY>
```

Save the OSD file. Switch back to your App-V client workstation and perform a publishing refresh request.

MANUALLY REFRESHING THE CLIENT

To perform a publishing refresh request from the command line, type **SFTMIME REFRESH SERVER:`<server display name configured in App-V client>`**.

To accomplish the same function using SCRIPTBODY, the script would look somewhat similar except for the doubling of the backslashes in the path and the \ns:

```
<DEPENDENCY>
        <SCRIPT TIMING="PRE" EVENT="LAUNCH" WAIT="TRUE" PROTECT="FALSE">
            <SCRIPTBODY>
                    NET USE Z: \\\\APP-V\\CONTENT \n
            </SCRIPTBODY>
        </SCRIPT>
        <SCRIPT TIMING="POST" EVENT="SHUTDOWN" WAIT="TRUE" PROTECT="FALSE">
            <SCRIPTBODY>
                    NET USE Z: /DELETE \n
            </SCRIPTBODY>
        </SCRIPT>
</DEPENDENCY>
```

One powerful option we could have used would be to call a previously created batch file to perform automated administrative functions:

```
<DEPENDENCY>
        <SCRIPT TIMING="PRE" EVENT="LAUNCH" WAIT="TRUE" PROTECT="TRUE">
            <HREF>\\APP-V\CONTENT\FOOSCRIPT.CMD</HREF>
        </SCRIPT>
</DEPENDENCY>
```

To execute a previously created VBS file with Windows Script Host, you can use the following code, which passes DoIt.bat as an input to the VB script:

```
<DEPENDENCY>
        <SCRIPT TIMING="PRE" EVENT="LAUNCH" WAIT="TRUE" PROTECT="TRUE">
                <HREF>wscript \\APP-V\CONTENT\TOOLS\CoolTrick.vbs \\APP-V\CONTENT\
TOOLS\DoIt.bat</HREF>
        </SCRIPT>
</DEPENDENCY>
```

Understanding Supported Deployment Scenarios

A very common misconception is to think that App-V is an all-or-nothing proposition *requiring* much complexity and architectural considerations. With the latest technologies built into the App-V client, it is possible to get your feet wet with App-V with no additional backend infrastructure whatsoever and achieve a very quick return on investment (ROI). In this scenario

App-V is reduced in complexity to that of a packaging technology. Chances are your organization is already packaging or repackaging MSI files, so packaging to an App-V standard requires little extra training because it is a very similar skill set. Be sure that the business justification for an App-V project plays a central role in determining which deployment scenario you choose. Figure 9.2 shows high-level descriptions of the relative complexity of three deployment models.

FIGURE 9.2
Supported App-V
deployment models

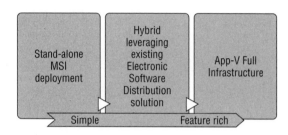

The first factor in choosing a deployment scenario is to understand which applications you will virtualize. Most corporations don't have a good understanding of which applications are actually being used in their environment. When starting an App-V deployment project an excellent source for this information can often be found in your inventory/application metering solution. If you are not currently capturing this information with your existing solution, you may want to consider enabling this function, if a metering solution is available, for several weeks. This should give you a good start on rationalizing your applications and will surely give you some surprises as to which applications users employ the most.

The second factor is to understand the physical locations of your users, the nature of their work, and the maturity of your network. Are most of your users mobile? How many remote offices are there, and how many users are at each? Some of the lesser-known but very important facts tend to be tribal knowledge. Do all of your users arrive at 8:00 a.m. and open all applications? Is this location primarily a help desk that will greatly benefit from free seating? Your answers to these questions will be essential in designing a right-fit architecture for App-V. Keep these answers in mind while reading the next few pages dealing with architecture design.

Stand-alone MSI Deployment

When the App-V client is put into stand-alone mode, it does not change the nature of the virtual application. The application still exists virtually, and all of the benefits of isolation between applications, packaging with dependencies, and others are still there. What is different, however, is that a sequencer-generated MSI file performs many of the functions of the management server, because in this model there is no management server or any other backend requirements. The MSI will copy the SFT file into cache, register file-type associations, and publish the shortcuts to their locations specified during sequencing.

A stand-alone MSI app is managed in a fashion similar to a locally installed application. It will register itself with Programs and Features (`appwiz.cpl`) and will be available to all users of that PC. Since there is no streaming server to update the virtual app, it is also updated as a physical MSI using your existing processes. Nearly any form of distribution can deploy an App-V MSI such as USB flash drive, DVD, UNC path, or Group Policy. A shrink-wrapped application installer to a deployed virtual application is essentially a three-step process, as shown in Figure 9.3.

FIGURE 9.3
Stand-alone MSI model

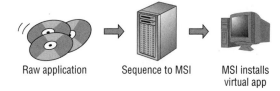

Raw application   Sequence to MSI   MSI installs
                                        virtual app

To configure an App-V client for stand-alone operation, first delete all applications listed in the Application Virtualization Client console and make the following dword value changes in the Registry:

```
[HKEY_LOCAL_MACHINE\SOFTWARE\Microsoft\SoftGrid\4.5\Client\Configuration]
"RequireAuthorizationIfCached"=dword:00000000

[HKEY_LOCAL_MACHINE\SOFTWARE\Microsoft\SoftGrid\4.5\Client\Network]
"AllowDisconnectedOperation"=dword:00000001
"Online"=dword:00000000

[HKEY_LOCAL_MACHINE\SOFTWARE\Microsoft\SoftGrid\4.5\Client\Permissions]
"ToggleOfflineMode"=dword:00000000
```

The last step is to reboot the machine. The machine is now configured as a stand-alone client. Remember that this can also be configured centrally via Group Policy with the Microsoft Application Virtualization Administrative Template.

To install an MSI-wrapped virtual application, launch the MSI file located in the same folder as the virtual application's SFT file (see Figure 9.4).

FIGURE 9.4
MSI Install of a virtual application

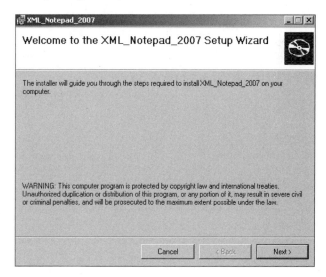

The stand-alone MSI deployment model is usually the best choice for the following scenarios:

◆ In rarely connected or severely bandwidth-limited situations

◆ Remote users or contractors who do not have access to Active Directory or to your App-V infrastructure

◆ In mature environments where existing application deployment processes are extremely efficient

The stand-alone MSI deployment model's considerations are

◆ No centralized reporting

◆ No package upgrade

Hybrid Model (Streaming)

The hybrid model (commonly known as the streaming or lightweight model) uses App-V streaming servers, SMB shares, or IIS servers to stream SFT files to clients. The MSI is used to "install" the virtual application and contains all of the virtualization files such as the ICOs and OSDs except for the SFT, which will remain on a central network location. The main benefit and limitation of this model is that no App-V management servers or SQL licenses are required. What this means is that App-V does not handle who has access to which applications — that is left up to your software distribution solution. Also missing are any reporting, licensing enforcement, or metering facilities. The hybrid model process is shown in Figure 9.5.

FIGURE 9.5
Hybrid deployment model

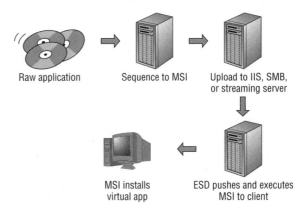

Raw application   Sequence to MSI   Upload to IIS, SMB, or streaming server

MSI installs virtual app   ESD pushes and executes MSI to client

---

INVENTORYING AND METERING AN INVISIBLE APPLICATION

Though stand-alone mode does not have its own inventory solution, the App-V client has a WMI provider that separate inventory solutions can query.

To configure your App-V client for the hybrid model be sure to modify the following Registry dword value:

```
[HKEY_LOCAL_MACHINE\SOFTWARE\Microsoft\SoftGrid\4.5\Client\Configuration]
"AllowIndependentFileStreaming"=dword:00000001
```

To deploy virtual application in a hybrid model you must use your software distribution solution to execute the MSIEXEC.EXE command on the target client machine with the following sample parameters:

```
MSIEXEC.EXE /I "\\app-v\content\XML_Notepad_2007\XML_Notepad_2007.msi" MODE=
STREAMING OVERRIDEURL="\\\\server\\share\\package.sft" LOAD=TRUE /q
```

MODE=STREAMING notifies the App-V client that it will need to stream the SFT from a remote streaming server defined in the OVERRIDEURL option. LOAD=TRUE indicates we want the SFT to be loaded into local cache, and the /q will execute this command silently. Everything but paths must be in capital letters. Notice that the backslashes also need to be doubled in the OVERRIDEURL path.

To stream apps from IIS you must configure the server first. Here are the steps:

1. Create a content folder on the IIS server (C:\content\, for example) and share it with default settings.

2. Open IIS Manager, expand <servername>\Sites\, right-click Default Web Site, and click Add Virtual Directory.

3. For the Alias type content and for the Physical path, browse to the local share you created (C:\content if you followed the example above) and click OK.

4. Highlight your newly created virtual directory called content, and double-click the Directory Browsing icon in the middle pane. In the right pane click Enable, and close IIS Manager.

5. On the client, change the OVERRIDEURL setting in the Registry to match the server URL.

Microsoft System Center Configuration Manager 2007 SP1 with R2 (SCCM) and newer has built-in support for deploying virtual applications using this deployment model. With a few check boxes you can begin streaming virtual applications directly from SCCM distribution points with inventorying and metering native in SCCM. For more information on SCCM integration, visit http://technet.microsoft.com/en-us/appvirtualization/cc843994.aspx.

The hybrid deployment model's strengths are as follows:

♦ Integration with existing technologies and practices makes it possibly a quicker deployment.

♦ It can work in an environment that has no SQL Server or Active Directory.

The hybrid deployment model's considerations are as follows:

♦ It requires command-line skill.

♦ Managing folder permission in IIS or NTFS ACLs is manual.

♦ Documentation is thinner than for other models.

Full Infrastructure Model

The full infrastructure model has the most robust feature set and consists of one or more management servers controlling policies and logging information. In chapter 7 we walked step-by-step through a basic full infrastructure deployment. The focus of the remainder of this chapter will be on how to scale this out to the enterprise.

When designing a large App-V full infrastructure deployment, one of the first things to consider is the number of publishing refresh requests that the SQL Server will need to handle. By default, the App-V client installer performs only a refresh at login. If your users need their applications more quickly, then you can set the refresh request to check with the server as often as every 30 minutes. Microsoft supports 12,000 publishing refresh operations per minute per SQL instance. If your organization requires more than this, you will need to create another SQL instance, which will essentially be a separate App-V environment with its own management servers, consoles, and other components. This number of requests was tested on a dual quad-core machine with 16 GB of RAM.

It is possible to have multiple management servers pointing to the same SQL instance. In fact, this is Microsoft's recommended path for increasing streaming and publishing refresh load capacity. A typical deployment would look like Figure 9.6.

FIGURE 9.6
Typical full
infrastructure design

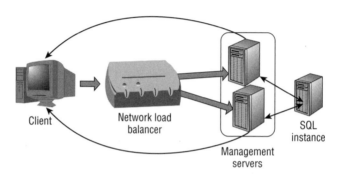

Client

Network load
balancer

Management
servers

SQL
instance

In this example the clients would be pointed to the virtual IP or hostname of the hardware or software network load balancer (NLB). The NLB would route incoming requests based on availability of the management servers. All management servers would then be pointed to the same SQL instance. Since significant SQL traffic will traverse the wire, it is a best practice to keep the management servers on the same subnet or VLAN as the SQL instance.

From Figure 9.6 you may notice that multiple management servers streaming virtual applications to clients require multiple content folders. The fact is that App-V does not automate replicating the content folders between management servers, IIS servers, streaming servers, and network shares. A common solution is to use Distributed File System Replication (DFSR) folder scopes to keep folders synchronized across multiple servers.

GOTCHAS

Be sure that your packages are replicated across all servers before provisioning applications to users. Otherwise, there could be a case where the user will receive an icon but there will be no SFT yet from which to stream. The client will throw an error in such a situation.

APPLICATION SOURCE ROOT

Most often, streaming applications over the WAN is not desirable because performance issues can occur when everyone at a branch location streams an application or an update for an application at once, such as on Monday mornings. This nightmare scenario spawned the Application Source Root (ASR) and its cousins the Icon Source Root (ISR) and the OSD Source Root (OSR).

In a nutshell, they allow the application authorization to still be obtained centrally from the management server located at a datacenter, but the SFT, ICO, and OSD files can stream from a local or distributed streaming source local to that branch office. This will enable the design illustrated in Figure 9.7.

FIGURE 9.7
Branch architecture

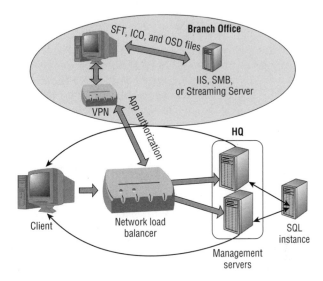

Even if you want to stream your applications across the WAN, you'll probably not want the ICO and OSD files copied from HQ each time a publishing refresh request occurs. Consider using the ISR and the OSR at the very least in this situation.

```
[HKEY_LOCAL_MACHINE\SOFTWARE\Microsoft\SoftGrid\4.5\Client\Configuration]

"IconSourceRoot"="\\\\branchserver\\content\\"
"ApplicationSourceRoot"="\\\\branchserver\\content\\"
"OSDSourceRoot"="\\\\branchserver\\content\\"
```

The ASR must always be used with the following Registry key configured on the clients:

```
[HKEY_LOCAL_MACHINE\SOFTWARE\Microsoft\SoftGrid\4.5\Client\Configuration]
"AllowIndependentFileStreaming"=dword:00000001
```

The full infrastructure deployment model's strengths are as follows:

- ◆ Free seating across the enterprise because applications are tied to user groups and act as network services

- ◆ Active upgrading of applications

- ◆ In-the-box rapid application application/icon publishing

- ◆ In-the-box reporting, metering, and license enforcement

- ◆ Very well documented by Microsoft

The full infrastructure deployment model's considerations are as follows:

◆ Network load balancers may be tricky to configure.

◆ Designing a very large App-V infrastructure well takes much planning.

◆ There's possibly a second infrastructure to manage if a software distribution solution is already in place.

These three models offer many choices in deciding the best route to design an App-V environment, and the best fit for a particular deployment will likely involve at least two models. For example, streaming may be used at corporate HQ, but retail stores with a single PC in each with 128Kbps connections will probably use the stand-alone mode. The deciding factors are the maturity of your current software distribution solution, how centralized your target PCs are from a networking perspective, and how important free seating and user-based targeting are to your business.

For an enterprise with a very mature software distribution solution, a hybrid model is usually best. If SCCM is present, then the determination becomes very clear because the integration is already present.

For a very decentralized enterprise, the stand-alone mode offers an easy deployment and a quick ROI because no additional servers are required since you are essentially deploying virtual applications using MSI actions.

For organizations that are interested in free seating, automatic application publishing, and granular application authorization, the App-V full infrastructure is usually the place to start.

The Bottom Line

Customize package behavior with OSD file scripting.   Customizing OSD files can greatly enhance a sequencing engineer's efficiency and effectiveness. Placing flags on a system for administrative purposes, setting an environmental variable, or even wiping out the user state upon application close can all be done with just a few lines of code.

Master It   You need to delete all hidden temp files that a virtual application creates in c:\myapp\temp\ each time the user shuts down an application.

Deploy a stand-alone MSI architecture.   The stand-alone MSI model is a powerful method of getting virtual applications to rarely connected computers and machines that are not domain joined.

Master It   You need to get an accounting application immediately to an auditor whose machine is not domain joined. What are the steps to accomplish this?

Deploy a hybrid architecture.   The hybrid model can be a good solution for mature software delivery environments. You get the benefits of streaming and package upgrades without designing a secondary infrastructure. If an organization already has System Center Configuration Manager SP1 with R2 deployed, there is little reason not to leverage it.

Master It   Your vice president of IT is leaning toward a hybrid environment because there are already IIS servers at all branch locations and the network has been very stable. Her only problem is that by regulation she needs to keep an accurate software inventory. Since App-V applications are not installed to the Registry or file system, how do you answer her?

Scale the full infrastructure model.   The full infrastructure model is a great solution for mid-size to large enterprises that do not have a streamlined application delivery process. Applications become network services and as such can be turned on or off on demand. Office 2007 "installs" in under 15 seconds. There is much business value in using the full infrastructure to dynamically manage your entire application life cycle.

Master It   You have designed a solution where clients get access to their App-V applications from your corporate headquarters, but the applications stream from their local branch offices. Several employees in your Denver branch need a new application, and your IIS server is not functioning. What is a temporary way to get your users their applications while you repair or replace their local IIS server?

Part 3

Remote Desktop Services

Chapter 10

Introduction to Remote Desktop Services

Microsoft Windows Server 2008, released in February 2008, ushered in many new features for Terminal Services. With the release of Microsoft Windows Server 2008 R2, Terminal Services has once again been enhanced with additional features and functionality. These enhancements fall into two main areas. The first area encompasses updates to the base functionality of the presentation virtualization capabilities offered by traditional Terminal Services. The second area of change involves the expansion of the role to include support for hosting a Virtual Desktop Infrastructure (VDI). Because of the change in functionality to offer both session-based and OS-based remote desktops, Terminal Services (TS) has been renamed Remote Desktop Services (RDS). This chapter and the three that follow will allow you to quickly master the new Remote Desktop Services functionality in Microsoft Windows Server 2008 R2. Previous experience with Terminal Services is not required because everything you need to set up a Remote Desktop Services environment will be presented.

In this chapter, you will learn to:

◆ Describe the Remote Desktop Protocol transport functionality and security

◆ Plan and size a Remote Desktop Services environment

◆ Configure a server to allow remote administration through Remote Desktop

What Is Remote Desktop Services?

Remote Desktop Services in Microsoft Windows Server 2008 R2 provides an execution environment wherein multiple distributed users can access a Windows desktop environment or application that is running on a centralized server or group of servers. Each user's desktop session or application utilizes the shared CPU and memory of the server. Then, using the Remote Desktop Protocol (RDP), the graphical output of that session is transferred to the user's client machine. The benefits of utilizing this technology are numerous:

◆ The IT administrator can easily deploy an application or set of applications to one or more servers composing a Remote Desktop Services farm to which authorized users then have access. This allows the IT administrator to provide access to an application for a great many users in as little as one installation of that application.

◆ The application upgrade process can be much more rapid because the IT administrator need only upgrade the application that was installed on the server or servers in the Remote Desktop Services farm. After that process is complete, all authorized users have access to the updated application.

◆ Each user's session information can be saved when the user disconnects. This gives users the ability to access an application or application set from a variety of devices. A user can move to a computer down the hall or one in an office in a different city and access the same application as if he had never left his desk. In addition, users can be granted remote access to the application, allowing them to work from nearly any device — even though that local device does not have the application installed.

◆ This technology solves an issue where insufficient bandwidth causes a client application installed locally on the user's device to perform poorly. By leveraging Remote Desktop Services, the previously poorly performing application can now utilize the very-high-speed connection that should exist between all of the servers in the datacenter. The end user is now just peeking in at the application as it executes on the centralized server and needs much less bandwidth in order to do so.

Of course, there are many other advantages to this technology. Your unique needs and requirements will determine which aspects of the Remote Desktop Services technology will benefit you the most.

History

Remote Desktop Services, formerly Terminal Services, was created in 1994, when Citrix licensed the Windows NT 3.51 source code and developed the first version of the product, WinFrame. Three years later, Microsoft licensed the technology back from Citrix, and Terminal Services made its debut as a product with an operational codename of Hydra, a multiheaded creature from Greek mythology. In September of 1998, Microsoft Windows NT Server 4.0, Terminal Server Edition became available. At this point, Microsoft had two distinct versions of Windows NT Server 4.0 — one with and one without Terminal Server functionality. Terminal Services was able to provide an execution environment wherein multiple users could utilize a shared desktop environment that executed on a centrally managed server. This allowed IT professionals to deploy the sometimes resource-heavy client portion of popular client/server technologies on a Terminal Server rather than directly on the end user's computer. Client computers that did not have the needed computational resources could continue to run business applications, and it also helped to overcome challenges associated with low-bandwidth network links that were common at the time.

In March 2000, Microsoft released Windows 2000 Server. It was at this point that the Terminal Server functionality was integrated into main operating system versions, and the Terminal Server Edition was dropped. With this release, Microsoft introduced encryption and a number of other enhancements for the Remote Desktop Protocol. When Windows Server 2003 was released in May of 2003, Terminal Services was once again vastly improved over the prior version. Management of the Terminal Servers and end-user environments via TS-specific Group Policy enhancements was a welcome feature. Remote Desktop Protocol — the protocol that is utilized to connect an end user's device to the Terminal Services environment — saw an increase in performance and flexibility. RDP could now support higher resolutions and deeper color along with better security. The 64-bit version of Microsoft Windows Server 2003 that was released in May of 2005 allowed for large increases in the number of users that could be serviced by a single Terminal Server due largely to the increased amount of RAM that could now be addressed in comparison to the 32-bit version. Now "scale up" as well as "scale out" were both viable options for larger Terminal Services deployments.

Microsoft Windows Server 2008, released in February of 2008, saw continued improvements to Terminal Services. The five major new enhancements are

◆ RemoteApp

◆ TS Web Access

◆ TS Gateway

◆ Easy Print

◆ Session Broker

In addition, a multitude of minor improvements such as support for multiple monitors, enhanced RDP security and RDP QoS, greater monitor resolution and color depth, IPv6 support, Network Access Protection (NAP) integration, and device redirection made for a very compelling product.

And now, Remote Desktop Services in Microsoft Windows Server 2008 R2 continues the trend with additional features, functionality and versatility.

What's New in Remote Desktop Services?

Remote Desktop Services in Windows Server 2008 R2 offers many new features as well as enhancements to features that existed in previous versions. And in keeping with the consistency of the name change from Terminal Services to Remote Desktop Services, Microsoft also changed the name of a few features:

◆ TS Gateway became RD Gateway

◆ TS Web Access became RD Web Access

◆ TS Session Broker became RD Connection Broker

◆ TS Licensing became RD Licensing

◆ TS RemoteApp became RemoteApp

Here are some of the new features of Remote Desktop Services:

◆ Remote Desktop (RD) Virtualization

◆ RD Gateway improvements

◆ RDS Provider for Windows PowerShell

◆ Enhanced functionality when using Microsoft Windows 7

◆ Remote Desktop Connection (RDC) 7.0 and RDP 7.0

◆ Remote Desktop IP Virtualization

◆ Windows Installer compatibility

- Fair Share CPU Scheduling
- Group Policy to manage roaming user profile cache
- Easier management of the client experience
- True multiple-monitor support
- Video and audio improvements

Remote Desktop Protocol

Remote Desktop Protocol (RDP) is a fundamental component of Remote Desktop Services (RDS). The Remote Desktop Connection (RDC) software that is included with Microsoft Windows operating systems is the actual application that a user invokes to connect to a server. RDC makes use of the Remote Desktop Protocol for its transport. By default, RDP operates on the Internet Protocol (IP) using TCP port 3389; however, this assignment can be changed if necessary. As a point of reference, the Internet Assigned Numbers Authority (IANA) has port 3389 registered as ms-wbt-server.

It's worth noting that RDP is a secure protocol that uses the RSA RC4 stream cipher encryption at either 56 bits or 128 bits and that can be configured to support the Federal Information Processing Standard (FIPS 140-1). By default, a Windows Server is configured to be "client-compatible" from an RDP encryption standpoint. This simply means that the server will first attempt a 128-bit RC4 encryption, and if the client does not support the 128-bit encryption, it will drop down to 56-bit RC4.

With the release of RDP 6.1 in Windows Vista and Windows Server 2008, Microsoft introduced additional security for RDC connectivity with Network Level Authentication (NLA). This mechanism reduces the risk of denial of service (DoS) attacks by completing the user authentication to the remote host prior to actually attaching the connection. NLA can also conserve resources on the RDS server because the server does not have to use as much processing power on users that do not have access to log on. Further security for the RDP connection can be gained by employing Transport Layer Security (TLS) to enable Server Authentication (SA). This will verify the authenticity of the server to which the client is connecting. Server Authentication can minimize the risk of man-in-the-middle attacks.

The RDS Gateway feature allows you to securely extend RDS to remote users outside the corporate firewall. With RDS Gateway, remote client machines connect to the RDS Gateway server using RDP encapsulated in HTTPS. The Gateway server then removes the SSL encryption and proxies RDP back to the RDS servers. The use of HTTPS here allows clients to connect even across firewalls that may be blocking RDP or other traditional VPN protocols. You can find out more about this feature in Chapter 12, "Deploying and Accessing Remote Desktop Services."

How Do I Obtain Remote Desktop Server?

Remote Desktop Server is included with the following operating systems:

- Microsoft Windows Server 2008 R2 Foundation Edition
- Microsoft Windows Server 2008 R2 Standard Edition
- Microsoft Windows Server 2008 R2 Enterprise Edition
- Microsoft Windows Server 2008 R2 Datacenter Edition

The ability to leverage RDC/RDP to remotely administer a Microsoft Windows Server is available in all versions. Note that all of the above editions except Foundation have a Server Core installation option. While remote desktop administration is available in the Core installation, full Remote Desktop Services is not.

System Requirements

System requirements to support Remote Desktop Server vary depending on a number of factors. Generally, the server resources that become taxed or exhausted are memory, processing, graphics, network, and storage. A user workload that presents a light resource footprint, Notepad, for example, on a server will allow more users to concurrently share that server. Resource-intensive applications such as CAD/CAM or Java-based applications weigh more heavily on a server and therefore allow far fewer concurrent users.

Memory

In most cases, RAM is the resource that presents the first bottleneck to be addressed in an RDS environment. The good news is that memory is relatively inexpensive. More good news is that since 2005, Microsoft has been offering Windows Server in both 32- and 64-bit versions. With the 64-bit versions of Windows Server, you can now take full advantage of any RAM above 4 GB in your servers. In discussing RDS, it's very important to understand the difference between a 32-bit and a 64-bit OS.

So what exactly is the difference between 32-bit and 64-bit operating systems? A 32-bit operating system can natively address up to 4 GB of RAM. After 4 GB of RAM, the operating system then uses a technology called Address Windowing Extensions (AWE) that works in conjunction with a technology on the server hardware called Physical Address Extensions (PAE). Together, these technologies allow Windows to swap memory out of the initial 4 GB into any additional RAM installed on the system. In fact, it's a bit like EMM386 in the DOS world. This swapping of memory is not nearly as efficient as using actual memory. In addition, the 32-bit Windows operating systems will run into bottlenecks in kernel memory, which are much harder to detect.

So, enter 64-bit Windows, or, more specifically, x64. The x64 architecture represents 64-bit memory extensions on the traditional x86 architecture, which serves to expand the memory capabilities of the server while maintaining compatibility with the 32-bit OSes. With the x64 architecture, Windows Server can natively address up to 2 TB of RAM with no swapping. Most kernel memory limits are raised to 128 GB, virtually eliminating kernel memory bottlenecks. Adding extra RAM to your systems will allow them to take advantage of all those processor cores you have in there. Remember, it's not enough to have x64 hardware; you also need to install a 64-bit OS.

While 64-bit RDS is great from a scaling perspective, before you deploy it on all your servers, there is one important caveat. Not all applications can run on 64-bit Windows. Clearly, native 64-bit applications will run, and the majority of 32-bit applications will run as well; however, some 32-bit apps are not compatible with the 64-bit OS. If your app falls into this category, you will need to deploy 32-bit Windows Server 2008 Terminal Servers, because Windows Server 2008 R2 is available only in a 64-bit version, and therefore RDS is available only in 64-bit. As we discussed, R2 will allow RDS to actually take advantage of all that extra memory you just purchased, but you may find that some of your applications will not run on the 64-bit OS. When sizing servers, you also need to take into account the particular edition of the Microsoft Windows Server 2008 R2 you choose, because the different versions have limitations on just how much RAM they can handle, as indicated in Table 10.1.

TABLE 10.1: Maximum RAM per server edition

SERVER EDITION	MAXIMUM RAM
Foundation	8 GB
Standard	32 GB
Enterprise	2 TB
Datacenter	2 TB

When it comes to determining how much RAM should be allocated per user on a server, use this very basic rule of thumb as a starting point. Set aside 2 GB for the server OS itself and the RDS role. Now you need RAM for each individual user session. Although this can vary depending on the number of applications and their footprint, allow 32 MB per user as a starting point. In this case, if you intend to support 64 users, add another 2 GB of RAM. At this point you're looking at 4 GB of RAM to allow 64 users to access your applications. Do not let these numbers either scare you or lull you into a false sense of security — they are merely a very conservative starting point. As you test your user scenarios and gauge performance, you will discover your actual memory needs. But memory sizing is only the first of your challenges. You can find some detailed scaling guides for RDS on Microsoft's website.

Processing

The second server resource typically vulnerable to depletion in an RDS environment is processing. Today's modern servers are capable of employing processors with six (soon to be eight) cores, across numerous sockets. Microsoft Windows Server 2008 R2 can support up to 256 cores in a single server. This is far more than any server hardware is able to currently provide. Most RDS servers are deployed with two or four processors, with today's standard being four cores per socket. This represents significant processing power, but if you begin to exhaust processor capacity and can no longer scale up, you need to begin considering scaling out through the use of an RDS farm. By utilizing a load-balanced RDS farm, you can continue to add servers as necessary to accommodate a growing number of users or more demanding workloads. Deploying an RDS farm in this manner also provides the benefits of redundancy and high availability.

Graphics

The remoting of graphics from the host server to the client can also become a limiting factor in overall application performance and the end-user experience. Enhancements in RDP have certainly mitigated this greatly, but there are a few things to keep in mind. RDS in R2 has provided new capabilities to improve the multimedia experience for RDP clients. These enhancements allow for smooth streaming of Windows Media Video (WMV) files, as well as improved performance of other video formats to the RDP client. However, this will require more processing on the server and more bandwidth to the client. While RDS will make the

WMV stream look great, it can't squeeze it into the bandwidth-efficient stream that you expect from RDS. In addition, graphically intensive applications like CAD/CAM or image-editing programs will consume more processing power than other applications, especially because servers are not typically equipped with powerful video cards to assist with graphical rendering. You should carefully evaluate each application for its suitability for graphic performance.

Network

Network requirements also play a critical part in a successful RDS implementation. The network is required not only to provide connectivity between the client and the RDS host server, but also to interact and communicate with other devices and services. Printing, file and database access, email, and Internet browsing all eat into the available network bandwidth that is available on each server. So be cognizant of applications that utilize the network heavily or require very-low-latency connections. As your user density increases with these particularly network-intensive apps, you may need to add additional network links or jump to faster connections such as 10Gbps Ethernet.

Storage

Finally, don't overlook storage, because it oftentimes becomes the weak link. For example, as the total number of concurrent users increases on a server, page files can become a real performance issue. Fast access to storage components can help make the end-user experience more satisfactory. Conversely, slow access to storage can marginalize the fastest processors, the largest amounts of RAM, and the speediest networks. The end-user experience will suffer greatly because of this, so ensure that you have not neglected your storage environment.

Unfortunately, there is no secret formula to determine exactly what your server environment should look like. Fully understanding the workloads you intend on deploying to users and the impact they will have on memory, processing, network, and storage will be your best guide to sizing the server hardware appropriately. To understand these workloads, it is important to monitor the applications while in use and perform thorough testing of the RDS environment prior to rolling into production.

Licensing

In order to appropriately deploy Microsoft Remote Desktop Services, the environment needs to be properly licensed. Every user or every device that connects to RDS must have a connection license. Microsoft offers two different Remote Desktop Services Client Access Licenses (RDS CALs) to accomplish this. The first is user-based and the second is device-based. You should purchase the RDS User CAL if you have a scenario wherein your users are accessing the RDS environment from more than one device or you have more devices than you do connecting users. Alternatively, acquire the RDS Device CAL if you have more users than devices. This is common in situations such as shift work, retail, and call centers. The RDS CALs must be purchased in addition to the standard Server CAL requirements for the base Microsoft Windows Server 2008 R2 product.

One of the roles available in Windows Server 2008 R2 is the Remote Desktop Licensing role service, which is designed to support the licensing of the RDS environment. The setup of this role service is discussed in Chapter 11, "Installing and Configuring Remote Desktop Services." This RD Licensing role service is essential to the operation of an RDS deployment. When using the RDS User CAL model, the RDS server will attempt to contact a license server when a user connects. If it can successfully locate a license server, the connection is allowed.

The licensing process for the RDS Device CAL is somewhat more complicated. The process is summarized here:

1. When an RDP client initially connects to an RDS server, it is granted a 90-day temporary license.

2. When the client connects for a second time, the server will attempt to locate a Remote Desktop Licensing server to obtain a CAL for the connecting user or device.

3. If a license server is found and a license is available, the client is assigned a license and is allowed to connect.

4. If no license servers are available or there are no free licenses, the client will be able to connect until the 90-day temporary license expires. After that, if there is still no license server available or available licenses, the client will no longer be allowed to access the RDS server.

Remote Desktop Administration

Remote Desktop Services serves two functions in the Microsoft Windows environment. It can act as a Remote Desktop Server providing many users with a centralized execution environment, or it can act as a very effective remote management mechanism. Microsoft allows up to two connections to a Windows Server for remote management and administration of that server. To use RDS for remote administration, you do not need to install the RDS role. You simply enable the Remote Desktop as shown in the following sidebar. Using the Remote Desktop Connection for administration does not require the purchase of an RDS CAL.

Remote administration allows an IT administrator to securely access and control a Windows Server from anywhere in the world utilizing the Remote Desktop Connection software that is included with Microsoft Windows operating systems. RDC makes use of the Remote Desktop Protocol for its transport.

Real World Scenario

CONFIGURING REMOTE ADMINISTRATION

Administrative Remote Desktop is disabled by default in Microsoft Windows Server 2008 R2. To enable the feature so that you can remotely administer the server, do the following:

1. Launch Server Manager by clicking its icon located in the taskbar. If you do not have a Server Manager icon, from the Start menu choose Administrative Tools ➢ Server Manager.

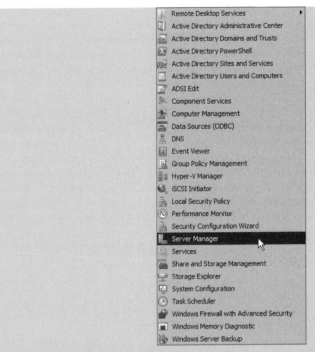

If it's not already there, you may want to consider adding a shortcut for Server Manager in the taskbar, because you will find yourself using it regularly. It will be there by default.

2. Once the Server Manager window opens, locate and select the Configure Remote Desktop link at the top right of the window.

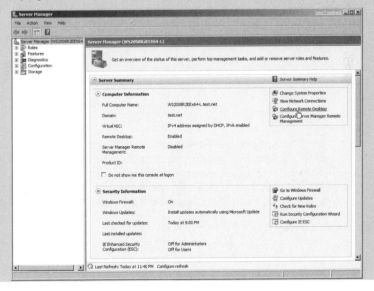

3. In the System Properties window under the Remote tab, you'll be offered three choices for regarding remote connectivity for administration. The first radio button is the default setting and will disable the ability to connect to the server remotely. The second radio button allows pre-RDP 6.0–based clients to connect. For instance, if you have a Microsoft Windows XP client with RDP 5.2, you will want to select this option. The third and final choice, which is recommended, leverages NLA, which was discussed earlier in the "Remote Desktop Protocol" section of this chapter. This selection will allow only RDP 6.0 and newer clients to connect. These include Microsoft Vista and Microsoft Windows 7 as well as Windows Server 2008 and 2008 R2. The RDP 6.0 client is also available as a download for Windows XP and Windows Server 2003. As stated, this provides a more secure connection mechanism.

Enabling either of the two connection choices will bring up a dialog box stating that a Remote Desktop Firewall Exception will be enabled. This is expected and welcome behavior, and all you need to do is click OK. At this point, Windows has created a rule in the integrated firewall called Remote Desktop (TCP-In) to allow RDP inbound.

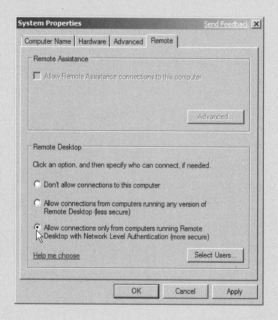

By default, the local administrator as well as any members of the Administrators group are authorized to connect if they successfully authenticate. If the server is joined to a domain, any members of the Domain Admins group are also authorized to connect if they successfully authenticate and you have not removed them from the local Administrators group. You may also click the Select Users button to manually add any user or group you want.

4. To complete this task, click OK.

You've now successfully enabled Remote Desktop to allow authenticated and authorized users to securely connect to and administer the server from any RDC client.

The Bottom Line

Describe the Remote Desktop Protocol transport functionality and security.   Having a well-developed understanding of the capabilities of Remote Desktop Services will allow you to evaluate a need within your organization and quickly determine if RDS is an appropriate solution.

> **Master It**   Take a current organizational need or find an example of an existing workload or application deployment. Leverage your understanding of the capabilities and features of RDS to determine if it would be a suitable platform to deploy the workload or application.

Plan and size a Remote Desktop Services environment.   Properly planning and specifying, or sizing, the RDS environment is critical to a successful deployment. An improperly sized RDS server or farm will most certainly lead to a poorly performing workload or application set.

> **Master It**   Using the example you selected above, plan for and size the appropriate server for your workload or application set based on the number of users for which you expect to provide access.

Configure a server to allow remote administration through Remote Desktop.   Leveraging the administrative mode of RDS, you can easily manage all of your Microsoft Windows Servers remotely using the full GUI as if you were in front of the device.

> **Master It**   Configure your Microsoft Windows Server 2008 R2 device to allow an administrator to remotely connect to and manage the server.

Chapter 11

Installing and Configuring Remote Desktop Services

Remote Desktop Services (RDS) provides the base functionality to deploy everything from individual applications to full server-based desktops for access by remote users. Through its Gateway feature, RDS also supports secure remote access to all of the internal applications that you are hosting on RDS servers, as well as to any servers that have Remote Desktop enabled for administration. In addition to providing remote applications and desktops, the Remote Desktop Session Host supplies the foundation on which additional software vendors such as Citrix can base their products.

Capabilities and functions provided by Microsoft Windows Server 2008 R2 are defined as either *roles* or *features*. Generally, roles are considered major functional components, referring to the function or purpose of the server, such as web server, file server, or print server. Features, although important, are regarded as supporting functions — for example, Failover Clustering is a feature that supports multiple roles. Remote Desktop Services (RDS) is defined as a role within Microsoft Windows Server 2008 R2.

In the earlier chapters of this book, you have seen a few new options for installing the Windows Server 2008 operating system itself — namely, in a Hyper-V virtual machine and using the Server Core installation option. When installing RDS, you will be able to take advantage of the Hyper-V technology; however, you cannot install RDS on a Server Core installation.

In this chapter you will learn to:

- ◆ Determine when to use an RDS Per User CAL and when to use an RDS Per Device CAL
- ◆ Identify which clients can utilize Network Level Authentication
- ◆ Determine when to enable Client Experience features
- ◆ Properly install applications on an RD Session Host

Preparing the Environment

Remote Desktop Services in Microsoft Windows Server 2008 R2 has a number of dependencies both within and outside the server on which it is being installed. The first of these is Active Directory Domain Services (ADDS).

ADDS?

Active Directory Domain Services (ADDS) is new nomenclature for what we all know as Active Directory. With the release of Windows Server 2008, Microsoft began using Active Directory as a branding moniker under which falls an associated suite of product features. When you see ADDS referenced, think AD with a lot of enhancements. Also, Active Directory Application Mode (AD/AM) is now referred to as Active Directory Lightweight Directory Services (ADLDS).

ADDS is critical for a properly functioning, well-performing, and flexible RDS deployment. For the purposes of this book, we will assume you have ADDS already up and running. Where necessary, we will indicate where and when RDS interacts with ADDS, what changes need to be made to ADDS, and the ramifications of such events. For more information on how to install, configure, and manage ADDS, refer to books such as *Mastering Active Directory for Windows Server 2008* (Sybex).

Although it is possible to configure RDS on the same server that is acting as a domain controller, this is not a good practice and not recommended for a number of reasons. Aside from the obvious security issues, performance and flexibility of the RDS environment become impacted negatively. In fact, if you attempt to install RDS on a domain controller, you will be greeted with a cautionary alert not to do so. If you are looking to set up RDS in a lab environment, make use of Hyper-V and configure two separate logical servers, one for ADDS and one for RDS, on the same host hardware.

The first thing we need to do in ADDS is to set up some groups so that we can manage access to the RDS environment. Open the Active Directory Users and Computers MMC and navigate to the Users OU. Create a new group here and name it **RDS Users**. This group will contain the users to whom we want to provide access to the RDS environment. Now right-click the RDS Users group, and select Add To Group. Type **Remote Desktop Users** in the blank field, and click Check Names. The Remote Desktop Users group name should now be underlined. Click OK. Creating this group will provide you more granularity and control going forward by allowing you to add users to a central Active Directory–managed group rather than to individual servers.

The second dependency of the RDS role is that of a Remote Desktop Licensing server. In a production deployment, in order to provide optimum flexibility, it is recommended that the RD Licensing server be placed on a separate server that is not functioning as an RD Session Host. Therefore, you will need a domain-joined Microsoft Windows Server 2008 R2 server to support this functionality. In many environments, the RD Licensing server could be deployed in a Hyper-V virtual machine. In a small test lab, you could co-locate the RD licensing server with the RD Session Host. For purposes of this book, we will be installing the RDS Licensing Server role on a separate server instance.

Finally, ensure that the server on which you are installing the RD Session Host has Microsoft Windows Server 2008 R2 installed and has been properly updated and joined to your domain. We will be using test.net as our domain. The specific edition of the server for RDS is not important from a feature standpoint but possibly from a resource standpoint. Standard, Enterprise, and Datacenter Editions of Windows Server 2008 R2 all support the RD Session Host feature but vary on the amount of computing resources supported. If you plan to support a large number of users and need a lot of RAM, Enterprise Edition can support up to 2 TB. That is substantially more than Standard Edition, which tops out at a comparatively meager 32 GB. Remember that Windows Server 2008 R2 is available only in a 64-bit edition, which is why the RAM limits are so high. However, if you are planning to deploy numerous RD Session Host nodes that will operate as constituents of a farm, Standard Edition may prove more than adequate.

The addition of two new components to the Standard Edition of Windows Server 2008 makes it a more compelling choice than Standard Edition in Windows Server 2003. The first new component is Windows System Resource Manager (WSRM). Previously only available in the Enterprise and Datacenter Editions, WSRM allows you to set policies for evenly distributing CPU and memory resources for services, users, and applications. In the RDS environment, WSRM allows you to balance computing resources evenly across user sessions. The other big change is the ability to participate in an RDS farm at all. Windows Server 2003 Standard Edition did not support participation in a farm. The inclusion of WSRM and the new ability to join a Session Broker farm make using Standard Edition as a base for multiserver RDS farms a great option.

Licensing

In preparation for the establishment of your RDS environment, you need to acquire all appropriate licenses from Microsoft. This includes not only licenses for the server operating systems but also the Remote Desktop Services Client Access Licenses (RDS CALs). The RDS CALs are offered in two versions — Per User and Per Device. The idea is to acquire and deploy whichever RDS CAL is the least expensive. Because both the user and device CALS cost the same, the least expensive route would be the method requiring the fewest number of RDS CALs. If you have an environment where there are more devices than users, you would typically select the RDS Per User CAL. This would be an environment wherein users had multiple unique devices, such as a laptop and desktop, that no one else used. Conversely, if you have far more users than devices, select the RDS Per Device CAL. A typical scenario for the Per Device CAL would be a manufacturing environment where a device is shared among workers across all shifts. After you have purchased the licenses, you will be able to install those licenses on your RDS License Server through a process described later in this chapter. Once installed in the environment, the RD Session Host servers will be able to retrieve licenses in order to initiate client connections.

Enabling the Remote Desktop Services Role

The first step in setting up a Remote Desktop Services environment is to enable the RDS role. This should be done on a domain-joined Windows Server 2008 R2 server. Joining the server to a domain will allow much greater control of the server through Group Policy and much more flexibility when dealing with users and groups for determining access. The server on which RDS is enabled is known as a Remote Desktop Session Host, or RD Session Host. Log on to the server that is going to be your RD Session Host as a user with local administrator privileges. On a new installation of Windows Server 2008 R2, Server Manager should start automatically after you log on. If it does not, launch Server Manager by clicking on its icon in the taskbar. If you do not have a Server Manager icon on your taskbar, you can click the Start menu and choose Administrative Tools ➢ Server Manager, as shown in Figure 11.1, or you can begin typing **Server Manager** in the instant search field.

In Server Manager, click Roles in the leftmost column, and then click Add Roles in the Roles Summary area, as indicated by Figure 11.2.

The Add Roles Wizard will launch and subsequently prompt you for the information needed to install RDS. Click Next on the Before You Begin page of the wizard (Figure 11.3).

> ### SKIP THIS PAGE?
>
> If you'd like, you can check the Skip This Page By Default box before you click Next. This will prevent the current page of the wizard from being displayed on all subsequent additions of any server roles.

FIGURE 11.1
Launching Server Manager

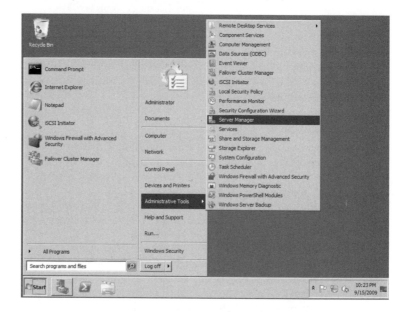

FIGURE 11.2
Adding a role

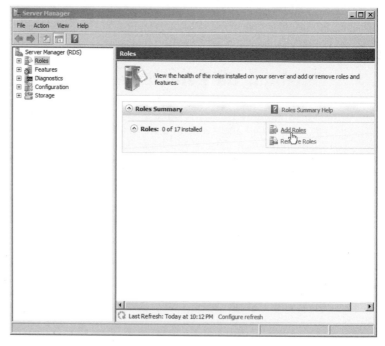

FIGURE 11.3

Before You Begin page

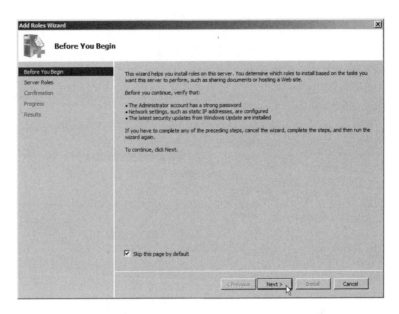

Now the wizard will display the Select Server Roles page, listing all available roles for this server. Select the check box next to Remote Desktop Services and click Next (see Figure 11.4).

FIGURE 11.4

Selecting the Remote Desktop Services role

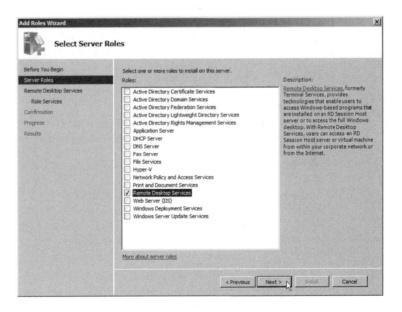

A Remote Desktop Services information page will be presented, providing you a brief explanation of RDS and a link to a local help file that will provide additional information. Click Next when ready to continue. The Select Role Services page that follows will outline all of the available role services pertinent to the RDS role. For the purpose of the chapter, we will be enabling the Remote Desktop Session Host. The Session Host role service is equivalent to what was previously known as Terminal Services, or Terminal Services Application Mode in Windows Server 2003. The RD Session Host role will furnish you with the ability to provide applications or entire desktops hosted on the server to remote users. In later chapters, we will be installing and configuring additional role services.

On this page, you can click on any one of the role services to see a brief description of that role service. In addition, you can follow the link at the bottom of the page to open a local help file with further information.

Click the Remote Desktop Session Host check box and then click Next (see Figure 11.5).

FIGURE 11.5
Selecting the Remote Desktop Session Host role service

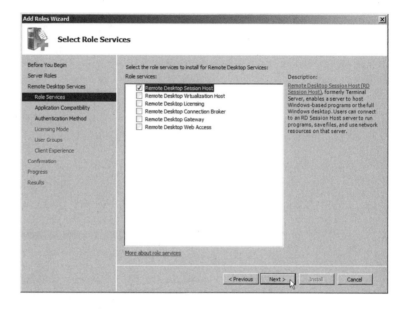

The next page, Uninstall And Reinstall Applications For Compatibility, presents a warning that should be well heeded. Applications that are to be delivered via an RD Session Host need to be installed in a very specific manner. Failure to do so may result in applications functioning poorly, erratically, or not at all. We will be covering the installations of programs onto an RD Session Host later. Since we're setting up a new server, no applications should already be installed. Click Next to advance the wizard.

As we discussed in Chapter 10, Microsoft introduced an additional security feature with the release of Windows Server 2008 known as Network Level Authentication (NLA). When enabled, NLA provides a more secure authentication method wherein the authenticity of the remote server can be verified by the client prior to connection. In addition, NLA decreases potential malicious attacks that could lead to a denial of service (DoS).

WHEN SHOULD I LEVERAGE NLA?

Network Level Authentication is a welcomed new security enhancement, but it does not come without drawbacks. In order to use NLA, the remote clients must also support NLA or they will be denied a connection to the host server. Microsoft has provided support for NLA in Windows XP SP3 and newer clients. Service Pack 3 (SP3) is required because it includes components necessary to enable NLA, such as the Credential Security Service Provider (CredSSP).

By default, NLA is not activated after SP3 for Windows XP is installed. You must enable CredSSP in order to activate NLA.

Understanding these client requirements from a connectivity perspective will allow you to confidently choose whether to use NLA. If you have clients such as Windows XP SP2, Windows 2000 Professional, or older Apple Macintoshes, enabling NLA on your RD Session Host is a certain way to deny connectivity for them.

Now that you're familiar with NLA and understand its ramifications, select whether to require NLA on the Specify Authentication Method For Remote Desktop Session Host page of the wizard, and click Next (see Figure 11.6).

FIGURE 11.6
Enabling NLA

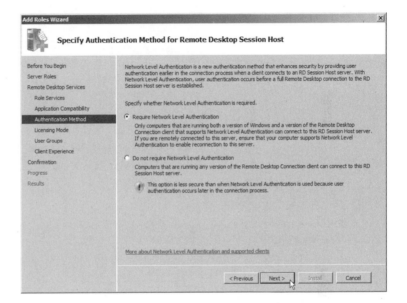

On the Specify Licensing Mode page, leave the default Configure Later radio button selected, as shown in Figure 11.7. We will, as indicated, be configuring this function at a later time. At this point, we are simply going to install and configure the server as an RD Session Host. As stated earlier, it is recommended that the RD Licensing server be placed on a separate server that is not functioning as an RD Session Host. The main reason for this is flexibility in building out an RDS farm, especially when considering a highly available environment. However, it is certainly possible to install both RD Licensing and a RD Session Host on the same server. This is attractive for small-farm or single-server deployments or in a lab or test environment.

We are now at the Select User Groups Allowed Access To This RD Session Host Server page. Here we will determine which users can connect to this server. By default, the local Administrators group is added and cannot be removed. Fortunately, we've already created a group in ADDS in the "Preparing the Environment" section of this chapter. Through membership in this group, we will grant access to this RD Session Host server. To add the group we created, click

Add and then enter **RDS Users** in the Select Users, Computers, Or Groups dialog box. Click Check Names to ensure you have made no syntax errors and that the group actually does exist in ADDS. The group name should become underlined to indicate everything is correct. Click OK to accept and continue (see Figure 11.8).

FIGURE 11.7
Postponing configuring
the Licensing server

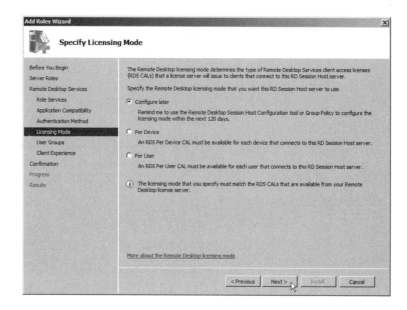

FIGURE 11.8
Choosing a Group
from ADDS

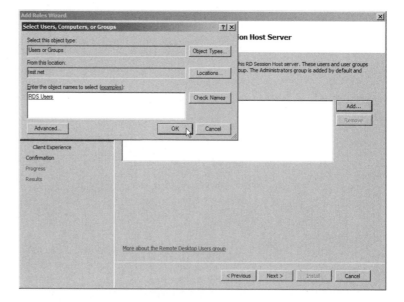

You should now show your RDS Users group as authorized users below the Administrators group, as shown in Figure 11.9. Click Next to continue with the wizard.

FIGURE 11.9
Adding an authorized users group

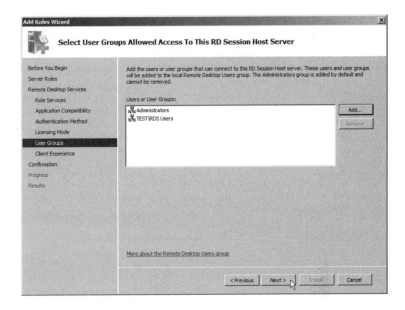

Next up is the Configure Client Experience page. Some decisions pertaining to how the RD Session Host will be leveraged are made here. The good news is that if you choose not to enable any of the features and realize you need them in the future, you can manually set them later. Enabling the client experience features will help to create a richer client experience; however, it is important to understand that enabling any or all of these features will take a toll on the resources of the host server. This manifests itself primarily on CPU and network resources and may degrade the end-user experience if not properly accommodated. For example, allowing audio and video playback will give the user a better multimedia experience, but it will require more processing power on the server to deliver the richer content.

ENABLING THE CLIENT EXPERIENCE

If you plan to deploy a full Microsoft Windows desktop to remote users, you should consider enabling at least the Desktop Composition and the Audio And Video Playback features. This is especially recommended when limited local resources exist, as when using a thin client device. But be keenly aware of the application set and workload that you will be deploying. If your applications or workloads have no use for video or audio playback, don't enable the feature. The same holds for Desktop Composition. Desktop Composition is an important feature that allows remote desktops and applications from the RDS host to display in the Windows Aero theme. This allows the RDS experience to mirror a local experience from a display perspective. However, if your users will not benefit from the Windows Aero look and feel, leave it disabled. You'll end up getting more users supported on a server with the Client Experience features off. Conversely, if your intended workload requires A/V playback or elements of Windows Aero, you'll need it enabled. Just size your physical servers appropriately. When working with the more graphically intensive Client Experience features like streaming video or Aero, be aware that some thin clients have scaled-back graphical capabilities and may not be able to support these features.

If you are not planning to deploy a full desktop but rather to deploy individual applications, you may not need any of the Client Experience features. For instance, applications delivered via RemoteApp may function perfectly and perform better with no Client Experience features enabled. Of course, if an individual application requires A/V playback, then certainly enable the functionality. To further complicate matters, video playback requires significant bandwidth, so you should take that into consideration as well, especially in remote locations.

For the sake of this chapter and those that follow, we will enable all of the Client Experience functionality. Check all of the boxes and then click Next (see Figure 11.10).

FIGURE 11.10
Enabling the Client Experience features

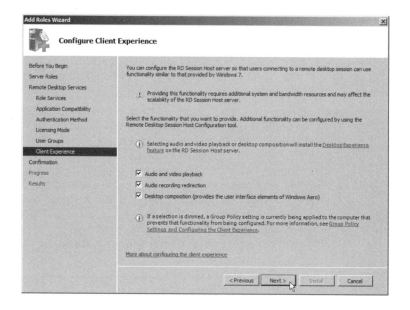

The Add Roles Wizard now presents the Confirm Installation Selections page. Here you can review everything that is about to happen once you click Install. If you find you've made an error or decide you want to change something, it is a simple matter of clicking the Previous button repeatedly until you locate the page containing the information you wish to modify. Note that the server will need to be restarted in order to complete the installation of RDS and the RD Session Host. Assuming everything is correct, click Install (see Figure 11.11).

After a very brief period, the wizard will display the Installation Results page. This indicates that both RDS and the Desktop Experience were installed and that the server is waiting to be restarted. You may either click one of the two lines stating "You must restart this server to finish the installation process" or click the Close button (see Figure 11.12). When the dialog box appears prompting you to restart the server, click Yes.

FIGURE 11.11
Confirm Installation
Selections

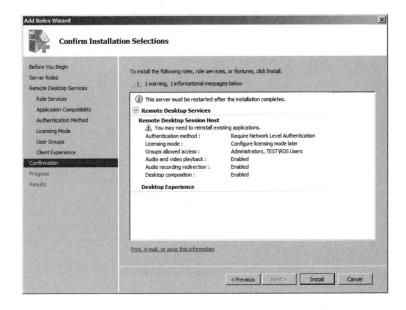

FIGURE 11.12
Installation Results
before restart

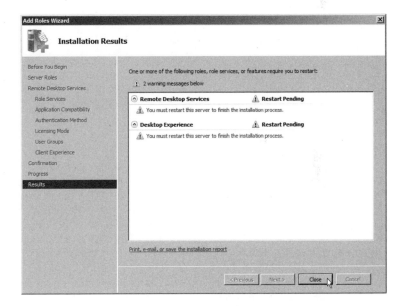

The server will begin a reboot sequence, and you will see a screen stating "Configuring Windows features x% complete Do not turn off your computer." After the reboot, a similar screen will appear as the RDS component installations are finalized.

When you log back into the server using the same account, you will notice that a new personalization process is executed for you. This is expected and is a result of the new RD

Session Host being installed. The final wizard page indicating Installation Results post-restart is displayed. It warns you that you need to configure an RD Licensing server. Failure to do so will cause clients to no longer connect after a period of 120 days. An informational link to a local help file prompts you to enable Windows 7 features for the recently installed RD Session Host. Don't worry about that because we've already installed the Desktop Experience features when we chose to enable Audio And Video Playback and Desktop Composition during the initial RDS install. A quick glance farther down the window will confirm that it was installed. Click Close to complete the installation process (see Figure 11.13).

FIGURE 11.13
Installation Results after restart

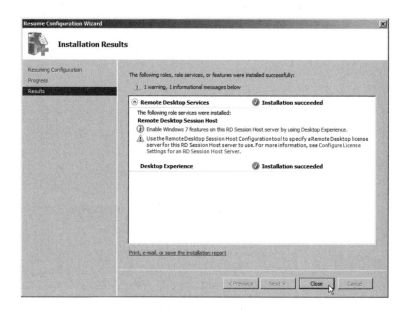

Post Installation

Once you've completed the RDS installation, open Server Manager. Expand the Roles heading in the left column, and then the Remote Desktop Services role. You can see that we now have on the RD Session Host server a RemoteApp Manager, an RD Session Host Configuration, and a Remote Desktop Services Manager available. We will be making use of these later.

Expand the Configuration heading located in the left column, just below the Diagnostics heading. Then expand the Windows Firewall With Advanced Security heading and select Inbound Rules. In the center section of the Server Manager window, scroll down until you see the entry Remote Desktop (TCP-In). As part of Windows Server role-based installation, the Windows Server Add Role Wizard ensured that Remote Desktop Protocol (RDP) on TCP port 3389 was automatically opened for us so that clients can connect to our RDS server.

In order to fully enable the remote client to get a desktop experience that is like Windows 7, we must complete one more step. Open Server Manager, expand the Configuration node, and select the Services node. In the right-hand pane, locate the Themes service, right-click it, and select Properties. Set the startup type to Automatic, start the service, and then click OK to accept. Minimize Server Manager, right-click on the desktop, and select Personalize. When the

Personalization window opens, choose one of the available Aero themes. Now, when your users log on to a Remote Desktop session, they will receive the Windows Aero theme.

Automated Installation and Configuration

In a large environment, there is a good chance that you will have an automated build process for your servers. In most cases, an automated build process will handle the base installation of the operating system but nothing more. Here are a few considerations when using automated deployment of the Windows Server 2008 R2 OS.

First, consider using a tool that integrates with Windows Server's role-based installation. A tool like the free Microsoft Deployment Toolkit 2010, or MDT, will allow you to install the RDS role as an automated task post-setup, as well as supply parameters for the installation.

Second, you should look to leverage Group Policy to configure your RDS servers. Group Policy can configure settings that are not available in the role installation process and make it easy to keep settings consistent across large numbers of RDS servers. Figure 11.14 shows some of the categories available for configuration in Group Policy. The Group Policies for RDS are found in the Group Policy Management Editor under Computer Configuration ➤ Administrative Templates ➤ Windows Components ➤ Terminal Services.

FIGURE 11.14
Configuring RDS servers with Group Policy

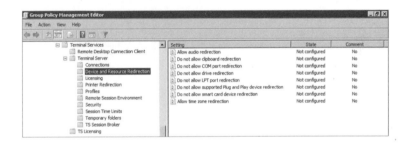

Connecting from a Remote Client

In order to test our newly configured RD Session Host, we should attempt to log in from a remote client. First we need to add a test user named John Doe to ADDS. Add him as a standard user with a logon name of jdoe. Once he is set up in ADDS, add him to the RDS Users group we created earlier. That's all there is to it. Bear in mind that this user has no administrative privileges anywhere.

From any client, launch the Remote Desktop Connection (RDC) program. On Microsoft Windows Vista and newer, you can click the Start icon, type **mstsc**, and press the Enter key. You can also click the Start button and begin typing **remote desktop** in the Search field, and Vista will quickly locate the program for you. Alternatively, you can click Start ➤ All Programs ➤ Accessories and locate the Remote Desktop Connection program there. Remember that if you chose to use NLA on the server, your client requirements are XP SP3 or newer.

When the RDC starts, enter the remote server's fully qualified domain name (FQDN) in the box next to Computer and click Connect. In our example, we would use rds.test.net. You will then be prompted for credentials for the remote server (Figure 11.15). Here you will see your current credentials, TEST\jdoe, for the user along with a space to enter your password. Enter the password you assigned to jdoe and click OK.

You should see a logon process that connects you to the session, after which you will be connected to a full Windows desktop that is being provided by the RD Session Host. Notice that with Desktop Experience enabled, you hear the Windows Logon sound and have the Windows Server Start menu replaced with the Windows 7 icon. This all aids in putting the end user at ease when using this new environment while reducing costs associated with retraining.

FIGURE 11.15
Connecting with RDC

You'll also notice a Server Manager icon in the taskbar. What's that doing there? For you security-conscience folks, don't be overly alarmed. Clicking the icon reveals that you must be an administrator to execute that program. A quick click on the Windows icon shows us that we are indeed logged on as John Doe, whom we know is not an administrator. So while our security is certainly intact, our environment may need some tweaking. Take care to ensure your remote users receiving a full Windows desktop see just the information you want them to have access to. This is one reason RemoteApp, which we will cover later, is such a powerful tool, because it will allow you to present a single application window to the user rather than a full desktop. The good news is that our RDS environment is up and running and ready to accept applications and remote user connections.

Installing Applications

The applications that are provided to remote RDS users from an RD Session Host need to be installed in a very particular manner. If applications are not installed as described, they will perform poorly, or possibly not at all. On an RD Session Host, you cannot always simply install an application from standard media as you have always done. If your application is packaged in a Windows Installer package, as many are, Windows Server 2008 R2 will automatically install that application in RD install mode. If the application does not come packaged in a Windows Installer package, you must either install applications via the Install Application On Remote Desktop Server Wizard or by first manually placing the RDS server into install mode. We'll explore both scenarios.

In versions of Terminal Services prior to Windows Server 2008, it was necessary to go through the process of putting the Terminal Server into install mode before installing any applications. Windows Server 2008 greatly simplified this process by automatically putting the server into install mode whenever the installation was being performed from a Windows Installer package (.msi). For applications that are not in the .msi format, you still have to follow one of the two traditional methods, which we will describe here.

To illustrate the methods for non-.msi applications, let's install a program to which we intend to provide our remote users access. We'll install the application using one method and then install it using the other method so that you understand both. You can choose any application you'd like, but for the examples that follow, we'll utilize the freely downloadable version of Adobe Reader. With any software you plan to deploy to remote users with RDS, please follow the publisher's distribution and licensing guidelines to ensure you are in compliance. It is also important to note that if operating system choices are available, as is the case with Adobe Reader, you need to choose the Windows Server 2008 version and not a client OS version. In many cases, a Windows Server 2008 version will not be available. If this is the case with your application, it is important to test the application thoroughly after installation to ensure that it performs as expected.

INSTALLING SOFTWARE WITH USERS CONNECTED

It is important to note that no remote users should be connected to the RDS server at the time software is being installed or it is manually placed into install mode.

Ensure your RDS server has been drained of all current users' connections and that no subsequent logons can occur. There are a few methods for preventing new logons. One option is to remove all the members of the RD Users group on the server except admins. You can also change the logon mode of the server to Allow Reconnections But Prevent New Logons. This serves to gradually drain the user connections so that you can perform maintenance. This setting is changed in the RD Session Host Configuration MMC, under User Logon Mode. Connections can also be inhibited by simply blocking the Remote Desktop Protocol to the server via the Integrated Firewall settings. Of course, totally blocking RDP will render remote connections unavailable even for administrators. In that case, you have to be logged in physically at a console to install software. But that's not a bad idea in case something goes wrong or you need to swap media.

Wizard-Based Installations

For the first method, locate Install Application On Remote Desktop Server in Control Panel (Figure 11.16).

When the initial Install Program From Floppy Disk Or CD-ROM page of the wizard presents itself, click Next (see Figure 11.17). If you are installing from CD, insert it now. By the way, who among you is still using floppy disks to install server applications?

FIGURE 11.16
Installing an RDS application using the wizard

FIGURE 11.17
Install Program Wizard

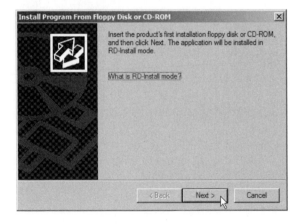

When you click Next, the wizard will scan any floppy drives you have for software installers, followed by a scan of any optical drives. If no drives are detected or no software installers are located, the wizard will default to a Run Installation Program page that prompts you to enter the location manually or browse to the location (Figure 11.18).

FIGURE 11.18
Locate the installer

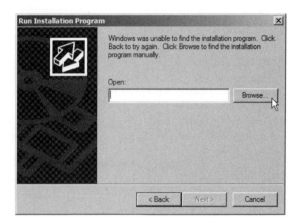

You will find that as your RDS farm grows even modestly in size, placing your application installers on a shared network drive becomes a fast and convenient method for installing applications onto the RDS servers. At this point, either enter the location of the application installer or browse to it, double-click the setup file, and click Next to begin the installation process. Once the application installation has completed, click the Finish button, as shown in Figure 11.19.

FIGURE 11.19
Complete the
installation wizard

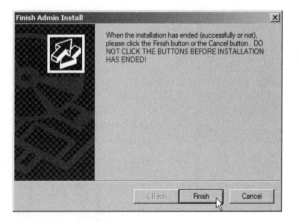

Congratulations! You've just installed an RDS application onto your RD Session Host that your remote users can now access. Go ahead and log into the RD Session Host from a remote client device as the John Doe user we set up earlier. Navigate the Start menu to locate Adobe Reader, and click to launch it. If everything completed successfully, our John Doe user now has the ability to run that application. Even better is the fact that whatever changes John Doe makes to his application, such as altering application-specific preferences, they persist across his sessions and do not affect those of any other user on that RD Session Host. To put it another way, the user can log on and launch an application. He can then alter the behavior of that application and then log off. The next time John Doe logs in and launches the application, all of the changes he made in his previous session will be remembered.

Manual Installations

The second method of installing applications into an RDS environment is a bit more manual but offers a level of installation flexibility. In the previous example, when we launched the wizard to install our application, the RDS server was basically expecting an application to be installed and made the appropriate preparations to accommodate the installation. And when the installation was complete, we closed the wizard and the RDS server knew the event was complete and again took the appropriate actions. This all ensured that whatever application we installed was done in such a manner that it could function properly in a multiuser environment.

But what if we have a more complex setup environment? What if we need to run multiple installations back to back or have an application set that has dependencies on other installers? In these cases we can leverage this second method of installation. We are going to manually place the RDS server into install mode and keep it there the entire time we are installing our applications. Once we have completed our installations, we are then going to manually place the RDS server back into execute mode.

Three commands support this RDS-specific behavior:

change user /install

change user /execute

change user /query

The first step prior to installing an application is to place the RDS server into install mode. We accomplish this by launching a command prompt (cmd.exe) as an administrator and entering the command **change user /install**. This will place the RDS server into install mode, and we can begin to install one or more applications or complex application sets. You are not required to install your application via the command line. Simply leave the Command Prompt window open and install your applications as you normally would. If you use this method, it is not necessary to use the Install Application On Remote Desktop Server Wizard as described previously. Figure 11.20 illustrates the command to enter.

FIGURE 11.20

Entering install mode

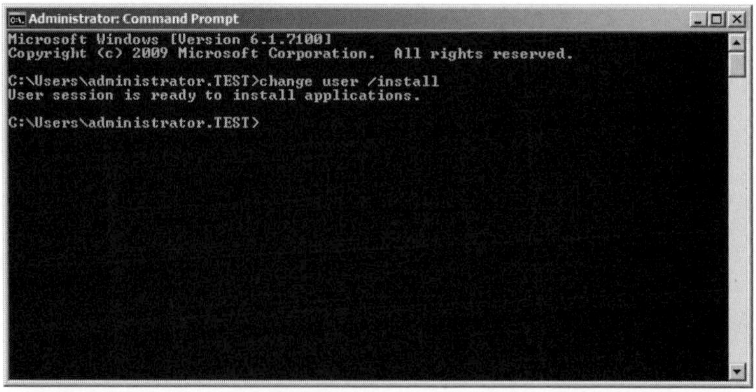

```
Administrator: Command Prompt                                         _|□|x|
Microsoft Windows [Version 6.1.7100]
Copyright (c) 2009 Microsoft Corporation.  All rights reserved.

C:\Users\administrator.TEST>change user /install
User session is ready to install applications.

C:\Users\administrator.TEST>
```

Once you have completed the installation of all of your applications, you need to place the server back into the normal operating mode of execute. This should be done prior to allowing any remote users to connect to the RD Session Host server. To place the server back into normal operation, enter the command shown in Figure 11.21, **change user /execute**. Once this is accomplished, you can then unblock RDP in the firewall, or reverse whatever method you utilized to inhibit RDP connections, to allow remote users to once again connect and gain access.

FIGURE 11.21
Entering execute mode

The change user /query command will display the current state of the RDS server. This is sometimes handy in case you forget what mode you are in or for troubleshooting efforts.

APP-V AS AN APPLICATION INSTALLATION METHOD

Microsoft's App-V is a product that provides the ability to virtualize an application and then execute that virtualized application on an RD Session Host.

This is a very powerful method of "installing" applications into an RDS environment, even though the applications are not actually installed into the Windows Server 2008 R2 OS.

For additional information, please review the chapters on App-V.

Licensing an RDS Environment

In order for your newly created RDS environment to continue to function longer than 120 days, you'll need to set up and configure an RD Licensing server. Although it is possible to install the RD Licensing server on the same server as an RD Session Host, in any production environment it is a best practice for it to be installed on a separate server. This gives the RDS farm more flexibility, especially when adding or deprecating RD Session Host servers within the farm. If you already have a Microsoft Windows Terminal Services Licensing server running in support of existing Windows Server 2008 Terminal Services, you can leverage that server for your Windows Server 2008 R2 RDS environment.

The RD Licensing server is fairly unique in the Microsoft ecosystem of operating systems and applications. Remote Desktop Services is one of the few Microsoft products that require a licensing server to issue and track consumption of a Client Access License (CAL). For instance, the Windows Server CAL, SQL CAL, and most others require no such construct. It is therefore important that your RDS environment be properly licensed and properly configured.

In addition, determining and acquiring the proper type of RDS CAL is also critically important. As discussed earlier in the "Preparing the Environment" section, choosing whether to deploy the Per User RDS CAL or the Per Device RDS CAL can impact the cost, and perhaps future flexibility, of a RDS environment.

Configuring an RD Licensing Server

The RD Licensing server can be installed on a domain-joined Windows Server 2008 or Windows Server 2008 R2 server. For the examples that follow, we will be setting up a new RD Licensing server on Windows Server 2008 R2. Log on as user with local administrator privileges to the Windows Server 2008 R2 server you plan on using. Server Manager should start automatically after you log on. After Server Manager starts, click Roles in the leftmost column and then click Add Roles in the Roles Summary area. As when we previously installed the RDS role, the Add Roles Wizard will launch and subsequently prompt you for the information needed to instantiate a new RDS role. Click Next on the Before You Begin page of the wizard. On the Select Server Roles page, click the check box for the Remote Desktop Services role and click Next, as illustrated in Figure 11.22.

FIGURE 11.22
Selecting the RDS role

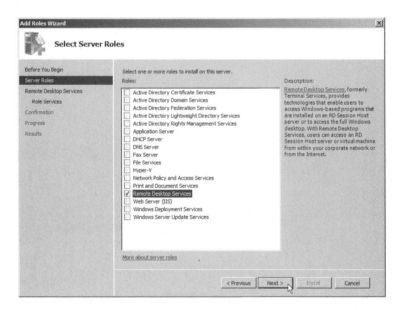

Click Next on the following Remote Desktop Services screen. You should now be at the Select Role Services screen. Click the check box to select the Remote Desktop Licensing role service and then click Next, as shown in Figure 11.23.

The next wizard page is Configure Discovery Scope For RD Licensing. The discovery scope option is disabled by default and is not required if you're using only RD Session Host servers on Windows Server 2008 R2. This is the case in our scenario, so we are not going to select this option. The reason it is not required for RD Session Hosts on Windows Server 2008 R2 is because automatic license discovery is no longer supported. Instead, the RD Licensing server now registers a Service Connection Point (SCP) within ADDS so that it can be selected and utilized when configuring the RD Session Host servers. If you need backward compatibility for earlier Terminal Services servers, then select and configure this option. Figure 11.24 displays the options that can be configured. Leave the preconfigured location for the RD Licensing database intact and click Next.

FIGURE 11.23
Selecting the RD
Licensing role service

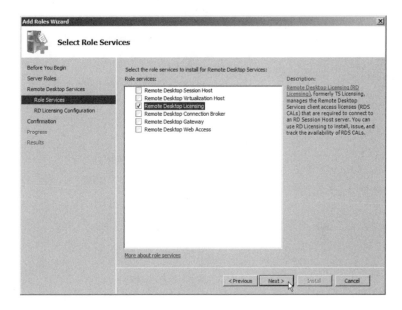

FIGURE 11.24
Configure Discovery
Scope

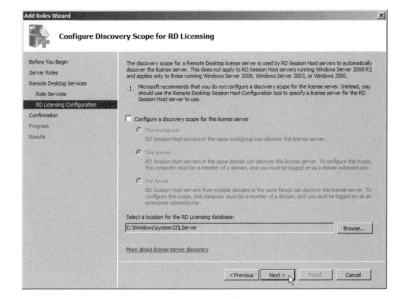

The next wizard page is Confirm Installation Selections. This provides you an opportunity to review and correct any setup errors prior to the installation of the role service. Click Install if everything looks good. No restart of the server should be required. The wizard will then present the Installation Results screen (Figure 11.25) when everything is completed. You will receive a warning letting you know to configure all of your RD Session Host servers to make use of this newly constituted RD Licensing server. Click Close.

FIGURE 11.25
Installation Results

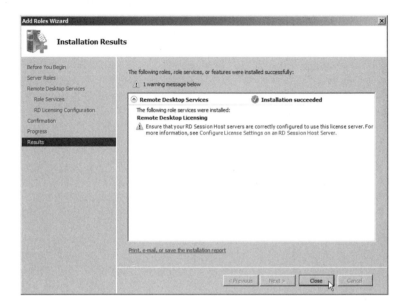

Now we need to activate and configure the RD Licensing server appropriately for the environment. In the far-left column of Server Manager, expand the Roles object and then select the Remote Desktop Services object. On the right column of Server Manager, scroll down until you find the heading of Advanced Tools, as indicated in Figure 11.26 and click the link to open Remote Desktop Licensing Manager. You can also click the Start menu and enter **licmgr.exe** in the Search Programs And Files box and press Enter. Entering **licensing** or **remote desktop licensing** in the Search Programs And Files field will also locate the application.

Once RD Licensing Manager opens, you will see your server listed by its NetBIOS name. We now need to activate the server so that it can begin to assign and track RDS CALs to our devices or users. Right-click the server and select Activate Server from the contextual menu, as shown in Figure 11.27.

The Activate Server Wizard will launch and take you through the process of activating your RD Licensing server. Click Next at the initial welcome screen. The following page will ask you for a connection method and defaults to Automatic Connection. This requires an Internet connection, but it's the most straightforward way of activating the server. You can also select to utilize a web browser or complete the activation via a telephone call. Phone calls are useful where no Internet connectivity exists because of a very restrictive, secure environment. Once you've selected your connection method, click Next. If you've selected Automatic, then the wizard will then contact a Microsoft Clearinghouse. If for some reason the wizard cannot contact a Clearinghouse server, you need to either correct the network connectivity issue or resort to one of the other two methods to activate the RD Licensing server. Once communication is established with the Clearinghouse server, the wizard will continue and prompt you for your company information. Provide the requested information and click Next. The next screen asks for additional information regarding the RD Licensing server's administrator. Please keep in mind that the information entered is kept confidential and is used in the event of problem resolution regarding RDS CALs and licensing that may occur in the future. Populate the fields as requested and click Next. The Activate Server Wizard will then be completed (Figure 11.28), and the RD Licensing server will be activated. Clicking Next will then launch another wizard that will guide you through entering the RDS CALs you acquired.

FIGURE 11.26
Starting RD Licensing Manager

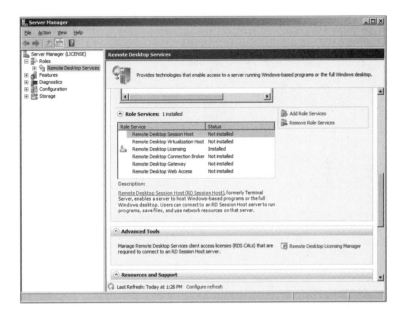

FIGURE 11.27
Activating the RD Licensing server

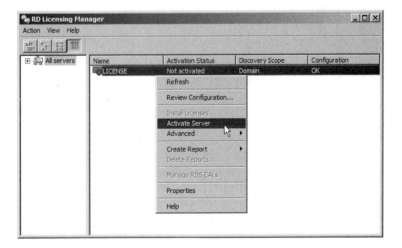

FIGURE 11.28
Completing the RD
Licensing server
activation

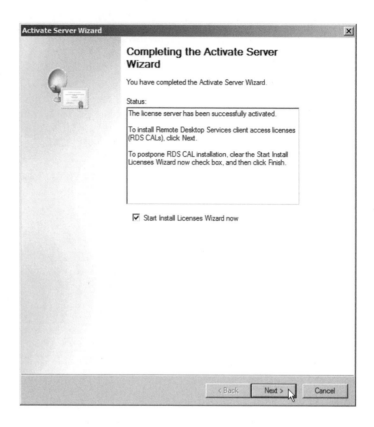

Complete the subsequent wizard to install any or all of your RDS CALs. RDS CALs can be acquired in a number of ways, and the wizard accommodates all of the purchase methods. Choose how you acquired the RDS CALs and then click Next. You will then be prompted to enter the license code, agreement number, or some other unique identifier that corresponds to the RDS CALs you acquired. Click Next when compete. The subsequent page will then ask for the product version. Select the appropriate version/server in the pull-down menu. Then you need to indicate whether the RDS CALs you acquired were Per Device or Per User and the total number acquired for that particular license. Click Next, and the wizard will complete the installation of the RDS CALs. Click Finish. The wizard will exit, and you will see that your RD Licensing server (Figure 11.29) now indicates that it is activated within the RD Licensing Manager. Double-clicking the server will show all of the RDS and TS CALs installed on that particular RD Licensing server.

That's it. You've finished! Well, almost. Now we need to go back to our RD Session Host server and configure it to use our newly configured RD Licensing server. Log on to the RD Session Host server and go into Server Manager. In Server Manager, expand the Roles object in the left column and then expand the Remote Desktop Services object. Figure 11.30 shows the options available for configuration. Select the RD Session Host Configuration object, and configuration information concerning the RD Session Host server will appear in the center column. In that column, under the Edit Settings ➤ Licensing section, you'll see that the RD Session Host server has nothing specified. Double-click Remote Desktop Licensing Mode.

FIGURE 11.29
Activated RD Licensing server

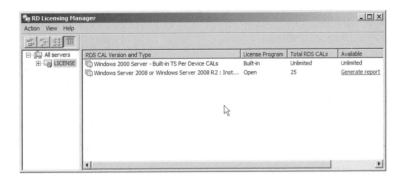

FIGURE 11.30
RD Session Host Configuration status

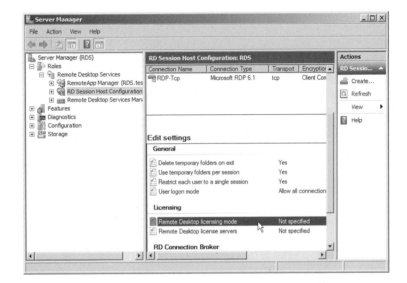

The Properties window will be displayed and the Licensing tab will be selected. You must select how your RD Session Host server is to be licensed — Per Device or Per User. The licensing mode should match the type of RDS CALs you acquired and installed on the RD Licensing server. A mismatch could result in users being unable to connect to the RDS server. Once you've selected the appropriate licensing mode, you will then be able to specify the RD Licensing server. Click Add, and the Add License Server dialog box will appear (Figure 11.31). It should already be populated with the RD Licensing server we previously set up. Select the server in the Known License Servers box on the left, and click Add to place it in the Specified License Servers box on the right. Complete this selection process by clicking OK.

You are then returned to the Properties window (Figure 11.32), which now indicates that that an RD Licensing server has been selected for the RD Session Host server. Click OK to continue.

When you now look at the RD Session Host Configuration screen in Server Manager, you'll see that the Remote Desktop licensing mode is either Per User or Per Device, and that the Remote Desktop Licensing server is Specified. Subsequent installation of RD Session Host servers now just need to be pointed to the existing RD Licensing server.

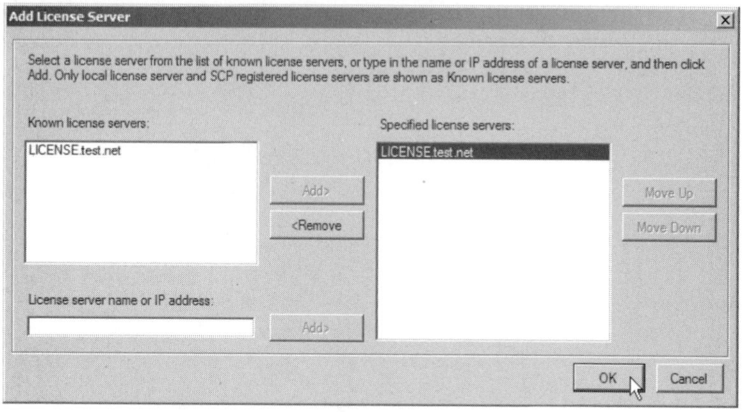

FIGURE 11.31
Selecting an RD
Licensing server

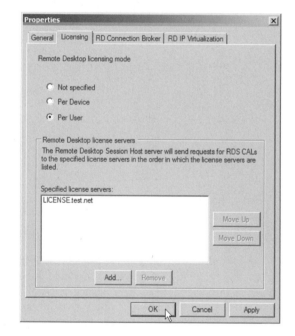

FIGURE 11.32
Completing the licensing
configuration for the RD
Session Host

The Bottom Line

Determine when to use an RDS Per User CAL and when to use an RDS Per Device CAL.
Understand how a Per User RDS CAL and a Per Device RDS CAL differ, when either should
be deployed in your environment, and how your choice can have an impact on the overall cost
of deploying an RDS solution.

> **Master It**   You are put in charge of standing up an RDS environment so that workers in
> your call center can access applications via new thin client devices. The call center operates

24/7 and is manned by three shifts of workers. Should you acquire and deploy Per User RDS CALs, or Per Device RDS CALs?

Identify which clients can utilize Network Level Authentication.   Understanding which clients or devices can or cannot make use of NLA is important, and you must determine your connectivity needs. The enhanced security of NLA comes at the cost of reducing the types of client devices that can connect.

> **Master It**   You are configuring an RD Session Host and have determined that Windows 2000 users will need to connect. Do you implement NLA?

Determine when to enable Client Experience features.   Enabling the Client Experience consumes additional server resources such as RAM and CPU, thus reducing the total number of remote users you can concurrently host on an RD Session Host.

> **Master It**   You are planning an RDS environment for knowledge workers who are fairly adept and comfortable with Microsoft client operating systems such as Windows Vista. Should you enable the Client Experience in your RDS environment?

Properly install applications on an RD Session Host.   When you are installing applications onto an RD Session Host, it is important that the server be placed in the proper state. If the server is not appropriately configured to accept new programs, unexpected results such as failure of programs to execute could result.

> **Master It**   You are about to install three major applications and two smaller supporting programs onto an RD Session Host. What is an appropriate procedure or course of action to ensure that the applications are installed in such a manner as to function correctly?

Chapter 12

Deploying and Accessing Remote Desktop Services

Now that we've set up and configured RDS with an RD Session Host and an RD Licensing server and installed an application within the environment, we need to explore some ways in which we can allow our end users to connect to the resources we're providing them. In this chapter, when we discuss deployment of RDS, we are referring not to the RDS environment itself but to the methods that are available with which we can distribute and make available access to the applications RDS is supporting. As you will see, there are a number of ways to accomplish this. We will also consider users accessing the RDS while on the corporate network and while outside of your network firewall over the Internet. Microsoft has improved deployment and access features first found in Windows Server 2008 Terminal Services that allow IT professionals to much more readily and securely deploy what is now called Remote Desktop Services (RDS).

In this chapter, you will learn to:

♦ Describe the differences between a full desktop provided by an RD Session Host and a remote desktop provided within a Virtual Desktop Infrastructure (VDI)

♦ Determine when to utilize the functionality provided by RemoteApp

♦ Configure access to RemoteApp programs via a web browser

♦ Deploy applications to only certain users or groups of users

Who and Where Are Your Users?

As you begin to deploy application resources to your end users based on the new RDS environment you set up, you first have to understand who these users are or, more specifically, what type of users they are and from where and on what device they will be connecting. Knowing this will allow you to determine the best way to deploy the RDS resources to those users. For instance, are your users office or clerical workers whose PCs are connected to your main network? Or are those same types of users spread out across your entire wide area network (WAN)? Do you have a need for users to connect when outside your firewall across the public Internet? And do they currently use a VPN connection to access your existing corporate resources? The more questions you can ask yourself regarding your constituents, the more detailed and clearer an idea you will have of which mechanisms to utilize in the deployment of RDS resources.

While we have offered some items for consideration, everyone's environment is unique, and their needs and requirements vary widely, so no complete list of questions can be offered to assist you in this matter. What we can do is get to the root of why these questions regarding why, who, and where the users are is important. Who your users are, or the user type, will help determine such things as whether they will be deployed a full Windows desktop or just the necessary applications to adequately complete their jobs. Where your users are located will assist in selecting connectivity mechanisms and deployment options for those full Windows desktops or individual applications.

For example, let's consider users who have full-fledged Windows desktops at their desks in the office. Everything those users need to accomplish their tasks is provided by those local computers. But when those users are away from the office, say, at home, they often need to connect into the corporate network to access a specific application. How can we deploy our RDS resources in the most effective way to accommodate these user types? Based on the who and where questions, we might determine that deploying that single application securely to remote users over the Internet without requiring the added prerequisite step of VPN connectivity is the best method. You may further find that as this is deployed, your internal users can also benefit from connecting to that single application in the same manner. And as you add similar user types across your organization who happen to be located across a slower WAN link on your network, this method will allow you to easily deploy this single application to those users with very little performance penalty.

An additional example would be users using thin-client devices to connect to your RDS environment while on the corporate network. In this case, the device itself limits how we deploy our RDS application resources. Thin clients are often short on computing power and run operating systems that do not support most applications. Thus, you will typically need to deliver a full remote desktop to users of these devices.

Get in the habit of conducting regular reviews or assessments of your organization's applications and how they are being deployed. You may discover that, in conjunction with the who and where of your user base, you can more effectively, securely, and economically deliver those applications by further leveraging your RDS environment. So go ahead and clearly define who your users are and from where they will be connecting, realizing that this exercise may result in deployment of RDS to only a subset or cross section of users and a handful of applications. That's fine. Consider it a place to start. In fact, your RDS environment may never grow past this initial deployment. RDS is a tool to help us as IT professionals best implement and deliver resources, and the environment can be as large or small as we see fit.

Deploying a Server-Based Desktop

Two options are available for deploying application resources in an RDS environment. One is on a per-application basis called RemoteApp, and the other is to deploy a full desktop to the user that contains and provides all of the applications the user requires. We will first discuss the deployment of a full server-based desktop to the users, and then later in this chapter we'll discuss deploying single applications via RemoteApp.

ISN'T THIS VDI?

Don't confuse a server-based full desktop in a Remote Desktop Session Host environment with a remote desktop in a Remote Desktop Virtualization Host environment. It's easy to do, as there are many similarities, so let's clarify the one main difference. One desktop is a shared environment based on a server OS, and the other is a unique and discrete desktop OS environment. A server-based full desktop provided to a user via an RD Session Host is a shared OS environment wherein computational resources are allocated and shared among all participating users connected to the RD Session Host. In other words, this is the classic Terminal Services environment that has existed for many years. A hosted virtual remote desktop, as you find in the RD Virtualization Host environment, is a unique computational environment wherein a separate desktop OS environment is installed for each user on a server running a hypervisor. This provides a greater level of segmentation between users because each user has their own OS instance whose applications will not conflict with any other instance. In addition, because you are running a client OS, more applications may be compatible with that OS. One of the downsides of virtual remote desktops comes in the form of reduced scalability, because fewer users can be serviced per physical host using a full remote desktop OS than can be supported when leveraging a shared OS for a full desktop based on an RD Session Host. You will learn more about virtual hosted remote desktops and Virtual Desktop Infrastructure (VDI) later in this book.

Deploying a full server-based desktop via an RD Session Host to your users is a fairly straightforward process. In fact, we did just that in Chapter 11. At the conclusion of that chapter, we successfully delivered a full server-based desktop to a user connecting to an RDS Session Host. What we did not consider was the actual configuration and deployment of the Remote Desktop Connection (RDC) client software to your end users. You could certainly explain to your users how to configure the RDC client to connect or possibly even promulgate very detailed instructions to do the same. Ambitious administrators may even personally visit their users to set up the connection for them. While that would work with a very small set of users, it obviously does not scale well. Our goal is to preconfigure a Remote Desktop Protocol (RDP) file for a specific RDC that will automatically connect the user to the appropriate RD Session Host. The user need not do anything more than double-click the appropriate file and, after authenticating, be connected to the correct server. There are a number of ways to accomplish this task.

The first and more complex method involves manually creating an RDP file that specifies all of the parameters required for a proper RDC client connection. By default, a single RDP file resides in the following directory in Windows 7 and Windows Vista:

```
C:\Users\%userName%\Documents\Default.rdp
```

Substitute the actual username in place of the *%userName%* variable. This is a hidden file, so you will need to enable the Show Hidden Files option to actually see the file. At this point, we need to open the document with WordPad, and we have two ways we can go about it from within the graphical user interface (GUI). The first is to right-click the document and select Open With from the contextual menu. In the ensuing dialog box, ensure that you uncheck the Always Use The Selected Program box or else you will run into problems very soon. Browse to the wordpad.exe application located in the Program Files\Windows NT\Accessories directory and open the document. The second method to open the document is to first open WordPad and then open the Default.rdp document from within that application.

Another option to get to the file is to open a command prompt window (**CMD.EXE**) and browse to it. For this method, it is not necessary to first enable the Show Hidden Files option. In the command prompt window enter the following command:

```
dir \users\%userName%\documents /A:H
```

Again, substitute the actual username for the variable *%userName%* in the above command. This should bring up a screen similar to the one shown in Figure 12.1. You can see the Default.rdp file that resides in the user's documents folder.

FIGURE 12.1
Exposing the
Default.rdp file

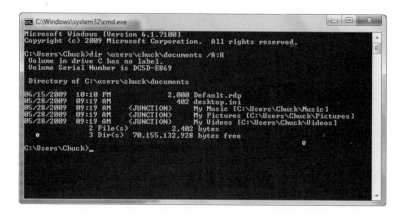

To open this hidden document in WordPad in one command line, enter the following:

```
"\program files\windows nt\accessories\wordpad.exe"
\users\%userName%\documents\default.rdp
```

Figure 12.2 shows this command entered in the command prompt window.

FIGURE 12.2
Opening the
Default.rdp file

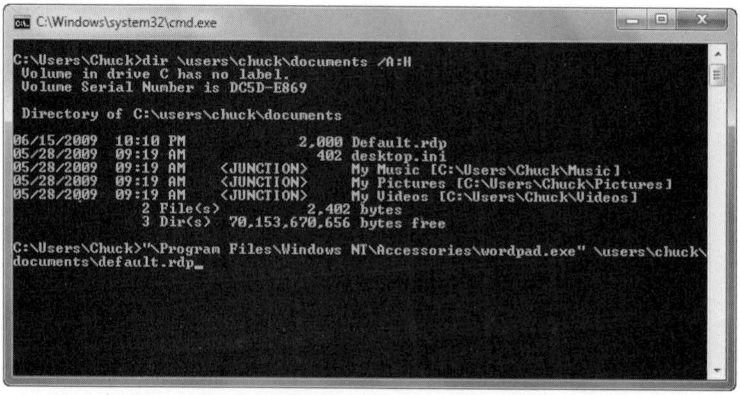

Entering this command will automatically open the `Default.rdp` document in WordPad for editing.

DEFAULT.RDP FILE CONTENTS

Here is an example of what a `Default.rdp` document might look like:

```
screen mode id:i:2
use multimon:i:0
desktopwidth:i:1680
desktopheight:i:1050
session bpp:i:32
winposstr:s:0,3,0,0,800,600
compression:i:1
keyboardhook:i:2
audiocapturemode:i:0
videoplaybackmode:i:1
connection type:i:2
displayconnectionbar:i:1
disable wallpaper:i:1
allow font smoothing:i:0
allow desktop composition:i:0
disable full window drag:i:1
disable menu anims:i:1
disable themes:i:0
disable cursor setting:i:0
bitmapcachepersistenable:i:1
full address:s:fe80::c13:298b:1eac:95db
audiomode:i:0
redirectprinters:i:1
redirectcomports:i:0
redirectsmartcards:i:1
redirectclipboard:i:1
redirectposdevices:i:0
redirectdirectx:i:1
autoreconnection enabled:i:1
authentication level:i:2
prompt for credentials:i:0
negotiate security layer:i:1
remoteapplicationmode:i:0
alternate shell:s:
shell working directory:s:
gatewayhostname:s:
gatewayusagemethod:i:4
gatewaycredentialssource:i:4
gatewayprofileusagemethod:i:0
promptcredentialonce:i:1
use redirection server name:i:0
```

As you can see, quite a bit of information is contained within the document.

While we will not cover in detail each of the items in the `Default.rdp` file, the important ones to get our users nicely connected are the following:

`screen mode id:i:` 2

`desktopwidth:i:` 1024

`desktopheight:i:` 768

`session bbp:i:` 32

`full address:s:` 10.1.1.10

The `screen mode` option can be a value of either 1 or 2. A value of 1 allows you to explicitly define the remote window resolution, while a value of 2 sets the resolution for full screen.

The `desktopwidth` and `desktopheight` values are set only when you indicated a value of 1 for `screen mode`. These desktop integer values are typically assigned for standard resolutions such as 800×600 or 1024×768. For most users who will be getting a full server-based desktop, it is a best practice to set their resolution to full screen or `screen mode` to a value of 2.

`session bbp` determines the color depth to which the user's remote session will be set. It is recommended that this value be set to 32, indicating a 32-bit color depth. Although you may think that reducing the color depth will improve performance on the remote server, that will not always be the case. In Windows Server 2008 R2, 32-bit color will typically perform better than 24-bit because of specific optimizations made for 32-bit color. Dropping to 16- or 15-bit color will reduce bandwidth but may also noticeably hurt the user experience. So, unless you have an application that cannot support 32-bit color, set it to 32. Other acceptable values are 24, 16, and 15.

Maybe the most important setting is `full address` because without it we have no way of knowing to where to connect. This value can be either a valid IPv4 or IPv6 address or a fully qualified domain name (FQDN). Using the FQDN is the best option, as it allows you the flexibility to change server IP addresses without breaking all of your RDP connections.

At a minimum, only the `full address` value needs to be present in the RDP file. If no other values are present, they will be set to defaults. The RDP file is never written back to by the remote server, so even after a successful connection, your minimal configurations are left untouched.

Now we have a means by which to manually create a very specific, customized RDP file that RDC will use to connect our users to the appropriate full server-based desktop on an RD Session Host. Go ahead and make changes to the `Default.rdp` document, and then do a Save As and save the modified document to the desktop. Make certain that the file is saved in a plain-text format and has .rdp as a file extension. Give it a name such as `My Remote Desktop` to make it obvious what the file is intended to be used for.

We're almost there, and all we need to do is get that newly created RDP file out to our intended users. This process can be automated through use of software distribution tools such as Microsoft System Center Configuration Manager (SCCM). Target an obvious location for the RDP file's final destination. Potentially this could be the user's desktop or in their Start menu. Wherever you place it, all you now need to do is let the users know it's there, and they can start connecting with no configuration effort on their part at all.

That was a lot of manual work, but hopefully it served to give you an idea of what is going on behind the scenes when a remote user establishes a connection to an RD Session Host. An easier way to accomplish the same task is to use the GUI RDC client configuration itself to create a new connection profile. Simply launch the Remote Desktop Connection (RDC) client software. The actual executable is called `mstsc.exe`. The very first time the RDC is launched on a computer, it will have no configuration information and will appear as indicated in Figure 12.3. If your window has something entered in the Computer section, clear it and you should be good.

In the Computer section, enter the FQDN or IPv4/IPv6 address of the RD Session Host to which you want users to connect. Next, click the Options button in the bottom-left corner of the window. This will expose all of the options you can set as we did manually in the previous examples (Figure 12.4).

Take some time to browse the RDC configuration tabs. You will see that you can set every-thing precisely to your requirements. When you've finished configuring the RDC client, click Save As under the Connection Settings section, as shown in Figure 12.5, and save your new RDP file with a recognizable name, as you did previously. Now you have an RDP file that can be deployed to your users through a software distribution tool.

For an additional layer of protection, you can leverage Group Policy to secure the client connection and workspace. For instance, there is a Group Policy (GP) that prevents a user from saving credentials in the RDP file. Others set cryptographic mechanisms or inhibit local user resources from being redirected to the RD Session Host. The complete list of GPs for RDS can be found in the Group Policy Management Editor console. In Figure 12.6, you can see a list of the Group Policy settings that are available for determining the RDC client behavior.

FIGURE 12.5
Saving the new RDP file

FIGURE 12.6
Group Policy Settings for
RDC Client

So now we have a method of creating and distributing a properly configured RDC client to our users, allowing them to easily connect to application resources provided by our RD Session Host server. When these users connect, they will be greeted with a full desktop. Next we will explore a deployment method that allows us to connect a user to a single application.

Deploying a Single Application

Something new that was introduced in Microsoft Windows Server 2008 and carried forward into Windows Server 2008 R2 was RemoteApp. This allows a single application executing on an RD Session Host server to be seamlessly displayed on the remotely connected user's device. This is a fantastic feature as it presents IT administrators with the ability to host and deploy a single critical application without the need to deliver a complete desktop environment. It's a very powerful feature, because it allows you to deliver an application via RDS that looks and acts just like any other locally installed application. This seamless integration with the desktop makes user adoption much easier. The first step is to get RemoteApp up and running. Log on as a server administrator to the RDS server that we configured in the last chapter to be an RD Session Host and open Server Manager. Under Roles you should see Remote Desktop Services. Expand that and you should find the RemoteApp Manager. This was installed automatically when we added the RDS role with the RD Session Host role service to the server. Select RemoteApp Manager, and the center section of the Server Manager MMC will display all pertinent information for RemoteApp. You can also launch RemoteApp Manager directly from the Start menu under Administrative Tools ➤ Remote Desktop Services.

Let's deploy the Adobe Reader application we previously installed as a single application using RemoteApp. To do this, click Add RemoteApp Programs in the Actions section, as indicated in Figure 12.7.

FIGURE 12.7

Add RemoteApp
Programs

This will start the RemoteApp Wizard, which will guide us through the necessary steps. On the initial screen of the wizard, click Next (Figure 12.8).

FIGURE 12.8

RemoteApp Wizard

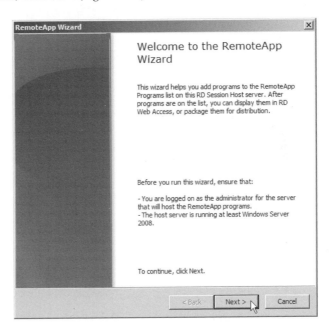

The next wizard screen allows you to select one or more applications to deploy using RemoteApp. Notice that every application that is installed on the RD Session Host is available, not just the applications we installed after configuring the RDS environment. If it's not selected already, highlight Adobe Reader by clicking the name of the application, and then click the Properties button, as indicated in Figure 12.9.

FIGURE 12.9
Selecting properties for an application

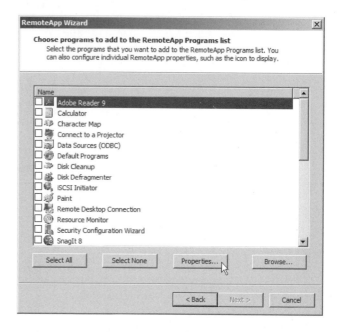

The RemoteApp Properties screen allows us to pass command-line arguments to the application upon its launch by a remote user. There is also a check box to allow or disallow the application in question from being made available through RD Web Access. We'll discuss RD Web Access a bit later in this chapter. But better yet, the User Assignment tab, as shown in Figure 12.10, provides the ability to mask particular applications from users based on group membership within ADDS. This is not just security through obscurity but rather a better interface and experience for the end user. Only the applications designated for a particular user will be presented to that user.

For our purposes, click Cancel and get back to the Choose Programs To Add screen. Click the check box next to Adobe Reader to select it to become a RemoteApp, and then click Next, as in Figure 12.11.

A final wizard screen will appear indicating what is about to occur. Click Finish (Figure 12.12).

You are then returned to the RemoteApp Manager. There you will see at the bottom of that screen, under the RemoteApp Programs section, the Adobe Reader application we selected. That's it. We have just configured RemoteApp to deliver a single application instead of an entire desktop environment. Now we need to provide a means for our users to connect to the RD Session Host and execute the application.

Deploying RemoteApp to Users

A couple of mechanisms exist to deploy the RemoteApp single application to the users. One is quite similar to the method we utilized to deploy a full RD Session Host–based desktop. RDS provides an automated means to create both an RDP file and a standard Windows Installer specific to the RemoteApp application. Once we create either of these files, we can once again use our distribution tools to disseminate it to the users.

FIGURE 12.10
RemoteApp Properties

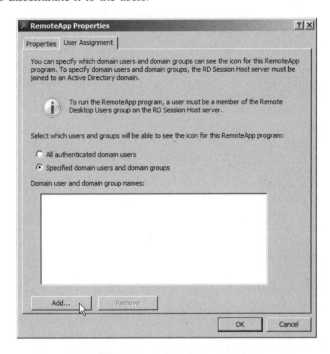

FIGURE 12.11
Selecting an application

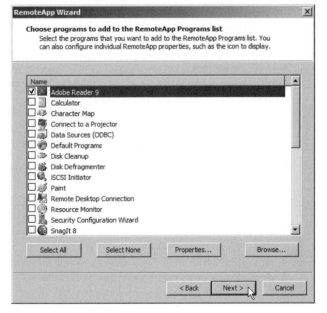

FIGURE 12.12
Completing the
RemoteApp Wizard

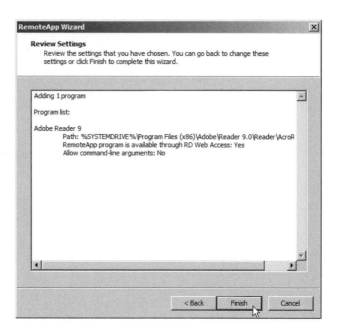

REMOTEAPP RDP FILE DEPLOYMENT

The first method we will review to deploy access to the RemoteApp program produces an RDP file. The final RDP file contains all of the requisite information to connect an end user to the RemoteApp single application. This RDP file, once created, can be sent using software distribution tools or even placed on a file share that users can access. Unlike the process outlined previously to allow access to a full RD Session Host desktop, RemoteApp provides automation for the creation of the RDP file. To begin, select a program such as Adobe Reader 9 in the RemoteApp Programs section of the RemoteApp Manager, as indicated in Figure 12.13.

In the Actions menu on the right, you will see that a contextual section for the selected Adobe Reader application appears. Click Create .rdp File, as shown in Figure 12.14, and the RemoteApp Wizard will launch.

This wizard will guide you through the creation and configuration of an RDP file that can be used to get users connected to the application delivered by RemoteApp. Click Next on the Welcome To The RemoteApp Wizard screen. The next screen, shown in Figure 12.15, will prompt you for a location to save the final RDP file as well as for other specific connection settings. For now, accept the defaults and click Next.

The next screen will show you what is about to happen. Click Finish to complete the wizard and create the RDP file. A window will open to the directory you specified, C:\Program Files\Packaged Programs by default, with the RDP file you just created. When our users double-click this RDP file, they will automatically be connected to the RemoteApp program, Adobe Reader 9 in our example. All that is left to do is to disseminate the file to users by a method of your choosing.

A closer examination of the file, by opening it in WordPad, for example, will provide you some insight into what the RemoteApp Wizard did when creating the RDP file. Our example is shown in Figure 12.16.

FIGURE 12.13
Select a RemoteApp
program

FIGURE 12.13
Select a RemoteApp
program

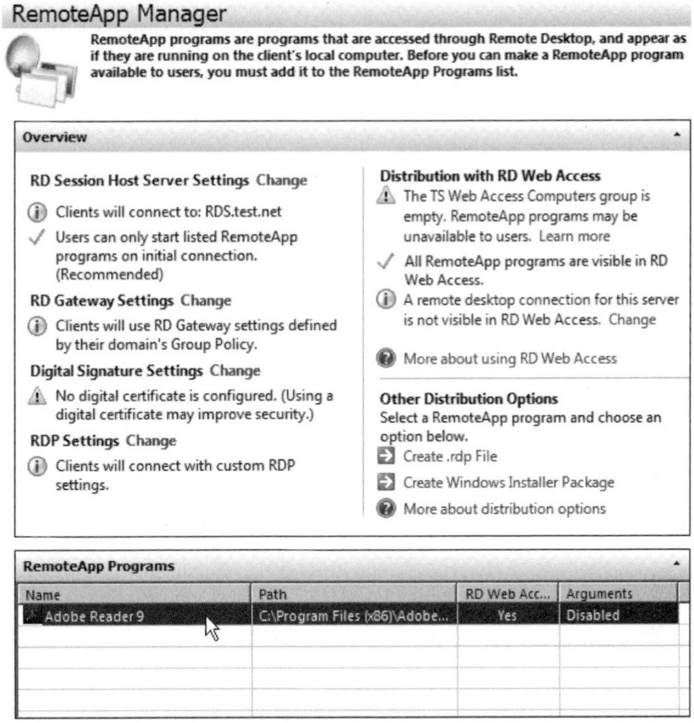

FIGURE 12.14
Create .rdp File

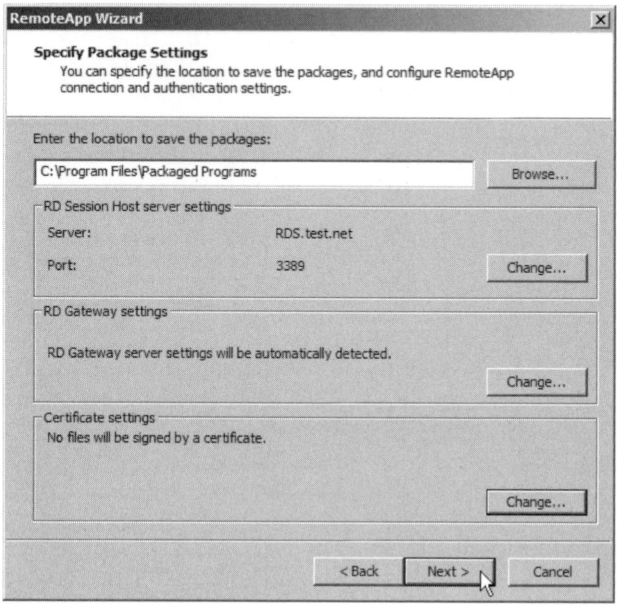

FIGURE 12.15
Specify Package Settings

FIGURE 12.16
RemoteApp RDP file
contents

```
redirectclipboard:i:1
redirectposdevices:i:0
redirectprinters:i:1
redirectcomports:i:1
redirectsmartcards:i:1
devicestoredirect:s:*
drivestoredirect:s:*
redirectdrives:i:1
session bpp:i:32
prompt for credentials on client:i:1
span monitors:i:1
use multimon:i:1
remoteapplicationmode:i:1
server port:i:3389
allow font smoothing:i:1
promptcredentialonce:i:1
authentication level:i:2
gatewayusagemethod:i:2
gatewayprofileusagemethod:i:0
gatewaycredentialssource:i:0
full address:s:RDS.test.net
alternate shell:s:||AcroRd32
remoteapplicationprogram:s:||AcroRd32
gatewayhostname:s:
remoteapplicationname:s:Adobe Reader 9
remoteapplicationcmdline:s:
```

REMOTEAPP WINDOWS INSTALLER PACKAGE DEPLOYMENT

The second method of deploying access to a RemoteApp program is to use a Windows Installer
Package. This format can be used in conjunction with software distribution tools such as
Microsoft System Center Configuration Manager to aid in the programmatic deployment of
RemoteApp access. The Windows Installer Package is typically a better choice than the RDP

file, because it allows much more flexibility in terms of how the RDP connection is integrated into the desktop environment.

For this method, choose Create Windows Installer Package in the Actions section for the selection application, as shown in Figure 12.14. This will again launch the RemoteApp Wizard to guide you through the process. On the first screen of the wizard, click Next. You will see an identical screen to the one you encountered when configuring the RDP file (Figure 12.15). Click Next to accept the defaults. The ensuing screen, shown in Figure 12.17, presents some intriguing options.

FIGURE 12.17

Configure Distribution Package

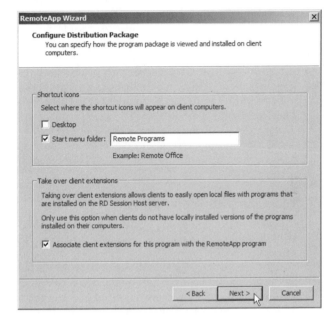

We can specify where on the end user's device we want the RemoteApp launch icon to appear. We can place it on the user's desktop or in a folder in the user's Start menu. Be cautious of placing too many icons on the user's desktop, if any at all. Many times, these will become lost in the clutter and overlooked if not accidentally deleted.

Also provided is the ability to take over client extensions. This is extremely handy for a user who will often use a RemoteApp program running on an RD Session Host to access data residing on his local machine or a remote share. For instance, we may have users who receive a large number of Adobe Acrobat documents via email. These documents have an extension of .pdf. Unfortunately for our user, he does not have any applications installed locally that can use to open these PDF documents. By selecting Associate Client Extensions For This Program With The RemoteApp Program, we allow this RemoteApp distribution package to essentially masquerade as a locally installed program that can open the user's PDF documents.

Make your selections and select Next to see a screen describing what the wizard is about to perform. Click Finish to complete the wizard and open a window to your newly created Windows Installer Package. Notice that this file is in a standard MSI format. This is a file that will run an installation routine when executed, unlike an RDP file that causes RDC to execute. When used in tandem with Microsoft System Center Configuration Manager or other such software distribution tools, this method of deploying access to the RemoteApp programs is more refined than the simple RDP method.

Using the Web to Access RDS

So far, we've configured our RDS environment to provide full RD Session Host desktops as well as individual programs through RemoteApp. We've also explored a few methods of deploying access to those resources for our users. But while these deployment methods for access aren't terribly difficult, they may not meet your needs. For example, both the RDP and MSI deployment methods require something to be installed on the client machine, and you may not always have access to do that, as in the case of an offshore contractor. To address this, Microsoft introduced TS Web Access in Windows Server 2008. Microsoft has improved and enhanced it in Windows Server 2008 R2, and the feature is now called RD Web Access.

To be clear, leveraging RD Web Access does not allow your applications to execute within a web browser as the original TSWeb application did in Windows Server 2003. Rather, RD Web Access provides an access deployment mechanism for both full RD Session Host–based desktops and RemoteApp programs. In this case, we use the Web to enumerate resources that are available in a RDS environment to our end users. The user can easily locate the appropriate application and connect without regard for a pre-positioned or previously distributed RDP file. This greatly simplifies the IT professional's tasks since she may no longer need to leverage software distribution tools to send out RDP files or Windows Installer Packages for RDS connections. Future changes to the RDS environment, such as the addition of applications, can then easily and rapidly be achieved and deployed to users. Let's examine how this would be accomplished.

Installing RD Web Access

We want to provide access to our RDS environment for our users with as little effort as possible while yet allowing a dynamic and agile situation. RD Web Access will permit us to accomplish this quite readily.

To begin, we need a Windows Server 2008 R2 server that will provide the RD Web Access role. This should be a separate, stand-alone server. Once this server is installed and configured, ensure that it is fully patched and updated and joined to the Windows domain.

We will now instantiate the RD Web Access role on this server to allow us to more easily deploy access to the RDS environment resources. Launch Server Manager and right-click the Roles icon in the left column. From the contextual menu, select Add Roles. An Add Roles Wizard will launch and open an initial Before You Begin screen. Click Next. RD Web Access is part of the RDS environment, so select the Remote Desktop Services check box, as indicated in Figure 12.18, and click Next.

The following screen of the wizard is an informational screen that you have seen before; click Next to continue. We now see all of the choices within the RDS environment, and we will select Remote Desktop Web Access. When you click the check box, another window will appear, prompting you to install additional roles services required to support RD Web Access. This is new functionality introduced in Windows Server 2008 designed to ensure all of the required components are installed when configuring new services. In this case, as shown in Figure 12.19, we are being asked to also install components of the Microsoft Internet Information Services (IIS7) web server. This makes sense since will be utilizing the Web to deploy access to our RDS environment. To confirm and continue, click Add Required Role Services and then click Next on the original wizard screen.

Windows Server now dynamically inserts the requisite IIS Web Server Installation Wizard seamlessly into our process to ensure all essential components are established. Click Next on the Introduction To Web Server (IIS) screen to advance the wizard. You are now presented with a detailed view indicating all of the individual IIS components that will be installed to support the RD Web Access role. Leave the default selections in place and click Next. The wizard screen that follows will provide you an overview of everything that is about to occur. Click Install to confirm and continue. A progress window appears, and a few minutes will be required for the installation to complete. Finally, the wizard will present an Installation Results window, as in Figure 12.20, showing exactly how things went and any errors that may have occurred. Notice that it even presents a warning that RD Web Access still needs attention for the role service to be fully operational. Click Close to exit the wizard.

FIGURE 12.18

Selecting the Remote Desktop Services role

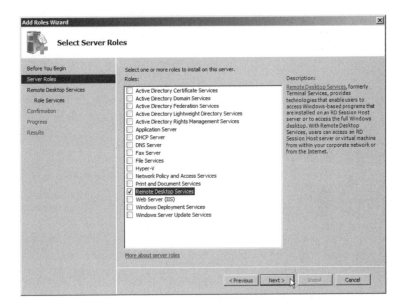

FIGURE 12.19

Adding the IIS Role Services

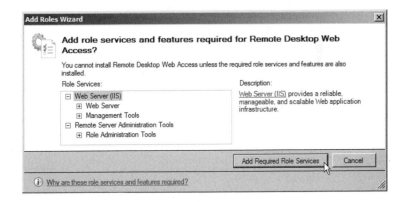

When the installation completes, you'll be returned to Server Manager, and you will see that the Remote Desktop Services role as well as the Web Server (IIS) role has been installed on the server. Expand Remote Desktop Services by clicking the plus sign next to the role name, and then again on Remote Desktop Services Manager. You will see the name of your server here, as shown in Figure 12.21.

FIGURE 12.20
Installation Results

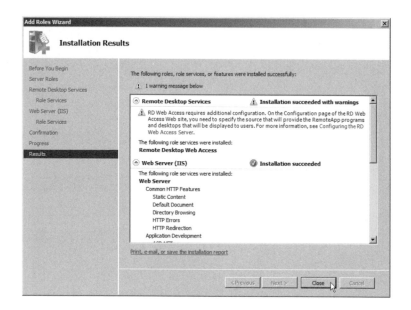

FIGURE 12.21
RD Web Access in Server
Manager

Establishing Authorization

Our next few tasks revolve mainly around security and establishing which users and computers can participate in the RDS environment via RD Web Access. For our examples, we already have John Doe (username: jdoe) properly configured as a member of the ADDS Security Group we named RDS Users. As you may remember, we created that group within the Users container and then added it to membership in the Remote Desktop Users security group located within the Builtin container. At a default minimum, all that is required to connect to RD Web Access is the user's membership within the Remote Desktop Users security group. If you do not already have a user who is a member of Remote Desktop Users, create one now or add an existing user to this group.

We also must define which RD Web Access computers can connect to the RD Session Host server or servers supporting our RemoteApp sources. To accomplish this, we need to add our RD Web Access server to the TS Web Access Computers local group on the RD Session Host server. Yes, the TS stands for Terminal Services and harkens back to the earlier name of what is now RDS. For compatibility reasons, Microsoft has left some directory and executable names unchanged. So where you see TS, assume RDS. On the RD Session Host server, you can locate the TS Web Access Computers local group by going to Start ➤ Administrative Tools ➤ Computer Management. When the Computer Management MMC opens, expand Local Users And Groups and then select Groups, as shown in Figure 12.22.

FIGURE 12.22
Local groups

In the center section of the screen you will see TS Web Access Computers, which you can double-click to open. Click on the Add button at the bottom of that window to add our RD Web Access server to this local group. A standard Select Users, Computers, Services Accounts, Or Groups dialog window will open, allowing you to enter the name of the RD Web Access server you want to allow to connect to this RD Session Host for RemoteApp access. Here you might notice that, by default, Computers is not included as an object type. To add it, click the Object Types button, select the Computers check box, and click the OK button, as indicated in Figure 12.23.

FIGURE 12.23
Adding the Computers object type

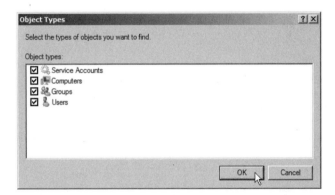

After you enter the name of the RD Web Access server, click the Check Names button to verify that you have entered a server that has a directory entry. If all is well, the computer name you entered should become underlined and no error message will appear, as illustrated in Figure 12.24. Click OK to proceed.

FIGURE 12.24
Selecting the RD Web Access Server

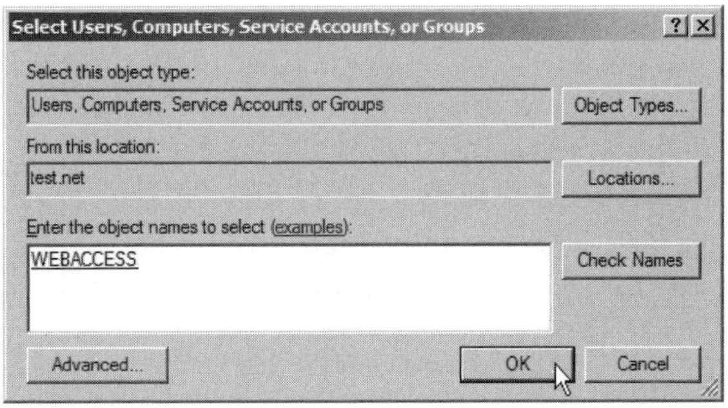

You now see the RD Web Access server as a member of the local TS Web Access Computers group, as shown in Figure 12.25. Click OK to commit this addition and close the window. If you want to manage this from an ADDS perspective to allow more flexibility, you can always create a security group in ADDS that will contain your RD Web Access servers and then add just that newly created group into the local TS Web Access Computers group. Then you can add the computer accounts for the RD Web Access servers to the group in ADDS. This will allow you to more readily move RD Web Access servers in and out of local membership across a large number of RD Session Host servers without actually modifying any of the local groups.

FIGURE 12.25
Adding the RD Web Access server to the group

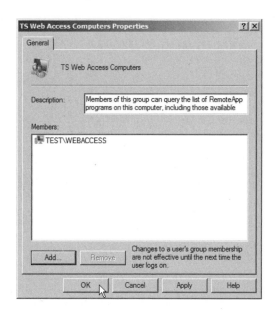

Finally, it is necessary to establish the users who have the ability to manage the RD Web Access server. This is accomplished on the RD Web Access server. Log onto the RD Web Access server and navigate to the local TS Web Access Administrators group by choosing Start ➢ Administrative Tools ➢ Computer Management. Double-click the TS Web Access Administrators group in the center section of the MMC to open it. Click the Add button to select which users will be members of this group. For our example, we will add the Domain Admins group to the TS Web Access Administrators group. If you need more granularity, you can add an individual user or a group you created in ADDS specifically for this task. Figure 12.26 represents what we will be doing in our example. Once you've added your user or group, click OK to commit and exit.

Configuring RD Web Access

Now we need to connect to the RD Web Access server and configure which RemoteApp programs will be made available to our users. On the RD Web Access server, go to Start ➢ Administrative Tools ➢ Remote Desktop Services ➢ Remote Desktop Web Access Configuration. Select RD Web Access Configuration to launch Internet Explorer. The first screen you see, similar to Figure 12.27, will be an error message indicating that the website's security certificate cannot be verified.

FIGURE 12.26
Adding users to
the TS Web Access
Administrators group

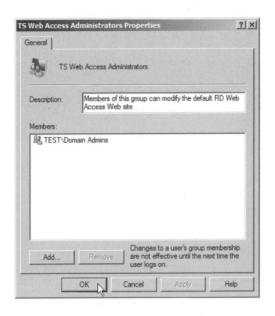

SECURITY CERTIFICATE?

This problem is caused by the server using a default self-signed X.509 certificate to provide the encryption. It is recommended as a best practice that you install and configure an X.509 certificate for this website from a trusted third party or from your own enterprise Public Key Infrastructure (PKI) certificate servers. This will enhance the RD Web Access server security and eliminate this error screen. Microsoft provides PKI functionality through the integrated Certificate Services in Windows Server products.

FIGURE 12.27
Website security
certificate error

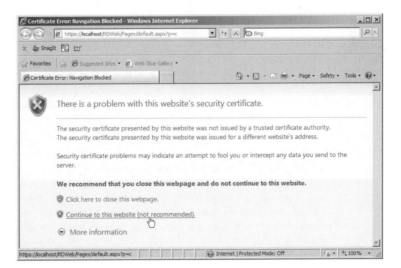

Before you do anything else, I recommend you change the URL that was automatically populated by the tool. The default URL is `https://localhost/RDWeb/Pages/default.aspx?p=c`. We will replace the `localhost` server name with the FQDN of the RD Web Access server. In our example, `localhost` will become `webaccess.test.net`. Type the change into the Internet Explorer (IE) address bar and press Enter. IE will connect to our RD Web Access server using the FQDN we entered instead of just the `localhost` name. We still have our certificate security error as expected. Click Continue To This Website (Not Recommended) to advance to the next screen.

The RD Web Access server will prompt us for credentials to authenticate and authorize us, as shown in Figure 12.28. Notice toward the top of the IE browser that the website may prompt you to install a Microsoft ActiveX control add-on. If so, select Run Add-on from the contextual menu and follow the instructions. At this point, I suggest you create a favorite for this site so that you can easily return to it, because this may become a frequently utilized tool. Enter your domain name/username and password for an Administrative account, and either leave the Security radio button at its default of This Is A Public Or Shared Computer or select This Is A Private Computer. If you choose the This Is A Private Computer radio button, the RD Web Access server will extend the period of time you can be inactive before automatically terminating your connection. For our purposes here, either choice is fine. Click Sign In.

FIGURE 12.28
Authenticating to RD
Web Access

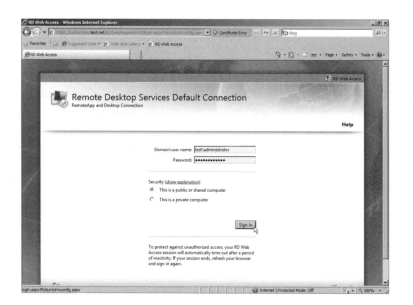

The Remote Desktop Services Default Connection Page that is displayed will be open to the Configuration tab. Leave the default One Or More RemoteApp Sources radio button selected beside Select The Source To Use. In the Source Name box, enter either the NetBIOS name or the fully qualified domain name of the RD Session Host server on which RemoteApp is installed and running. FQDN provides the greatest flexibility. If you are going to have two or more RemoteApp sources, you can enter them all in the box, separated by semicolons. If you are deploying an RDS farm or two or more servers and intend to make use of a hardware load balancer, enter the FQDN of the farm itself and not the individual servers. For our example, we will enter **rds.test.net**, as indicated in Figure 12.29. Click OK to proceed.

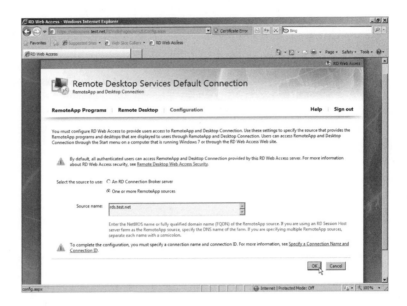

FIGURE 12.29

Configuring a RemoteApp source

IE will automatically refresh, and you will be taken directly to the RemoteApp Programs tab. At this point, you should see that the Adobe Reader 9 application that we set up earlier is available. To verify that everything is working properly, let's test access to this application via the Web. Log on to your end-user desktop and launch Internet Explorer. In the IE address bar, enter the URL that corresponds to your RD Web Access server followed by /rdweb. In our example, we will enter **http://webaccess.test.net/rdweb**. Notice that if you fail to append the /rdweb directory to FQDN, you will land on the default IIS7 web server page.

SIMPLIFY THE URL FOR RD WEB ACCESS

If you want to make the URL a bit more memorable and easier to enter, here is a way to circumvent the need to enter the /rdweb as part of the URL. If your RD Web Access server is not being utilized to serve any additional websites other than for access to your RDS environment, you can implement a simple line of code to accomplish our goal. On your RD Web Access server, navigate to C:\inetpub\wwwroot. In this directory, you will see a file called iisstart.htm. Right-click that file and select Open With ➢ Notepad from the contextual menu. Notepad will open and display the default HTML code. Under the File menu, select Save As, and save the unmodified document as **iisstart-original.htm**. Make sure you select All Files under the Save As Type selection box and click Save. This will ensure you can always revert to our default HTML code. Close Notepad, and again right-click the iisstart.htm file and select Open With ➢ Notepad. Under the Edit menu, choose Select All, and then press the Backspace key. In this now clean slate of a document, enter the following HTML code all on one line:

```
<meta http-equiv="refresh" content="0;url=https://webaccess.test.net/rdweb">
```

Obviously, replace our example of webaccess.test.net with the FQDN of your RD Web Access server. Under the File menu, select Save, and close the Notepad application. Now all the end user has to remember is the name of the RD Web Access server. Our code will automatically invoke the requisite /rdweb directory.

Back to our client testing — once we've entered the URL for our RD Web Access server into IE, we'll be connected and greeted by the expected certificate security warning. Click the Continue To This Website (Not Recommended) link to proceed. As before, you may be prompted to accept a Microsoft ActiveX add-on. If so, click the prompt and follow the instructions to get the ActiveX control installed. As mentioned earlier, RD Web Access is different from the TSWeb page that came with Windows Server 2003. In TSWeb, the ActiveX control ran the RDP session inside the browser window. With RD Web Access, the ActiveX control simply launches the local RDP application on the client machine. This provides a much better user experience. At the authentication screen, enter the credentials for a standard, non-administrative user who has access to the RDS environment. In our example, we will use our John Doe (jdoe) account, as shown in Figure 12.30.

FIGURE 12.30
Client authenticating to RD Web Access

Once you log on, you will be taken to the RemoteApp Programs page and presented with the Adobe Reader 9 application, as in Figure 12.31. Notice that the Configuration page we utilized earlier is unavailable to nonprivileged users.

Clicking once on the Adobe Reader 9 application will begin the process wherein the user is connected via RDP to the application as it is being executed on the remote RD Session Host server. By default, the user will see the screen shown in Figure 12.32.

There are two things to point out about this window. The first is the glaring security warning stating that the publisher of the RemoteApp program cannot be identified. This, much like the initial certificate security warning on the RD Web Access website, can be corrected by implementing an X.509 digital certificate to sign the RDP file. In order to assign a digital certificate for use by RemoteApp, log onto the RD Session Host and launch RemoteApp Manager. Click the Change link next to Digital Signature Settings. As represented in Figure 12.33, the RemoteApp Deployment Settings window opens to the Digital Signature tab. Once you have a certificate available on the server, you can choose to sign RemoteApp RDP files and select the available certificate. By signing the RDP file, you allow the client to validate the RDS server and the RDP file. Signing the file also allows the user to save their connection settings and avoid being prompted to confirm every connection to the server.

FIGURE 12.31
Client applications via
RD Web Access

FIGURE 12.32
RDP connection
configuration

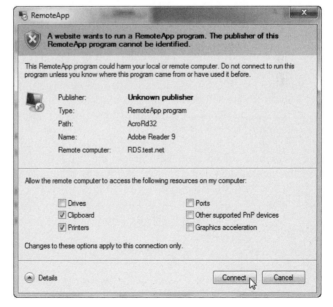

FIGURE 12.33
Digitally signing RDP
files

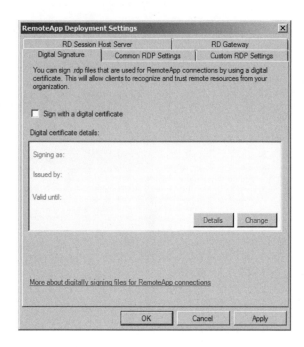

The second item to note is all of the check boxes the user can select to connect local resources to the remote RD Session Host supporting the RemoteApp program. We can restrict these selections directly on the RDS server within the same RemoteApp Deployment Settings windows we had open for digital signatures. Select the Common RDP Settings tab, and you will be able to uncheck specific resources that you do not want your end users to utilize when connecting to the remote server. These check boxes will remove all but a few of the choices presented in our connection example in Figure 12.32. To remove the remaining two, Ports and Graphics acceleration Redirection, you will need to manually add them into the Custom RDP Settings tab, as detailed in Figure 12.34. Note that Authentication Level:i:2 is there by default. Of course, you need to do this only if you never want your users to connect such local resources to the remote server. The settings we put into the Custom RDP Settings field follow the same format as the custom RDP file we built earlier in the chapter. You can also configure these settings programmatically via Group Policy as indicated in Chapter 11.

Returning to the end-user client device, click the Connect button. The end user is now prompted for credentials to access the application. Enter the credentials that were added in Figure 12.34 and click OK. After a brief moment, the user will be connected to the RD Session Host RemoteApp program and Adobe Reader 9 will appear on the user's client device as if had been launched locally. Congratulations! You've now successfully deployed access to RemoteApp programs hosted on your RD Session Host servers via a web interface.

FIGURE 12.34
Adding custom RDP
settings

SIMPLIFYING USER LOGON TO RDS

In all of our examples so far, we have explained how to enter credentials to establish connections with the RDS servers. In Windows Server 2008, Microsoft introduced the ability for users on Windows Vista machines to do single sign-on when connecting to Windows Server 2008 Terminal Servers. That capability also exists for Windows 7 clients and Windows Server 2008 R2 servers. Single sign-on for RDS is enabled through a local policy on the client. This is most easily modified using Group Policy.

To enable single sign-on, start by opening the Group Policy Management Console. In the console, locate an existing policy that applies to your client machines, or create a new one and link it to an appropriate OU. Now edit the group policy, where you will add the settings for single sign-on. In the Group Policy Management Editor, locate the GPO setting for Credentials Delegation.

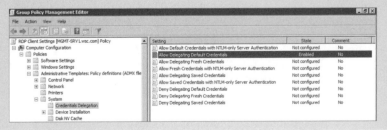

Double-click Allow Delegating Default Credentials. Click the radio button to enable the policy, and then click the Show button. Click Add and enter **termsrv/***.

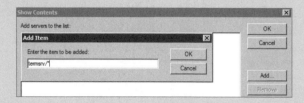

Click OK, OK, and OK again to apply the setting. Now, either wait for Group Policy to refresh on the client, or open a command prompt, type **gpupdate**, and hit Enter. Now any Windows Vista or Windows 7 client receiving the policy will automatically send its default credentials to any Windows Server 2008 or 2008 R2 RDS server and will sign on with no prompts.

Security Trimming RemoteApp Access

We can also determine to which individual RemoteApp programs users have access via the web browser interface. RemoteApp Manager provides a mechanism to specify individual users or groups who will be able to view a particular application icon. This is an invaluable way to present a particular set of applications to certain users and also lower possible confusion on the users' part. For instance, let's assume that user John Doe (jdoe) can have access to the Adobe Reader 9 application, but another user, Jane Smith (jsmith), cannot.

Log on to the RD Session Host server running RemoteApp, and launch RemoteApp Manager. Right-click the Adobe Reader 9 application and select Properties from the contextual menu. When the RemoteApp Properties window opens, click the User Assignment tab. Now select the radio button for Specified Domain Users And Domain Groups, and click the Add button. A standard Select Users Or Groups dialog window appears in which you should enter your test user. In our case, we will enter John Doe (jdoe). Click Check Names to verify accuracy and then click OK. You should now see a screen similar to Figure 12.35; click the OK button to enable that user to see the Adobe Reader 9 application icon in the web browser.

To test this from the client device, we need a different user account than our John Doe (jdoe) account. For our example, we will create a new user account in ADDS called Jane Smith (jsmith) and add her to our RDS Users security group we previously created. If you recall, our RDS Users group is a member of the Remote Desktop Users located in the Builtin container.

From the client device, launch IE and access the RD Web Access URL. Hopefully, you created a favorite for this site already on your client device. Our example URL is http://webaccess.test.net. Accept the certificate security warning and log in as the new user. As expected, our user Jane Smith cannot see the icon for the Adobe Reader application in the browser window.

Keep in mind that this feature becomes very powerful when properly configured domain groups are leveraged in RemoteApp. For instance, if we decided we did want Jane Smith to have access to the Adobe Reader 9 application, we could simply add her as a specified user in

RemoteApp Manager. This, however, would not be very scalable. Creating a group in ADDS called Adobe Reader 9 Users would allow IT administrators to easily deny or allow access to that application by simple ADDS group membership. You could take that a step further by nesting various groups for application usage into a larger group that determines application set access by a user's role within the organization.

FIGURE 12.35

Adding Specific Users for RemoteApp Access

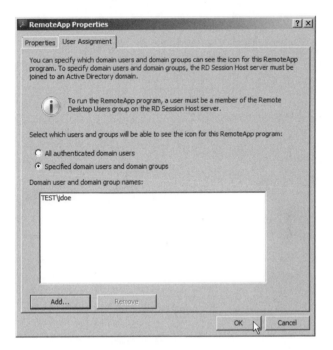

 Real World Scenario

RAPID APPLICATION DEPLOYMENT

Now that we have set up our RDS environment with RemoteApp, let's investigate how quickly we can deploy a new application to our users. In this example, we'll assume that we have been asked to deploy the extremely critical application called Paint.

Log on as an administrator to the RD Session Host server that supports RemoteApp and launch RemoteApp Manager. Since the Paint application is already installed on the RD Session Host by default, we will not need to go through that process. Remember that if you do need to install a program on the RD Session Host, and the application is not packaged as an MSI, the server has to be put into install mode, as discussed in Chapter 11. Choose Add RemoteApp Programs in the Actions column of the RemoteApp Manager.

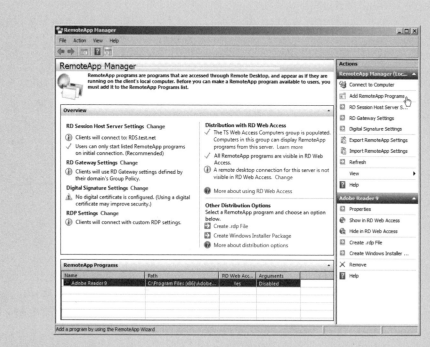

As before, the RemoteApp Wizard will launch and bring up a welcome screen on which you can click Next. The screen that follows will enumerate all of the applications currently installed on the RD Session Host. Click the check box to select the Paint application, and then click the Properties button.

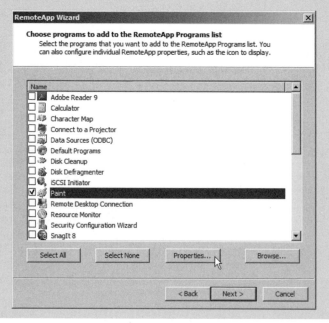

Leave the default settings under the Properties tab and click the User Assignment tab. Select the radio button for Specified Domain Users And Domain Groups and then click the Add button. For this example, we will add our Jane Smith (jsmith) user account only. Your RemoteApp Properties window should look like this, and you can click OK to confirm and continue with the RemoteApp wizard.

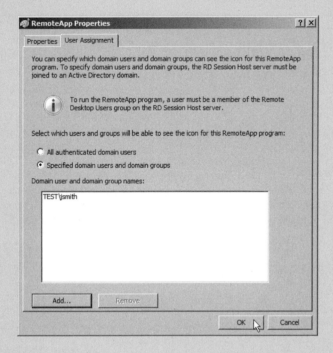

Click the Next button on the RemoteApp wizard to proceed to the Review Settings screen, and click Finish to complete the process. You have now added Paint as a RemoteApp program that is accessible by users via the web browser. In our case, we specified that only one user has access to the Paint application, but you know how easily that can be reconfigured.

To test end-user access to this newly deployed application, log on to the client device and launch Internet Explorer. Browse to the previously configured RD Web Access URL. Our example will be http://webaccess.test.net. We will authenticate as the new user Jane Smith. When the browser refreshes, we will be presented with all of the applications to which Jane Smith has access. In this case, it is only the Paint application, because that is all that we have assigned to her. Notice that the Adobe Reader 9 application has been security-trimmed and does not appear as an icon for this user. Click the Paint icon in the browser to begin the connection process, and you will be given a warning regarding digital signatures as well as remote resources to connect as before. Accept the defaults and click Connect. If this is the first time the user has connected to the RD Session Host, it may take a bit longer than normal. This is because the server needs to generate a profile for the user. While this happens, a first-time user will see a notification regarding personalization of the RDS environment.

Once this completes, the Paint application will appear on the client devices as if it had been launched locally. Subsequent launches of this and other applications will occur more rapidly.

With that, you have successfully, rapidly, and easily deployed an application to a specified set of users leveraging Remote Desktop Services.

Keeping RemoteApp up to Date

To this point, we have discussed multiple methods for users to access remote desktops and RemoteApp applications. Each method has its own strengths. Distributing an RDP file is simple and requires no installation but doesn't scale well over many clients. MSI is a great deployment option, offering great desktop and Start menu integration, but it requires that you push packages every time you have a new application. The RD Web Access method offers great flexibility for accessing the applications, and new RemoteApp applications appear immediately. With Windows Server 2008 R2 and Windows 7 clients, there is one more method for accessing RemoteApps (and desktops), known as RemoteApp and Desktop Connections feeds. What this method allows you to do is subscribe to an RDS server, or connection broker, and receive a dynamic stream of applications from the RD Web Access server directly to the Start menu.

To subscribe to a feed, log on to a client machine, click the Start button, and type **RemoteApp** into the Search box. You should see a RemoteApp and Desktop Connections icon appear. Click the shortcut to launch the RemoteApp and Desktop Connections configuration tool (Figure 12.36). You can also access the tool through Control Panel.

FIGURE 12.36
RemoteApp and Desktop
Connections

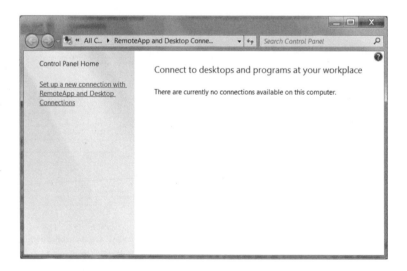

After the tool launches, click Set Up A New Connection on the left-hand side of the window. A dialog box will appear, prompting you to enter a URL (Figure 12.37). The URL will point to the same server as your RD website, with a slightly different URL. In our case, enter **https://webaccess.test.net/RDWeb/Feed/webfeed.aspx**. Click Next, and click Next again.

FIGURE 12.37
Adding the RemoteApp
feed

Now, click the Start button, select All Programs, and click RemoteApp feed. You should see all of the RemoteApp programs that are available on the RD web page in the Start menu. If anyone updates the RD web server applications, the client will automatically add the RemoteApp icon to the folder in the Start menu (Figure 12.38).

FIGURE 12.38
RemoteApp feed in Start
menu

Once you have established the connection to the RemoteApp feed, it will create a scheduled task that will update the feed once a day. If you need to update manually, simply open the RemoteApp And Desktop Connections console again, select the Properties button for the connection that you want to update, and on the following screen, select Update Now. This feature is very powerful, as it allows you add new applications to the RDS farm and have all of your clients receive updated Start menu shortcuts in an automated fashion.

The Bottom Line

Describe the differences between a full desktop provided by an RD Session Host and a remote desktop provided within a Virtual Desktop Infrastructure (VDI).   Understanding these differences becomes critical when determining how to deploy a server-based desktop session to an end user in your environment.

Master It   Your assessment of business needs and associated costs has led you to consider deploying a server-based desktop to a larger portion of your end users. These particular users are task-based and utilize a finite set of applications in the normal course of their workday. They are not allowed to install their own applications, nor are the applications they utilize resource-intensive. Would it be best to deploy the user's desktop using the functionality of a RD Session Host, or through leveraging a desktop provided by a Virtual Desktop Infrastructure?

Determine when to utilize the functionality provided by RemoteApp.   RemoteApp is a fantastic mechanism to deploy applications to end users. There are certain instances when RemoteApp is more suitable than other methods.

Master It   A target group of task workers is moving to thin-client devices and will be accessing their application workloads hosted on RD Session Host servers. Should you implement RemoteApp for these users?

Configure access to RemoteApp programs via a web browser.   Enabling access to RemoteApp programs via a web browser is a very effective and nimble method of providing access to the hosted resources to end users.

Master It   Many applications have already been installed on your RD Session Host server. Assuming that RD Web Access is properly configured as well, what is the process to allow end users to access a RemoteApp program via a web browser?

Deploy applications to only certain users or groups of users.   In order to increase security and reduce user confusion, RemoteApp provides a mechanism to security trim access to applications based on individual users or groups of users.

Master It   You are deploying RemoteApp in conjunction with RD Web Access and want to implement more granular security. To this end, you want to present only certain application icons in the browser to specific users. What process would you follow to accomplish this?

Chapter 13

Load Balancing Remote Desktop Services

As your Remote Desktop Services (RDS) environment grows and begins to support more applications and users, you will need to be able to ensure a high degree of uptime of that RDS environment for those users. The most popular method for achieving high availability in an RDS environment is through the use of load balancing. In addition to providing for a highly available RDS environment, we can leverage load-balancing features to scale out our RDS environment to eventually consist of many servers and support greater numbers of users. When multiple RDS Session Host servers are configured to host the same set of applications, this is most often referred to as a *farm*. Although there are several methods to provide load balancing for an RDS environment, we will be specifically focusing on the Microsoft RD Connection Broker.

In this chapter you will learn to:

◆ Describe why you would want to implement load balancing in an RD Session Host environment

◆ Identify the key feature that an RD Connection Broker provides that other stand-alone load balancers do not

◆ Share an end user's server-based session so as to provide assistance in real time

Load Balancing and High Availability

Load balancing provides a mechanism for IT professionals to somewhat evenly distribute a data processing workload across two or more computing devices. In the case of Remote Desktop Services (RDS), the workload we are distributing is the user application set that will be executing on an RD Session Host server. High Availability (HA) is the capability of a specific data processing workload to maintain a continuous functional state. This can be achieved through a combination of technologies and depends on where the workload needs the HA functionality. For example, to ensure a physical server is highly available, we would need to include fault-tolerant items such as RAID, redundant power supplies, link-aggregated network interfaces, and so on. High Availability can also be achieved at application layers through the use of clustering technologies such as Microsoft Failover Clustering or Network Load Balancing. The exact method you choose to employ depends largely on the application workload you intend to make highly available.

In the case of RDS, Microsoft has provided a specific mechanism to load balance two or more RD Session Hosts — the Remote Desktop Connection Broker. In this manner, we gain the ability to scale out the number of RD Session Host servers to support many users and simultaneously make those services highly available. If an RD Session Host server fails, the user can be reconnected to another RD Session Host in the farm and continue to work.

ALTERNATIVES TO THE RD CONNECTION BROKER

You are not limited to utilizing the RD Connection Broker when it comes to load balancing your RDS environment. You can use the basic Network Load Balancing (NLB) functionality that Microsoft includes with Windows Server. You could also employ a dedicated hardware load balancer, which would give you much better performance and more control than Microsoft's integral NLB.

However, the RD Connection Broker has one very compelling feature above basic load balancing designed specifically for the RDS environment. When you load balance an RD Session Host farm using the RD Connection Broker, you can enable an end user to reconnect to an existing session from which he had previously disconnected.

For instance, if a user is connected to a session on an RD Session Host and suddenly finds their network connection severed, the session will continue to execute on the server. When the user corrects the issue, they will be reconnected to their session exactly as they left it. This is true even if the user connects from a different machine in a different location. This capability is particularly important in an environment where users are constantly moving between devices, such as doctors or nurses in a hospital, and allows the session to follow the user wherever they go.

Configuring an RD Connection Broker for RD Session Host

We will be installing an RD Connection Broker and other required components into the RDS environment you set up in the previous chapters. In all, you will need to set up an additional RD Session Host server for a minimum of two RD Session Host servers and a server to support the RD Connection Broker functionality. We require at least two RD Session host servers so that we can implement load balancing across multiple hosts. The RD Connection Broker server is a role service and is available in the Standard, Enterprise, and Datacenter editions of the Microsoft Windows Server 2008 R2 product.

If you do not yet have at least two RD Session Host servers configured, do this first. Follow the steps outlined in Chapter 11, "Installing and Configuring Remote Desktop Services." Once you have two RD Session Host servers identically configured with licensing servers specified, you can proceed.

RD Connection Broker Role Service

Now that you have at least two RD Session Host servers, you can set up the RD Connection Broker server. This function should typically be installed and configured on a separate server from the other RDS environment servers, such as the RD Session Host servers and the RD Web Access servers.

To begin, configure a server and install Microsoft Windows Server 2008 R2. Ensure all updates are installed and join it to the domain. Log on to the server as a user with administrative privileges. Launch Server Manager if it does not launch automatically when you log on. Server Manager can be found under Start ➢ Administrative Tools.

In Server Manager, right-click the Roles icon and select Add Roles, as shown in Figure 13.1. You can also select Roles by clicking the icon and then clicking the Add Roles link on the right side of the Roles Summary screen.

FIGURE 13.1

Adding a new role

The Add Roles Wizard will launch. Click Next on the Before You Begin screen. We need to install the Remote Desktop Services role in order to have access to the RD Connection Broker role service, so select the Remote Desktop Services check box and click Next, as in Figure 13.2.

FIGURE 13.2

Selecting the Remote Desktop Services role

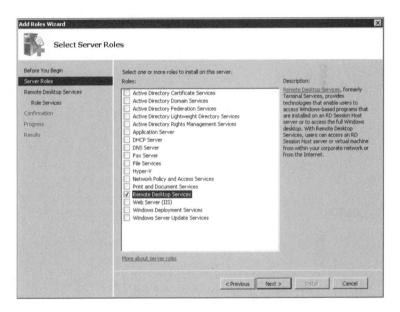

You'll be shown a screen that you've seen in a previous chapter welcoming you to RDS and providing a link to further information. Click Next. On the Select Role Services screen, choose Remote Desktop Connection Broker and click Next, as indicated in Figure 13.3.

The subsequent screen will inform you of what is about to be installed and indicate that a restart may need to occur. Click the Install button to continue. After installation is complete, an Installation Results screen will appear. Click Close to complete the installation.

Now that we have installed the RD Connection Broker role service, we need to configure it so that all of our RD Session Host servers can participate in the farm. To accomplish this, we will need to add the RD Session Host servers that are to be members of the load-balanced farm to the Session Broker Computers group on the RD Connection Broker server. Launch Computer Management by choosing Start ➢ Administrative Tools. When Computer Management opens, expand Local Users And Groups and then select Groups, as shown in Figure 13.4.

FIGURE 13.3
Choosing the RD
Connection Broker role
service

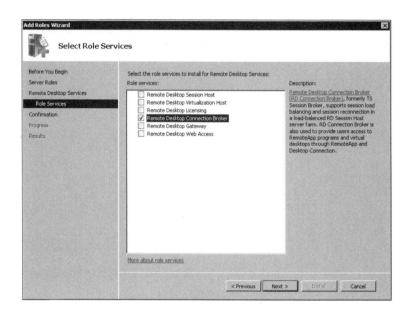

FIGURE 13.4
Displaying local groups

You will see toward the bottom of the middle section the Session Broker Computers group.

> ### SESSION BROKER OR CONNECTION BROKER?
>
> You may find it interesting that the local group on our RD Connection Broker into which we will place all of our participating RD Session Host servers is called Session Broker Computers. This is a holdover from the previous version of Microsoft Windows Server 2008 Terminal Services wherein this functionality was called the Session Broker. In Windows Server 2008 R2, along with Terminal Services becoming Remote Desktop Services, the Session Broker has become the RD Connection Broker. This is to more accurately reflect its expanded role. However, to maintain backward compatibility with scripts and the like, the local group has retained the original name.

Double-click this group to open it, or right-click and select Properties from the contextual menu. As shown by Figure 13.5, a Properties window will open. Click the Add button.

FIGURE 13.5
Session Broker
Computers Properties

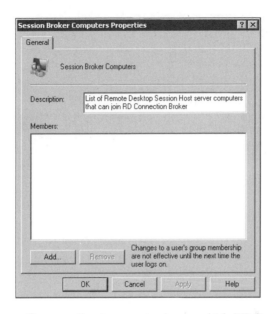

A standard selection dialog box will open, allowing you to choose which RD Session Host servers you want to participate in the farm that's load balanced by the RD Connection Broker. Before entering your server computer names into the dialog box, you need to click the Object Types button. When the Object Types window appears, as in Figure 13.6, select the check box for Computers and uncheck the other three objects. Click OK. If you forget to do this, the selection dialog box will return an error because it will not be looking for computer accounts in the directory. This will also ensure that we are presented with only computer accounts and can reduce confusion in subsequent screens. As an example, if you have named an RD Session Host server RDS as we have, you will be prompted to select from a list that contains groups that also have RDS in their names.

FIGURE 13.6
Selecting the Computers
object type

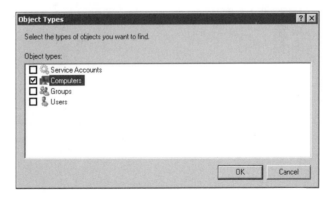

Enter the computer account names of your RD Session Host server that you want to participate in the farm into the dialog box. I would recommend that you click the Check Names button after every entry you make in the dialog box. This will ensure you are properly selecting the correct resources to add to the group. For instance, if you have two or more similarly named RD Session Host servers, you'll prompted to select the correct resource. The good news here is that if you named all of your RD Session Host servers in a similar vein or pattern, the Multiple Names Found dialog box will show all of your servers, and you'll be able to Ctrl-click or Shift-click them all at once, saving you from repeating this step for every server. This is shown in Figure 13.7.

FIGURE 13.7
Selecting multiple
computer accounts

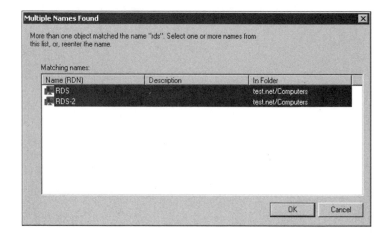

Once you have entered all of the RD Session Host server computer accounts into the dialog box and checked their names, click OK to continue. As in Figure 13.8, the Session Broker Computers Properties window should now be populated with all of the RD Session Host servers you intend to have load balanced by the RD Connection Broker. Click OK, and then close Computer Management to complete this portion of the process.

FIGURE 13.8
RD Session Host servers
grouping

RD Session Hosts

Now that the RD Connection Broker has been properly set up, you need to configure each RD Session Host server you plan to have as a member of the farm. These would be the RD Session Host servers that you previously placed into the RD Connection Broker's local Session Broker Computers group. Log on to the first RD Session Host server as a user with administrator privileges, and launch Remote Desktop Services Host Configuration. Choose Start ➤ Administrative Tools ➤ Remote Desktop Services. Double-click Member Of Farm In RD Connection Broker under the Edit Settings section of the window, as indicated in Figure 13.9.

FIGURE 13.9

Locating the RD Connection Broker settings

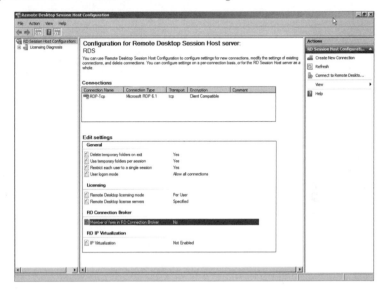

You will be presented with the RD Connection Broker tab in a Properties screen, as shown in Figure 13.10. Click the Change Settings button.

In the ensuing RD Connection Broker Settings window, we will be making three changes. These are all shown in Figure 13.11. First, we will select the radio button for Farm Member. Next, we need to enter the name of the server that is acting as our RD Connection Broker into the RD Connection Broker Server Name box. I recommend using a fully qualified domain name (FQDN) whenever possible. Finally, in the Farm Name box, enter a new name by which the farm will be known and accessed. Again, use a FQDN here for clarity. The farm name should be the name that you want users to see when they are connecting to the server. You will eventually publish this name in DNS so that users and administrators can use it to connect to the farm. Also, I highly recommend that this be a unique name that is not currently in use elsewhere within your network because this will lessen the chance for confusion and errors down the road. When you have completed the entries on this screen, click OK.

That screen will close, bringing you back to the previous Properties screen. Notice that you can now select the Participate In Connection Broker Load-Balancing check box. Check that box at this time. That box also allows you to easily remove a server from participation in the load-balanced farm. You may need to do this when routine or scheduled hardware maintenance or software upgrades are required. In this manner, the RD Connection Broker will no longer direct new incoming user connections to that particular RD Session Host server. When you designate the server to participate in the load balancing, another choice becomes available. This is the Relative Weight Of This Server In The Farm setting, and it is purely optional.

FIGURE 13.10
Edit RD Connection
Broker properties

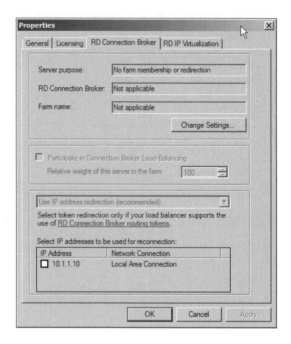

FIGURE 13.11
RD Connection Broker
settings

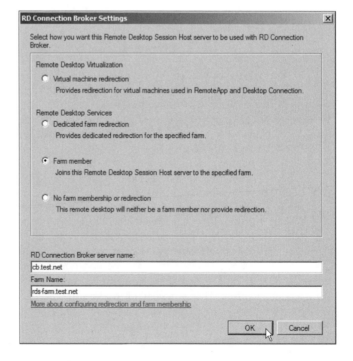

RELATIVE WEIGHTING

The default value for relative weighting is 100. These values are relative to all of the RD Session Host servers participating in the load-balanced farm. If all servers maintain the value of 100, they will all equally receive user sessions. The weighting is useful in an environment where the physical server hardware varies to a wide degree. For instance, three of four RD Session Host servers have 32 GB of RAM and four processor cores. But one of the servers in the farm has only 8 GB of RAM and a single processor core. We would want to enter a weight of 25 for that server. Think of it as a percentage. That one server has roughly one quarter of the computational resources of the other systems, so we want it to receive only a quarter of the incoming user sessions. The key here is that you can use this feature to optimize the number of users' sessions directed to each server. You can monitor your environment and adjust the weightings accordingly. This weighting number can be changed while the RD Session Host is online, participating in the load-balanced farm and servicing users.

Leave the default selection of Use IP Address Redirection (recommended). This method will be applicable in almost every situation. The other choice, Use Token Redirection, is used only if the client cannot directly communicate with the RD Session Host server via IP and you are employing a network load balancer that supports the RD Connection Broker routing tokens. Select the check box for the addresses to which users will reconnect with their existing sessions in the Select IP Addresses To Be Used For Reconnection section. These can be IPv4 or IPv6 addresses if available and can be all addresses on the server or just one. Figure 13.12 shows an example of the completed Properties screen. Click OK to continue.

FIGURE 13.12
Completing RD Connection Broker properties

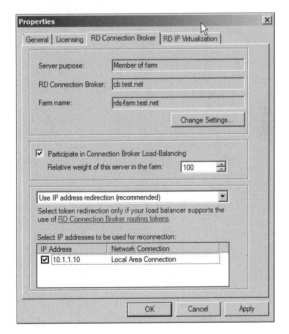

Repeat the above instructions for all of the remaining RD Session Host servers you plan to have participate in the load-balanced farm. After all of your RDS Session Host servers have been configured, proceed to the next section.

DNS Server

The final portion in the overall setup of our RD Connection Broker load-balanced RD Session Host farm is to configure DNS properly to support a DNS round-robin mechanism. While this DNS method can be accomplished on any modern DNS server, we will be utilizing a Microsoft Windows Server 2008 R2 domain controller that is leveraging AD Integrated DNS. By default, DNS in Windows Server 2008 R2 will respond to queries in a round robin fashion. We must log in as a user with Domain Admin credentials or similar credentials that can modify DNS. Once you're logged into the DNS server, launch DNS Manager. You can access this via Server Manager under Roles or by clicking Start ➢ Administrative Tools ➢ DNS. Expand the server name and then Forward Lookup Zones. Click the domain name once to select it, and then right-click the domain name. In the contextual menu that appears, select New Host (A or AAAA), as shown in Figure 13.13.

FIGURE 13.13
DNS Manager

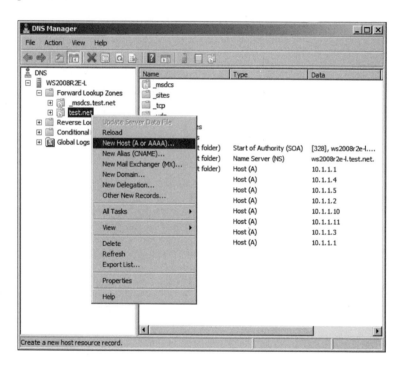

A New Host screen will appear. Enter the host portion of the FQDN of the new RDS farm name into the Name (Uses Parent Domain Name If Blank) box. As noted earlier, it is highly recommended, but not required, that you enter the same name here as you assigned to the farm when configuring the RD Session Hosts. Note that only the host portion of the FQDN should be entered. For instance, we earlier used `rds-farm.test.net` as the name of our farm when configuring the RD Session Hosts. So in this current dialog box, we would enter only rds-farm. The wizard will automatically append the domain name as you type and display it in the box directly below your entry. This will be the FQDN that users will use to connect to the load-balanced RD Session Host farm. In the IP Address box, enter the IP address of one of the RD Session Host servers that is participating in the load-balanced farm. Your screen should look similar to Figure 13.14. Click Add Host when finished.

FIGURE 13.14

Adding a new host

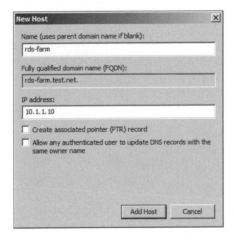

You will be greeted with a dialog box indicating that the host or Address Resource record was successfully created in the forward zone. Click OK to dismiss the dialog box. Notice that the New Host screen remains and is ready for additional input. This is perfect because we need to enter similar host records for every RD Session Host server that will be participating in the farm. It is important to note that the name will remain constant for every record. In our example, that name is rds-farm. The only item that will change is the IP address of each RD Session Host. Once you have finished entering all of your RD Session Hosts, finalize the process by clicking Done on the New Host window.

Looking now at the forward zone detail in our DNS Manager window, we should see all of our newly added RD Session Host servers. Each unique server IP address should have the same exact farm name associated with it. See Figure 13.15 for an example. You can now exit DNS Manager.

Now that we have configured the load balancing, what happens when a client tries to connect to the farm? First, the client will initiate a remote desktop session to rds-farm.test.net either through RDWeb or through the Remote Desktop client. At this point, the client will perform a DNS lookup and receive an IP address for one of the servers in the farm. As additional clients connect, the DNS server will cycle through the addresses that are associated with the farm, thus load balancing the initial connections to the farm. Now, you may be saying that DNS round-robin is not load balancing, because it doesn't take into account the sessions that are already on the different servers. This is absolutely correct. The initial DNS round-robin is done only to spread out the initial connections. Once the client makes its connection to an RDS server based on DNS, the actual Connection Broker load balancing kicks in. When the client is referred to the RDS server via the farm name, the RDS server will query the Connection Broker server to determine how to handle the connection.

First, the RDS server will look for an existing connection for the user who is attempting to connect. This would happen if a user signed on to RDS and disconnected and reconnected or changed computers. If the user already has an active session on one of the servers in the farm,

FIGURE 13.15
DNS round-robin entries

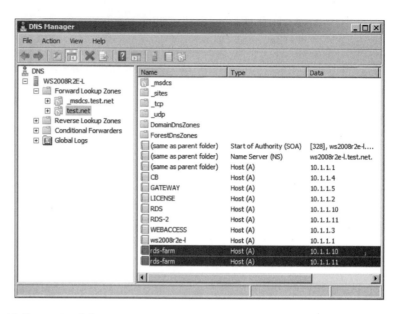

the RDS server that initially received the connection attempt will then redirect the user to their existing session. If the user does not have an existing session, the RDS server will then query the RD Connection Broker server to find the RD Session Host server with the fewest active RDP connections. At this point any weighting values would come into play in terms of deciding where to redirect the new session. The user will then be redirected to the least-loaded server. So, by keeping track of active RDP sessions, the RD Connection Broker can load balance the farm by redirecting new sessions to the least-used servers.

Managing the Connections

In a large RDS environment, it is important to be able to monitor and manage user connections across the servers in the farm. To this end, Microsoft has provided a mechanism through which we can observe and manage all of the user sessions across the entire farm or group of farms from a single console. This functionality is available from both the server side and the client side through the Remote Server Administration Tools (RSAT) for Microsoft Windows 7. The tool is called Remote Desktop Services Manager. Log on to an RD Session Host server as an administrator and then choose Start ➤ Administrative Tools ➤ Remote Desktop Services. There you will find Remote Desktop Services Manager. When you launch the program, you will see a screen similar to Figure 13.16. It will have the local server that you logged on to as its default server.

FUNCTIONALITY LIMITATIONS

If you launch Remote Desktop Services Manager from the actual physical console, the RSAT, or a Hyper-V console, you will be presented with an informational dialog box. This is basically a notice that you will be unable to utilize the Remote Control feature and the Connect feature while doing so. If you desire to use these two features, you must log on to the RD Session Host server via a Remote Desktop Connection (RDC).

FIGURE 13.16
Default RD Services
Manager

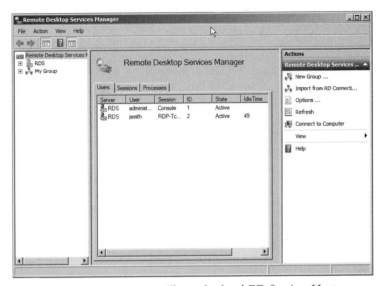

In the default RD Services Manager screen, you will see the local RD Session Host server to which you connected and any current user sessions. We can customize this program, and it will retain our settings upon subsequent launches. If you log on to a different RD Session Host server, however, you will need to customize the program for that particular server. This is one of the benefits of utilizing the RSAT on a Windows 7 client workstation — your customization will always be a part of your profile on your workstation. To begin our customization, right-click the Remote Desktop Services Manager icon on the left, and select Import From RD Connection Broker from the contextual menu. Enter the name of the RD Connection Broker server here and press the Enter key. The Remote Desktop Services Manager tool will then query the RD Connection Broker server and return the names of all of the farms that it is hosting and display them in the left-hand column. Expand the RD Connection Broker group and you will see, as shown in Figure 13.17, all of the RD farms. Expanding any of the farms will display the individual servers that make up that farm. Clicking any individual server in that group will display all of the user sessions currently being hosted. In addition, clicking the icon for the farm itself will provide a complete list of all user sessions across all servers in the farm.

FIGURE 13.17
Customized RD Services
Manager

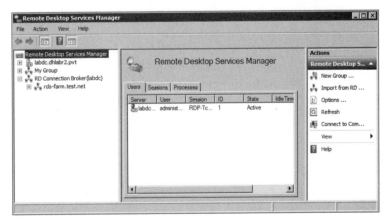

 **Real World Scenario**

CONTROLLING USER SESSIONS

Using the Remote Desktop Services Manager, you can exercise a great deal of control over the users' sessions spread across the RD Session Host farm. Right-clicking any particular connection will bring up a contextual menu that will allow you perform tasks such as disconnecting a user, sending a user a message, getting the user's status, as well as logging off a user — very powerful. For an example, let's consider that you will need to perform maintenance on a few servers. You want to ensure your users are as productive as possible, but you also want them to know that those servers will need to be taken offline soon. In order to give them a chance to complete and save their work, you can send them a message stating that a maintenance window is coming up and that they need to log off. Here's how to accomplish this. In Remote Desktop Services Manager, you can Ctrl-click multiple users to select them. After selecting the appropriate users, right-click any one of them to bring up the contextual menu shown below. Then select Send Message. Type your message in the dialog box and click OK.

Instantly, a dialog box containing the message and sender information will appear on top of whatever the user is currently doing in the session. The user can click OK to dismiss the dialog box. Similarly, you can select multiple sessions, right-click one, and choose the option to reset or log off users individually or in bulk as the situation requires.

In addition, when connected to an RD Session Host via RDC and running Remote Desktop Services Manager, you can take remote control of a user session with that user's permission. Open Remote Desktop Services Manager, right-click a user session, and select Remote Control. You will be asked to provide a key combination that you will later use to terminate the remote control session. Select a key combination and click OK. At this point, the user will see a dialog box on their screen notifying them that someone is attempting to take control of their session. The user can respond either Yes to allow the control or No to decline. If you wish, you can also create a Group Policy that will allow you to take control of a user session without prompting the user for permission. This is a great technology that allows someone to guide a user through a particular program feature or some other remote assistance scenario.

Configuring an RD Connection Broker for RemoteApp

In the previous section, we installed and configured a Remote Desktop Connection Broker server to provide load balancing and session reconnection to a collection of RD Session Host servers known as a farm. Now we will perform a similar configuration for a collection of RD Session Host servers that are supporting RemoteApp functionality. The goal is to provide two or more load-balanced servers so that users can be ensured of accessing their RemoteApp-provided application. Since much of this effort has previously been accomplished, we will leverage that work instead of duplicating it here. To that end, we will use the existing RD Connection Broker you set up earlier. If you have not yet done this, follow the section titled "RD Connection Broker Role Service" earlier in this chapter. Once that is complete, come back and pick it up here. We will continue to use the same RD Session Host servers.

The first thing that we will need to do is allow the RD Connection Broker server to access all of the RD Session Host servers in the farm. To do this, log on to an RD Session Host server as an administrator and choose Start ➢ Administrative Tools ➢ Computer Management ➢ Local Users And Groups ➢ Groups. In the center pane of the window, right-click the TS Web Access Computers group and choose Add To Group from the contextual menu, as indicated in Figure 13.18. Note that in this section you will see several references to TS, or Terminal Services, in the group names. This is simply an artifact of the original name for Remote Desktop services that was not removed by Microsoft in the upgrade from Windows Server 2008 to R2.

FIGURE 13.18
Selecting the TS Web Access Computers group

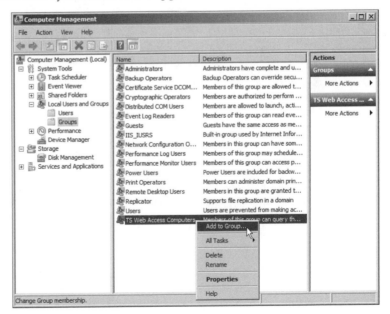

In the ensuing TS Web Access Computers Properties screen, click the Add button. This will invoke a standard object-selection dialog box. Click the Object Types button and select the Computers check box in the subsequent screen. Click OK. Enter the computer name of the RD Connection Broker and click Check Names. If everything is valid, click OK to accept and continue. As shown in Figure 13.19, you will see that the RD Connection Broker is now a member of the TS Web Access Computers local group. Click OK, and then close the Computer Management window to complete. Do this for every RD Session Host in the load-balanced farm.

FIGURE 13.19
RD Connection Broker
added to group

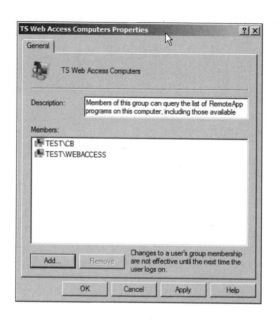

In Chapter 12, we configured a couple of programs to be hosted by RemoteApp. We will use those programs for the balance of this procedure. Our next step is to configure the RD Connection Broker. The first task is to add the RD Web Access server to the TS Web Access Computers group on the RD Connection Broker server. Log on to the RD Connection Broker as a user with administrative privileges. Choose Start ➢ Administrative Tools ➢ Computer Management ➢ Local Users And Groups ➢ Groups. In the center section of the screen, right-click TS Web Access Computers and select Add To Group, as shown in Figure 13.20.

In the TS Web Access Computers Properties window, click Add to get the RD Web Access server into this group. You will again need to click Object Types to select Computers before entering the server name. Enter the server name, and click OK. Click OK again and exit Computer Management to complete the addition of the RD Web Access server to the local TS Web Access Computers group on the RD Connection Broker.

Now that we have the RD Web Access server and the RD Connection Broker introduced and trusting each other, we need to configure the RemoteApp source to make use of our RD Connection Broker. Previously in Chapter 12, we configured RD Web Access to use a single RemoteApp source. Now that we have an RD Connection Broker server established, we are going to modify that configuration to make use of the RD Connection Broker.

Log on to the RD Web Access server as a user with administrative credentials and click the Start menu. To access the configuration, browse to the URL for RD Web access — typically `https://servername/RDWeb`. Alternatively, you can choose Administrative Tools ➤ Remote Desktop Services ➤ Remote Desktop Web Access Configuration. With either method, if you are using a self-signed SSL certificate, you will be presented with a web page warning you about the security status of the site. This issue can be resolved at a later time by employing either a trusted third-party certificate or a certificate issued by your own trusted certificate authority. For now, click the link Continue To The Website (not recommended). On the next page, enter user credentials that have administrative privileges and click Sign In. The next page will be the Configuration page. Midway down the page you will see the Select The Source To Use radio buttons; select An RD Connection Broker Server. Then, in the Source Name box, enter the FQDN of the RD Connection Broker server. Our example is shown in Figure 13.21. Click OK.

FIGURE 13.20

Selecting the TS Web Access Computers group

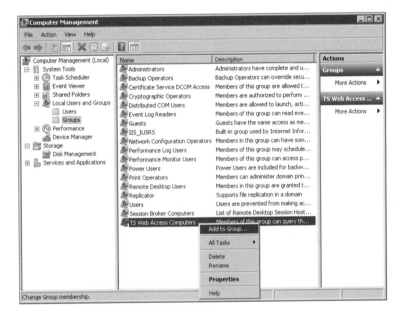

FIGURE 13.21

Configuring RD Web Access to utilize an RD Connection Broker

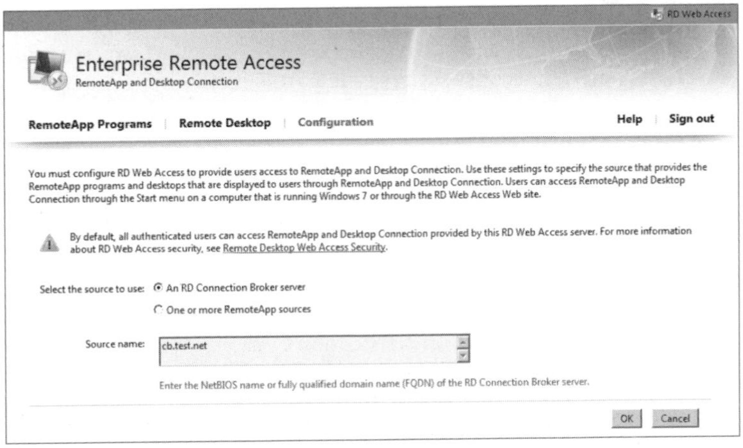

Skipping around one last time, we now need to log on to the RD Connection Broker server with administrative credentials. Here, we are going to make a RemoteApp source available to the RD Connection Broker. On the RD Connection Broker, click Start ➢ Administrative Tools ➢ Remote Desktop Services ➢ Remote Desktop Connection Manager.

Right-click the RemoteApp Sources icon on the left pane of the screen and choose Add RemoteApp Source from the contextual menu, as shown in Figure 13.22.

FIGURE 13.22
Selecting Add
RemoteApp Source

An Add RemoteApp Source dialog box will open. Enter the FQDN of the RD Session Host farm name you configured earlier in this chapter. In our example, this will be rds-farm.test.net, as shown in Figure 13.23. Click the Add button to complete.

FIGURE 13.23
Adding the FQDN of the
load-balanced farm

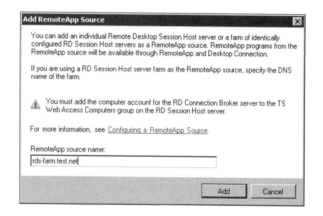

To test, launch Internet Explorer on a client computer and browse to the website we set up earlier. If you recall in Chapter 12, we created a simple URL to remember: http://webaccess.test.net. You will be greeted with a sign-in page where you should use one of the nonadministrative user accounts we created, such as test\jdoe or test\jsmith. Observe that the per-user restrictions we placed on the application serviced by RemoteApp are still enforced even in the load-balanced configuration. It's also worth pointing out that the RD Connection Broker is simultaneously supporting user session reconnection to an RD Session Host load-balanced farm as well as supporting a load-balanced RemoteApp farm with an RD Web Access front end. That's it! You've created a load-balanced farm of RD Session Host servers that now provides a much higher degree of availability to your end users.

Now that your RD Connection Broker server is providing load balancing and High Availability to your RD Session Host servers, you should also consider the availability of your RD Connection Broker server. This server now is the point of entry for all of your RD servers and thus a very important piece of infrastructure. Unlike the RD Session Host servers, the Connection Broker cannot be load balanced. Luckily, in Windows Server 2008 R2, Microsoft added support for the RD Connection Broker role in Failover Clustering. So, to really improve the availability of your RD environment, you should look into clustering your RD Connection Broker Hosts.

The Bottom Line

Describe why you would want to implement load balancing in an RD Session Host environment. Understanding benefits that load balancing provides to an RD Session Host farm is essential in ensuring a successful implementation that can scale with your future needs.

> **Master It** Your colleagues and manager are curious as to why you want to expend a bit more effort, and possible additional hardware and software, to configure load balancing for your new RDS environment. How would you justify your decision?

Identify the key feature that an RD Connection Broker provides that other stand-alone load balancers do not. Even if you have the budget for expensive hardware load balancers or already have them in production, an RD Connection Broker plays a unique role in the RD Session Host farm.

> **Master It** Your network counterpart approaches you and comments that you won't need to configure an RD Connection Broker because she will be providing load balancing via dedicated hardware load balancers. What would be your explanation as to why you still believe it to be a good idea to stand up an RD Connection Broker?

Share an end user's server-based session so as to provide assistance in real time. Ensuring a productive user experience when participating in a server-based session on an RD Session Host should be a top priority for us as IT professionals. Any mechanism that can abet us toward that goal is welcome.

> **Master It** A user contacts you and states that he is confused about how to complete a few tasks and is becoming frustrated. Unfortunately, this user is located across town, so you can't just visit him at his desk. What is the best way to proceed?

Part 4

Desktop Virtualization

Chapter 14

Introducing Microsoft Desktop Virtualization

Virtualization is one of the hottest topics and trends in the information technology industry, and desktop virtualization is becoming a more important component of an organization's overall virtualization strategy. Even though less than 1 percent of all desktops are virtualized, companies are very interested in exploring the potential benefits of implementing desktop virtualization. They have benefited greatly by using server virtualization to reduce costs, improve utilization, strengthen security, and increase agility. Because of the high cost of provisioning, deploying, managing, and supporting the desktop environment, companies are looking to receive similar benefits from desktop virtualization. They also want to improve desktop security, agility, and the overall user experience.

This chapter introduces you to Microsoft desktop virtualization products, technologies, and solutions, more specifically Microsoft Virtual Desktop Infrastructure (VDI) and Microsoft Enterprise Desktop Virtualization (MED-V). We begin with identifying best practices to improve an organization's desktop environment and an overview of Microsoft's approach called the Windows Optimized Desktop. Next we review different types of centralized desktop architectures, looking at the benefits and disadvantages of each. We then discuss desktop virtualization solutions, reviewing client-hosted and server-hosted architectures. MED-V and Microsoft VDI are two types of desktop virtualization solutions and are the focus of the rest of the chapter.

In this chapter, you will learn to:

◆ Identify Microsoft Windows Optimized Desktop best practices

◆ Describe different types of desktop virtualization solutions

◆ Define VDI, its benefits, architecture, and components

◆ Understand the Microsoft Enterprise Desktop Virtualization solution and its architecture

◆ Understand the Microsoft VDI solution and its architecture

The Pursuit of a Better Desktop

The pursuit of a better desktop, in terms of increasing IT control and improving user experience, has been going on since the early eighties. This effort has seen many evolutionary steps over the years. Sometimes these steps created unwanted dependencies along the way, increasing complexity and management costs and reducing organizations' agility. These negative effects have led companies to seek better ways to design, deploy, and manage the desktop environment. Desktop virtualization is seen by many organizations as a technology solution that has the potential to help them address many of their business and IT needs, significantly and rapidly improving their desktop environment.

Microsoft also believes that desktop virtualization can be beneficial to organizations and has incorporated this technology into its virtualization strategy and solution offering. Desktop virtualization represents one solution and best practice that is included in Microsoft's Optimized Desktop approach. It is available for companies to leverage in an effort to improve the overall desktop environment.

The Microsoft Optimized Desktop

The Microsoft Optimized Desktop is a vision for enhancing the overall desktop environment. This vision is enabled by a collection of products, technologies, solutions, and best practices that assist organizations in improving their desktop environment, leading to reduced deployment and management costs, improved security, and more agile environment.

Microsoft Optimized Desktop best practices focus on eight main areas:

◆ Minimizing the number of desktop OS images

◆ Deploying electronic software distribution

◆ Securing the PC environment

◆ Centrally managing user settings and data

◆ Extending the life cycle of legacy PCs

◆ Centrally managing and deploying applications when appropriate

◆ Centrally managing and deploying desktop operating system environments when appropriate

◆ Supporting flexible work scenarios

The Microsoft solutions used with these best practices include the following:

◆ Microsoft Windows 7 Enterprise

◆ Windows Fundamentals for Legacy PCs (WinFLP) — a benefit of Microsoft Software Assurance (SA)

◆ Microsoft Application Virtualization (APP-V) — part of Microsoft Desktop Optimization Pack

◆ Microsoft Enterprise Desktop Virtualization (MED-V) — part of Microsoft Desktop Optimization Pack

◆ Microsoft Windows Server 2008 R2

◆ Microsoft System Center Management Suite

◆ Microsoft Forefront Security Suite

MICROSOFT DESKTOP OPTIMIZATION PACK

The Microsoft Desktop Optimization Pack (MDOP) is a Microsoft product available to customers with Microsoft Software Assurance on their Windows Desktops. MDOP includes six products that assist an organization in optimizing their desktop environment and reducing the total cost of ownership (TCO). The six products are

◆ Diagnostics and Recovery Toolset

◆ Asset Inventory Service

◆ Microsoft Advanced Group Policy

◆ Microsoft System Center Desktop Error Monitoring

◆ Microsoft Application Virtualization (APP-V)

◆ Microsoft Enterprise Desktop Virtualization (MED-V).

Microsoft APP-V is discussed earlier in this book, and Microsoft MED-V is discussed later in this chapter and in Chapter 16. More information about MDOP can be found at www.microsoft.com/mdop.

Each Microsoft Optimized Desktop best practice is enabled through the use of Microsoft infrastructure products and technologies. Table 14.1 is an overview of the mapping of the Microsoft Optimized Desktop best practices, products, and technologies.

TABLE 14.1: Microsoft Optimized Desktop best practices, products, and technologies

BEST PRACTICES	PRODUCTS	TECHNOLOGIES
Minimizing the number of desktop OS images	Windows 7 Enterprise	ImageX
Deploying electronic software distribution	System Center Configuration Manager	Electronic software distribution (ESB)
Securing the PC environment	Microsoft Forefront Windows 7 Enterprise Windows Server 2008 R2	Antivirus software BitLocker Drive Encryption Rights Management solution Network Access Protection (NAP)
Centrally managing PC settings and data	Windows 7 Enterprise Windows Server 2008 R2	Redirected folders Offline folders Roaming profiles
Extending the life cycle of legacy PCs	Windows Fundamentals for Legacy PCs	Based on Windows XP Embedded SP2 OS

TABLE 14.1: Microsoft Optimized Desktop best practices, products, and technologies *(CONTINUED)*

BEST PRACTICES	PRODUCTS	TECHNOLOGIES
Centrally managing and deploying applications when appropriate	App-V Remote Desktop Services	Application virtualization Presentation virtualization
Centrally managing and deploying desktop operating system environments when appropriate	MED-V Remote Desktop Services Microsoft VDI	Client- and server-hosted desktop virtualization
Support of flexible work scenarios	Windows 7 Enterprise, MDOP Windows Server 2008 R2	BitLocker Direct Access Roaming profiles Redirected folders Offline folders APP-V MED-V Microsoft Remote Desktop Services Microsoft VDI

Some of the products and technologies that are used by the Microsoft Desktop Optimization best practices are appropriate for the entire organization, while others should be implemented to meet the specific business needs.

For a company to use the Microsoft Optimized Desktop approach, they first need to evaluate their desktop environment, reviewing its current capabilities, challenges, and needs. Microsoft has a tool that can assist companies with this evaluation process called the Microsoft Windows Optimized Desktop Scenario Assessment Guide. More information about this guide and a free download can be found at http://technet.microsoft.com/en-us/library/dd334417.

Some of the solutions employed in the Microsoft Optimized Desktop include using centralized desktop solutions and virtualization technologies. Let's now review both of these solution and technology areas.

Centralized Desktop Solutions

Centralized desktops have been used for some time, but the architectures and approaches have changed over the years. Today companies have several solution options to choose from, each with its own benefits and disadvantages. Each of these can be implemented as a stand-alone solution or combined with others, creating a hybrid solution, depending on the company's business needs.

Today companies use four main centralized desktop solution options to deliver a remote desktop to an endpoint device. These solution options include diskless PCs, presentation virtualization, blade PCs, and Virtual Desktop Infrastructure (VDI). Let's review each of these solution options and its architectures, benefits, and disadvantages.

THE DISKLESS PC

The diskless PC is just that, a PC that has no drives. The diskless PC connects to a server on the network via a Preboot Execution Environment (PXE)–enabled endpoint device. It then downloads or streams the operating system from the appropriate server on the network, booting and running the operating system in the diskless PC's memory. Figure 14.1 illustrates a diskless PC.

FIGURE 14.1
Diskless PC solution

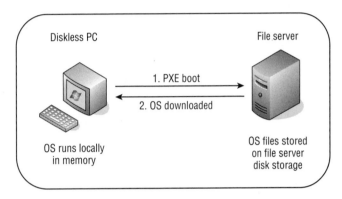

The benefits of a diskless PC solution are improved security and management, since the operating system, applications, and data are stored, updated, and managed centrally on servers in the datacenter. The disadvantage of this solution is that you are downloading or streaming a large amount of data over the network and require a high-bandwidth network connection to effectively download the operating system to the PC in a timely manner so that it doesn't negatively impact the user experience.

A MANUFACTURING PLANT IN THE EIGHTIES

Back in the 1980s, I was designing and implementing diskless PCs in large manufacturing plants across the United States. There were two main reasons for implementing this type of centralized desktop solution. The first was to minimize the cost of implementing a PC into this environment; PCs without hard drives were less expensive to procure and support. The second was related to centralizing applications and data, which improved security and manageability. These benefits are still relevant to companies today, contributing to the renewed interest in centralized desktop solutions and strong interest in investigating VDI.

PRESENTATION VIRTUALIZATION

Presentation virtualization provides a centralized desktop solution by creating multiple user sessions running in the Windows Server operating system environment. The remote desktop session is delivered to the endpoint device via the Microsoft Remote Desktop Protocol (RDP). To the end user, the session on their display looks like a local desktop operating system. The end user interacts and controls the environment with their keyboard and mouse, even though the session is running on the server.

Some of the benefits of a presentation virtualization solution are rapid application delivery, improved security, central management, and efficient network utilization, in addition to it being a mature and lower-cost solution as compared to VDI. These benefits are enabled by the operating system, applications, and data being stored and accessed centrally on servers running in the datacenter.

Application delivery is more agile and rapid because applications are installed once on the server and can be accessed by the user without having to install the application locally. In addition, the user can access applications from any endpoint device that supports the presentation virtualization solution.

Security of the user environment is improved because the user's applications and data are stored, secured, executed, and accessed centrally instead of being located on the user's local desktop device.

Management of the user environment is easier than for a distributed desktop environment because of the centralization of the operating system environment, applications, and data settings and its configuration on servers in the datacenter. For example, adding a new user environment is completed without having to install an operating system or applications on the local endpoint device. Software updates, patches, and upgrades are also completed on servers in the datacenter instead of on the user's endpoint device.

This solution provides efficient use of network bandwidth, making it appropriate to use over low-bandwidth networks. This is possible because the presentation virtualization session is just sending display, keyboard, and mouse data over the network instead of having to provide data exchange between the datacenter and the user's endpoint device.

Presentation virtualization is a mature technology, is easy to implement, and scales well as compared to a VDI solution. A presentation virtualization solution can support more users per server than a VDI solution. For example, a typical presentation virtualization solution can support 250 or more users per server as compared to a typical VDI solution supporting 30–45 users per server. Presentation virtualization is also less expensive to implement in terms of initial acquisition cost and supporting infrastructure. This is due to the solution being included into the Microsoft Windows Server operating system instead of having to purchase additional software and requiring fewer servers to implement the solution.

The main disadvantages of this solution are that some applications are incompatible with presentation virtualization, administrative privilege is not recommended in user sessions, and user sessions are less isolated than in other centralized desktop solutions like blade PCs or VDI. Figure 14.2 shows a presentation virtualization solution.

FIGURE 14.2
Presentation virtualization solution

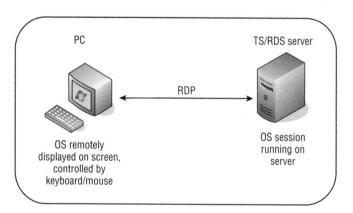

Application incompatibility issues are related to desktop applications running in a Windows Server operating system environment instead of a Windows desktop operating system.

In addition, an application may require specialized hardware that is not typically on the server, such as high-end graphics cards or security devices.

If administrative permissions are required for the user's desktop environment, presentation virtualization would not be the best option. This is because Microsoft doesn't recommend providing users administrative permissions to the presentation virtualization environment. Since this solution shares a single-server operating system, a user who makes an administrative change can adversely affect all the users running in the presentation virtualization environment.

If a business need requires a user's desktop to be isolated on a separate hardware or operating system environment, presentation virtualization would not provide this capability since multiple user sessions share a single-server operating system.

DELIVERING LINE OF BUSINESS APPLICATIONS EFFECTIVELY

Microsoft Windows Server Terminal Services has been around since the 1990s. Back then, it was common to see companies using Terminal Services to deploy enterprise resource planning or customer relationship management applications in a more effective and rapid way. For example, an organization could rapidly make their new line of business (LOB) application available to users without having to upgrade or refresh hardware and install the application on their local desktop. This was especially valuable for users on low-bandwidth networks. These benefits and others are still driving factors for organizations deploying Terminal Services today.

BLADE PC

The blade PC centralized desktop solution is based on deploying enclosed blade PCs stored in the datacenter. Each blade PC runs an operating system such as Windows XP, Windows Vista, or Windows 7 and is dedicated to a single user session. The remote desktop is delivered to the user's endpoint device via RDP or another protocol. An example of a popular solution in this space is the HP Consolidated Client Infrastructure (CCI).

The benefits of the blade PC centralized desktop solution are similar to those of the Terminal Services solution. In addition, since each user session is dedicated to an individual PC, this solution has good performance and strong user session isolation, and users can be given administrative privileges.

The disadvantages of this solution are higher cost and increased management, since individual blade PCs still need to be managed separately, even though they are centralized in the datacenter. Figure 14.3 illustrates a blade PC solution.

VIRTUAL DESKTOP INFRASTRUCTURE

The Virtual Desktop Infrastructure (VDI) centralized desktop solution utilizes servers to host individual desktop operating system environments running as virtual machines. Each hosted desktop virtual machine (VM) is running an operating system such as Windows XP, Windows Vista, or Windows 7 and is dedicated to a single user session. The remote desktop is delivered to the user's endpoint device via RDP or another protocol like Citrix's Independent Computing Architecture (ICA).

The benefits of this solution are very similar to the combined benefits of the presentation virtualization and blade PC solutions.

FIGURE 14.3
Blade PC solution

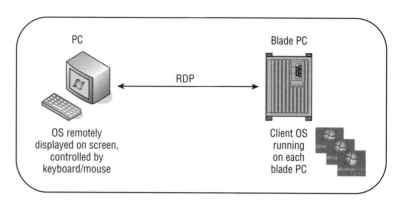

The disadvantage of this solution is that the technology is new and rapidly evolving. In addition, this solution is more complex than the centralized desktop solutions, requires a significant investment in hardware and software to build out the backend infrastructure to implement this solution, provides less density per server than presentation virtualization, and doesn't offer the dedicated performance of blade PCs. Figure 14.4 illustrates a VDI solution.

ALL THE VDI EXCITEMENT, BUT ONE SIZE DOESN'T FIT ALL

You may have heard the saying, "When all you have is a hammer, everything looks like a nail." Sometimes I am reminded of this phrase when hearing discussions about VDI. VDI looks like it could be beneficial to companies for particular use-case scenarios, such as for call center workers or contractor/offshore workers, but it may be impractical and too expensive to implement throughout the entire organization. In some cases, presentation virtualization, application virtualization, and client-hosted desktop virtualization may be more appropriate solutions. The decision to use VDI really depends on your business requirements and whether they can be met by using more-proven and less-expensive solutions. Think of VDI as one of the tools in your tool belt that can be used when needed, along with other solutions in a hybrid strategy to incrementally improve the overall desktop environment.

FIGURE 14.4
VDI solution

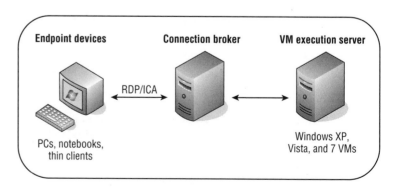

Client Virtualization

Client virtualization is the decoupling of computer resources on the client endpoint device, such as hardware, operating system, applications, and user settings and data. Virtualization solutions including desktop virtualization, application virtualization, and user-state virtualization enable the decoupling or separation of client computing resources. This separation provides a more flexible or agile environment, reducing complexity and costs and improving deployment, security, and manageability. All of these benefits have the potential to improve the overall desktop environment. A model of the traditional client endpoint device and virtualized client architecture is illustrated in Figure 14.5.

FIGURE 14.5
Traditional and virtualized desktop model

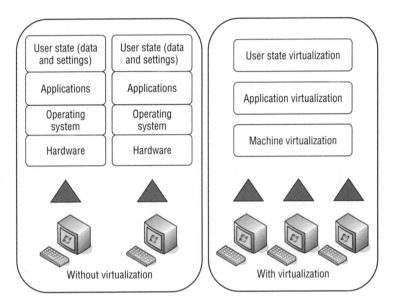

Without virtualization

With virtualization

DESKTOP VIRTUALIZATION

Various types of desktop virtualization solutions are available to companies today. The two main types are client-hosted desktop virtualization and server-hosted desktop virtualization. In most cases, these solutions use hypervisors to provide the virtualization solution to host the desktop VM. Let's review each type of desktop virtualization solution further.

Client-Hosted Desktop Virtualization Client-hosted desktop virtualization is a software solution that allows a single desktop to run multiple operating system environments at the same time. Each operating system environment is running in its own VM on the desktop. The operating system and applications running in the VM are unaware that they are sharing a single personal computer.

One common use case for desktop virtualization is a user with Windows 7 on their desktop and unable to run an application because of compatibility problems with the operating system. In this example, the user could solve the application-compatibility problem by running desktop virtualization software on their desktop, allowing them to run the application in a compatible operating system like Windows XP in a VM.

Client-hosted desktop virtualization implementations can be unmanaged or managed. The unmanaged client-hosted desktop virtualization solution runs hypervisor-based software on the endpoint device. Each endpoint device may have one or more VMs and their corresponding operating system, applications, user settings, and data. Each VM on the endpoint device is individually installed, configured, secured, updated, and managed. In addition, each VM environment has its own desktop environment that the end user must navigate and interact with. This type of desktop virtualization solution may create management and security challenges for organizations and additional complexity and training for the user. The managed client-hosted desktop uses a backend infrastructure and tools that enable administrators to centrally provision, configure, deploy, manage, update, and decommission the desktop VMs and provide a seamless desktop environment to the user. We will cover more details about both types of client-hosted desktop virtualization solutions in the Microsoft desktop virtualization overview section.

Server-Hosted Desktop Virtualization   There are also two types of server-hosted desktop virtualization: presentation virtualization and VDI. Both of these solutions provide the ability to host centrally managed desktop environments and deliver them remotely to the user's endpoint devices via a remote desktop protocol, but they have different architectures, benefits, disadvantages, and use cases, as we discussed earlier.

Virtual Desktop Infrastructure Overview

Virtual Desktop Infrastructure (VDI) refers to the hosting of a desktop operating system running in a VM on the server. The server-hosted desktop virtualization solution approach is also sometimes called virtual desktop environment (VDE). As mentioned before, VDI allows a user to access a remote desktop environment from an endpoint device via a remote desktop protocol. For the user, the experience is very similar to using the presentation virtualization solution, except that the desktop operating system is running in a VM hosted on a server instead of a remote user session on a Windows Server operating system. The hosted remote operating system and associated applications are shown on the user's endpoint device display and controlled via the endpoint device's keyboard and mouse.

VDI Architecture

The VDI architecture consists of several infrastructure components that work together to provide an end-to-end solution. The main components are endpoint devices, a connection broker, VM hosting servers, management servers, application servers, and other infrastructure services. Figure 14.6 illustrates the VDI architecture and main components.

Let's review each of the main VDI components, describing its specific role and functionality.

Virtual Machine Hosting Servers

The VM hosting servers are responsible for hosting the desktop VMs that are remotely delivered to the endpoint devices. Each server runs virtualization software or hypervisor and stores the desktop VMs on local (DAS) or shared storage (SAN or NAS). Type 1 hypervisors, like Microsoft Hyper-V, are most suitable for this type of solution because of their performance and scalability benefits, and they support a greater number or density of VMs than type 2 hypervisors.

FIGURE 14.6
VDI architecture and
components

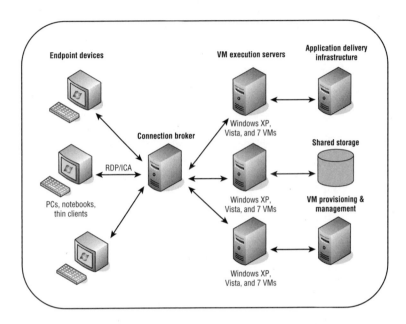

The number of VMs a single server can support depends on several variables and factors, including hardware and software types and configurations, user workloads of the desktop VMs, storage, and network.

The desktop VMs can be running any desktop operating system supported by the server virtualization solution, like Windows XP, Windows Vista, and Windows 7. In a server-hosted desktop virtualization solution, each VM can be dedicated to a specific user or allocated in a pool.

A VM pool shares VMs for concurrent use by many users. VM pools have the potential to save VM disk storage requirements. The savings come from not dedicating VMs for every individual user. For example, if an organization had 100 users, but only 50 were concurrent at any one time, they could preprovision 50 VMs in a pool and allocate them as administrators or users request. In theory, this deployment option could save 50 percent of the VM storage required for individual operating systems and applications.

Each VM can be preprovisioned for later use or dynamically provisioned at the time of use. When provisioning a VM, a template or image can be used as a basis for the creation of the VM, settings, and disk. Advanced provisioning technology allows a VM to be provisioned using a single image. An example of this technology is the Citrix XenDesktop Provisioning Server solution. Instead of allocating a complete disk image for every user VM, only a single image is used to provision the VM dynamically when the administrator or user requests the VM. This provisioning solution option has the potential to save a significant amount of VM disk storage. The savings results from provisioning a VM from a single image and not requiring a full VM disk image for every virtual machine running.

Each VM approach, dedicated or pooled, preprovisioned or dynamically provisioned, has its own benefits and disadvantages. Organizations should choose the most appropriate option based on their business needs and requirements.

ENDPOINT DEVICES

End users employ endpoint devices to access the VM running on the hosting server via a remote desktop protocol. Endpoint devices can be desktops, laptops, netbooks, thin devices, and even mobile devices.

Various remote desktop protocols can be used depending on the type of device and VDI solution used. Two of the most popular remote desktop delivery protocols are Microsoft's RDP (Remote Desktop Protocol) and Citrix's ICA (Independent Computing Architecture).

VDI solutions can be implemented using a mixture of different endpoint devices, such as a laptop running a local Windows operating system and/or a thin client running a Windows embedded operating system or another operating system environment. Each type of endpoint device has its own advantages and disadvantages. Organizations should carefully review these and select the appropriate solution based on their business needs and requirements. For example, a rich PC endpoint device has more computing power than a thin device and can also be used offline. In comparison, a thin PC endpoint device has lower hardware acquisition costs and uses less energy than a traditional PC.

CONNECTION BROKER

The connection broker is responsible for establishing and managing the user session between the endpoint device and the desktop VM that is running on the VM hosting server. It can have manageability, security, reliability, and scalability benefits in large and complex VDI environments.

A connection broker is generally needed as part of the VDI solution for a larger or more complex environment. One example where a connection broker would be needed is with VM pools. In this case the connection broker would connect the user to an available VM in the pool. There are some cases where a connection broker may not be needed for a VDI solution. One example would be when an organization dedicates VMs to each user. In this case, the user would be configured to connect directly to the same VM by computer name or IP address.

It's important to determine whether the connection broker is compatible and supports the type of server virtualization software or hypervisor you are using for your VM hosting servers, endpoint devices, and related remote desktop protocols.

The connection broker typically uses Microsoft Active Directory Services to facilitate session authentication, authorization, and management. In addition, the connection broker may require other services, such as Microsoft Internet Information Services for its web client to access the desktop VMs and a SQL Server database to store metadata, logging, and reporting information.

MANAGEMENT INFRASTRUCTURE

The management infrastructure includes services for managing the complete VDI infrastructure environment and desktop VM life cycle. These services include VM creation/provisioning, configuration, deployment, management, updating, health monitoring, backup and recovery, and retirement.

APPLICATION DELIVERY AND EXECUTION INFRASTRUCTURE

In a VDI solution, an organization can choose different ways to deliver applications to users as well as where each application will run or execute. When determining which application delivery and execution methods to use, an organization should carefully review all the options, mapping the most appropriate option that meets their business needs and requirements.

There are many options for delivering an application to a user. For example, applications can be delivered to the local endpoint device or server-hosted VM or via presentation virtualization. If the application is delivered to the local endpoint device, it would be placed on the host or guest operating system. If the application is delivered to the server-hosted VM, it would be placed on the operating system running in the VM. If the application is delivered by presentation virtualization, it would be placed on the server operating system running the presentation virtualization solution.

An additional option that could complement these delivery options is to use application virtualization technology such as Microsoft's Application Virtualization (APP-V) solution. Application virtualization runs the applications in a container that is hosted on the targeted operating system environment, that is, Windows client or server. The virtualization application is packaged and deployed to the end user without the application needing to be installed on the operating system. In addition, the application is cached on the operating system environment. More information about application virtualization and the Microsoft APP-V solution can be found in chapters 7, 8, and 9.

Applications can run or execute on different platform locations of a VDI solution. For example, applications can run on the local endpoint device, on either the host OS or VM guest OS. Applications can also run on the server-hosted desktop VM. Another option is for applications to run on a presentation virtualization server OS. Application virtualization can also be used to complement each of these options.

An organization has many options and combinations to choose from for delivering and running applications to users in a VDI environment. Choosing the right solution or combination of solutions will require an organization to review their business needs and map them to the products and technologies that can best meet their requirements. This process can take time, analyzing their application portfolio, IT, and user needs and requirements and reviewing available solutions, some that they may own and others that may require acquiring new hardware and software and investing in additional training and support. As mentioned before, the Microsoft Windows Optimized Desktop Scenario Assessment Guide may be a helpful resource in assisting an organization in the early planning process of this effort. More information about this guide and a free download can be found at `http://technet.microsoft.com/en-us/library/dd334417`. Listed below is a summary of different application delivery and execution options that can be used in a VDI solution.

Endpoint device

- Installed and run locally

- Virtualized and run locally

- Provided via presentation virtualization

Client-hosted virtual machine

- Installed and run within the VM

- Virtualized and run within the VM

- Provided via presentation virtualization within the VM

Server-hosted client virtual machine

- Installed and run within the VM

- Virtualized and run within the VM

◆ Provided via presentation virtualization within the VM

◆ Virtualized and run via desktop virtualization within the VM (Note that this is not a very common approach due to overhead limitations but is an available option.)

OTHER SERVICES

Other infrastructure services may be required in a VDI solution. Examples include directory services for authentication and authorization services, web servers to host remote desktop access websites, database servers for storing configuration and log information, shared storage (SAN and NAS) services for storing VM hard disks and configuration files, and client-hosted desktop virtualization for complementing the VDI solution. The prerequisites and requirements of other services that may be needed will depend on the VDI solution and components an organization selects.

Benefits and Disadvantages of a VDI Solution

Like any technology solution, a VDI solution has benefits and disadvantages. Right now in the IT industry, the benefits and disadvantages of VDI are debatable. One of the most controversial areas is the TCO benefits of VDI and where they come from. The main problem is that there is little unbiased data and analysis that proves there are substantial TCO benefits associated with a VDI solution. One area that most agree on is the security and flexibility benefits of this type of solution. But all these benefits come at a cost of having to make a significant upfront infrastructure investment to implement the solution. The bottom line is that there are benefits and disadvantages with VDI, and the importance of each one is related to what an organization is trying to accomplish. Here is a summary of some of the main benefits and disadvantages.

VDI BENEFITS

What are the specific benefits an organization may receive from implementing a VDI solution? Perhaps more important questions might be why an organization is interested in VDI and what type of problems they are trying to solve. These are important questions that an organization will need to think about and answer. A VDI solution is not a silver bullet to solve all the challenges in a desktop environment. It is only one tool in your desktop optimization tool belt that can be very useful for supporting specific business needs and use-case scenarios. For example, VDI can help an organization that requires tight security and is highly regulated. The use-case scenarios that have most benefited from VDI are specific industry knowledge workers (for example, financial services, healthcare, government) and remote workers (for example, contract, offshore, and work-from-home users). Organizations should carefully assess the value of using a VDI solution in their environment as compared to other desktop optimization solutions prior to making a decision to implement.

Potential desktop optimization benefits a VDI solution may deliver to an organization include improved deployment agility, management efficiency, improved security, and better business continuity and disaster recovery. Let's review each of these benefits in more detail.

Improved Deployment and Management VDI has the potential to improve desktop operating system deployment agility and management efficiency. Deployment agility improvements come from centralizing the desktop operating system images on servers in the datacenter and creating virtual images of the operating systems. A VDI environment can enable rapid desktop operating system environment provisioning and deployment. This is enabled by virtualizing the desktop environment, decoupling the operating system environment from the physical hardware desktop device. Desktop operating system environments are provisioned from preconfigured VM templates and images and then deployed by distributing the VM files to the appropriate hosting server, where they will run and be accessed by the user.

A VDI environment can be more efficient to manage than a distributed, nonvirtualized desktop environment. The increased management efficiency comes from the desktop operating system environment being centralized on hosting servers in the datacenter, where it can be more effectively managed by IT staff.

Improved Security   VDI can also provide security benefits for the desktop environment. The benefits come from storing and running the desktop operating system environment on centralized servers located in the datacenter, instead of on distributed desktops or endpoint devices. By storing the desktop data and applications in the datacenter instead of on local desktops, the data and applications can be better secured and controlled. If the desktop or laptop is lost or stolen, the user's desktop environment is still protected. In addition, the centralization of the desktop environment on servers in the datacenter, along with good management practices and software, can make it more efficient to implement security software updates. This is especially true if the desktop operating system and applications that run in the VM are provisioned from a single image or application package.

Better Business Continuity and Disaster Recovery   Desktop business continuity and disaster recovery can be improved by implementing VDI. Business continuity improvements are enabled by centralizing the desktop operating system, applications, and data in the datacenter, where administrators can more easily perform backup and recovery operations. Business continuity is also improved by implementing a highly available (HA) solution for the VDI solution to support maintenance operations and responses to hardware failures. If the desktop or laptop has a failure, the user's desktop environment is still available to them since their workspace is provided by the VDI solution and resides in the datacenter.

Disaster recovery for the desktop environment can be improved by VDI in two ways. In the event of a disaster that affects a user's work location, a new endpoint device can be brought up at an alternative location and the user can gain access to their same desktop workspace as before. If the disaster affects an organization's primary datacenter, the VDI solution can be brought up quickly at the secondary datacenter to support users. This is accomplished by regularly replicating the VDI desktop VMs from the primary datacenter to the secondary datacenter, where they are available to be run if necessary.

VDI DISADVANTAGES

A VDI solution has some disadvantages an organization will need to consider. These include the reliance on a network connection, unsuitability for high-end graphic applications, the need for additional infrastructure, and the significant acquisition costs of required hardware and software. In some cases, these disadvantages outweigh the potential benefits and impact an organization's decision to implement a VDI solution.

Reliance on a Network Connection   A VDI solution relies on a network connection in order to work. If the user's endpoint device cannot connect to hosting server, the user will be unable to access their desktop, applications, and data. In addition, the network connection should be reliable and have suitable bandwidth and low latency to provide a good user experience.

Unsuitable for High-End Graphic Applications   Typically, a VDI solution is not suitable for users who require the use of high-end graphic applications. This is mainly due to the remote desktop protocols being used in a VDI solution not being able to provide a suitable level of performance for this type of application. A lot of work is being done to improve remote desktop protocols in an effort to overcome this limitation, so I don't expect this disadvantage to be long lasting. For example, Microsoft acquired RDP-related technologies from a company called Calista in 2008 and has plans to incorporate these technologies into future products to better support high-end multimedia and graphics applications.

Additional Infrastructure Required   As mentioned in an earlier section of this chapter, a VDI solution requires additional servers, storage, and networking infrastructure. The amount of additional infrastructure required depends on the scale, performance, and service levels an organization needs for the solution. A VDI solution can potentially introduce a significant number of new servers and added storage into the datacenter. For example, if an organization is planning to support 5,000 dedicated users with their VDI solution, hosting 50 users per server, they would need 100 additional servers just to run the VMs. Additional shared storage would also be needed for this solution, and the amount depends on the VM provisioning methods used. If an organization used a nondynamic provisioning method for their 5,000 dedicated users and each VM was 5 GB, the additional amount of shared storage required would be 25 TB.

Additional Hardware and Software Costs   Since a VDI solution requires additional infrastructure, an organization would need to acquire new servers, storage, and networking to support this solution. In addition, VDI software would need to be acquired to support the server and endpoint devices. Organizations looking at VDI to reduce their software licensing costs will be disappointed since they will need to acquire additional software licenses for the VDI software solution.

VDI Use-Case Scenarios

As mentioned earlier, various use-case scenarios may benefit from a VDI solution. The three most common scenarios for a VDI solution are industry-specific knowledge workers, contractor and offshore workers, and work-from-home users. Let's review some examples of these use-case scenarios and their use of a VDI solution.

Hospital Doctors and Nurses   In this scenario, the users are doctors and nurses who work in various clinics and hospitals throughout a metro area. These users work in different shifts and use multiple PCs or endpoint devices to access the healthcare applications they use to do their job. PCs are distributed throughout the clinics and hospitals and placed where doctors or nurses perform patient care. Most PCs have a core set of applications, and others are used only to access specialized applications. Some applications are provided via presentation virtualization, but not all of their needed applications are compatible with this solution.

Doctors and nurses working in this environment have many requirements. For example, they need access to their desktop environment, applications, and data across multiple endpoint devices, regardless of where they are located throughout the work environment. They also require their user state to follow them as they move from one endpoint device to another. When accessing their applications and data they need very quick access (less than a few seconds) to their desktop environment. The solution must also be compatible with the suite of applications they currently use. The IT group who supports these users would like a more agile and flexible desktop environment to manage.

This healthcare knowledge worker use-case scenario could benefit from using a VDI solution to meet their business needs and requirements. A VDI solution is used to create a pool of VMs that would be used to deliver their desktop environment to doctors and nurses and associated applications to distributed endpoint devices. Since this desktop environment is centralized, they are able to use any endpoint device in a clinic or hospital while performing patient care. Applications are provided by presentation virtualization and application virtualization from the VDI VM. User access to the desktop environment is very quick, since the VM is already running and ready for the user to access. Since the desktop environment is now centralized, running as VMs on servers in the datacenter, IT has a more agile and flexible environment to manage and support.

Contracted Offshore Developers   This scenario consists of a financial services organization that is using contracted offshore developers to work on important IT projects. The contracted developers work from their remote location in India using their own Windows PCs.

In order for the offshore contractors to perform their development work, they need access to project applications and data that reside in the financial services organization's datacenter. In addition, each developer requires administrative rights on their desktop environment. The financial services organization has security and regulatory requirements that prevent offshore contractors from accessing corporate applications and data from non-corporate-owned desktops.

This scenario can also benefit from using a VDI solution to meet the offshore developers' and the financial services organization's requirements. The solution uses VDI to deliver developer desktops to the offshore contractor–owned Windows PCs. Each offshore contractor will have their own dedicated VM running in the organization's datacenter. Each developer has administrative rights for their assigned VM. Applications, user settings, and data are stored in the developer's dedicated VM running on servers located in the organization's datacenter. The financial services organization can provide the required level of control and security to meet their regulatory requirements and effectively manage the desktop environment.

 **Real World Scenario**

REDUCING DESKTOP HARDWARE COSTS

In an effort to reduce capital costs and improve overall desktop manageability, a retail company in the United States chose to implement VDI to support their developers who required more than one PC. VDI allowed them to significantly reduce their desktop hardware costs by enabling developers to access multiple operating system environments on one Windows PC device. Other benefits included reducing the time to provision and deploy new desktop environments and improved manageability. The business case for this solution was very compelling, and total cost of ownership (TCO) was realized in the first year of implementation. It is worth noting that their decision to implement VDI was made prior to the Microsoft Enterprise Desktop Virtualization (MED-V) product being available to customers.

Work-from-Home Call Center Agents   This scenario consists of call center agents who are employed at a travel and hospitality company. These workers perform their job from home, using their own personal computers.

They require remote access to the corporate call center applications and their data. Corporate security and regulatory policies require call center applications to run from the datacenter and not on remote or employee-owned PCs. And they require user desktop environments to be running in a tightly isolated desktop environment. Because of the seasonal nature of the business and dynamic employee staffing levels, corporate IT would like to implement a centralized desktop environment to provide more agility and efficiency in deploying, managing, and supporting call center agents' desktops.

This work-from-home scenario benefits from using a VDI solution to meet all of the organization's business needs. The VDI solution uses server-hosted VMs in a pool to deliver the call center agents an isolated desktop environment and applications. The agents use their own home-based Windows PC and broadband Internet connection to access the VDI desktop environment. User settings and data are centrally stored on servers running in the datacenter. Call center applications are provided to the agents via applications that are installed on the hosted VM and via presentation and application virtualization. Because the desktop environment is centralized, running on servers in the datacenter, this VDI solution provides corporate IT a more agile and flexible way to provision, deploy, manage, and support call center agent desktops.

INCREASING BUSINESS AGILITY WHILE REDUCING FACILITY COSTS

A telemarketing company in the United States had a requirement to add another call center facility, but in the midst of an economic downturn they needed to control costs as much as possible. This need led them to investigate alternative approaches to support call center agents. One of the alternatives they looked at was to avoid building or leasing another facility and having their call center agents work from their homes using their own PCs. Implementing a VDI solution for this business requirement allowed them to avoid facility and desktop hardware costs. Since the desktop images, applications, and data were centrally stored in the datacenter, the desktop environment could be well managed and secure. And since this environment was delivered via RDP, the broadband Internet connection in their homes was adequate to meet the connectivity needs.

Microsoft Desktop Virtualization Overview

Microsoft provides a comprehensive offering of desktop virtualization solutions. These solutions can be grouped into two categories, client- and server-hosted desktop virtualization.

For client-hosted desktop virtualization Microsoft provides two solutions that work together to provide a centrally managed environment: Microsoft Virtual PC and Microsoft Enterprise Desktop Virtualization (MED-V).

For server-hosted desktop virtualization Microsoft provides two solutions that are included in Microsoft Windows Server 2008 R2, leveraging Hyper-V and Remote Desktop Services. The Microsoft RDS solution provides session-based remote applications and desktops (presentation virtualization) and server-hosted VM desktops (VDI) using Hyper-V. More information about the RDS's session-based application and desktop services is provided in chapters 10 to 13. RDS's VDI-based solution is discussed in the "Microsoft VDI" section later in this chapter.

Client-Hosted Desktop Virtualization

Microsoft offers three client-hosted desktop virtualization solutions: Microsoft Virtual PC, Microsoft Enterprise Desktop Virtualization (MED-V), and Windows 7 XP Mode. Each product has its own benefits and is positioned to solve specific business problems. Let's briefly review

Microsoft Virtual PC and Windows 7 XP Mode, and then I'll provide a more detailed overview of MED-V.

MICROSOFT VIRTUAL PC

Microsoft Virtual PC is a client-hosted desktop virtualization solution that runs alongside the Windows desktop operating system. The solution utilizes a type 2 hypervisor that provides virtualization capabilities via hardware emulation. Microsoft Virtual PC was first released in 2004 after the technology was acquired from Connectix in 2003. The current version is Virtual PC 2007 SP1 and is used by millions of users. Common use-case scenarios for Microsoft Virtual PC are development and test, IT support, and application-to-OS compatibility remediation.

Microsoft Virtual PC supports a wide variety of host and guest operating systems and is available as a free download on the Microsoft website. More information about Microsoft Virtual PC, its system requirements, and other resources can be found at www.microsoft.com/virtualization.

WINDOWS 7 XP MODE

Windows 7 Professional, Enterprise, and Ultimate Editions provide a free add-on called Windows XP Mode. Windows XP Mode is a desktop virtualization solution that can help small businesses with application-compatibility issues that may arise during desktop operating system upgrades. It allows a user to run an application in a Windows XP SP3 VM and provides a seamless interface experience for accessing the virtualized application via the Windows 7 Desktop Start menu. It also provides support for USB 2.0 devices and access to the host OS's file shares and printers.

Windows XP Mode uses a new version of Virtual PC called Windows Virtual PC. The new version requires a PC to have hardware-assisted virtualization (Intel-VT or AMD-V) enabled in the BIOS. It supports Windows 7 and Vista host operating systems and Windows XP SP3 as a guest OS. More information about Windows XP Mode and Windows Virtual PC can be found at www.microsoft.com/windows/virtualpc.

MICROSOFT ENTERPRISE DESKTOP VIRTUALIZATION

Microsoft Enterprise Desktop Virtualization, or MED-V, is a managed client-hosted desktop virtualization solution that is part of the Microsoft Desktop Optimization Pack (MDOP) product offering. MED-V can help medium and large businesses with application-compatibility issues that may arise during desktop operating system upgrades. Unlike Windows XP Mode, MED-V enhances a Microsoft Virtual PC environment by centrally managing the client-hosted desktop virtualization environment. It provides centralized provisioning, deployment, control, management, and support of Virtual PC VMs running on a PC. Like Windows XP Mode, it also provides the user seamless integration access to the local virtualized OS and applications via the Windows 7 Desktop Start menu. The secret sauce that MED-V uses to provide these benefits is called a *workspace*. A workspace consists of a service and policies that wrap around the Virtual PC software and image, defining the usage polices of the VM and who can use it. Let's review in more detail how MED-V enhances the Microsoft Virtual PC environment.

Image Creation, Delivery, and Update Virtual PC images are stored in MED-V's central repository. MED-V associates the Virtual PC image with a workspace (that is, usage policies for the VM). The workspace can then be packaged and delivered to an endpoint device via the Web, electronic software distribution, or removable media (DVD or USB). MED-V workspaces can be updated centrally and distributed to an existing deployment.

Centralized Management and Monitoring   The MED-V environment can be centrally managed and monitored through the MED-V Management Console. The Management Console is used to create, configure, deploy, and manage the MED-V workspace. It is also used to monitor MED-V clients and create status, activity, and error reports.

Usage Policy and Data Transfer Control   A MED-V workspace controls the access and use of the Virtual PC image running on the desktop. MED-V uses Microsoft Active Directory Domain Services to provide authentication and authorization services. In addition, workspace usage settings like offline use, browser behavior, copy and paste rights, access to removable devices, and the expiration period are configured via the Management Console and controlled by the Management Server.

End-User Experience and Usability   A key end-user benefit of the MED-V solution is its ability to provide seamless access to the Virtual PC VM. An end user can access the MED-V workspace and its applications via the Windows Start menu or via a desktop shortcut. The end user is unaware that they are running an additional operating system environment or virtual machine on their PC. This transparency is enabled by the MED-V software and configured in the workspace policy settings.

MED-V Architecture   The MED-V architecture consists of a four main components: the Repository Server, Management Server, Management Console, and client software. The MED-V components work together to provide a MED-V solution called an *instance*. A diagram of the MED-V architecture is shown in Figure 14.7.

Repository Server   The Repository Server is responsible for storing Virtual PC images that are utilized in the MED-V solution. It stores the images on a Microsoft Windows Server 2008 file server, and they can be accessed via Microsoft Internet Information Server Web Server. There can be more than one repository per MED-V instance depending on the specific business and IT needs of the solution. For example, if you have a distributed environment, you may want to deploy MED-V Repository Servers close to the users to minimize the impact on the network and improve performance during the initial deployment process and future updates.

Management Server   The Management Server provides services for the creation, configuration, and updating of the Virtual PC images and MED-V workspaces. It uses the repository server to store and access the Virtual PC images. The MED-V workspace properties and usage settings are stored on the Management Server as XML files. The Management Server is also responsible for managing MED-V client access to workspaces via Microsoft Active Directory authentication and authorization.

Management Console   The Management Console is the administrative tool for managing the entire MED-V environment and the life cycle of the MED-V workspace. These tasks include creating and testing Virtual PC images; creating, configuring, assigning, and deploying MED-V workspaces; monitoring client activity and events; and creating reports. The MED-V management console can be installed only on a Windows client and not on a Windows Server. There can be more than one management console installed in a MED-V instance, but a management console can manage only one MED-V instance at a time.

FIGURE 14.7
Med-V architecture

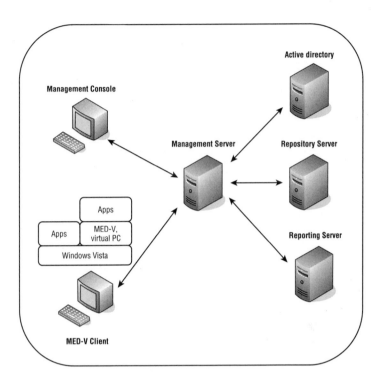

Client Software The client software is responsible for managing the Virtual PC environment and the MED-V workspaces on the desktop based on settings it retrieves from the Management Server. It can be installed along with Virtual PC via electronic software distribution, or removable media (DVD, USB). Once the client software is installed, it can communicate with the management server to view and download available workspaces that the user has been given access to. After the workspace has been downloaded to the desktop, it seamlessly integrates into the host OS desktop and Start menu. To access applications that are being hosted by a MED-V instance, a user would select Start ➤ All Programs ➤ MED-V Applications. Each time the workspace starts up, the client software will try to connect and authenticate with the management server. If the management server is not available, the workspace can run in offline mode if its settings allow for this type of operation. The MED-V client software will also regularly check with the management server to look for updates for the workspace settings and image, and send client activity and event information for support and reporting activities.

System Requirements The MED-V solution uses Virtual PC 2007 and does not require hardware-assisted virtualization (Intel-VT and AMD-V), unlike XP Mode. MED-V version 1 supports 32-bit versions of Windows Vista and XP as the host operating system and 32-bit Windows XP and 2000 as guest operating systems. MED-V version 2 will support Windows 7 as a host and a guest and is planned for release in 2010. The system requirements for the MED-V version 1 solution are shown in Table 14.2. For the latest MED-V information, please review the Microsoft MED-V website at www.microsoft.com/medv.

TABLE 14.2: MED-V version 1 system requirements

MANAGEMENT SERVER	
Processor	Dual processor, 2.8 GHz.
Memory	4 GB RAM.
Operating system	Windows Server 2008 Standard or Enterprise.
Database	Microsoft SQL Server 2005 Enterprise SP2 or Microsoft SQL Server 2008 Express, Standard, or Enterprise.
REPOSITORY SERVER	
Web server	Microsoft IIS.
File server	Windows Server 2008 disk space requirements are determined by the size and number of VM images that will be stored in the repository.
CLIENT SYSTEM	
Memory	1 GB for Windows XP, 2 GB for Windows Vista
Disk space	Disk space requirements are determined by the size and number of guest VMs.
Host OS	Windows XP SP2/SP3 (32-bit), Windows Vista SP1 (32-bit).
Client OS	Windows 2000 SP4 (32-bit), Windows XP SP2/SP3 (32-bit).
Desktop virtualization software	Microsoft Virtual PC 2007 SP1.

We will continue the review of MED-V version 1 in more detail in Chapter 16, with a focus on the deployment of this solution. Let's now move on to reviewing Microsoft server-hosted desktop solutions.

Server Hosted

As discussed earlier in this chapter, there are two main types of server-hosted desktop virtualization solutions: presentation virtualization and Virtual Desktop Infrastructure (VDI). Let's review Microsoft's solutions for these two types of server-hosted desktop virtualization.

MICROSOFT WINDOWS SERVER REMOTE DESKTOP SERVICES

Microsoft's solution for presentation virtualization has traditionally been called Terminal Services. In Windows Server 2008 R2, Terminal Services has been renamed to Remote Desktop Services (RDS) to better reflect the solution's abilities to deliver both presentation virtualization and VDI services.

Microsoft Windows Server 2008 R2 RDS can be used to deliver a desktop environment to an endpoint device via RDP. This can be accomplished via the Microsoft Remote Desktop

Connection, with a web browser via (RD) Web Access and via the Windows 7 Start menu. In addition, the RD gateway can also be used to provide remote access to an organization's RDS applications and remote desktops via RDP over HTTPS.

MICROSOFT VDI

With the addition of Windows Server 2008 R2, Microsoft now has a complete Virtual Desktop Infrastructure solution. The solution is simply called Microsoft VDI, and it leverages many of Microsoft's virtualization products and technologies to provide a robust, scalable, end-to-end solution. Let's look at the Microsoft VDI solution, its architecture and components, how they work together, and can be complemented by using partner solutions.

MESSAGE FROM THE MICROSOFT PRODUCT TEAM

"We are very excited about the features we have worked hard to implement, and the benefits they will bring to organizations that are considering VDI today. VDI is part of an enterprise's cohesive, holistic virtualization strategy across its IT infrastructure; as such, it supports Microsoft's vision of Dynamic IT. Microsoft VDI is a carefully-matched combination of Virtualization Technology and Licensing. It offers the best combination of performance and price. Its features include a scalable, stable and high performance hypervisor, an integrated management suite, application virtualization technology, a connection broker, and a subscription based licensing model."

George Zhu, Product Manager, Microsoft Corporation

The Microsoft VDI Solution

Microsoft VDI is not a single product but a set of products and technologies that are well integrated, creating an end-to-end solution. The solution can be implemented using only Microsoft technologies or a hybrid approach, leveraging partner solutions that complement and add value to Microsoft's offering. The Microsoft VDI solution includes the following core technologies and products:

- Microsoft Windows Server 2008 R2 with Hyper-V

- System Center Virtual Machine Manager 2008 R2

- Windows Server 2008 R2 Remote Desktop Services (RDS)

- Windows 7, Vista, and XP

- Microsoft Application Virtualization 4.5

The cornerstone of Microsoft's VDI offering is its server virtualization solution called Hyper-V. Hyper-V is the main platform where the hosted desktop VMs run. The hosted desktop VMs are provisioned and managed through Microsoft's System Center Management tools. The Microsoft Remote Desktop Connection (RDC) runs on the endpoint device and desktop VM. Microsoft RDC uses the Microsoft Remote Desktop Protocol (RDP) to deliver the remote Windows Desktop interface to the endpoint device. The Microsoft RD Connection Broker establishes and manages the connection between the endpoint device and the appropriate hosted desktop VM. All of these products work together to provide a scalable, secure, and well-managed VDI environment, as shown in Figure 14.8. Let's now map the Microsoft product and technology to the appropriate VDI component.

FIGURE 14.8
Microsoft VDI
architecture

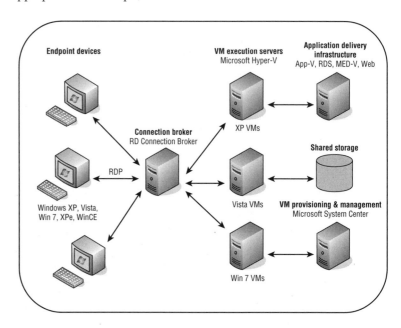

Endpoint Devices

Microsoft provides the following products that can be utilized on traditional or rich PCs and thin devices and that are available through hardware OEMs, such as Dell, HP, and Wyse.

Traditional or rich PC

◆ Windows XP and Vista

◆ Microsoft Windows XP and Windows Vista users will be able to access the Microsoft VDI environment via the RemoteApp and Desktop web access page. Note: One of the significant advantages of using a traditional or rich PC versus a thin device is in its ability to work offline and still be very useful without a network connection.

◆ Windows Fundamentals for Legacy PCs (WinFLP)

◆ WinFLP is a version of Windows based on Windows XP Embedded SP2 OS that has minimal system requirements. It is available to customers who have Software Assurance (SA) on their Windows clients and is used to extend the life of legacy PCs.

◆ Windows 7

◆ Microsoft Windows 7 users access the Microsoft VDI solution via the RemoteApp and Desktop Connection application. This application is configured in Control Panel; it provides dynamic updates of the resources available on the Microsoft VDI environment and seamlessly integrates into the Windows 7 Start menu.

Thin device

- Windows Embedded XP

  - Microsoft Windows Embedded XP is a special version of Windows XP that is prein-stalled by OEMs on thin and specialized devices such as point of sale (POS) and med-ical devices. The Windows XP Embedded thin device typically comes with Microsoft RDP or another remote desktop protocol such as Citix's ICA and Internet Explorer. Users would access the VDI environment from this device using their browser and navigating to a website to select their available resources. More information about Win-dows Embedded XP can be found at www.microsoft.com/windowsembedded.

- Windows CE

  - Microsoft Windows CE is also a special version of the Windows operating system; it is based not on Windows XP but on another version of Windows made especially for small computing devices. Windows CE is preinstalled on many computing devices, ranging from mobile phones, to entertainment solutions in automobiles, to thin devices. The Windows CE thin device also comes with Microsoft RDP or another remote desktop protocol such as Citix's ICA and Internet Explorer. Users would access the VDI environment from this device using their browser and navigating to a website to select their available resources. More information about Windows CE can be found at www.microsoft.com/windowsembedded.

Virtual Machine Hosting Servers

Microsoft's solution for the VM hosting server is provided by its family of server virtualization products. Microsoft Windows Server 2008 R2 with Hyper-V and Microsoft Hyper-V 2008 R2 are Microsoft's latest server virtualization solutions. All of these products run on the Intel and AMD 64-bit based servers, and all have their own system requirements that can be found in chapter 1 of this book.

Provisioning and Management

Provisioning and management services are provided by Microsoft's System Center Manage-ment tools. The tools include four products that support the management of the physical and virtual environments, desktop, and servers and heterogeneous hypervisor platforms. These products are System Center Configuration Manager, System Center Operations Manager, System Center Virtual Machine Manager, and System Center Data Protection Manager. Let's review each of these solutions and their potential management benefit in a VDI environment.

SYSTEM CENTER CONFIGURATION MANAGER

System Center Configuration Manager (SCCM) provides the infrastructure to support electronic software distribution, updates and patching, and software and hardware asset management for the entire desktop environment, whether it is a physical device, VM, or application. More information regarding SCCM can be found at www.microsoft.com/sccm.

SYSTEM CENTER OPERATIONS MANAGER

System Center Operations Manager (SCOM) monitors the health of the desktop environment, operating system, and applications. It creates events and alerts when there is a problem or condition with the desktop device or VM and can take automated actions to resolve the problem. In addition, SCOM can send its information to System Center Virtual Machine Manager to automatically move VMs from one host to another for load-balancing purposes or because of host health–related issues. All of this information can be collected and aggregated to create reports for the desktop environment. More information regarding SCOM can be found at www.microsoft.com/scom.

System Center Virtual Machine Manager

System Center Virtual Machine Manager (SCVMM) provides Hyper-V host and VM life cycle management. This includes Hyper-V host and VM provisioning, configuration, management, and retirement of the VDI environment. SCVMM is responsible for provisioning and deploying the server-hosted desktop VMs to the Microsoft Hyper-V hosting server. SCVMM would also be used to manage and configure the VMs. SCVMM works with SCOM to provide health monitoring and reporting of the VDI environment. More information regarding SCVMM can be found at www.microsoft.com/scvmm.

Systems Center Data Protection Manager

System Center Data Protection Manager (SCDPM) provides data backup and recovery for desktop environments whether a physical device or VM. SCDPM utilizes Volume Shadow Copy Service (VSS) to provide online backups of the Windows Server hosts and Windows VMs. Data can be backed up from disk to disk and disk to tape. More information regarding SCDPM can be found at www.microsoft.com/scdpm.

Profile Virtualization

Microsoft Windows Server 2008 R2 and Windows 7 provide support for profile virtualization. Profile virtualization is the abstraction of user data and settings from the hardware and operating system. It allows users to move from one endpoint device to another and have their user settings and data follow them around. This capability is very useful in a VDI environment and allows the unbundling of the user settings and data from the operating system running in the VDI VM. Microsoft provides profile virtualization support by using roaming profiles, redirected folders, and offline folders or client-side caching. Roaming profiles allow user settings to be stored centrally and follow the user from device to device. Redirected folders allow user data created locally to be stored on a network server instead of the local device. Offline folders or client-side caching provides support for local caching and synchronization of data that is stored on a network server.

Connection Broker

The Remote Desktop (RD) Connection Broker is an RDS role service included in Windows Server 2008 R2. It can be used as the connection broker for the Microsoft VDI solution and is positioned as a solution for low-complexity VDI environments. It provides session management services for remote applications and remote desktops. Specifically the RD Connection Broker orchestrates VMs running on Hyper-V, publishes VMs on the RemoteApp and Desktop Connection website, and establishes and ends user sessions to desktop VMs running on Hyper-V. The RD Connection Broker is extensible and serves as a platform for VDI partners and customers to build on to complement this solution.

Some Microsoft partners also provide connection broker services. Companies that provide connection broker services for the Microsoft VDI solution include Citrix, Unisys, Ericom, and Quest. More information on third-party connection brokers is provided in a later section in this chapter.

Application Delivery

Microsoft provides several options for the delivery of applications in a VDI environment. Which application delivery option or combination of options to choose will depend on the specific user, business and IT needs, and requirements of an organization. Some examples of Microsoft application delivery options are listed in Table 14.3.

TABLE 14.3: Microsoft application delivery options

DELIVERY OPTION	MICROSOFT SOLUTION
Web application	ASP.Net
Presentation virtualization	RDS RemoteApp and Web Access
Application virtualization	APP-V
Client-hosted VM	Virtual PC/MED-V, Windows 7 XP Mode
Server-hosted VM	Microsoft VDI

Microsoft VDI Licensing

Microsoft has two licensing products that are related to a Microsoft VDI solution: the Windows Virtual Enterprise Centralized Desktop and the Microsoft VDI Suite license. Let's review each of these licensing products.

VIRTUAL ENTERPRISE CENTRALIZED DESKTOP

Microsoft Virtual Enterprise Centralized Desktop (VECD) is not a technology but rather a licensing product. Microsoft VECD provides a customer the licensing rights to access a Windows Desktop operating system in a VDI environment, regardless of the hypervisor solution being used (i.e., Hyper-V, ESX, XenServer). Microsoft VECD is subscription based and licensed by endpoint device. The Microsoft VECD license allows a user using an endpoint device to access up to four concurrent VMs running in a VDI environment. There are two types of Microsoft VECD licensing products: VECD for Software Assurance (SA) and VECD. The VECD for Software Assurance license is for Windows PC devices that are licensed by Software Assurance. The VECD license is for endpoint devices (PCs or thin clients) that are not licensed by SA or do not qualify for SA. This VECD license is also used for licensing third-party PCs or thin-client devices in an organization's VDI environment. More information about VECD can be found at www.microsoft.com/vecd.

MICROSOFT VDI LICENSE

In October of 2009 Microsoft introduced a new licensing option that makes purchasing the Microsoft VDI solution much easier. The new option is called the Microsoft VDI Suite and includes the infrastructure and management components of the Microsoft VDI solution. The new license option is subscription based and available to customers who have Software Assurance on their Windows clients. The license comes in two flavors: Microsoft VDI Standard Suite and Microsoft VDI Premium Suite. The Standard Suite license provides Hyper-V, RD

Connection Broker, APP-V (from MDOP), Virtual Machine Manager, Operations Manager, and Configuration Manager. The Premium Suite license includes everything from the Standard Suite plus the RDS Session Host and APP-V for RDS Session Host. These two options add session-based remote application and desktop publishing. More information about the Microsoft VDI license can be found at www.microsoft.com/virtualization/products/desktop.

How Microsoft VDI Works

VDI is a complex infrastructure solution with many moving parts, but to the end user, the experience can be fairly transparent. Let's review the process of an end user using a VDI session, both from the user experience and what is taking place behind the scenes.

  1. User logs in and connects to the RemoteApp and Desktop Connection website.

    User Experience The end user logs into the endpoint device, launches Internet Explorer, navigates to the RemoteApp and Desktop Connection login screen, and enters their login credentials, as shown in Figure 14.9.

FIGURE 14.9
RemoteApp and Desktop
Connection login screen

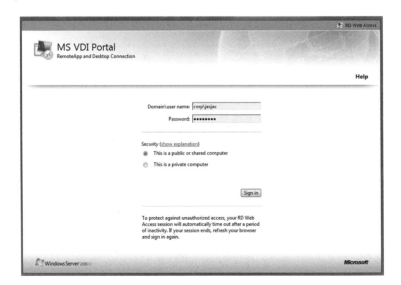

    Behind the Scenes Active Directory authenticates and authorizes the user. Internet Explorer connects to the RemoteApp and Desktop Connection login screen. RD Web Access talks to the RD Connection Broker. The RD Connection Broker queries the Hyper-V/RD Virtualization Server for VMs that the user is authorized to use and sends the results back to RD Web Access to present on the RemoteApp and Desktop Connection website.

  2. User selects their remote desktop.

    User Experience The end user selects the appropriate desktop operating system (i.e., Windows XP, Windows Vista, or Windows 7) from the RemoteApp and Desktop Connection web page, as shown in Figure 14.10.

FIGURE 14.10
RemoteApp and Desktop
Connection web page

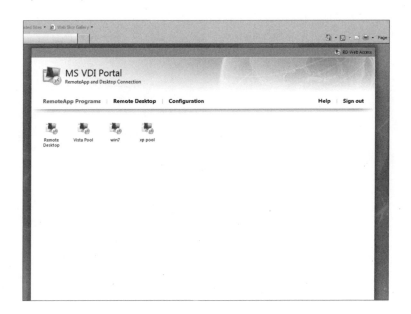

Behind the Scenes   The RD Connection Broker communicates with the Hyper-V/RD Virtualization Server to deliver the appropriate VM to the user's endpoint device. If the selected VM is in a saved state, the RD Connection Broker will send a command to the Hyper-V server to start the VM.

3. The user's remote desktop is delivered to endpoint device.

User Experience   A new window is opened on the end user's desktop that contains the remote Microsoft Windows operating system environment, prompting the user to log on.

Behind the Scenes   Remote Desktop Connection connects to the RD Connection Broker. The Connection Broker connects to the Hyper-V/RD virtualization server, and an RDP session is established between the user's endpoint device and the selected desktop.

4. The user's remote desktop session is active.

User Experience   The user interacts with the remote desktop Windows session, using available applications, services, and data. See Figure 14.11.

Behind the Scenes   Windows Server 2008 R2 Hyper-V is hosting the running VM. The VM is remotely displayed and controlled from the endpoint device via the Remote Desktop Connection application using RDP.

5. The user ends the remote desktop session.

User Experience   The user ends the remote desktop session by logging off the remote Windows desktop session and closing the Remote Desktop Connection application.

FIGURE 14.11
Remote desktop session

Behind the Scenes The connection broker ends the remote desktop session. Since this session was from a personal desktop, the VM would remain running unless it had been configured to hibernate, in which case it would be put in a saved state. If this was a VM from a pool, two behaviors could take place at the end of a session. If the user doesn't log out of the operating system, the VM is still running and available to the user for a short period of time. If the user logs out of the OS and ends the RDP session, the VM will be restarted to be available for the next user request.

MICROSOFT VDI PARTNERS

Microsoft is known for its large and healthy partner ecosystem and is leveraging this community to complement and add value to Microsoft's overall virtualization solution. Examples of Microsoft virtualization partners that complement the Microsoft VDI solution are provided here:

CITRIX

Citrix provides a connection broker and provisioning server that complement the Microsoft VDI solution. Both of these products are included in the Citrix XenDesktop solution and support Microsoft Windows Server 2008 Hyper-V and System Center Virtual Machine Manager. More information about this solution and the Microsoft partnership can be found at www.citrix.com.

QUEST

Quest provides a connection broker that complements the Microsoft VDI solution. This Quest product is called vWorkspace. More information about this solution and the Microsoft partnership can be found at www.quest.com.

UNISYS

Unisys provides a connection broker that complements the Microsoft VDI solution. This Unisys product is called Unisys Session Manager and is included in the Unisys Consolidated Desktop solution. More information about this solution and the Microsoft partnership can be found at www.unisys.com.

ERICOM

Ericom provides a connection broker that complements the Microsoft VDI solution. This Ericom product is called PowerTerm WebConnect DeskView. More information about this solution and the Microsoft partnership can be found at www.ericom.com.

The Bottom Line

Identify Microsoft Windows Optimized Desktop best practices.   Microsoft's approach to improving the desktop environment is called the Windows Optimized Desktop.

Master It   List five technologies that contribute to a Microsoft Windows optimized desktop.

Describe different types of desktop virtualization solutions.   There are two different types of desktop virtualization solutions: client-hosted and server-hosted.

Master It   How are the architectures of presentation virtualization and Virtual Desktop Infrastructure (VDI) different?

Define VDI, its benefits, architecture, and components.   A VDI solution has several benefits and disadvantages an organization will need to consider carefully.

Master It   What are some benefits and disadvantages of a VDI solution?

Understand the Microsoft Enterprise Desktop Virtualization solution and its architecture. Microsoft has three different types of client-hosted desktop virtualization solution: Virtual PC, Windows XP Mode, and Microsoft Enterprise Desktop Virtualization.

Master It   How does MED-V enhance a Virtual PC environment?

Understand the Microsoft VDI solution and its architecture.   The Microsoft VDI architecture consists of many server and client components that work together to provide a single solution.

Master It   What are the main server components of the Microsoft VDI solution?

Chapter 15

Deploying Microsoft VDI

Chapter 14 presented an overview of desktop virtualization and Microsoft's offerings for client- and server-hosted desktop virtualization. In this chapter we will review deploying Microsoft's VDI solution. The chapter includes an overview of considerations for planning a VDI deployment, a review of specific Microsoft server and client components used in this solution, and guidance and step-by-step instructions for installing and configuring the Microsoft VDI solution in a test environment.

In this chapter, you will learn to:

◆ Install and configure the Microsoft Remote Desktop Connection Broker

◆ Create and assign a personal virtual machine

◆ Create and assign virtual machines to a pool

◆ Install and configure the Microsoft Remote Desktop Web Access server

◆ Configure Windows 7 for RemoteApp and Desktop Connection

Planning for a Microsoft VDI Deployment

The process of planning a Microsoft VDI deployment consists of several steps: assessing the current environment, determining the requirements of your organization and its users, defining the scope of the deployment project, creating the solution design and architecture, implementing a test or proof of concept (POC) environment, conducting a pilot, and moving forward with a full-scale deployment. Let's review each of these planning steps at a high level.

Assessing Your Environment

When considering implementing a VDI solution, you should conduct an assessment of an organization's environment to review the current desktop infrastructure in terms of hardware, operating systems, applications, and user settings and data. In addition, identifying the types of users who are in the organization (for example, task, office, offshore/contractors, mobile, and home), their workload or applications, and technology needs is very important in mapping the most appropriate solution and technologies to the right user or group of users. Accessing your current desktop management solutions and capabilities is also important in determining if there are challenges that need to be addressed before moving to a virtualized desktop environment. Microsoft has assessment tools to assist an organization with this effort. The Microsoft Assessment and Planning Toolkit can be found at http://technet.microsoft.com/en-us/solutionaccelerators.

Determining Requirements

The information collected from the assessment can be used to help determine the desktop requirements of the IT organization and its users. Several solutions and technologies can address the needs of an organization, helping them optimize their desktop environment. An organization should take a holistic approach in their desktop optimization efforts and not try to make a single solution fit everywhere. Once the organization determines its desktop requirements, a list of solutions and technologies that address these requirements can be made and mapped to the corresponding user types. As discussed in the previous chapter, Microsoft's Windows Optimized Desktop Scenario Selection Tool can assist an organization with this effort. The tool can be found at http://technet.microsoft.com/en-us/library/dd334417.aspx.

Defining Project Scope

Determining the scope for an initial VDI project and future efforts is very important. Instead of trying to boil the ocean, some organizations have decided to implement a walk-before-run strategy. For example, they may target the most important requirements, like reducing desktop management costs or addressing security and regulatory requirements. Once an organization has determined the goals for the project, they can further develop the project scope to include which group of users to target, what solution capabilities will be delivered, and when the solution will be delivered.

An organization may choose to implement their VDI solution project in phases, with each phase expanding the scope of target groups or users and capabilities provided. For example, they may decide to implement a VDI solution to improve desktop management efficiency and agility. The project scope for the first phase could implement dedicated virtual machines that include the current desktop image and applications, targeting users in their IT desktop management group, and roll out the solution over six months, increasing the number of users every month. The project scope for the second phase could move to a pooled virtual machine architecture and expand the deployment to the help desk or call center. The project scope for the third phase could add application virtualization to the solution and further expand the solution deployment to the most appropriate user groups in the organization.

Microsoft Consulting Services and Partners can assist organizations with all of these planning efforts. More information regarding MCS and Partner offerings can be found at www.microsoft.com/services/microsoftservices and www.microsoft.com/virtualization/partners.

Creating a Solution Design and Architecture

The solution design and architecture should closely align with the organization's goals for their VDI effort, project scope, and IT and user needs as well as provide a solid foundation for future plans and growth of the organization. Sometimes this can be part science and part art, especially considering that VDI is a new virtualization solution and evolving rapidly. We discussed in the previous chapter the main server and client components of a VDI solution, which consisted of a hosting server to run the virtual desktops, a connection broker to connect and manage the remote desktop session between the endpoint device and hosting server, and the endpoint devices. The scope of your VDI project will determine the number of servers that would be required for each component in order to fulfill the performance and reliability needs of an organization.

One critical part of the design and architecture for a VDI solution is the sizing of the servers that will host the desktop virtual machines. A key consideration in determining this sizing is the number of users an organization is planning to support with this solution. The million-dollar question that everyone asks is how many users a server can support in a VDI solution. Finding the answer to this question helps an organization determine the number of servers they will require in the architecture. The answer to this question is like many answers to technical questions: It depends. For example, if an organization wants to support 200 task worker users with this solution, and if a hosting server can support 45 concurrent task worker users, in theory you would need 5 desktop virtualization hosting servers. If you wanted to support 500 task worker users, in theory you would need 12 hosting servers. And if you wanted to support 1000 users, in theory you would need 23 hosting servers, and so on. The number of users that can be supported on a hosting server depends on factors such as user work load, virtual desktop image size, operating system version, the configuration of the server, and other variables.

One of the most important server configuration factors on a hosting server is the amount of memory it has. For example, a server with 32 GB of memory, supporting virtual machines that require 1 GB of memory, in theory would be able to support 30 virtual machines, using 30 GB of memory for the desktop virtual machines and 2 GB for the hosting server.

Another important factor to consider is the number of processor cores you have on the server. A conservative rule of thumb related to this factor is to map 4–6 users per core, so if a server has 16 cores, in theory and with an adequate amount of memory you could support 64–96 users on a single server. In addition, networking and storage variables come into play for determining the number of users a single server can support and the performance or user experience of the VDI solution. Designing a hosting server to have dedicated network adapters for the desktop virtual machines and using fast shared storage (SAN) is also recommended. The bottom line is that an organization will need to do their own thorough testing to determine how many hosting servers they will need to support their unique solution goals and environment. See Chapter 6 to review Hyper-V performance recommendations.

Another area an organization will likely need to address is providing High Availability (HA) for the VDI solution. The Microsoft VDI solution can provide High Availability through the use of Failover Clustering and load-balancing services. It supports Failover Clustering of the Hyper-V servers that host the desktop VMs. In addition, desktop VMs running on one host can be migrated to another host without any service interruption to the user by using Microsoft Live Migration. Microsoft Failover Clustering is also supported for the RD Connection Broker, but only one RD Connection Broker per RD Session Host (Redirector) farm can be used at the same time, requiring an active/passive cluster configuration. The solution can also use multiple RD Session Host (Redirector) servers and RD Web Access servers to provide load balancing. For more information regarding architecting and implementing a highly available Microsoft VDI solution, see Chapter 6 (Hyper-V) and Chapter 13 (RDS).

Implementing a POC

Once the solution design and architecture are completed, the next step is to test the solution in a proof of concept (POC) lab environment. A POC is where the rubber meets the road and can vary in goals, scope, time frame, and outcome. It's important to conduct a well-organized POC, defining success criteria, focusing on only the goals and scope agreed upon, involving the right resources, and documenting the entire process from start to finish, so that this information can be reviewed and utilized to support later project efforts. During the POC an organization should evaluate the functionality of the solution and compare the findings to their solution requirements. In addition, the solution's performance and capacity assumptions should also be evaluated and validated.

Depending on the goals of the POC, the architecture and server configuration of this environment can be implemented on a much smaller scale than a pilot or production deployment of the solution. For example, a typical VDI POC involves two physical servers and three to five endpoint devices. One server would support the hosting of the desktop virtual machines, and the other server would support the connection broker service and provision/management services. A mixture of endpoint devices can be used, mapping to the organization's current desktop environment, running Windows XP, Windows Vista, and Windows 7. An example VDI POC server configuration is shown along with the VDI POC architecture example in Figure 15.1.

FIGURE 15.1
Microsoft VDI POC architecture example

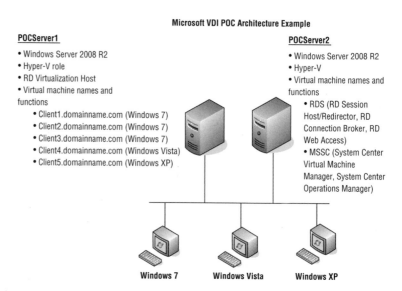

Microsoft VDI POC Architecture Example

POCServer1
- Windows Server 2008 R2
- Hyper-V role
- RD Virtualization Host
- Virtual machine names and functions
  - Client1.domainname.com (Windows 7)
  - Client2.domainname.com (Windows 7)
  - Client3.domainname.com (Windows 7)
  - Client4.domainname.com (Windows Vista)
  - Client5.domainname.com (Windows XP)

POCServer2
- Windows Server 2008 R2
- Hyper-V
- Virtual machine names and functions
  - RDS (RD Session Host/Redirector, RD Connection Broker, RD Web Access)
  - MSSC (System Center Virtual Machine Manager, System Center Operations Manager)

Windows 7   Windows Vista   Windows XP

At a high level, you can break the POC into four areas: preparation, installation and configuration, testing and knowledge transfer, and review and analysis. Each area is important and will have an effect on the success of the POC and preparation for a production deployment. The knowledge transfer and testing area should be well defined in terms of what the POC team wants to learn and evaluate regarding the Microsoft POC solution.

VDI POC ACTION PLAN EXAMPLE

Here is a simple but effective one-week POC action plan as an example of a real-world POC engagement.

POC planning activities

- ◆ Conduct initial meeting.

   Determine goals, scope, expected outcome, time frame, resources involved, location(s), IT infrastructure needs (hardware, software, services, networking, storage, etc.).

- Conduct a pre-VDI POC meeting.

  - Include all the required IT and business resources.

  - Review the POC areas described above.

  - Identify potential project showstoppers.

  - Create an itinerary for the one-week POC activities along with the responsibilities of IT and business resources participating.

POC activities

- Day 1 — Install Windows Server 2008 R2, Hyper-V, and RDS components.

  1. Conduct a VDI POC kickoff meeting the first day of the POC. Verify that POC prerequisites are completed and the organization is ready to begin.

  2. Review POC project and planned day 1 activities.

  3. Begin Microsoft VDI software installation.

     a. Install and configure two Windows Server 2008 R2 Servers with Hyper-V called POCServer1 and POCServer2.
     b. Install Remote Desktop Virtualization role service on POCServer1 running Hyper-V.
     c. Create five Windows client virtual machines on POCServer1 for use as personal and pooled virtual machines. Name the VMs with fully qualified names, for example, client1.*domainname*.com, client2.*domainname*.com, and so on. Install Windows 7 on VMs client1–client3, Windows Vista on VM client4, and Windows XP on VM client5.
     d. Create a VM on POCServer2 called RDS, running Windows Server 2008 R2.
     e. Create another VM on POCServer2 called MSSC, running Windows Server 2008 R2.
     f. Install RD Session Host (Redirector), RD Licensing, RD Connection Broker, and RD Web Access role services on the VM called RDS on POCServer2.
     g. Install System Center Virtual Machine Manager and System Center Operations Manager on the VM called MSSC on POCServer2.

  4. Conduct daily status meeting.

- Day 2 — Configure Windows Server 2008 R2 and RDS components.

  1. Review planned day 2 activities.

  2. Configure and test Microsoft VDI environment.

     a. Configure RD Session Host on the VM called RDS on POCServer2.
     b. Configure the RD licensing on the VM called RDS on POCServer2.
     c. Configure the RD Session Host (Redirector) on the VM called RDS on POCServer2.
     d. Configure the RD Web Access on the VM called RDS on POCServer2.
     e. Configure the RD Connection Broker on the VM called RDS on POCServer2.
     f. Configure the five Windows client virtual machines on POCServer1 for use as personal and pooled virtual machines.
     g. Assign client1, client4, and client5 VMs as personal VMs. Test access to the personal VMs from supported Windows client endpoint devices.

      h. Assign client2 and client3 VMs as pooled virtual machines. Test access to the virtual machine pool from supported Windows client endpoint devices.

    3. Conduct daily status meeting.

◆ Day 3 — Set up and configure RDS RemoteApp, System Center VMM, and Operations Manager.

    1. Review planned day 3 activities.

    2. Install appropriate desktop applications to be used as RDS RemoteApps on the VM called RDSH on POCServer2 and configure them to be available to Microsoft VDI users.

    3. Install and configure Microsoft System Center Virtual Machine Manager on the VM called MSSC on POCServer2.

    4. Install and configure Microsoft System Center Operations Manager on the VM called MSSC on POCServer2.

    5. Conduct daily status meeting.

◆ Day 4 — Transfer knowledge and test Microsoft VDI environment.

    1. Review planned day 4 activities.

    2. Review and test Microsoft VDI environment.

    3. Conduct daily status meeting.

◆ Day 5 — Transfer knowledge and test Microsoft VDI environment.

    1. Review planned day 5 activities.

    2. Review and test Microsoft VDI environment.

    3. Conduct daily status meeting.

Post-POC activities

◆ Prepare report on POC activities completed, including highlights and lowlights and key findings.

◆ Develop an action plan for moving forward with the project.

Conducting a Pilot

Implementing the Microsoft VDI solution in a POC is different from implementing it in a pilot. The most significant difference in a pilot is that the solution is being implemented in a production environment instead of a lab, using production infrastructure services such as Active Directory and management tools and applications. Another important difference is that the solution is deployed on a server architecture that can be built upon and scaled to meet the future needs of the organization. Conducting a pilot further evaluates the solution, testing reliability, performance, user experience, and supportability. Some organizations will begin a pilot by targeting their own IT group or help desk to gain some experience, minimize risk, train support staff, and provide an opportunity to gradually increase the numbers of test users, evaluating and refining the solution as they go. After the initial pilot deployment, further refinement of the solution can be done, better positioning the solution for future phased deployments. Outlined below is an example of a phased Microsoft VDI solution pilot deployment. The phases in the pilot span a six-month period that gradually adds users and broadens deployment across two groups. Months 1 through 3 focus on IT users, starting out with 40 test users and moving to 120. Months 4 through 6 continue testing the 120 IT test users and extend the deployment to business users, starting out with 40 test users and moving to 120. During each month the testing results will be analyzed to determine if the pilot is meeting the organization's solution criteria and if it should continue or be paused to make any changes related to architecture, infrastructure, components, configuration, or process. An example of a Microsoft VDI pilot deployment plan follows:

Microsoft VDI solution pilot deployment plan

Month 1   Deploy solution to 40 IT test users.

Month 2   Deploy solution to 80 IT test users.

Month 3   Deploy solution to 120 IT test users.

Month 4   Continue support of 120 IT test users. Deploy solution to 40 business users.

Month 5   Continue support of 120 IT test users. Deploy solution to 80 business users.

Month 6   Continue support of 120 IT test users. Deploy solution to 120 business users.

Conducting a Full-Scale Deployment

After all the necessary steps have been completed to verify the VDI solution meets an organization's goals and requirements, they are ready to begin a full-scale deployment in the environment. A Microsoft VDI enterprise deployment plan can be implemented in phases, spanning several months or multiple years. In addition, each phase may implement additional capabilities or functionality throughout the project life cycle. For example, the organization may choose to implement a less-complex solution first and move to a more complex environment over time.

SAMPLE MICROSOFT VDI SOLUTION PHASED DEPLOYMENT PLAN

This example of a phased deployment approach implements additional capabilities in each phase.

Phase 1   A VDI solution implemented with dedicated virtual machines. Applications are installed directly on the virtual machine, and presentation virtualization is used via RDS.

Phase 2   A VDI solution implemented with dedicated and pooled virtual machines. Applications are installed directly on the virtual machine, and presentation virtualization is used via RDS.

Phase 3   A VDI solution implemented with dedicated and pooled virtual machines. Applications are delivered from the virtual machine, via presentation virtualization, and via application virtualization.

Installing the Microsoft VDI Solution

The process of implementing the Microsoft VDI solution consists of installing and configuring several services on servers running Windows Server 2008 R2 and endpoint devices running the Windows client operating system.

As discussed in previous chapters, Microsoft Remote Desktop Services provides support for session management and publishing of the remote applications and desktops. Microsoft Remote Desktop Services includes five role services that support the Microsoft VDI solution. In the next two sections we will review the main installation steps required to be performed on the servers and clients that make up the VDI solution. Figure 15.2 shows an example of the Microsoft VDI solution architecture we will be installing.

SAMPLE MICROSOFT VDI SOLUTION ARCHITECTURE

The architecture used for this Microsoft VDI solution example consists of four servers and three clients. A key assumption is made regarding the existence of infrastructure services that are needed to support this solution, for example, AD, DNS, and DHCP.

SERVERS

Server A   A Remote Desktop Virtualization Host server running Windows Server 2008 R2 with the Hyper-V role and Remote Desktop Virtualization Host role service.

Server B   A Remote Desktop Session Host (Redirector) server running Windows Server 2008 R2 with the Remote Desktop Session Host role service configured only as the Redirector and not used for RemoteApp publishing.

Server C   A Remote Desktop Connection Broker running Windows Server 2008 R2 with the Remote Desktop Connection Broker role service.

Server D   A Remote Desktop Web Access server running Windows Server 2008 R2 with the Web Server (IIS) role and Remote Desktop Web Access role service.

ENDPOINT DEVICES

Endpoint Device 1   Running Windows 7 client operating system.

Endpoint Device 2   Running Windows Vista SP1 client operating system.

Endpoint Device 3   Running Windows XP SP3 client operating system.

Server Components Overview

The Microsoft VDI solution environment consists of five main architecture tiers that include the Windows endpoint devices, the Web Access server, Session Host, Connection Broker, and Desktop Virtual Machine Hosting server. With Windows Server 2008 R2, Microsoft now has all the necessary server components for implementing a virtual desktop solution in an enterprise environment. The previously missing component, the connection broker, is now provided in Windows Server 2008 R2. The Microsoft connection broker is called Remote Desktop (RD) Connection Broker and is a role service of the Remote Desktop Services role. In addition, improvements in Remote Desktop Services, Windows 7, and RDP solidify and enhance the overall solution. We'll go through the necessary steps to implement a Microsoft VDI solution using Windows Server 2008 R2 with Hyper-V, Remote Desktop Services, Windows XP, Windows Vista, and Windows 7.

FIGURE 15.2
Microsoft VDI solution architecture example

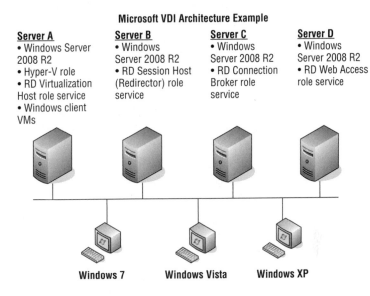

Microsoft VDI Architecture Example

Server A
• Windows Server 2008 R2
• Hyper-V role
• RD Virtualization Host role service
• Windows client VMs

Server B
• Windows Server 2008 R2
• RD Session Host (Redirector) role service

Server C
• Windows Server 2008 R2
• RD Connection Broker role service

Server D
• Windows Server 2008 R2
• RD Web Access role service

Windows 7   Windows Vista   Windows XP

The Microsoft Windows Server 2008 R2 components that are needed to support this VDI solution include Windows Server 2008 R2, the Hyper-V role, the Remote Desktop Services role, and the following Remote Desktop Services role services: RD Session Host, RD Virtualization, RD Licensing Server, RD Web Access, and RD Connection Broker. In addition, the RD Gateway role service may also be needed if access to this environment from the Internet is required.

This architecture example uses four servers to provide the VDI solution. Even though the entire solution could be implemented on one server (using VMs) or two servers, I wanted to provide an example that would isolate the main VDI components by running them on separate servers. Note that the RD Virtualization Host role service and RD Connection Broker role service cannot be installed on the same physical or virtual server.

In addition, other Microsoft products, technologies, and updates may also be needed before or during the installation of the solution components. Examples include Microsoft Active Directory Domain Services, Web Server (IIS), DNS, DHCP, System Center management tools, and Windows server and client operating system updates. For more information regarding system requirements, see Chapter 2 (Hyper-V) and Chapter 11 (RDS).

Let's review each of the servers in this architecture example and the VDI-related services installed.

SERVER A — REMOTE DESKTOP VIRTUALIZATION HOST

Server A runs the Hyper-V role and the RD Virtualization Host role service. It provides the platform to host and run the Windows Desktop operating systems in virtual machines that endpoint devices connect to for accessing remote desktops. One hosting server is used for this architecture example, but more servers may be added to support the organization's performance and scalability needs. See Chapter 6 for more information regarding Hyper-V scalability and performance.

SERVER B — REMOTE DESKTOP SESSION HOST (REDIRECTOR)

Server B runs the RD Session Host role service and acts as a Redirector, redirecting RDP sessions to the RD Virtualization Host server. A RD Session Host role service can be used either for RemoteApp publishing or as a Redirector for the Microsoft VDI solution but not both. If an organization requires both capabilities, they can install separate instances of RD Session Host role service on different servers or VMs. A single Remote Desktop Session Host can support redirection to pooled virtual machines and personal virtual machines. In addition, multiple RD Session Host (Redirector) servers can be used to provide load balancing.

SERVER C — REMOTE DESKTOP CONNECTION BROKER

Server C runs the RD Connection Broker role service and provides the session management services that connect the user to the correct remote personal or pooled desktop virtual machine. When a user connects to the RemoteApp and Desktop Connection web page, the RD Connection Broker queries Active Directory Domain Services to see if that user has a personal VM and also queries the RD Virtualization Host for VM pools and publishes this information back to the RD Web Access web page. When the user makes a VM selection from the web page, the RD Connection Broker checks to see if the user has an existing session or if a new session needs to be established.

SERVER D — REMOTE DESKTOP WEB ACCESS SERVER

Server D runs the RD Web Access role service and provides a web page called RemoteApp and Desktop Connection. After the user navigates to this web page and logs on, the page displays available VM resources that the user can access. Microsoft RD Web Access also supports the RemoteApp and Desktop Connection web feed that provides seamless access to remote applications and desktops via dynamically updated links in the Windows 7 Start menu.

Client-Side Component Overview

The client-side components needed for the Microsoft VDI solution include the Windows client operating system with appropriate service packs and Remote Desktop Connection (RDC) 6.1 or later. RDC 7.0 has many improvements that enhance the user's remote desktop experience. These include improved support for rich multimedia, bidirectional audio, Aero Glass remoting, multiple monitors, and 2D/3D remoting for DirectX 10.1. RDC 7.0 is included in Windows 7 and is planned to be available for Windows Vista and XP. For more information about RDC 7.0 and its enhancements, see Chapter 10.

Supported operating systems for the Microsoft VDI solution include Windows 7, Windows Vista SP1 or later, and Windows XP SP3. Endpoint devices access the Microsoft VDI environment in two primary ways, depending on the Windows client operating system version used. If the endpoint device is Windows 7, access to remote applications and desktops can be provided by using RemoteApp and Desktop Connection via the Windows 7 Start menu and by using the RemoteApp and Desktop Connection web page. If the endpoint device is Windows Vista or

Windows XP, access to remote applications and desktops is provided via the RemoteApp and Desktop Connection web page.

This architecture example uses three Windows client endpoint devices, with endpoint device 1 running Windows 7, endpoint device 2 running Windows Vista, and endpoint device 3 running Windows XP.

Let's review each of the endpoints in this architecture example and the VDI-related services that are installed.

Endpoint Device 1 — Windows 7   Endpoint device 1 is running Windows 7 and uses the RemoteApp and Desktop Connection feature to gain access to the Microsoft VDI environment via the Windows Start menu.

Endpoint Device 2 — Windows Vista   Endpoint device 2 is running Windows Vista SP2 and uses the Internet Explorer 7 browser to access the Microsoft VDI environment via the RemoteApp and Desktop Connection web page. Figure 15.3 shows a screen shot of options for accessing a remote desktop via the Windows Start menu.

Endpoint Device 3 — Windows XP   Endpoint device 2 is running Windows XP and uses the Internet Explorer 7 browser to access the Microsoft VDI environment via the RemoteApp and Desktop Connection web page.

FIGURE 15.3
Accessing a remote desktop via the RemoteApp and Desktop Connection web page

Installation of the Microsoft VDI Solution Server Components

The server architecture used for this Microsoft VDI solution example includes four servers. Each server requires the installation of Microsoft Windows Server 2008 R2 and specific server roles and role services. The installation process begins with installing the Hyper-V role and Remote Desktop Virtualization role service on Server A, which is the Remote Desktop Virtualization Host server. The next step is to install the Remote Desktop Session Host role service on Server B. We then install the Remote Desktop Connection Broker role service on Server C and Remote Desktop Web Access role service on Server D. Administrator rights are required for all of these operations. As mentioned before, a key assumption made regarding the installation environment is the existence of AD and that it is configured at the Windows 2008 functional level. Another assumption is that DNS and DHCP infrastructure services are available in the environment. A flowchart of the installation process is shown in Figure 15.4.

FIGURE 15.4
Microsoft VDI installation process flowchart

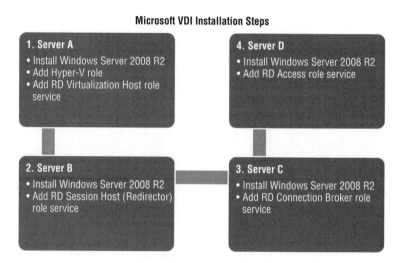

Microsoft VDI Installation Steps

1. Server A
- Install Windows Server 2008 R2
- Add Hyper-V role
- Add RD Virtualization Host role service

4. Server D
- Install Windows Server 2008 R2
- Add RD Access role service

2. Server B
- Install Windows Server 2008 R2
- Add RD Session Host (Redirector) role service

3. Server C
- Install Windows Server 2008 R2
- Add RD Connection Broker role service

Creation of VDI Users and Group in Active Directory

To support the installation and use of the Microsoft VDI test environment, we will create five users and one group in Active Directory Domain Services. The names of the users are rdvuser1, rdvuser2, rdvuser3, rdvuser4, and rdvuser5, and the group is rdvusers. The created users will be added to the rdvusers group. Here are the steps for creating these users and group in AD:

Create VDI users

1. Log on with administrator rights, and open Active Directory Users and Computers from the Start menu ➤ All Programs ➤ Administrator Tools.

2. Select the domain that is supporting your VDI test environment and double-click Users.

3. On the Active Directory Users and Computers Action drop-down menu, select New ➤ User.

4. Under the First Name and User Logon Name fields, enter **rdvuser1** and click Next.

5. Enter a password and select the preferred password options.

6. Review the New Object–User summary screen and click Finish.

7. Repeat these steps for adding rdvuser2 through rdvuser5, substituting rdvuser1 with the appropriate username in the First Name and User Logon Name fields.

Create a VDI group and add VDI users to the group

1. Log on with administrator rights, and open Active Directory Users and Computers from the Start menu ➢ All Programs ➢ Administrator Tools.

2. Select the domain that is supporting your VDI test environment and double-click Users.

3. On the Active Directory Users and Computers Action drop-down menu, select New ➢ Group.

4. Under the Group Name field enter **rdvusers** and click OK.

5. Double-click the group rdvusers.

6. Choose the Members tab in the rdvusers Properties window, and click Add.

7. Under the Enter The Object Names To Select field, enter **rdvuser1**, **rdvuser2**, **rdvuser3**, **rdvuser4**, **rdvuser5** and click Check Names to verify. Click OK, and click OK again to close the rdvuser Properties window.

8. Close the Active Directory Users and Computers tool.

Server A — Remote Desktop Virtualization Host Server

The first installation step is to install Windows Server 2008 R2 with Hyper-V on this server. Please follow the instructions for installing and configuring Windows Server 2008 R2 and Hyper-V that are provided in Chapter 2.

The next installation step is to add the Remote Desktop Services role with only the Remote Desktop Virtualization Host role service selected and installed. Here are the steps for installing the Remote Desktop Virtualization Host:

1. Log on with administrative rights, and open Windows Server 2008 R2 Server Manager on Server A or the server you are adding the Remote Desktop Virtualization Host role service on.

2. Select Roles on the Server Manager hierarchy.

3. On the Roles Summary page, select Add Roles, review the Before You Begin screen, and click Next.

4. On the Select Server Roles page, select the Remote Desktop Services check box and click Next. Note that if you have already installed the Remote Desktop role on this server, you will need to add this role service from the Roles Summary page under the Remote Desktop Services section of Server Manager.

5. On the Introduction To Remote Desktop Services page, click Next.

6. On the Select Role Services page, select the Remote Desktop Virtualization Host role service and click Next.

7. On the Confirm Installation Selections page, review the results and click Install. The installation process will begin.

8. On the Installation Results page, review the results and click Close.

The installation steps for Server A, the Remote Desktop Virtualization Host server, are now complete. The configuration steps for this server are provided in the upcoming section called "Configuration of the Microsoft VDI Solution Server Components."

Server B — Remote Desktop Session Host (Redirector) Server

The first installation step is to install Windows Server 2008 R2 on this server. Please follow the instructions for installing Windows Server 2008 R2 in Chapter 2.

The next installation step is to add the Remote Desktop Services role with only the Remote Desktop Session Host role service selected and installed. As a reminder, this server will be used only as an RD Session Host Redirector and not for RemoteApp purposes. Here are the steps for installing the Remote Desktop Session Host role service:

1. Log on with administrative rights, and open Windows Server 2008 R2 Server Manager on Server B or the server you are adding the Remote Desktop Session Host role service on.

2. Select Roles on the Server Manager hierarchy.

3. On the Roles Summary page, select Add Roles, review the Before You Begin screen, and click Next.

4. On the Select Server Roles page, select the Remote Desktop Services check box and click Next. Note that if you have already installed the Remote Desktop role on this server, you will need to add this role service from the Roles Summary page under the Remote Desktop Services section of Server Manager.

5. On the Introduction To Remote Desktop Service page, click Next. Note that you skip this step if RDS has already been installed.

6. On the Select Role Services page, select the Remote Desktop Session Host role service and click Next.

7. On the Uninstall And Reinstall Applications For Compatibility page, review the text and click Next. Note that the purpose of installing the RD Session Host role service for this solution is for it to act as a Redirector and not for RemoteApp publishing. For more information regarding the installation of RD Session Host role service for RemoteApp publishing, see Chapter 11.

8. On the Specify Authentication Method For Remote Desktop Session Host page, select the type of network-level authentication your organization requires and click Next.

9. On the Specify Licensing Mode page, select the type of licensing mode that is appropriate for your organization and click Next. Note that if you don't know the correct licensing type to select at this time, you can select Configure Later, and you will have 120 days to properly configure it.

10. On the Select User Groups Allowed Access To This RD Session Host Server page, add the rdvusers group and click Next. To accomplish this task, click Add, type **RDV Users**, click Check Names, click OK, and then click Next.

11. On the Configure Client Experience page, select the organization's preferred configuration options and click Next.

12. On the Confirm Installation Selections page, review the results and click Install. The installation process will begin. Click Close on the Installation Results window. In the pop-up Add Roles Wizard dialog box, click Yes if you want to restart the server now.

13. After rebooting the server, log on with the same administrator account, review the Installation Results page, and click Close.

The installation steps for Server B, the Remote Desktop Session Host (Redirector) server, are complete. The configuration steps for this server are provided in the upcoming section called "Configuration of the Microsoft VDI Solution Server Components."

Server C — Remote Desktop Connection Broker

The first installation step is to install the Windows Server 2008 R2 on this server. Please follow the instructions for installing Windows Server 2008 R2 that are provided in Chapter 2.

The next installation step is to add the Remote Desktop Server role with only the Remote Desktop Connection Broker role service selected and installed. Note for future installations that the Remote Desktop Connection Broker role service cannot be installed on the same physical server or virtual machine as the Remote Desktop Virtualization Host role service, but it can coexist with other Remote Desktop role services. Here are the steps for installing the Remote Desktop Connection Broker role service:

1. Log on with administrative rights, and open Windows Server 2008 R2 Server Manager on Server D or the server you are adding the Remote Desktop Connection Role Service on.

2. Select Roles on the Server Manager hierarchy.

3. On the Roles Summary page, select Add Roles, review the Before You Begin screen, and click Next.

4. On the Select Server Roles page, select the Remote Desktop Services check box and click Next. Note that if you have already installed the Remote Desktop role on this server, you will need to add this role service from the Roles Summary page under the Remote Desktop Services section of Server Manager.

5. On the Introduction To Remote Desktop Services page, click Next. Note that you skip this step if RDS has already been installed.

6. On the Select Role Services page, select the Remote Desktop Connection Broker role service and click Next.

7. On the Confirm Installation Selections page, review the results and click Install. The installation process will begin.

8. On the Installation Results page, review the results and click Close.

The installation steps for Server C, the Remote Desktop Connection Broker server, have been completed. The configuration steps for this server are provided in the upcoming section called "Configuration of the Microsoft VDI Solution Server Components."

Server D — Remote Desktop Web Access Server

The first installation step is to install Windows Server 2008 R2 on this server. As before, the instructions for installing Windows Server 2008 R2 are provided in Chapter 2.

The next installation step is to add the Remote Desktop Service role with only the Remote Desktop Web Access role service selected and installed. The Remote Desktop Web Access role service requires the Web Server (IIS) and Remote Server Administration tools to be installed during this process. The steps for installing the Remote Desktop Web Access role service follow:

1. Log on with administrative rights, and open Windows Server 2008 R2 Server Manager on Server D or the server you are adding the Remote Desktop Service role service on.

2. Select Roles on the Server Manager hierarchy.

3. On the Roles Summary page, select Add Roles, review the Before You Begin screen, and click Next.

4. On the Select Server Roles page, select the Remote Desktop Services check box and click Next. Note that if you have already installed the Remote Desktop role on this server, you will need to add this role service from the Roles Summary page under the Remote Desktop Services section of Server Manager.

5. On the Introduction To Remote Desktop Services page, click Next. Note that you skip this step if RDS has already been installed.

6. On the Select Role Services page, select the Remote Desktop Web Access service and click Next. Note that if IIS is not already installed, the Add Role Services window will pop up asking you to install Web Server (IIS) and the Remote Server Administration tools. Click Add Required Role Services. Click Next on the Select Role Services page.

7. On the Web Server (IIS) introduction page, review the information and click Next.

8. On the Select Role Services For Web Server (IIS) page, accept the default settings and click Next.

9. On the Confirm Installation Selections page, review the results and click Install. The installation process will begin.

10. On the Installation Results page, review the results and click Close.

The installation steps for Server D, the Remote Desktop Web Access server, are complete. The configuration steps for this server are provided in the upcoming section called "Configuration of the Microsoft VDI Solution Server Components."

Installation of the Microsoft VDI Solution Client Components

The client architecture used for this Microsoft VDI solution example includes three endpoint devices. Each endpoint device requires the installation of a supported Microsoft Windows client operating system. The installation process begins with installing Windows 7 on endpoint device 1, followed by installing Windows Vista SP1 on endpoint device 2 and Windows XP SP3 on endpoint device 3. If you already have Microsoft VDI–supported Windows client operating systems installed on your endpoint devices, you can move to the configuration section of this chapter. The following installation steps are basic and presented at a high level. For more detailed instructions on the installation of a Windows client operating system, please refer to the Microsoft TechNet website at `http://technet.microsoft.com`.

Endpoint 1 — Windows 7

The steps for preparing Endpoint 1 are listed below.

1. Install Windows 7 Business, Enterprise, or Ultimate Edition.

2. Create the computer name.

3. Secure the Windows 7 client.

4. Configure the network.

5. Join the AD domain.

6. Activate the Windows 7 client.

Endpoint 2 — Windows Vista

The steps for preparing Endpoint 2 are listed below.

1. Install Windows Vista Business, Enterprise, or Ultimate Edition with SP1 or later.

2. Create the computer name.

3. Secure this Windows Vista client.

4. Configure the network.

5. Join the AD domain.

6. Activate the Windows Vista client.

Endpoint 3 — Windows XP

The steps for preparing Endpoint 3 are listed below.

1. Install Windows XP Professional with SP3.

2. Create the computer name.

3. Secure this Windows XP client.

4. Configure the network.

5. Join the AD domain.

6. Activate the Windows XP client.

The installation steps for the Windows endpoint devices are complete. The configuration steps for the endpoint devices are provided in the upcoming configuration section of this chapter.

Configuration of the Microsoft VDI Solution Server Components

Once the Microsoft VDI solution server and client components have been installed, they need to be configured to work properly with each other. The order in which the components are configured is important, so follow these instructions carefully. A flowchart of the configuration process is shown in Figure 15.5.

FIGURE 15.5
Microsoft VDI
Configuration Process
Flowchart

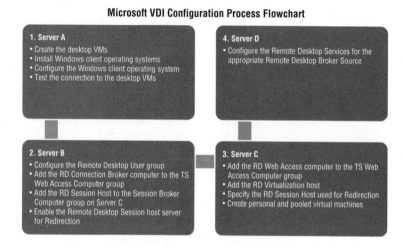

Microsoft VDI Configuration Process Flowchart

1. Server A
- Create the desktop VMs
- Install Windows client operating systems
- Configure the Windows client operating system
- Test the connection to the desktop VMs

4. Server D
- Configure the Remote Desktop Services for the appropriate Remote Desktop Broker Source

2. Server B
- Configure the Remote Desktop User group
- Add the RD Connection Broker computer to the TS Web Access Computer group
- Add the RD Session Host to the Session Broker Computer group on Server C
- Enable the Remote Desktop Session host server for Redirection

3. Server C
- Add the RD Web Access computer to the TS Web Access Computer group
- Add the RD Virtualization host
- Specify the RD Session Host used for Redirection
- Create personal and pooled virtual machines

Server A — Remote Desktop Virtualization Host Server

The process for configuring Server A, the Remote Desktop Virtualization Host server, is executed in four procedures: creating the desktop VMs, installing the Windows client operating system in the desktop VMs, configuring the Windows client operating system in the desktop VMs, and testing the connection to the desktop VMs. Each procedure and its configuration steps are provided below.

The steps for creating desktop VMs are as follows:

1. Log on with administrator rights, and open the Windows Server 2008 R2 Server Manager on Server A or the server you are configuring Hyper-V and the Remote Desktop Virtualization Host role service on.

2. Select the Hyper-V role ➤ Hyper-V Manager ➤ Server A (or your server name) on the Server Manager hierarchy.

3. In this step we will create five VMs. Three VMs will be running Windows 7, one VM will be running Windows Vista SP2, and one VM will be running Windows XP. The VMs will be configured with the following settings:

   Windows 7

   Names: client1.*domainname*.com, client2.*domainname*.com, client3.*domainname*.com

   Number Of Processors: 1

   Memory: 1024 MB

Network Connection: Local Area Connection - Virtual Network

Hard Disk Size: Accept default for creating a virtual hard disk, 127 GB

Windows Vista

Names: client4.*domainname*.com

Number Of Processors: 1

Memory: 1024 MB

Network Connection: Local Area Connection - Virtual Network

Hard Disk Size: Accept default for creating a virtual hard disk, 127 GB

Windows XP

Names: client5.*domainname*.com

Number Of Processors: 1

Memory: 512 MB

Network Connection: Local Area Connection - Virtual Network

Hard Disk Size: Accept default for creating a virtual hard disk, 127 GB

4. Under the Actions pane, select New Virtual Machine. Follow the New Virtualization Wizard to create and configure the desktop virtual machines that will be used to host the Windows client operating system using the configuration settings listed above. Repeat these steps for each new desktop virtual machine.

   Note that if a virtual machine will be used in a virtual machine pool, each virtual machine in the pool should be identical in terms of the operating system, configuration, and applications to provide a consistent experience for users who are using remote desktop VMs in the pool.

   The name of the virtual machine for a personal VM or VM pool needs to match the fully qualified name of the computer name running inside it, for example, client1.*domainname*.com.

The steps for installing the Windows client operating systems in VMs are as follows:

1. Install Windows 7 on VMs client1–client3, Windows Vista SP1 or SP2 on VM client4, and Windows XP SP3 on VM client5.

2. Install Hyper-V Integration Services on each Windows client operating system running in the desktop virtual machines. For more information regarding installing Hyper-V Integration Services see Chapter 3.

The steps for configuring the Windows client operating systems are listed below. Repeat these steps for each desktop virtual machine.

1. Log on with administrator rights, and open the Windows Server 2008 R2 Server Manager on Server A or the server you are configuring Hyper-V and the Remote Desktop Virtualization Host role service on.

2. Select the Hyper-V role ➤ Hyper-V Manager ➤ Server A (or your server name) on the Server Manager hierarchy.

3. Connect to the desktop VM by selecting the VM and clicking Connect on the Actions pane.

4. Start the VM if needed by clicking the green start button.

5. Log on to the desktop operating system with administrative rights.

6. The following steps configure the Windows client operating system to allow remote access and assign the appropriate users and groups to the Remote Desktop User group.

   a. Open Control Panel, choose the system applet, and select Remote Settings. Note that Remote Settings is located under the Task menu in Windows 7 and Vista and on the Remote tab in Windows XP.

   b. Under the Remote Desktop settings, select the Allow Connections Only From Computers Running Remote Desktop With Network Level Authentication (More Secure) option.

   c. Click Select Users and add the rdvusers group. Click OK, and click OK on the System Properties window.

7. The following steps configure the Windows client operating system firewall to allow Remote Service Management.

   a. Open Control Panel and the Windows Firewall applet. For Windows 7, the applet is located in Control Panel ➤ System And Security. For Windows Vista, the applet is located in Control Panel ➤ Security. And for Windows XP, the applet is located in Control Panel ➤ Firewall.

   b. Add an exception to allow Remote Service Management.

   c. Close Control Panel.

8. The following steps configure the Windows client operating system to allow remote procedure calls (RPC).

   a. Open a command prompt and run `regedit.exe`. Use caution when using the regedit application and making changes to the Registry. Making unwanted changes could adversely affect the normal operation of the Windows operating system.

   b. Navigate to `Computer\HKEY_LOCAL_MACHINE\SYSTEM\CurrentControlSet\Control\Terminal Server`.

   c. Set the Allow Remote RPC Registry setting to a value of **1**.

   d. Close regedit.

9. The following steps configure the Windows client operating system for each virtual machine to grant RDP security privileges for the Remote Desktop Virtualization Host server (Hyper-V and Remote Desktop Virtualization Host role service) to access the Remote Desktop virtual machine. Run the following commands, replacing ***domainname*** with your domain name and the ***servername*** with the name of the Remote Desktop Virtualization Hosting server.

   a. Open a command prompt window.

   b. On the command prompt enter the following commands.

```
wmic /node:localhost RDPERMISSIONS where ↵
TerminalName="RDP-Tcp" CALL AddAccount  "domainname\servername$",1

wmic /node:localhost RDACCOUNT where
"(TerminalName='RDP-Tcp' or TerminalName='Console') ↵
andAccountName='domainname\\servername$'" CALLModifyPermissions 0,1

wmic /node:localhost RDACCOUNT where
"(TerminalName='RDP-Tcp' or TerminalName='Console') ↵
andAccountName='domainname\\servername$'" CALLModifyPermissions 2,1

wmic /node:localhost RDACCOUNT where
"(TerminalName='RDP-Tcp' or TerminalName='Console') ↵
andAccountName='domainname\\servername$'" CALLModifyPermissions 9,1

Net stop termservice

Net start termservice
```

  c. Exit the command prompt, and log off the Windows client operating system running in the remote desktop VM.

Test access to the remote desktop VM from a Windows client endpoint device via the Remote Desktop Connection application. Repeat this process for each remote desktop VM.

  1. Log on to one of the endpoint devices.

  2. Open the Remote Desktop Connection application from the Windows Start menu.

  3. In the Computer field, input the computer name or the IP address of the remote desktop VM, and click Connect.

  4. Provide your security credentials and click OK

  5. The desktop session will display. Log in to the Windows operating system running on the remote desktop session.

  6. Log off the remote Windows desktop operating system.

Server B — Remote Desktop Session Host (Redirector) Server

The process for configuring Server B, the Remote Desktop Session Host (Redirector) server, is executed in four procedures: configuring the Remote Desktop User group, adding the RD Connection Broker computer to the TS Web Access Computer group, adding the RD Session Host to the Session Broker Computers group on Server C, and enabling the Remote Desktop Session Host server for Redirection. Each procedure and its configuration steps are provided below.

The steps for configuring the Remote Desktop Users group are as follows:

  1. Log in with administrator rights, and open Windows Server 2008 R2 Server Manager on Server B or the server you are configuring the Remote Desktop Session Host role service on.

2. Select Server Manager on the Server Manager hierarchy, and click Change System Properties on the right pane.

3. On the System Properties window, select the Remote tab.

4. Under Remote Desktop, select the Allow Connections Only From Computers Running Remote Desktop With Network Level Authentication (More Secure) option to allow connections, and click Select Users.

5. Click Add, enter **rdvusers**, and click OK. Click OK on the System Properties window.

The steps for adding Server C, the RD Connection Broker computer, to the TS Web Access Computer group on the Remote Desktop Session Host server are listed below:

1. Log on with administrator rights, and open Windows Server 2008 R2 Server Manager on Server B or the server you are configuring the Remote Desktop Session Host role service on.

2. Under Configuration, select Local Users And Groups ➢ Groups.

3. Double-click the TS Web Access Computer group and click Add.

4. Click the Object Types button, select the check box next to the Computers object, and click OK.

5. Enter the RD Connection Broker computer name in the Enter The Object Names To Select field, and click OK. Click OK again in the Computer Properties window.

The steps for adding Server B, the RD Session Host, to the Session Broker Computers group on Server C are listed below. This procedure is required to provide proper rights for the RD Session Host server.

1. Log on with administrator rights, and open Windows Server 2008 R2 Server Manager on Server C or the server you are configuring the Remote Desktop Connection Broker role service on.

2. Under Configuration, select Local Users And Groups ➢ Groups.

3. Double-click the Session Broker Computers group and click Add.

4. Click the Object Types button, select the check box next to the Computers object, and click OK.

5. Enter the RD Session Host (Redirector) computer name (Server B) in the Enter The Object Names To Select field, and click OK. Click OK again in the Computer Properties window.

The steps for configuring the Remote Desktop Session Host server for virtual machine redirection are listed below:

1. Log on with administrator rights, and open Windows Server 2008 R2 Server Manager on Server B or the server you are configuring the Remote Desktop Session Host role service on.

2. Under Roles, select Remote Desktop Services ➢ RD Session Host Configuration, as shown in Figure 15.6.

FIGURE 15.6
RD Session Host
Configuration

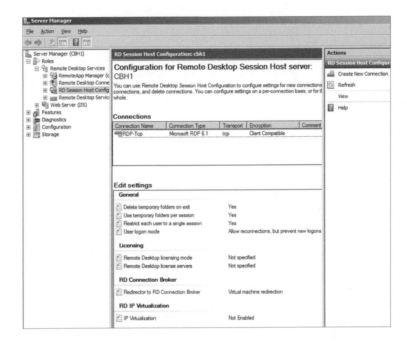

3. On the Configuration For Remote Desktop Session Host Server pane, scroll down to Edit Settings, select RD Connection Broker, and right-click Properties.

4. On the Properties window, click Change Settings. Under Remote Desktop Virtualization, select Virtual Machine Redirection and enter the name of the RD Connection Broker server (Server B). Click OK.

5. Click OK in the Properties window and close Server Manager.

Server C — Remote Desktop Connection Broker

The process for configuring Server C, the Remote Desktop Connection Broker server, is executed in four procedures: adding the RD Web Access server to the TS Web Access Computer group, adding the RD Virtualization host, specifying the RD Session Host used for Redirection, and creating personal and pooled virtual machines. Each procedure and its specific configuration steps are provided below.

The steps for adding Server D, the RD Web Access server, to the TS Web Access Computers group follow. This procedure is required to provide the proper rights for the RD Web Access server.

1. Log on with administrator rights, and open Windows Server 2008 R2 Server Manager on Server C or the server you are configuring the Remote Desktop Connection Broker role service on.

2. Under Configuration, select Local Users And Groups ➤ Groups.

3. Double-click the TS Web Access Computers group, and click Add.

4. Click the Object Types button, select the check box next to the Computers object, and click OK.

5. Enter the RD Web Access computer name (Server D) in the Enter The Object Names To Select field, and click OK. Click OK again in the Computer Properties window.

The steps for adding the RD Virtualization Hosts and RD Session Host for Redirection are listed below:

1. Log in with administrator rights, and open Windows Server 2008 R2 Server Manager on Server C or the server you are configuring the Remote Desktop Connection Broker role service on.

2. On the Server Manager hierarchy pane, navigate to Remote Desktop Services ≻ Remote Desktop Connection Manager, as shown in Figure 15.7.

FIGURE 15.7
Remote Desktop
Connection Manager

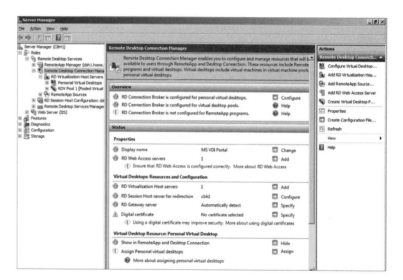

3. In the middle pane under the Virtual Desktops: Resources And Configuration, locate RD Virtualization Host Servers and click Add.

4. Enter the RD Virtualization Host server (Server A) name in the RD Virtualization Host Server Name field, and click Add.

5. Continue to use Remote Desktop Connections Manager, locate RD Session Host Server For Redirection in the Virtual Desktops: Resources And Configuration section, and click Configure.

6. Enter the name of the RD Session Host (Redirector) server (Server B). If you will be supporting endpoint devices with Remote Desktop Connection (RDC) version 6.1 or earlier,

select the check box for enabling Redirector for earlier RDC versions and provide an alternative server name. The name is arbitrary, but it needs to be unique in your environment. In addition, you will need to enter this name in DNS as a DNS host resource record. Please refer to the DNS section on techNet.microsoft.com for instructions for adding a DNS host resource record. Click OK.

The steps for creating personal virtual machines are shown here:

1. Open the Remote Desktop Connections Manager tool on Server D, the Remote Desktop Connection Broker server.

2. Select Configure Virtual Desktops from the Actions pane located on the right side of the window.

3. In the Configure Virtual Desktops Wizard, review the Before You Begin screen and click Next.

4. Verify that Server A, the Remote Desktop Virtualization Host server running Hyper-V, is listed in under RD Virtualization Host Servers. If it is not, enter this server in the Server Name field and click Add.

5. Verify that Server B, the Remote Desktop Session Host that will be the Redirector, has already been specified. If it has not, enter this server in the Server Name field and click Next.

6. Verify that Server D, the Remote Desktop Web Access server, has already been specified. If it has not, enter this server in the Server Name field and click Next.

7. Confirm these changes and click Apply.

8. Review the summary page, select the check box for Assign Personal Virtual Desktop, and click Finish.

9. On the Assign Personal Desktop page, click the Select User button, enter the rdvuser1 user account name, and click OK.

10. Select the virtual machine called client1.*domainname*.com.

11. On the Confirm Assignment page, review the information and click Assign.

12. Repeat this process for the username rdvuser2 and VM client4.*domainname*.com and for the username rdvuser3 and VM client5.*domainname*.com.

13. On the Assignment Summary page click Finish.

The steps to create a virtual machine pool are listed below:

1. Open the Remote Desktop Connections Manager tool on Server C, the Remote Desktop Connection Broker server.

2. Select Create Virtual Desktop Pool from the Actions pane located on the right side of the window.

3. On the Create Virtual Desktop Pool Wizard page, review the welcome information and click Next.

4. On the Select Virtual Machines page, select the client2.*domainname*.com and client3.*domainname*.com virtual machines. Note that the virtual machines used in the same pool should be identical in terms of Windows operating system, configuration, and applications. Click Next.

5. On the Set Pool Properties page, enter a display name for the pool called **RDV Pool 1** and a Pool ID of **RDVP1**, and click Next.

6. Review and verify the information on the Results page, and click Finish.

Server D — Remote Desktop Web Access Server

The process for configuring Server D, the Remote Desktop Web Access server, is executed in one procedure: configuring Remote Desktop Services for the appropriate Remote Desktop Connection Broker source. This procedure and its configuration steps are provided below:

1. Log on with administrative rights, and open the Remote Desktop Web Access Configuration tool from the Windows Server 2008 R2 Start menu ➤ Administrator Tools ➤ Remote Desktop Services. This task can also be accomplished by opening your browser and entering **https://serverd/rdweb**.

2. Log in to the Remote Desktop Connection web page.

3. On the Remote Desktop Connection web page, select the Configuration menu, as shown in Figure 15.8.

FIGURE 15.8
RD Connection configuration

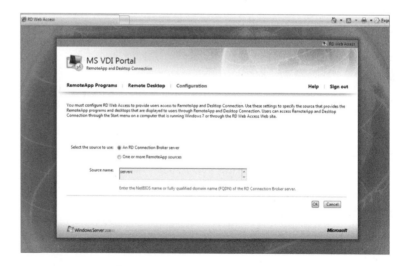

4. Select an RD Connection Broker server as the source to use, and enter the name of the RD Connection Broker server (Server C) in the Source Name field. Click OK and sign out.

Configuration of the Microsoft VDI Solution Client Components

Once the Microsoft VDI client components have been installed on endpoint devices 1, 2, and 3, they will need to be configured to work properly with the Microsoft VDI solution. This procedure and its specific configuration steps follow.

Endpoint Device 1 — Windows 7

The process of configuring the Windows 7 endpoint includes configuring the operating system to support the RemoteApp and Desktop Web Feed connections in Control Panel.

1. Log on to the Windows 7 endpoint device with administrative rights.

2. Select the Start menu and enter **RemoteApp and Desktop Connection** in the Search Programs And Files field. Under the Control Panel search results, select RemoteApp And Desktop Connection. This will open the RemoteApp And Desktop Connection Control Panel applet.

3. On the RemoteApp And Desktop Connection applet window, select Set Up A New Connection With RemoteApp And Desktop Connection.

4. In the Connection URL field enter `\\serverd\rdweb\feed\webfeed.aspx` in the Data field.

5. Select the Start menu, select RemoteApp And Desktop Connection, and select an available remote desktop to confirm the RemoteApp and Desktop Connection web feed is working correctly.

Endpoint Device 2 — Windows Vista SP1 or 2

The process of configuring the Windows Vista endpoint includes opening Internet Explorer, entering the URL for the RemoteApp and Desktop Connection web page, and downloading and installing a Microsoft ActiveX control.

1. Open Internet Explorer and connect to the RD Web Access website, `\\serverd\rdweb`.

2. When prompted, download and install the Microsoft ActiveX control.

3. Access the RD Connection web page.

Endpoint Device 3 — Windows XP SP3

The process of configuring the Windows XP endpoint device 3 is the same as for the Windows Vista endpoint, device 2, described above.

Managing the Microsoft VDI Solution

The Microsoft VDI solution can be managed using Microsoft management tools included in Windows Server 2008 R2 and System Center. The Windows Server 2008 R2 Remote Desktop Services tools are described in the following sections.

Server Management

The Microsoft VDI solution can be managed by using Server Manager or by launching the Remote Desktop Server applications from the Windows Server Start menu.

You can use Server Manager to manage the RDS roles and role services that support the Microsoft VDI solution from a management user interface. An example of the RDS management tools available through Server Manager is shown in Figure 15.9. Let's review the management tools included in Remote Desktop Services.

FIGURE 15.9

Managing RDS through Server Manager

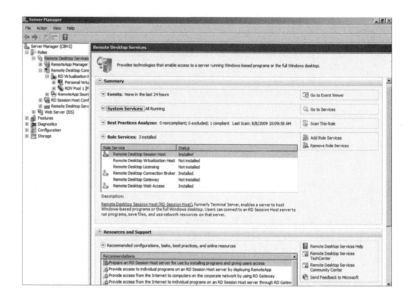

REMOTE DESKTOP SERVICES MAIN SUMMARY PAGE

The Remote Desktop Services Main Summary page offers a number of useful tools and information for managing your Microsoft VDI environment. The main page includes Events, System Services, Best Practice Analyzer, Role Services, and Resources And Support. This tool can be accessed through Server Manager, by selecting the Remote Desktop Services role. A brief description of each tool is given below.

Events   The Events section displays events related to the RDS implementation including the event level, ID, date, time, and source.

System Services   The System Services section displays RDS-related services and their status. Examples include IIS Admin Service (iisadmin), Remote Desktop Virtualization Host Agent (VMHostAgent), Remote Desktop Connection Broker (tssdis), Remote Desktop Services (TermService), RemoteApp and Desktop Connection Management (tscpubrpc), and World Wide Web Publishing Service (w3svc).

Best Practice Analyzer   The Best Practice Analyzer scans a server, reviews the configuration of an RDS implementation, and makes recommendations based on best practice information that was collected from Microsoft Support and Consulting Services.

Role Services   The Role Services section displays the six role services and indicates which ones have been installed on that server. When you select a role service in this list, it will display a short description of the service and a link you can click for more information. It is also the place where you would add or remove an RDS role service.

Resources And Support   The Resources And Support section displays a list of recommended configurations, tasks, best practices, help, and online resources like RDS TechCenter and Community Center, and it includes a link for you to provide feedback to Microsoft.

REMOTE DESKTOP CONNECTION MANAGER

The Remote Desktop Connection Manager is an important tool for creating and configuring the Microsoft VDI environment. This tool is used to create personal virtual desktops and virtual desktop pools. It is also used to add the RemoteApp source and the RD Web Access server. This tool can be accessed through the Windows Server Start menu ➤ Administrative Tools ➤ Remote Desktop Services and through Server Manager under the Remote Desktop Services role.

RD SESSION HOST CONFIGURATION

RD Session Host Configuration is used for configuring RDP connections and settings for sessions, licensing, RD Connection Broker, and RD IP virtualization. This tool can be accessed through the Windows Server Start menu ➤ Administrative Tools ➤ Remote Desktop Services and through Server Manager under the Remote Desktop Services role.

RD WEB ACCESS CONFIGURATION

RD Web Access Configuration is used for selecting the RD Connection Broker and RemoteApp source(s) that will be made available by RD Web Access. This tool can be accessed through the Windows Server Start menu under Administrative Tools ➤ Remote Desktop Services or on the RD Web Access web page.

CONTROL PANEL, REMOTEAPP, AND DESKTOP CONNECTIONS

Windows 7 clients can use the RemoteApp and Desktop Connection applet in Control Panel to set up connections to the Microsoft VDI environment and access these resources through the Windows Start menu.

Each server in this VDI solution can leverage the management tools mentioned above. Let's review some examples of this for each server.

SERVER A: REMOTE DESKTOP VIRTUALIZATION HOST SERVER

The Microsoft management tool used to manage the Remote Desktop Virtualization Host server running Microsoft Hyper-V is Hyper-V Manager or System Center Virtual Machine Manager to manage the server-hosted desktop virtual machines.

SERVER B: REMOTE DESKTOP SESSION HOST SERVER (REDIRECTOR)

The Microsoft management tools used to manage the Remote Desktop Session Host server (Redirector) are Server Manager and RDS Main, RD Session Host Configuration, and RemoteApp Manager. Note that these tools can be accessed via Server Manager and also through the Start menu ➤ All Programs ➤ Administrator Tools.

SERVER C: REMOTE DESKTOP CONNECTION BROKER SERVER

The Microsoft management tools used to manage the Remote Desktop Connection Broker server are Server Manager, RDS Main, and RDS Remote Desktop Connection Manager. Note that these tools can be accessed via Server Manager and also through the Start menu ➢ All Programs ➢ Administrator Tools.

SERVER D: REMOTE DESKTOP WEB ACCESS SERVER

The Microsoft management tools used to manage the Remote Desktop Web Access server are Server Manager, RDS Main, RD Session Host Configuration, RemoteApp Manager, and RD Web Access Configuration. Note that these tools can be accessed via Server Manager and also through the Start menu ➢ All Programs ➢ Administrator Tools.

ENDPOINT DEVICE 1 — WINDOWS 7

The Microsoft tools used to manage the Windows 7 endpoint device include Microsoft System Center Configuration Manager, System Center Operations Manager, and the RemoteApp and Desktop Connection applet in Control Panel. This last tool is used to set up a new connection to the Microsoft VDI solution so that it will appear in the Windows Start menu under Programs ➢ RemoteApp And Desktop Connection.

ENDPOINT DEVICE 2 — WINDOWS VISTA SP1 OR SP2

The Microsoft tools used to manage the Windows Vista SP1 or SP2 endpoint device include System Center Configuration Manager and System Center Operations Manager.

ENDPOINT DEVICE 3 — WINDOWS XP SP3

The Microsoft tools used to manage the Windows XP SP3 endpoint device include System Center Configuration Manager and System Center Operations Manager.

Testing the Microsoft VDI Solution

After you have installed and configured the required Microsoft VDI solution server and client components, it is time to test the end-to-end solution to make sure it is working properly. The initial testing process of the VDI solution focuses on successful user access to the server-hosted VMs via the RemoteApp and Desktop Connection web page and web feeds. The testing process is shown below. If you run into errors during testing, please review the Microsoft Windows Server 2008 R2 event logs, carefully review the installation instructions to verify that all necessary steps were completed, and refer to the TechNet website to research these issues at http://technet.microsoft.com.

VDI SOLUTION USER ACCESS TESTING PROCESS

Repeat this testing process for each Windows client endpoint device.

RemoteApp and Desktop Connection website

1. From a supported Windows client endpoint device, navigate to the RemoteApp and Desktop Connection web page, for example, //server d/rdweb.

2. At the login page, provide the appropriate user credentials.

3. On the RemoteApp and Desktop Connection web page, select a VM pool and provide the appropriate user credentials.

4. When the remote desktop session is displayed on the Windows endpoint device, log in to the Windows client operating system running on the remote desktop VM, and interact with the session to make sure the Windows client OS is working properly.

5. Log off the Windows client operating system.

6. On the RemoteApp and Desktop Connection web page, select your personal VM and provide the appropriate user credentials.

7. When the remote desktop session is displayed on the Windows endpoint device, log in to the Windows client operating system running on the remote desktop VM, and interact with the session to make sure the Windows client OS is working properly.

8. Log off the Windows client operating system.

Repeat this testing process for each Windows 7 client endpoint device.

RemoteApp and Desktop Connection web feed

1. From a Windows client 7 endpoint device, select the Start menu ➤ All Programs ➤ RemoteApp And Desktop Connection.

2. Under the RemoteApp And Desktop Connection menu, select a VM pool, and provide the appropriate user credentials.

3. When the remote desktop session is displayed on the Windows 7 endpoint device, log in to the Windows client operating system running on the remote desktop VM, and interact with the session to make sure the Windows client OS is working properly.

4. Log off the Windows client operating system.

5. Under the RemoteApp And Desktop Connection menu, select a personal VM and provide the appropriate user credentials.

6. When the remote desktop session is displayed on the Windows 7 endpoint device, log in to the Windows client operating system running on the remote desktop VM, and interact with the session to make sure the Windows client OS is working properly.

7. Log off the Windows client operating system.

COMMON INSTALLATION ISSUES AND RESOLUTION

I have been with the Remote Desktop Virtualization team at Microsoft for four years. Many of the software components that I develop are part of our VDI solution that allows users to connect to pooled or personal VMs. Several common installation mistakes or issues became clear to our team while debugging issues. Here is a list of top issues and debugging techniques:

◆ Unable to connect to a Personal or Pooled desktop. The user sees a message about waking up the VM and this hangs for 20 minutes or more.

This almost always is an issue with the VM Guest OS not being configured properly, which is generally the trickiest part of configuring an end-to-end system. We support XP SP3, Vista, and Windows 7 as the guest OS and then verify the following:

- Remote Desktop Connections are enabled and the firewall rules are enabled for RDP.

- The Registry key is configured properly: HKEY_LOCAL_MACHINE\SYSTEM\Current-ControlSet\Control\Terminal Server\AllowRemoteRPC is 1.

- Remote Service Management firewall rule is enabled.

- The VM Host machine account is added to the RDP Listener permissions:

  http://technet.microsoft.com/en-us/library/dd883257(WS.10).aspx

- If you are not seeing a Personal VM desktop Icon in RD Web Access, then you check for the following issues:

  - The RD Web Access machine is part of the "TS Web Access Computers" security group on the Connection broker server.

  - On the connection broker server, the "TS Web Access Computers" group is allowed remote DCOM permissions and has permission for Remote on the "TerminalServer" WMI namespace. These can be checked using mmc snapins. This tends to get broken when syspreping an installed machine to be pushed out to several machines.

  - That the Server can connect to the Domain Controller. This can be checked by looking at the Eventlog and looking for access denied or other errors. Without this connection the service can't query for what desktop is assigned to a user.

  - That TCP port 5504 and the WMI ports are open in the firewall.

- Additional information that helps in debugging issues:

  - All Pool and Personal VM RDP files are stored at: %WINDIR%\RemotePackages|RemoteDesktops. The Personal desktop RDP file is PersonalDomain Desktops.rdp. All VM pool RDP files use their Pool ID as their name: poolid.rdp. These are the same files that are passed back to RD Web Access, and you can use these to determine if a setting is not configured properly.

Kevin London, Software Design Engineer, Microsoft Corporation

Summary

In this chapter we covered a lot of material related to deployment of a Microsoft VDI solution. We discussed the planning steps and considerations in preparing for a deployment, how to plan and conduct an effective POC and pilot, and the steps for installing and configuring a Microsoft VDI solution server and client components. I hope this information gave you a greater understanding of the Microsoft VDI solution and laid the groundwork to implement a POC and pilot in your environment.

In the next chapter we will explore the deployment of Microsoft Enterprise Desktop Virtualization (MED-V) version 1.0, which is a client-hosted desktop virtualization solution that utilizes Microsoft Virtual PC VMs. We will review the main architectural server and client components, look at an example POC architecture and itinerary, and walk through the steps for installing the MED-V solution in a test environment.

The Bottom Line

Install and configure the Microsoft Remote Desktop Connection Broker. The Microsoft Remote Desktop connection Broker provides session management services for the Microsoft VDI solution.

Master It Can the RD Connection Broker be installed on the same physical or virtual server as the RD Virtualization Host?

Create and assign a personal virtual machine. The Microsoft VDI solution can support personal and pooled virtual machines.

Master It Can the same VM be used as a personal VM and a pooled VM at the same time?

Create and assign virtual machines to a pool The Remote Desktop Connection Manager tool is used to create a virtual machine pool.

Master It What are the four main configuration steps for preparing a Windows operating system for running in a VM that will be used in a Microsoft VDI solution?

Install and configure the Microsoft Remote Desktop Web Access server. The Remote Desktop Web Access web page provides access to RemoteApp and Desktop resources.

Master It How do you configure RD Web Access to use a RD Connection Broker server?

Configure Windows 7 for RemoteApp and Desktop Connection Windows 7 supports accessing the RemoteApp and Desktop Connection from the desktop start menu.

Master It How do you set up a new connection for RemoteApp and Desktop Connection on Windows 7?

Chapter 16

Deploying Microsoft Enterprise Desktop Virtualization

In the previous chapter we reviewed deploying Microsoft VDI, a server-hosted desktop virtualization solution. In this chapter we will review deploying Microsoft Enterprise Desktop Virtualization (MED-V), a managed client-hosted desktop virtualization solution. The chapter includes a review of considerations for planning a deployment, guidance for conducting a Proof of Concept (POC), an overview of required server and client solution components, and step-by-step instructions for installing and configuring MED-V in a test environment.

In this chapter, you will learn to:

- ◆ Install and configure the MED-V Management Server

- ◆ Create and prepare a MED-V test image

- ◆ Create and configure a MED-V Workspace image

- ◆ Deploy a MED-V Workspace image

- ◆ Generate MED-V reports

Planning Considerations for a MED-V Deployment

At a high level, the process and steps of planning for a MED-V deployment are similar to the approach we took in our last chapter, but the specific details for each step are different. As a review, the planning steps included assessing the current environment, determining needs and requirements, defining the project scope, creating an architectural design, conducting a POC, and continuing on with a pilot and later a full deployment. Let's review these planning steps and their specific MED-V considerations.

Assessing Your Environment

Before an organization deploys a MED-V solution, it's important that they conduct an assessment of their current desktop environment. The assessment would include reviewing desktop hardware, operating systems, applications, user data and settings, network infrastructure, and management tools.

A review of the desktop hardware environment, the processor family and type, memory configuration, and hard disk storage of each desktop should be made and recorded. In addition, the Windows client operating system and versions running on each desktop, either physically or as virtual machines, needs to be identified and recorded. All of this information is required in determining whether the current desktops meet the MED-V client system requirements and if a hardware or software upgrade may be needed.

Another necessary step is to review which corporate applications are running on each desktop, along with their specific hardware and software dependencies. Each application will need to be evaluated to determine if it can run in a virtual machine and the application vendor supports it.

An assessment of the desktop network environment is also important. Understanding where the desktops are located (main, distributed, or home office) and their associated network bandwidth and latency will help in determining the location of MED-V server infrastructure and how images will be initially deployed and updated.

Understanding what processes and tools are used to manage the desktop environment along with identifying current management challenges are essential. An organization will need to determine if their existing management process and tools can be used to manage the MED-V client environment or if new processes or tools will need to be evaluated and implemented. In addition, current desktop management challenges should be addressed prior to introducing a new desktop solution into the environment.

As mentioned before, Microsoft has assessment tools that can be used to assist an organization in this effort. The Microsoft Assessment and Planning Toolkit can be found at `http://technet.microsoft.com/en-us/solutionaccelerators`.

Determining Needs and Requirements

The next step for the organization is to determine their requirements for a MED-V implementation. The data collected during the assessment step can help with this process. An organization will need to ask what problem or problems they are trying to solve. For example, is the organization planning to migrate from the Windows XP to Windows 7 operating system and does it need a solution to remediate potential application-to-OS compatibility problems? Are they considering deploying corporate-managed VMs to nonmanaged or employee-owned PCs? Maybe they would like to improve their desktop business-continuity and disaster-recovery capabilities by having the ability to rapidly and easily move a desktop PC image from one PC device to another in the event of a hardware failure, stolen PC, or disaster. This analysis will help an organization determine whether MED-V is the most appropriate solution to meet their requirements and help guide the architecture design and implementation of the solution.

Defining Project Scope

After the organization has conducted an assessment of their environment and identified the problem(s) they are trying to solve and their specific needs, the next step is to define the scope of the MED-V deployment project. Some of the areas to consider when defining the project scope include which scenario(s) to implement first, the type and number of users and groups to target, which locations to include, and whether this effort should be part of a larger project. All of these questions should be answered to help develop the initial, mid-, and long-term scopes of the MED-V deployment project.

An organization may choose to implement the MED-V deployment project in phases, with each phase targeting a specific solution scenario and expanding the scope of users and groups over time. They may decide to initially implement a MED-V solution as a way to improve the disaster-recovery capabilities of the organization. They may also choose to use MED-V to remediate application-to-operating system compatibility issues to support a Windows Vista or Windows 7 deployment project. In this case, the MED-V project would be part of the larger

Windows migration project and closely aligned with that project scope. A future plan could also include implementing a MED-V solution as a more agile way to deploy corporate desktop images to employee-owned or unmanaged desktops. Whatever the reason(s) for deploying a MED-V solution, the organization will need to define and closely align the scope of the project with its goals and needs.

Microsoft Consulting Services and Microsoft Partners can assist organizations with defining the MED-V project scope and overall planning efforts. More information regarding Microsoft Consulting Services and Partner offerings can be found at http://www.microsoft.com/services/microsoftservices and http://www.microsoft.com/virtualization/partners.

Creating a Solution Design and Architecture

Once an organization has completed the above steps, from conducting the assessment to defining the project scope, they are ready to design the MED-V solution architecture. A MED-V architecture consists of multiple server components that make up the overall solution. The number of servers needed to support a MED-V solution will depend on the organization's current IT environment and requirements. The architectural design factors include the number of users, location of users, Active Directory domain design, number of Workspace images, existing management infrastructure, security and regulatory requirements, and High Availability needs. Let's explore some of these factors and their effect on designing a MED-V solution architecture.

Today, Microsoft MED-V v1 is positioned and supported only for desktops that are part of an Active Directory Domain Services environment. Microsoft is planning to support nondomain, unmanaged desktops with the next version of MED-V planned for release in 2010. A MED-V solution is called an *instance* and consists of a Management Server, Image Repository Server, and Reporting Server. A MED-V Management Server can belong to only one MED-V instance at a time, but the MED-V Repository Server and Database Server can be shared across multiple MED-V Management Servers. Microsoft recommends no more than 5,000 concurrent users be supported per MED-V instance. If an organization is planning to support more than 5,000 concurrent users, another MED-V instance will need to be added for each additional 5,000 users. In addition, if the organization has security or regulatory requirements that mandate the separation of specific MED-V Workspace images, they can implement additional MED-V instances to support those requirements.

The MED-V Management Server should be centrally located to provide reliable network access for its clients. A MED-V client regularly connects to the MED-V Management Server to send status and event information once a minute. The MED-V client also checks with the MED-V Management Server for Workspace updates every 15 minutes and image updates every four hours. If a client is unable to connect to a MED-V Management Server, the status and event information is queued on the client until it is able to reconnect. Microsoft does not support using Failover Clustering for MED-V Management Server, so it's important to create a standby MED-V Management Server that can be brought online in the case of server failure. This is especially true if the MED-V Workspace is configured to require the client to be online and authenticated in order to use the MED-V Workspace. It is possible to implement MED-V Management Server on two servers. More information about implementing this type of failover support can be found in the MED-V manual.

The MED-V Management Server stores Workspace configuration metadata, which is 30 KB per Workspace. To determine the disk storage requirements for storing Workspace metadata on the MED-V Management Server, multiply the number of Workspaces by 30 KB. For example, if you have 20 Workspaces, you would multiply 20 by 30 KB, which equals

600 KB. The MED-V Management Server can be backed up and restored to the same server or a backup server using Microsoft System Center Data Protection Manager (SCDPM) or another backup and restore solution. Four XML files make up the server configuration files: `ClientSettings.xml`, `ConfigurationFiles.xml`, `OrganizationalPolicy.xml`, and `WorkspaceKeys.xml`. The location for the data to back up is *drive letter*:\microsoft enterprise desktop Virtualization\servers\serverconfiguration.

As mentioned earlier, a Repository Server consists of a Web Server (IIS) and a file server that stores the images on a file share. The number of Web Servers (IIS) and file servers used in a MED-V solution instance will depend on the number of concurrent users, the size and number of the MED-V images, deployment and update frequency, the user location, network bandwidth, and other factors. Multiple Web Servers (IIS) can be used for a MED-V solution instance and load balanced to provide the appropriate level of scalability and performance. The placement of the Repository Servers should be close to the clients, avoiding WAN connections. This is important for the initial deployment of the MED-V image and also image updates. The disk storage requirements for the Image Repository are determined by identifying the number and size of MED-V images that will be supported on a given repository. Backing up the MED-V images is also important and can be accomplished by using SCDPM or another backup and restore solution.

The Med-V Database Server stores client activity and event information. The size of an event sent by a client is around 200 bytes. The MED-V Database Server database storage requirements are determined by the number of MED-V clients, multiplied by the number of events sent by each client per day. Other database size factors include how long the data will be stored and the allocation of additional space for unknown events or circumstances.

Organizations will need to determine how the MED-V client software and images will be deployed and updated on the client. There are different options to choose from, including using the MED-V solution infrastructure, existing client management solutions, and removable media (DVD and USB storage). For example, an organization could deploy the MED-V client software by making it part of their corporate Windows image, deploying it using ESD or with removable media. The initial MED-V image can be deployed to the client by using the MED-V Management Server, prestaging it to the client using ESD or by removable media (DVD and USB storage). The Med-V images will also need to be updated, which can be accomplished by using the MED-V Management Server. Some organizations may also decide to update the client operating system and applications running in the MED-V image by using their corporate ESD solution.

Implementing a MED-V POC

Once the solution design and architecture are completed, the next step is to test the solution in a Proof of Concept (POC) lab environment. POCs are where the rubber meets the road and can vary in goals, scope, time frame, and outcome. It's important to conduct a well-organized POC, focusing only on the goals and scope agreed on, involving the right resources, and documenting the entire process from start to finish, so that this information can be reviewed and utilized to support later project efforts.

Depending on the goals of the POC, the architecture and server configuration of this environment can be implemented on a much smaller scale than a pilot or production deployment of the solution. For example, a typical MED-V POC involves one physical server and one to two PCs. The server would support the MED-V Management Server and Image Repository, and the PCs would support the MED-V Management Console and MED-V Client. An example MED-V POC server configuration is shown along with the MED-V POC architecture example in Figure 16.1.

FIGURE 16.1

MED-V POC architecture example

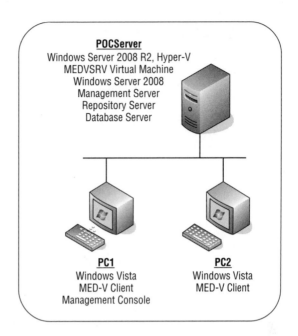

POCServer
Windows Server 2008 R2, Hyper-V
MEDVSRV Virtual Machine
Windows Server 2008
Management Server
Repository Server
Database Server

PC1
Windows Vista
MED-V Client
Management Console

PC2
Windows Vista
MED-V Client

At a high level, you can break the POC into four areas: preparation, installation and configuration, testing and knowledge transfer, and review and analysis. Each area is important and will have an effect on the success of the POC and preparation for a production deployment. The knowledge transfer and testing area should be well defined in terms of what the POC team wants to learn and evaluate regarding the Microsoft POC solution. A simple but effective one-week POC action plan follows.

MED-V POC ACTION PLAN EXAMPLE

POC PREPLANNING ACTIVITIES

◆ Conduct an initial meeting.

   ◆ Determine goals, scope, expected outcome, time frame, resources involved, location(s), IT infrastructure needs, and prerequisites (hardware, software, services, networking, storage, and so forth).

◆ Conduct a pre-MED-V POC meeting.

   ◆ Include all the required IT and business resources.

   ◆ Review the POC areas described above.

   ◆ Identify potential project showstoppers.

   ◆ Create an agenda for the one-week POC activities along with the responsibilities of IT and business resources participating.

POC ACTIVITIES

◆ Day 1 — Kickoff meeting, installation of Windows Server 2008 R2, Hyper-V, Web Server (IIS), SQL Server, and MED-V server and client components.

  ◆ Conduct a MED-V POC kickoff meeting the first day of the POC. Verify that the POC prerequisites are completed and the organization is ready to begin.

  ◆ Present an overview of the POC project and planned day 1 activities.

  ◆ Begin MED-V solution server software installation.

    1. Install and configure a Windows Server 2008 R2 Server with Hyper-V called POCServer.

    2. Create a VM on POCServer called MEDVSRV.

    3. Install Windows Server 2008 (32- or 64-bit) and prerequisite software on the VM called MEDVSRV on POCServer.

    4. Install the Web Server (IIS) role on the VM called MEDVSRV on POCServer.

    5. Install BITS Server Extensions feature on the VM called MEDVSRV on POCServer.

    6. Install SQL Server 2008 Express on the VM called MEDVSRV on POCServer.

    7. Install MED-V Management Server V1 on the VM called MEDVSRV on POCServer.

  ◆ Conduct daily status meeting.

◆ Day 2 — Installation of MED-V client components, and creation and testing of MED-V Workspace image.

  ◆ Present an overview of the planned day 2 activities.

  ◆ Install the MED-V client components.

    1. Install MED-V client V1 and Management Console and prerequisite software on PC1 running Windows Vista (32-bit).

    2. Install MED-V client V1 and prerequisite software on PC2 running Windows Vista (32-bit).

  ◆ Create and test MED-V Workspace images.

    1. Prepare Virtual PC images for MED-V.

    2. Add MED-V test images.

    3. Create and configure MED-V Workspaces.

    4. Test MED-V Workspaces.

    5. Pack tested MED-V images.

  ◆ Conduct daily status meeting.

- Day 3 — Deployment of MED-V Workspace.
  - Present an overview of planned day 3 activities.
  - Continue to create and test MED-V Workspace images.
  - Deploy MED-V Workspace.
    1. Deploy MED-V Workspaces using the MED-V Server.
    2. Update MED-V Workspaces using the MED-V Server.
    3. Deploy MED-V using Deployment package on removable media.
    4. Deploy MED-V using ESD for prestaged deployment.
  - Conduct daily status meeting.
- Day 4 — Continuation of MED-V Workspace deployment activities and knowledge transfer.
  - Present an overview of planned day 4 activities.
  - Continue MED-V Workspace deployment activities.
  - Conduct knowledge transfer activities.
  - Conduct daily status meeting.
- Day 5 — Knowledge transfer and testing of MED-V environment.
  - Present an overview of planned day 5 activities.
  - Review MED-V troubleshooting tools.
    1. Generate and review MED-V reports.
    2. Run and review MED-V diagnostics.
  - Lead MED-V Q & A discussion.
  - Conduct end-of-POC status meeting.

POST-POC ACTIVITIES

- Prepare report on POC activities completed, including highlights and lowlights and key findings.
- Develop an action plan for moving forward with the project.

Installing the MED-V Solution

The process of implementing the MED-V solution consists of installing and configuring several Microsoft software services on servers running Windows Server 2008 and personal computers running Windows Vista or Windows XP operating system. In the next two sections we will review the main installation steps required to be performed on the servers and clients that make up the MED-V solution. Figure 16.2 shows an example of the MED-V solution architecture that we will be installing.

FIGURE 16.2
Simple MED-V solution architecture

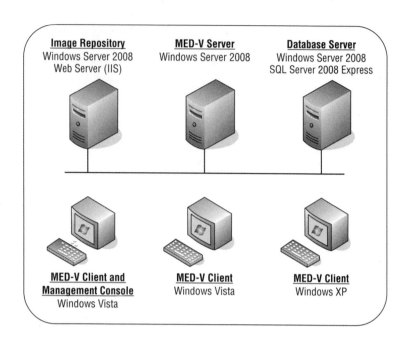

The architecture used for this MED-V solution example consists of three servers and three clients. The reason for using three servers is to provide an example of how to isolate the required server components — MED-V Management Server, Web/Repository Server, and SQL Server — on separate servers. This may be useful in supporting scenarios that require higher performance, greater scalability, and distributed client locations. It is possible to implement all of the MED-V server components on one server running on a single instance of the server operating system or distributed on VMs, as we did for our POC.

The system requirements for the MED-V version 1 are listed in Table 16.1. For the latest MED-V information, please review the Microsoft MED-V website at www.microsoft.com/medv.

We're making a key assumption regarding the existence of infrastructure services that are needed to support this solution, that is, AD, DNS, and DHCP. A list of the servers and clients used in this installation example is provided below. In addition, other Microsoft products, technologies, and updates may also need to be installed either before or during the installation of the solution components. Examples of these include .NET Framework 3.0 SP 1, Windows Installer 4.5, and the SQL Server Native Client and SQL Server Management Objects. Please refer to the Microsoft Windows Server 2008, MED-V, Windows Vista, and Windows XP installation instructions related to prerequisites for more information.

Servers

For this solution example, we will use three Windows Servers named ServerA, ServerB, and ServerC. A description of each server follows.

ServerA Image Repository Server, running Windows Server 2008 (32- or 64-bit), Web Server (IIS), and BITS Server Extensions. This server provides the platform to store and deploy MED-V Workspace images to MED-V clients.

ServerB Database Server, running Windows Server 2008, SQL Server 2008 (32- or 64-bit). This server provides the database that is used to store MED-V client information that is collected by the MED-V Management Server. Reports can then be created from this data.

ServerC MED-V Server, running Windows Server 2008 (32- or 64-bit), MED-V Management Server V1. This server stores MED-V Server settings and Workspace policies, communicates with Active Directory to assign users and groups to Workspace images, authenticates and authorizes MED-V clients, and manages policy and Workspace deployment and updates.

TABLE 16.1:   MED-V system requirements

MANAGEMENT SERVER	
Processor	Dual processor, 2.8 GHz.
Memory	4 GB RAM.
Operating system	Windows Server 2008 Standard or Enterprise.
Database	Microsoft SQL Server 2005 Enterprise SP2 or Microsoft SQL Server 2008 Express, Standard, or Enterprise.
REPOSITORY SERVER	
Web server	Microsoft IIS.
File server	Windows Server 2008. Note that disk space requirements are determined by the size and number of VM images that will be stored in the repository.
CLIENT SYSTEM	
Memory	1 GB for Windows XP, 2 GB for Windows Vista.
Disk space	Note that disk space requirements are determined by the size and number of guest VMs.
Host OS	Windows XP SP2/SP3 (32-bit), Windows Vista SP1/SP2 (32-bit).
Guest OS	Windows 2000 SP4 (32-bit), Windows XP SP2/SP3 (32-bit).
Desktop virtualization software	Microsoft Virtual PC 2007 SP1.

Personal Computers

For this solution example, we will use three Windows PCs named PC1, PC2, and PC3. A description of each PC is provided below.

PC1 MED-V Client and Management Console, running Windows Vista SP2 (32-bit) and MED-V Client and Management Console software. This personal computer will be used to manage the MED-V environment and test MED-V Workspace images.

PC2 MED-V Client running Windows Vista SP2 (32-bit) and MED-V Client software. This personal computer will be used to download and run MED-V Workspaces.

PC3 MED-V Client running Windows XP SP3 (32-bit) and MED-V Client software. This personal computer will be used to download and run MED-V Workspaces.

Installation of the MED-V Solution Server Components

The server architecture used for this MED-V solution example comprises three servers: ServerA, the Image Repository Server; ServerB, the Database Server; and ServerC, the MED-V Management Server. The installation process begins with installing IIS and BITS Server Extensions on ServerA. The next step is to install SQL Server 2008 Express on ServerB. We then install the MED-V Management Server on ServerC. Administrator rights are required for all of these operations. As mentioned before, a key assumption made regarding the installation environment is the existence of AD, DNS, and DHCP infrastructure services that are required to support this solution. A flowchart of the server installation process is shown in Figure 16.3.

FIGURE 16.3
MED-V Server installation process flowchart

Microsoft MED-V Installation Steps

ServerA — Image Repository Server

The first installation step is to install the Windows Server 2008 (32- or 64-bit) on this server. Installation instructions for Windows Server 2008 can be found on `technet.microsoft.com`.

The second installation step is to add the Web Server/Internet Information Service (IIS) role. The instructions for installing Internet Information Server are listed below:

1. Open Windows Server 2008 Server Manager on ServerA.

2. Select Roles on the Server Manager hierarchy.

3. On the Roles Summary page, select Add Roles.

4. Review the Before You Begin page and click Next.

5. On the Select Server Roles page, select the Web Server (IIS) check box. Click the Add Required Features For Web Server (IIS) pop-up screen, and click Next.

6. Review the Introduction To Web Server (IIS) page, and click Next.

7. On the Select Role Services page, under the Security section, select Basic Authentication, Windows Authentication, and Client Certificate Mapping Authentication, and click Next.

8. On the Confirm Installation Selections page, review the results and click Install. The installation process will begin.

9. On the Installation Results page, review the results and click Close.

The third installation step adds the BITS Server Extensions feature to the server. The steps for installing this feature are as follows:

1. Open Windows Server 2008 Server Manager on ServerA.

2. Select Features on the Server Manager hierarchy.

3. On the Features Summary page, click Add Feature.

4. On the Select Features page, select the BITS Server Extensions check box. The Add Role Services Required For Background Intelligent Transfer Service (BITS)? pop-up screen will appear. Click Add Required Role Services, and then click Next.

5. On the Introduction To Web Server (IIS) page, click Next.

6. On the Select Role Services page, click Next.

7. On the Confirm Installation Selections page, review the results and click Install. The installation process will begin.

8. On the Installation Results page, review the results and click Close.

The installation steps for ServerA, the Image Repository Server are now complete. The configuration steps for this server are provided in the upcoming section called "Configuration of the MED-V Solution Server Components."

ServerB — Database Server

The first step is to install the Windows Server 2008 (32- or 64-bit) on this server. Installation information for Windows Server 2008 can be found on technet.microsoft.com.

The second step is to install SQL Server. For this installation example we will use SQL Server 2008 Express. Note that SQL Server 2005 Enterprise and SQL Server 2008 Standard and Enterprise may also be used and are a better choice for production deployments. The steps for installing the SQL Server 2008 Express are listed below:

1. Install .NET Framework 3.0 SP 1. SQL Server 2008 Express Setup requires .NET Framework 3.0 SP1 to be installed. .NET Framework 3.0 SP1 can be downloaded at www.microsoft.com/downloads.

2. Install Windows Installer 4.5. SQL Server 2008 Express Setup requires Windows Installer 4.5 to be installed. Windows Installer 4.5 can be downloaded at www.microsoft.com/downloads.

3. The next step is to install SQL Server 2008 Express. SQL Server 2008 Express can be downloaded from www.microsoft.com/downloads. Follow these installation steps:

    a. Run SQL Server Express Setup.
    b. On the SQL Server Installation Center page, select Installation.
    c. Select New SQL Server Stand-alone Installation or Add Features To An Existing Installation. The Setup Support Rules process will run and identify any problems. If any failures are identified, correct the issues and rerun this process. If no problems are identified, click OK.
    d. On the Product Key page, click Next since SQL Server Express is a free product.

    e. Review the License Terms, and if you accept them, select the I Accept The License Terms check box.

    f. On the Setup Support Files page, click Install.

    g. For the Setup Support Rules step, see if failures were identified. If failures were identified, correct the issues and rerun this process. If no problems were identified, click Next.

    h. For the Feature Selection step, select the Database Engine Services check box and click Next.

    i. For the Instance Configuration step, accept the default settings and click Next.

    j. For the Disk Space Requirements step, review the disk usage summary and click Next.

    k. For the Server Configuration step, there are two tabs: Service Accounts and Collation. For Service Accounts, select NT Authority ➤ System from the Account Name drop-down list. Accept the default setting for SQL Server Browser. For the Collation settings, accept the defaults. Click Next.

    l. For the Database Engine Configuration, Account Provisioning, select Mixed Mode, and enter a password for the built-in SQL Server administrator account (SA). Specify SQL Server administrators by clicking Add Current User. Accept the default settings for Data Directories, User Instances, and FILESTREAM, and click Next.

    m. For the Error And Usage Reporting step, accept the default settings and click Next.

    n. For the Installation Rules step, see if failures were identified. If failures were identified, correct the issues and rerun this process. If no problems were identified, click Next.

    o. Review the Ready To Install information and click Install. The installation process will begin.

    p. When the installation has completed successfully, click Next.

    q. Review the information on the completed page, and click Close.

The installation steps for ServerB, the Database Server are now complete. The configuration steps for this server are provided in the upcoming section called "Configuration of the MED-V Solution Server Components."

ServerC — MED-V Management Server

The first step is to install Windows Server 2008 (32- or 64-bit) on this server. Installation instructions for Windows Server 2008 can be found on `technet.microsoft.com`.

The next step is to install the MED-V Management Server. The steps for installing the MED-V Management Server V1 are listed below.

1. Run the appropriate MED-V Server Windows Installer package, `MED-V_serverx_86_1.0.72.msi` for x86 or `MED-V_server_x64_1.0.72.msi` for x64.

2. Review the MED-V Server Installation Wizard Welcome screen, and click Next.

3. Review the MED-V License Agreement. If you accept the licensing terms, click Next.

4. Review the Install Destination Folder setting, and click Next.

5. On the Ready To Install The Program screen, click Install.

6. On the MED-V Wizard Completed screen, deselect Launch MED-V Server Configuration Manager, and click Finish.

7. The next steps are to install the SQL Server Native Client and SQL Server Management Objects. The Microsoft SQL Server 2008 Feature Pack includes SQL Server Native Client and SQL Server Management Objects and can be downloaded at `www.microsoft.com/downloads`.

    a. Install SQL Server Native Client by running the file `sqlcli.msi`. Follow the Installation Wizard instructions, accepting all defaults.

    b. Install SQL Server Management Objects by running the file `SharedManagementObjects.msi`. Follow the Installation Wizard instructions, accepting all defaults.

The installation steps for ServerC, the MED-V Management Server, are now complete. The configuration steps for this server are provided in the upcoming section called "Configuration of the MED-V Solution Server Components."

Installation of the MED-V Solution Client Components

The client architecture used for this MED-V solution example includes three personal computers: PC1, PC2, and PC3. Each personal computer requires the installation of a supported Microsoft Windows Client operating system along with the MED-V Client software.

PC1 — Windows Vista MED-V Client and Management Console

The installation process for PC1 includes installing Windows Vista SP 2 and the MED-V Client and Management Console software. Follow the installation steps listed below.

1. Install Windows Vista SP 2 (32-bit).

2. Install Microsoft Virtual PC 2007 SP1 and KB 958162 Update. You can download these from `www.microsoft.com/downloads`.

3. Install the MED-V Client and Management Console software.

    a. Run the MED-V Client Windows Installer package named `MED-V_1.0.72.msi`.

    b. Review the MED-V Client Installation Wizard Welcome screen, and click Next.

    c. Review the MED-V License Agreement. If you accept the licensing terms, click Next.

    d. Review the Install Destination Folder setting, and click Next.

    e. On the MED-V Settings screen, put checkmarks next to Install The MED-V Management Application, Load MED-V When Windows Starts, and Add A MED-V Shortcut To My Desktop. Enter the correct server address and port for your MED-V Server. Accept the default directory to store the MED-V virtual machines. Click Next.

    f. On the Ready To Install The Program screen, click Install. The MED-V Client and Management Console software will now be installed.

    g. On the MED-V Wizard Completed screen, deselect Launch MED-V Enterprise Desktop Virtualization, and click Finish.

PC2 — Windows Vista MED-V Client

The installation process for PC2 will include installing Windows Vista SP 2 and MED-V Client software. Follow the installation steps listed here:

1. Install Windows Vista SP 2 (32-bit).

2. Install Microsoft Virtual PC 2007 SP1and KB 958162 Update.

3. Install the MED-V Client.

   a. Run the MED-V Client Windows Installer package named `MED-V_1.0.72.msi`.
   b. Review the MED-V Client Installation Wizard Welcome screen, and click Next.
   c. Review the MED-V License Agreement. If you accept the licensing terms, click Next.
   d. Review the Install Destination Folder setting, and click Next.
   e. On the MED-V Settings screen, put checkmarks next to Load MED-V When Windows Starts and Add A MED-V Shortcut To My Desktop. Enter the correct server address and port for your MED-V Server. Accept the default directory to store the MED-V virtual machines. Click Next.
   f. On the Ready To Install The Program screen, select Install. The MED-V Client software will now be installed.
   g. On the MED-V Wizard Completed screen, deselect Launch MED-V Enterprise Desktop Virtualization, and click Finish.

PC3 — Windows XP MED-V Client

The installation process for PC1 will include installing Windows XP SP3 and MED-V Client software. Follow the installation steps listed below.

1. Install Windows XP SP 3 (32-bit).

2. Install Microsoft Virtual PC 2007 SP1 and KB 958162 Update.

3. Install the MED-V Client, and follow the instructions listed under PC2.

The installation steps for the personal computers are now complete. The configuration steps for the Windows personal computers are provided in the upcoming configuration section of this chapter.

Configuration of the MED-V Solution Server Components

After the MED-V solution server and client components have been installed, they need to be configured to work properly with each other. Instructions for configuring the server and client components are provided in the following sections.

ServerA — Image Repository Server

The configuration process for ServerA, the Image Repository Server, includes configuring the Web Server (IIS). The steps for configuring this server are listed below.

1. Open Windows Server 2008 Server Manager on ServerA.

2. Select the Web Server (IIS) role on the Server Manager hierarchy.

3. Select Internet Information Services (IIS) Manager.

4. In the Internet Information Services (IIS) Manager pane under Connections, select Default Web Site.

5. Right-click the Default Web Site, and select Add Virtual Directory.

6. In the Add Virtual Directory screen, enter **MEDVImages** in the Alias field and **C:\MEDV Server Images** in the Physical Path field, and click OK. Note that the MEDV Server Images directory was created during the installation of MED-V.

7. Under Default Web Site, select the MEDVImages folder. In the MEDV Images Home pane, scroll down to the IIS section and select MIME Types ➢ Open Feature from the Actions pane. The following steps will add the MED-V required filename extensions and MIME types:

   a. Select Add from the Actions pane. On the Add MIME Type window, enter .ckm in the File Name Extension field and **application/octet-stream** in the MIME Type field. Click OK.

   b. Select Add from the Actions pane. On the Add MIME Type window, enter .index in the File Name Extension field and **application/octet-stream** in the MIME Type field. Click OK.

8. Under Default Web Site, select the MEDVImages folder. In the MEDV Images Home pane, scroll down to the Other section and select BITS Upload ➢ Open Feature from the Actions pane. Select the check box Allow Clients To Upload Files. Select Apply from the Actions pane.

9. Under Default Web Site, select the MEDVImages folder. In the Actions pane, select Edit Permissions. On the MED-V Server Images Properties screen, choose the Security tab. Select Edit, add the appropriate groups, and select Allow Read Permissions. In this instance we will use the group Everyone.

ServerB — Database Server

The configuration process for ServerB, the Database Server, was conducted during the time of the installation. Other database settings related to this server are located in the MED-V Server Configuration Manager.

ServerC — MED-V Management Server

The configuration process for ServerC, the MED-V Management Server, includes configuring Client Connections, Image Management, Management Permissions, and Database Settings. The steps for configuring this server are listed below. The MED-V Server Configuration Manager is shown in Figure 16.4.

FIGURE 16.4
MED-V Server
Configuration Manager

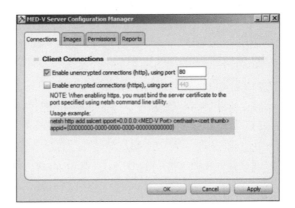

1. Open MED-V Server Configuration Manager from the Start menu on ServerC.

2. The Connections Tab will be selected by default.

    a. Select the type of connection. MED-V Server provides two types of connections options: unencrypted connections using port 80 and encrypted connections using port 443. In this instance we will use the default setting, Enable Unencrypted Connections (http), Using Port 80.

3. Select the Images tab.

    a. Enter the VMs Directory location. In this instance we will use the default directory location, **C:\MED-V Server Images**. Earlier we configured the Web Server (IIS) to use the same directory.
    b. Enter the VMs URL In this instance the URL is **http://ServerC/medvimages**.

4. Select the Permissions tab.

    a. Add the preferred domain users or groups who will need permissions to manage the MED-V Management Server. If the group Everyone has been added by default, remove it by selecting the group and clicking Remove.

5. Select the Reports tab.

    a. Select the Enable Reports check box.
    b. Enter the appropriate value in the Database Server Connection String field. In this instance the connection string would be **DataSource=ServerB\SQLEXPRESS;Initial Catalog=MEDV;UID=SA;PWD=P@ssword1**. A complex password was used to meet the Windows Server password policy requirement.
    c. Click the Create Database button. Click the Test Connection button.

6. Click the OK button. When prompted to restart the MED-V Management Server, click Yes.

Configuration of the MED-V Solution Client Components

After the MED-V Client components have been installed on personal computers 1, 2, and 3, they will need to be configured properly to work with the MED-V solution. The steps for configuring MED-V Client components are listed below. The MED-V Client Settings screen is shown in Figure 16.5.

PC1 — Windows Vista MED-V Client and Management Console

The process of configuring the Windows Vista MED-V Client and Management Console includes the following steps:

1. Launch the MED-V Client software.

2. Right-click the MED-V icon on the system tray and select Settings.

3. Under Start Options, verify that the Load Med-V After Windows Logon check box and Start Workspace When Med-V Starts check box have been selected.

4. Under Server Properties, enter the appropriate Server Address and Port data. In this instance, the server would be ServerC. Select Encrypt Connections (HTTPS) if applicable.

5. Click OK.

FIGURE 16.5
MED-V Client settings

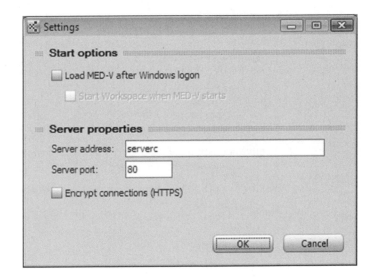

PC2 — Windows Vista MED-V Client

The steps for configuring the Windows Vista MED-V Client are the same as those performed on PC1. Please refer to the MED-V Client configuration instructions for PC1.

PC3 — Windows XP MED-V Client

The steps for configuring the Windows XP MED-V Client are the same as those performed on PC1. Please refer to the MED-V Client configuration instructions for PC1.

Preparing, Deploying, and Updating MED-V Images and Workspaces

Now that the MED-V solution components have been installed and configured on the required servers and clients, the environment is ready to create and prepare VPC images, create test MED-V Workspace images, and deploy MED-V workspace images. The following sections provide an overview of this process.

Create and Prepare a VPC Image for MED-V

A MED-V Workspace image consists of a Virtual PC (VPC) virtual machine that has been properly prepared for the MED-V environment. The preparation consists of the following steps:

1. Create the virtual machine image with the Microsoft Virtual PC Console. As mentioned before, Microsoft Virtual PC 2007 SP1 with KB 958162 update is required. In this instance, we will use VM configuration settings of 512 MB memory and hard disk size of 65 GB.

2. Start the new virtual machine and install Windows XP SP2/SP3 or Windows 2000 SP4 in the VPC virtual machine. Note that the MED-V solution requires this Windows client operating system to use a Volume License Key (VLK).

3. Install the VPC Virtual Machine Additions on the virtual machine.

   a. On the Virtual PC VM Console menu, select Action ➤ Install Or Update Virtual Machine Additions.

   b. On the Would You Like To Install Or Update The Virtual Machine Additions Now? window, click Continue.

   c. On the Welcome To Setup For Virtual Machine Additions window, click Next, and the installation process will begin.

   d. On the Setup Completed window, click Finish and Yes to restart Windows.

4. Install Microsoft .NET Framework 2.0 SP1 on the virtual machine. Microsoft .NET Framework 2.0 SP 1 can be downloaded from www.microsoft.com/downloads.

5. Install any additional software, such as utilities and applications.

6. Install MED-V Workspace software, and run the VM Prerequisites tool on the virtual machine.

   a. Run the MED-V installation file MED-V_Workspace_1.0.72.msi in the virtual machine.

   b. On the Welcome To The InstallShield Wizard For MED-V screen, click Next.

   c. Review the License Agreement screen, and if you accept the terms, select I Accept The Terms In The Agreement, and click Next.

   d. On the Ready To Install Program screen, click Install.

   e. On the InstallShield Wizard Completed screen, select the check box for launching the VM Prerequisites tool and click Finish. Note that you can also run this tool from Start ➤ All Programs ➤ MED-V ➤ MED-V VM Prerequisites Wizard.

   f. Review the MED-V VM Prerequisite Wizard Welcome screen, and click Next.

   g. Review the Windows Settings screen, accept the default settings, and click Next.

   h. Review the Internet Explorer screen, accept the default settings, and click Next.

   i. Review the Windows Services screen, accept the default settings, and click Next.

   j. On the Windows Auto Logon screen, select the check box for Enable Windows Auto Logon, enter a valid username and password, and click Apply.

   k. On the MED-V pop-up screen, when asked if you want to apply all the changes now, click Yes.

7. Review the Summary screen, and click Finish.

8. Test the newly created VPC image to ensure that the virtual machine, Windows operating system, and applications are running properly.

9. The next step is to run the System Preparation Utility (Sysprep) on the Windows operating system. In this instance we will follow the steps below. For more information on how to use Sysprep, please refer to technet.microsoft.com.

   a. Create a directory called Sysprep on the root directory of the Windows XP VM.

   b. From the Windows XP media or www.microsoft.com/downloads, copy the Deploy Cabinet file to the VM. This file is located on the Windows XP media in the \support\tools directory.

   c. Extract the setupmgr, sysprep, and setupcl files from to the sysprep directory.

   d. Run the extracted setupmgr (Microsoft Setup Manager Wizard) file. Follow the Setup Manager Wizard, and create a new answer file, choose Sysprep setup, choose the correct product version, accept the terms of the licensing agreement (only if you agree to them), enter the name and organization, accept the default display settings, enter the time zone, enter the Volume Licensing Key (VLK) product key, select to auto generate the computer name, enter an administrator password, select network components, enter the workgroup or domain, enter Telephony settings, enter Regional settings, select a language, install printers, and enter additional commands and an identification string if appropriate. Click Finish, and save the answer file by clicking OK. Once Setup Manager is complete, close the Completing Setup Manager window.

e. Run the extracted `sysprep` file. Follow the Sysprep wizard, clicking OK to run Sysprep, selecting to use Mini-Setup, and clicking the Reseal button. Click OK to regenerate SIDs. The Sysprep process will begin and when completed will shut down Windows and stop the VM.

Creating a MED-V Image

After the VPC virtual machine has been created and prepared for the MED-V environment, you can upload it into the Image Repository. The process for creating a test image, packing the tested image, and uploading or extracting the image is described next.

The first step to adding our newly created VPC virtual machine into the MED-V environment is to create a test image. The steps for creating a test image are as follows:

Creating a Test Image

1. From PC1 client launch the MED-V Management Console from Start ➤ All Programs ➤ MED-V ➤ MED-V Management or from the MED-V Management desktop shortcut.

2. Select the Images icon.

3. Under Local Test Images, select New.

4. On the Test Image Creation dialog box, click Browse, select the Windows VM Settings file for the Windows XP image we just created, and click Open. Enter an image name and click OK. The Image Creation dialog box is shown in Figure 16.6. The process will create a new directory on the Management Console's local hard disk at `C:\MED-V_Images\`*imagename*. The directory includes a `GlobalImageData` XML file and `Test` directory. The `Test` directory includes an `ImageState` XML file and the image's Virtual Machine Settings file.

After a test image has been created and tested, you can further prepare the image by packing it. The packing process compresses the image and stores it on the Management Console's local hard disk at `C:\MED-V_Images\PackedImages`. Two packed image files are created: the Kidaro Compressed Machine (*imagename*`.ckm`) file and the Index file (`imagename.ckm.index`) file.

Packing an Image

1. In the MED-V Management Console, select the Images icon.

2. Under Local Test Images, select the test image we created earlier and click Pack.

The packing process will begin with the Packing The Image Files screen displaying the process and status, as shown in Figure 16.7. This process may take several minutes to complete.

Once a MED-V image has been packed, it can be uploaded. The uploading process copies the packed image files to the Repository Server, where it is available for client deployments.

Uploading a Packed Image

1. In the MED-V Management Console, select the Images icon.

2. Under Local Packed Images, select the image we just packed and click Upload.

3. The action will begin with the Uploading screen displaying the process and status, as shown in Figure 16.8.

FIGURE 16.6
Test Image Creation
dialog box

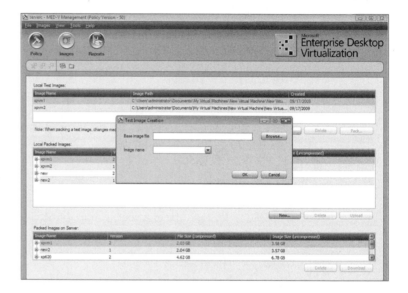

FIGURE 16.7
Packing The Image Files
screen

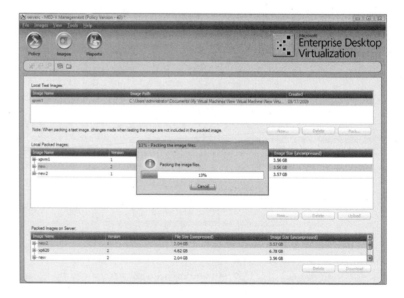

FIGURE 16.8
Uploading the image

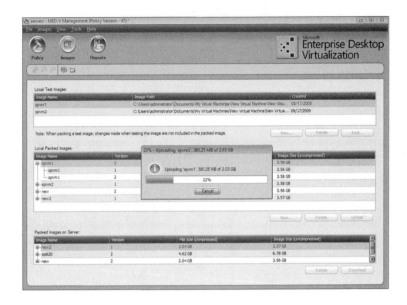

Creating a MED-V Workspace

The process to create a MED-V Workspace requires creating the Workspace in the MED-V Management Console and configuring settings in eight areas: General, Virtual Machine, Deployment, Applications, Web, VM Setup, Network, and Performance. The process for creating and configuring a MED-V Workspace is provided below:

1. Launch the MED-V Management Console.

2. Select the Policy icon.

3. Under the Workspaces pane on the right side of the console, click the Add button to create a new Workspace, which we will configure in the following steps.

4. Configure the General settings. The General configuration settings include areas for defining Workspace Properties, Workspace UI, and Host Verification.

   a. Click the General tab.
   b. Under the Workspace Properties settings, enter the name of the Workspace, its description, and support contact information. In this instance, we will accept the default name of Workspace.
   c. For the Workspace UI settings, you can choose Seamless Integration or Full Desktop. Accept the default settings of Seamless Integration and Draw A Frame Around Each Workspace Window.
   d. For Host Verification, accept the default settings, leaving the command line blank. Don't select the check box for not starting the Workspace if the verification fails. This setting enables a command to be run and verified on the host prior to starting the Workspace.

   The General tab is shown in Figure 16.9.

FIGURE 16.9
General tab

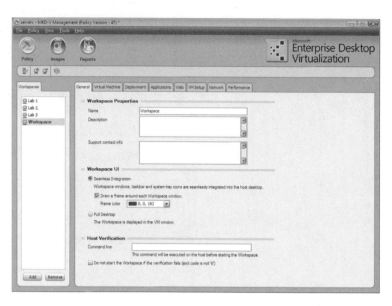

5. Configure the Virtual Machine settings. The Virtual Machine configuration settings include areas for defining Virtual Machine Settings, Lock Settings, and Image Update Settings.

   a. Click the Virtual Machine tab.

   b. For the Virtual Machine Settings, select the Windows XP image that we created in an earlier step as the Assigned Image. Select the Workspace Is Revertible radio button. A revertible VM is a MED-V Workspace image that returns to its original state after each session. Leave the Synchronize Workspace Time Zone With Host option at its default setting of being selected.

   A Workspace can also be configured to be persistent. A persistent VM is a MED-V Workspace image that saves its state after each session. Other options for a persistent Workspace include shutting down the VM when stopping the Workspace, logging into Windows, running in the VM, and using MED-V credentials to support Single Sign-on (SSO).

   c. Under Lock Settings, accept the defaults of not enabling the Workspace to be locked during host standby or hibernation and the related option to lock the Workspace after a specific amount of idle time.

   d. Accept the default Image Update Settings of not enabling the Keep Only (#) Old Image Versions and Suggest Update When A New Version Is Available. Also accept the default setting of enabling Clients Should Use Trim Transfer When Downloading Images For This Workspace. Trim Transfer is a MED-V technology that optimizes the process of deploying or updating a Workspace image to a client. Prior to MED-V deploying an image to a client, Trim Transfer indexes the client hard drive and compares this data to the Workspace image, looking for duplicated operating system and application data. Once this process is complete, Trim Transfer will transfer only image data from the Repository Server that doesn't already reside on the client hard disk, minimizing the amount of data transferred, optimizing network bandwidth, and reducing deployment and update time.

   The Virtual Machine tab is shown in Figure 16.10.

FIGURE 16.10
Virtual Machine tab

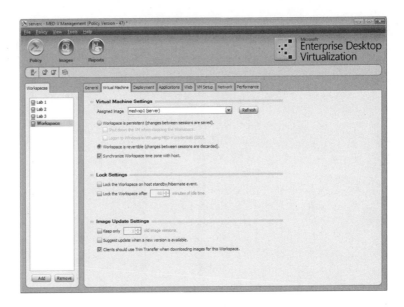

6. Configure the Deployment settings. The Deployment configuration settings include areas for defining which users and groups have access to the Workspace, Workspace expiration data, offline restriction, data transfer behavior, and device control.

   a. Click the Deployment tab.

   b. For the General settings, select Enable Workspace For 'Everyone.' You can add or remove users and groups by clicking the Add or Remove button under the Users / Groups pane on the left. Leave the check boxes for Workspace expiration and offline work restriction unchecked.

   c. For the Data Transfer settings, select the check boxes for Support Clipboard Between Host And Workspace and Support File Transfer Between The Host And Workspace. Note that we are enabling these settings for the purpose of evaluating these features in a MED-V test environment. If you are deploying MED-V in a production environment, configure these settings based on your organization's guidelines and policies.

   d. For the Device Control settings, select the check box for Enable Printing To Printers Connected To The Host and Enable Access To CD / DVD. We are enabling these settings for the purpose of evaluating these features in a MED-V test environment. If you are deploying MED-V in a production environment, configure these settings based on your organization's guidelines and policies.

   The Deployment tab is shown in Figure 16.11.

7. Configure the Applications settings. The Applications configuration settings include areas for defining which applications and menus that exist on the image are published for this MED-V Workspace.

   a. Click the Applications tab.

   b. Add published applications. Click the Add button under the Published Applications area and type **Notepad** in the Description field and **notepad.exe** in the Command Line field. You can enter other applications in a similar manner.

FIGURE 16.11
Deployment tab

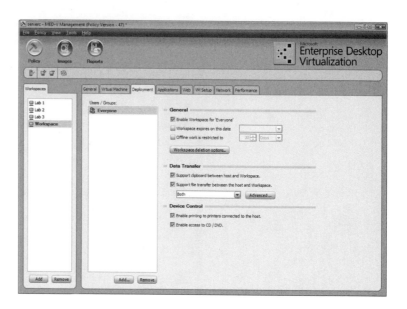

c. Enter the appropriate menus in the Published Menus section. Click the Add button under the Published Menus area and type **Accessories** for the Description and Folder In Workspace fields. Note that you can include all folders by entering a backslash (\) in the Folder In Workspace field. Leave the Start Menu Shortcuts Folder field with the default entry of MED-V Applications.

Application shortcuts can also be created for MED-V Workspace published applications on the host desktop by using the following command: `"drive letter:\program files\microsoft enterprise desktop virtualization\manager\ kidarocommands.exe" /run "published application name" "MED-V Workspace name"`. You can find more information about the use of Kidaro commands by typing `"drive letter:\program files\microsoft enterprise desktop virtualization\manager\kidarocommands.exe" /help`.

The Applications tab is shown in Figure 16.12.

8. Configure the Web settings. The Web configuration settings include areas for defining web-browsing behavior for the Workspace and host.

a. Click the Web tab.
b. For the Web Browsing settings, select the check box Browse The List Of URLs Defined In The Following Table. In The Workspace will be selected by default. Click the Add button located in the lower-right side of the Web Browsing area. We will leave the Type field with the default setting of Domain. Note that this field can be set to Domain Suffix, IP Suffix, or All Local Addresses. Enter **www.microsoft.com** in the Value field.
c. Select the check box Browse All Other URLs and the radio button In The Host.
d. Leave the check box Always Browse "Mailto" Links blank.

The Web tab is shown in Figure 16.13.

FIGURE 16.12
Applications tab

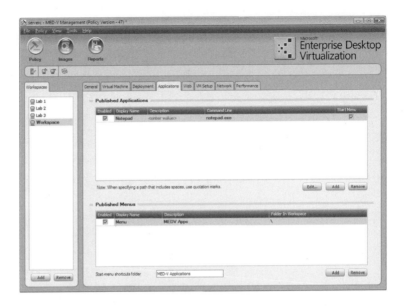

FIGURE 16.13
Web tab

9. Configure the VM Setup settings. The VM Setup configuration settings include areas for defining Persistent VM Setup, Revertible VM Setup, VM Computer Name Pattern, and Script Actions. For this test environment, we will set up the MED-V Workspace image for a revertible setup. This setup process further configures the Workspace image and is run once on the initial deployment after the Sysprep mini-setup is completed.

   a. Click the VMSetup tab.
   b. Under Revertible VM Setup, select the check box Rename The VM Based On The Computer Name Pattern.

c. For the VM Computer Name Pattern settings, click the Insert Variable list box and select Host Name. Other choices include User Name, Domain Name, Workspace Name, and Virtual Machine Name.

Note that if our MED-V Workspace image was configured to be persistent, we would have the option to run a script as part of the MED-V VM setup process. To create a VM setup script, select Run VM Setup and click the Script Editor button. The script editor includes prebuilt scripts to restart Windows, join a domain, check network connectivity, run a command from a command line, rename a computer, and disable auto logon. To add and configure a prebuilt script action, click the Add button under the Script Actions Pane. Once the script is complete, click OK.

The VM Setup tab is shown in Figure 16.14.

FIGURE 16.14
VM Setup tab

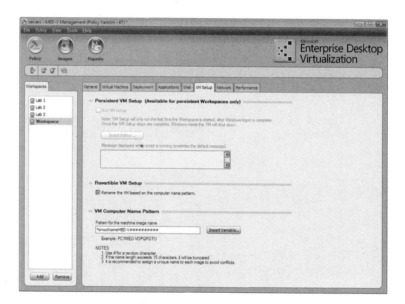

10. Configure the Network settings. The Network configuration settings include areas for defining TCP/IP Properties and DNS Options.

   a. Click the Network tab.
   b. Accept the default TCPIP Properties setting Use Host's IP Address (NAT). If the Workspace requires its own IP address, you can enable this by selecting Use Different IP Address Than Host (Bridge).
   c. Accept the default DNS Options settings to use the host's DNS address. Options are also available for changing the configured DNS setting in the image or using a specific DNS address. Also accept the default setting for Assign DNS Suffixes, which is Append Host Suffixes.

   The Network tab is shown in Figure 16.15.

11. Configure the Performance setting. This setting defines a specific amount of memory that will be available to the MED-V Workspace based on the host's memory configuration.

Note that this is a valuable setting for legacy applications that require a specific amount of memory to run.

a. Click the Performance tab.
b. Enter the appropriate VM Memory Allocation settings.

The Performance tab is shown in Figure 16.16.

12. After the Workspace has been created and configured properly, in the top menu bar select Policy ➢ Commit to save your changes.

FIGURE 16.15
Network tab

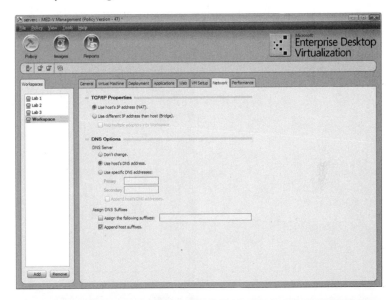

FIGURE 16.16
Performance tab

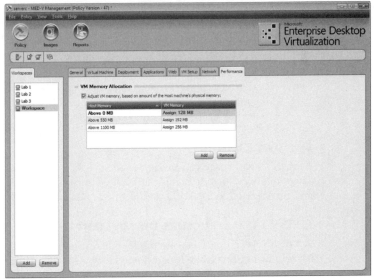

Testing a Med-V Workspace

After you've created a Workspace in the MED-V Management console, you can test it on the local Management Console workstation prior to deploying it to users. The steps for this process follow:

1. Launch the MED-V Client on the Management Console workstation.

2. Enter the administrator username and password on the Start Workspace screen.

3. On the Workspace selection screen, select the Workspace we just created. A Confirm Running Test dialog box will display, as shown in Figure 16.17. Click the Use Test Image button.

FIGURE 16.17
Confirm Running Test dialog box

4. The selected test image will start. You can now test the workspace on the workstation.

5. If you need to make Workspace setting changes to the test Workspace, such as for behavior or memory, stop the Workspace and launch the MED-V Management Console to reconfigure the test Workspace, save your changes, and test again.

Deploying a MED-V Workspace

A Med-V Workspace can be deployed to a user's personal computer in one of three ways. These methods include using the MED-V infrastructure, Electronic Software Distribution (ESD), and removable media (DVD or USB). Let's review each type of deployment and its process.

MED-V INFRASTRUCTURE DEPLOYMENT

A MED-V Workspace can be deployed to user's personal computers using the MED-V Management Server, the Image Repository, and Client software. All of these MED-V infrastructure components must be installed and configured prior to the deployment of the Workspace, including the installation of the MED-V Client software and prerequisite software. The process for deploying a MED-V Workspace using MED-V Infrastructure is provided in the following steps.

1. Create the MED-V Workspace and upload the packed image to the repository using the MED-V Management Console using the steps above.

2. Launch the MED-V Client software on the personal computer targeted for the Workspace deployment.

3. Provide the appropriate username and password on the Start Workspace screen.

4. If the user has been assigned to more than one Workspace, select the desired Workspace from the list. The Workspace Download process screen will display and carry out the following steps:

   a. Index the local hard disk.
   b. Download the image.

5. The Starting Workspace screen will display the progress, as shown in Figure 16.18, and will disappear once the Workstation has started properly. A Windows Notification icon will be displayed on the taskbar. The MED-V Workspace is now ready to use.

FIGURE 16.18
Starting Workspace screen

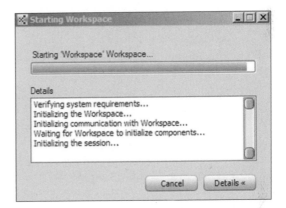

ELECTRONIC SOFTWARE DISTRIBUTION DEPLOYMENT

An Electronic Software Distribution tool such as Microsoft System Center Configuration Manager can also be used to initially deploy a MED-V Workspace. This method may be appropriate if an organization already has an ESD infrastructure in place and uses it as their standard method for distributing software. An advantage of using ESD in a WAN environment is the initial MED-V Workspace image deployment and the ability to distribute the image once to a remote site and then transfer the image locally to prestaged directories on each client. A disadvantage of ESD is not being able to use MED-V's Trim Transfer technology. The process for deploying a MED-V Workspace using Electronic Software Distribution is provided in the following steps.

1. Create the MED-V Workspace, and upload the packed image to the repository using the MED-V Management Console. You can skip this step if you have already created the MED-V Workspace and image.

2. Download the image to the desired Management Console workstation using the MED-V Management Console. The image files will be downloaded to the C:\MED-V_Images\PackedImages*imagename* directory on the local hard disk of the Management Console. You can skip this step if you have already downloaded the MED-V Workspace and image.

3. Create an Electronic Software Distribution package that includes the two MED-V packed image files (Compressed Machine file and Index file) that were downloaded.

4. Distribute the packed image files to the targeted user's personal computer's hard disk in the prestaged images directory located at C:\Med-V Images\PrestagedImages.

5. Launch the MED-V Client software on the personal computer targeted for the Workspace deployment.

6. Provide the appropriate username and password on the Start Workspace screen.

7. If the user has more than one Workspace assigned, choose the desired Workspace.

8. The Starting Workspace screen will display the progress and disappear once the Workstation has started properly. A Windows Notification icon will be displayed on the taskbar. The MED-V Workspace is now ready to use.

REMOVABLE MEDIA DEPLOYMENT

Removable media such as a DVD or USB storage device can also be used to initially deploy a MED-V Workspace. The process for deploying a MED-V Workspace using removable media is provided in the following steps:

1. Create the MED-V Workspace, and upload the packed image to the repository using the MED-V Management Console. You can skip this step if you have already created the MED-V Workspace and image.

2. Download the image to the desired Management Console workstation using the MED-V Management Console. The image files will be downloaded to C:\MED-V_Images\ PackedImages*imagename* directory on the local hard disk of the Management Console. You can skip this step if you have already downloaded the MED-V Workspace and image.

3. To prepare for the Packaging Wizard deployment package process, create a local or network directory with separate subdirectories for the MED-V client, Virtual PC, and .NET Framework installation files, and copy the associated setup files into these directories. The Packaging Wizard will ask for the location of these installation files during this process.

4. On the MED-V Management Console top menu bar, select Tools ≻ Packaging Wizard.

5. On the Packaging Wizard Deployment Package screen, click Next.

6. On the Workspace Image screen, mark the check box to include the image in the package. Select the image we just downloaded and click Next.

7. On the MED-V Installation Settings screen, select the path where we located the MED-V installation files, enter the MED-V server address and port, select Install MED-V Using Default Installation Settings if appropriate, and click Next.

8. On the Additional Installations screen, select the appropriate check boxes and installation path for Virtual PC 2007 SP1, Virtual PC QFE, and .NET Framework 2.0, and click Next.

9. On the Finalize screen, enter the path for the package destination and package name, and click Finish.

10. Copy the contents of the MED-V deployment package to the removable media (DVD or USB storage device).

    a. On the personal computer targeted for the Workspace deployment, insert the DVD or USB storage device that has the deployment package files that we previously copied.

    b. Open the removable media device, and launch the `MedvAutorun.exe` application. The MED-V screen will appear, asking if you would like to install the MED-V package now. The Installer screen will be also be displayed and will provide progress information for the installation of Virtual PC 2007 SP1, Virtual PC 2007 SP1 Update, MED-V Client, and the importing of the Workspace image. At the end of the process, the MED-V Installer window will display a message saying that MED-V was successfully installed.

    c. The MED-V Workspace is now ready to use.

Managing the MED-V Solution

The Microsoft MED-V solution can be managed using Microsoft management tools that are included in MED-V, Windows Server 2008, and System Center. The MED-V Management and Server Manager tools are discussed below, along with a mapping of the tools for each server and client in the solution.

The MED-V solution or instance can be managed by using Server Manager/IIS Manager, MED-V Server Configuration Manager, and MED-V Management Console.

Server Manager, IIS Manager

Server Manager is used to manage the Web Server (IIS) role that supports the MED-V Image Repository solution. The IIS Main Summary page offers a number of useful tools and information for managing your MED-V environment. The main page includes System Services, Best Practice Analyzer, Role Services, and Resources And Support. You can access this tool through Server Manager, by selecting the IIS role or by using IIS Manager.

MED-V Server Configuration Manager

The MED-V Server Configuration Manager runs on the MED-V Server and is used to initially configure the MED-V Server environment settings. These settings include client connections, location for storing images in the repository, management permissions, and database settings. If you need to change any of these configuration settings, you would use the MED-V Server Configuration Manager tool.

MED-V Management Console

The MED-V Management Console is the primary management tool for the MED-V and supports the life cycle of the Workspace images. It provides management of MED-V Workspaces, images, and reports. The Management tool supports the creation and configuration of MED-V Workspaces, image creation, and deployment and generation of status, activity, and error reports.

MED-V Logs and Events

You can review MED-V logs and events using the MED-V Management Console reports to view the status, activity, and error log information. This information can be viewed within the Management Console or exported into Microsoft Excel. Figure 16.19 show the MED-V Diagnostic tool.

FIGURE 16.19
MED-V client activity report

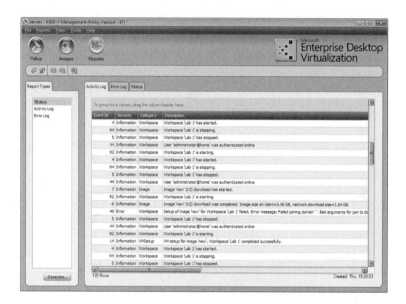

In addition, the MED-V Client software includes MED-V Diagnostics, which can gather comprehensive log information related to that MED-V client. You can access this tool through the Program menu under MED-V Management ➢ Tools ➢ MED-V Diagnostic Tool or by selecting the MED-V Notification icon under Help.

MED-V Client Tool

The MED-V Client tool is used to start MED-V, open Help, run Diagnostics, configure the MED-V client Start options and Server Connection properties, and start or stop a Workspace. You can access this tool by selecting the MED-V Notification icon.

MED-V Diagnostics

The MED-V Diagnostics tool is used to review system, policy, Workspace, and image store information on the MED-V client. In addition, you can use the tool to gather diagnostic logs, update a policy, enable diagnostic mode, and browse the local image store. A screen shot of the MED-V Diagnostics tool is provided in Figure 16.20.

ServerA: MED-V Image Repository Server

The MED-V Solution Management tools required to manage the MED-V Image Repository Server includes Server Manager\IIS Manager, MED-V Server Configuration Manager, and the MED-V Management Console.

FIGURE 16.20
MED-V Diagnostics tool

ServerB: MED-V Database Server

The MED-V Solution Management tools required to manage the MED-V Database Server includes SQL Server Configuration Manager and Management Studio, MED-V Server Configuration Manager, and the MED-V Management Console.

ServerC: MED-V Management Server

The MED-V Solution Management tools required to manage the MED-V Management Server includes Server Manager, SQL Server Configuration Manager and Management Studio, MED-V Server Configuration Manager, and the MED-V Management Console.

PC1 — Windows Vista MED-V Client and Management Console

The MED-V Solution Management tools required to manage the Windows Vista personal computer include the MED-V Client tool and MED-V Diagnostics.

PC2 — Windows Vista SP1 MED-V Client

The MED-V Solution Management tools required to manage the Windows Vista personal computer include the MED-V Client tool and MED-V Diagnostics.

PC3 — Windows XP SP3 MED-V Client

The MED-V Solution Management tools required to manage the Windows XP SP3 personal computer include the MED-V Client tool and MED-V Diagnostics.

Summary

In this chapter we reviewed considerations for planning a MED-V deployment, provided guidance for conducting a POC, identified and defined required server and client solution components, and provided step-by-step instructions for installing, configuring, and deploying MED-V in a test environment.

The Bottom Line

Install and configure the MED-V Management Server. A MED-V solution consists of a Management Server, Repository Server, Management Console, and Client software.

Master It What Windows operating systems does MED-V support for the host and guests?

Create and prepare a MED-V test image. MED-V uses Microsoft Virtual PC 2007 SP1 to create its VM images.

Master It How do you prepare a Virtual PC virtual machine for MED-V?

Create and configure a MED-V Workspace image. A MED-V Workspace can be assigned only one image, but an image can support more than one MED-V Workspace.

Master It Where do you configure the amount of memory that is available to a MED-V Workspace?

Deploy a MED-V Workspace image. Trim Transfer is a MED-V data transfer technology that minimizes the amount of data, bandwidth, and time it takes to deploy or update a MED-V image to a client.

Master It What are three methods to deploy a MED-V Workspace image to a client?

Generate MED-V reports. MED-V uses Microsoft SQL Server to store reporting data collected from MED-V clients.

Master It What tool is used to generate and view MED-V client reports? What types of reports are available?

Appendices

In this section you will find:

◆ Appendix A: The Bottom Line

◆ Appendix B: Microsoft Virtualization Tools and Resources

Appendix A

The Bottom Line

Each of The Bottom Line sections in the chapters suggest exercises to deepen skills and understanding. Sometimes there is only one possible solution, but often you are encouraged to use your skills and creativity to create something that builds on what you know and lets you explore one of many possible solutions.

Chapter 1: Understanding Microsoft's Hypervisor

Microsoft's history in virtualization   Microsoft has introduced multiple products for virtualizing the x86 architecture.

Master It   List the three products that Microsoft has released that provide the capability to virtualize the x86 or x64 architecture.

Solution

- ◆   Virtual Server (Virtual PC)
- ◆   Windows Server 2008 Hyper-V
- ◆   Hyper-V Server 2008

Monolithic versus microkernelized virtualization architectures   Monolithic and microkernelized are the two primary approaches to creating hypervisors. The difference is the amount of code between the virtual machine and the physical hardware on which it is running.

Master It   List the components that exist in the monolithic hypervisor. List the components that exist in the microkernelized hypervisor.

Solution   Monolithic

- ◆   Scheduler
- ◆   Memory management
- ◆   Storage stack
- ◆   Network stack
- ◆   VM state machine
- ◆   Virtualized devices

◆ Binary translators

◆ Drivers

◆ Management APIs

Microkernelized

◆ Scheduler

◆ Memory management

Hardware requirements Not all systems are capable of running Hyper-V.

Master It List the minimum requirements of the host system for installing and running Hyper-V.

Solution

◆ A Designed for Windows x64-based processor. Hyper-V is available in x64-based versions of Windows Server 2008 — specifically, the x64-based versions of Windows Server 2008 Standard, Windows Server 2008 Enterprise, and Windows Server 2008 Datacenter.

◆ Hardware-assisted virtualization. This is available in processors that include a virtualization option; specifically, Intel-VT or AMD Virtualization (AMD-V).

◆ Hardware Data Execution Prevention (DEP) must be available and be enabled. Specifically, you must enable Intel XD bit (execute disable bit) or AMD NX bit (no execute bit).

◆ Enough memory (RAM) to run the Windows kernel (at least 1 GB, but 2 GB is better) and to run one or more virtual machines.

Chapter 2: Installing, Configuring, and Managing the Hyper-V Host

Installing the Hyper-V role Windows Server 2008 has been highly modularized when compared to previous versions of Windows Server. The modularization has resulted in the definition of distinct roles that can be separately installed without affecting any other role on the system.

Master It Install the Hyper-V role on a Windows Server 2008 Full installation.

Solution

1. Click Start, and then click Server Manager.

2. In the Roles Summary area of the Server Manager main window, click Add Roles.

3. The Before You Begin page comes up. Click Next to continue to the next step in the wizard.

4. On the Select Server Roles page, click Hyper-V.

5. On the Create Virtual Networks page, click one or more network adapters that you want to use for virtual machines.

6. On the Confirm Installation Selections page, click Install.

7. The computer must be restarted to complete the installation. Click Close to finish the wizard.

8. Click Yes to restart the computer.

9. After you restart the computer, log on with the same account you used to install the Hyper-V role. This ensures that the Resume Configuration Wizard completes the installation. Click Close to finish the wizard.

10. Install KB950050 to update to the final bits of Hyper-V.

Hyper-V is now ready for configuration.

Remotely administering Hyper-V Server   Microsoft provides a set of tools that can be installed on a system administrator's workstation for managing Windows Server 2008 hosts and all the roles that can be installed on them.

Master It   Set up a server for remote administration by using commands instead of the GUI interface. Install the Hyper-V management console on your workstation. Select the remote Hyper-V system to manage.

Solution   Command lines to execute.

```
;
; Set up to support WinRS/WinRM - this requires a response
winrm quickconfig
;
; Set up for remote administration
netsh advfirewall firewall set rule group="remote administration" new enable=yes
;
; Enable remote admin mode (Terminal Services)
cscript c:\windows\system32\scregedit.wsf /ar 0
;
; Enable ping
netsh firewall set icmpsetting 8 enable
```

1. Download the remote Hyper-V management tool from www.microsoft.com/downloads/details.aspx?familyid=BF909242-2125-4D06-A968-C8A3D75FF2AA&displaylang=en.

2. Install the update.

3. When managing from Windows Server 2008 choose Start ➢ All Programs ➢ Administrative Tools ➢ Hyper-V Manager.

4. When managing from Windows Vista, choose Control Panel ➢ Administrative Tools ➢ Hyper-V Manager (Windows Vista SP1).

5. In the Actions menu, click Connect To Server.

6. Enter the server name to manage.

Backing up Windows Server Windows Server 2008 comes with a built-in backup utility that can take backups of running virtual machines if the operating system environment running in that virtual machine supports Volume Shadow Copy Services.

Master It Set up your Hyper-V Server host to enable the use of Windows Server Backup.

Solution First, turn on the feature within the host operating system. Then follow these steps:

1. In Server Manager, click Features in the left-hand column.

2. In the right-hand column, click Add Feature.

3. On the Select Features page, expand Windows Server Backup Features and select the check boxes for Windows Server Backup and Command-Line Tools.

Next, set the Registry value to enable Windows Server Backup, and follow these steps:

1. Click Start, click Run, type **regedit**, and then click OK.

2. Locate the following Registry key: HKEY_LOCAL_MACHINE\SOFTWARE\Microsoft\ Windows NT\CurrentVersion.

3. Right-click CurrentVersion and select Export. Save the .reg file in a safe location in case you need to go back to it.

4. Right-click CurrentVersion, point to New, and then click Key.

5. Type **WindowsServerBackup**, and then press Enter. This renames the New Key #1 value.

6. Right-click WindowsServerBackup, point to New, and then click Key.

7. Type **Application Support**, and then press Enter. This renames the New Key #1 value.

8. Right-click Application Support, point to New, and then click Key.

9. Type **{66841CD4-6DED-4F4B-8F17-FD23F8DDC3DE}**, and then press Enter. This provides the GUID for the VSS writer.

10. Right-click {66841CD4-6DED-4F4B-8F17-FD23F8DDC3DE}, point to New, and then click String Value.

11. Type **Application Identifier**, and then press Enter.

12. Right-click Application Identifier, and then click Modify.

13. In the Value data box, type **Hyper-V**, and then click OK.

14. On the File menu, click Exit.

Chapter 3: Creating and Managing Virtual Machines

Managing the Hyper-V parent When Hyper-V is installed on a physical system, you interact with the physical system through the parent partition. Besides providing the host management environment, the parent partition is also used for setting up an environment in which the virtual machines will run.

Master It   What are some of the components that the parent partition manages that affect all virtual machines running on that host and are unique to the virtual environment?

Solution   The parent partition has physical ownership of the hardware.

◆   Virtual hard disks — default folder in which to store virtual hard disks

◆   Virtual machines — default folder in which to store virtual machine configuration files.

◆   Keyboard — how you want to use Windows key combinations when running the VMconnect utility

◆   Mouse release key — what key combination you want to use to release the mouse when Integration Components are not installed

◆   User Credentials — whether you want to use your default credentials automatically with the VMconnect utility to connect to a running virtual machine

Managing the Hyper-V guests or children   Working with virtual machines, or guests, is very similar to working with physical systems. Most of the software that works on the physical host also works in a virtual machine. But there are a variety of physical functions or actions that you may execute on a physical machine, such as pressing a physical power button, that do not exist on a virtual machine.

Master It   List the actions that you can take on a virtual machine and compare them to actions you might take on a physical machine.

Solution   Though they may not be called the same, these actions performed on virtual machines are similar to physical equivalents.

◆   Start — This is the same as pressing the power button on a physical machine. If the machine is powered off, the machine boots up. If the machine is in a hibernate state (saved state in a virtual machine), the machine reloads its saved memory and starts from the point it was at when it was hibernated (saved).

◆   Shutdown — This is same as issuing the Shutdown command to a physical machine. It performs a graceful shutdown (stops running services, and so on) and then turns the power to the machine off. This function is available only on virtual machines that have the Integration Services installed and where the operating system supports a shutdown action.

◆   Save — This is the same as hibernating a physical machine. The contents of memory are written to a hibernate file (the system VHD in the case of the virtual machine) to be used for restarting at that point when the system is restored. Unlike the Shutdown action, this works for any running operating system; that is, it is not dependent on any special function of the operating system because it is handled entirely by Hyper-V.

◆   Pause — This is the same as the sleep function. On a physical operating system that supports this, the sleep function stops the execution of the operating system and turns off all power to the system except for a trickle needed to keep memory in its current state. In the virtual machines, this works for any operating system because it is handled entirely by Hyper-V. If the physical machine loses electricity for memory (for example, the battery on a laptop fully discharges while the machine is in a sleep state), the state of the machine is lost. In Hyper-V, if host machine is turned off or restarted, any virtual machine in a pause state loses its state.

◆ Reset — This is the same a reset button on a physical machine. The contents of memory are lost as the machine reboots itself.

◆ Snapshot

◆ Revert

Using some common tools for virtual machines   As I have stated many times, managing virtual machines is very much like managing physical machines. In fact, many of the tools you use in a physical environment, like backup and your patch-management tools, will be deployed in much the same way for your virtual environment as for your physical environment.

Master It   Some common tools that come with the Windows operating system have been modified to recognize the fact that a virtual machine is another operating system environment on the physical host. What are some of these tools?

Solution   Though there are many tools that can be purchased to assist in managing virtual machines, these are part of the operating system.

◆ Windows Management Instrumentation — Hyper-V classes, methods, and properties to manage the Hyper-V roles have been provided for access by scripting and programming languages.

◆ Perfmon — Performance counters specific to individual virtual machines can be monitored.

◆ Authorization Manager — This provides an environment for application developers to create a roles-based delegation model for performing different types of operations in the Hyper-V environment.

◆ Scripting languages like PowerShell and VBscript — These have not actually been modified, but they can be used to call the application programming interface provided by Hyper-V in order to work with the virtual machines. Using these scripting environments allows the creation of command-line access to Hyper-V functions.

Chapter 4: Storage and Networking for Hyper-V

Planning storage on your host   The Hyper-V host platform supports all the storage options that are supported by the Windows Server 2008 platform. This means that USB, IDE, SATA, SAS, Fibre Channel, and iSCSI disks are all available for use by the host. This provides a significant amount of flexibility in storage options for your host environment.

Master It   List the various storage options that you would consider to fall into the low-end, midrange, and datacenter-class solutions. Explain why you think they belong where you placed them and what you would consider a typical usage for that solution.

Solution

◆ Low-end solutions

USB and IDE because they tend to have slower speeds (5400/7200 rpm) so their performance is lower. Some SATA and SAS drives could also fall into this lower category because of performance.

Low-end solutions could be development and test environments or small businesses that do not require the higher levels of performance.

◆ Midrange solutions

Direct attached SAS and SATA drives with or without host-based RAID controllers and software-based iSCSI Targets because they provide a higher level of performance and options that address a broader range of applications.

Midrange solutions could be departmental solutions, medium-sized businesses, or large development environments. These solutions may require the benefits of RAID for redundancy and higher availability, and they will require reasonable performance.

◆ High-end solutions

Fibre Channel and iSCSI SAN because they provide the highest levels of performance and the most flexibility in configurations for different business needs.

High-end solutions could be used in datacenters of companies that have storage specialists who specialize in managing storage for varying business needs.

Configuring storage for virtual machines   Hyper-V virtual machines can utilize either physical disks (pass-through) or virtual hard disks, and the virtual hard disks can be created in different ways. Each selection has various advantages and disadvantages from both management and performance aspects.

Master It   List some advantages and disadvantages of each type of disk that a virtual machine can use.

Solution

1. Pass-through disk

   Advantages

   Near-native disk performance. Easy to move from physical use to virtual use. No reformatting of physical disk to use in virtual environment. Large volume size. Access to any disk that is connected to the host.

   Disadvantages

   Does not support snapshots or differencing capabilities.

   Note that iSCSI disks have similar advantages and disadvantages as pass-through disks. But because Hyper-V virtual machines access them directly over the network, they are not considered pass-through disks.

2. Fixed VHD

   Advantages

   Highest performing of the virtual formats. Similar performance to physical disk. Can use snapshots and/or differencing capabilities. Highly portable across multiple hosts — simple file copy or export/import.

   Disadvantages

   Limited to 2040GB maximum size. Must have all requested space available on the host disk to create. Creation time includes time required to write the entire volume.

3. Dynamic VHD

   Advantages

   Can use snapshots and/or differencing capabilities. Highly portable across multiple hosts — simple file copy or export/import. Minimal storage required to create; allocates storage as needed.

   Disadvantages

   Slowest performing due to regular requests to allocate more storage. Can cause runtime errors if there is not enough space to allocate the requested storage.

4. Differential VHD

   Advantages

   Highly portable across multiple hosts. Minimal storage required because it is created as a dynamic disk. Create multiple children off a common base.

   Disadvantages

   Same disadvantages as the dynamic disk because it is a dynamic disk. Changing the base image will invalidate all children.

Planning your network configuration for the host   The Hyper-V host systems provide access for the virtual machines to the physical network resources you have in your organization. Because you will most likely now have more than one system communicating over each physical NIC, you will need to plan accordingly.

Master It   Describe some considerations about the number of NICs you should have on a host machine.

Solution   Use a minimum of two NICs on the host platform. The first NIC should be dedicated to managing the physical environment.

Determine what sort of network access will be required by the virtual machines and the network traffic required for each access. For example, you might have a backup network or an iSCSI network.

Consider isolating the differing access needs to separate NICs if the traffic volume dictates it.

Consider the speed of your NICs and network infrastructure to determine whether you can continue operating with your current environment or you need to upgrade the speed. For example, if you plan to use iSCSI storage, you may want to upgrade to 10Gbps Ethernet if you need that level of performance.

Configuring virtual switches for virtual machines   Hyper-V can operate in a complex networking environment. It accomplishes this by creating virtual switches that are used for connecting into either the physical or the virtual environment.

Master It   There are three types of virtual switches that can be defined and used. List the three types and what their normal usage is.

Solution

◆   External

An external switch is created to bind virtual NICs to a physical NIC on the host. By assigning this virtual switch to a physical host NIC, virtual machines can also gain access to the external network. Only a single external switch can be configured for each physical NIC.

◆   Internal

An internal switch is created to provide a line of communication between the Hyper-V host and any virtual machine running on that host that attach to this virtual switch. It also provides a means of communication between virtual machines running on the Hyper-V host. An unlimited number of internal switches can be created.

◆   Private

A private switch is created to provide communications among the virtual machines attached to this switch running on a single Hyper-V host. The host cannot communicate over this switch with any virtual machine. An unlimited number of private switches can be created.

Chapter 5: High Availability and Hyper-V

Setting up a highly available environment on physical machines hosting virtual machines

Master It   In Windows Server 2008 pre-R2 and R2 and in Microsoft Hyper-V Server 2008 R2, it is possible to set up Hyper-V as a highly available service in a Microsoft Failover Cluster. This ensures that if a Hyper-V server hosting virtual machines fails for whatever reason, the virtual machines on that failed host are failed over, or restarted, on a surviving node of the Failover Cluster. The hardware configuration has several requirements in order to create a Failover Cluster that is fully supported by Microsoft. List the requirements of the configuration.

Solution   You must have two (or more, up to 16) 64-bit servers with AMD-V or Intel VT technology and Data Execution Prevention enabled. Servers must all be either AMD or Intel. You cannot mix AMD and Intel servers in the same cluster. (www.windowsservercatalog .com has a category of servers that support Hyper-V.)

All individual components must come from the list of products already certified through the Failover Cluster Configuration Program (www.microsoft.com/windowsserver2008/en/us/failover-clustering-program-overview.aspx).

Server systems must have enough RAM to support the parent partition (recommended to start with 2 GB) plus the memory for the virtual machines expected to be run. Servers must be running the Enterprise or Datacenter Edition of Windows Server 2008 or Windows Server 2008 R2. Microsoft Hyper-V Server 2008 R2 could also be used. Microsoft Hyper-V Server cannot be clustered with Windows Server.

It is recommended to have at least three NICs in each server, each on its own unique IP subnet: one NIC for host management, one NIC for network access to the virtual machines, and one NIC for cluster communication. The use of iSCSI for storage would increase the number of recommended NICs to four. Your workload requirements will be the final arbiter of the proper number of NICs.

The names of the virtual networks used within the virtual machines must be spelled exactly the same across all nodes of the virtual machine cluster.

There is no restriction on the operating system environment that can run in the virtual machines running on the Hyper-V hosts.

The complete cluster configuration must pass the validation wizard with no errors.

Setting up an environment with the ability to move running virtual machines from one server to another with no downtime

Master It   A new capability provided in Windows Server 2008 Hyper-V R2 and Microsoft Hyper-V Server 2008 R2 is the ability to move a running virtual machine from one node in a Failover Cluster to another node with no loss of machine state and no loss of network connections to the virtual machine as it is moved. This capability is known as Live Migration. It is built on top of the Failover Cluster feature. Since the previous question defined the base configuration for a Failover Cluster, list the recommended new components that are required to upgrade the configuration to support Live Migration.

Solution   You must have Enterprise or Datacenter Edition of Windows Server 2008 R2 running as the parent partition. Microsoft Hyper-V Server 2008 R2 can also be used to create a Failover Cluster.

Optionally you can install the Cluster Shared Volume feature. Though this is not a requirement for Live Migration, it does enable multiple virtual machines to be stored on a single LUN and give the individual machines the ability to be migrated live to another node of the cluster without impacting any of the other virtual machines that are stored on that same LUN.

Setting up a highly available environment on virtual machines

Master It   Not only is it possible to create highly available host environments with Failover Clusters, but it is also possible to create highly available virtual machines, regardless of whether the virtual machines hosts are members of a Failover Cluster. Describe the recommendations to create a Failover Cluster between two virtual machines.

Solution   The virtual machines must be running the Enterprise or Datacenter Edition of Windows Server 2003 SP2, Windows Server 2008, or Windows Server 2008 R2.

If shared storage is used between the nodes, the storage must be on iSCSI.

It is recommended to have at least four virtual NICs for each virtual machine: one each for system management, cluster communication, client access, and iSCSI (if shared storage is used).

The complete virtual cluster configuration must pass the Cluster validation wizard with no errors.

Chapter 6: Planning a Virtual Infrastructure with Hyper-V

Defining the scope of your project   Projects often tend to take on a larger number of requirements if the end goals are not carefully defined. One of best ways to protect against project creep is to define the specific problems that are to be solved.

Master It   Define two classes of specific problems to be addressed by a project. Give an example of each.

Solution   Business problem statements are statements that define a business problem to be solved and quantifiable measurements of the success of the proposed solution.

Problem statement: During the testing phase of developing a new application, it takes one or two hours to rebuild or reset a test environment to run a new series of tests.

Goal: Reduce the reset time to less than 15 minutes and allow the tester to return to any one of multiple known points in time for different tests.

Technical problem statements are statements that define a technical problem to be solved and quantifiable measurements that can be used to measure the success of the proposed solution.

Problem statement: Cooling capacity in the datacenter is about to reach its maximum.

Goal: Reduce the cooling requirements in the data center by 25 percent.

Discovering what you have to work with   Before you can start a successful project, you need to know what you have to work with. For an infrastructure virtualization project, you need to be able to identify which physical machines are good candidates for virtualization.

Master It   List some of the capabilities of the Microsoft Assessment and Planning Toolkit that make it a key tool for taking an inventory of your environment to determine virtualization candidates.

Solution   Does not require any software to be installed on the machines being surveyed.

Operator does not need to know the exact machines to be discovered. Discovery can be accomplished via IP address range, Active Directory groups (forest, domain, organization unit, container), Windows networking protocols, list of known computers, or manually entered.

Provides hardware (CPU, memory, disk, network) utilization statistics.

Provides a list of installed applications and operating systems per surveyed machine.

Provides a list of hardware configuration for each surveyed machine.

Data can be exported for use in a Return on Investment tool available from Microsoft.

Assessing what you can accomplish with your resources   Once you have discovered what you have in your environment, you can make better judgment calls about which physical machines should be moved first into a virtual environment. This requires an understanding of your specific business goals defined in the envisioning phase.

Master It   List some of the ways you could decide which physical machines to select for virtualization and why you might use each method.

Solution   Age of physical machine — older machines are most likely the most expensive to run and they are most likely less powerful than current hardware technologies.

Low CPU utilization — these machines use a lot more electrical power than is required to accomplish their job.

Single- or dual-processor machines — these are most likely older machines, so they could fit into the first category. Also, Hyper-V can support a maximum of four virtual cores in a virtual machine, so physical machines that are not pushing that limit are likely candidates.

Financially justifying a virtualization project   If you cannot prove that your project saves the company money or brings in significantly more money than it costs to implement, it generally does not make sense to proceed. Virtualizing an infrastructure is one method that often proves a return on the investment in a very short period of time.

Master It   List some ways that virtualization can save expenditures now or in the future.

Solution   Server consolidation — run the same application workload on fewer servers. Can reduce the expense of purchasing additional servers and reduce the monthly expense of power and cooling.

Retirement of older hardware — remove maintenance contracts on older hardware that can be retired by moving application workload to a virtual environment.

Quick response to business needs — deploy server infrastructure for new projects in a timelier manner. Save cost of personnel required to build physical environment and get the new application workload into production faster to start making money from the application earlier.

Delay or put off expansion — consolidation of multiple servers into less rack space could delay or even negate the requirement to expand a datacenter.

Chapter 7: Understanding Microsoft Application Virtualization and Streaming

Understand and apply App-V terminology.   App-V introduces many new concepts to traditional application deployment and requires new language.

> **Master It**   A key concept in understanding App-V streaming is the minimum launch threshold. Describe the minimum launch threshold and how this is important in a free-seating scenario.

> **Solution**   The minimum launch threshold is the runtime of an application (typically 5–15 percent of the total disk footprint of an application) that streams down initially to a user. Having to load only this threshold to launch and use an application reduces the time an application takes to load the first time it is launched on a computer. This can enable free seating on highly connected computers because application shortcuts are automatically published to users, and only this threshold needs to be streamed for users to become productive with their applications.

Learn the core benefits of App-V.   App-V offers many benefits with regard to an enterprise's application life cycle. These benefits include simplifying and stabilizing your applications and at the same time making your applications more accessible.

> **Master It**   An old version of an Oracle client needs to be deployed alongside a locally installed newer version. The user still needs the newer version for production testing purposes. How can App-V help in this scenario?

> **Solution**   Virtualize the older version and deploy it alongside the locally installed newer version. App-V can help resolve issues by isolating applications so they can work well on the same device even when traditionally installed the two applications would contend for the same resources.

Set up an App-V environment where applications will be provisioned to users based on Active Directory group membership.   Tying applications to users rather than to computers can make sense in many situations. The simplicity of changing group membership in Active Directory and the applications appearing on users' desktops without the possibility of interfering with other applications is driving a revolution in the way modern enterprises view application deployment.

> **Master It**   You've just provisioned both Visual Studio 2008 and AutoCAD 2009 to a user, and the user has called the help desk and complained of not yet receiving the applications. What is a likely reason the user does not have the applications?

> **Solution**   The App-V client has probably not yet completed a publishing refresh request. Ask the user to right-click the App-V icon in the Windows system tray and click Refresh Applications.

Chapter 8: Creating Virtual Applications

Understand sequencing concepts. Sequencing and provisioning applications can take a few times to get the process down completely. The great thing is that once you are familiar with the process, packaging is nearly identical for both easy applications and those that are normally difficult to package using traditional technologies. In the previous example, the application was delivered instantly and on demand surrounded by policy and control.

Master It Which two of the following is correct syntax for an 8.3 package root directory?

1. C:\fooapp.v01

2. Q:\fooapp.v01

3. Q:\foo_app_2009\

4. Q:\fooapp

Solution

2. Q:\fooapp.v01

Install and configure a Sequencer workstation. Properly configuring your Sequencer workstation can lead to much more reliable and predictable sequences. A few minutes spent up front can save many hours of troubleshooting when the applications are streamed enterprisewide to clients.

Master It Your packaging team has reported that sequencing applications takes too much time to process. What is the best way to speed up the process?

Solution The Sequencer process gains the most performance typically by increasing disk I/O. The best solution would be to add a second hard disk to the workstation and relocate the Sequencer software's %tmp%, %temp%, and the scratch directory in Tools ➤ Options.

Sequence an application with middleware. One of the benefits of virtual applications is the ability to bundle middleware with the application that requires it. This can lead to efficiencies in deployment because you no longer have to check whether the dependency is deployed to your target machine because the application has all it needs in its virtual environment.

Master It Part of your App-V deployment is a requirement to deploy to contract workers who have PCs that are not domain joined. Realizing that you can deploy a virtual application by MSI, you look in the virtual application folder in \\App-V\content\<appname> and don't see any MSI files. Think of a way in which you might be able to create these MSIs.

Solution Open the package in the Sequencer software on the Sequencer workstation. On the Deployment tab, click Generate Microsoft Windows Installer (MSI) Package. Click File and then Save. This will automatically generate the MSI.

Publish an application to users. Publishing applications to users is a powerful feature of App-V. Simply changing a group membership in Active Directory can entitle users to a range of applications.

Master It Many users have complained that icons for virtual applications placed on their desktops keep reappearing even after they delete them. How can you centrally prevent this from happening?

Solution Open the App-V Management Server console, expand the Applications node, and find the application record. Double-click the application record, click the Shortcuts tab, and uncheck the Publish To User's Desktop option.

Chapter 9: Deploying Virtual Applications

Customize package behavior with OSD file scripting. Customizing OSD files can greatly enhance a sequencing engineer's efficiency and effectiveness. Placing flags on a system for administrative purposes, setting an environmental variable, or even wiping out the user state upon application close can all be done with just a few lines of code.

Master It You need to delete all hidden temp files that a virtual application creates in `c:\myapp\temp\` each time the user shuts down an application.

Solution

```
<DEPENDENCY>
        <SCRIPT TIMING="POST" EVENT="SHUTDOWN" WAIT="TRUE" PROTECT="FALSE">
                <SCRIPTBODY>
                        DEL /AH /Q c:\\MYAPP\\TEMP\\*.* \n
                </SCRIPTBODY>
        </SCRIPT>
</DEPENDENCY>
```

Deploy a stand-alone MSI architecture. The stand-alone MSI model is a powerful method of getting virtual applications to rarely connected computers and machines that are not domain joined.

Master It You need to get an accounting application immediately to an auditor whose machine is not domain joined. What are the steps to accomplish this?

Solution

1. Be sure that an MSI was created when the application was sequenced.

2. Copy the entire App-V application folder containing the MSI, SFT, and all other virtualization files to a USB flash drive or DVD.

3. Install the App-V client and change the Registry settings to put the client in stand-alone mode.

4. Reboot the computer.

5. Complete the MSI install from the App-V folder.

Deploy a hybrid architecture.   The hybrid model can be a good solution for mature software delivery environments. You get the benefits of streaming and package upgrades without designing a secondary infrastructure. If an organization already has System Center Configuration Manager SP1 with R2 deployed, there is little reason not to leverage it.

Master It   Your vice president of IT is leaning toward a hybrid environment because there are already IIS servers at all branch locations and the network has been very stable. Her only problem is that by regulation she needs to keep an accurate software inventory. Since App-V applications are not installed to the Registry or file system, how do you answer her?

Solution   App-V virtual applications, though not installed locally, register themselves with a local WMI provider, which can be queried using first- and third-party inventory solutions.

Scale the full infrastructure model.   The full infrastructure model is a great solution for midsize to large enterprises that do not have a streamlined application delivery process. Applications become network services and as such can be turned on or off on demand. Office 2007 "installs" in under 15 seconds. There is much business value in using the full infrastructure to dynamically manage your entire application life cycle.

Master It   You have designed a solution where clients get access to their App-V applications from your corporate headquarters, but the applications stream from their local branch offices. Several employees in your Denver branch need a new application, and your IIS server is not functioning. What is a temporary way to get your users their applications while you repair or replace their local IIS server?

Solution   Using the App-V Group Policy ADM template, temporarily change their Application Source Root (ASR) to either their closest branch or to an IIS server at headquarters.

Chapter 10: Introduction to Remote Desktop Services

Describe the Remote Desktop Protocol transport functionality and security.   Having a well-developed understanding of the capabilities of Remote Desktop Services will allow you to evaluate a need within your organization and quickly determine if RDS is an appropriate solution.

Master It   Take a current organizational need or find an example of an existing workload or application deployment. Leverage your understanding of the capabilities and features of RDS to determine if it would be a suitable platform to deploy the workload or application.

Solution   Users in manufacturing facilities around the world access an enterprise resource planning (ERP) system to drive order fulfillment. The application is a WinForms application that connects to a back-end database server. The application is frequently updated, and delivering updates to remote facilities is difficult. Users consistently complain of slow response.

This is an ideal workload for RDS. By putting the application on an RDS server, you eliminate the slow response times but place the client application in close network proximity to the database server, and only display is pushed over the network. You can also alleviate pains associated with updates because you need to update only the small number of central RDS servers rather than many distributed workstations.

Plan and size a Remote Desktop Services environment. Properly planning and specifying, or sizing, the RDS environment is critical to a successful deployment. An improperly sized RDS server or farm will most certainly lead to a poorly performing workload or application set.

Master It Using the example you selected above, plan for and size the appropriate server for your workload or application set based on the number of users for which you expect to provide access.

Solution The ERP application has some components that make it memory intensive — about 200 MB per user. A standard server has two quad-core processors and 16 GB of RAM. The application is not graphically intensive.

Based on RAM utilization, we expect to support up to the following:

(16 GB (Server standard) − 2GB (for OS)) / 200 MB = 71 users per server

Total concurrent users for the system will be about 500, so we will deploy seven RDS servers with Windows Server 2008 R2 x64 to start.

Configure a server to allow remote administration through Remote Desktop. Leveraging the administrative mode of RDS, you can easily manage all of your Microsoft Windows Servers remotely using the full GUI as if you were in front of the device.

Master It Configure your Microsoft Windows Server 2008 R2 device to allow an administrator to remotely connect to and manage the server.

Solution Open Server Manager and select Configure Remote Desktop. In the System Properties window under the Remote tab, select either of the Allow Connections radio buttons. A dialog box will appear informing you that a firewall exception will be made to allow RDP. Click OK to dismiss the dialog box, and then click OK again to complete the process and close the System Properties window.

Chapter 11: Installing and Configuring Remote Desktop Services

Determine when to use an RDS Per User CAL and when to use an RDS Per Device CAL. Understand how a Per User RDS CAL and a Per Device RDS CAL differ and when either should be deployed in your environment and how your choice can have an impact on the overall cost of deploying an RDS solution.

Master It You are put in charge of standing up an RDS environment so that workers in your call center can access applications via new thin client devices. The call center operates 24/7 and is manned by three shifts of workers. Should you acquire and deploy Per User RDS CALs or Per Device RDS CALs?

Solution   Because there are more users than devices, you would be best served by acquiring and deploying Per Device RDS CALs. You would need to buy three times as many Per User RDS CALs as Per Device RDS CALs. Deploying Per Device RDS CALs in this environment is the most cost-effective solution.

Identify which clients can utilize Network Level Authentication.   Understanding which clients or devices can or cannot make use of NLA is important, and you must determine your connectivity needs. The enhanced security of NLA comes at the cost of reducing the types of client devices that can connect.

Master It   You are configuring an RD Session Host and have determined that Windows 2000 users will need to connect. Do you implement NLA?

Solution   Because NLA supports only Microsoft Windows XP SP3 and newer, your Windows 2000 users will not be able to connect. So you would not want to implement NLA on your RD Session Host server.

Determine when to enable Client Experience features.   Enabling the Client Experience consumes additional server resources such as RAM and CPU, thus reducing the total number of remote users you can concurrently host on an RD Session Host.

Master It   You are planning an RDS environment for knowledge workers who are fairly adept and comfortable with Microsoft client operating systems such as Windows Vista. Should you enable the Client Experience in your RDS environment?

Solution   Those knowledge workers who are largely confident and experienced with existing Microsoft Windows client operating systems may revolt if suddenly they are presented with an unfamiliar environment. Not only may productivity suffer, but support incidents may also increase. In this case, definitely invoke the Client Experience and plan for additional resources as necessary.

Properly install applications on an RD Session Host.   When you are installing applications onto an RD Session Host, it is important that the server be placed in the proper state. If the server is not appropriately configured to accept new programs, unexpected results such as failure of programs to execute could result.

Master It   You are about to install three major applications and two smaller supporting programs onto an RD Session Host. What is an appropriate procedure or course of action to ensure the applications are installed in such a manner as to function correctly?

Solution   For any applications with Windows Installer packages, install the applications as you normally would on a client machine, by running the package. Prior to installing any applications that are not in the Windows Installer format on an RD Session Host, the server needs to be placed into install mode. For this to occur, the server should be drained of all currently connected users. Set the RDS logon mode to "Allow reconnections but prevent new logons" in RD Session Host Configuration. Once all users have logged off and you have inhibited new users from connecting, you can issue the command **C:\change user /install**. This will place the server into install mode, and you can begin to install all of the applications. After the programs are installed and configured, place the server back into service by issuing the command **C:\change user /execute**. Finally, allow users to connect to the server again.

Chapter 12: Deploying and Accessing Remote Desktop Services

Describe the differences between a full desktop provided by an RD Session Host and a remote desktop provided within a Virtual Desktop Infrastructure (VDI).   Understanding these differences becomes critical when determining how to deploy a server-based desktop session to an end user in your environment.

Master It   Your assessment of business needs and associated costs has led you to consider deploying a server-based desktop to a larger portion of your end users. These particular users are task based and utilize a finite set of applications in the normal course of their workday. They are not allowed to install their own applications, nor are the applications they utilize resource intensive. Would it be best to deploy the user's desktop using the functionality of a RD Session Host or through leveraging a desktop provided by a Virtual Desktop Infrastructure?

Solution   Because the group of users in question is task workers and not power users who require complete OS isolation, you should deploy the desktops utilizing the RD Session Host functionality. A benefit of this approach will be much greater density of users per similarly configured host servers. You will also have less of a management burden since you have only the smaller number of server OSes to manage as opposed to many clients.

Determine when to utilize the functionality provided by RemoteApp.   RemoteApp is a fantastic mechanism to deploy applications to end users. There are certain instances when RemoteApp is more suitable than other methods.

Master It   A target group of task workers is moving to thin-client devices and will be accessing their application workloads hosted on RD Session Host servers. Should you implement RemoteApp for these users?

Solution   Because the thin-client devices may not have a robust environment in which to deploy any locally executed applications, you will most likely need to provide a full desktop for these users. RemoteApp is the choice for a single or targeted set of applications that users can access from their existing rich-client devices, where they can coexist with other local applications.

Configure access to RemoteApp programs via a web browser.   Enabling access to RemoteApp programs via a web browser is a very effective and nimble method of providing access to the hosted resources to end users.

Master It   Many applications have already been installed on your RD Session Host server. Assuming that RD Web Access is properly configured as well, what is the process to allow end users to access a RemoteApp program via a web browser?

Solution   To make an installed application available as a RemoteApp program accessible via a web browser, you first need to add an installed application using the RemoteApp Wizard. By default and if your RD Web Access is properly configured, the application will dynamically be made available to all authorized users when they next access the RD Web Access website.

Deploy applications to only certain users or groups of users. In order to increase security and reduce user confusion, RemoteApp provides a mechanism to security trim access to applications based on individual users or groups of users.

Master It You are deploying RemoteApp in conjunction with RD Web Access and want to implement more granular security. To this end, you want to present only certain application icons in the browser to specific users. What process would you follow to accomplish this?

Solution On the RD Session Host server, launch RemoteApp Manager. Right-click a listed RemoteApp program and select Properties. Under the User Assignment tab, add the users or groups that you want to allow access to the RemoteApp program. Upon subsequent logon to the RD Web Access website, the end users will not see the application icon in the browser if they were not specifically allowed access.

Chapter 13: Load Balancing Remote Desktop Services

Describe why you would want to implement load balancing in an RD Session Host environment. Understanding benefits that load balancing provides to an RD Session Host farm is essential in ensuring a successful implementation that can scale with your future needs.

Master It Your colleagues and manager are curious as to why you want to expend a bit more effort, and possible additional hardware and software, to configure load balancing for your new RDS environment. How would you justify your decision?

Solution Although load balancing requires a bit of additional effort at the outset, it sets the foundation for an RDS environment that can scale out easily in the future. As far as additional hardware is concerned, that expenditure may be well worth it — but you can always implement an RD Session Host farm consisting of only one RD Session Host server. At that point, future RD Session Host servers can be much more readily added to the farm.

Identify the key feature that an RD Connection Broker provides that other stand-alone load balancers do not. Even if you have the budget for expensive hardware load balancers or already have them in production, an RD Connection Broker plays a unique role in the RD Session Host farm.

Master It Your network counterpart approaches you and comments that you won't need to configure an RD Connection Broker because she will be providing load balancing via dedicated hardware load balancers. What would be your explanation as to why you still believe it to be a good idea to stand up an RD Connection Broker?

Solution An RD Connection Broker has the unique ability to track user sessions across all of the RD Session Host servers in the farm. If a user purposefully or accidentally disconnects from his session, the RD Connection Broker can automatically reestablish that connection on the user's subsequent logon. The great news about this capability is that it can be used in conjunction with your dedicated hardware load balancers if you so choose.

Share an end user's server-based session so as to provide assistance in real time. Ensuring a productive user experience when participating in a server-based session on an RD Session Host should be a top priority for us as IT professionals. Any mechanism that can abet us toward that goal is welcome.

Master It   A user contacts you and states that he is confused about how to complete a few tasks and is becoming frustrated. Unfortunately, this user is located across town, so you can't just visit him at his desk. What is the best way to proceed?

Solution   Since the user is running a full session of an RD Session Host server, you have a very useful option available. Ask the user if you can join him in his session and take remote control of his mouse and keyboard. He will be able to watch everything you do on his screen and show you exactly where he is having problems. This is a quick resolution of a problem, and no one has to leave their desk.

Chapter 14: Introducing Microsoft Desktop Virtualization

Identify Microsoft Windows Optimized Desktop best practices.   Microsoft's approach to improving the desktop environment is called the Windows Optimized Desktop.

Master It   List five technologies that contribute to a Microsoft Windows optimized desktop.

Solution   These technologies include ImageX, ESD, antivirus software, BitLocker, rights management, NAP, roaming profiles, redirected folders, offline folders, direct access, application virtualization, desktop virtualization, and WinFLP.

Describe different types of desktop virtualization solutions.   There are two different types of desktop virtualization solutions: client-hosted and server-hosted.

Master It   How are the architectures of presentation virtualization and Virtual Desktop Infrastructure (VDI) different?

Solution   Presentation virtualization uses a single Windows Server operating system to deliver session-based remote desktops to users. VDI uses server virtualization to host individual VMs that the user remotely connects to.

Define VDI, its benefits, architecture, and components.   A VDI solution has several benefits and disadvantages an organization will need to consider carefully.

Master It   What are some benefits and disadvantages of a VDI solution?

Solution   Benefits include deployment agility, management efficiency, improved security and better business continuity and disaster recovery. Disadvantages include reliance on a network connection, unsuitability for high-end graphic applications, the requirement for additional infrastructure, and the significant acquisition costs of required hardware and software.

Understand the Microsoft Enterprise Desktop Virtualization solution and its architecture. Microsoft has three different types of client-hosted desktop virtualization solution: Virtual PC, Windows XP Mode, and Microsoft Enterprise Desktop Virtualization.

Master It   How does MED-V enhance a Virtual PC environment?

Solution   MED-V provides an enterprise solution to centrally provision, configure, deploy, and update Virtual PC images and a seamless user experience through a single desktop environment.

Understand the Microsoft VDI solution and its architecture.   The Microsoft VDI architecture consists of many server and client components that work together to provide a single solution.

Master It   What are the main server components of the Microsoft VDI solution?

Solution   The main components are Windows Server 2008 R2, Windows Server 2008 R2 Hyper-V, RD Virtualization, RD Connection Broker, RDS Session Host, RD Web Access, System Center Management tools, and APP-V.

Chapter 15: Deploying Microsoft VDI

Install and configure the Microsoft Remote Desktop Connection Broker.   The Microsoft Remote Desktop connection Broker provides session management services for the Microsoft VDI solution.

Master It   Can the RD Connection Broker be installed on the same physical or virtual server as the RD Virtualization Host?

Solution   No. Microsoft does not support installing the RD Connection Broker and RD Virtualization Host on the same physical or virtual server.

Create and assign a personal virtual machine.   The Microsoft VDI solution can support personal and pooled virtual machines.

Master It   Can the same VM be used as a personal VM and a pooled VM at the same time?

Solution   No, a VM can only be used as a personal VM or as part of a pool.

Create and assign virtual machines to a pool   The Remote Desktop Connection Manager tool is used to create a virtual machine pool.

Master It   What are the four main configuration steps for preparing a Windows operating system for running in a VM that will be used in a Microsoft VDI solution?

Solution   The four main configuration steps for preparing a Windows operating system for running in a VM that will be used in a Microsoft VDI solution are allowing remote access, setting an exception for the Windows firewall to allow Remote Service Management, using regedit to allow Remote RPC, and granting RDP security privileges.

Install and configure the Microsoft Remote Desktop Web Access server.   The Remote Desktop Web Access web page provides access to RemoteApp and Desktop resources.

Master It How do you configure RD Web Access to use a RD Connection Broker server?

Solution Connect to the RD Web Access web page with administrator privilege, select the Configure tab, select the source as an RD Connection Broker server, enter the name of the RD Connection Broker server in the Source field, and click OK.

Configure Windows 7 for RemoteApp and Desktop Connection Windows 7 supports accessing the RemoteApp and Desktop Connection from the desktop start menu.

Master It How do you set up a new connection for RemoteApp and Desktop Connection on Windows 7?

Solution Using the Control Panel applet RemoteApp and Desktop Connection, select Create A New Connection, and enter the connection URL to the RD Web Access server, for example, `//Web Access Server/rdweb/feed/webfeed.aspx`.

Chapter 16: Deploying Microsoft Enterprise Desktop Virtualization

Install and configure the MED-V Management Server. A MED-V solution consists of a Management Server, Repository Server, Management Console, and Client software.

Master It What Windows operating systems does MED-V support for the host and guests?

Solution MED-V supports the following host operating systems: Windows XP SP2/SP3 and Windows Vista SP1. MED-V supports the following guest operating systems: Windows 2000 SP4, Windows XP SP2/SP3, and Windows Vista SP1/SP2.

Create and prepare a MED-V test image. MED-V uses Microsoft Virtual PC 2007 SP1 to create its VM images.

Master It How do you prepare a Virtual PC virtual machine for MED-V?

Solution The steps for preparing a Virtual PC virtual machine for MED-V include the following: Create the virtual machine image with the Microsoft Virtual PC Console. Start the new virtual machine and install Windows. Install the VPC Virtual Machine Additions. Install Microsoft .NET Framework 2.0 SP1. Install any additional software (utilities and applications). Install the MED-V Workspace software. Test the VPC image. Run Setup Wizard and Sysprep. Shut down the VPC image.

Create and configure a MED-V Workspace image. A MED-V Workspace can be assigned only one image, but an image can support more than one MED-V Workspace.

Master It Where do you configure the amount of memory that is available to a MED-V Workspace?

Solution   This setting is configured in the MED-V Management Console under Workspace Performance settings.

Deploy a MED-V Workspace image.   Trim Transfer is a MED-V data transfer technology that minimizes the amount of data, bandwidth, and time it takes to deploy or update a MED-V image to a client.

Master It   What are three methods to deploy a MED-V Workspace image to a client?

Solution   A MED-V Workspace image can be deployed by using the MED-V Client to stream the image to the desktop, by using Electronic Software Distribution to prestage an image to the desktop hard disk, or by copying an installation package to a DVD or USB storage device.

Generate MED-V reports.   MED-V uses Microsoft SQL Server to store reporting data collected from MED-V clients.

Master It   What tool is used to generate and view MED-V client reports? What types of reports are available?

Solution   The Reports section of the MED-V Management Console is used to generate and view MED-V client reports. Reports can be generated and viewed for client status, activity log, and error log.

Appendix B

Microsoft Virtualization Tools and Resources

Microsoft provides a comprehensive collection of virtualization resources that include websites and blogs, whitepapers and guides, webcasts and podcasts, training and certification tests, solution accelerators, return on investment (ROI) calculators, case studies, partners and licensing information. A list of these resource categories is provided below along with their locations.

Websites

Microsoft has several website locations for finding information about their virtualization products and technologies depending on the type of virtualization solution you are looking for. The following Microsoft websites include general and technical virtualization information as well as information about Microsoft VDI, Microsoft Virtual PC, and Microsoft Desktop Optimization Pack.

- ◆ Main Virtualization
  www.microsoft.com/virtualization

- ◆ Technical Virtualization
  http://technet.microsoft.com/en-us/virtualization

- ◆ Window Server 2008 R2 Hyper-V
  www.microsoft.com/hyperv

- ◆ System Center Virtual Machine Manager R2
  www.microsoft.com/systemcenter/virtualmachinemanager

- ◆ Microsoft Virtual Desktop Infrastructure
  www.microsoft.com/windows/enterprise/solutions/virtualization
  www.microsoft.com/rds

- ◆ Windows XP Mode and Windows Virtual PC
  www.microsoft.com/virtual-pc

- ◆ Microsoft Desktop Optimization Pack (APP-V & MED-V)
  www.microsoft.com/mdop
  www.microsoft.com/technet/mdop

- ◆ Microsoft Virtualization Product Downloads
  www.microsoft.com/virtualization/tryit/product-downloads/default.mspx

Blogs

Here are some good Microsoft virtualization blogs authored by Microsoft product groups. Reading these blogs regularly is a great way to learn about and stay abreast of the latest Microsoft virtualization information and news.

```
http://blogs.technet.com/virtualization
http://blogs.msdn.com/virtual_pc_guy
http://blogs.technet.com/wincat
http://blogs.technet.com/roblarson
http://blogs.technet.com/rakeshm
http://blogs.msdn.com/rds
http://blogs.technet.com/softgrid
http://blogs.technet.com/windowsserver
```

Whitepapers and Guides

Microsoft has virtualization whitepapers and guides that can help you better understand their products and how to implement them. The following Microsoft Virtualization whitepapers and guides on virtualization may be useful to review and can be found at www.microsoft.com/virtualization/resources.

- ◆ Datacenter Virtualization–Enabling a Dynamic Datacenter with Microsoft Virtualization
- ◆ Microsoft Virtualization from Datacenter to Desktop
- ◆ Hyper-Green Seven Steps in Virtualization System White Paper
- ◆ Virtualization for Windows: A Technology Overview
- ◆ Desktop Virtualization Strategy White Paper
- ◆ Hyper-V Security Infrastructure Planning and Design Guides for Virtualization

Webcasts and Podcasts

Microsoft virtualization webcasts and podcasts are great resources for learning about Microsoft Virtualization strategy, products, and technologies. They cover many virtualization subjects and are offered at different technical levels.

- ◆ Webcasts
  www.microsoft.com/events/series
- ◆ Podcasts
  www.microsoft.com/events/podcasts

Training and Certification

Microsoft provides virtualization training resources, classes, and certification on the website below. Resources and classes are available on Windows Server 2008 Hyper-V R2, System Center Virtual Machine Manager R2, Remote Desktop Services, Microsoft Enterprise Desktop Virtualization and Microsoft Application Virtualization. In addition, information about Microsoft training organizations and their locations are also provided.

www.microsoft.com/learning/virtualization

Virtualization Solution Accelerators

Microsoft Solution Accelerators are guides and tools that can assist customers and partners with their implementation of Microsoft solutions. Listed below are six Microsoft Virtualization Solution Accelerators and guides that may be useful to review and utilize. They can be downloaded at the following location:

`http://technet.microsoft.com/en-us/solutionaccelerators`

- Microsoft Deployment Toolkit 2010
- Hyper-V Security Guide
- Microsoft Assessment and Planning Toolkit
- Offline Virtual Machine Servicing Tool
- Infrastructure Planning and Design Guides for Virtualization
- Security Compliance Management Toolkit Series

Virtualization Calculators

Microsoft has a virtualization calculator that can assist an organization in determining the ROI of implementing a Microsoft virtualization solution.

- Virtualization ROI Calculator

  `www.microsoft.com/virtualization/roitool`

Customer Case Studies

Microsoft has thousands of customers using and benefiting from its virtualization solutions, products, and technologies. Many of these customers are showcased on the website listed below, describing their business problem, solution implemented, and business and technical benefits received.

`www.microsoft.com/virtualization/casestudies`

Partners

There are many partners that support and complement the Microsoft virtualization solution offering. These partners include independent hardware and software vendors, system integrators, and training companies. A listing of the Microsoft virtualization partners can be found at the following location.

`www.microsoft.com/virtualization/partners`

Licensing Information

Licensing information for Microsoft products and their use in a virtualized environment can be found in the following locations.

- Overview

  `www.microsoft.com/licensing/about-licensing/virtualization`

- Windows Server

  `www.microsoft.com/windowsserver2008/en/us/licensing-overview`

◆ System Center

www.microsoft.com/systemcenter/en/us/pricing-licensing

◆ VDI Suite

www.microsoft.com/windows/enterprise/solutions/virtualization/
improve-flexibility

◆ Virtual Enterprise Centralized Desktop

www.microsoft.com/windows/enterprise/solutions/virtualization/licensing

◆ Microsoft Desktop Optimization Pack

www.microsoft.com/windows/enterprise/products/mdop

◆ Enrollment for Core Infrastructure

www.microsoft.com/licensing/licensing-options/enrollments

Index

Note to the Reader: Throughout this index **boldfaced** page numbers indicate primary discussions of a topic. *Italicized* page numbers indicate illustrations.